MEDIEVAL LYRIC
Genres in Historical Context
EDITED BY WILLIAM D. PADEN

Medieval genres of lyric poetry have long been accepted as self-evident categories that define the literature. *Medieval Lyric* reveals the importance of investigating the historicity of genres themselves as a means of coming to grips with the evolution of the poems they were meant to characterize and the cultures they attempted to serve.

An essential volume for medievalists and scholars of comparative literature, *Medieval Lyric* opens up a reconsideration of genre in medieval European lyric. Departing from a perspective that asks how medieval genres correspond with twentieth-century ideas of structure or with the evolution of poetry, this valuable collection argues that the development of genres should be considered as a historical phenomenon, embedded in a given culture and responsive to social and literary change.

An array of widely respected scholars draw from French, Italian, German, Latin, Catalan, Spanish, Galician-Portuguese, Arabic, and Hebrew literature to address questions about what genre could have meant to medieval poets and poet-musicians and what distortions result when modern ideas of genre are applied to medieval lyric. Essays explore the relations of medieval lyric genres, such as love songs and satires, to their historical contexts and consider genres in relation to rhetoric and music. Contributors also challenge the concept of genre itself, clarifying what we do when we read in genres and demonstrating the hazards of applying concepts of genre to an age that did not think in those terms.

WILLIAM D. PADEN, a professor of French at Northwestern University, is the author of *Introduction to Old Occitan* and the editor of numerous collections.

A VOLUME IN THE SERIES ILLINOIS MEDIEVAL STUDIES

MEDIEVAL LYRIC

Illinois Medieval Studies

EDITORIAL ADVISORS

Karen Fresco
Anne D. Hedeman
Megan McLaughlin
Janet Smarr
Charles D. Wright

A list of books in the series appears at the end of this book.

Medieval Lyric

GENRES IN HISTORICAL CONTEXT

Edited by William D. Paden

UNIVERSITY OF ILLINOIS PRESS

Urbana and Chicago

FRONTISPIECE: Paris, BN, lat. 1118, fol. 114r. Cliché
Bibliothèque nationale de France, Paris.

The Northwestern University Research Grants Committee has
provided partial support for the publication of this book.
We gratefully acknowledge this assistance.

© 2000 by the Board of Trustees of the University of Illinois
Manufactured in the United States of America
All rights reserved.
∞ This book is printed on acid-free paper.

Library of Congress Cataloging-in-Publication Data
Medieval lyric : genres in historical context / edited by
William D. Paden.
p. cm. — (Illinois medieval studies)
Includes bibliographical references and index.
ISBN 0-252-02536-9 (alk. paper)
1. Poetry, Medieval—History and criticism.
2. Lyric poetry—History and criticism.
I. Paden, William D. (William Doremus), 1941–
II. Title. III. Series.
PN691 .M39 2000
809.1'40900902—dc21   99–050897

C 5 4 3 2 1

Contents

Introduction   1
   WILLIAM D. PADEN

Part 1: Genres in History

1. The System of Genres in Troubadour Lyric   21
   WILLIAM D. PADEN

2. "Cobleiarai, car mi platz": The Role of the *Cobla* in the Occitan Lyric Tradition   68
   ELIZABETH W. POE

3. The Place of Secular Latin Lyric   95
   WINTHROP WETHERBEE

4. On the Conventionality of the *Cantigas d'amor*   126
   JULIAN WEISS

5. Traditional Genres and Poetic Innovation in Thirteenth-Century Italian Lyric Poetry   146
   MICHELANGELO PICONE

6. *Decir canciones:* The Question of Genre in Fifteenth-Century Castilian *Cancionero* Poetry   158
   ANA MARÍA GÓMEZ-BRAVO

Part 2: Genre and Rhetoric

7. The Poem as Art of Poetry: The Rhetoric of Imitation in the *Grand Chant Courtois* 191
   DOUGLAS KELLY

8. The Old Occitan Arts of Poetry and the Early Troubadour Lyric 209
   RUPERT T. PICKENS

9. Genre and Demonstrative Rhetoric: Praise and Blame in the *Razos de trobar* and the *Doctrina de compondre dictats* 242
   JOHN DAGENAIS

10. "Wa-hiya taklifu ghannat": Genre and Gender in Hispano-Arabic Poetry 255
    VICENTE CANTARINO

Part 3: Genre and Music

11. Genre as a Determinant of Melody in the Songs of the Troubadours and the Trouvères 273
    ELIZABETH AUBREY

12. Intergeneric Play: The Pastourelle in Thirteenth-Century French Motets 297
    SYLVIA HUOT

Part 4: Questioning Genre

13. "The Fire of Love Poetry Has Kissed Me, How Can I Resist?" The Hebrew Lyric in Perspective 317
    ROSS BRANN

14. Thwarted Expectations: Medieval and Modern Views of Genre in Germany 334
    HUBERT HEINEN

    CONTRIBUTORS 347
    INDEX 349

Introduction

WILLIAM D. PADEN

The image of a dancing woman which serves as the frontispiece of this volume comes from an eleventh-century collection of prose passages intended to be sung during Mass at the Abbey of Saint-Martial in Limoges.[1] As she dances she displays a pair of green bells connected by a cord. Her mantle is blue, her bodice yellow. Her orange skirt balances the orange color with which she has dyed four fingers of both her hands; her yellow chemise, which flounces out beneath her skirt, matches the color of her bodice; her green shoes balance the color of the bells. We know she is dancing because she bends her legs sharply at the knee, and she supports her weight on her right foot as she raises the left; her posture requires movement to sustain equilibrium. Her mantle and chemise sway outward from her body, allowing us to infer that she twirls before us; but as she turns she maintains her upper body, her arms, and her head in what appears to be a stable position. She holds the bells at arm's length, describing a horizontal axis in contrast with the vertical axis of the triangles of color: green in her bells and shoes, orange in her hands and skirt, yellow in her bodice and chemise. These three triangles all stand on their apexes, which are located in her dancing legs and feet. The scale of the drawing seems to expand as it goes up, as though to suggest that her small feet are peripheral to the focus of the drawing, which falls on her large, intelligent eye.

The dancing woman seems to be at once light-footed and steady in her gaze. By her combination of dynamically balanced balletic qualities, as well as the apparently secular note she introduces into a liturgical manuscript,[2] she may be thought to anticipate the eventual career of Occitan poetry and, perhaps, of medieval lyric poetry in general—the freedom of its inspiration and its intellectual acuity, as well as its evolution from the secular spirit of Guilhem IX toward eventual merger with ecclesiastical ethics. The songs are like her dance; the genres are like her gaze, paradoxically steady even as she pirouettes before us.

In making this assertion, I claim that the genres move with the songs, that they participate in their rhythm, in time, in history. The earliest troubadour songs show no awareness of genre. Beginning at this generic degree zero, or tabula rasa, the genres appeared at first as distinctive traits; they gradually evolved into institutions of voluntary coherence; then, in the arts of poetry, they became prescriptions for composition; finally, they linked together as a taxonomic grid in manuscript rubrics and eventual scholarly tradition. In our retrospective view this final stage, in which the genres serve as instruments of taxonomy, naturally obscures the more distant preceding stages and threatens to efface the historicity of the genres. Taxonomic effects have also been claimed for genres in other lyric traditions of medieval Europe, with varying degrees of accuracy and justification. Without wishing to sacrifice the real advantages of taxonomy, we need to question its historical basis in order to understand what it does and does not tell us about the poetry itself. In order to understand the multiple rhythms of the dance we must follow both the dancer's feet and her eye.

Genres are strange, and medieval lyric genres stranger still.[3] Nominalists from Giordano Bruno to Croce have regarded genres as meaningless, declaring that "There are as many genres of poetry as there are poets."[4] It could be argued that there are as many genres as poems, since every poem is in some sense unique, or perhaps even more, since a poem may participate in more than one genre.[5] Since Romanticism the dissolution of the neoclassical genres has come to seem a normal state of affairs. In our time many authors, readers, and critics have felt, with Maurice Blanchot, "that impetuous impulse of literature that no longer tolerates the distinction of genres and wants to shatter the limits."[6] For Derrida any law of genre is madness.[7]

Despite such post-Romantic hostility toward genre criticism, however, it has been claimed on broad theoretical grounds that genre is intrinsic in artistic creation. E. H. Gombrich argues that "images are not made from nothing; one has to begin somewhere, with something."[8] Gombrich offers the term "schema" for that first something; when we make a snowman, for example, "we feel tempted to work the snow and balance the shapes till we recognize a man. The pile of snow provides us with the first schema, which we correct until it satisfies our minimum definition."[9] We cannot build a snowman without starting with the snow. Similarly, in this view, we cannot make a poem without beginning with poetic materials, not simply words but the whole diffuse mindset from which the poem will emerge. In a traditional culture that mindset may include an institutional and conventional genre. To avoid the abstraction of Platonic forms and keep our footing firmly in history, however, Gombrich insists that the schema must be not rigid but elastic, loose, and flexible.[10] The fundamental process of schema (the pile of snow) and correction (our shaping of the snow) continually evolves; the flexibility of the schema is essential to the historical process. Gombrich extends the model of schema and correction beyond the production of art to the perception of it (which always involves an expectation, that is, a schema), beyond perception of art to the history of art, and beyond the history of art to the history of science,[11] in which the schema corresponds to what Thomas Kuhn called the paradigm with which the scientist approaches his experiment. Neither scientists nor historians of art, neither artists nor poets, create from nothing. Genres in this fundamental, dynamic sense are essential to creativity.[12]

For the critic of modern literature, genre is an explanatory critical instrument, and the discovery or invention of a new genre has become a familiar critical performance.[13] Adena Rosmarin has translated Gombrich's schemata into genres of nineteenth- and twentieth-century lyric poetry such as the dramatic monologue. She observes that when a critic of modern literature juxtaposes a genre to a text in order to explain it, the text will always go beyond the genre; in the comparison the genre will always seem relatively incomplete, the text complete or full.[14] By exceeding the genre, the text is enhanced.

The freewheeling scene of embattled genres in criticism of modern poetry is very different from the lay of the medieval land. For the reader of medieval lyric, especially of the troubadours, the genre of a text may be evidenced by a rubric in the manuscript, and was presumably anticipated by the poet (the late poet, if not the early one) in composing the piece. The medieval genre differs from modern ones, too, in the degree of its coincidence with the text. A genre may resemble the finished work more or less closely, leaving more or less work for the artist to do in creating the work, for the reader to do in understanding it, and for the critic to do in explaining it. Gombrich's pile of snow does not look much like a snowman; the realist novel, in general, is very different from *War and Peace;* but a *canso* is an Occitan composition of five to seven rhymed verse stanzas in which the first-person speaker expresses his desire for a distant and unresponsive beloved woman—or so the grammarians say. The explicit definitions of genres in medieval arts of poetry and rhetoric threaten to explain the text so fully as to leave it empty, incapable of eluding us, containing no more than we know.[15] Genres may be necessary to poetry, but in this way they can also become inimical to poetic achievement. The system of the medieval genres, insofar as it has been accepted by modern readers on the authority of medieval writers, has undoubtedly had a depressing effect on our esteem for medieval poetry.[16]

The familiar division of poetry into epic, dramatic, and lyric genres cannot be found in Plato and Aristotle, but first emerged in the sixteenth century when Minturno included "melic," that is, song, as one of the three macrogenres.[17] Lyric, meaning poetry sung to the accompaniment of the lyre, had been recognized by Dionysius Thrax in the second century B.C. among other genres including tragedy, comedy, elegy, epic, lyric, and lamentation; but the overview which was destined to predominate was first expressed by Diomedes in the fourth century A.D., when he distinguished the active genre or tragedy, the narrative genre or narrative, and the mixed genre or epic. Although Friedrich Schlegel proposed to abolish all definitions and classifications by genre, his brother August Wilhelm envisioned a tripartite system of poetry including subjective (lyric), objective (epic), and the synthesis of the two (drama).

Following such models one may consider the lyric genres of the Middle Ages in relation to the chanson de geste, the romance, or encyclopedic narratives such as the *Roman de la Rose,* the *Divine Comedy,* and the *Canterbury Tales.*[18] History tells us, however, that medieval people did not do so; rather they considered what we call the lyric genres in relation to themselves and to each other, treating song as a world apart.[19] The medieval lyric genres, encased in the chansonnier manuscripts and theorized in treatises on lyric practice, remained discontinuous from narrative forms, except when they influenced romance in the form of lyric insertions or amorous motifs.[20] They were even more discontinuous from their classical predecessors and their successors in the Renaissance. Neoclassical theorists had little interest in them.[21]

Although it is undoubtedly true that poetry must involve some sort of structural genre (Gombrich's snowman), it is not true that consciously held, historical genres or genre-systems are ubiquitous. H. Ansgar Kelly asserts the contrary: "In my study of the occurrences and meanings of the word tragedy over the centuries, I have been struck by how rare the term was and how seldom it was used as a genre in the Middle Ages. But when I broaden my view to take in genres as a whole, I conclude that generic thinking of all kinds was comparatively rare."²² And Kelly adds evidence for this claim from the traditions of commentary and rhetoric, which taught invention independently of genre.²³ In some times and places—the Iceland of the skalds, the Midi of the earliest troubadours—we find production of lyric poetry in the absence of any genres at all.²⁴ But there is no doubt that medieval lyric genres could become institutions, voluntary practices of coherence among poets who imitated their antecedents for motives of traditional mentality.²⁵ Such is the case in the later troubadours and in poets who chose to imitate them in other languages. These genres could also become prescriptive or authoritarian in intent, as they did in the fourteenth century—but this is not to say that they were necessarily obeyed. To the contrary, it appears that the codification of traditional troubadour genres in Middle Occitan did not produce imitation but instead inspired departure into new modulations of generic structure.

Because of such a range in the historical record, to ask how medieval lyric genres corresponded with real, or rational, or twentieth-century concepts of structure is not, I believe, the most pressing question, although we certainly need to know what kinds of poetry the poets actually wrote, whatever their concepts of genre. Nor do I think it the most profitable avenue to accept the medieval genres as our critical givens and to study the evolution of poetry in relation to them.²⁶ Rather we should investigate the historicity of the genres in themselves, as terms and concepts. We should consider genre not as a natural class but as an artificial classifying statement.²⁷ The nominalism of our age may serve to set the realism of medieval practice in relief, to enable us to appreciate its dynamism, its pulls and tugs, rather than, simply and thoughtlessly, to accept its static results. How did these concepts arise? How did the various concepts enter into relations with each other? How did these relations evolve into the pedagogical grid which they became, and remain today? And perhaps the most interesting question, because the most difficult: why?

The essays that follow are organized into four groups. The first group explores the relations of medieval lyric genres to their historical context; the second considers genres in relation to rhetoric, and the third to music; while the fourth challenges the concept of genre itself, proposing modifications in the way we understand it. It is a mark of the coherence of the collection that many of the essays participate in more than one of these foci. They range broadly over the lyric production of medieval Europe, centering on the Occitan troubadours but circling out toward French, Italian, German, Latin,

Catalan, Spanish, Galician-Portuguese, Arabic, and Hebrew. Their geographic and linguistic range assures the diversity of the problems they analyze and highlights their common concern with genres as historical phenomena.

In the first group genres are securely tied to their historical settings in Occitan, Latin, Galician-Portuguese, Italian, and Spanish. I survey the array of genres which inform our reading of the Occitan troubadours. These genres constitute a system in the sense that they include all the extant poems, and that each poem is treated as a member of just one genre; certain pairs of genres have special relations between them, and all the genres make up a list which characterizes troubadour production. Analysis of the total output shows that there are three numerically major genres, the *canso* or love song, the *sirventes* or satire, and the *cobla* or independent stanza, which include, respectively, about 40 percent, 20 percent, and 20 percent of the extant poems. Numerically minor genres such as the *partimen*, the *tenso*, the *planh*, the *pastorela*, and the *alba* account for the rest. The *canso* dominated production in the twelfth century, but was then supplanted by the *cobla* and the *sirventes*, while minor genres too waxed and waned. But these generalizations, based as they are on the genres as instruments of taxonomy, mask the fluidity underlying the genres themselves. Since the earliest troubadours made no distinctions among lyric genres at all, the system grew from nothing during the time when the troubadours sang. Its growth corresponded to many other symptoms of the elevation of vernacular language from speech to writing, from oral to cultural medium, from low language, subservient to Latin, to high language in competition with it. On one hand this dynamic may be taken to define the Middle Ages; on the other it assures that the genre system as it gradually evolved, despite its usefulness, was always anachronistic in application to earlier production. A case study of what may be the earliest *canso* by a trobairitz, Azalais de Porcairagues, demonstrates the fluidity of the genre concept in the original version by Azalais and its evolution through subsequent adaptations.

Elizabeth Poe describes the history and function of the little-studied Occitan genre called the *cobla* or "independent stanza." As the name of a genre, the word applies to four types: inserted *coblas*, which were added to a preexisting work by another poet; extracted *coblas*, selected from longer poems by anthologists; *coblas esparsas* ("scattered stanzas"), which the composer intended to stand alone; and *cobla*-exchanges among two or more poets. The genre came into practice during the decade of the 1190s: the earliest known example is a *cobla esparsa* by Folquet de Marseilla, soon followed by three *cobla*-exchanges in which troubadours and patrons trade insults. The term *cobla* entered technical usage during the same decade, though both its meanings, "representative of the genre" and simply "stanza" (of a poem in any genre) continued to occur. Unambiguous occurrences as the name of a genre occur in poetry of the second half of the thirteenth century and in the *Doctrina de compondre dictats*. The word was compounded in *cobleiar* (to make *coblas*) and in *cobleiador* (one who makes *coblas*). *Coblas* provide evidence both for composition in writing and for improvisation. The genre flourished in the thirteenth and fourteenth centuries in southern France, where it tended toward a moralizing tone, and in Italy, where it was more satirical and figured significantly in the creation of florilegia, or collections of *coblas* extracted from the songs of the great troubadours. The *cobla* was always regarded as an inferior genre, but its undemanding form enabled people who were not great poets to compose it; by imitating various other genres, it contributed to the relaxation of an increasingly rigid system, and its often earthy eroticism released the tension of the *canso*.

Winthrop Wetherbee argues that the learned tradition made twelfth-century Latin lyric a "sustained ironic gloss" on vernacular love poetry. He traces the poetics of this lyric to the *Cosmographia* of Bernardus Silvestris (circa 1147–48), in which a divine ordering principle collaborates with primordial matter to make the world more beautiful at the risk of reverting to chaos. Alan of Lille, in his *De planctu Naturae* (before 1171), focused on the role of human language, specifically of vernacular courtly poetry, which he saw from the perspective of the monumental Latin tradition. Geoffrey of Vinsauf, in his *Poetria Nova* (circa 1208–13), alludes to a *nova causa* or "strange cause" that separates learning from passion and Latin lyric from lyric in the vernacular. Such a poetic informs lyrics of Peter of Blois and the *Carmina Burana* which take "a detached, ironic perspective on the idealism generated by the courtly fantasy," as does the figure of Genius in Jean de Meun's *Roman de la rose* (about 1270). In his *De vulgari eloquentia* (about 1305) Dante rewrote the myth of poetic language in *De planctu Naturae,* implying that the vernacular had absorbed and transcended the Latin tradition.

Julian Weiss sees the conventionality of the Galician-Portuguese *cantigas d'amor* (love songs in the male voice) as a creative conformity by which poets asserted their participation in their social class. The *cantigas d'amigo* (love songs in the female voice), which, like the *cantigas d'amor,* were written only by men, seem more concrete and specific; the female voice boasts that a man loves her, whereas the male voice never boasts that a woman loves him. By refusing to give details about his unique lady, the male voice maintains his stylistic conformity and maintains his edge in homosocial competition. Poets like Vaasco Praga de Sandin (active 1200–1225) mark their work by repetition of formulaic expressions which gain the effect of personal mottos, similar to heraldic devices, and insist on the present moment in the poetry as the scene of constant self-renewal. A poet like Roy Queimado, on the other hand, who employed the conventions with flagrant insincerity, was seen as threatening the basis of genre and gender. Conformity conferred status, but was vulnerable to imitation by those who were not legitimate members of the group. The poet asserted his membership in the group and sought to exclude his competitors by the superiority of his feelings and the uniqueness of his lady. Thus conventionality became a means of asserting subjectivity. By historicizing the genre we rediscover its social and esthetic functions.

Michelangelo Picone traces the development of troubadour genres into Italian, where they fused in the Petrarchan book of poetry, a codification of lyric form destined to endure for five hundred years. Picone traces five factors that contributed to the distinctive character of Italian poetry in the thirteenth century: the rediscovery of Aristotle, the spirituality of the new mendicant orders, the rise of the universities, the study of classical authors, and the development of bourgeois society. Within this dynamic social context, lyric genres developed into a system distinct from that of the troubadours. The number of genres was reduced by the eclipse of the *sirventes*, which had balanced the *canso* in Occitan; without it, Italian lyric focused on themes of love to the exclusion of all others. Furthermore in Dante's *Vita Nuova* the theme of *fin' amor* overshadowed other forms of love, with the result that the eroticism of the *alba* and the obsessive desire of the *sestina* lost their place. Personified Love became the object of the poet's quest. The genres which remained in use came together and lost the sharpness of their distinctions within the macrogenre of Dante's *libro di poesia* or Petrarch's *canzoniere*, the narrative of the poet's life as a lover and artist. At the same time the divorce between poetry and music changed public performance into internal adventure. Guittone d'Arezzo left a highly structured songbook in which, after his conversion, he rewrote his earthly desire as divine. Thus the author of the whole book came into conflict with himself as earthly lover, and lyric became narrative. In Dante's *Vita Nuova* the traditional genres inherited from the troubadours were adapted to poetic autobiography; in his own view Dante realized and fulfilled the aims of his predecessors, as Christ fulfilled the aims of the Old Testament, and produced a book modeled on the Bible.

Ana M. Gómez-Bravo challenges the conventional distinction of fifteenth-century Castilian poetry into *cantigas* or *canciones* (songs) and *decires* (recited poems), musical versus nonmusical. She argues that the musical aspect of earlier poetry had diminished with a corresponding increase in the importance of rhetoric, and further adduces chronological distinctions among the terms in use. These distinctions arose from fundamental cultural changes such as the specialization of music and the consequent divorce between music and poetry; increasing literacy, which corresponded to growth of silent reading, more visual page setup in manuscripts, and a shift to silent prayer; and the increasing contributions to poetry by professionals with rhetorical training. Gómez-Bravo provides philological evidence of the close relation of *decir* to *dictar*, related to Latin *dictamen*, the rhetoric of composition in either prose or verse. She shows that the term *cantiga*, current in the thirteenth and fourteenth centuries, was supplanted by *canción* in the fifteenth and sixteenth, while early usage of *dictado* yielded to *decir* in the latter fourteenth and early fifteenth centuries, and *decir* in turn was replaced by *coplas*. (For similar evolution in another system, compare Paden on Occitan.) All these terms were used erratically. Thus, instead of the usual image of genre contrasts simplified to the point of caricature, Gómez-Bravo comes closer to reality by evoking a complex and dynamic history.

The essays in the second section relate lyric to rhetoric in Occitan, French, Catalan, and Arabic. Douglas Kelly posits that the most prestigious genre of vernacular poetry, the *canso* of the troubadours or the *grand chant courtois* of the trouvères, functioned in terms analogous to those of traditional Latin rhetoric, exemplified in the dialogues of Andreas Capellanus. Where Wetherbee sees ironic gloss in the relation of Latin to vernacular, Kelly sees analogy in the way the poems work. Poets were inescapably acquainted with both Latin tradition, from their schooling, and vernacular tradition, from their art. Like Latin poetry, the *grand chant courtois* was founded upon treatises, models, and imitation: the poet learned principles of composition in the treatises, studied the work of his predecessors, and imitated them with originality. He or she invented topoi in terms of "material style," which "classes persons, things, and actions according to a social hierarchy and typology." Kelly shows that these principles apply to early troubadours such as Bernart de Ventadorn, early trouvères such as the Châtelain de Couci, thirteenth-century figures such as Thibaut de Champagne, and fourteenth-century poets such as Machaut and Charles d'Orléans.

Rupert Pickens begins, like Paden, with the observation that generic distinctions did not appear in the early troubadour repertoire, but Pickens moves in another direction, proposing a modern rhetoric of genre. He shows that only seven of the generic concepts in the arts of poetry, the *vidas* and the *razos*, may be used to describe songs written before 1180, in the period of the *usanza antiga* or "old usage." In this usage *vers* was applied to any song, with no generic specificity whatsoever, as *dictatz* would be used later in the arts of poetry. *Canso* was first introduced in the 1170s as a synonym of *vers,* and only later became narrowed to the specific genre of the song of love. Since no other specific genres were named in the early style, moreover, Pickens argues that it is antihistorical to apply the genres defined in the arts of poetry retrospectively. Instead, he proposes a structuralist paradigm of three genres: (1) pure lyric, the genre of here and now, in which the speaker self-consciously addresses a courtly audience and, beyond that audience, the lady; (2) reciprocal discourse, in which two voices engage in dialogue while excluding the audience from their address; and (3) narrative, the genre of there and then. Generic variants within pure lyric arise when the singer's contemplation is deflected from himself onto the world, including anticipations of the *planh,* or funeral lament, and the *sirventes,* or satire. Thus the *usanza antiga* offers lyric prototypes of the *canso,* the *sirventes,* and the *planh;* in dialogue form, protoypes of the *tenso* and *partimen;* and in narrative, a prototype of the *pastorela.* But none of the classical genres was yet actually present.

John Dagenais shows that the arts of poetry saw troubadour genres as acts of demonstrative rhetoric in which the poet praised or blamed a topic such as love, his lady, or his lord. This retrospective rhetoricizing revived troubadour songs by treating them as living acts of persuasion. Dagenais finds praise and blame as early as Raimon Vidal's *Razos de trobar,* around 1200, since Raimon sets out to correct misguided praise or blame of troubadour compositions, and thus locates the lyric moment not in the fiction of the lover's anguish but in the reality of the performer's interaction with his audience. Around 1290–1300 the *Doctrina de compondre dictats* constructed a system of genre definitions built largely in terms of praise or blame of whatever subject matter the poet might choose. This system joined a long tradition that began in Aristotle and continued in twelfth-century *accessus ad auctores,* or introductions to classical authors and biblical texts such as the lyric Song of Songs. In the mid-thirteenth century, Hermann the German translated Averroës' "Middle Commentary," which asserts that Aristotle viewed every poem as "either praise or blame." In the fourteenth century analysis of praise and blame was applied again to troubadour genres in the *Leys d'amors,* written in Toulouse, and to individual Occitan compositions in the rubrics of Occitan manuscript *H,* compiled in Italy. In the rhetorical understanding of the written page—which was normally read aloud—the reader was compelled to analyze the author's intention to praise or blame, and so became engaged in a revived rhetorical presence of the text.

Examining a possible relation of genre to gender, Vicente Cantarino considers the lyric poetry of Moslem Spain, asking whether feminine gender found distinctive expression either in verse by women or in the language of female personae in verse by men. In the popular fiction of the *Thousand and One Nights* and in anthologies of poetry compiled later, women of all social classes, from slaves to the daughter of a caliph, played important roles as authors and performers from the late eighth century to the fourteenth. Anthologists provided biographical background for the poetry, but the accuracy of such information is doubtful. Poems written by women or attributed to female personae show the same gender-neutrality that is observable in poems by men. Such neutrality is expressed in stereotyped rhetoric, vocabulary, role distribution, or cultural forms; in conflicting attributions to a woman or a man; and in grammatical usage which permits masculine forms in address to a woman. Most situations, actions, and phrases were gender-free, and can be interpreted in relation to gender only with the greatest care. The clearest female personae occur in the *kharjas,* but we do not know if their authors were women or men; moreover the *kharja* is joined to its *muwashsha* by formal features of verse, rhyme, and rhythm rather than by lyrical content, so that the lyricism of the *kharja* remains divorced from that of the *muwashsha.* The *kharja,* marked for gender, is not itself a genre but an element of a genre which remains gender-neutral like the other Arabic genres. In a larger way, though, gender is expressed in classical Arabic poetry as a whole, since the physical gender of the beloved has a decisive influence on the poetic gender of the speaker, whether author, performer, or persona. In poetry addressed to a beloved man, the speaker takes on a feminine quality. Gender becomes instrumental in the production of genre.

The third section relates genres in Occitan and French to music. Elizabeth Aubrey casts troubadour song within a rhetorical perspective in order to analyze the relation between word and melody. In the work of the late thirteenth-century Parisian music theorist Johannes de Grocheio she finds a clear statement that while the text provides matter, the melody offers form; matter and form are conceived inseparably in relation to the song's theme or subject matter; since theme is the basis of genre, genre determines the song's structure, language, function, and melody. She finds this Aristotelian view also in the Occitan arts of poetry from Raimon Vidal around 1200 to Jofre de Foixà and the anonymous *Doctrina de compondre dictats* a century later. The *Doctrina* prescribes qualities in the melody suitable for the various genres, particularly whether the melody should be new or an old one, borrowed from an earlier composition. The *canso,* the *lay,* the *alba,* the *retroncha,* the *dansa,* and the *estampida* call for new melodies; the *descort* melody must be unexpected; the *planh* may have any tune except one from a *dansa;* the *sirventes* usually took a borrowed tune, as did the *tenso;* the *pastora* melody may be either new or borrowed, possibly from traditional folk song.

Sylvia Huot studies the interaction, or "intergeneric play," between the genre of the pastourelle, already well established in the thirteenth century, and the newly developing motet. The monophonic pastourelle was essentially narrative, while the polyphonic motet featured two or more voices singing simultaneously. The tenor usually performed a word, sometimes a syllable, from liturgical chant in Latin; the motetus, or duplum, sang a second text, either in Latin or French; the triplum and the quadruplum offered further possibilities of simultaneous performance and juxtaposition. By juxtaposing two or more very brief texts, each one comprising a stanza or two at the most, the motet opened up new possibilities of dialogue between sacred and secular, Latin and vernacular. Huot studies how the motet highlights the contrasts between the sexuality of the pastourelle world and the restraint of the courtly *chanson,* between variations on the plot of the traditional pastourelle, and between secular and sacred, in motets which allegorize the pastourelle as a narrative of divine love. The interaction between these two genres is one example, among others such as lyric insertions in narrative and lyric contrafacta, of thirteenth-century experimentation with lyric forms.

In the last section, scholars in Hebrew and German challenge the very idea of genre. Ross Brann describes genre in medieval Hebrew lyric from Spain. Beginning in the tenth century, this poetry appropriated Arabic thematic types such as wine poetry, love poetry, and lyrical complaint, as well as the verse forms of the mono-rhymed ode (*qasida*) and the strophic *muwashsha,* or "girdle poem." Such thematic genres were implicit in parodies and in the organization of poets' work, although scribal glosses sometimes applied the terms erratically, and composite poems, such as the ode, defied thematic classification. Modern critics have differed in their assessments, some seeing generic convention as the ultimate source of meaning, while others have recognized an element of personal expression interacting with generic form. Some genres were relatively conventional while others were more personal. The tension between tradition and creativity prevented genres from becoming rigid and kept them in a state of flexibility. Love poems addressed to a man have come to be read in terms of a pervasive gender-neutrality (compare the essay by Cantarino), which attaches little importance to gender except in the *muwashsha,* which entered Hebrew practice in the eleventh century, a hundred years after it had developed in Arabic, and was characterized in Hebrew by melodic borrowing or con-

Introduction

13

trafaction. The *muwashsha* could be erotic or panegyric, secular or liturgical, like the French motet (see Huot); devotional *muwashshahat,* imitating secular love songs, were performed during service in the synagogue, and secular love songs influenced epithalamia (wedding songs). Thus while both the *qasida* and the *muwashsha* accommodated thematic genres, "Hebrew lyric resists efficient generic mapping."

Hubert Heinen argues that in Middle High German taxonomic genres of lyric song are attested furtively at best, while a more dynamic kind of genre underlies the play with audience expectations which characterizes the lyric. German poets who did, exceptionally, produce texts consistent with static concepts of genre did so out of a desire to imitate their more inspired colleagues. We have the names of a few genres such as the *Leich* (lay), *Tagelied* (dawn song), and *Kreuzlied* (crusading song), "subsets of the broad spectrum of song that are discernibly different from the remainder of the song corpus." Others such as the *Tanzweise* (dance song) and the *Reie* (dance) have names but no discernible difference except the use to which they were put, while yet other types widely discussed by scholars, such as the *Spruch* (didactic song), the *Frauenlied* (women's song), the *Wechsel* (dialogue), and the *Botenlied* (song of a messenger), had no names in medieval language. Not even song, in contrast with spoken or chanted forms, had an unambiguous name, though there is no doubt that scribes and auditors knew the difference. Heinen illustrates the play of thwarted expectations in the dawn song. Around 1170 Dietmar von Aist cultivated the *Tagelied* as a genre already well known; about 1200 Wolfram von Eschenbach turned its conventions upside down; in the thirteenth century Bruno von Hornberg wrote imitative verse which fulfilled "a social need for a fixation of poetic norms," while Ulrich von Singenberg violated the conventions of the dawn song in a "reverie on the joys of mutual love." But Germany never developed a system of lyric genres.

The architecture critic Herbert Muschamp, praising the Guggenheim Museum in Bilbao, Spain, designed by Frank Gehry (1997), has written of "the increasing awareness that art resides only partly within individual artworks": "It also lives in the spirit of risk and experimentation that works of art help sustain. This awareness is a central characteristic of the post-industrial city, as well as a theme of contemporary art. Art has spilled out of its classical containers into performance, the media, fashion and other ephemeral forms of expression. By the same token, at least since the advent of conceptual art, the task for many artists has been not only to create objects but also to escape their confining dimensions."[28] In literature such "classical containers" have been the genres, either on the large scale of epic, drama, and poetry, or on the smaller scale of the lyric genres, often called "subgenres," which are the subject of this book.

If Muschamp is right—and a host of witnesses, older than the Bilbao Guggenheim, say he is—then readers today can hardly take lyric genres as the self-evident reading instruments that they once were considered to be, in obedience to the prescriptive grammarians who first endowed them with didactic force. In our age genres are not self-evident at all, but rather unexpected. Their ostensible stability is surprising, if not astonishing, in a cultural landscape of continual experimentation. For us, to historicize genres, to grasp their contingency, is a preliminary step necessary to any understanding of what they once could mean. If we manage to see them as the historical phenomena they were, we can begin to explore their contingency in various ways and in various contexts. Genres appear as second-order artworks in their own right, as critical performances, as reading and writing strategies which could be more or less effective in grasping the evolving forms of poetic expression. By study of genres in history we come to grips with the evolution of the poems they served to characterize and the changing culture, or cultures, in which they played their part.

NOTES

1. Paris, Bibliothèque Nationale, lat. 1118, fol. 114r; see Ph. Lauer, ed., *Catalogue général des manuscrits latins*, vol. 1 (Paris: Bibliothèque Nationale, 1949), 408–9. Color reproductions in Jean Porcher, *Medieval French Miniatures* (New York: Abrams, [1960?]), plate XVI, and in Tilman Seebass, *Musikdarstellung und Psalterillustration im früheren Mittelalter: Studien ausgehend von einer Ikonologie der Handschrift Paris Bibliothèque Nationale fonds latin 1118* (Bern: Francke, 1973), Bildband, plate 9. For details concerning dress I have followed Eunice Rathbone Goddard, *Women's Costume in French Texts of the Eleventh and Twelfth Centuries* (Baltimore: Johns Hopkins Press, 1927), 81, 94, 103, 201.

2. Seebass (*Musikdarstellung*, 162–63) discusses inconclusively her possible relation to Mary the prophetess, sister of Aaron, who "took a timbrel in her hand: and all the women went forth after her with timbrels and with dances" (Exodus 15:20, Douai version), or to Salome, the daughter of Herodias, who "danced before them and pleased Herod" (Matthew 14:6, cf. Mark 6:22).

3. For a well-informed survey of genre criticism in relation to modern lyric poetry, see Adena Rosmarin, *The Power of Genre* (Minneapolis: University of Minnesota Press, 1985), 3–51.

4. Bruno, quoted by G. N. G. Orsini, "Genres," *Princeton Encyclopedia of Poetry and Poetics*, ed. Alex Preminger and others (Princeton: Princeton University Press, 1965), 308.

5. "Works need not coincide with categories, which have merely a constructed existence; a work can, for example, manifest more than one category, more than one genre" (Tzvetan Todorov, *The Fantastic: A Structural Approach to a Literary Genre* [Cleveland: Press of Case Western Reserve University, 1973], 22).

6. Quoted by Tzvetan Todorov, "The Origin of Genres," *New Literary History* 8 (1976): 159–70, at 159.

7. Jacques Derrida, "La loi du genre/The Law of Genre," *Glyph* 7 (1980): 176–232.

8. As paraphrased by Rosmarin, *Power of Genre*, 14.

9. E. H. Gombrich, *Art and Illusion: A Study in the Pyschology of Pictorial Representation*, 2d ed. (Princeton: Princeton University Press, 1961), 100.

10. Ibid., 88, 100.

11. Ibid., 271, 316–17, 321.

12. For a linguistic approach to genre, "spoken or written, with or without literary aspirations," see John M. Swales, *Genre Analysis: English in Academic and Research Settings* (Cambridge: Cambridge University Press, 1990), 33–67. Among the many kinds of spoken genres mentioned by Swales are the presidential press conference, the sermon, the lecture, the telephone conversation, and ordering a meal in a restaurant. Swales develops a model for the relation between genres and schemata, or "prior knowledge structures" (83–92), observing that "Human beings consistently overlay schemata on events to align those events with previously established patterns of experience, knowledge, and belief" (83).

13. "Empson puts together, as versions of pastoral, As You Like It, The Beggar's Opera, Alice in Wonderland. The Brothers Karamazov is put with other murder mysteries" (René Wellek and Austin Warren, "Literary Genres," in *Theory of Literature*, 3d ed. [New York: Harcourt, Brace & World, 1956], 227).

14. Rosmarin, *Power of Genre*, 44. "Une transgression (partielle) du genre est presque requise: sinon, l'œuvre manquera du minimum d'originalité nécessaire (cette exigence-là a beaucoup varié suivant les époques)" (A partial transgression of genre is almost required: otherwise the work will lack the necessary minimum of originality. This requirement has varied greatly from period to period) (Oswald Ducrot and Tzvetan Todorov, "Genres littéraires," in *Dictionnaire encyclopédique des sciences du langage* [Paris: Seuil, 1972], 195).

15. "The more stereotypically a text repeats the generic, the more inferior is its artistic character and its degree of historicity" (Hans Robert Jauss, "Theory of Genres and Medieval Literature," *Toward an Aesthetic of Reception*, trans. Timothy Bahti [Minneapolis: University of Minnesota Press, 1982], 89).

16. "Genre has in recent years become associated with a disreputably formulaic way of constructing (or aiding the construction of) particular texts—a kind or writing or speaking by numbers. This association characterizes genre as mere mechanism, and hence is [read "as"?] inimical to the enlightened and enlightening concept that language is ultimately a matter of *choice*" (Swales, *Genre Analysis*, 33; his italics).

17. Frederick Garber, G. N. G. Orsini, and T. V. F. Brogan, "Genre," *The New Princeton Encyclopedia of Poetry and Poetics*, ed. Alex Preminger and T. V. F. Brogan (Princeton: Princeton University Press, 1993), 457. In the original *Princeton Encyclopedia of Poetry and Poetics*, the article by Orsini ("Genres") claimed that Plato and Aristotle

recognized lyric poetry implicitly as one member of the tripartite system, but that their attention focused more sharply on the other two. Ducrot and Todorov also attribute the tripartite concept to Plato (*Dictionnaire encyclopédique des sciences du langage,* 198).

18. Jauss, in "Theory of Genres and Medieval Literature" (83), developed a partial system of generic functions for the epic, the romance, and the novella. Paul Zumthor, in his *Essai de poétique médiévale* (Paris: Seuil, 1972), took the trouvère love song, which he called the *grand chant courtois,* as the cornerstone of his analysis of genre in Old French, including narrative genres and theater. Simon Gaunt has analyzed gender ideology in four Old French genres (epic, romance, saints' lives, fabliaux) and the Occitan *canso,* but does not address the problem of generic status as such: see his *Gender and Genre in Medieval French Literature* (Cambridge: Cambridge University Press, 1995). For a sweeping vision of literary kinds in western tradition see Northrop Frye, *The Anatomy of Criticism: Four Essays* (Princeton: Princeton University Press, 1957); for an overview of "systems of genre," see Alastair Fowler, *Kinds of Literature: An Introduction to the Theory of Genres and Modes* (Cambridge, Mass.: Harvard University Press, 1982), 235–55.

19. This is not to say that they called it lyric, which is an eighteenth-century term; see my essay following.

20. On such intergeneric effects see Nancy Freeman Regalado, "Gathering the Works: The 'Oeuvres de Villon' and the Intergeneric Passage of the Medieval French Lyric into Single-Author Collections," *Esprit créateur* 33, no.4 (1993): 87–100.

21. Joachim du Bellay begged the aspiring poet to abandon "toutes ces vieilles poësies francoyses . . . comme rondeaux, ballades, vyrelaiz, chantz royaulx, chansons et autres telles episseries, qui corrumpent le goust de nostre langue, et ne servent si non à porter temoingnaige de notre ignorance" (all those old French poems . . . like rondeaux, ballades, virelais, *chants royaux,* songs, and other such spices, which corrupt the taste of our language and serve only to bear witness to our ignorance) (*La deffence et illustration de la langue francoyse* [1549], book 2, chap. 4, ed. Henri Chamard [Paris: Albert Fontemoing, 1904], 201–3). On the evolution of French genre systems from Old French to Middle French and into the French Renaissance, see my "Christine de Pizan and the Transformation of Late Medieval Lyrical Genres," in *Christine de Pizan and Medieval French Lyric,* ed. Earl Jeffrey Richards (Gainesville: University of Florida Press, 1998), 27–49.

22. H. Ansgar Kelly, "Interpretation of Genres and by Genres in the Middle Ages," in *Interpretation: Medieval and Modern,* ed. Piero Boitani and Anna Torti (Cambridge: D. S. Brewer, 1993), 107–22. On tragedy and comedy in Dante see Amilcare A. Iannucci, "Dante's Theory of Genres and the *Divina Commedia,*" *Dante Studies* 91 (1973): 1–25. Iannucci argues that Dante's statements about genre must be considered diachronically; "Dante articulates different theories of genres depending on when he is writing, and for what purpose. His views on art are not static but dynamic and expanding, and they undergo major revisions as his experience grows and his outlook on life changes" (3–4).

23. On commentary see A. J. Minnis, *Medieval Theory of Authorship: Scholastic Literary Attitudes in the Later Middle Ages,* 2d ed. (Philadelphia: University of Pennsylvania Press, 1988), which makes slight mention of genre. On rhetoric, see James J. Murphy, "Poetry without Genre: The Metapoetics of the Middle Ages," *Poetica: An*

International Journal of Linguistic-Literary Studies (Tokyo) 11 (1979): 1–8. For a study of rhetorical variation within romance see Scott D. Troyan, "Rhetoric without Genre: Orality, Textuality and the Shifting Scene of the Rhetorical Situation in the Middle Ages," *Romanic Review* 81 (1990): 378–95.

24. In Kentucky bluegrass music, the only distinctions readily made are those between tunes (instrumental pieces without words) and songs (with words); gospel songs are recognized, but there are no terms for other kinds (John Wright, personal communication).

25. On genre as institution see Wellek and Warren, *Theory of Literature*, 226.

26. The concept of intergenre represents an attempt to break away from the constraints of traditional genres, but assumes their independent status as a point of departure and rarely goes beyond synchronic analysis to recognize the fluidity of genres in history. See the useful essays published in *Esprit Créateur* 33, no.4 (1993), especially Sara Sturm-Maddox and Donald Maddox, "*Genre* and *Intergenre* in Medieval French Literature" (3–9); Kathryn Gravdal, "Poem Unlimited: Medieval Genre Theory and the Fabliau" (10–17); Jeff Rider, "Genre, Antigenre, Intergenre" (18–26). An outstanding contribution combining intergenre with diachrony is Regalado, "Gathering the Works."

27. Cf. Rosmarin, *Power of Genre*, 46.

28. Herbert Muschamp, "The Miracle in Bilbao," *New York Times Magazine*, Sept. 7, 1997, 54+.

PART 1

Genres in History

CHAPTER 1

The System of Genres in Troubadour Lyric

WILLIAM D. PADEN

In what sense may we speak of a system of the troubadour lyric genres? I first encountered the system myself when I began to study the troubadours in the *Anthology* edited by Hill and Bergin, with its heading over each poem identifying the poem's genre and its table of "genres of lyrics" at the end.[1] That table lists twenty-five genres, from the most numerous, the *canso* (love song) with thirty-two examples in Hill and Bergin, and the *sirventes* (satire) with twenty-five, to the *tenso* (debate) with twelve; the *vers*, an early term for song, with seven; the *alba* (dawn song) and the *planh* (lament), with six apiece; the crusade song and the *pastorela* (song about a shepherdess), with four apiece; down to the *dansa* (dance song), with two. Quite a few types are represented in this anthology by only one example, running alphabetically through the *descort* (song of discord), the *enueg* (song of annoyance), the *escondich* (excuse), the *esdemessa* (effort), the *estampida* (perhaps uproar, racket), the *estribot* (of uncertain meaning), the *fabla* (fable), the *flabel* (little fable), the letter, the *miei-sirventes* (half-sirventes), the *no-sai-que-s'es* (I-don't-know-what-it-is), the *plazer* (song of pleasure), a poem to the Virgin, the *serena* (evening song), the *sestina* (a metrical form involving the repetition of rhyme-words through various positions in succeeding stanzas), and the *vanto* (boast). Although this list seems to include a lot of rather disparate notions, as a student I did not pause to reflect long on the provenance or utility of each one, but simply accepted them all, provisionally at least, on the authority of the editors.

This list implies that each troubadour poem belongs to a genre, since there seem to be no poems that defy generic categorization (not even the *no-sai-que-s'es* by Raimbaut d'Aurenga). Furthermore it implies that each poem belongs unambiguously to only one genre, since there seem to be no messy overlaps, cross-references, or parentheses among the genres named. The list categorizes all the poems selected by the editors into a sort of pigeon coop, with no difficulty over which pigeonhole to put any poem into and no difficulty over holes that might connect with other holes, or contain no pigeons, or pose other problems. Although the genres in the list are ranged in alphabetical order, the student learns soon enough that there are interesting relations among certain ones among them. Thus the *canso* on love usually adopts a new metrical form, and the *sirventes* on politics or morality frequently imitates the specific metrical form of a *canso*. The *vers* seems to be an early form of the *canso*.[2] Genres in dialogue include the *tenso* and the *pastorela*. We have paired sets of genres such as the *sirventes* and the *miei-sirventes,* the *enueg* and the *plazer,* the *alba* and the *serena*. Some genres are musical, such as the *dansa* and the *estampida*. The system offers variety of theme within a stable and inclusive pattern.

The same impression is fortified by reference to compendia of information on troubadour lyrics such as the *Bibliographie der Troubadours* of Pillet and Carstens or the *Répertoire métrique* of István Frank.[3] In both these works the full listing of all troubadour lyrics known to the editor includes a generic identification of each one. In what follows I shall first explore the taxonomic implications of the more recent of the two works, Frank's *Répertoire*. Second, I shall turn to a historical view, asking how the system developed. I shall argue that the concept of genre grew up simultaneously with the poems themselves, starting at ground zero with the earliest troubadours, and that therefore many poems we categorize in this or that genre cannot have been so intended, since the concepts of the genres did not yet exist when the poems were written. Third, I shall attempt to place the development of genres within the larger context of poetic and cultural practice. Finally I shall make a case study of one poem, the *canso* by the trobairitz Azalais de Porcairagues, attempting to show that the sense of genre which informs it—very different from the concept later codified in the arts of poetry—provides a key to understanding the song.

Evolving Generic Practice

Although Frank may well have intended his generic identifications as no more than a set of handy tags, their sum total constitutes an all-embracing characterization of the generic structure of troubadour lyric. By computerizing the Pillet-Carstens number of each poem with its genre according to Frank, we may make that characterization visible, as though we were developing an exposed film into a photograph.

Table 1.1 shows, first, that there are 2,552 troubadour poems listed by Frank—and not 2,542, as he said himself.[4] I can explain the discrepancy only by observing that Frank had no computer at his disposal. As we see in figure 1.1, the *chanson,* as Frank calls the *canso,* accounts for about 1,000 poems, or approximately 40 percent of the total; the *sirventes* for a few more than 500, actually 21 percent; the *cobla* for a few less, actually 19 percent; and all the rest of the genres account for the the remaining 500-odd poems, the last 20 percent.[5] These relative proportions are not what we might have expected, considering that the *cobla* has been discussed and analyzed far less than the *sirventes* or the *canso*—so much less that it is conspicuously (but understandably) absent from the table of genres in Hill and Bergin.[6]

Nor might we have expected that only three genres would prove so dominant in numerical terms, and that the others would turn out to be so much less frequent. The three major genres—the *canso,* the *sirventes,* and the *cobla*—account for 80 percent of the extant troubadour poetry. The remaining

Figure 1.1. Occitan Genres

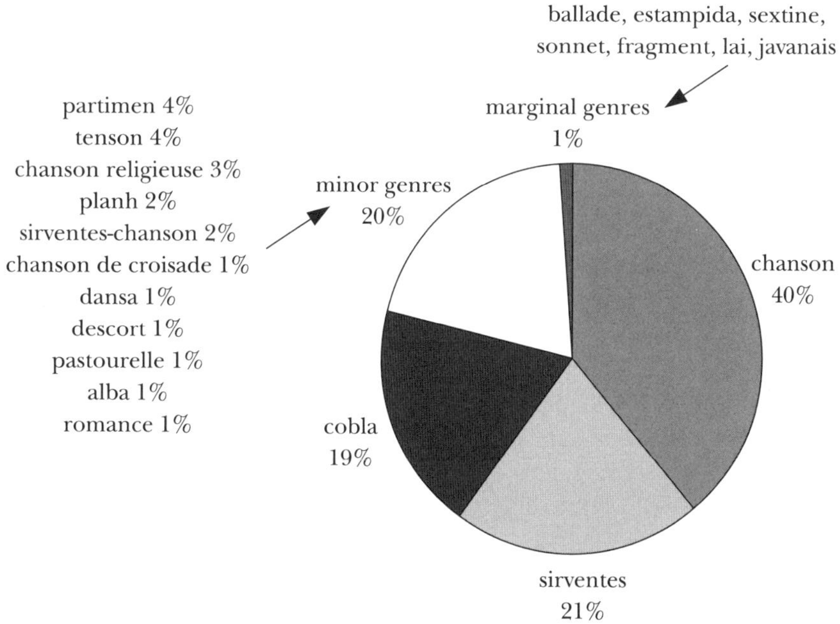

ballade, estampida, sextine,
sonnet, fragment, lai, javanais

partimen 4%
tenson 4%
chanson religieuse 3%
planh 2%
sirventes-chanson 2%
chanson de croisade 1%
dansa 1%
descort 1%
pastourelle 1%
alba 1%
romance 1%

marginal genres
1%

minor genres
20%

chanson
40%

cobla
19%

sirventes
21%

20 percent includes eleven genres which I shall call "minor" on strictly numerical grounds; they are, in Frank's terms and in descending order of frequency, the *partimen*, the *tenson*, the *chanson religieuse*, the *planh*, the *sirventes-chanson*, the *chanson de croisade*, the *dansa*, the *descort*, the *pastourelle*, the *alba*, and the *romance*. After another leap to a lower range of frequencies we find a third subset of genres which I shall call "marginal," represented by under ten examples apiece. They include the *ballade*, the *estampida*, the *sextine*, the *sonnet*, the *fragment* (of an unrecognizable genre), the *lai*, and the *javanais*.[7] Frank characterized the entire troubadour corpus in terms of twenty-one genres, three which I call major, eleven minor, and seven marginal.[8]

We may push our analysis a step further by introducing a chronological feature for each poem. I suggest doing so by determining the midpoint of the author's career. This technique accommodates cases in which we know only a single year for some of the obscure troubadours, as well as cases in which we have a period of poetic activity or, more rarely, dates of birth and death. Once having determined the midpoint of an author's career, we may place his or her work in an appropriate segment of forty years, five of which make up the two centuries of troubadour practice. I shall call these periods 1 through 5; they may be illustrated by reference to Guilhem IX (period 1), Raimbaut d'Aurenga (period 2), Bertran de Born (period 3), Peire Cardenal (period 4), and Guiraut Riquier (period 5).[9] Of course a single poem may have been written long before or after the midpoint of the author's career, perhaps in a preceding or following period of forty years; but any attempt to specify the chronology of 2,552 individual poems would soon embroil us in difficulty. In any case it is unlikely that a poem was actually written two periods away from the midpoint of the author's career, that is, at least forty-two years sooner or later.[10] This technique is therefore unlikely to err in dating a given poem by more than one period. It offers a practical means to form an overview of the chronological evolution of the genre system.

Figure 1.2 presents an outline of troubadour production broken down into five periods. As you see, production begins with a small number, rises rapidly to the very productive third period, and then falls off less rapidly. The rise from period 1 to period 3 represents the conundrum of origins: do we have so few texts from the earliest periods because few were composed, or because few were preserved? The fall from period 3 to period 5 represents the problem of decline: it has often been said that the troubadours gradually slowed their production because of the effects of the Albigensian Crusade in 1209–29, at the end of period 3 and the beginning of period 4 (but I doubt it, for reasons I have explained elsewhere); perhaps the decline was an effect of inanition, the internal exhaustion of their lim-

Figure 1.2. Genres in Periods 1-5 (Poems)

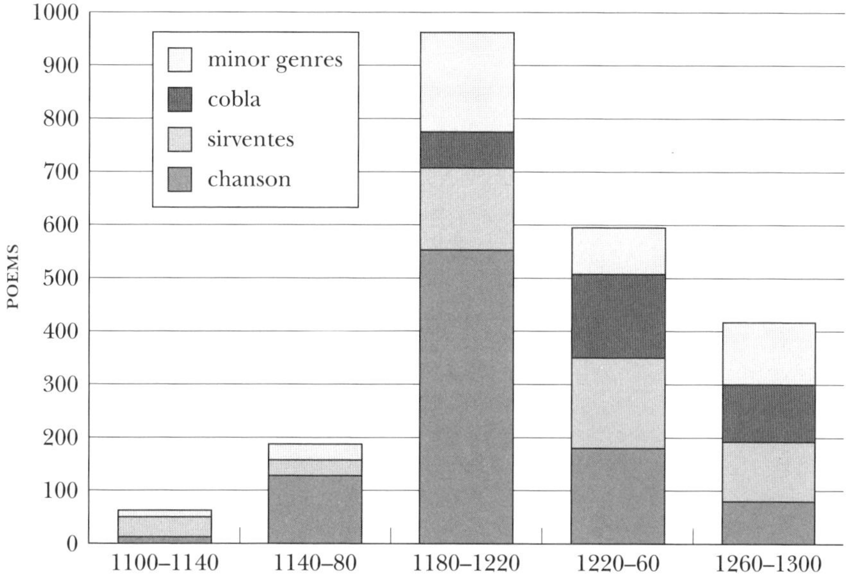

ited range of themes; more likely it was caused by a shift in linguistic prestige to French.[11]

Figure 1.3 further details the relative importance of the three major genres within each period. The relative dominance of the *sirventes* within period 1 reflects the work of Marcabru, whose activity is dated 1130–49; the midpoint of his career falls at 1139.5, barely within period 1. In period 2 the *canso* accounts for the majority of all poems, with over 70 percent; it still does so, but with less than 60 percent of all production, in period 3; in period 4 the *canso* is reduced to about a quarter of all poems, and in period 5 to about a fifth. The successive losses to the *canso* are made up in period 3, in part, by the gain of the *sirventes,* which grows stronger yet in period 4, then somewhat weaker in period 5, though it still remains important. But it is the *cobla* which registers the most spectacular gains after negligible presence in periods 1 and 2, winning a significant impact in period 3, greater yet in period 4, and almost as great in period 5. The minor genres, too, become suddenly numerous in period 3 and continue almost as strong in periods 4 and 5. It appears that the *canso* dominated all other genres in periods 2 and 3, to be supplanted by the combined effect of the *sirventes,* the *cobla,* and the minor genres in periods 4 and 5. As the thirteenth century progressed,

Figure 1.3. Genres in Periods 1-5 (Percentages)

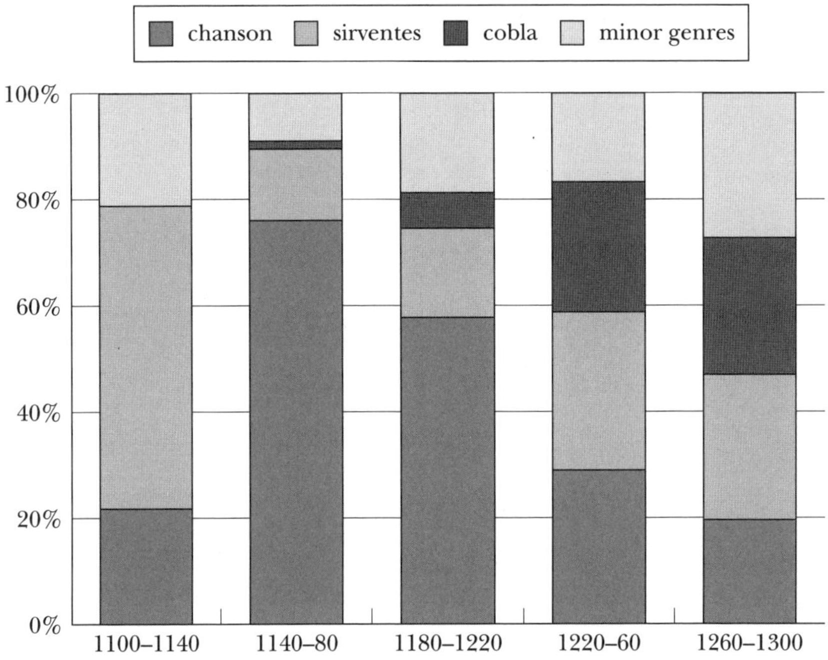

■ chanson ■ sirventes ■ cobla □ minor genres

troubadour production became less focused on *fin' amor* and opened onto a broader range of themes.

Table 1.1 presents the full range of data on all of Frank's twenty-one genres, broken down into periods 1 through 5, plus a period 6 for the work of some few poets whose midpoints fall in the fourteenth century, and period X for works I have found it impossible to locate chronologically.[12] The next-to-last column gives the total number of poems in each genre in descending order, and so underlies the composition of figure 1.1. The next-to-bottom row gives the totals per period, and so underlies figures 1.2 and 1.3.

The impression one gets from figure 1.3 regarding the evolution of dominance among genres becomes more specific and concrete in table 1.2. I have adapted a technique, standard in statistical analysis, by which one compares an observed result, here the observed number of poems in a given genre and period, with the result that might have been expected. One's expectation would be that the total number of poems in a given genre, say the thousand or so *cansos,* should be distributed across the various periods in proportion to the distribution of all poems in all genres across the periods.[13] For table 1.2 I have focused on periods 2 through 5 in order to see

Table 1.1. Genres by Periods

	Period 1	Period 2	Period 3	Period 4	Period 5	Period 6	Period X	Totals	% of N = 2552
Major Genres									
Chanson	13	136	546	178	80	3	55	1,011	40
Sirventes	34	25	162	175	114	5	18	533	21
Cobla	0	2	61	151	107	4	156	481	19
	47	163	769	504	301	12	229	2,025	79
Minor Genres									
Partimen	0	1	48	24	19	0	14	106	4.2
Tenson	0	6	39	19	12	0	13	89	3.5
Chanson religieuse	1	6	5	13	27	0	18	70	2.7
Planh	0	2	18	9	11	0	3	43	1.7
Sirventes-chanson	1	4	28	2	8	0	0	43	1.7
Chanson de croisade	2	1	17	6	9	1	0	36	1.4
Dansa	0	0	0	14	5	0	9	28	1.1
Descort	0	0	13	3	4	0	8	28	1.1
Pastourelle	2	0	7	0	14	0	3	26	1.0
Alba	0	0	6	2	5	0	4	17	0.7
Romance	7	1	2	0	2	0	1	13	0.5
	13	21	183	92	116	1	73	499	19.6
Marginal Genres									
Ballade	0	0	0	0	3	0	6	9	0.35
Estampida	0	0	1	0	5	1	0	7	0.27
Sextine	0	0	2	0	1	0	1	4	0.16
Sonnet	0	0	0	0	3	0	0	3	0.12
Fragment	0	0	1	0	0	0	1	2	0.08
Lai	0	0	0	0	0	0	2	2	0.08
Javanais	0	0	0	1	0	0	0	1	0.04
	0	0	4	1	12	1	10	28	1.10
Grand totals	60	184	956	597	429	14	312	2,552	
Percentage of N = 2552	2	7	37	23	17	1	12		

Key: Period 1 = 1100–1140; Period 2 = 1140–1180; Period 3 = 1180–1220; Period 4 = 1220–1260; Period 5 = 1260–1300; Period 6 = 1300–1340; Period X = unknown. *Note:* Columns may not add up because of rounding off.

more clearly what happened to the relative frequency of genres. Hence I have eliminated period 1, period 6, and period X, and I have also eliminated all the marginal genres and the *romance* because they are too few in number to provide meaningful statistical information. Because I was interested in an evolution from the middle of the troubadour era to the end, I combined periods 2 and 3 on the one hand, and periods 4 and 5 on the other. I then calculated the expected frequency of the remaining genres in each period, subtracted the expected number from the number observed, and organized the table in descending order of the results.

Table 1.2 shows that the genre system rotated from dominance by the *canso* and some of the minor genres to dominance by the *cobla*, the *sirventes*, and other minor genres. The *canso* was produced in far more than expected numbers in periods 2 and 3 (observed minus expected = 185). Its preeminence shifted in periods 4 and 5 most of all to the *cobla* (observed minus expected = 107), and rather less to the *sirventes* as well (observed minus expected = 65). Minor genres do not show so violent a shift, but rotate around the *partimen*, which appears in exactly the expected numbers in both these longer periods. Earlier the *sirventes-chanson*, the *tenson*, the *descort*, and the *chanson de croisade* were somewhat favored along with the *canso*. Later they were displaced by the *alba*, the *planh*, the pastourelle, the *dansa*, and the *chanson religieuse*, along with the *sirventes* and the *cobla*.

This result demonstrates that from one eighty-year period to another (from 1140–1220 to 1220–1300), the genre system shifted from one well-

Table 1.2. Rotating the System

Periods	Observed			Expected		Observed-Expected	
	2 and 3	4 and 5	Total 2–5	2 and 3	4 and 5	2 and 3	4 and 5
Chanson	682	258	940	497	443	185	–185
Sirventes-chanson	32	10	42	22	20	10	–10
Tenson	45	31	76	40	36	5	–5
Descort	13	7	20	11	9	2	–2
Chanson de croisade	18	15	33	17	16	1	–1
Partimen	49	43	92	49	43	0	0
Alba	6	7	13	7	6	–1	1
Planh	20	20	40	21	19	–1	1
Pastourelle	7	14	21	11	10	–4	4
Dansa	0	19	19	10	9	–10	10
Chanson religieuse	11	40	51	27	24	–16	16
Sirventes	187	289	476	252	224	–65	65
Cobla	63	258	321	170	151	–107	107
	1,133	1,011	2,144				

defined set of preferences to another. The domination by the *canso,* which continues to this day in our association of the troubadours with *fin' amor* above all other themes, yielded in the last eighty years to a more diverse tonality. This analysis contradicts the perpetually haunting suspicion that all troubadours were really alike, and that their production had no history.[14]

Development of the Genre Concept

The foregoing analysis, though diachronic in the breakdown of periods, was resolutely synchronic in the tools it used to sort the songs into genres. The names Frank used for the genres grew out of history in many different ways but became instruments for his taxonomy, presumably, because they struck him as coherent, unambiguous, and therefore useful. He selected names from among those suggested by history, excluding a number of those listed by Hill and Bergin: the *esdemessa,* the *estribot,* the *fabla,* the *flabel,* the letter, the *miei-sirventes,* the *no-sai-que-s'es,* the *plazer,* the poem to the Virgin, the *serena,* the *vanto,* and the *vers.* Each of these terms has some sort of origin in troubadour composition; each of the poems identified with these terms in Hill and Bergin turns up in Frank's list with one of his twenty-one names. I could also point out that there are cases in which Frank put the pigeon into a different hole from the one chosen by Pillet and Carstens in the *Bibliographie.* There are uncertainties, for example, over the difference between the *tenso* and the *partimen.*[15] Furthermore some of the names Frank uses are conspicuously postmedieval. The term *romance* corresponds, in Old Occitan, neither to *roman* (novel) nor to *romans* (vernacular language, written in vernacular language).[16] *Chanson de croisade* depends on the modern distinction of crusade from pilgrimage, and even as seemingly self-evident a genre as the *chanson religieuse* actually corresponds to no term in troubadour usage.[17] The clarity of our figures was purchased at the price of a certain truth to history.

I am interested, however, in a more radical infidelity. In historical consciousness the system of the genres evolved with dramatic rapidity after beginning at a generic tabula rasa, as Pierre Bec demonstrated in 1982.[18] Bec showed that among the earliest troubadours, Guilhem IX, Jaufre Rudel, Marcabru, and Cercamon, there occur no operative terms or concepts of genres within the domain of lyric song. Marcabru did not call his own poems *sirventes,* although they are generally known as *sirventes* among scholars like Frank who apply the later term; rather he called them simply *vers* (songs).[19] The fundamental distinction between *canso* and *sirventes* appeared fleetingly in Bernart Marti in the mid-twelfth century,[20] but remained innocent at first of its eventual authority. Bernart de Ventadorn used *canso* and *vers* synonymously for "song" in general, with no generic distinction intended.[21] Bertran de Born applied the term *sirventes* to exactly the poems to which Frank applies it in Bertran's own work, but Bertran has no distinctive term for love songs, even though he wrote a significant number of them (five according to Frank). He identifies his love songs as *canso* or *chan* (exceptionally as *d'amor chan* [a song of love]) or *chantar,* and applies both *sirventes* and *canso* (song) to two of his poems without the slightest contradiction.[22] If Bertran did not contrast *sirventes* to *canso,* we cannot say he intended the term *sirventes* just as later writers, both medieval and modern, have intended it. If the *canso* and the *sirventes* were not distinct in the practice of Bertran de Born, one need scarcely ask whether he entertained opinions about a hybrid form which some scholars call the *sirventes-canso,* or whether he intended to write one.[23] The expression *partir un joc* evolved into the generic term *joc partit* only late in the twelfth century.[24] The *albas,* with their generic marker in the word itself, appear to have been composed from the late twelfth to the mid-thirteenth century.[25] The *cobla,* which would eventually become as numerous as the *sirventes* or the minor genres altogether, seems to have been recognized as a genre in the 1190s.[26]

The orderly list of genres which modern readers bring to their reading of troubadour lyric song may be found emerging into clarity in the evolution of the Occitan poetic treatises. In the earliest, the *Razos de trobar* written at the beginning of the thirteenth century (perhaps in period 3) by Raimon Vidal de Besalù in Catalonia, there is no extensive discussion or analysis of the lyric genres, although Raimon declares the Occitan language better suited than French for composing "vers e cansons et serventes."[27] Elsewhere Raimon applies *canso* in passing to two love poems, but he nowhere explains what any of these terms means. It therefore comes as a pointed corrective when, in the second half of the century (in period 4 or 5), the anonymous Catalan author of the *Doctrina de compondre dictats* devotes his treatise entirely to "the content and the form, both metrical and musical, of the various poetic genres," beginning with assurances that the attentive reader will learn to compose correctly no fewer than sixteen distinct types: "canço, vers, lays, serventesch, retronxa [or song with a refrain], pastora, dança, plant [the planh, or lament], alba, gayta [or song of a watchman, doubtless akin to the alba], estampida, sompni [dream], gelozesca [song of jealousy], discort, cobles esparses [individual stanzas], tenso."[28] Perhaps independently of the *Doctrina de compondre dictats,* another Catalan author composed an anonymous treatise contained in a manuscript from

Ripoll, "in the last decade of the thirteenth century or the first half of the fourteenth" (in period 5 or 6), in which he expounded the differences between eight genres: "cançons, tençons, sirventesch, cobles, vers, dançes [songs of love to please a lady], desdançes [songs of anger to displease a lady], e viaderes [a kind of dance song]."[29] Such doctrines demonstrate the central position of a system, or at least a list, of genres in the critical and poetic mentality of the time.

About 1340 Guilhem Molinier, author of the *Leys d'amors,* proposed eleven principal genres and seventeen nonprincipal ones ("no-principals").[30] He failed to mention the *cobla,* with its 481 extant examples, or Frank's *chanson religieuse, sirventes-chanson, chanson de croisade, alba, romance, ballade, sextine, sonnet, fragment, lai,* or *javanais.* To the remaining nine terms employed by Frank he added, as principal genres, the *vers,* the *retroncha* (song with a refrain), and the *escondig* (excuse); as nonprincipal ones he added the *somi* (dream), the *vezio* (vision), the *cossir* (song of care), the *reversari* (song of antitheses), the *enueg* (annoyance), the *desplazer* (displeasure), the *desconort* (discomfort), the *plazer* (pleasure), the *conort* (comfort), the *rebec* (of uncertain meaning, perhaps a musical form), the *relay* (moment of respite), the *gilozesca* (song of jealousy), the *bal* (ball, a dance song), the *garip* (a type of melody without words), the *redondel* (rondeau), and the *viandela* (a dance song).

Guilhem distinguished significantly between what he called the "principal genres" and the "nonprincipal" ones in terms of liberty of the poet. His definitions of the principal genres are consistently authoritarian in tone.[31] For example, the *canso:*

> Chansos . . . deu tractar principalmen d'amors o de lauzors. . . . En chanso no deu hom pauzar deguna laia paraula. . . . Hom que·s red enamoratz, no solamen en sos faytz se deu mostrar cortes, ans o deu far ysshamens en sos digz et en son parlar. Chansos deu haver so pauzat.[32]
>
> A *chanson* must deal principally with love or with praise. . . . In a *chanson* one must not put any unseemly word. . . . A man who falls in love must not only show himself to be courtly in his deeds, but must do likewise in his words and in his speech. A *chanson* must have a stately melody.

But Guilhem defines the nonprincipal genres in terms of freedom of will, *voluntat:*

> Autres dictatz pot hom far et ad aquels nom enpauzar segon la voluntat de cel que dicta, e segon que requier le dictatz. . . . Et en aytals dictatz no trobam cert nombre de coblas, per que en aytals dictatz pot hom far aytantas coblas quo·s vol. . . . Hom fa lo dictat de bal, tractan d'amors o

> de lauzors or d'autra materia honesta, segon la volontat del dictayre....
> Aytals dictatz no-principals pot haver tornada o no; e pot hom en loc de tornada repetir la una cobla del comensamen o de la fi.[33]

> One may compose other genres and give them names according to the will of the one who writes, and according to what the genre requires.... And in such genres we do not find a set number of stanzas, because in such genres one may compose as many stanzas as one chooses.... One composes the genre of the *bal*, dealing with love or praise or another decorous subject, according to the will of the poet.... Such a nonprincipal genre can have a *tornada* or not; and one may, instead of a *tornada*, repeat a stanza from the beginning or the end.

Thus, on the one hand, the system of the principal genres became an authoritative, retrospective generic grid, while on the other, the nonprincipal genres opened possibilities of free invention which implied a different concept of genre altogether, genre as a means of description rather than one of prescription, as a characterization rather than a category in a system.

All this means that if we look back to our figures, we realize that they are radically ahistorical. By the time of the *Doctrina de compondre dictats* eleven of Frank's twenty-one genres had crystallized, including his three major ones and half of his minor ones, but not the other half, comprising the *partimen*, the *chanson religieuse*, the *sirventes-chanson*, the *chanson de croisade*, and the *romance*. Earlier on, however, at the time when many troubadour songs were composed, the genres into which we sort them were not functional concepts. Figure 1.2 broke the major genres into periods, but we cannot be sure that the *canso, sirventes,* and *cobla* were distinctive concepts in the minds of the troubadours or their public until at least as late as period 3. Figure 1.1, innocent of the attempt at periodization, nevertheless counts many poems as members of this or that genre, even though the idea of the genre did not exist at the time when the songs were composed. A figure of troubadour songs composed intentionally as members of various genres would have to show the genre concepts themselves becoming distinct with the passage of time; if it did not, but only showed poems composed intentionally as members of the genre system, it would represent perhaps half or less of the songs we have been discussing, and might look very different from the figures we have seen. The system of the genres is not intrinsic in all the material being systematized or contemporary with all the songs. It grew up during the activity of the later troubadours and continued to develop after they had ceased to compose.

Furthermore the slender production of poetry in Middle Occitan, which was contemporary with the codification of troubadour genres in the *Leys d'amors*, appears to have favored the freedom of the nonprincipal genres rather than the authority of the principal ones.[34] In this poetry genre terms sometimes revert to their early, undifferentiated usage, as when "canso" is used of a *sirventes* (469,1), or when "vers" is used of a *chanson* (482,2 etc.), a *chanson religieuse* (463,1 etc.), a *sirventes* (464,2 etc.), or a *tenso* (558,9). In such cases "canso" and "vers" seem to be synonymous general terms for "song." Other genre terms are used loosely: "sirventes" is applied to a *chanson religieuse* (472,1 etc.) or a *chanson de croisade* (544,1), "planh" to a *sirventes* (474,4), "pastorela" to a *chanson de croisade* (474,3). Middle Occitan poems are frequently identified in the manuscripts not only by genre but also in terms of their metrical technique, as in a "canso de Nostra Dona, retrogradada" (a song of Our Lady with retrograde rhymes") (473,1); a "canso de Nostra Dona, ams rims maridatz, alias dirivatius" (a song of Our Lady with married rhymes, also known as derivative) (491,1); or a "canço retrogradada per diccios e per bordos e per coblas" (a song with retrograde words, rhymes, and stanzas) (518,11). Individual songs are identified with terms such as *complanh moral* (moral complaint), *conseyll* (counsel), *corona* (crown, a type of computus, or poem of astronomical computation), *gardacors de mal* (bodyguard against harm), *gesta* (song of deeds), *porquiera* (song about a pig-girl), *truffa* (trifle), which do not categorize them within a generic system but simply describe them.[35] These terms reflect the freedom endorsed by Guilhem Molinier for nonprincipal genres. A freer, more supple and expressive practice threatened to supplant the system of the principal genres, based on a conventionalization of subject matter, at the very time when the system reached its most rigid formulation.

We look back at the troubadours and their world through a kaleidoscope of more recent lenses. Medieval studies, we are told, were founded in the period from 1895 to about 1965.[36] The nineteenth century saw the coinage of the words "medieval" and "medievalist," the invention of the concept of the Romance languages, and the distinction in architectural history between Gothic and Romanesque.[37] The nineteenth century also saw the term "Renaissance" first established as the general designation for that period.[38] In the eighteenth century the word "lyrique" was first applied to poetry in the modern manner.[39] The seventeenth century witnessed the birth of the modern notion of literature; during that period, too, vernacular lyric was treated as great literature for the first time, as it had not been by Petrarch or Shakespeare.[40] The sixteenth century, more or less, invented the concept of the Middle Ages.[41]

In their own time, therefore, the world of the troubadours had no notion of a Middle Age or of a distinction between Romanesque and Gothic, much less an inkling of medieval studies or the Renaissance. Medieval people had no idea of the Romance languages. The troubadours lacked our concepts of literature and of lyric poetry. And yet we apply these notions to the study of the troubadours. When we look back onto a distant past, we have no choice but to commit anachronism, whether flagrant or subtle, deliberate or unintended. Hence the partial, staggered anachronism of the genre system does not undermine it or expose it as invalid. Rather, by realizing its ahistoricity we may learn to understand better what we do when we read in genres, and to judge better their usefulness. We need to ask how and why this system came to be built.

A Dynamic Context

The troubadour experience rode the cultural groundswell which we call the Middle Ages. Elsewhere I have suggested defining the Middle Ages as the period of sociolinguistic transition between an early stage, when the high language throughout Western Europe was Latin while the low language in each place was the local vernacular, and a late stage when newly prestigious vernaculars rose up to challenge Latin for authority.[42] Such a definition can shed light, I believe, on the development of the genre system within the larger evolution of troubadour practice.

The gradual monumentalization of vernaculars required them to pass from orality to literacy and enabled them to assume the many functions of written language. This process may be traced in the troubadours themselves from Guilhem IX's jocular claim to the title of *maistre certa* (a sure master, in song and in sex) to Guiraut Riquier's heartfelt petition for the degree of *doctor de trobar* (a Ph.D. in composition).[43] Intermediate steps, or processes, which developed during the twelfth century included the creation of *trobar clus* (closed style) as distinct from *trobar leu* (easy style); the progressive institutionalization of contrafacture (metrical imitation) as the principle of the *sirventes;* and the differentiation of the genres. In the thirteenth century a new stage was reached when lyric technique became the object of book-length study in the *Razos de trobar* and the *Donatz provensals,* and when the poets and their texts began to inspire *vidas* and *razos.*

The movement which had begun in the anticlericalism of Guilhem IX eventuated in the development of the *chanson religieuse* and the ecclesiastical outlook of the *Breviari d'amor,* in which Matfre Ermengau asserted, around 1288, that *fin' amor* naturally culminated in marriage and love of children. Matfre pioneered in the anthologizing of troubadour lyric, along with his Italian contemporary Ferrari de Ferrara. In his day the first dated troubadour chansonnier, MS *D* at Modena (dated 1254 in the colophon), was several decades old; other manuscripts would soon be compiled which we date at the end of the thirteenth century or the beginning of the fourteenth. Most of these anthologies are organized according to genre, beginning with the *canso*, which corresponds to the Italian *canzone*, the most prestigious lyric form in the peninsula at the time when the manuscripts were produced; others are organized according to author. As Marshall points out, "we have extant sources which transmit this poetry to us precisely from the moment when the poetry itself was ceasing to be a living thing in its native land."[44] These manuscripts provide the first systematic identification of individual songs by genre, and so anticipate the listings by Hill and Bergin, Pillet and Carstens, and Frank.

Scholars differ in their views of transmission before the compilation of the surviving manuscripts, but musicologists tend to regard it as obvious that an original oral artform had yielded to written transmission. I have argued that we have another form of indirect evidence in the troubadours' frequent instructions to a *joglar* to perform the song.[45] Analysis of the incidence of such instructions reveals a steady decline over the twelfth and thirteenth centuries. If, as seems likely, the *joglars* were mostly illiterate, this steady decline in mentions made of them would correspond to a decline in memorial transmission and a corresponding increase in transmission through writing.

This sweeping process of monumentalization, to use Zumthor's term (or classicization if you prefer), brought the foundation in fourteenth-century Toulouse of the Consistori de la Subregaya Companhia del Gay Saber, with its annual contests in imitation of the classical troubadour genres. These contests, in which winners were crowned with a silver violet for the best imitation of a *canso*, a wild rose for the best *sirventes*, or a marigold for the best *dansa*, required a set of rules for accurate judgment, and these rules required prescriptive definitions of the genres. To these rules we owe the system of the lyric genres. In the manuscripts the genres represent a reading strategy; for the Consistori they became a writing strategy that locked into the systematic relation which has endured in the didactic tradition down to the present time.

As the art of the troubadours rose from the status of an oral entertainment and assumed increasing cultural authority, the system of the genres developed as one means of rationalizing, organizing, and enhancing their songs. The system remains available today, and useful for grasping the overall proportions of the subject. But we must take care not to invest it with factitious authority over our reading, and in particular we must avoid reading the early troubadours as though they were subservient to a genre system which in fact they were in the process of creating.

Azalais de Porcairagues

But what about the poets?

All that I have said means that the individual troubadour or trobairitz found himself or herself in a dynamic situation as regards genre. It is difficult for us to reconstruct with confidence and detail just what that situation was. The beginning of the evolution at generic point zero and its culmination in the *Leys d'amors* are clear, but the particular circumstances of an individual act of composition along the way can be ascertained, if at all, only by careful investigation. I will offer an example.

If, as the *Leys d'amors* declare, the *canso* expresses the feelings of a man in love,[46] then the genre must have undergone a significant inflection when first it was written by a woman. Such may have been the case when the trobairitz Azalais de Porcairagues composed her single surviving song, "Ar em al freg temps vengut" (Now we have come to the cold season).[47] Sakari has established that Azalais participated in a poetic exchange with the troubadour Raimbaut d'Aurenga and that in this song she grieves for his death, which occurred in May, 1173.[48] This is the earliest specifically datable trobairitz composition. It is the only one which we can be certain was written in the twelfth century, although several others may have been as well.[49]

In the tornada Azalais identifies her song as a *chanson,* balancing the opening stanza in which she laments that it is winter and no birds sing: "us de *chantar* non s'afraingna" (see Appendix: Version 1, lines 4 and 51). The *vida* which introduces this song in three manuscripts says that Azalais "fez . . . mantas bonas cansos,"[50] which may be taken to imply, since this is the only song we have by her, that the author of the *vida* considered it a *canso*. It is so identified by Pillet and Carstens (43,1) and by Frank (382:107).

But what did Azalais mean when she called this poem a *chanson?* Did she use the term as a general one, meaning simply "song," as Bertran de Born would do a few years later, or did she intend to describe this song, which focuses on mingled feelings of grief and love, as a *canso* in the specific sense, as a song of love? The problem is a general one, since, as Poe demonstrates in this volume, the term *cobla,* too, had both a general sense (stanza) and a specific one (member of the genre identified as the *cobla*). *Vers,* too, seems to have meant either "song" or "love song." *Tenso* could always mean either "dispute, quarrel" or "member of the genre called the *tenso*."[51] The interpretation of these words involves the whole history of genre among the troubadours and trobairitz.

For lack of other poems by Azalais we may turn to those by Raimbaut d'Aurenga as her most immediate context. We have forty-one poems by Raimbaut, listed by Frank as thirty-one *chansons,* six *sirventes,* two *tensos,* and two *sirventes-chansons.* One of those Frank identifies as a *sirventes* is the *No-sai-que-s'es,* and begins on the theme of lyric genres:

> Escotatz, mas no say que s'es
> Senhor, so que vuelh comensar.
> Vers, estribot, ni sirventes
> Non es, ni nom no·l sai trobar;
> Ni ges no say co·l me fezes
> S'aytal no·l podi'acabar,
>
> Que ia hom mays non vis fag aytal ad home ni a femna en est segle ni en l'autre qu'es passatz.[52]
>
> Listen, gentlemen, but I don't know what this which I am beginning is. It is not a *vers, estribot,* or *sirventes,* nor can I find a name for it; I do not know how I should construct it if I weren't able to finish it in such a way that one never saw its equal made by man or woman in this century or in the other which has passed.

Raimbaut declares flatly that his song is not a *sirventes,* as Frank calls it over the poet's protest. Nor is it anything else that Raimbaut can name; in Gombrich's terms, Raimbaut claims to have no schema in mind.[53] But we have learned from Gombrich that all creativity must involve a schema; even Raimbaut's denial implies that he has some idea that terms for kinds of lyric exist, so it may be legitimately taken as evidence that by the 1170s the idea of lyric genres was in the air. To be in the air, however, is far from having crystallized as the genres would do many years later in the arts of poetry. Raimbaut's terms *estribot* and *sirventes* were obviously in the air too—but if this passage offers an embryonic genre system it is a curious one, or very embryonic, since Raimbaut never used *estribot* or *sirventes* again in any of his extant works.[54] He never called his own songs *sirventes* (as Frank calls six of them); remember that Marcabru did not do so either.[55] In the present song Raimbaut is playing with the idea of lyric genre, most pointedly when he ends the stanza by breaking the bonds of lyric versification altogether and prattling on in prose.

Elsewhere Raimbaut uses the word *vers* to identify ten of his poems that Frank calls *chansons,*[56] in seeming anticipation of Frank's system. However, Raimbaut says in one of these poems that even though it is a *vers* he will call it a *canso,* because it has easy words, an easy melody, and a common, plain rhyme.[57] This statement seems to imply two things: first, that *vers* is the more general term and *canso* more specific, unless Raimbaut is simply lying, in a playful way, when he calls this song by both names; and second, that the *canso* is easier and the *vers* more difficult. Elsewhere he calls two poems *cansos* in contrast with *vers,* one a *canso* that is easy to dance to even though it has subtle rhymes (no. 4, lines 1–3), and the other an easy *canso* in contrast with more difficult *vers* (no. 18, lines 1–6).[58] It is not clear, then, whether the term *vers* can be more general than *canso*, but it is clear that Raimbaut makes a stylistic distinction between the two terms. We would be wrong to assume that either term, or both, is limited to singing of love, though, since he calls another song a *vers* twice, at the beginning and the end (no. 37, lines 3 and 58), which is a song of invective against the *lauzengiers,* identified as a *sirventes* by both Frank (item 160:3) and Pillet and Carstens (389,5). We recall that Raimbaut uses *sirventes* only once in his extant work, and then only to deny that the *No-sai-que-s'es* is a *sirventes.* In another text he says that he would like to make a *vers* (no. 7, line 3), but his lady doesn't want him to, so he gives the song in question no name at all.

Insofar as Raimbaut may be said to display a system of genres, then, it is based on a stylistic distinction between the easy *canso* and the more challenging *vers.* It is not truly a system, however, since he does not apply it systematically to all his songs but only to some of them, while leaving others nameless. Since Raimbaut does not distinguish love songs from satires, his concept is radically different from the system elaborated in the later arts of poetry and enshrined in our scholarly compendia. Raimbaut uses some of the terms which later became systematized in description of genres, although he does not use others such as *cobla, tenso, partimen, planh, dansa, descort, alba, balada, estampida,* or *sestina.* The use to which he puts them, however, is to make stylistic distinctions which are more closely related to terms such as *trobar leu*—compare his term *chanson leu* (no. 4, line 2, and no. 18, line 4)—and *trobar clus* than to what we call genre.[59]

If we may read Azalais de Porcairagues in the context provided by Raimbaut, therefore, it would appear that when she calls her single song a *chanson*, if she means anything more than that it is a song, she must mean that it is easy to perform—that it has easy words, an easy melody, and easy rhymes, to paraphrase Raimbaut. (In fact the rhymes of her song include none of those usually characterized as *rimas caras,* heavy with consonants.)[60] She does not define it generically in terms of theme, whether amorous, satirical, or something else. This correction in our sense of genre as Azalais may have intended it can contribute, I believe, to our understanding of her song in both historical and aesthetic ways.

Up to this point we have simplified matters by referring to Azalais's song as though it were simply one. In fact we have it in three distinct versions:[61]

—Version 1, represented in manuscripts *CDIKd* and fragmentarily in *H* (folio 57), comprises fifty-two lines which constitute six stanzas of eight lines apiece and one tornada of four lines.
—Version 2, in manuscript *N*, runs to fifty-six lines forming six stanzas and two tornadas.
—Version 3, in manuscript *H* (folio 46), has just sixteen lines comprising two stanzas.

In order to assess Azalais's sense of genre we must sort out the relations among these versions. The short one (Version 3) is found in manuscript *H*, which was compiled near Treviso in the last quarter of the thirteenth century.[62] These two stanzas with the rubric identifying them as *doas coblas* represent no doubt the practice of excerpting stanzas from preexisting songs which Poe identifies in this volume as "extracted *coblas*," one of four subtypes of the genre. This practice implies that the short version is a late one. The implication is supported by the chronology of the *cobla*, since the genre came into practice in the 1190s and Azalais's song must have been composed originally in 1173, the year when Raimbaut d'Aurenga died.[63]

Disentangling the relation between the two longer versions, 1 and 2, requires more care. Version 1 is represented in six manuscripts including the oldest specifically dated troubadour chansonnier, *D*, apparently compiled in 1254.[64] Version 2 occurs in manuscript *N*, perhaps compiled in the period 1285–1300, if not as late as the mid-fourteenth century.[65] Four of the manuscripts of Version 1 (*DIKd*) attribute the poem to Azalais, while it is anonymous in three manuscripts representing all three versions (*C*, containing Version 1; *N*, containing Version 2; and *H*, containing Version 3). A web of implications suggests that Version 1 is the original: it is attested by more manuscripts, including the earliest manuscript concerned, and by manuscripts informed about the authorship of the song, whereas Version 2 is attested only once, later, and anonymously.

It is easy to imagine the scribe of *N* (or the scribe of an earlier manuscript which led to *N*) adapting Version 1 to suit his judgment. To do so he created his first tornada out of four lines in the second stanza (Version 1, lines 13–16), while replacing those lines with four new ones. To compose these new lines he used two rhyme words already present in his exemplar (*fenida*, Version 2, lines 15 and 55 = Version 1, line 51; *garida*, Version 2, lines 16 and 32 = Version 1, line 32). He also introduced two new rhyme words (*esmai*, Version 2, line 13; *morai*, Version 2, line 14). These new rhyme words modified the pattern of rhymes in Version 1, where stanzas 1–4 are *coblas doblas*. In Version 2 the c-rhyme varies irregularly, -*ais* in stanzas 1 and 7, -*ai* in stanzas 2–6 and 8, so only stanzas 3 and 4 are true (but apparently accidental) *coblas doblas*. Version 2's first tornada varies from the usual pattern, too, since its first rhyme, *-ais,* is not identical to the rhyme *-ai* in corresponding position in the preceding stanza.

On this interpretation the original author, Azalais, came close to sustaining the form of *coblas doblas* throughout Version 1, though she did not do so completely since stanza 6 departs from the rhymes in stanza 5. The creative scribe of Version 2 lost sight of that principle altogether. This is not the only possible interpretation, since Azalais could have written Version 2, which would then have been regularized to a degree by an innovative scribe of Version 1. On balance, however, this view seems more plausible.

If Azalais wrote Version 1 and called it *ma chanson,* she contrasted it with the *chansons* of Raimbaut, for whom she grieved. The form of the piece resembles that of the *vers* Raimbaut said he would call a *canso* (Pattison no. 30). Raimbaut used a stanza of seven lines:

a7, a7, b7', c7, c7, d7, d7

And Azalais, one of eight:

a7, b7', a7, b7', c7, c7, d7', d7'

Azalais has adapted Raimbaut's form by inserting her eighth line in second position as a b-rhyme of seven syllables feminine, like Raimbaut's preexisting b-rhyme, and by substituting feminine rhymes for Raimbaut's masculine ones at the d-rhyme.

Her song also resembles another by Raimbaut (no. 15), a song without a generic name in the text which he addressed to *Joglar* (line 60)—presumably Azalais herself. It too has a stanza of seven lines:

a7, b7', c7', c7', d8, d8, d8

Here the metrical resemblance to Azalais's song is looser, since Raimbaut used octosyllabic lines for the d-rhyme, and the two rhyme schemes diverge more sharply. However, this poem begins with language that may have suggested words used by Azalais:

> Entre gel e vent e fanc
> E giscl'e gibr'e tempesta
> E·l braus pensars que·m turmenta
> De ma bella dompna genta
> M'an si mon cor vout en pantais . . .
> (Raimbaut, no. 15, lines 1–5)

The freezing cold and wind and mud and squalls and frost and storm and the grievous thought, concerning my beautiful, gentle lady, which torment me, have so agitated my heart . . .

Raimbaut's *gel* and masculine *fanc* may have inspired Azalais's *gel* and feminine *faingna* (Version 1, line 2).[66] The foul weather makes Raimbaut worry about his lady; Azalais, citing the foul weather, complains of her grievous disappointment and observes that we lose sooner than we gain. As she makes clear later, what she has lost is Raimbaut. When she says "D'Aurenga me moc l'esglais" (My grief began in Orange) (line 14), she echoes Raimbaut's use of *esglais* twice in this same poem, including once at the rhyme (no. 15, lines 23, 34).

Raimbaut would no doubt have called "Entre gel e vent e fanc" a *vers*, with its hard rhymes (*-anc, -esta, -enta, -ais*) and hard words (*giscle, gibre, pantais, biais*). He dwells on his vertiginous desire but digresses to curse the *lauzengiers* (no. 15, lines 27–31). Near the end he reveals his desire "to undress myself so I should be with you without vestment in that guise in which you are most gentle" (trans. Pattison, lines 51–53). Such outspoken eroticism creates a humorous effect which is foreign to the *canso* as defined in the arts of poetry, and reminiscent of similar effects in the love poetry of other self-confident lords such as Guilhem IX and Bertran de Born. In Raimbaut's other *vers* (no. 30, the one he said he would call a *canso*), in a form similar to that of Azalais's song, he upbraids the fools, the *fatz*, who criticize his hard words, and goes on to dispute the uncongenial view that a lady does wrong to love a powerful man—the theme of Azalais's stanza 3—before ending with praise of his lady, praise which will be especially deserved, he says, if she gives him what she should.

The variety of theme, both amorous and satirical, in these two poems by Raimbaut contrasts with the uniformity recommended for the *canso* in the arts of poetry, and confirms that Raimbaut intended their coherence to be more stylistic than thematic. As context for Azalais's song, they imply that we should expect something similar from her, and that is what we find. In her song Azalais blends two very different emotional registers. The wintry grief of stanza 1, which silences all the elements of the amorous spring setting, moves into the disconsolate sense of loss in stanza 2, the grief that came from Aurenga. Then, unexpectedly, we hear that a lady should not love a wealthy man (stanza 3), but that the lady speaking has a wonderful "amic" who "sobre toz seignoreia" (lords it over everyone [stanza 4]); in stanza 5 she addresses this *amic* directly, expressing her confidence that he will be considerate of her. Then in stanza 6 she reverts to the register of grief sounded in stanzas 1 and 2, apostrophizing the castle where Raimbaut d'Aurenga may have died, his city, his tower, his castle, his lord, and the Roman triumphal arch of Orange, and declaring that she will be aggrieved forever by his death. The poem combines elements suggestive of the *planh* in stanzas 1, 2, and 6 with a central passage like the *canso* (as described in the arts of poetry) in stanzas 3, 4, and 5.

The *canso* sequence refers to the speaker's lover, a man different from Raimbaut. The troubadour was her friend, perhaps her relative, but not her lover.[67] According to the *vida* her *amic* was Gui Guerrejat (the warrior). We know independently that Gui Guerrejat was a cousin of Raimbaut d'Aurenga, and that he held castles located within 25 or 30 kilometers of Portiragues (Hérault), Azalais's home near Béziers; as the youngest of five brothers he was a vavasor (Version 1, line 19).[68] So Azalais grieves for her friend Raimbaut but consoles herself that she loves a vavasor, as a lady should.[69]

She intertwines her feelings for the two men, blending the themes of the *planh* and the *canso*, and the combination is tangentially suggestive of what critics have called the *comjat* (leave-taking") or *chanson de change*.[70] Rather than celebrate changing from an old love to a new one, however, Azalais laments the death of her friend (stanzas 1–2); reasons that a woman should not love a powerful man like him (stanza 3); expresses satisfaction with her *amic* (stanza 4), if only he will not be too demanding (stanza 5); says goodbye to Raimbaut (stanza 6); and sends the song to Ermengarde de Narbonne, the viscountess who ruled that city in her own name for half a century (stanza 7). The theme unfolds gradually, as is characteristic of the songs of Raimbaut.[71] As I read the song, Azalais expresses the complexity of real feelings at a time of bereavement and love. In comparison to such a work of genuine emotion, the *chanson de change* is a playful entertainment; the *canso* of the treatises is a pedagogical device, a template designed to assist students in learning the art of poetry.

The diversity of theme in this song has been cited by Tilde Sankovitch as evidence for "a female aesthetics . . . an aesthetics not of well-constructed forms, of linear development, and of logical unity, but of fluidity, of multiplicity, of simultaneity; an aesthetics of disruption and impropriety." Sankovitch sees Azalais proceeding "from her agile mimicry of the nature opening into a just as adept mimicry of *planh* and *canso* in which two stanzas of the former genre frame three stanzas of the latter"; "Azalais usurps both genres in a catachrestic way."[72] My approach would modify this formulation, since I see emergence of genres, and of the concept of genre itself, rather than a catachresis, or strained union, forced upon preexisting genres.[73] I would point out, however, that the trobairitz seem to have participated in composition for less than a hundred years, and to have fallen silent by midthirteenth century. It may be that during this time generic expectations were fluid enough to accommodate a female aesthetics of disruption; the age of the arts of poetry, in the latter half of the thirteenth century, may have imposed generic forms so rigid that they discouraged participation by nonconformists. However that may be, a flexible approach to genre in the time of Azalais has the great advantage of allowing us to read her song as a varied and stimulating whole, rather than compelling us to reduce it to a conglomerate of fragments.[74] The fluid, nascent genres with which she worked allowed her the freedom, as a poet and a woman, to express the particularity of her feelings.[75]

As for Version 2 of Azalais's song, which Rieger finds more coherent than the version I regard as the original,[76] I suggest that this coherence may reflect the gradual clarification of genre. By rewriting the second half of stanza 2, the reviser eradicated its foreshadowing of the *planh* in stanza 6 and concentrated on the grief of the speaker, intensified to the point of a death wish which anticipates the somber tones of Castelloza. Indeed, such intensification of grief may reveal Castelloza's influence on the scribe of MS *N*, who apparently intended to make the trobairitz whose work he included sound like one and the same woman.[77] In stanza 5, at the high point of the *canso* sequence, instead of stating that she *is* with the *bel amic*, the speaker of Version 2 wishes she *were* (*fos*) with him, casting their togetherness into the realm of hypothesis, again like Castelloza. The first tornada, coming right after the statement of the *planh* in stanza 6, is undoubtedly clearer as a gloss than it was, in the earlier version, as a foreshadowing.

Finally, Version 3, excerpted as *doas coblas* in *H*, reverses the order of stanzas 3 and 4, strips away the song's dramatic passion, and turns it into an erudite *bon mot*. Now the speaker boasts that her lover lords it over others *en ditz d'amor* ("in words of love" [line 2]) and attributes the opinion that ladies should not love wealthy men to no less a source than Ovid (line 13). This compact and coherent statement would appeal to a collector of memorable sayings.[78]

The three versions of Azalais's song allow us to glimpse the complex evolution in the sense of genre between the beginning of the troubadour era and the end. Another example that comes to mind is Bertran de Born, a few years later, who used *canso* to mean any kind of song including *sirventes*, and who blended themes of war and love throughout his work.[79] A more obscure example is Guilhem d'Autpol with his alter ego "Daspol," perhaps one and the same man or perhaps two different men, who, in the late thirteenth century, systematically wrote religiously oriented versions of four well-defined genres, the *alba*, the *pastorela*, the *tenso*, and the *planh*.[80] By the time of Guilhem d'Autpol the concept of genre had come into sharp focus. The crossing of these genres with the religious perspective, however, anticipated the religious poetry of the fourteenth century rather than the secular categories of the Consistori.

The system of genres in troubadour lyric was never a Platonic form. It grew and developed from nothing at all into the set of requirements for prizes awarded by the Consistori, with the avowed purpose of maintaining a generic practice which the Consistori had in fact invented. To gauge the relation of individual songs to the evolving sense of genre provides a challenge to our historical imagination. When we insist too sharply on the restrictions imposed upon the troubadours and trobairitz by the system of genres—or, more broadly, by the system of the courtly code, or by tradition—we reduce their stature as poets in our own eyes. By realizing the dynamism of their genres, we can rediscover a measure of their freedom and dignity.

APPENDIX

Azalais de Porcairagues, "Ar em al freg temps vengut"

VERSION 1

Six MSS: *C* 385r–v; *D* 190r–v; *H* 57r (lines 37–52); *I* 140r; *K* 125v–126r; *d* 314r–v. Base *D*. The late seventeenth- or early eighteenth-century manuscript known as the Béziers chansonnier is a copy of *I*.[81] I have consulted *D* in facsimile[82] and the rest of the manuscripts in microfilm.

Attribution: Nalasais de porcaragues *rubric D* 190r, *identical in table of contents D* VIIr; Nazalais de porcarages *vida I* 140r, . . . porcaraiges *table of contents I* 1r, . . . porcarages *I* 6v; Nazalais de porcairagues *vida K* 125v, *table K* VIv, . . . porcaragues [?] *K* Ir; Nazalais de porcairagues *d* 314r. *Anonymous CH.*

Versification: a7 b7' a7 b7' c7 c7 d7' d7'. Frank[83] describes the form as *coblas doblas* without pointing out that the a- and b-rhymes in stanza 6 fail to match those in stanza 5.

Major editions: Schultz[-Gora], "Die provenzalischen Dichterinnen,"[84] 16–17; Sakari, "Azalais," 181–98; Riquer, *Trovadores*, 1:459–62; Rieger, *Trobairitz*, 480–504; Bec, *Chants d'amour*, 65–70; Bruckner and others, *Songs*, 34–37, 154–57.

Vida *IKd*, with miniatures in *IK*.[85] In both miniatures Azalais stands within the initial letter *A* of the *vida;* in *I* she wears a blue gown and a lined cape with a clasp around her neck, and gestures with her right hand; in *K* she wears a red gown and gestures with her left. In both she has brown hair; the rouge on her cheeks, fainter in *I*, is more pronounced in *K*. The *vida* in *I* was copied into the Béziers chansonnier, where a miniature depicts Azalais as a prostitute.[86]

Text

1
Ar em al freg temps vengut
que·l gells e·l neus e la faingna . . .
e l'auçellet estan mut,
c'us de chantar non s'afraingna;
e son sec li ram pels plais, 5
que flors ni foilla no·i nais;
ni rrossignols no i crida,
que l'am'e mai me rreissida.

2
Tant ai lo cors deseubut
per qu'eu soi a toz estraigna, 10
e sai que l'om a perdut
molt plus tost que non gasaingna;
e s'ieu faill ab motz verais
d'Aurenga me moc l'esglais,
per qu'eu m'estauc esbaïda 15
e·n pert solatz en partida.

3
Dompna met mot mal s'amor
que ab ric ome pladeia,
ab plus aut de vavasor,
e s'ill o fai il folleia; 20
car so diz om en Veillai
que ges per ricor non vai,
e dompna que n'es chauzida
en [t]enc per envilanida.

4
Amic ai de gran valor 25
que sobre toz seignoreia,
e non a cor trichador
vas me, que amor m'autreia.
Eu dic que m'amors l'eschai,
e cel que dis que non fai— 30
Dieus li don mal'esgarida,
qu'eu m'en teing fort per guerida.

5
Bels amics, de bon talan
son ab vos toz jorz en guaje,
corteza, de bel semblan, 35
sol no·m demandes outraje.

       Tost en veirem a l'assai,
       qu'en vostra merce·m metrai.
       Vos m'aves la fe plevida
       que no·m demandes faillida.   40

       6
       A Dieu coman Belesgar
       e plus la siutat d'Aurenga
       e Gloriet'e·l caslar
       e lo seignor de Proenza,
       e tot cant vol mon ben lai   45
       e l'arc on son fag l'assai.
       Cellui perdiei c'a ma vida,
       e·n serai toz jorz marrida.

       7
       Joglar que aves cor gai,
       ves Narbona portas lai   50
       ma chanson a la fenida
       lei cui jois e jovenz guida.

Rejected readings in *D:* 3 e li auçellet. 24 [t]enc renc.
Variants: 2 que·l *DCIKd*, qu'es *N*. 3 e li auçellet (+1) *DC*, e·ill auscellet *IKNd*. 4 non] *omitted I*. 8 lam e mai me *DIKd*, lan en mai nos *N*, lau [lan?] en may me *C;* rreissida *D*, reissida *KNd*, ressida *I*, tissida *C*. 9 cors *DIKd*, cor *CN*. 10 soi totz estranigna *d*. 12 nom *C*. 15 n'estauc *CIKd*. 16 pantida *d*. 18 qu'ab trop ric *C*. 21 diz om] dison *CIKd*. 24 [t]enc renc *D*, tenc *CHIKNd*. 28 s'amors *C*, s'amor *IKd*. 37 veirem *DI*, venrem *CHKd*, annarem *N*. 49 cors *IKd*.
Orthographic changes from *D:* 15 esbaida. 34 iorz . . . guaie. 35 outraie. 48 iorz. 49 Ioglar. 52 cuj iois e iouenz. The distinction between *u* and *v*, capitalization, spacing between words, and punctuation have been modernized.

Translation

       1
       Now we have come to the cold season
       when [there are] frost and snow and mud
       and the little birds are mute,
       for not a one breaks into song;
       and the branches in the hedges are dry,   5
       for neither flower nor leaf buds;
       nor does the nightingale sing,
       which awakens my soul in May.

       2
       I have been so surprised
       that I am a stranger to everyone,   10

and I know that a man has lost
much sooner than he wins;
and if I am astounded by true words
my grief began in Orange,
which is why I stand astonished   15
and lose joy in part.

3
A lady commits her love very badly
who deals with a powerful man,
with anyone higher than a vavasor,
and if she does so she acts like a fool;   20
for they say in Le Velay
that it [love] doesn't go according to wealth,
and a lady who is chosen for this reason
I consider reduced to a peasant.

4
I have a friend of great worth   25
who lords it over everyone,
and he does not have a deceiving heart
toward me, for he grants me love.
I say that my love belongs to him,
and he who says it doesn't—   30
God give him ill fortune,
for I consider myself honored by him.

5
Fair friend, with a good will
I am always engaged with you,
courteous and welcoming,   35
if only you won't ask me for anything outrageous.
Soon we shall see about it in action,
for I shall put myself at your mercy.
You have sworn to me your faith
that you won't ask me [to do] wrong.   40

6
To God I commend Beauregard
and also the city of Orange
and Glorieta and the château
and the lord of Provence,
and whatever wishes my good there   45
and the arch where the assaults are made.
I lost him who has my life,
and I shall be forever aggrieved by it.

7

Joglar, [you] who have a merry heart, 50
carry there, to Narbonne,
my *chanson* at the end [with the tornada?]
to her whom joy and youth guide.

Notes to Version 1

2–3 Ellipsis of a verb, perhaps *son vengut* by extension from *em vengut* in line 1 (Lewent, cited by Sakari, "A propos," 526), or "q*ue* es" (Version 2), unless we prefer to understand syllepsis (as in "He lost his coat and his temper"), since frost and snow and mud cannot be described as mute in the same sense as little birds. Sakari ("Azalais," 187–88) proposed a special sense of *mut*, "inanimé," but to say that mud is inanimate is not to say much. The wintry landscape is silent, in part because birds do not sing. Translated loosely by Rieger as "mit Schnee und Eis and Matsch" (with snow and ice and mud); by Bec as "avec le gel, la neige et la boue" (with frost, snow, and mud); best by Bruckner and others as "when there's snow and ice and sludge."

4 s'afrain*gn*a] Normally *afranher* ("*v. réfl.* se fléchir; . . . se pencher, s'incliner, se tourner vers" [*PD* 10],[87] here *afranhar* with change of conjugation [*S-W* 1: 29]);[88] cf. Rieger, 485.

5 "*Plais, s.m.* haie" (*PD* 296).

8 l'am'e mai me] Thus MSS *DIKd;* compare the variants. The interpretation of *am'* as a form of *anm'*, *anma* (soul) ("*arma, anma, s.f.* âme" [*PD* 28]) is due to Sakari; see his "Azalais," 188–89; "A propos," 525–26; and "Un vers." The form *ama* occurs in MS *a¹* as a variant of *arma* in MS *D*, in *Ben grans avoleza intra* (P-C 233,2, line 3), attributed to Bertran de Born in *a¹* and Guilhem de Saint Gregori in *D;* see Paden, Sankovitch, and Stäblein, eds., *Poems of Bertran de Born*, no. 39, and the earlier edition by Giulio Bertoni, "La 'sestina' di Guilhem de Saint Grigori," *Studj romanzi* 13 (1917): 31–39. Occitan *ama* is attested in 1521, and in Lyons and Forez in the fifteenth century, by the *FEW* (24: 582).[89]

In "A propos," Sakari cites Lewent's objection: "I doubt that a medieval person used the word 'soul' when speaking of his feelings" (525); Lewent suggested changing *lam* to *la* or *lai,* as Bec does. For parallels to the use of reflexes of *anima* to refer to emotions, see Sakari, "Un vers," 215–31; for further examples see Psalm 30:10 ("Conturbatus est in ira oculus meus, anima mea, et venter meus" [My eye is troubled with wrath, my soul, and my belly (Douay-Rheims Version)]), and also Psalms 6:4, 87:4, 93:19, 142:8 (Vulgate). Compare also Propertius 2.10.11, "Surge, anima, ex humili; iam, carmina, sumite uires" (Arise, [my] spirit, from low [language]; now, [my] songs, take on strength).[90]

Edited by Rieger rather freely as "que *am s'*en mai me reissida," but she provides the translation only of the version in *N*: "die ich liebe, wenn sie uns im Mai erweckt" (which I love when it wakes us in May). Rieger deletes *l,* conjectures *s'*, and translates *nos* from *N* instead of *me* in *D,* but produces a smooth translation. Bec gives the text as "Que *lai* en mai me reissida," "lui qui là-bas, en mai, me réveille" (which wakes me over there in May), changing only one letter (the *i* in *lai*, represented in the manuscripts as *m, n,* or possibly *u*), but produces a pedestrian reading. Bruckner and others read "que l'am'e*n* mai me rreissida" (who wakes my soul in May). Their emendation of one letter in "e*n*" is unnecessary, since *e* before a nasal is a well attested form of *en.* Given the choice between a surprisingly poetic reading in the manuscripts and a pedestrian reading by emendation, we should not hesitate to choose the manuscripts.

"*Reisidar, v.a.* réveiller" (*PD* 321).

9 cor] The reading *cors* (body, self, person [*DIKd*]), suggests an opposition with *am'* (soul) in line 8. "*Cors, s.m.* corps; ... *mos cors* moi; *ieu mos cors* moi en personne" (*PD* 98). The emendation to *cor* (heart) (as in *CN*), accepted by Rieger, Bec, and Bruckner and others, is a *lectio facilior.* deseubut] "*Decebre, v.a.* décevoir, tromper; faire tort à, ruiner; surprendre" (*PD* 106).

11–12 Proverbial; Cnyrim,[91] item 851, p. 48.

13 faill] "*Falhir, v.n.* faillir, commettre une faute; ... se tromper; être trompé dans son attente, être désappointé" (*PD* 183). ab motz verais] The report of Raimbaut's sudden death, possibly caused by "a wave of influenza which swept over Europe in 1173" during which, according to one chronicler, "many people coughed out their souls" (Pattison, *Life and Works of Raimbaut d'Orange,* 25). Raimbaut was born in 1146–48 (Pattison, 12), so he died at about the age of twenty-six.

14 esglais] "*Esglai . . . s. m.* effroi, horreur; crainte; douleur" (*PD* 167).

16 en partida] Prepares for the transition from the subject of the speaker's bereavement (stanzas 1–2) to her love (stanzas 3–5). She is bereaved in part and in part joyful. Glossed "en partie" by Sakari and *PD* 280; "am Ende, schließlich" (*a la partida*) by Schultz (quoted by Rieger, 487).

18 "*Plaidejar . . . v.n.* plaider, intenter un procès; traiter, conclure un accord" (*PD* 296).

19 vavasor] "Arrière-vassal" (*Petit Robert*), the vassal of a vassal.

21 Veillai] "The region of Le Velay (Haute-Loire)."[92] Perhaps a reference to the troubadour Guilhem de Saint-Leidier, from Le Velay; but Guilhem does not make such a statement in his extant songs. Cf. Sakari, "Azalais," 56–65; Sakari, *Poésies du troubadour Guillem de Saint-Didier* (Helsinki: Société Néophilologique, 1956), 78–79; Sakari, "A propos," 523–24; Rieger, 488.

22 Elliptical form of a proverb: "Ges amors segon ricor no vai" (Love scarcely goes according to wealth), Bernart de Ventadorn, "Bel m'es qu'eu chan," Appel, *Bernart von Ventadorn,* no. 10, line 35; for further parallels see Cnyrim, *Sprichwörter,* items 17–22, p. 25. Whether or not powerful men, *rics omes,* deserved a lady's love was a question debated by numerous troubadours. See Sakari, "Azalais," 56–69; Costanzo Di Girolamo, *I trovatori* (Turin: Bollati Boringhieri, 1989), 91–99.

23–24 "Je tiens pour avilie une dame qui se distingue ainsi" (I think a woman who distinguishes herself that way demeans herself) (Bec); "If a lady's known for that / I consider her dishonored" (Bruckner and others). Rieger (489) takes *n* as the negative particle, and translates "eine Frau, die einem *ric ome* nicht abgeneigt ist, halte ich deshalb für schändlich/schimpflich" (I consider a woman who is not ill-disposed toward a *ric ome* as shameful). For elision of *no* as *n'*, see *S-W* 5:413–14.

29 eschai] "*Escazer, v.n.* échoir; arriver; revenir, appartenir" (*PD* 161).
31 Anacoluthon. esgarida] "*Escarida, s.f.* destinée, fortune" (*PD* 160).
34 guaje] "*Gatge, s.m.* gage; testament; amende; gages, solde" (*PD* 204); cf. *se metre a gatges* "sich anwerben lassen, Dienste nehmen" (*S-W* 4:80). Not translated by Rieger, since she translates only the text in *N* (my Version 2). Bec translates "Je me suis pour toujours engagée à vous"; Bruckner and others, "I am at all times promised to you." The literal meaning of *gatge* is commercial (English "wage"); *son ab vos en guaje* appears to mean, literally, "I am in service, employed, with you," where "you" might represent a fellow worker or an employer. Azalais veils the relationship to which she refers. (It is not at all clear that the expression *eser en gatge ab* can refer to an engagement to marry, as English "engagement," "to be engaged to" might suggest.)
36, 40 demandes] Present subjunctive after *sol no* (36) and the expression of promise (39).
37 assai] "*Asag, -ai . . . s.m.* essai, épreuve, entreprise" (*PD* 29). Nelli's controversial concept of the *assag*, which he saw as a ritual in which the lover and his lady would lie together naked but chaste, is today largely abandoned. For bibliography see Rieger, 490–91 and 503, n. 863; Städtler, *Altprovenzalische Frauendichtung*, 158; Zaganelli, "Trovatori e 'trobairitz,'" 102.
41–48 Rieger (491, 495), following Sakari ("Azalais," 193; "A propos," 527–28), takes this stanza as an interpolation added after the death of Raimbaut d'Aurenga to a preexisting love song.
41 coman] "Azalais prie le Seigneur d'administrer par intérim les domaines du défunt" (Azalais prays to the Lord to administer the dead man's properties temporarily) (Sakari, "Azalais," 194). Belesgar] The castle of Beauregard (Vaucluse, canton of Jonquières), near Courthézon, residence of Raimbaut d'Aurenga (Chambers, *Proper Names*, 70). Sakari asked if Raimbaut might have died there ("Azalais," 193–94); on May 10, 1173, Raimbaut, in his last illness ("in ultima infirmitate"), drew up his will at Courthézon (Pattison, *Life and Works of Raimbaut d'Orange*, 218).
42 Aurenga] Orange (Vaucluse) (Chambers, *Proper Names*, 59). If pronounced in the dialect of Le Velay, *Aurenga* might provide a true rhyme with *Proenza* in line 44 with both words ending in [-tsa] (Rieger, 491). Indirect support for this hypothesis is provided by the Latin form *Aurenca* in acts of January 1171 (Sakari, "Azalais," 38) and September 1171 (Pattison, *Life and Works of Raimbaut d'Orange*, 217).
43 Glorieta] "The former palace of the princes of Orange" (Chambers, *Proper Names*, 142); "le nom de la tour d'Orange dans les chansons de geste du cy-

cle de Guillaume au Court Nez" (A. Thomas, cited by Rieger, 492); Sakari, "Azalais," 194–95. "*Caslar,* s.m. château" (*PD* 71); on the château of Orange, destroyed in 1673, see Sakari, "Azalais," 195.

44 lo seignor de Proenza] Either Raymond V of Toulouse, lord of both Raimbaut d'Aurenga and Azalais de Porcairagues (Sakari, "Azalais," 195), to whom Raimbaut did homage in 1154 (Pattison, *Life and Works of Raimbaut d'Orange,* 216), or Alfonso II of Aragon, marquis of Provence, whose court Raimbaut attended in 1162 and 1170 (Pattison, 9; Riquer, *Trovadores,* 1:462n). Cf. Version 2.

46 l'arc on son fag l'assai] The triumphal arch at Orange, apparently restored by Tiberius in A.D. 26–27, depicts scenes of battle between legionnaires and Gauls during a revolt in A.D. 21. See Robert Amy, *L'arc d'Orange* (Paris: Centre National de la Recherche Scientifique, 1962), 1:157; Michel-Edouard Bellet, *Orange antique: monuments et musée* (Paris: Imprimerie nationale, 1991); and James Bromwich, *The Roman Remains of Southern France: A Guidebook* (London: Routledge, 1993), 183–86. Amy (1:12) and Bellet (46) assert that the history of the arch is unknown from its founding to the thirteenth century, but overlook this mention by Azalais in 1173. The violence of combat depicted on the frieze of the arch may have expressed for Azalais the violence of Raimbaut's death, whether by influenza (see note to line 13 above) or some other cause, or perhaps it expressed the violence of her bereavement. "Les visages sont convulsés, les corps contortionnés: c'est la fureur de la bataille!" (Bellet 58).

"Et l'arc (de triomphe) sur les faces duquel sont figurés des assauts" (and the arch of triumph on the sides of which assaults are portrayed) (Sakari, "Azalais," 187, cf. 195–96); "und den Triumphbogen, auf dem die Heldentaten abgebildet sind" (and the triumphal arch on which heroic deeds are depicted) (Mölk, cited by Rieger, 492). Rieger continues, "Der plötzlich verstorbene Raimbaut—so es um ihn handelt—wäre dann auf irgendeinem Kriegsschauplatz (oder Turnierplatz?) umgekommen" (If the line does refer to Raimbaut, it may imply that his sudden death occurred in a theater of war or in a tournament).

47–48 Interpreted more weakly by Lewent as "I lost the one for whom I shall always mourn in my life" (cited by Sakari, "A propos," 524; cf. Rieger, 492).

49 Joglar] Cannot refer to Raimbaut d'Aurenga, since Raimbaut has died (stanza 6), unless we read stanza 6 as an interpolation; if the song in Version 1 is an organic whole, *Joglar* must refer, as it ordinarily does, to the *joglar* to whom the song is entrusted for delivery.[93] The description "q*ue* aves cor gai," following immediately on "marrida" (line 48), continues the blending of grief and joy which characterizes the song. *Joglar* was identified by Sakari, Kolsen, and Delbouille as a reciprocal senhal exchanged between Azalais and Raimbaut (Rieger, 493).

51 "*Fenida, s.f.* fin; fin de la vie; mort; glas funèbre" (*PD* 186); also a synonym of tornada (Rieger, 493).[94] Here both meanings seem possible.

52 lei] Assumed to refer to Ermengarde, who inherited the title of viscountess of Narbonne in 1143, ruled until 1192 (when she abdicated in favor of her nephew), and died in 1197.[95]

VERSION 2

One MS: *N* 233r–v. Anonymous.
Edition: Rieger, *Trobairitz*, 481–84.

Text

1
[A]r em al freit tems vengut
q*ue* es neus e gels e faigna,
e·ill auselet estan mut,
qu'us de cantar non se laigna;
ez son sec li ram pels plais 5
que flors ni fuoilla no·i nais,
ni·l rusignols non [i] crida
que l'a[m]'en mai nos reissida.

2
[T]ot ai lo cor deseubut
per qu'eu sui si tot'estraigna; 10
e sai que l'om a perdut
molt plus tost c'om non gazaigna,
per qu'eu sui en gra*n* esmai
car sai que·m aissi morai;
e s'eu fos enans fenida, 15
ben me tengra per garida.

3
[D]ompna met molt mal s'amor
que ab ric home plaideia,
a plus aut de varvasor;
e s'il o fai ill foleia, 20
car so diz hom sai e lai,
"Amor per ricor non vai";
e dompna qu'e[n] es chauzida
en tenc per envilanida.

4
[A]mic ai de gran valor 25
que sobre totz seingnoreia,
e no*n* a cor trichador
ves me, que s'amor m'autreia.
Eu dic que m'amor l'eschai,

e cel que diz que non fai— 30
Deus li don mal'escarida,
qu'eu m'en teing ben per garida.

5
[B]els amics ses cor truan,
car me fos ab vos en gatge,
cortes'e de bel semblan, 35
sol no·m dissessez oltrage.
Tost annarem a l'assai,
qu'e[n] vostra merce·m metrai.
Vos m'avez la fe plevida
que no·*m* demandez faillida. 40

6
[A] Dieu coman Belesgar
e puois la ciuptat d'Aurenga
e Gloriet' e·l caslar
e·l seingnoriu de Proensa,
ez tot ca*n*t vol mon be lai. 45
Mas lai on son fait l'assai
perdiei celui c'a ma vida,
e·n serai toz jorn[z] marida.

7
[E] s'ieu fail ab motz verais
d'Aurenga me mou l'esglais, 50
per qu'eu n'estau esbaïda
en'n pert solatz en partida.

8
[J]oglar, vos c'avez cor gai,
ves Nerbona portez lai
ma chanso a la fenida 55
leis cui jois capdel'e guida.

Rejected readings in *N:* The first letter of every stanza, left by the scribe for the rubricator, was never inserted; for these letters I follow Version 1. 4 queus. 7 non crida (-1). 8 lan. 10 tota. 11 e] er. 23 queu. 29 Eu o dic (+1). 32 *conteing* (+1). 34 fos *N,* fes *Rieger.* 38 queu. 40 no·m demandez faillida (-1) *Rieger.* 48 iorn. 55 chansos. 56 iois capdella e. 56 *Rieger indents.*

Translation

1
Now we have come to the cold season
which is frost and snow and mud,
and the little birds are mute,

for not a one complains;
and the branches in the hedges are dry,
for neither flower nor leaf buds;
nor does the nightingale sing,
which awakens our soul in May.

2
My heart has been utterly wronged,
which is why I am utterly estranged,
and I know that a man has lost
much sooner than he wins;
which is why I am in great dismay,
for I know that thus I shall die;
and if I had [only] died first,
[then] I would consider myself cured.

3
A lady commits her love very badly
who deals with a powerful man,
with anyone higher than a vavasor;
and if she does so she acts like a fool,
for they say here and there,
"Love doesn't go according to wealth";
and a lady who is chosen for this reason
I consider reduced to a peasant.

4
I have a friend of great worth
who lords it over everyone,
and he does not have a deceiving heart
toward me, for he grants me his love.
I say that my love belongs to him,
and he who says it doesn't—
God give him ill fortune,
for I consider myself honored by him.

5
Fair friend, with a good will
I wish I were engaged with you [?],
courteous and welcoming,
if only you wouldn't tell me anything outrageous.
Soon we shall go to the test,
for I shall put myself at your mercy.
You have sworn to me your faith
that you don't ask me [to do] wrong.

6
To God I commend Beauregard
and then the city of Orange

and Glorieta and the château
and the lordship of Provence,
and whatever wishes my good there.   45
But where the assaults are made
I lost him who has my life,
and I shall be forever aggrieved.

7
And if I am deceived with true words
my grief begins in Orange,   50
which is why I stand astonished
and lose joy in part.

8
Joglar, [you] who have a merry heart,   55
carry there, toward Narbonne,
my *chanson* at the end [with the tornada?]
to her whom joy leads and guides.

Notes to Version 2

4 "*Lanhar, v. réfl.* se plaindre" (*PD* 221).

12–16 Compare the language of death in Castelloza; see Paden and others, "Poems of the *Trobairitz* Na Castelloza," 166–67.

19 varvasor] "*Valvasor, vav-*" (*PD* 377); forms in *val-, va-,* and *vas-* are recognized by *LR* (5:470)[96] and *S-W* (8:580), but forms in *var-* are attested for Catalan, Italian, and French (dialect of Gondecourt, near Lille) by *FEW* (14:201–2), so no emendation is necessary.

29 amor] Rieger emends to *amors* with the other manuscripts, but *amor* could also be nominative.[97]

34 In this version Azalais wishes she were engaged (employed) with her *amic*, possibly either as a fellow worker or as her employer; cf. note to Version 1, line 34.

35 Rieger takes *cortes* as referring to *amics* 33; her interpretation of the passage is undermined, however, by her erroneous reading of *fos* 34 as *fes*.

44 Refers to the territory of the lord of Provence, the culmination of the places named in lines 41–43, instead of invoking the lord himself as in Version 1 (Rieger, 492).

49–52 Rieger asserts that these lines (from Version 1, lines 13–16) make sense only following stanza 6 as here, "als Ausdruck der Trauer um den Verlust des Geliebten aus Orange, in dem wohl tatsächlich Raimbaut d'Aurenga zu sehen sein wird" (as an expression of grief for the loss of the beloved from Orange, in whom we should indeed probably see Raimbaut d'Aurenga) (493). I see no reason, however, why Version 1 does not make the same sense in a more elaborate structure: first (lines 13–16) the poet alludes to the reason for her grief, then she explains it more fully (lines 41–48).

49–50 "Und wenn ich fehlgehe, in wahren Worten / erreicht mich aus Aurenga die schreckliche Kunde" (and if I go wrong, in true words the terrible news reaches me from Aurenga) (Rieger, 483), linking *ab motz verais* to *esglais;* "même si je pêche par ma franchise" (even if I err by my candor) (Sakari, "Azalais," 196), linking the phrase to *fail.*

VERSION 3

One MS: *H* 46r.

Text

Rubric: Aqestas doas coblas porten lor raisons.

1
Amic ai de gran valor
q'en ditz d'amor seignoreia,
e non a cor trichador
vas mi, qe s'amor m'autreia.
Eu dic qe m'amors l'eschai,   5
e cil qe ditz qe no*n* fai—
Dieus li don mal'es[c]arida
q*u'e*u m'en teing p*er* garida.

2
Dompna met mout mal s'amor
c'ab trop ric home plaideia,   10
ab plus aut de vavasor;
e cil qi o fai folleia,
qe Ovidis o retrai
c'amors per ricor non vai,
e dompna qe n'es causida   15
ne tenc p*er* envilanida.

Rejected reading in *H:* 7 esp*er*arida.

Translation

Rubric: These two coblas carry their subject.

1
I have a friend of great worth
who lords it in words of love,
and he does not have a deceiving heart
toward me, for he grants me his love.
I say that my love belongs to him,   5
and he who says it doesn't—

God give him ill fortune,
for I consider myself honored by him.

2
A lady commits her love very badly
who deals with too powerful a man,   10
with [anyone] higher than a vavasor;
and she who does so acts like a fool,
for Ovid says
that love doesn't go according to wealth,
and a lady who is chosen for this reason   15
I consider reduced to a peasant.

Notes to Version 3

Rubric] That is, "These *coblas*, being self-explanatory, call for no external gloss" (Poe, *Compilatio*). Rieger (489) interprets the rubric as "Their *razos* carry these two coblas," i.e., the excerptor has taken them from *razos* we do not have. Krispin points out both interpretations but seems to lean toward the first ("La tradition manuscrite des trobairitz," 234).

13 The same attribution to Ovid was made by Arnaut de Maruelh, "Mout eron doutz miei cossire": "Mas Ovidis retrais / qu'entre·ls corals amadors / non paratgeia ricors" (P-C 30,19, lines 28–30)[98] (But Ovid said that among sincere lovers wealth is not esteemed). Cf. Ovid: "Non bene conveniunt nec in una sede morantur / majestas et amor" (Majesty and love do not go well together, nor tarry long in the same dwelling-place [*Metamorphoses* 2:846–47]); "Non ego divitibus venio praeceptor amandi . . . Pauperibus vates ego sum, quia pauper amavi" (I come not to teach the rich to love . . . I am the poet of the poor, because I was poor when I loved [*Art of Love* 2:161, 165]); "Ecce, recens dives parto per vulnera censu / praefertur nobis sanguine pastus eques!" (Behold a newly rich knight, fed fat on blood, who won his rating by dealing wounds, is preferred to me! [*Amores* 3:8:9–10]).

NOTES

1. Raymond Thompson Hill and Thomas Goddard Bergin, eds., *Anthology of the Provençal Troubadours* (New Haven: Yale University Press, 1941), [364].

2. See the *vida* of Marcabru: "Et en aquel temps non appellava hom cansson, mas tot qant hom cantava eron vers" (And in that time one did not call [anything] a *canso*, but everything that was sung were *vers*); Jean Boutière and A.-H. Schutz, *Biographies des troubadours,* 2d ed., rev. by I.-M. Cluzel (Paris: Nizet, 1964), 12. For recent discussions of the meaning of *vers* see Frank M. Chambers, *An Introduction to Old Provençal Versification* (Philadelphia: American Philosophical Society, 1985), 26, and index, 299; Erich Köhler, "'Vers' und Kanzone," in *Grundriss der romanischen Literaturen des Mittelalters,* vol. 2: *Les genres lyriques,* ed. Erich Köhler, Ulrich Mölk, and

Dietmar Rieger (Heidelberg: Carl Winter, 1979–90), tome 1, fascicle 3, 45–176; Gérard Gonfroy, "Les genres lyriques occitans et les traités de poétique: de la classification médiévale à la typologie moderne," *Actes du XVIIIe Congrès International de Linguistique et de Philologie Romanes, Université de Trèves (Trier) 1986*, ed. Dieter Kremer (Tübingen: Max Niemeyer, 1988), 6:121–35, at 128–29; Mieke de Winter-Hosman, "La naissance d'une terminologie de genres chez les premiers troubadours," *Amsterdamer Beiträge zur älteren Germanistik* 30 (1990): 139–49, at 142–45; and Pickens in this volume.

3. Alfred Pillet and Henry Carstens, *Bibliographie der Troubadours* (Halle: Niemeyer, 1933); István Frank, *Répertoire métrique de la poésie des troubadours* (Paris: Champion, 1953–57). The *Grundriss der romanischen Literaturen des Mittelalters*, vol. 2, lists fifteen genres, including the three I call major, the eleven I call minor, and the *salut d'amor* (which Frank does not regard as lyric because it is not composed in stanzas, but in rhymed couplets). For discussion of the system of troubadour genres see Dietmar Rieger, "Einleitung: Das trobadoreske Gattungssystem und sein Sitz im Leben," in *Grundriss der romanischen Literaturen des Mittelalters*, vol. 2, tome 1, fascicle 3, 15–28; Gonfroy, "Genres lyriques occitans et les traités de poétique"; de Winter-Hosman, "Naissance d'une terminologie de genres."

4. Frank, *Répertoire*, 1:xvi, n. 1. For the sake of accuracy I have entered the data from the *Répertoire* on two occasions in two separate operations and reconciled the discrepancies between the two. The result may, I believe, be considered reliable. An earlier census with very similar results was reported by Rupprecht Rohr, "Zur Interpretation der altprovenzalischen Lyrik: Hauptrichtungen der Forschung (1952–1962)," in *Der provenzalischen Minnesang*, ed. Rudolf Baehr (Darmstadt: Wissenschaftliche Buchgesellschaft, 1967), 111.

5. In the figures and tables I use Frank's names for the genres, since the data are his and since, as I shall explain in "Development of the Genre Concept," below, several of them can be questioned.

6. See Christiane Leube, "Cobla," in *Grundriss der romanischen Literaturen des Mittelalters*, 2, part 1, fascicle 4 (1980): 67–72 and fascicle 7 (1990): 384–421; Angelica Rieger, "La *cobla esparsa* anonyme: phénoménologie d'un genre troubadouresque," in *Actes du XVIIIe Congrès International de Linguistique et de Philologie Romanes, Université de Trèves (Trier) 1986*, ed. Dieter Kremer (Tübingen: Niemeyer, 1988), 6:202–18; and Poe in this volume.

7. Frank applies "javanais" to P-C 434a,66, "= 434a,68 en 'javanais'" (*Répertoire*, 2:177). *Javanais*, "argot conventionnel consistant à intercaler dans les mots les syllabes *va* ou *av*" (a conventional slang in which the syllable *va* or *av* is inserted into words [*Petit Robert*]). The incipit of 434a,68, "Tart fa hom" (a *sirventes*), becomes, in the *javanais* version, "Taflamart."

8. Subtypes which Frank recognizes include religious varieties (*alba religieuse, pastourelle religieuse, sirventes religieux*); polyglot forms (*chanson plurilingue, sirventes plurilingue*); parodies (*dansa parodique, romance parodique*); and fragments (*albas, chansons, coblas,* and *dansas fragmentaires*). He regularly distinguishes between *tenson, tenson fictive,* and *tenson avec un inconnu* (therefore perhaps a *tenson fictive*); *partimen* and *partimen avec un inconnu; cobla, échange de coblas,* and *échange de coblas avec un inconnu.* On rare occasions he observes generic blends such as a *dansa-pastourelle* (244,8), a *sextine* (*sirventes*) (233,2), or a *sirventes* (*tenson fictive*) (339,3).

9. For the chronology of the troubadours I have drawn on Alfred Jeanroy, "Liste bio-bibligraphique des troubadours des origines au milieu du XIVe siècle," *La poésie lyrique des troubadours* (Toulouse: Privat, 1934), 1:326–436, supplemented by Martín de Riquer, ed., *Los trovadores: historia literaria y textos* (Barcelona: Planeta, 1975). It is true that our knowledge of chronology is uncertain in many cases; for example, Bernart de Ventadorn's activity is usually dated 1147–70 (period 2), but it is possible that he died as abbot of Tulle about 1237, that he was born about 1150, and so that the midpoint of his career fell in 1194 (period 3). For an exploration of this hypothesis see William D. Paden, "Bernart de Ventadour le troubadour devint-il abbé de Tulle?" in *Mélanges de langue et de littérature occitanes en hommage à Pierre Bec* (Poitiers: Centre d'études supérieures de civilisation médiévale, 1991), 401–13.

10. For example, if the midpoint of a troubadour's activity fell in 1181 (period 3), he may easily have composed an otherwise undatable song at some time in period 2 (1140–80), but it is less likely that he actually composed it in period 1 (1100–1140). Peire Cardenal, the longest-lived troubadour, was active from 1205 to 1272; the midpoint of his activity was 1239, hence in period 4 (1220–60); but he began to write in period 3 and ended in period 5.

11. I have argued against the crusade hypothesis in "The Troubadours and the Albigensian Crusade: A Long View," *Romance Philology* 49 (1995): 168–91; for further implications of this claim see my study, "The Chronology of Genres in Medieval Galician-Portuguese Lyric Poetry," *La Corónica* 26, no. 1 (1997): 183–201.

12. Frank defines the domain of the *Répertoire* as "les textes contenus dans les chansonniers provençaux proprement dits, et uniquement ceux-là" (the texts contained in the Provençal chansonniers properly speaking, and only in those) (1:xvi), thus including a small number of fourteenth-century poems which are found in the troubadour manuscripts but excluding fourteenth-century poems of the School of Toulouse. For present purposes (other than table 1.1) I have ignored the small number of fourteenth-century poems included by Frank.

13. Therefore in table 1.2, to calculate the expected occurrence, for example, of the *chanson* in periods 2 and 3, one multiplies the total number of *chansons* in periods 2 through 5 (940) by the proportion of poems in periods 2 and 3 (1,133) to the total number of poems in the chart (2,144). The result is 497.

14. The charge was laid by Friedrich Diez, whose encounter with Goethe at Weimar in 1818 led to the foundation of troubadour studies. In a celebrated passage of his book *Die Poesie der Troubadours*, published in 1826, Diez asserted that "If you compare a number of poems by various troubadours, you will notice at once that they all express one and the same poetic character. This entire literature could be considered as the work of a single poet, merely spoken in various voices" ("Vergleicht man eine Reihe von Gedichten verschiedener Verfasser, so wird man sogleich die Wahrnehmung machen, dass sie sämmtlich einen und denselben poetischen Charakter offenbaren. Man könnte sich diese ganze Litteratur als das Werk eines Dichters denken, nur in verschiedenen Stimmungen hervorgebracht" [Diez, *Die Poesie der Troubadours* (Zwickau: Gebrüder Schumann, 1826), 122–23; 2d ed. (Leipzig: Johann Ambrosius Barth, 1883), 107]). Jeanroy declared in 1934 that Diez's work remained "sur bien des points, la base de toute recherche" (on many points the base for all research [*Poésie lyrique,* 1:22]).

15. In general Pillet and Carstens use the term *Tenzone* for Frank's *tenson, Tenzone*

(*Partimen*) for his *partimen*, and *Fingierte Tenzone* for his *tenson fictive*. Occasionally, however, one of Frank's *tensons* is identified by Pillet and Carstens as a *Tenzone* (*Partimen*) (8,1; 129,3; 248,77) or as a *Coblaswechsel* (12,1); several of Frank's *partimens* are identified as *Tenzonen* (12b,1; 413a,1; 414,1; 435,1; 436,1; 436,2; 437,11); one of his *tensons fictives* is identified as a "Fabel... der Tenzone angenähert" (a fable closely related to the *tenso*) (305,13), another as an "Allegorische Darstellung eines Streites" (an allegorical representation of a debate) (398,1), yet another as a "Traum von einem Streit (*tenzo*)" (a dream of a debate, or a *tenso*) (282,4).

16. See Erich Köhler, "Romanze," in *Grundriss der romanischen Literaturen des Mittelalters*, vol. 2, tome 1, fascicle 5 (1979): 55–59 and fascicle 7 (1990): 502–8. The *romance* is, in my opinion, the nongenre *par excellence*.

17. The sole metapoetic reference to troubadour religious poetry occurs in the *vida* of Lanfranc Cigala, who "trobava volontiers de Dieu" (composed willingly about God). See Boutière and Schutz, *Biographies*, 569; Francisco J. Oroz Arizcuren, ed., *La lírica religiosa en la literatura provenzal antigua: Edición crítica, traducción, notas y glosario* (Pamplona: Excma. Diputación Foral de Navarra, Institución Príncipe de Viana, 1972), 21–34.

18. Pierre Bec, "Le problème des genres chez les premiers troubadours," *Cahiers de civilisation médiévale* 25 (1982): 31–47; reprinted in Pierre Bec, *Ecrits sur les troubadours et la lyrique médiévale (1961–1991)* (Caen: Paradigme, 1992), 87–103. For Ulrich Mölk the system of genres crystallized in the years around 1170, but this is a simplification—recall that the *cobla* was born in the 1190s; see Mölk, *Trobadorlyrik: Eine Einführung* (Munich: Artemis, 1982), 99. More satisfactorily, Mieke de Winter-Hosman dates the birth of genre terms around 1150–70, and posits their development in later troubadours, culminating in the Occitan *arts poétiques* ("Naissance d'une terminologie de genres," 145–46).

19. See J.-M.-L. Dejeanne, ed., *Poésies complètes du troubadour Marcabru* (Toulouse: Edouard Privat, 1909), "Glossaire."

20. Bec, "Problème des genres," 46; Chambers, *Introduction*, 85. According to Chambers (91), the "earliest known Provençal poet to designate his compositions (both of them) by the name *sirventes*" was Marcoat, active in the third quarter of the twelfth century according to Riquer (*Trovadores*, 1:258). On Marcoat's *sirventes* as contrafacta of a *vers* by Peire d'Alvernhe, see my review of Dietmar Rieger's *Gattungen und Gattungsbezeichnungen der Trobadorlyrik* (Tübingen: Niemeyer, 1976) in *Romance Philology* 34 (1981): 510.

21. Carl Appel, ed., *Bernart von Ventadorn: Seine Lieder* (Halle: Niemeyer, 1915), nos. 6, line 24, and 8, line 1. In his extant poems Bernart de Ventadorn did not use *sirventes* at all, whether because he did not know the term or simply because he found no occasion to use it.

22. Bertran de Born's poems 27 and 33 are identified as both *cansos* (27, line 3; 33, line 3) and *sirventes* (27, line 43; 33, line 43). See William D. Paden, Tilde Sankovitch, and Patricia H. Stäblein, eds., *The Poems of the Troubadour Bertran de Born* (Berkeley: University of California Press, 1986), 46.

23. Frank identifies both P-C 80,37 and 80,38 as *sirventes-chansons*. See also Erich Köhler, "Die Sirventes-Kanzone: 'genre bâtard' oder legitime Gattung?" *Mélanges offerts à Rita Lejeune* (Gembloux: Duculot, 1969), 1:159–83.

24. F. R. P. Akehurst, "The Computer Takes Up the Challenge: Thoughts on the

Joc-partit," in *Studia Occitanica in Memoriam Paul Remy,* ed. Hans-Erich Keller and others (Kalamazoo: Medieval Institute Publications, Western Michigan University, 1986), 2:235–41.

25. See Eliabeth Wilson Poe, "New Light on the *Alba:* A Genre Redefined," *Viator* 15 (1984): 139–50.

26. Frank, like Pillet and Carstens, identifies as *coblas* poems by Peire de Valeira (362,3) and Uc Catola (451,2, an *échange de coblas* with an anonymous lady), both active in period 2, but perhaps we should understand them as "stanzas," the original sense of the word *coblas,* rather than as members of the constituted genre. Elizabeth Poe, in her essay in this volume, argues that the *cobla* became "well enough established as a genre to be considered part of the standard repertoire of troubadour songs" in the 1190s.

27. J. H. Marshall, ed., *The "Razos de trobar" of Raimon Vidal and Associated Texts* (London: Oxford University Press, 1972), 6.

28. Ibid., xciii, 95. Marshall ascribes the text to Jofre de Foixà and dates it accordingly in the last decade of the thirteenth century (lxxv–lxxviii). A translation of the *Doctrina de compondre dictatz* has been provided by Marianne Shapiro, *De vulgari eloquentia: Dante's Book of Exile* (Lincoln: University of Nebraska Press, 1990), 127–31.

29. Marshall, *"Razos de trobar" of Raimon Vidal,* 101; on the date, lxxviii–lxxix.

30. Carl Appel, ed., *Provenzalische Chrestomathie,* 6th ed. (Leipzig: Reisland, 1930), 197–201; Adolphe-F. Gatien-Arnoult, ed., *Las flors del gay saber, estier dichas "Las leys d'amors"* (Toulouse: J.-B. Paya, 1841–43), 1:338–65. See Alfred Jeanroy, "Les *Leys d'amors,*" *Histoire littéraire de la France* 38 (1949): 139–233.

31. "Il semble les considérer comme des formes rigides, soumises à des règles immuables" (He seems to consider them as rigid forms subject to unchangeable rules) (Jeanroy, *"Leys d'amors,"* 185).

32. Appel, *Provenzalische Chrestomathie,* 198.

33. Ibid., 200–201.

34. The following examples are documented by reference to François Zufferey, *Bibliographie des poètes provençaux des XIVe et XVe siècles* (Geneva: Droz, 1981).

35. Ibid., 568,2; 518,1; 558,12; 558,27; 558,34; 569,29; 558,8.

36. Norman F. Cantor, *Inventing the Middle Ages: The Lives, Works, and Ideas of the Great Medievalists of the Twentieth Century* (New York: William Morrow, 1991), 7.

37. "Mediaeval" appeared in English in 1827, "médiéval" in French in 1874; "médiéviste" appeared in French in 1868, "mediaevalist" in English in 1874 (in the sense "one who studies . . . mediaeval history"). See the *Oxford English Dictionary,* 2d ed. (1989), and the *Trésor de la langue française.* On the concept of Romance languages, see Iorgu Iordan, *An Introduction to Romance Linguistics, Its Schools and Scholars,* trans. John Orr, rev. R. Posner (Oxford: Blackwell, 1970), 3–13. On Gothic and Romanesque, see Stephen G. Nichols, "Periodization and the Politics of Perception: A Romanesque Example," *Poetics Today* 10 (1989): 127–54, and Nichols, "Romanesque Imitation or Imitating the Romans?" in *Mimesis, from Mirror to Method: Augustine to Descartes,* ed. John D. Lyons and Stephen G. Nichols, Jr. (Hanover: University Press of New England, 1982), 36–59.

38. William Kerrigan and Gordon Braden, *The Idea of the Renaissance* (Baltimore: Johns Hopkins University Press, 1989), 9.

39. "Se dit des poésies qui expriment les sentiments intimes du poète" (used of

poems that express the intimate feelings of the poet) since 1755, according to the *Trésor de la langue française*. In English since 1664 or 1778 (*Oxford English Dictionary*, 2d ed.). "The word 'lyric' is not typically medieval"; see Margaret Switten and Howell Chickering, eds., *The Medieval Lyric: A Project Supported by The National Endowment for the Humanities and Mount Holyoke College* ([South Hadley, Mass.: Mount Holyoke College], 1987–89), *Commentary Volume*, 3.

40. Timothy J. Reiss, "The Invention of Literature," *The Meaning of Literature* (Ithaca: Cornell University Press, 1992), 70–96; Mark Jeffreys, "Ideologies of Lyric: A Problem of Genre in Contemporary Anglophone Poetics," *PMLA* 110 (1995): 196–205, at 198.

41. See Nathan Edelman, "The Early Uses of Medium Aevum, Moyen Age, Middle Ages" and "Other Uses of Moyen Age and Moyen Temps," *The Eye of the Beholder: Essays in French Literature* (Baltimore: Johns Hopkins University Press, 1974), 58–85.

42. William D. Paden, "Europe from Latin to Vernacular in Epic, Lyric, Romance," in *Performance of Literature in Historical Perspectives*, ed. David W. Thompson (Lanham, Md.: University Press of America, 1983), 67–105.

43. Guilhem IX, poem 6, line 36; see Gerald A. Bond, "The Structure of the *Gap* of the Count of Poitiers, William VII," *Neuphilologische Mitteilungen* 79 (1978): 162–72. Valeria Bertolucci [Pizzorusso], ed., "La supplica di Guiraut Riquier e la risposta di Alfonso X di Castiglia," *Studi mediolatini e volgari* 14 (1966): 9–135.

44. J. H. Marshall, *The Transmission of Troubadour Poetry* [London: Westfield College, 1975], 5.

45. William D. Paden, "The Role of the Joglar in Troubadour Lyric Poetry," in *Chrétien de Troyes and the Troubadours: Essays in Memory of the Late Leslie Topsfield*, ed. Peter S. Noble and Linda M. Paterson (Cambridge: St. Catharine's College, 1984), 90–111; and Paden, "Manuscripts," in *A Handbook of the Troubadours*, ed. F. R. P. Akehurst and Judith M. Davis (Berkeley: University of California Press, 1995), 307–33.

46. "Hom que's red enamoratz" (Appel, *Provenzalische Chrestomathie*, 198).

47. For an edition of this song in its three versions see the appendix to this essay. A thorough review of scholarship on Azalais and an edition of her song were provided by Angelica Rieger, *Trobairitz: Der Beitrag der Frau in der altokzitanischen höfischen Lyrik, Edition des Gesamtkorpus*, Beihefte zur Zeitschrift für romanische Philologie, vol. 233 (Tübingen: Niemeyer, 1991), 480–504. More recent editions have relied heavily on Rieger's, as have I; see Pierre Bec, *Chants d'amour des femmes-troubadours: Trobairitz et "chansons de femme"* (Paris: Stock, 1995), 65–70, and Matilda Tomaryn Bruckner, Laurie Shepard, and Sarah White, *Songs of the Women Troubadours* (New York: Garland, 1995), 34–37, 154–57.

48. Aimo Sakari, "Azalais de Porcairagues, le Joglar de Raimbaut d'Orange," *Neuphilologische Mitteilungen* 50 (1949): 23–43, 56–87, 174–98; Sakari, "A propos d'Azalais de Porcairagues," *Mélanges de philologie romane dédiés à la mémoire de Jean Boutière*, ed. Irénée Cluzel and François Pirot (Liège: Soledi, 1971), 1:517–28; Sakari, "Un vers embarrassant d'Azalais de Porcairagues," *Cultura neolatina* 38 (1978): 215–22; Sakari, "Azalais de Porcairagues, interlocutrice de Raimbaut d'Orange?" in *Atti del Secondo Congresso Internazionale della Association Internationale d'Etudes Occitanes*, ed. Giuliano Gasca Queirazza (Turin: Dipartimento di Scienze Letterarie e Filologiche, 1993), 1:369–74.

49. See William D. Paden, "The Chronology of the Trobairitz," in *The Voice of the*

Trobairitz: Perspectives on the Women Troubadours, ed. Paden (Philadelphia: University of Pennsylvania Press, 1989), 23–25. The comtessa de Dia, perhaps attested in 1212 (Paden, "Checklist of Poems by the Trobairitz," in *Voice*, 231), was dated at the end of the twelfth or beginning of the thirteenth century by Riquer (*Trovadores*, 2:791), but in the second half of the twelfth century by Rieger (*Trobairitz*, 614). Rieger argued that the comtessa imitated songs of Bernart de Ventadorn and Azalais de Porcairagues; aside from the uncertainty regarding the dates of Bernart, however, contrafacture does not provide reliable chronology, since an imitation need not be contemporary with its model. On this conjectured network of songs see also Gioia Zaganelli, "Trovatori e 'trobairitz': voci provenzali a confronto (su Azalais de Porcairagues, la Contessa di Dia, Castelloza, Raimbaut d'Aurenga e Bernart de Ventadorn)," *Messana*, n.s. 4 (1990): 89–120, at 107; further on Azalais and the comtessa de Dia, see Zaganelli, 115–16. Castelloza was active in the early thirteenth century (Paden, "Checklist," 230; Riquer, *Trovadores*, 3:1325; Rieger, 562). Other *cansos* were composed by Clara d'Anduza (1200–1250 [Rieger, 577]), Beatritz de Romans (uncertain [Rieger, 509]), and an anonymous trobairitz (P-C 461,206: after the comtessa de Dia [Rieger, 639]). Tibors left a fragmentary *cobla*, perhaps from a *canso* (1200–1233 [Rieger, 651]).

50. Boutière and Schutz, *Biographies*, 341.

51. William D. Paden with Linda H. Armitage, Olivia Holmes, Theodore Kendris, Audrey Lumsden-Kouvel, and Terence O'Connell, "The Poems of the Troubadours Guilhem d'Autpol and 'Daspol,'" *Romance Philology* 46 (1993): 407–52, at 419.

52. Walter T. Pattison, *The Life and Works of the Troubadour Raimbaut d'Orange* (Minneapolis: University of Minnesota Press, 1952), no. 24, lines 1–7; trans. Pattison.

53. On Gombrich see the introduction to this volume.

54. I base this negative assertion on the computerized text of Pattison's edition provided by Professor F. R. P. Akehurst of the University of Minnesota, and accessible on the Internet through ARTFL (American Research on the Treasury of the French Language), at <http://humanities.uchicago.edu/forms/PROV.form.html>.

55. The *estribot* does not figure in Frank's terminology; we have only two poems to which the term is applied in their own texts, both thirteenth-century satires against monks. See Chambers, *Introduction*, 85–86.

56. Pattison, *Life and Works of Raimbaut d'Orange*, nos. 1, line 64; 5, lines 1, 55; 10, lines 47, 58; 11, line 1; 17, line 71; 20, line 60; 35, lines 4, 50; 36, line 4; 38, line 63; 39, line 41.

57. "A mon vers dirai chansso / Ab leus motz ez ab leu so / Ez en rima vil'e plana" (Pattison, *Life and Works of Raimbaut d'Orange*, no. 30, lines 1–3).

58. Linda Paterson renders no. 4, line 2, as "a light *chanso* for jousting"; see her *Troubadours and Eloquence* (Oxford: Clarendon Press, 1975), 171–72. The connotation of easiness in *canso* can also be expressed in the diminutive *cansoneta*: Raimbaut offers to make *una chansoneta gaia* (no. 9, line 7) and a *chansoneta ... laner'a dir*, "a little song ... easy to sing" (no. 3, lines 1–2, trans. Pattison in *Life and Works of Raimbaut d'Orange*) or "to be sung in a low way" (Paterson, 163–64). He identifies three songs with the term *chanso* (nos. 16, line 57; 19, line 57; 21, line 43) which are *chansons* to Frank.

59. On *trobar leu* and *trobar clus* in general see Paterson, *Troubadours and Eloquence;* on these ideas in Raimbaut d'Aurenga, 145–85. "Raimbaut ... seems to distinguish

between *vers* and *chanso* according to whether a composition belongs to the *trobar leu* or not" (Paterson, 173).

60. For a list of *rimas caras* see Gianluigi Toja, ed., *Arnaut Daniel: Canzoni* (Florence: Sansoni, 1960), 42–44.

61. Rieger (*Trobairitz*, 481–84) edits Versions 1 and 2 but translates only Version 2. She is aware, of course, that Version 3 exists.

62. Elizabeth W. Poe, *Compilatio: Lyric Texts and Prose Commentaries in Troubadour Manuscript H (Vat. Lat. 3207)*, forthcoming. Beginning of the fourteenth century or end of the thirteenth according to Arno Krispin, "La tradition manuscrite des trobairitz: le chansonnier *H*," *Atti del Secondo Congresso Internazionale della Association Internationale d'Etudes Occitanes,* ed. Giuliano Gasca Queirazza (Turin: Dipartimento di Scienze Letterarie e Filologiche, 1993), 1:231–42, at 231.

63. Rieger sees this history in the opposite order: "Sie [the two *coblas* in *H*] bilden in der Tat in dieser umgekehrten Reihenfolge eine abgeschlossene, sinnvolle Einheit, so daß die 'doas coblas' durchaus auch als *cobla dobla* zum Thema *ric ome* konzipiert und erst später in die *canso* interpoliert worden sein könnten" (The two *coblas* in *H* form, in this reversed order, a well-defined unit of meaning, so that the *doas coblas* could only have been conceived as a *cobla dobla* on the theme of the *ric ome*, and first interpolated later into the *canso*) (*Trobairitz*, 495). On the chronology of the *cobla* see Jeanroy, *Poésie lyrique*, 2:274; Leube, "Cobla," 69; and Poe in this volume.

64. See Paden, "Manuscripts," 308–9.

65. For various opinions on the date of *N* see Michel-André Bossy and Nancy A. Jones, "Gender and Compilational Patterns in Troubadour Lyric: The Case of Manuscript *N*," *French Forum* 21 (1996): 261–80, at 275, n. 1, and add, for 1285–1300, Stephen G. Nichols, "'Art' and 'Nature': Looking for (Medieval) Principles of Order in Occitan Chansonnier *N* (Morgan 819)," in *The Whole Book: Cultural Perspectives on the Medieval Miscellany*, ed. Stephen G. Nichols and Siegfried Wenzel (Ann Arbor: University of Michigan Press, 1996), 83–121, at 91.

66. *Fanc* and *fanha* are synonyms; both are glossed as "fange" (mud) in the *PD* (183–84). Sakari ("Azalais," 83) pointed out verbal parallels to Azalais's song in Raimbaut's winter settings in other poems: "Er quant s'embla·l foill del fraisse" (Pattison, *Life and Works of Raimbaut d'Orange*, no. 13), "Ar s'espan la flors enversa" (no. 39), and "Non chant per auzel ni per flor" (no. 27). Maria Luisa Meneghetti added "Ara non siscla ni chanta" (no. 14); see *Il pubblico dei trovatori* (Modena: Mucchi, 1984), 119–21.

67. Azalais was a relative of Raimbaut according to Rieger (*Trobairitz*, 501–2), who cites Pattison, *Life and Works of Raimbaut d'Orange*, no. 15, lines 36–40, addressed to Joglar: "I cannot remember that I ever had a sister, cousin, or female relative who, if she wished to love in gentle fashion ever refrained from it or remained silent on account of me" (trans. Pattison). Riquer has described Azalais's relation to Raimbaut as "más confidente que amada" (more a confidante than a lover [*Trovadores*, 1:421]); cf. Sakari, "Azalais," 81.

68. Sakari, "Azalais," 29, 68; Rieger, *Trobairitz*, 500.

69. In this reading Azalais identifies herself with the *dompna* of line 17. The opposite view was taken by Sarah Kay in *Subjectivity in Troubadour Poetry* (Cambridge: Cambridge University Press, 1990), 106–7. For Kay (111), the encounter with a repressive gender system "silenced or oppressed" the subjectivity of the trobairitz. For

Simon Gaunt, the trobairitz rather represented their subjectivity as inexpressible; see *Gender and Genre in Medieval French Literature* (Cambridge: Cambridge University Press, 1995), 165. I grant that the gender system was oppressive to women, of course, but not that they failed to express themselves—as Azalais did, and eloquently, in the present poem.

70. On the *comjat* or *chanson de change* see A. Jeanroy and J.-J. Salverda de Grave, eds., *Poésies de Uc de Saint-Circ* (Toulouse: Privat, 1913), xxx–xxxi; Jeanroy, *Poésie lyrique*, 1:121–22, 2:163–64, 328–29. Christiane Leube-Fey identifies thirty examples in *Bild und Funktion der dompna in der Lyrik der Trobadors* (Heidelberg: Winter, 1971), 74–75; Köhler discusses them in "'Vers' und Kanzone," 167–76. A more diffuse and general parallel is to the themes of joy and grief in *cansos* such as those of Bernart de Ventadorn, on which see Pierre Bec, "La douleur et son univers poétique chez Bernard de Ventadour," *Cahiers de civilisation médiévale* 11 (1968): 545–71, 12 (1969): 25–33, reprinted in Bec, *Ecrits*, 165–200; and Bec, "L'antithèse poétique chez Bernard de Ventadour," *Mélanges de philologie romane dédiés à la mémoire de Jean Boutière* (Liège: Soledi, 1971), 1:107–37, reprinted in Bec, *Ecrits*, 201–31.

71. Paterson, *Troubadours and Eloquence*, 155, 162.

72. Tilde Sankovitch, "The *Trobairitz*," in *The Troubadours: An Introduction*, ed. Simon Gaunt and Sarah Kay (Cambridge: Cambridge University Press, 1999), 118–19. On mimicry or borrowed speech see also Doris Earnshaw, *The Female Voice in Medieval Romance Lyric* (New York: Lang, 1988), and Kathryn Gravdal, "Metaphor, Metonymy, and the Medieval Women Trobairitz," *Romanic Review* 83 (1992): 411–26.

73. The *planh* begins with the prototype by Cercamon, "Lo plaing comenz iradamen" (1137), which is as true to the eventual concept of the genre as Marcabru's prototypical *pastorela* is true to that one. But a prototype does not constitute a genre until it inspires imitation; that the *planh* was not fully constituted at the death of Guilhem X of Aquitaine, for whom Cercamon lamented, is shown by the incidental mention of Guilhem's death in Marcabru's "Pax in nomine Domini," where it is introduced quite unexpectedly, almost as an afterthought. For Cercamon's poem see George Wolf and Roy Rosenstein, eds., *The Poetry of Cercamon and Jaufre Rudel* (New York: Garland, 1983), no. 1; Marcabru's poem is edited in my *Introduction to Old Occitan* (New York: MLA, 1998), 106–11. For a *planh* by an anonymous trobairitz for her *amic*, dated conjecturally in mid-thirteenth century, see Rieger's no. 42 (on the date see *Trobairitz*, 670). On prototypes of various genres in the *usanza antiga*, see Pickens in this volume.

74. "Möglicherweise ist sie [the song] ein Konglomerat aus mehreren, formal nahezu identischen, alle nur fragmentarisch überlieferten Werken der trobairitz, einer *canso*, einer *cobla dobla* nach deren Muster und einer *cobla* aus einem Raimbaut d'Aurenga betreffenden *planh* oder *sirventes*-artigen Stück" (Possibly the song is a conglomerate of several works of the trobairitz, formally almost identical, all fragmentary—a *canso*, a *cobla dobla* on the model of the *canso*, and a *cobla* from a *planh*- or *sirventes*-like piece belonging to Raimbaut d'Aurenga) (Rieger, *Trobairitz*, 495); see also Rieger, 503–4; Bec, *Chants d'amour*, 66.

75. I hesitate to regard the songs of the trobairitz as a blend of the troubadour *canso* and the *chanson de femme*, better attested in Old French than in Occitan but named as a genre only in Galician-Portuguese (the *cantiga de amigo*), because such an algebra of genres assumes that the genres themselves had more reality at the time

than we can show they did. For this approach see Pierre Bec, "'Trobairitz' et chansons de femme: contribution à la connaissance du lyrisme féminin au moyen âge," *Cahiers de civilisation médiévale* 22 (1979): 235–62, reprinted in Bec, *Ecrits*, 283–310; Bec, "Trobairitz occitanes et chansons de femme françaises," *Perspectives médiévales* 5 (1979): 59–76, reprinted in Bec, *Ecrits*, 283–310; Matilda Tomaryn Bruckner, "Na Castelloza, *Trobairitz*, and Troubadour Lyric," *Romance Notes* 25 (1985): 239–53, at 251; Gravdal, "Metaphor, Metonymy, and the Medieval Women Trobairitz," at 413–14; Caroline A. Jewers, "Loading the Canon: For and against Feminist Readings of the Trobairitz," *Romance Quarterly* 41 (1994): 134–47, at 144–45. Ulrich Mölk points out that Bec "n'a pas coupé tous les liens qui l'attachent à la théorie romantique de l'origine de la poésie européenne, car il considère la 'chanson de femme,' 'ce type lyrique (je le cite) bien défini, archaïsant et traditionnel' comme 'l'archétype générateur de nombreux genres et sous-genres médiévaux'" (Bec has not cut all the ties that bind him to the romantic theory of the origin of European poetry, since he considers the "chanson de femme," "this lyric type" [I quote him] "well defined, archaizing and traditional," as "the generating archetype of many medieval genres and subgenres"); see "Chansons de femme, trobairitz et la théorie romantique de l'origine de la poésie lyrique européenne," in *Atti del Secondo Congresso Internazionale della Association Internationale d'Etudes Occitanes,* ed. Giuliano Gasca Queirazza (Turin: Dipartimento di Scienze Letterarie e Filologiche, 1993), 1:243–54, at 250.

76. Rieger, *Trobairitz,* 496.

77. For this interpretation see Bossy and Jones, "Gender and Compilational Patterns." As Bruckner has observed, MS *N* "seems to have made numerous small variations in its representation of Na Castelloza's songs that lead to a more negative reading" ("Na Castelloza, *Trobairitz,* and Troubadour Lyric," 252, n. 22). However, key passages in which Castelloza seems to say she takes pleasure in pain are essentially the same in *N* and the other manuscripts. Compare the version of poems 1, line 36; 2, lines 22–23; and 3, lines 16–17, as edited by Rieger in *Trobairitz* (520, 529, 539), with the edition from *N* by William D. Paden with Julia C. Hayes, Georgina M. Mahoney, Barbara J. O'Neill, Edward J. Samuelson, Jeri L. Snyder, Edwina Spodark, Julie A. Storme, and Scott D. Westrem, "The Poems of the *Trobairitz* Na Castelloza," *Romance Philology* 35 (1981): 158–82 (analysis of this point, 166). If the scribe of *N* enhanced Castelloza's dark tones and extended them to Azalais de Porcairagues, he nevertheless found his point of departure in Castelloza's own work.

78. "The introduction of Ovid into this stanza represents the intervention of an intellectual.... The *H* scribe (or his predecessor) changed the whole thought in a manner revealing more scholarly imagination than scribal integrity.... [The form of MS *H* is that of] a collection of authoritative writings accompanied by commentary" (Poe, *Compilatio*). For Krispin the scribe of *H* was "un érudit," "un dilettante éclairé," "un collectionneur ou un chroniqueur de la vie mondaine" (a scholar ... an enlightened dilettante ... a collector or a chronicler of fashionable life) ("Tradition manuscrite des trobairitz," 231, 232, 233).

79. See Paden, Sankovitch, and Stäblein, *Poems of Bertran de Born,* 33–44.

80. Paden and others, "Poems of the Troubadours Guilhem d'Autpol and 'Daspol'"; for detailed discussion of the generic status of the four poems, see 415–23.

81. See Geneviève Brunel-Lobrichon, "Images of Women and Imagined Trobair-

itz in the Béziers Chansonnier," in *Voice of the Trobairitz*, ed. Paden, 211; transcription of the poem, 223–24.

82. *Il canzoniere provenzale estense, riprodotto per il centenario della nascita di Giulio Bertoni*, 2 vols. (Modena: STEM Mucchi, 1979–82).

83. Frank, *Répertoire*, 382:107.

84. Oscar Schultz[-Gora], ed., "Die provenzalischen Dichterinnen," in *Einundachtzigste Nachricht von dem Friedrichs-Gymnasium zu Altenburg* (Altenburg: Bonde, 1888), 1–36.

85. Color reproductions in Martín de Riquer, *Vidas y retratos de trovadores* (Barcelona: Círculo de Lectores y Galaxia Gutenberg, 1995), 184.

86. Brunel-Lobrichon, "Images of Women," 217; the miniature is reproduced on 214.

87. Emil Levy, *Petit dictionnaire provençal-français*, 4th ed. (Heidelberg: Winter, 1966).

88. Emil Levy and Carl Appel, *Provenzalisches Supplement-Wörterbuch* (Leipzig: Reisland, 1894–1924).

89. Walther von Wartburg, *Französisches etymologisches Wörterbuch* (Bonn: Klopp, 1928–).

90. H. E. Butler and E. A. Barber, eds., *The Elegies of Propertius* (Hildesheim: Olms, 1964).

91. Eugen Cnyrim, *Sprichwörter, sprichwörtliche Redensarten und Sentenzen bei den provenzalischen Lyrikern* (Marburg: Elwert, 1888).

92. Frank M. Chambers, *Proper Names in the Lyrics of the Troubadours* (Chapel Hill: University of North Carolina Press, 1971), 265.

93. "A *joglar*" for Joan M. Ferrante, "Notes toward the Study of a Female Rhetoric in the Trobairitz," in *Voice of the Trobairitz*, ed. Paden, 64. "Wahrscheinlich ein Senhal für einen weiteren Freund in der Runde" (probably a senhal [code name] for another friend in the circle) for Katharina Städtler, *Altprovenzalische Frauendichtung (1150–1250)* (Heidelberg: Winter, 1990), 160.

94. See also Riquer, *Trovadores*, 1:44; Amelia E. Van Vleck, "Reciprocating Composition in the Songs of Castelloza," in *Voice of the Trobairitz*, ed. Paden, 103–4.

95. See Jeanroy, *Poésie lyrique*, 1:165–66; Sakari, "Azalais," 177–78; Hans-Erich Keller, "Ermengarda of Narbonne and Beatrice of Este: A Study in Contrasts," *Tenso* 10 (1994): 9–17; further references in Bossy and Jones, "Gender and Compilational Patterns," 280, n. 54. Städtler points out, however, that *lei* could also refer to some other friend of Azalais (*Altprovenzalische Frauendichtung*, 160n.).

96. François-Just-Marie Raynouard, *Lexique roman* (Paris: Silvestre, 1844).

97. Paden, *Introduction to Old Occitan*, 360.

98. R. C. Johnston, ed., *Les poésies lyriques du troubadour Arnaut de Mareuil* (Paris: Droz, 1935), 148.

CHAPTER 2

"*Cobleiarai, car mi platz*": The Role of the Cobla in the Occitan Lyric Tradition

ELIZABETH W. POE

It is paradoxical that we classify the genre that accounts for fully 19 percent of all troubadour poems as minor.[1] Only the *canso* and the *sirventes* are better represented than the *cobla*. As far as form is concerned, we are right to assign the *cobla* a relatively low rank in the hierarchy of troubadour genres. In contrast to the *canso* and, to a lesser extent, the *sirventes*, which pride themselves on metrical complexity and originality, the *cobla* is short and essentially derivative. From the standpoint of theme as well, we are justified in not taking the *cobla* very seriously, since it tends to deal with trifles, including parody, personal satire, and reports of recent tavern brawls.[2] Historically too, we are on solid ground in relegating the *cobla* to the "kitchen"[3] inasmuch as the troubadours themselves seem to have regarded it as inferior to the three major courtly genres, namely, the *canso, sirventes*, and *tenso*. It is in the domain of function, however, that we need to reevaluate the accepted appraisal of the *cobla*. Clearly, any genre that was practiced and preserved with as much diligence as the *cobla* must have played a major role both in society and within the system of troubadour lyric genres.

There are essentially four types of *cobla:* inserted *coblas*, extracted *coblas*, *coblas esparsas*, and *cobla*-exchanges.[4] The first type, consisting of stanzas inserted by one person into someone else's poem, is the hardest to spot, when it is well done. The *C*-scribe's rendering of Guillem IX's famous red-cat poem,[5] which omits some stanzas and substitutes new ones, represents a blatant instance of such unauthorized intervention. Somewhat subtler is the

RT-version of Giraut de Bornelh's *alba*, "Reis glorios" (P-C 242,64), which, with its seventh stanza, betrays the tampering of a literal-minded interpreter.

The second type, or extracted *cobla*, is made up of one, two, or three stanzas taken by one person from the poem of another and allowed to function, either anonymously or under the name of their author, as an independent entity. In MS *H*, for example, we encounter on fol. 46a two stanzas introduced by the heading: "Aquestas doas coblas porten lor raisons." Although they are presented as a unit unto themselves in *H*, we know from other manuscripts that they are an integral part (specifically, stanzas 4 and 3) of Azalais de Porcairagues's only surviving *canso* (P-C 43,1).[6] Extracted *coblas* typically occur in florilegia, in troubadour biographies (especially those in MS *P*), and in the "Perilhos tractat" section of Matfre Ermengaud's *Breviari d'Amor*.[7] In some codices, however, they are simply mixed in with anonymous *coblas esparsas*.

The third type, or *cobla esparsa*, is a stanza composed by an individual poet, who conceived of it as an entity that could stand alone.[8] Although the *cobla esparsa* can treat any subject, we usually associate it with the assertion of bourgeois values thanks to its most prolific practitioners, Bertran Carbonel of Marseille and Guillem Olivier of Arles.[9] Bertran's unabashed admonition (P-C 82,72) to distrust one's neighbor is characteristic of the practical but not very Christian advice found in at least one kind of *cobla esparsa*.

> Per fol tenc qui s'acompanha
> Ab sel a qui a fach mal;
> Car non es c'ades non planha
> Dins son cor l'ira mortal;
> Que coratje sert, sapchatz,
> Non a ben tro qu'es venjatz;
> Per que totz hom deu refudar la pacha
> D'ome, cant mal ni anta li a facha.[10]

> I hold him for a fool who keeps company with someone whom he has harmed; for it is impossible for that person not to hold a mortal resentment in his heart; it will be calmed only when he has avenged himself; that is why everyone should refuse to have dealings with anyone whom he has harmed or shamed.[11]

The fourth type, or *cobla*-exchange, consists of a series of stanzas by two or more poets. It distinguishes itself from the *tenso* both by its brevity and by the fact that it does not necessarily raise a question. Most often it begins when one person insults another, either addressing him or her directly or speaking in the third person. If the injured party replies (and it is not always clear that a response is expected or even welcome), the result is a *cobla*-exchange;[12] otherwise the original stanza remains a *cobla esparsa*.[13] In the example that I have chosen (P-C 457,33 = 185,3), Uc de Saint Circ, who is doing very well for himself, makes fun of his patron, the count of Rodez, for having fallen on hard times. The count answers in a manner typical of such exchanges. He does not deny the allegation that he is having financial difficulties, for he is clever enough to see that if he contradicts the disrespectful jongleur on this point, he will no longer have such a ready excuse for not giving him anything. Instead, he argues that if he is poor, Uc, with his insatiable greed, is partly to blame.

> Seign'en coms, no·us cal esmaiar
> Per mi ni estar cossiros,
> Q'ieu non sui ges vengutz a vos
> Per ren querre ni demandar,
> Que ben ai so que m'a mestier,
> E vos vei que faillon denier;
> Per que non ai en cor qe·us qieira re;
> Anz si·us dava, faria gran merce.

> N'Uc de Sain Circ, be·m deu grevar
> Q'ie·us veja, que ogan sai fos
> Paubres e nutz e sofraitos
> E eu vos fi manen anar,
> Que mai·m costetz que dui archier
> Non feiron o dui cavallier;
> Pero ben sai si·us dava un palafre,
> Dieus que m'en gart, vos lo penriatz be.[14]

Lord Count, there is no need for you to worry or be upset on my account, for I did not come to you to seek or ask for anything, for I have all that I need. But I see that you are short of money; therefore I do not intend to ask you for anything; on the contrary, if I were to give to you, I would be doing an act of mercy.

Sir Uc de Saint Circ, I am right to be sorry to see you come, for the last time you were here, you were poor and naked and lacking in everything and I saw to it that you went away rich. You cost me more than two archers or two knights would have done; and yet I know for sure that if I were to give you a palfrey—perish the thought!—you would indeed take it.

Dividing the *coblas* into four types, while useful, represents the attempt of modern scholars to impose order on a sometimes unruly body of texts. Such classifications cannot tell us how the genre developed. In order to determine at what point the troubadours became aware of the potential of the *cobla* to function as a distinct genre, we need to examine what they themselves have to say on the matter. The *vida* for Uc de Saint Circ provides us with an important clue for establishing the approximate date of the emergence of the *cobla* as genre. The biographer, probably Uc himself, reports that, while he was studying in Montpellier, he learned "cansos e vers e sirventes e tensos e coblas."[15] What this tells us is that by the first quarter of the thirteenth century, the *cobla* was well enough established as a genre to be considered part of the standard repertoire of troubadour songs. We can assume, then, that the genre must have been recognized and practiced, at the very latest, among the poets of the generation immediately preceding Uc's, that is, those active in the last decade of the twelfth century.[16] And indeed the manuscript tradition supports this hypothesis, for it preserves one *cobla esparsa* and several *cobla*-exchanges that can be dated to the early 1190s.

The first is a *cobla esparsa* by Folquet de Marseilla (P-C 155,35), which was probably composed late in 1189.[17] This stanza was meant as a follow-up to the *canso* "Mout i fetz gran pechat Amors" (P-C 155,14), which had been completed some months before. In the *cobla* Folquet complains to Vermillion, whom we can take to be a jongleur, that a certain painted lady has been going around telling everyone that Folquet's latest *canso* was dedicated to her. She has spread the word that the "High Branch," which the troubadour had begged Mercy to bend toward him, refers to her.[18] Folquet counters that he would never touch a branch that bends and breaks so easily or that would smudge his hands with make-up.

> Vermillon, clam vos faç d'un' avol pega pencha
> qe m'a una chançon degolad' et estencha
> qe di qe fi de lei, e s'es vanad' e feincha
> q'eu l'appellei Aut-Ram don il s'es aut empencha:
> il men, q'eu non plei ram qi tan leu fraing ni·s trencha
> ni voil branca tochar de qe leu ma man tencha.[19]

> Vermillion, I am complaining to you about an evil, stupid, painted lady who has destroyed and ruined my song by saying that I composed it about her, and she has boasted and pretended that I called her High Branch, on account of which she raised her status considerably: she lies, for I do not bend a branch that so easily breaks or splits, nor do I want to touch a branch from which my hand would get easily smudged.

As Folquet's editor, Stronski, has remarked, it is impossible to determine what claims this vulgar hussy may have had on the troubadour.[20] Maybe he really was involved with her. In any event, this *cobla* is an amusing monument to the risks of concealing the identity of the intended recipient of one's *canso* and to the new practice of composing one- and two-stanza poems.

Besides Folquet's *cobla esparsa,* three *cobla*-exchanges can reasonably be situated in the last decade of the twelfth century.[21] The first, "Ben auria ops pas e vis" (P-C 136,2 = 167, 13), consists of an exchange of insults between Gaucelm Faidit and Elias d'Uisel (1192 or 1193).[22] Elias teases Gaucelm for having lived extravagantly while he was off on a crusade. He mocks him for his corpulence, which kept him from being a threat to the Turks. Gaucelm retaliates, making fun of Elias for his boasting and poverty. He has managed to reduce his noble family to such destitution that the only things that one can expect to receive at their castle are *cansos* and *sirventes.* They have no food or clothing to bestow on their guests. Elias does not let Gaucelm's charges go unanswered: he admits that he is poor in contrast to Gaucelm, who has profited from his association with Guillelma, a woman of questionable reputation.[23] In MS D^a the exchange includes a fourth *cobla,* in which Gaucelm, conceding that he is fat, renews his attack on poor Elias.

The second early *cobla*-exchange, "Tuit me pregon, Engles, qu'eu vos don saut" (P-C 392,31; 209,1; 392,15a), involves Raimbaut de Vaqueiras and Guillem del Baus.[24] Like the piece by Gaucelm Faidit and Elias d'Uisel, this one is a volley of innuendoes, but, in this case, it is even harder than in the first to make sense of the allusions. Raimbaut taunts Guillem for having made a foolish journey from which he has returned none the wiser. He makes an obscure reference to a gift denied to Guillem by the king of France. Guillem reacts by expressing his surprise that Raimbaut should be so upset with him, since Raimbaut himself is known for his foolishness as well as for his greed. Raimbaut's retort, which portrays Guillem as being caught like a fish and then deceived by a burgher who presented a counterfeit seal, is uninterpretable without a context. While the precise meaning of the image may escape us, its tone of disdain is nonetheless unmistakable.[25]

The third extant *cobla*-exchange that may have been composed as early as the 1190s consists of two *coblas* directed by Lanza Marques against Peire Vidal, followed by one *cobla* of rebuttal from Peire (P-C 285,1 = 364,19).[26] Borrowing the metrical pattern and an identifying phrase, "sen ni membransa," from Peire Vidal's *canso,* "Quan hom honratz torna en gran paubreira" (P-C 364,40),[27] Lanza characterizes the troubadour as a debauched emperor—stupid, drunk, cowardly, but harmless. The D^a version of the exchange contains a second *cobla* in which Lanza goes on to enumerate the various injuries that he wishes this "emperor" to suffer, among others, that he be jabbed in the eyes and given a stick in place of a lance. Recognizing himself as the object of Lanza's scorn, Peire responds by accusing his opponent of being like a blind man who, having lost all sense of propriety, urinates in the middle of the road. With a play on the verb *vens*, Peire implies that Lanza sells castles just as the hag does her capons.[28]

These three early *cobla*-exchanges resemble one another to a degree that cannot be merely coincidental: all three consist of insults hurled back and forth between a professional troubadour and someone who was essentially a patron and only occasionally a poet; all three are preserved in the same two manuscripts, namely *H* and D^a, both of which were compiled in the second half of the thirteenth century in northern Italy. All three of these poems were well known to Uc de Saint Circ, who chose to include them in the collection of songs that he compiled for Alberico da Romano (= D^a)[29] and to incorporate material from them into his prose commentaries.[30]

The first troubadour to experiment systematically with the *cobla* as genre was Guillem de Berguedan. Among his twenty-two extant poems are a *cobla*-exchange, a *cobla esparsa*, and a pair of *coblas*. All three of these pieces can be situated in the early 1190s. Guillem's *cobla*-exchange (P-C 210,10b) with a certain Gauceran, who is otherwise unknown to us, is more technically speaking a *devinalh*, or riddle poem.[31] Through a series of paradoxes, Guillem describes the weight (*lo pes*) which he bears but cannot touch. The further away from him it is, the more it weighs on him. The weight is called wolf and yet is not a wolf: "Lop es nommat lo pes e lop no es." Gauceran responds without giving away the answer for those slower-witted than he, but nevertheless makes it obvious to his partner that he has caught onto the joke. The *pes*, as Dietmar Rieger has recently clarified, is love, for which the wolf is often a metaphor.[32]

In the other two pieces, Guillem forgets about love and focuses on the bishop of Urgel, whom he despises. In the *cobla* beginning "Ben fo ver qu'en Berguedan" (P-C 210,4),[33] Guillem lambastes the bishop, citing various offenses and defects. He criticizes him for forcing the construction of the lookout at Avian, which cost over a hundred lives and which he is using as a convenient place for sodomizing men and boys. Guillem presents the bishop as physically repulsive with his horse's face. He explains that the bishop has been castrated, which, given his favorite pastime, makes him a laughable figure. Guillem concludes this *cobla* with a punch: "Per c'ausels vola mal ses ploma e pauc val cell'ab meinz d'arzos, e mal fot bisbes ses coillos" (Just as a bird has trouble flying without feathers and a room cannot stand without supports, a bishop has trouble fornicating without testicles). The *cobla*-pair beginning "Mal o fe lo bisbe d'Urgel" (P-C 210,15)[34] tells us nothing new, except that the bishop (and one can hardly blame him) has excommunicated Guillem. Once again the troubadour makes fun of him, for, as he puts it bluntly, "not having testicles in his scrotum" (q'el non a coillos en la pel), for his expressionless face and his nose like a monstrous fish. As in the single *cobla,* Guillem portrays the bishop in this text as a lecherous homosexual. Both pieces come to a climax of sorts in their final verse with a conjugated form of *fotre.*

In addition to the compositions that Guillem intended to be short, the manuscript tradition has apparently shortened two others. One of these pieces, "E fetz una mespreison" (P-C 210,10a), is a single *cobla* recorded as part of a *razo* about Bertran de Born.[35] The biographer quotes this *cobla,* which he identifies as coming from a *sirventes* by Guillem de Berguedan, to help justify Bertran's hatred for Alfonso II, king of Aragon. In the verses cited, Guillem criticizes someone whom we can take to be the king of Aragon for burning two Christians—a jongleur and his companion—on account of a Jew. Obviously this *cobla,* which is explicitly described as part of a longer poem and which does not specify the subject of the opening predicate "fetz mespreison," was not meant by its author to stand alone. The other is a two-stanza *sirventes,* "Ara voill un sirventes far" (P-C 210,3), which Guillem's editor, M. de Riquer, maintains is incomplete.[36] In these verses Guillem rages against an unnamed count thanks to whom the poet almost lost his life. Riquer's claim that these two *coblas* are part of a longer composition is substantiated by the fact that the only collection in which they are preserved is D^c, which is the florilegium of Ferrari de Ferrara, who did not record whole poems but one-, two-, or three-stanza excerpts. Thus, partly through his own doing, partly through the caprices of transmission, Guillem de Berguedan's surviving corpus includes examples of all three kinds of *cobla* that acquired status as a genre.

The oldest attestation of the word *cobla* used as a technical term occurs in a poem by Guillem de Berguedan (P-C 210,6), which can be dated to the early 1190s and which, in any event, predates 1194.[37] In these verses Guillem praises a certain Bernart de Baseill, who has decided to become a troubadour. No one from his hometown should be surprised by this decision, since he knows how to compose well and lace up words and *coblas.*

> Bernartz diz de Baseill
> Que·s fara trobaire
> E no s'en meraveill
> Hom de son repaire;
> Car ben e gen sap trobar
> E moz e coblas laçar.[38]

> Bernart de Baseill says that he will become a troubadour, and let no one from his hometown be surprised by this, for he knows how to compose well and fine and bind together words and *coblas.*

Cobla in this instance means "stanza within a poem," and not a poem unto itself. This is clear not only by its being paired with *motz* but also by its association with the verb *lassar*.[39] Already in the poetry of the earliest known troubadour, *lassar* is a technical term. Guillem IX uses it to explain how he laces up the verse that he produces in his workshop; Marcabru laces the theme with the poem ("razon e·l vers"); Bernart Marti speaks of lacing and tying words ("motz"); Giraut de Bornelh joins and laces finely locked words ("menutz motz serratz"); Peire Vidal boasts of his skill at assembling and lacing words and melody ("motz e son").[40] By setting *coblas* in the context of *motz* and *lassar*, Guillem acknowledges the term's technical meaning, but gives no indication that it denotes anything other than stanzas as components of a longer poem.

The word *cobla* occurs in another text from the 1190s, namely in the Monk of Montaudon's fictive *tenso* with God beginning "L'autrier fui en Paradis" (P-C 305,12), whose composition can be fairly firmly set in 1194. In this "conversation" with the Almighty, the Monk expresses his concern that composing *coblas* and *cansos* is sinful, since anyone who knowingly lies loses God's love.

> "Senher, ieu tem que falhis
> s'ieu fas coblas e cansos,
> qu'om pert vostr'amor e vos
> qui son escien mentis."[41]

> Lord, I fear that I am at fault if I compose *coblas* and *cansos,* for one loses Your love and You if one knowingly lies.

Although the phrase "coblas e chansos" could mean that the *cobla* is a lyric genre, just like the *canso,* it could also mean that the composition of *coblas* is a necessary step in composing a *canso*. One cannot make a *canso* without first making *coblas*.

We find another relatively early instance of *cobla* used as a technical term in the opening verses of Guillem de Saint Didier's *canso,* "Aissi cum es bella cill de cui chan" (P-C 234,3). Because his lady and everything about her is so *bella,* Guillem intends to start every stanza of this poem with the word *bel:*

> Aissi cum es bella cill de cui chan,
> E bels sos noms, sa terr' e siei chastel,
> E beill siei dich, siei faich e siei semblan,
> Vuoill mas coblas movan totas en *bel.*[42]

> Since the one about whom I sing is beautiful, and her name, her land, and her castles are beautiful as well, and beautiful are her speech, her deeds, and her appearance, I want all of my stanzas to begin with "beautiful."

In this instance, the meaning of *cobla* is unquestionably "stanza," as a part of a longer composition.

Guillem Ademar, too, while indulging in a bit of verbal acrobatics in the song beginning "Comensamen comensarai" (P-C 202,4), employs the term *cobla* in a straightforward way. Having committed himself to the pattern of reusing one word from the final verse of each stanza in every verse of the next, the troubadour gets himself into a bind when he has to build a whole stanza around the word *deniers* (money). But, as he explains, he has no choice, given the ending of his *cobla lay*.

> Deniers—pus "deniers" mentaurai
> Tan soven—per deniers, no·m plai;
> Mas quar fenisc ma cobla lay
> En "deniers," dic tans "deniers" sai.[43]

> Money—since I will mention money so often—does not please me because it is money; but because I ended my *cobla* there in "money," I say "money" so much here.

As in the example from Guillem de Saint Didier, *coblas* in Guillem Ademar's poem can only mean "stanzas" as building blocks of *cansos*.

Indeed, the only instance before a very late date where the word *cobla* within a lyric poem might refer to *coblas esparsas* (with the possible exception of the Monk of Montaudon's fictional *tenso* with God) occurs in a *cobla esparsa* by Guillem Magret (P-C 223,6), a jongleur active around the turn of the thirteenth century. Magret, who, as his name suggests, was not getting fat from his verses, laments the fact that money will get the jongleur further than songs.

> Non valon re coblas ni arrazos
> ni sirventes; tan es lo monz deliz
> qe per dos solz serai meillz acollitz,
> si·ls port liatz en un de mos giros,
> que per cent vers ni per doz cenz cansos.[44]

> *Coblas* and *arrazos* and *sirventes* are not worth a thing; the world is so degenerate that for two cents I will be better received if I carry them tucked in one of my pockets, than for a hundred *vers* or two hundred *cansos*.

Although I assume that *coblas* here denotes what, by the early thirteenth century, had come to be regarded as a lyric genre in its own right, even in this instance the meaning of the term is equivocal because of its association with *arrazos*. If *arrazos* refers, as it could, to the prose commentaries that were recited by the jongleur to introduce individual *cansos* and *sirventes*, then *coblas* could easily designate the isolated stanzas that he sang at the end of his performance as he passed the hat.⁴⁵ If, however, *razo* means "theme," then *coblas* and *razos* together could be construed as the constitutive components of the *sirventes*. I am inclined toward the first interpretation; but the uncertainty of *arrazos*, which seems to have disturbed the medieval scribes as well, leaves the question open.

After the year 1200 the word *cobla* shows up with greater frequency in lyric poems. Uc de Saint Circ, for example, begins a piece (P-C 457,5), which happens to be a pair of *coblas,* by explaining that his fellow troubadour Aimeric de Peguillan "used to make *coblas* about a prostitute" (Antan fez coblas d'una bordeliera).⁴⁶ Gui de Cavaillon opens one of his songs (P-C 192,2) with the words: "Doas coblas farai en aqest son."⁴⁷ The troubadour Izarn, having been presented by someone named Rofian with the choice of making love with his lady and dying upon completion of the act or loving her indefinitely without getting any signal from her that the feeling is reciprocated, chooses *amor de lonh* and life over the alternative. Confident that he has made the better choice, he predicts that his partner, Rofian, if he manages to worm his way out of this debate, will never propose another exchange of *coblas* with him:

> E dic vos ben: Qan d'aqesta tenso
> M'escapares, mais non aures talen
> De far coblas ab mi nullas sazos.⁴⁸

> And I tell you indeed: When you escape from me in this *tenso,* you will never again be inclined to compose *coblas* with me.

What is striking in all of these examples of *cobla* is the lingering ambiguity of the term. The song "Dieus m'a dada febre tersana dobla" (P-C 401,5), composed by Raimon Gaucelm of Béziers in the second half of the thirteenth century, reveals the various meanings that *cobla* had assumed by that relatively late date.⁴⁹ The theme of the poem is quite simply that the troubadour believes that God has struck him with a violent fever in order to make him remember Him. In each of the five stanzas, Raimon places the word *dobla* at the rhyme in the first verse and *cobla* in the third. Every time, of course, he must use *dobla* and *cobla* in a slightly different meaning from before. With *dobla,* his task is not so complicated because the word can function as either adjective or verb and because, not being a technical term, it can be applied to a wide range of situations. *Cobla* is trickier. Raimon meets the challenge that he has set for himself in the following manner. In stanza one he refers to "la premeira cobla," by which he means *cobla* as stanza, building block of a longer lyric poem. In the second stanza he uses *cobla* in the phrase "tensos, dansa ni cobla" to designate an independent lyric genre. It has a neutral connotation. In the third stanza the poet speaks of how everyone wants to make "sa cobla e sos esquerns et sos malvays dechatz" about God. Levy understands *dechat* as a song of scorn.[50] We surmise from the context that *cobla* here means a "worthless poem." In the fourth stanza Raimon uses the word metaphorically to predict the damnation of the hypocrites who will hear *mala cobla* from God on the day of their judgment. Raynouard translates this as: "il en entendra mauvaise chanson."[51] In the fifth stanza Guillem prays that God will hear *esta cobla,* by which he means not just this stanza but the whole poem. When *cobla* is linked, as in the second stanza, to other recognized lyric types, we can be sure that it has gained status as a designation of genre. Nevertheless we observe that it has retained its original meaning (stanza 1), "stanza" as the basic unit of composition for all kinds of lyric poems, and has also acquired a new meaning (stanza 5) as a synonym for a whole poem regardless of length.

Within the *vidas* and *razos,* too, *cobla* can denote either a stanza within a longer poem or a specific lyric genre. When the biographer quotes Raimbaut de Vaqueiras, "si com el dis en una cobla de la stampida" (as he said in a *cobla* from the *stampida*), he uses the term in the one sense; when he says about Guillem Magret, "e fez bonas cansos e bons sirventes e bonas coblas" (and he composed good *cansos* and good *sirventes* and good *coblas*), he uses it in the other. It should be remarked that phrases like "e saub ben far coblas e sirventes e chansos" (and he knew well how to compose *coblas* and *sirventes* and *cansos*) are not empty formulas.[52] There is a high degree of coincidence between those poets whom the biographer describes as composing *coblas* and those for whom one- and two-stanza compositions survive.[53]

As one might expect, the grammars and poetic treatises of the thirteenth and fourteenth centuries reflect the two meanings of *cobla*. The *Razos de trobar* uses *cobla* to denote a stanza within a *canso;* the *De doctrina de compondre dictats* treats *cobla esparsa* as a genre, which it defines as follows:

> Si vols fer cobles esparses, potz les far en qual so te vulles. E deus seguir les rimes del cant de que trayras lo so; e atressi les potz far en altres rimes. E deven esser dues o tres cobles e una o dues tornades.[54]

> If you want to compose *coblas esparsas,* you can compose them to whatever melody you want. And you should follow the rhymes of the song from which you take the melody; moreover, you can compose them using other rhymes. And they should consist of two or three *coblas* and one or two *tornadas.*

The anonymous author of this guide to composing lyric verse confirms, through the vagueness of his instructions on how to write *coblas,* that the genre was fairly amorphous. Unperturbed by the ambiguity of the word, he explains that *coblas* (*esparsas*), the genre, consist of *coblas,* or stanzas. This definition, as has been noted by J. H. Marshall, is "curious" in its failure to mention the "common practice of exchanging *coblas* or to admit the existence of the single *cobla esparsa*."[55] Nevertheless, it is useful to the extent that it emphasizes that the *cobla* is meant to be sung and that the tune is to be borrowed from an existing song.[56]

The most important contribution of the grammatical tradition to our understanding of the *cobla* comes from an entry found in the Occitan-Latin word list in the *Donatz proensals*. The author, Uc Faidit, who may well have been Uc de Saint Circ,[57] lists *cobleiar,* which he renders in "Latin" as *coblas facere* (to make *coblas*).[58] The fact is significant that he either knows no Latin equivalent for Occitan *cobla* or assumes that his readers will understand the Occitan word better than any Latin term that he might use to translate it. Even more significant, however, is the transformation of *cobla* into a new verb indicative of the creative process. *Cobleiar,* which appears to be an Italian invention, is attested in the poems of Bertolome Zorzi and Lanfranc Cigala, both troubadours active in northern Italy in the mid-thirteenth century, thus contemporaries of Uc Faidit.[59] The verb retains the ambivalence of the noun on which it is based. When Lanfranc Cigala instructs a certain Thomas (P-C 282,22) "prec que cobleian respondatz ad aquestas coblas qu'eu fatz" (I ask that you respond, by making *coblas,* to these *coblas* that I have made), he implies that *cobleiar* is to compose lyric poems belonging to the genre *cobla,* but when he opens a multistanza love song (P-C 282,18) with the announcement "pensius de cor e marritz, cobleiarai, car mi platz" (heavy of heart and sorrowful, I will make *coblas* because it pleases me), he understands the term *cobleiar* to refer to the composition of *coblas* that will gradually result in a *canso*. Thus, *cobleiar* is practically a synonym for *trobar.*

There is even some evidence for the coinage, again in Italy, of an agentive noun *cobleiador* from the verb *cobleiar.* Raynouard lists it, citing only the instance "Ren non valgra om cobleiador," which he attributes with singular imprecision to the anonymous troubadour of a *cobla esparsa*.[60] This example of *cobleiador,* which may be an unicum, comes from a variant version of the opening verse of Guillem Magret's *cobla,* "Non valon re coblas ni arrazos" (P-C 223,6).[61] The substitution of *cobleiador* for *arrazos* attests, on the one hand, to the troublesome nature of *arrazos,* mentioned earlier, and, on the other, to the existence of the noun *cobleiador*. The only manuscript containing this variant is the fourteenth-century Italian MS *T,* which lists the text anonymously among its *coblas esparsas*.

Finally, the *Leys d'Amors*, which defines every kind of *cobla* imaginable on which to build a lyric poem (*estrampa, multiplicativa, serpentina, retrogradada*, to name only a few) also recognizes the *cobla esparsa* as a genre in its own right.[62] It does not, however, make any mention of *cobla*-exchanges.

The headings in certain of the manuscripts provide additional proof that by the late Middle Ages *cobla* could mean a variety of things. In Italy, the late thirteenth-century MS *H* uses "cobla de lauzor" (fol. 48a) and "cobla de rancura" (fol. 49b) to introduce stanzas taken from *cansos* by Peire Vidal and Uc de Saint Circ, respectively, and "aquestas doas coblas" (fol. 46a) to announce two stanzas from the *canso* by Azalais de Porcairagues; the fourteenth-century MS *P* contains rubrics such as "cobla de messer Sordel qera malad," "cobla de Folket e den Porcer del cont de Tolosa," and "cobla de Marchabrun per lo rei Aduard e per lo rei A.," in all of which *cobla* designates what we would more properly call a *cobla*-exchange; it does not provide any headings for its *coblas esparsas*.[63] The fourteenth-century MS *T* uses the rubric *coblas esparsas* to identify stanzas that stand alone either because they were composed to be independent or because they have been extracted from longer poems. The fifth stanza of Uc de Saint Circ's *canso*, "Ses dezir e ses razo" (P-C 457,35), for example, is sandwiched between two anonymous *coblas* that appear to be true *coblas esparsas* (P-C 461,95 and P-C 461,129).[64]

In southern France, the fourteenth-century MS *J*, which undoubtedly drew its *coblas* from the same source as the Italian MSS *GQT*, begins the section in question with the heading "Aisi comenson las coblas esparsas," and adds above most of the entries the label *cobla*.[65] The *coblas esparsas* in *J*, like those in *T* (and *GQ* as well, though these manuscripts contain no rubrics marking the *coblas* as such) represent a mixture of extracted *coblas* and one-stanza compositions. MS *f* introduces its collection of *coblas* by Bertran Carbonel by identifying both the author and the genre of the texts to follow: "Bertran Carbonel coblas esparsas." It also uses the term *coblas* to refer to stanzas that belong to poems recorded earlier in the codex: "Aquestas coblas fes P. Vidal e son en .xxxiij. que son d'aquelas: Can homs honratz" (These *coblas* were composed by P. Vidal to the melody of number 33, which begins "Can homs honratz").[66] The fourteenth-century MS *R*, which, like *f*, devotes a whole section to *coblas* by Bertran Carbonel, contains the heading "Aiso son coblas triadas esparsas d'en Bertran Carbonel," and a similar one before the collection of *coblas* by Guillem Olivier d'Arles.[67] "Coblas triadas" here denotes *coblas esparsas* that have been selected for inclusion in the codex from a larger collection of *coblas esparsas* by Bertran Carbonel. Although modern scholars use *coblas triadas* to refer to stanzas extracted from longer poems, I have found no medieval attestation of the term with this meaning.[68] The fourteenth-century MS *C* contains at least one heading pertinent to this discussion: "So son coblas que fes Raymon Gaucelm quan fo malautes." What follows, of course, is the poem in which Raimon plays on the word *cobla*. The scribe could be using the identifying refrain-word simply as a convenient title for the entry.[69]

Whether as the basic compositional unit of a multistanza poem or as a short text unto itself that tended to borrow its metrical pattern and melody from a well-known *canso,* the *cobla* raises the question of how troubadours composed. Proponents of the improvisation theory argue that *cobla*-exchanges devised on the spot (with possible pauses between stanzas to give the respondent time to think) represent the origin of the *tenso* and *joc partit*.[70] Those, on the other hand, who are convinced that the troubadours did not invent even the simplest poems in their heads can produce evidence that *coblas,* just like longer, more complicated works, were written and sent. The following anonymous *cobla* (P-C 461,142) is the most compelling piece of testimony in the case made by those arguing for a continuous written tradition from the moment of composition to the moment of entry into the great chansonniers:[71]

> Gioglaret, quant passarez
> Garda no moill ta cappa verz,
> Que fols fora si noi laiderz;
> Qu'eu darr' un moi de segle,
> S'en carta qu'eu te regle
> Poi scriver' una tal cobla
> S'un d'aquestz motz non s'i dobla.[72]

> Gioglaret, when you pass, watch that you do not get your green cape wet, for he would be a fool who didn't try to mess it up; for I would give a measure of rye, if on the sheet that I rule for you, you would then write a *cobla* such that none of these words is repeated.

When Gui de Cavaillon announces (P-C 192,2): "Doas coblas farai en aqest son, q'eu trametrai a 'N Bertram d'Avignon" (I will compose two *coblas* to this tune that I will send to Sir Bertran of Avignon), he suggests that he is transmitting his verses in written form directly to their addressee.[73] The biographer, too, tells of *coblas* being sent, most notably in the case of Bernart Arnaut, who went off without seeing his lady Lombarda but leaving behind a pair of *coblas* (P-C 54,1), to which she replied (P-C. 288,1).[74] In all of these instances improvisation is out of the question. Unfortunately, however, close examination of the *cobla* alone will not tell us whether the troubadours were in the habit of composing on a tablet or in their heads. The fact that the anonymous author of *Gioglaret* is willing to give the jongleur a chance to write out his response in the extraordinarily challenging rhymes assigned to him or that the biographer occasionally goes out of his way to report that *coblas* could be exchanged over a distance does not prove that written composition was the rule. In extreme cases (and I believe that this was exceptional), such as the following verse-by-verse exchange between Aimeric de Peguilhan and Guillem Raimon (P-C 10,35 = 229,2), improvisation is likely. Despite its easy rhymes, this text must have been considered a tour de force.[75]

> N'Aimeric, qe·us par d'aqest novel marqes?
> Guillelm Raimon, be me par aizo qe n'es.
> N'Aimeric, meill volgra vos en pareges.
> Guillelm Raimon, et eu ben, s'esser poges.
> N'Aimeric, lo bon paire volgra sembles o·l fraire.
> Guillelm Raimon, et eu be, mas fils es de sa maire.[76]

> "Sir Aimeric, what do you think of this new marquis?" "Guillem Raimon, I think of him as he is." "Sir Aimeric, I would like it if he appeared better to you." "Guillem Raimon, I would too, if it were possible." "Sir Aimeric, I would like for him to be like his good father or his brother." "Guillem Raimon, I would too; but he is his mother's son."

Coblas of all kinds were quite popular throughout the thirteenth century and well into the fourteenth in both southern France and northern Italy. At the court of Raimon Berenger, count of Provence (1209–45), the genre was cultivated with enthusiasm.[77] The count himself engaged in several *cobla*-exchanges and encouraged the troubadours whom he was patronizing to do the same. In the second half of the century Peire Cardenal, Bertran Carbonel, and Guillem Olivier produced dozens of moralizing *coblas*. Matfre Ermengaud (late thirteenth century) organizes his *Perilhos tractat d'amor de donas* around *coblas* that he has drawn from the songs of the "old" troubadours.[78] And the compilers of MSS *JRf* devoted whole sections of their chansonniers to the preservation of *coblas esparsas*.

Meanwhile, in Italy the genre was practiced with equal if not greater vigor. Most of the early *cobla*-exchanges were produced by troubadours residing in Italy in the first few decades of the thirteenth century. Many of the *coblas esparsas* and *cobla*-exchanges of personal satire mocking people for their physical deformities or their moral weakness emerged from within this milieu. The author of the biographies as they are preserved in MS *P* incorporated whole *coblas* extracted from *cansos* and *sirventes* to substantiate his stories.[79] In the middle of the century Lanfranc Cigala composed a number of *coblas* and repeatedly used the verb *cobleiar*, thus emphasizing the prominent place that the *cobla* had come to occupy. The scribe of H^3

(late thirteenth century), who was working somewhere close to Treviso, compiled the largest surviving collection of *cobla*-exchanges, including the oldest ones that we know of. The scribe of the fourteenth-century MS *P* provides us with the biggest collection of *coblas esparsas* (165 entries). And the compilers of *FGQT* made sure to include some *coblas esparsas* in their chansonniers. The cultivation of the *cobla* in Italy distinguished itself from the analogous movement in southern France by its greater emphasis on personal satire and its disinclination to moralize.

The unique contribution of the Italians to the *cobla* tradition was the creation of florilegia, or collections of *coblas* extracted from the songs of the great troubadours. The florilegium compiled by Ferrari de Ferrara and preserved in the final section of *D* (=*D^c*) is the most famous and most extensive illustration of this two-stage process of selection: first, of deciding which of the troubadour poems to pass on to posterity and then, for each of the chosen songs, which *cobla*s to record:[80] "E fes un estrat de tutas las cançoss des bos trobadors del mon; e de chadaunas cançoss o serventes tras .I. cobla o .II. o .III., aqelas che portan las sentenças de las cançoss e o son tuit li mot triat" (And he made an extract from all the *cansos* of the good troubadours in the world; and from each *canso* or *sirventes*, he drew one *cobla* or two or three, those which carry the meaning of the *cansos* and in which all the words are select).[81]

A second major florilegium is preserved in the Italian MS *F*. This collection, as well as a recently discovered fragment of a third florilegium compiled in Italy, is based on the same source as Ferrari's.[82] The scribe of *H³* records prose commentaries for a set of *coblas* extracted from the *cansos* of the troubadours typically represented in the florilegia, namely, Raimon de Miraval, Arnaut de Maroill, Peire Vidal, Folquet de Marseilla, and Uc de Saint Circ. The florilegium of *H* (fols. 47–49) is unparalleled not only because it is equipped with *razos* but also because most of the *coblas* are not recorded in full but are identified simply by their initial verse.[83]

Despite its widespread practice, the *cobla* never gained much prestige as a genre. The biographer Uc de Saint Circ, who himself authored several *coblas*, criticizes Peire Guillem de Toloza for composing too many of them: "E fez ben coblas, mas trop en fazia; e fez sirventes joglarescs e de blasmar los baros" (And he composed *coblas* well, but he composed too many of them; and he composed *sirventes joglarescs* in order to blame the barons).[84]

In a *cobla*-exchange with Bertran (d'Alamano?), a jongleur called Javare (P-C 75,4 = 263,1) implies that in composing *coblas* one opens oneself up to abuse. By *coblas* he undoubtedly means *coblas* of personal satire, the idea being that you had better learn to take it as well as you dish it out:

> E pois coblas sabes faire,
> E per gazagnar mal traire,
> En aital point si ez vos sai venguiz
> Com eu lo iorn qan fui acoseguiz.[85]

> And since you know how to compose *coblas* and to suffer injury in order to make a profit, you have arrived at the point where I was the day I got caught.

Lanfranc Cigala (P-C 282,13) confirms that the *cobla* is a genre that lends itself, at least in some hands, to the thematization of indelicate matters:

> Lantelm, qui·us onra ni·us acuoill
> A pauc de scienza,
> Q'en vos no trob'om mais orgoill
> Ab desconoissenza;
> E comtatz de Gui de Nantoill
> En loc de Valenza
> Ez enpastatz coblas ab soill
> De descovinenza.[86]

> Lantelm, whoever honors you or receives you has little knowledge, for in you one finds only arrogance with ingratitude; and you tell tales about Gui de Nantoill instead of Valenza and you thicken your *coblas* with the mud of impropriety.

Hacks like Bertran Carbonel (P-C 82,25), intent on using the *cobla* for didactic purposes, had to fight the perception that it was an inferior genre: "E tug aquel que sabon coblas faire son fol tengut" (Those who make *coblas* are held for fools).[87] Guiraut Riquier ranks *coblas* with *dansas, sirventes, albas,* and *partimens* as secondary lyric genres practiced by those whom he would call "troubadours," whereas he would reserve the noble title of "doctor" for those capable of writing *cansos* and *vers*.[88] The anonymous poet of one *cobla* (P-C 461,223) articulates his reluctance to compose *coblas* because they don't sell well and those who compose them are held for fools.

> Si gais solatz ab bels ditz
> Fos aissi com sol grazitz
> E q'om no·n fos escarnitz
> Per faire coblas ses venda,
> Jeu·n fera; mas sui marritz,
> Car non sai com m'en defenda
> Qe li vilan, descortes,
> Glot de raub' e de totz bes,
> Cui Deus merme de lor renda,
> Dizon d'ome qe fols es,
> Q'en coblas faire s'entenda.[89]

> If pleasant conversation with fine words were appreciated the way it used to be, and if one were not scorned for composing *coblas* that won't sell, I would compose some; but I am distressed, for I do not know how to protect myself against the base, uncourtly people, greedy for clothes and all goods (may God reduce their income!) who say that anyone who devotes himself to composing *coblas* is a fool.

Not only the fact that this thought is virtually identical to that expressed by Bertran Carbonel in the *cobla* cited above but also the fact that the author of P-C 461,223 ends up doing exactly what he declares that he will not do, that is, compose a *cobla,* makes us think that there is more topos than truth in the complaint that producing *coblas* can be harmful to one's reputation. Raimon Gaucelm of Béziers opens one of his poems (P-C 401,3) by declaring unequivocally that he is proud to be known for his *coblas*. And yet one wonders why he feels compelled to make the point in the first place unless it is to defend himself against those who look down on the genre.

> A penas vauc en loc qu'om no·m deman:
> "Raimon Gaucelm, avetz fag res novel?";
> e ieu a totz respon ab bon talan,
> quar totas ves m'es per ver bon e bel,
> e·m plai quant aug dir de mi: "Aqest es
> tals que sab far coblas e sirventes";
> e no per so qu'ieu volha qu'om del mon
> me don raubas, qu'ieu n'ai pro e sai don.[90]

> I can scarcely go anyplace without being asked, "Raimon Gaucelm, have you composed anything new?"; and I answer everyone quite willingly, for it is always, in truth, to my advantage, and I like it when I hear it said about me, "He is the one who knows how to compose *coblas* and *sirventes*"; and not because I want anyone at all to give me clothes, for I have plenty of them and I know where they came from.

It is also possible that *coblas* here does not refer to *coblas* as genre at all but to the word *coblas* that was the distinctive refrain-word of Gaucelm's poem about the fever. The *C*-scribe at least (and why not Gaucelm himself?) seemed to regard *coblas* as an appropriate title for that particular song.

Even if never highly esteemed, the *cobla* served a wide range of functions within thirteenth-century society. It was used for moral instruction, propaganda, entertainment, and solicitation. A genre that typically presents real situations in a less than idealized way, the *cobla* offers, among other things, what Jeanroy has called "une sorte de chronique de la société courtoise."[91] Because it could be short and easy, the *cobla* was practiced not only by troubadours but also by jongleurs, patrons, women, foreigners and scribes.[92]

Thanks to the *cobla* the various recipients of troubadour verse could participate actively in the creative process. In a sense, then, the rise of the *cobla* epitomizes the gradual democratization of an initially elitist phenomenon.

Within a more strictly literary context, the versatile *cobla* could imitate the function of any of the other lyric genres. Indeed, virtually all of the lyric types—*canso, sirventes, tenso, descort, alba, salut, ensenhamen*—are represented in miniature in the *cobla*.[93] With its formal and thematic flexibility, the *cobla*, which did not establish itself as a distinctive genre until the last decade of the twelfth century, can be viewed as a relaxing of the rigid system of genres operative at the time[94] and, specifically, as a release of the tension inherent in the dominant genre, the *canso*.[95]

The *cobla* counterbalances the *canso* either by parodying a particular text or by undermining the force of one of the constitutive elements of the whole *fin' amors* paradigm.[96] The following *cobla* (P-C 461,202), which is obviously a spoof on a famous *canso* by Bernart de Ventadorn (P-C 70,37), offers a clear example of one of the ways in which the *cobla* brings the high-flown *canso* down to earth:

Bernart de Ventadorn	Cobla
Quan la freid' aura venta	Quan lo petz del cul venta
Deves vostre païs,	Dont Midonz caga e vis,
Vejaire m'es qu'eu senta	Vejaire m'es qu'eu senta
Un vent de paradis	Una pudor de pis
Per amor de la genta	D'una orrida sangnenta
Vas cui eu sui aclis,	Que tot jorn m'escarnis,
On ai mesa m'ententa	Qu'es mais de petz manenta
E mon coratge assis,	Que de marabodis,
Car de totas partis	E quan jatz sus son pis,
Per leis, tant m'atalenta.[97]	Plus put d'autra serpenta.[98]

Bernart de Ventadorn:
When the cool breeze blows from the direction of your country, it seems to me that I smell a wind from paradise on account of (my) love for the noble lady toward whom I am drawn, in whom I have placed my devotion and set my heart, for I would leave all other women for her, so greatly does she please me.

Cobla:
When the fart blows from the asshole out of which my lady shits and releases gas, it seems to me that I smell a stench of piss from a dirty bleeder who always scorns me, for she is richer in farts than in coins, and when she lies on her piss, she stinks more than any other serpent.

An anonymous stanza (P-C 461,245), in which the frustrated knight sublimates his desire for the inaccessible lady both by dreaming about her and by having intercourse with another woman, illustrates the other way in which the *cobla* can effectively undo the *canso:*

> Un cavaler conosc qe l'altrer vi
> Una domna bel' e precios' a fi,
> E plac li ben, qan lo mantel l'obri
> E vi son cors, sa cara e sa cri,
> E songet la la noit, can el dormi.
> E dirai vos com del somni gari ?
> Ab un' altra q'estava pres de si.[99]

> I know a knight who saw a fine and perfectly exquisite lady the other day, and she pleased him greatly when she opened her cloak for him and he saw her body, her face, and her hair, and he dreamed about her at night when he was asleep. And I will tell you how he recovered from the dream—with another woman who happened to be near him.

As the misfit which refused to be bound by social or literary constraints, the *cobla* enabled the troubadour lyric to evolve and thus to revitalize itself both in the bourgeois society of southern France and in the courts of northern Italy in the thirteenth century, when the idealistic system of values celebrated by Jaufre Rudel and Bernart de Ventadorn no longer seemed to ring true.

NOTES

1. Christiane Leube, "Cobla," in *Grundriss der romanischen Literaturen des Mittelalters*, ed. Hans Robert Jauss and Erich Köhler, vol. 2: *Les genres lyriques* (Heidelberg: Winter, 1979–90), 1: 4: 67.

2. Alfred Jeanroy, *La poésie lyrique des troubadours* (Toulouse: Privat, 1934), 2:276. Jeanroy believes that such *coblas* are to be taken seriously: "ce n'étaient pas là de vaines menaces: certaines *coblas* ne sont qu'un tissu d'imputations blessantes, d'infamantes révélations, d'allusions . . . à un passé chargé de méfaits et de vilenies." Leube says just the opposite: "Es sind in den seltensten Fällen ernst gemeinte Attacken, sondern viel eher als Jongleur weltkämpfe vorgetragene Spottgesänge" ("Cobla," p. 68).

3. The expression comes from Angelica Rieger, "La *cobla esparsa* anonyme: phénoménologie d'un genre troubadouresque," in *Actes du XVIIIe Congrès International de Linguistique et de Philologie Romanes, Université de Trèves (Trier) 1986*, ed. Dieter Kremer (Tübingen: Niemeyer, 1988), 6:215. In considering how and where *coblas* were performed, Rieger suggests that they were "condamnés à la clandestinité dans les cuisines, les arrière-boutiques et les tavernes."

4. For some highly suggestive remarks about inserted and extracted *coblas* see Maria Luisa Meneghetti, "Les florilèges dans la tradition lyrique des troubadours," in *Lyrique romane médiévale, la tradition des chansonniers: Actes du colloque de Liège, 1989*, ed. Madeleine Tyssens (Liège: Faculté de Philosophie et Lettres de l'Université de Liège, 1991), 43–44.

5. Alfred Pillet and Henry Carstens, *Bibliographie der Troubadours* (Halle: Niemeyer, 1933), item 183, 12. Henceforth abbreviated P-C.

6. [These stanzas in *H* are treated as a distinct version of the poem in the essay by Paden.—Ed.]

7. These *coblas* have been edited by Reinhild Richter, *Die Troubadourzitate im Breviari d'Amor* (Modena: Mucchi, 1976).

8. Cesare De Lollis suggests that the *cobla esparsa* modeled itself on extracted *coblas* ("Appunti dai MSS. provenzali vaticani," *Revue des langues romanes* 33 [1889]: 173). Angelica Rieger, on the other hand, sees the *cobla esparsa* as deriving from *cobla*-exchanges ("*Cobla esparsa*," 203).

9. For a complete edition of the *coblas* of these two poets see Karl Bartsch, ed., *Denkmäler der provenzalischen Litteratur* (Stuttgart: Litterarischer Verein, 1856), 5–50.

10. Alfred Jeanroy, "Les *coblas* de Bertran Carbonel," *Annales du Midi* 25 (1913): 170.

11. All translations, unless otherwise indicated, are mine.

12. Jeanroy cites the example of Peire Bremon's response to a (lost) *cobla* by Gui de Cavaillon, "Pois Guis m'a dit mal, eu lo dirai autressi," and remarks that Peire must have considered it possible that Gui's text remain unanswered, but that the outrageousness of the insults prompts him to speak up. See Alfred Jeanroy, "La tenson provençale," *Annales du Midi* 2 (1890): 455.

13. Angelica Rieger sees the *cobla esparsa* as deriving from the *cobla*-exchange ("*Cobla esparsa*," 203). She bases this hypothesis on what she regards as the essentially dialogic nature of many of the surviving *coblas esparsas*, including, among other things, a predilection for difficult rhymes that makes a response more challenging. The establishment of a difficult rhyme scheme in the first stanza seems to me, however, more of a deterrent than an incentive to the would-be respondent. Indeed, Bertran de Carbonel criticizes Bertran lo Ros on precisely this point. See Jeanroy, "*Coblas*," 165.

14. Alfred Jeanroy and Jean-Jacques Salverda de Grave, eds., *Poésies de Uc de Saint-Circ* (Toulouse: Privat, 1913), 122–23.

15. Jean Boutière and A.-H. Schutz, eds., *Biographies des troubadours*, 2d ed., rev. by Jean Boutière and Irénée-Marcel Cluzel (Paris: Nizet, 1973), 239.

16. Both Folena and Meneghetti set Uc's arrival in Italy around the year 1220. At the latest, then, Uc studied in Montpellier sometime between 1210 and 1215. He was already an established poet when he arrived in Italy. According to the *vida* about him, he composed all of his *cansos* while he was still in France. See Gianfranco Folena, "Tradizione e cultura trobadorica nelle corti e nelle città venete," in *Storia della cultura veneta*, ed. Gianfranco Folena, vol. 1: *Dalle origini al trecento* (Vicenza: Pozza, 1976), 520; and Maria Luisa Meneghetti, "Uc de Saint Circ tra filologia e divulgazione (su data, formazione e fini del Liber Alberici)," in *Il Medioevo nella Marca: trovatori, giullari, letterati a Treviso nei secoli XIII e XIV: Atti del Convegno*, ed. Maria Luisa Meneghetti and Francesco Zambon (Treviso: Edizioni Premio Comisso, 1991), 115.

17. Stanislaw Stronski dates this *cobla* to 1189 or 1190 (ed., *Le troubadour Folquet de Marseille* [Kraków: Académie des Sciences, 1919; Geneva: Slatkine, 1968], 74).

18. P-C 155,14; Stronski, *Folquet de Marseille*, 40–43, lines 18–20: "pero·l mals mi fora doussors, sol l'aut ram a qu'era·m sui pres mi plejes, mercejan, Merces" (How-

ever, the pain would be sweetness to me if only Mercy, showing mercy, would bend for me the high branch to which I am now so attached).

19. Stronski, *Folquet de Marseille,* 72.

20. Ibid., 46*-47*.

21. Jeanroy cites these and several others (*Poésie lyrique,* 2:275, n. 1).

22. Mouzat believes that these *coblas* must have been composed before 1193, while Saladin was still alive; see Jean Mouzat, ed., *Les poèmes de Gaucelm Faidit* (Paris: Nizet, 1965), 478–81.

23. Guillelma is described as a *soudadeira* by both Elias and the biographer (Boutière and Schutz, *Biographies,* 192), the latter of whom takes the word from the former. Raynouard, citing Elias, defines the word as "prostitute." See François-Just-Marie Raynouard, *Lexique roman* (Paris: Silvestre, 1844; reprint, Heidelberg: Winter, n.d.), 5:250. Angelica Rieger interprets *soudadeira* as referring to a female jongleur (*Trobairitz: der Beitrag der Frau in der altokzitanischen höfischen Lyrik, Edition des Gesamtkorpus* [Tübingen: Niemeyer, 1991], 105–8). In either case, the word has a negative connotation.

24. Joseph Linskill lists this piece under "Poems of Doubtful Attribution" (ed., *The Poems of Raimbaut Vaqueiras* [The Hague: Mouton, 1964], 268–71).

25. The biographer, whom I take to be Uc de Saint Circ, attempts to explain these allusions through a rather far-fetched *razo* preserved only in *H.* See Boutière and Schutz, *Biographies,* 485–87.

26. D'Arco Silvio Avalle, ed., *Peire Vidal: poesie* (Milan: Ricciardi, 1960), 2:415–22.

27. The phrase "membransa ni sen" came to be identified with Peire Vidal. The Monk of Montaudon, in his commentary on different poets, writes: "Que anc, puois si fetz cavaliers, non ac puois membransa ni sen" (for ever since he became a knight, he has not had any memory or sense) (lines 89–90). See Martín de Riquer, *Los trovadores: historia literaria y textos* (Barcelona: Planeta, 1975), 2:1044.

28. "Plus sovent venz chastels e domejos no fai veilla gallina ni capos" (He sells castles and dungeons more often than an old lady does hens and capons) (lines 19–20). *Vens* can be the second person singular of either *venser* (conquer), or *vendre* (sell). Line 19 alone might make one assume that Lanza conquers castles, but the unflattering comparison of line 20 makes it clear that *vens* means "sell." The motif of selling castles occurs commonly in such poems of insult. See Avalle, *Peire Vidal: poesie,* 2:421–22.

29. Folena, "Tradizione," 458, 534.

30. Boutière and Schutz, *Biographies,* 192–95, 485–87, 351–55. In the case of Peire Vidal and Lanza Marques, there is no surviving commentary on this specific text, but, as Boutière and Schutz (354, n. 1) point out, the *vida* for Peire incorporates some information that appears to have been gleaned from Lanza's verses, specifically the "fact" that the troubadour married the emperor's niece and called himself emperor.

31. Martin de Riquer describes it as "dos coblas" (ed., *Guillem de Berguedà* [Poblet: Abadía de Poblet, 1971], 2:267). István Frank calls it an "échange de *coblas*" (*Répertoire métrique de la poésie des troubadours,* vol. 2 [Paris: Champion, 1966], 126).

32. Dietmar Rieger, "'*Lop es nomnat lo pes, e lop no es*': un *devinalh* sans solution?" in *Mélanges de langue et de littérature occitanes en hommage à Pierre Bec* (Poitiers: C.E.S.C.M., 1991), 501–3.

33. Riquer describes it as a "poesia o estrofa de una poesia más larga no conservada" (*Guillem*, 2:93). Frank calls it a *cobla* (*Répertoire*, 2:126).

34. Riquer calls it a "sirventés" (*Guillem*, 2:87). Frank also calls it a *sirventes* (*Répertoire*, 2:126).

35. Boutière and Schutz, *Biographies*, 117–20. What is significant about this example is that although Guillem probably intended this *cobla* as an integral part of a longer piece, the biographer felt free to remove it from its context and let it function as an independent entity, which is the only form in which it has survived.

36. Riquer, *Guillem*, 2:209.

37. Walther von Wartburg remarks that in Occitan the word *cobla* is attested with the meaning "couplet d'une poésie" as of the thirteenth century, but he does not identify the earliest attestation (*Französisches etymologisches Wörterbuch* [Bonn: Klopp, 1922–], 2:1159).

38. Riquer, *Guillem*, 2:167–71. In the second line I used the *H* variant *trobaire* instead of the *DIK* reading *chantaire*.

39. These examples of *lassar* are cited by Riquer (ibid., 1:187–88).

40. Gerald A. Bond, ed., *The Poetry of William VII, Count of Poitiers, IX Duke of Aquitaine* (New York: Garland, 1982), 24; J.-M.-L. Dejeanne, ed., *Poésies complètes du troubadour Marcabru* (Toulouse: Privat, 1909), 37; Riquer, *Trovadores*, 1:257; Adolf Kolsen, ed., *Sämtliche Lieder des Trobadors Giraut de Bornelh* (Halle: Niemeyer, 1910–35), 1:142; Avalle, *Peire Vidal: poesie* 1:37.

41. Riquer, *Trovadores*, 2:1036–38.

42. Aimo Sakari, ed., *Poésies du troubadour Guillem de Saint-Didier* (Helsinki: Société Néophilologique, 1956), 54–67.

43. Kurt Almqvist, ed., *Poésies du troubadour Guilhem Adémar* (Uppsala: Almqvist and Wiksells, 1951), 164–69.

44. Fritz Naudieth, ed., *Der Trobador Guillem Magret*, Beihefte zur Zeitschrift für romanische Philologie, vol. 52 (Halle: Niemeyer, 1914), 123–25; Riquer, *Trovadores*, 2:924.

45. Angelica Rieger, "*Cobla esparsa*," 216.

46. Jeanroy and Salverda de Grave, *Poésies*, 91–92.

47. Boutière and Schutz, *Biographies*, 505–6.

48. Adolf Kolsen, *Trobadorgedichte* (Halle: Niemeyer, 1925), 42–44.

49. Francisco J. Oroz Arizcuren, ed., *La lírica religiosa en la literatura provenzal antigua* (Pamplona: Institución Príncipe de Viana, 1972), 404–9.

50. Emil Levy and Carl Appel, *Provenzalisches Supplement-Wörterbuch* (Leipzig: Reisland, 1894–1924), 2:118 (under *dechat*).

51. Raynouard, *Lexique*, 2:422. Cerveri de Girona also uses *cobla* metaphorically in one of his poems, "Totz homs deu far aquo que·l veyll sers fa" (P-C 434,15), line 32. See Martin de Riquer, ed., *Obras completas del trovador Cerverí de Girona* (Barcelona: Instituto Español de Estudios Mediterráneos, 1947), 257–62.

52. Boutière and Schutz, *Biographies*, 465, 493, 559.

53. According to the *vidas*, the following poets composed *coblas:* Sordel (Boutière and Schutz, *Biographies*, 562), Peire de la Mula (560), Albert Marques (559), Bertran d'Alamano (517), Cadenet (500), the Monk of Montaudon (307), Peire de Maensac (301), Guillem Magret (493), Raimbaut de Vaqueiras (447 and 451), Peire Guillem de Tolosa (436), Pons de Capdoill (315), Dalfi d'Alvernhe (284), Uc de

Saint Circ (239), Bertran de Born (132), Gaucelm Faidit (193), Elias d'Ussel (192), Ferrari de Ferrara (581), Gui de Cavaillo (505), Bernart Arnaut (417), the bishop of Clermont (286), Bertran de la Tor (289), the count of Rodez (250), Guillem del Baus (485), Gaudairenca (380), Tibors (498), Almuc and Iseut (422), Lombarda (416–17). The manuscript tradition has preserved *coblas* for all of these except Albert Marques, Cadenet, Peire de Maensac, Peire Guillem de Tolosa, Pons de Capdoill, and Gaudairenca.

54. J. H. Marshall, ed., *The "Razos de trobar" of Raimon Vidal and Associated Texts* (London: Oxford University Press, 1972), 97.

55. Ibid., 140, nn. 87–89.

56. Bertran Carbonel emphasizes the importance of the melody in a *cobla*. See Jeanroy, "*Coblas*," 176:

> Cobla ses so es enaissi
> Co'l molis que aigua non a;
> Per que fai mal qui cobla fa
> Si son non li don' atressi;
> C'om non a gaug pas del moli,
> Mas per la moutura que'n tra.

A *cobla* without a melody is like a mill that has no water; therefore, the person who composes a *cobla* does badly if he doesn't give it a melody too; for one has no pleasure from the mill itself but from the meal that one gets out of it.

[See also Aubrey in this volume for discussion of this *cobla* in regard to music.—Ed.]

57. It was Gustav Gröber who first proposed that Uc Faidit and Uc de Saint Circ were the same person, in "Der Verfasser des *Donat proensal*," *Zeitschrift für romanische Philologie* 8 (1884): 112–17, and "Zur Widmung des *Donat proensal*," *Zeitschrift für romanische Philologie* 8 (1884): 290–93. This hypothesis has been recently supported by Diether Janzarik, "Uc de St. Circ—auteur du *Donatz proensals*?" *Zeitschrift für romanische Philologie* 105 (1989): 264–75.

58. J. H. Marshall, ed., *The "Donatz Proensals" of Uc Faidit* (London: Oxford University Press, 1969), 156.

59. Bertolome Zorzi, "Mout fai sobreira folia," line 38, in Emil Levy, ed., *Der Troubadour Bertolome Zorzi* (Halle: Niemeyer, 1883), 62. Lanfranc Cigala, "Amics Symon, si·us platz, vostra semblanza," line 75; "Per o car vos fegnetz de sotilment entendre," line 5; "Seigne'n Thomas, tan mi plai," line 30; "Pensius de cor e marritz," line 2; in Francesco Branciforti, ed., *Il canzoniere di Lanfranco Cigala* (Florence: Olschki, 1954), 166, 170, 193, and 229.

60. Raynouard, *Lexique*, 2:422, lists *cobleiaire, cobleiador*. He illustrates the nominative form with the first verse of Lanfranc Cigala's "Pensius de cor e marritz cobleiaire" (P-C 282,18), but Branciforti, *Lanfranco Cigala*, 229, has emended *cobleiaire* to *cobleiarai*, which is the first-person future of the verb *cobleiar*. For the oblique, Raynouard cites the variant version of the first verse of Guillem Magret's *cobla*. Although he obviously knew this *cobla* quite well, recording it in *Choix des poésies originales des troubadours*, 6 vols. ([Paris: Didot, 1816–21], 2:201–2), and giving it as an example under *arrazos*, he failed to recognize MS *T*'s rendering of the text for what it was.

61. The text is preserved in four mss, *FJQT*. *FQ* give *arrazos;* *J* gives *artexos;* *T* gives *cobleiador*. The source was evidently hard to read, and the word must have been something other than what the scribe anticipated.

62. Joseph Anglade, ed., *Las Leys d'Amors* (Toulouse: Privat, 1919–20), 2:132.

63. See the diplomatic edition of *H* in L. Gauchat and H. Kehrli, "Il canzoniere provenzale H (Cod. Vaticano 3207)," *Studj di filologia romanza* 5 (1891): 341–558, and Edmund Stengel's edition of *P*, "Die provenzalische Liederhandschrift Cod. 42 der Laurenzianischen Bibliothek in Florenz," *Archiv für das Studium der neueren Sprachen und Literaturen* 50 (1872): 241–84.

64. For a list of the contents of *T*, see Camille Chabaneau, "Le chansonnier provençal T (Bibliothèque Nationale, fonds fr., no. 15211)," *Annales du Midi* 12 (1900): 194–208.

65. P. Savj-Lopez, ed., "Il canzoniere provenzale J," *Studj di filologia romanza* 9 (1903): 571–88.

66. The first four stanzas of the poem are recorded on fol. 37v, and stanzas 5–7 are recorded on fol. 69v, under the rubric cited.

67. For a list of the contents of *f* and *R*, see Paul Meyer, *Les derniers troubadours de la Provence* (Paris: Franck, 1871; Geneva: Slatkine, 1973).

68. Meneghetti, "Florilèges," 44; Maria Careri, *Il canzoniere provenzale H (Vat. Lat. 3207): struttura, contenuto e fonti* (Modena: Mucchi, 1990), 293. I have no objection to the term, but note only that it would seem never to have acquired any official status in the Middle Ages as a designation for *coblas* extracted from longer poems.

69. On the question of "titles" for troubadour poems see István Frank, "Du rôle des troubadours dans la formation de la poésie lyrique moderne," in *Mélanges de linguistique et de littérature romanes offerts à Mario Roques* (Paris: Didier, 1950), 1:68.

70. Rudolph Zenker makes an interesting distinction between the method of composing at least certain *cobla*-exchanges and that of composing a *tenso* (*Die provenzalische Tenzone* [Leipzig: Hirschfeld, 1888], 18). See also De Lollis, "Appunti," 180.

71. Gustav Gröber, "Die Liedersammlungen der Troubadours," *Romanische Studien* 2 (1875–77): 337–44; Dietmar Rieger, "*Senes breu de parguamina*? Zum Problem des 'gelesenen Lieds' im Mittelalter," *Romanische Forschungen* 99 (1987): 17–18; Dietmar Rieger, "*Chantar* und *faire*: zum Problem der trobadoresken Improvisation," *Zeitschrift für romanische Philologie* 106 (1990): 432–33. Amelia Van Vleck tries to use this example to prove just the opposite (*Memory and Re-Creation in Troubadour Lyric* [Berkeley: University of California Press, 1991], 56–60). She takes *carta* metaphorically as the tablet of the jongleur's mind. She considers Gröber's emendation of *en* to *eu* in the fifth verse (which I have accepted) unnecessary. Her position is weakened by her translation of *poi* as "I can" and *scriver'* as an infinitive. It is, I would argue, Gioglaret, not the author of the initial stanza, who is supposed to write the follow-up.

72. Gröber, "Liedersammlungen," 338; Friedrich Witthoeft, "*Sirventes joglaresc*": *ein Blick auf das altfranzöisische Spielmannsleben* (Marburg: Elwert, 1891), 65–66. The text also has a second stanza, which is presumably Gioglaret's proof that he can meet the challenge posed by the author of the stanza recorded here. As Dietmar Rieger has pointed out, Gioglaret succeeds only by making up nonsense words (*dintegle, lintegle*) ("*Chantar* und *faire*," 433; "*Senes breu*," 18). Van Vleck reads meaning into this second stanza, finding in it a "monumentalist metaphor . . . describing the poem

as a fortress that can withstand the assault of the common throng" (*Memory*, 58). I agree with Rieger, however, that the stanza is not meant as anything more than a playful rise to the challenge.

73. Boutière and Schutz, *Biographies*, 505–6.

74. Ibid., 416–17.

75. De Lollis argues that verse-by-verse exchanges like this one are the most primitive form of *cobla* ("Appunti," 177).

76. William P. Shepard and Frank M. Chambers, eds., *The Poems of Aimeric de Peguilhan* (Evanston, Ill.: Northwestern University Press, 1950), 180–81. My translation is similar to theirs. The text continues with a second stanza, where, just as in the first, the voices alternate.

77. Jeanroy, *Poésie lyrique*, 1:174, 2:275; and Irénée Cluzel, "Princes et troubadours de la maison royale de Barcelone-Aragon," *Boletín de la Real Academia de Buenas Letras de Barcelona* 27 (1957–58): 336.

78. See Peter T. Ricketts, who, in contrast to Richter, gives the narrative verses surrounding the lyric inserts (ed., *Le Breviari d'Amor de Matfre Ermengaud* [Leiden: Brill, 1976–]).

79. Meneghetti offers some interesting observations about the biographies in *P* ("Florilèges," 58).

80. Maria Luisa Meneghetti, "Il florilegio trobadorico di Ferrarino da Ferrara," in *Miscellanea di studi in onore di Aurelio Roncaglia a cinquant' anni dalla sua laurea* (Modena: Mucchi, 1989), 3:853–71; and Meneghetti, "Florilèges"; see the complete edition of Ferrari's florilegium in H. Teulié and G. Rossi, "L'anthologie provençale de Maître Ferrari de Ferrare," *Annales du Midi* 13 (1901): 60–73, 199–215, 371–88, and 14 (1902): 197–205, 523–38.

81. Boutière and Schutz, *Biographies*, 581–82.

82. See Edmund Stengel, *Die provenzalische Blumenlese der Chigiana* (Marburg: Elwert, 1878) for a complete transcription of the florilegium in *F*; and Laura Allegri, "Frammento di antico florilegio provenzale," *Studi medievali*, 3d ser., 27 (1986): 319–51, for the edition of the recently discovered fragment C^m.

83. For an edition and discussion of the annotated florilegium in *H*, see Careri, *Canzoniere*, 293–318.

84. Boutière and Schutz, *Biographies*, 436.

85. J.-J. Salverda de Grave, ed., *Le troubadour Bertran d'Alamanon* (Toulouse: Privat, 1902), 145.

86. Branciforti, *Lanfranco Cigala*, 181.

87. "Aras puesc ben conoisser sertamen," in Jeanroy, "Coblas," 149.

88. Joseph Linskill, ed., *Les épîtres de Guiraut Riquier, troubadour du XIIIe siècle* (Liège: Association Internationale d'Etudes Occitanes, 1985), 230.

89. Adolf Kolsen, *Zwei provenzalische Sirventes nebst einer Anzahl Einzelstrophen* (Halle: Niemeyer, 1919), 29.

90. Riquer, *Trovadores*, 3:1537–39.

91. Jeanroy, *Poésie lyrique*, 2:281.

92. De Lollis speculates that one of the reasons that the *cobla* was so popular in Italy was that it was a genre that non-native speakers could readily practice ("Appunti," 183). Most remarkable, in my view, is how many of the trobairitz made a name for themselves through their *coblas*.

93. For the *cobla* as miniature *alba*, see P-C 461,203, in Riquer, *Trovadores*, 3:1697; and P-C 461,99a, in Hermann Suchier, *Denkmäler provenzalischer Literatur und Sprache* (Halle: Niemeyer, 1883), 318. For *cobla* as *descort*, see Cerverí de Girona's *cobla* in six languages (P-C 434a,40), in Riquer, *Trovadores*, 3:1571–73. For *cobla* as miniature *tenso*, see the exchange between Gui and Eble d'Uisel (P-C 129,2 = 194,5), recorded in Jean Audiau, ed., *Les poésies des quatre troubadours d'Ussel* (Paris, 1922; Geneva: Slatkine, 1973), 76. For an example of the *cobla* as *sirventes*, see stanza 4 of Falquet de Romans's *sirventes*, "Qan cuit chantar, eu plaing e plor" (P-C 156,11), which is recorded as a *cobla esparsa* in MSS *PQSg;* see Raymond Arveiller and Gérard Gouiran, *L'œuvre poétique de Falquet de Romans, troubadour* (Aix-en-Provence: C.U.E.R.M.A., 1987), 85–97.

94. Mölk believes that it was around the year 1170 that the major genres were taking shape. See Ulrich Mölk, *Trobadorlyrik: eine Einführung* (Munich: Artemis, 1982), 99.

95. Erich Köhler notes in *Trobadorlyrik und höfischer Roman* "das späte Auftreten der Coblas, die in der Tat nicht als eine frühe Erscheinung anzusehen sind, sondern sich viel eher, bei ihrem mannigfaltigen gedanklichen Inhalt, als Lockerung einer erstarrenden Formalisierung, als literarische Streungserscheinung erklären lassen" ([Berlin: Rütten und Loenig, 1962], 155). Leube defines its "Stellenwert" as a "Modifikation der Kanzone, der Dominanten des Systems" ("Cobla," 71).

96. Leube accounts for the thematic complexity of the *cobla* in that individual elements of the *canso* are removed from the dialectical context of the "paradoxe amoureux" and are "herausgelöst" ("Cobla," 71).

97. Carl Appel, ed., *Bernart von Ventadorn: seine Lieder* (Halle: Niemeyer, 1915), 212–13.

98. Pierre Bec, *Burlesque et obscénité chez les troubadours* (Paris: Stock, 1984), 173–75.

99. Adolf Kolsen, "25 bisher unedierte provenzalische Anonyma," *Zeitschrift für romanische Philologie* 38 (1914): 296.

CHAPTER 3

The Place of Secular Latin Lyric

WINTHROP WETHERBEE

Criticism of the medieval Latin lyric has not kept pace with the study of lyric poetry in the vernacular. Where it has been studied at all, the emphasis has tended to be on its role in the transmission and adaptation of particular themes and motifs, in the development of accentual meter, or as providing models for the stanzaic form of the vernacular lyric. Hymnody aside, it is still possible to say, as Peter Dronke did almost thirty years ago, that the Latin lyric is seldom studied as poetry, and almost never placed in the context of medieval lyric in general.[1]

Dronke himself, unquestionably the major scholar and critic of this material over the last thirty years, has done a great deal to establish the Latin lyric as a field worthy of study in its own right, not only offering readings that set a new standard of rigor and seriousness for criticism of these poems but identifying significant themes and relationships, and significant milieux for the production of twelfth-century Latin poetry. Any serious approach to the Latin lyric must be founded on his. But even Dronke's invaluable and often brilliant work has its limitations. As a pioneering project, it is largely homegrown in its methodology and untheoretical in its aims. As a critic, moreover, Dronke tends to be most attracted by what he considers the individuating element in a particular poem and to deal only on an ad hoc basis with questions of form, or such issues as that of Latin-vernacular relations.

In most respects, to be sure, this avoidance of the systematic is probably a good thing. Though the Latin poets deploy many of the same themes and conventions found in contemporary vernacular lyric, their work is nearly impossible to classify in terms of genre, beyond the identification of obvious types like the pastourelle or the *Streitgedicht* and certain kinds of Goliardic parody and satire.² As I will suggest, a number of the finest Latin love-lyrics seem to be loosely modeled on the *canso* or *chanson,* the "grand chant courtois" of the troubadour and trouvère, but they are at the same time manifestly school-poetry, exercises which only occasionally distance themselves from their scholastic origins. They tend by their nature to bear only an allusive and incomplete resemblance to vernacular lyric forms, and as I will suggest, this oblique relation to identifiable genre is important to their poetic character.

However, if Dronke's eclectic approach is thus in one aspect an accurate reflection of the character of his material, and has undeniably generated a new appreciation for its expressive capacities, criticism like his can also lead to a somewhat reductive view of that material, for much of it is governed by convictions which not all readers will share. Dronke's own *Medieval Latin and the Rise of European Love-Lyric* (1965), still the single most important contribution to the field, shows very convincingly that the experience of "courtly love" has been a recurrent element in the poetry of cultures widely separated in space and time, but Dronke does not always take sufficient account of the radically conventional nature of courtly poetry, and shows little interest in the formal and theoretical concerns of critics who have addressed this issue.³ For Dronke the most significant common element in twelfth-century courtly poetry is the belief that the human emotion which expresses itself as a worship of the beloved has in it something divine, that there is a "unity between earthly and heavenly love in which the values of *courtoisie* are ultimately grounded."⁴ Repeatedly he discovers in complex and ambiguous poetic texts images of "serenely perfect love," "the divine totality of beauty and life," an "extreme faith that love-longing and the lady together can realize a sublime ideal in the lover," "a solemn intimation of universal love." This dominating conception of the courtly ideal produces a marked tendency to emphasize the element of personal experience in poems, Latin or vernacular, which may or may not be so personal, to find sincerity where others may see detachment and irony. In the case of the Latin lyric, moreover, though Dronke is acutely aware of its capacity for intellectual play and the witty deployment of classical learning, these qualities are seen as complemented by a fundamental "innocence" that distinguishes the typical Latin poem from what Dronke rightly regards as the often more probing, self-analytical treatment of experience in vernacular lyric.⁵

Though questions about Dronke's approach arose early on,[6] little has been offered in the way of alternatives. Stephen Nichols, starting from Dronke's argument that the idea of a self-transcending love is a central element in the courtly tradition, showed that this is not only a theme but a convention of troubadour lyric, that there exists a "rhetoric of subjective involvement" that constitutes a refinement on Ovid's analyses of metamorphosis.[7] Jeffrey Peterson has demonstrated the presence of a similar self-awareness in "Stetit puella," seemingly one of the slightest and most simply charming of the *Carmina Burana*.[8] Peter Godman and Robert Edwards, reexamining the twelfth-century erotic lyric in terms of its relation to ancient lyric and elegy, have discovered in the medieval poems something harder, at once more classical and more modern, than Dronke's readings tend to allow.[9] And in what follows, while considering ways in which Latin poets deliberately engage, explore, and comment on the themes and motifs common to Latin and vernacular lyric, I will attempt to demonstrate another way in which the Latin poems distance themselves from a simply playful or idealizing treatment of courtly experience. Many of the finest of these poems are distinguished by an ironic perspective of their own, and while they only rarely attain the extreme subtlety of nuance and argument which the flexible and highly refined idiom of the vernacular lyric makes possible, they take full advantage of their own linguistic status. The learned Latin in which they are couched is inescapably imbued with a history and knowledge carried forward from the classical past which implicitly question and often work to undermine the very courtly aspirations and ideals which provide their subjects. At times their relation to the forms and themes of the poetry of *courtoisie* is effectively that of a sustained ironic gloss, pointing up the constraints and contradictions inherent in the closed world of the lyric and its preoccupation with subjective experience.

In attempting to support these contentions I will first place the Latin lyric in relation to the poetics that informs it. Like Douglas Kelly, I see the conception of writing that bears most significantly on the poetics of Latin lyric as having been expressed first and foremost in the *Cosmographia* of Bernardus Silvestris, a work which is only now beginning to be assessed at its true value as a model for the literary activity of the later twelfth century.[10] Bernardus's masterpiece is a cosmology, modeled on Boethius, Martianus Capella, Ovid, and others, and at the same time a highly self-conscious literary exercise that amounts to an *ars poetica*.[11] Bernardus's account of the *ornatus elementorum,* a common twelfth-century term for the ordering of the created universe, is simultaneously an exercise in rhetorical *ornatus* and *dispositio,* charged with wordplay and full of images of the disciplining of an unruly *subiecta materia*. (Bernardus is in fact the source of the language in which Geoffrey of Vinsauf, whose *Poetria nova* is perhaps the most authoritative of the *artes poeticae* of the period, will describe the literary version of the same process.)[12] Throughout the *Cosmographia* there is a fascinating dialogic relationship between the divine ordering principle, or *Nous*, and the personification of primordial matter, *Silva*, whose chaotic fecundity has been well characterized by Linda Lomperis as a figure for the productive capacities of poetic language.[13] The universe at large, conceived in terms of the cosmology of Plato's *Timaeus*, presents a model of coherent rationality. The nuances and complexities of human nature, represented metaphorically by the waywardness and near intractability of *Silva*, threaten continually to disrupt or transgress this supreme pattern, as the gratuitous play of language resists the aspiration of human art to embody the ideal. Human fulfillment consists in recognizing that the macrocosm mirrors the ordering activity of *Nous*, a recognition which simultaneously confirms that man's mind is created in the image of the Divine Wisdom; but human experience is always a compromise between this reconstitutive vision and the aberrant, potentially subversive tendencies of human *ingenium*, imagination and appetite.

The implications of Bernardus's cosmic model inform the literary activity of the later twelfth century in various ways. The great project in which *Nous* enlists the aid of *Silva*, "that the world be made more beautiful,"[14] has rightly been recognized as a sustained metaphor for the collective aspiration of twelfth-century art and culture, courtly and religious,[15] but it also provides a sobering perspective on that enterprise. For Bernardus's cosmogony is pervaded by images and signs which portend the uneven course of world history, and the forces which will work to undermine the attempts of human societies to achieve order and harmony are foreshadowed in the unruly play of the elements themselves. Bernardus conveys a strong sense of the heroic in his treatment of man the creator, but equally strong is the recurrent pessimism with which he reminds us of the constant threat of a reversion to chaos.

The implicit precariousness of Bernardus's literary cosmology becomes explicitly a problem of poetics in the *De planctu Naturae* of Alan of Lille, a dialogue between a poet-narrator and the goddess *Natura* in which Bernardus's broad concern with the place of humanity in the natural order is recast in terms of the status of human language.[16] As in the *Cosmographia*, the project is informed by an ironic historical awareness: an extended discussion of the history of human sexual behavior and its aberrations becomes the occasion for an analysis of linguistic *proprietas*, the primordial relationship between language and Nature that has been disrupted by human sin.[17] And as for Bernardus, so for Alan the theme is one which has a special relevance to his own time. R. Howard Bloch and Alexandre Leupin agree in viewing Alan's conception of the "fall" of language from pristine purity into "perverse" wordplay, stylistic eccentricity, and wanton allusion as less a moral than a cultural phenomenon: what Alan is describing is the diffusion of language into metaphoricity and textuality—the birth, in short, of literature.[18] And Bloch suggests that Alan may be adverting specifically to the rise of the vernacular, with its secular orientation and freedom to coin new cultural images.[19] I think this is indeed the case, that Alan's engagement with the vernacular is quite specifically focused on the poetry of *courtoisie,* and that the issues that concern him are highly relevant to the ventures of Latin lyric in the later twelfth century.

Amid the sexual-linguistic anarchy that the poet of the *De planctu* bemoans, there are hints of a vestigial capacity for regeneration. He rails at a degenerate mankind who pursue base desires while allowing kisses to "lie untasted on virgin lips," but he himself can imagine enjoying such kisses, and making himself immortal through them:

> Spiritus exiret ad basia, deditus ori
>   Totus et in labiis luderet ipse sibi,
> Ut dum sic moriar, in me defunctus, in illa
>   Felici uita perfruar, alter ego.[20]

> My spirit, wholly committed to my mouth, would issue forth in response to such kisses, and delight itself in playing about her lips; hence, though I should thus die, once dead unto myself I should enjoy a happy life, a new state of being, in her.

This intuition of an ideal, supersexual significance in feminine beauty remains dislocated within the argument of the *De planctu.* The erotic and the religious blend in these lines to produce a *tertium quid,* a synthesis which resembles the primal integration of values that Nature and her poet seek to restore, yet remains wholly "other" relative to the economy of Nature.[21] But the lines are not just an isolated moment of fantasy. In such a passage we see Alan, and in his person the Latin literary and pedagogical tradition, acknowledging a new literary mode, a new way of speaking about love that draws on Latin religious forms and the rhetorical traditions of the Latin schools, but finds its most striking expression in vernacular courtly poetry.[22] The transformative power here imputed to the maiden's beauty corresponds to the high point on a scale of powers attributed by Bernart de Ventadorn to a lady whose "saving" grace is sometimes envisioned as concretely sexual, or as capable of making a poor man rich, but at times seems almost to impart a kind of *vita nova:*

> Per la bocha·m feretz al cor
> D'un doutz baizar de fin'amor coral
> Que·m torn en joi e·m get d'ira mortal![23]

> May your mouth strike my heart with a sweet kiss of heartfelt *fin' amor* that leads me to joy and frees me from mortal sadness!

> C'ab sol lo bel semblan que·m en fai
> Can pot ni aizes lo·lh cossen,
> Ai tan de joi que sol no·m en sen.[24]

> Just by the beautiful face she shows me, when she is able or the opportunity presents itself, I have such joy that I am no more myself.

Like the many passages in which troubadours deploy the terms of prayer and adoration to express their responsiveness to the lady's power, the lines I have quoted, at once transparent and subtly allusive, embody a promise which constantly eludes the dreamer-poet of the *De planctu Naturae*. He is acutely aware that the Latin in which he seeks to express his complex desire is the monument to a fundamental disjunction in human history, an awareness expressed in the dialogue's pervasive concern with the opposition between "fallen" human language and an innocent, "integral" language toward which his poetry continually yearns, and which the lyric of *fin' amor* can seem to embody.[25] Elsewhere in the *De planctu* other motifs reminiscent of vernacular lyric appear. The long, oxymoronic "definition of love" with which Nature seeks to "demonstrate the indemonstrable" and delimit what cannot be bounded suggests a destabilized counterpart to the balanced oppositions that structure the lyrics of Bernart and other vernacular poets,[26] and Alan's representation of the relations of Nature and her "priest," Genius, alludes in various ways to the bond between the troubadour and his lady.[27]

Alan, then, is clearly responsive to a number of the essential properties of the contemporary vernacular lyric, but he has also placed them in a perspective which is distinctly that of school-poetry, and differs fundamentally in its address to *courtoisie* and its implications. Though the vernacular draws on many of the same traditional resources,[28] the poetry of the schools is Latin poetry, a vehicle for the preservation and transmission of the classical tradition. One consequence of this legacy is what Paul Zumthor has called "monumentarisation," a burden of associations which invest this poetry with a certain authority, while depriving it of the spontaneity of the vernacular and restricting its capacity to fully engage emotional experience.[29] It is emphatically Ovidian poetry. From beginning to end of the *De planctu* Alan's language, the language of *Natura* as well as that of the poet-narrator, is pervaded by classical mythology, in particular images of metamorphosis and of sexual promiscuity among the gods. Indeed the dialogue could hardly take place without this classical lore, which confounds Nature's attempts to present an orderly view of love, but at the same time provides her with exempla and imagery essential to her analysis of the human condition in erotic terms.

Leupin has shown how this Ovidian sense of poetry informs Geoffrey's *Poetria nova*. The *Natura* of Alan and Bernardus is a sort of extended background metaphor in Geoffrey's treatise, and in her capacious function as Leupin describes it, she "assembles and 'metaphorizes' all of the topoi bequeathed by ancient literature . . . *Nature is first and foremost a text*—it is always an articulation—and poetry functions to transform one articulation into another."[30] The texts of Alan and Geoffrey posit a literary universe that is both closed, cut off from the larger cosmic economy that Alan's Nature seeks to recover, and, within the limits of its own self-contained economy, in a state of perpetual flux. And it is mythological formulas that define this universe, as a passage from the *De planctu* may serve to suggest:

> Poete tamen aliquando hystoriales euentus ioculationibus fabulosis quadam eleganti sutura confederant, ut ex diuersorum conpetenti iunctura ipsius narrationis elegantior pictura resultet. Sed tamen, cum a poetis deorum pluralitas sompniatur uel ipsi dii Venereis ferulis manus subduxisse dicuntur, in his falsitatis umbra lucescit. Nec in hoc poeta a sue proprietatis genere degener inuenitur.[31]

> Poets often join historical events to their own playful fabulations by a sort of elegant stitching, in order that from the artful conjoining of these diverse materials a more elegant narrative pattern may emerge. But when poets dream of a plurality of gods, or when the gods themselves are said to have undergone the tyranny of Venus, here the shadow of falsehood is brought to light. Yet in such things the poet is not deviating from his proper character.

The gods are first conceded only an imaginary existence, then allowed sufficient reality so that they must be defended against the charge of promiscuity. Then the contradiction is underlined by the oxymoronic linkage of light and shadow ("falsitatis umbra lucescit"), and the concluding assertion that such ambiguities are proper to poetry confirms the self-defining character of Alan's chronically "fallen" poetic universe. Alan's invocation of the lost purity of prelapsarian love is more than a flight of fancy, but it remains an elusive promise, and one purpose of the *De planctu Naturae* is to account for its unattainability in historical terms. The very idiom is charged with an ironic knowledge that enables it to express the paradoxical effects of something like original sin, while at the same time rendering it incapable of full participation in the idyllic and idealizing attitudes of the poetry of *fin' amors*.

Geoffrey of Vinsauf, illustrating the function of digression in his *Poetria nova*, touches this aspect of the Latin lyric:

> Unius astringit duo pectora nodus amoris;
> Corpora disjungit nova causa. Sed ante recessum
> Oscula praefigit os ori; cingit utrumque
> Mutuus et stringit amplexus . . .
> Veri cedit hiems. Nebulas diffibulat aer
> et caelum blanditur humo. Lascivit in illam
> Humidus et calidus; et quod sit masculus aer
> Femina sentit humus. . . .
> Hoc tempus titillat aves. Haec temporis hora,
> Quos nondum divisit amor, divisit amantes.[32]

> The knot of one love bound two hearts; an unknown cause separated their bodies. But before departing mouth pressed kisses upon mouth, a mutual embrace held both of them fast bound. . . . Winter yields to spring. The air throws open its cloudy robe and heaven smiles on earth, sporting with her, moist and warm: and feminine earth learns that air is masculine. . . . It is a time that arouses the birds. It was this time that separated those lovers whom love itself still held together.

It is in effect the presence of the unnamed *nova causa*, a disjunctive force thwarting the attempts of rhetoric and nature alike to establish harmony, that defines the situation of sophisticated Latin lyric, charged with an awareness of its own circumscribed and ambiguous status and generating an irony that is programmed by its inescapably allusive language. Thus, for example, in a lyric from the *Codex Buranus* which tells the story of Dido's love for Aeneas, a narrative pervaded by allusions to Dido's reckless generosity and forebodings of her destruction ends abruptly with a celebration of the union of the lovers:

> Et sic amborum in coniugio leta
>   resplenduit etherea regia—
>   nam ad amoris gaudia
>   rident, clarescunt omnia![33]

> And thus rejoicing at the marriage of the pair, the court of heaven shone resplendent. For at the joys of love all things smile and become radiant.

Virtually every word in this passage stands in telling contradiction to some ominous detail in the Virgilian source, where *coniugium* is a function of

Dido's willful self-delusion, heavenly radiance is the flashing of lightning, and the only laughter expresses Venus's foreknowledge that the plans of *pronuba Iuno* will be destroyed, and with them Dido herself.[34] As in Bernardus's *Cosmographia*, the universe of this lyric is indelibly inscribed with the history of human error, and its seeming beneficence and harmony are deeply ambiguous.

It is a version of this poetic universe that frames the early ventures in "serious" Latin lyric that I would like to turn to now. I have chosen to consider first some poems that are almost certainly by Peter of Blois, who, as Dronke has shown, was a central figure in the literary culture inspired by the court of Henry II.[35] At Henry's court he might well have met vernacular poets,[36] and in any case his interest in vernacular lyric seems to me unmistakable. But Peter's poetry expresses his own milieu, and he uses the conventional resources of school-poetry to construct lyrics which, true to the Ovidian tradition of the schools,[37] articulate and analyze the paradoxes of a kind of *fin' amors* in the process of imitating it. Many features of twelfth-century vernacular lyric are evoked in his poems: its autonomy, the "circular" character of the emotional experience it defines,[38] the intimation of larger harmonies in the courtly vision of love. But the experience is always self-conscious, conditioned by an awareness of the cosmic and historical problems discovered by Alan's *Natura*, and nearly always ends with an acknowledgment of defeat or dislocation.

I will not argue for precise connections between any of these lyrics and specific vernacular models, but their sustained tracing of lyric and erotic effects, though probably influenced by the Ovidian experiments of Baudri of Bourgueil and other French precursors in school-poetry,[39] has no real precedent in the medieval Latin tradition, and seems to be most readily explicable as a response to the vernacular *chanson*, an appropriation of the resources of the Latin tradition to the creation of a new kind of poem in emulation of the most significant new departures in vernacular poetry. Thus the presentation of the lady of Peter's "A globo veteri" (appendix 1), who embodies the ideal preconception of earthly beauty which once inspired the primal creativity of Nature, is reminiscent of Bernardus's cosmogony and the *descriptiones puellae* (descriptions of a girl) prescribed by Matthieu de Vendôme on the one hand, and at the same time responsive to the presentation of the *Dompna*, the all-powerful woman in troubadour lyric. Peter's lady is an archetype, an expression of all that is divine in the handiwork of Nature:

> A globo veteri
> cum rerum faciem

> traxissent superi
> mundique seriem
> prudens explicuit
> et texuit
> Natura,
> iam preconceperat
> quod fuerat
> factura.[40]

> When the higher powers had drawn forth the face of creation from the ancient mass, and Nature in her wisdom unfolded and wove together the sequence of world history, she had already formed a preconception of that which she was to create.

In a lyric of Raimbaut d'Orange, "mi donz" becomes, like Peter's lady, or like Nature herself in Alan's *De planctu Naturae*, the vice-regent of God on earth:

> C'a mi donz laisset en patz
> C'a seignoriu vas totz latz,
> Qe·l mons totz li deu servir
> E sos volers obezir.[41]

> For God left my lady to enjoy in peace sovereignty over all about her. So all the world must serve her and obey her wishes.

As Raimbaut's lady elsewhere becomes the model to whom other ladies bear a tentative, figural relation,[42] Peter's exhibits in herself all the beauties that Nature distributes more sparingly among other women: she is that creature in which Nature's artistry expresses itself most clearly. But in a fallen world this very splendor is a source of peril. As Raimbaut contrives to make the beauty of his lady an argument for promiscuity, since his love of others is inspired by their partial embodiment of the ideal most fully realized in her, so the consummate artistry of Peter's *Natura* finally serves the interests of Venus, in that the effect of his lady's perfect beauty is to render him prey to the snares of desire. Peter's allusions to Bernardus thus serve to frame an ironic humor very close to that latent in Raimbaut's idealizations. School-poetry and vernacular lyric are here brought together by a common *clergie*, the vernacular drawing on the learned topoi of the Latin tradition.[43] But in Peter's poem the irony is more sustained, and ends by bringing to the surface a deeper irony, latent in the initial references to the artistry of Nature. "Rapit michi me Coronis" (Coronis steals me from myself), he declares, and this line, with its disturbing hint at a kind of Ovidian transformation,[44] is in effect the poem's punch line. To contemplate the primal perfection embodied in his lady is only to be made finally more keenly aware of the disjunction in human nature and human experience which, like the *nova causa* in Geoffrey's specimen love-idyll, renders perfect communion unrealizable.

The world of Peter's "Dionei sideris" ("Star of Venus," appendix 3) is framed in the opening stanzas by mythological topoi: in the first stanza the loves of the gods are ordered by a hierarchy of generation, and terms like "spondet" (betroths), "salutat" (greets), "obtemperat" (obeys) define the collaboration of celestial powers in a process of renewal which expresses the benign planetary influence of Venus. Stanzas 2 and 3 repeat the same conventional idea in terms that become steadily more evocative of mythic history: the banishment of the "triste senium" ("grim old age") of winter is allusively linked to Jove's violent overthrow of Saturn, and the new dominion of "amor" which that defeat portends surfaces explicitly in stanza 4, where the tyranny of Cupid is set off by images of slavery and bestialization. In stanza 5 the combined influence of Cupid and Venus is conveyed in language which, by invoking the binding force, the "nexus" (bonds) and "amplexus" (embraces) from which human lovers are powerless to escape, reminds us of how readily Boethian cosmic *amor,* as it bears on human life, can become necessity.

The evolution and transformation of the view of love presented by this poem, as the beneficent cosmic order of the early stanzas is displaced as the poem's controlling metaphor by a kind of goading determinism, is in effect a compressed version of what will happen to the quest of the Lover in Jean de Meun's portion of the *Roman de la Rose.* Finally in stanza 6 the poet-lover is introduced, his subjection to love expressed as a futile orbiting ("ambiebam" [I went around]; "ambitu" [circle]; "ambicio" [lit. "going about"]) around the beloved. This is followed by the abrupt and ambiguous concluding declaration that he has at last come to know Venus's "clementia," a conclusion which resembles those of many troubadour lyrics in its somewhat equivocal claim to have discovered a kind of satisfying alternative to erotic fulfillment. But the claim to have been blessed by Venus would seem to be called into question by everything the poem has told us about the bearing of history and nature on his love, and even if true, only confirms his haplessness in the face of the larger forces determining his situation.

"Amor habet superos" ("Love possesses the gods," appendix 4) is not by Peter, but the poem manifests its own version of the knowingness which distances the Latin tradition from the vernacular. It presents itself as a straightforward celebration of continent love, the song of a lover whose pride it is to be free of the taint and tyranny that he sees as attendant on the consummation of love: "virgino cum virgine," he asserts, and therefore "pecco sine crimine" (I sin without blame). As a frame for this rather unappealing posture, the poet posits a state of nature in which love collaborates with cosmic order, causing Jove and the other gods to keep to their proper spheres, and a world where virginity possesses a talismanic power which keeps lust and its disruptive power at bay.

All of this is the common stuff of many lyrics, Latin and vernacular. But the point of the poem depends on our recognizing how far, and how self-consciously, this picture is at odds with the underlying worldview of Latin lyric. In treating the topoi of purity which chasten and exalt desire in other lyrics, and which constitute the essence of Alan's evocation of a lost Edenic condition in the *De planctu Naturae*, the poet of "Amor habet superos" has reduced that purity to a fetish, and there is a leering undertone in the refrain, "pecco sine crimine," which resists the smugness with which the speaker insists on his own youth and innocence.[45]

"Iam ver oritur" (Now spring emerges), an anonymous lyric from the *Codex Buranus* which exhibits a number of similarities and verbal correspondences with poems of Peter's, deals with the irony latent in the closed, circular structure of sophisticated lyric. It begins by describing the complex effect of the song of the nightingale in terms which make that song a metaphor for the autonomous, self-regulating economy of the sophisticated lyric:

1.
Iam ver oritur.
veris flore variata
tellus redimitur.
excitat in gaudium
cor concentus avium   5
voce relativa
Iovem salutantium.
In his philomena
Tereum reiterat,
et iam fatum   10
antiquatum
querule retractat.
sed dum fatis obicit
Itym perditum
merula   15
choraulica
carmina
coaptat.

2.
Istis insultantibus
casibus   20

fatalibus
in choree speciem
res reciprocatur.⁴⁶

> Now spring is come. The earth is adorned with [redeemed by?] many kinds of spring flowers. A chorus of birds, heralding Jove with harmonizing voices, arouses the heart to joy. Among these, the nightingale tells again [retells?] of Tereus, and now, plaintively, retells [revises? withdraws? undoes?] the ancient tragedy. But while she thus challenges the fates over the loss of Itys, the flute-playing blackbird adapts his song to hers. And as these two mock the disastrous power of fate, the affair is answered [turned back on itself? requited?] by means of a ritual dance.

As my tentative rendering of these lines is intended to suggest, the effect of the bird's song is to hold a number of possible "readings" in suspension, subject to the mood or experience of the listener. The wordplay defies any single translation, but by bringing lyric circularity into implicit confrontation with a narrative world of history that is ostentatiously undone or suppressed, it clearly suggests the sense in which the integrity, the flawless coherence of the song exists in a dialectical relation to the violation of purity that in mythic terms is the cause of that song.⁴⁷

Lyric and narrative come together again in one of the most direct addresses by the Latin tradition to vernacular literary culture, and at the same time one of the hardest to assess, the well-known "Si linguis angelicis" from the *Carmina Burana*. Like the portion of the *Roman de la Rose* attributed to Guillaume de Lorris,⁴⁸ it is a translation into narrative terms of an experience that is manifestly the stuff of lyric, and as such it represents one of the points of closest affinity between the Latin and vernacular lyric traditions.⁴⁹ The poem describes the narrator's encounter with a young lady for whom he has long felt an undeclared desire. She is accompanied by her duenna, and he prays that the old woman may be struck by lightning. For whatever reason, the old woman disappears at this point,⁵⁰ leaving the lover free to address to the beloved a long, rapturous appeal, reviewing the history of his love for her in terms that at times seem to accord it the status of a quasi-mystical experience.⁵¹ She then replies, revealing that she too has long harbored a desire for him. After some witty play, they embrace, and "Quis ignorat, amodo cuncta que secuntur?" (30:1) (Who does not know all that happened after that?).

The poem has been subject to widely divergent interpretations.⁵² I would argue that it is best taken as providing a detached, ironic perspective on the idealism generated by the courtly fantasy at its center—an idealism which evanesces rather abruptly in the last few stanzas. (In this respect the poem anticipates Jean de Meun as well as Guillaume de Lorris.) I would compare its critique of masculine courtly idealism to that implicit in the elaborate dialogues of Book 1 of the *De amore* of Andreas Capellanus. The lover's appeal in the "Si linguis" is less obviously self-promoting than the discourse of Andreas's male lovers, but it is comparably narcissistic in that the lady's role is wholly programmed by it. Moreover, the fact that the talk of Andreas's gentlemen achieves nothing, while the situation of the lover of "Si linguis" is somehow resolved, is less important than the underlying fascination of the speakers in both texts with their own eloquent lucidity. What Toril Moi observes of Andreas's speakers is true also of the hero of "Si linguis": "By dominating the word, [the lover] gains a kind of phallic power that contradicts his seemingly humble stance toward his lady."[53] This aristocratic mastery is in some sense an end in itself, but Andreas's probing mockery exposes within it a jealous anxiety about the lady's "otherness." Here as in so much courtly poetry, it is hinted that the aristocrat-lover is a slave to the very discourse he seems to have mastered. The same suggestion is strong in "Si linguis." One of the most striking moments in the poem is that in which the lady, finally allowed to speak, reminds the lover that she, too, has an emotional life: "sed que pro te tulerim, numquam somniasti" (24:3), deflating in an instant his claim to be the sole suffering center of his world. But this potentially devastating moment is quickly over, and with the coming together of the lovers in the poem's final stanzas all of the tension so crucial to the lyric situation is wholly dissolved. The arbitrariness with which the lover of "Si linguis" is vindicated in his desire is only another way of representing the hapless subjectivity of that desire. The two Latin writers are at one in their awareness of a fundamental irony at the heart of courtly literature.

The Latin tradition I have been tracing appears once again in Jean de Meun's portion of the *Roman de la Rose*, where the worlds of school-poetry and lyric *fin' amors*, the idealized aspirations of Guillaume's courtly lover and the exhortations of Alan's *Natura*, are together subjected to Jean's powerful irony. Here as in so many areas, Jean's *summa* provides a comprehensive reflection on the dialogue of Latin and vernacular, and the dilemma of his "Genius," the priest of Nature who brings the Latin tradition to bear on a crisis of *courtoisie*, and attempts to resolve the crisis of the poem with an authoritative discourse on the divine purpose and destiny of human sexuality, will continue to preoccupy vernacular poets.[54] But to deal adequately with Jean's version of my subject would exceed the scope of this essay, and I will end instead by noting what seems to me an attractive symmetry in the history of Latin-vernacular relations.

Like the emergence of vernacular poetry in the twelfth century, the new renaissance of vernacular lyric represented by the Italian *stilnovisti* of the later thirteenth century is acknowledged by a Latin treatise, the *De vulgari eloquentia* of Dante, a work which recalls in various ways the concern of Alan's *De planctu* with the "nature" of language, the language proper to nature. Alan's *poeta* had yearned to recover his lost status as the "secretary" and "familiar" of Nature. The poet posited by the *De vulgari eloquentia* is properly the *domesticus* and *familiaris* of his own vernacular, a language which is itself a "nature," aspiring to full articulation through the discipline of a *grammatica* which orders the different strains of the *volgare* in their common impulse toward the recovery of a primal speech.[55] The confirmation of this insight into language is the *canzone* as developed by Dante and his contemporaries, a poem whose vernacular medium has attained the learned density and allusiveness of Latin. It is a measure of Dante's extraordinary sense of the capacities of vernacular poetry that his semi-mythical treatment of the *volgare* is in effect a rewriting of the myth of poetic language in the *De planctu,* a rejoinder on behalf of the vernacular which confirms how completely the Latin tradition has been assimilated, and conveys as well the implicit suggestion that it has been transcended.

APPENDIXES

Texts of Lyrics Discussed

1. Peter of Blois, "A globo veteri," *Carmina Burana,* no. 67, ed. Alfons Hilka and Otto Schumann, vol. 1: 2 (Heidelberg: Winter, 1941), 31–32.

> 1a
> A globo veteri
> cum rerum faciem
> traxissent superi
> mundique seriem
> prudens explicuit
> et texuit
> Natura,
> iam preconceperat
> quod fuerat
> factura.
>
> 1b
> Que causas machine
> mundane suscitans,
> de nostra virgine
> iamdudum cogitans,
> plus hanc excoluit,

plus prebuit
honoris,
dans privilegium
et premium laboris.

2a
In hac pre ceteris
totius operis
Nature lucet opera.
tot munera
nulli favoris contulit,
sed extulit
hanc ultra cetera.

2b
Et que puellulis
avara singulis
solet partiri singula:
huic sedula
impendit copiosius
et plenius
forme munuscula.

3a
Nature studio
longe venustata,
contendit lilio
rugis non crispata
frons nivea.
simplices siderea
luce micant ocelli.

3b
Omnes amantium
trahit in se visus,
spondens remedium
verecunda risus
lascivia.
arcus supercilia
discriminant gemelli.

4a
Ab utriusque luminis
confinio
moderati libraminis
iudicio
naris eminentia
producitur venuste

quadam temperantia:
nec nimis erigitur
nec premitur
iniuste.

4b
Allicit verbis dulcibus
et osculis,
castigate tumentibus
labellulis,
roseo nectareus
odor infusus ori.
pariter eburneus
sedet ordo dentium
par niveum
candori.

5a
Certant nivi, micant lene
pectus, mentem, colla, gene;
sed, ne candore nimio
evanescant in pallorem,
precastigat hunc candorem
rosam maritans lilio
prudentior Natura,
ut ex his fit aptior
et gratior
mixtura.

5b
Rapit michi me Coronis
privilegiata donis
et Gratiarum flosculis.
nam Natura dulcioris
alimenta dans erroris,
dum in stuporem populis
hanc omnibus ostendit,
in risu blando retia
Veneria
tetendit.

1a. When the gods had drawn forth the visible universe from ancient chaos, and wise Nature was unfolding and coordinating the order of things, she had already preconceived all that she would fashion.

1b. As she gave energy to the motive forces of the world system, she was thinking long in advance about [creating] my lady. She endowed her with extra refinement and beauty, offering her as the seal and mark of value on her handiwork.

2a. In her, beyond all other creatures, the craft of Nature shines forth. On no other did she confer so many special gifts, but raised this one above the rest.

2b. And though she stingily parcels out her gifts one at a time to young girls, on this one she eagerly bestowed a full abundance of the gifts of beauty.

3a. Beautified by zealous Nature, her snow-white forehead, unmarked by wrinkles, rivals the lily. Her modest eyes shine with a starry light.

3b. She draws to herself all lovers' gazes, proffering the balm of her smile in playful modesty. Twin arcs define her eyebrows.

4a. From the inner corners of her eyes, with a nicely calculated inclination, her charmingly formed nose extends forth to a moderate extent; it is neither extended too far nor unduly recessive.

4b. She charms with the sweet words and kisses of her chastely swelling lips, her rosy mouth suffused with the odor of nectar. Her ivory teeth are arranged in perfect order, and as white as snow.

5a. Her breast, chin, neck, cheeks, gently glowing, rival the snow. But lest they seem too faint and pallid by an excessive whiteness, Nature prudently limits this whiteness, marrying the rose to the lily, that a more appropriate, more pleasing blending may take place.

5b. Coronis steals me from myself, licensed by the flourishing gifts with which she is graced. For Nature, who lets us feed on the sweets of folly, by showing forth this maiden to the astonishment of all, sets the traps of Venus through that fair smile.

2. Peter of Blois, "Vacillantis trutine," ed. Peter Dronke, *The Medieval Poet and His World* (Rome: Storia e Letteratura, 1984), 298–300.

> 1a
> Vacillantis trutine
> libramine
> mens suspensa fluctuat
> et estuat,
> in tumultus anxios
> dum se vertit
> et bipertit
> motus in contrarios.
> *O, O, O, O langueo—*
> *causam languoris video,*

nec caveo:
videns et prudens pereo!

1b
Me vacare studio
vult Ratio,
sed <dum> Amor alteram
vult operam,
in diversa rapior:
Ratione
cum Dione
dimicante crucior.
O, O, O, O langueo . . .

2a
Sicut in arbore
frons tremula,
navicula
levis in equore
dum caret anchore
subsidio,
contrario
flatu concussa fluitat—
sic agitat,
sic turbine sollicitat
me dubio
hinc Amor, inde Ratio.
O, O, O, O langueo . . .

2b
Sub libra pondero
quid melius,
et dubius
mecum delibero,
nunc menti refero
delicias
venerias,
que mea michi Florula
det oscula,
qui risus, que labellula,
que facies,
frons, naris, que cesaries!
O, O, O, O langueo . . .

3a
His invitat
et irritat

Amor me blandiciis,
sed aliis
Ratio sollicitat
et excitat
me studiis.
O, O, O, O langueo . . .

3b
Nam solari
me scolari
cogitat exilio.
Sed Ratio,
procul abi! vinceris
sub Veneris
imperio!
O, O, O, O langueo . . .

1a. My mind floats, suspended in the balance of the fluctuating scale, and seethes in anxious tumult, as it shifts and is divided by contrary motions.

Refrain. O, how feeble I am! I see the cause of my weakness, but do not shun it; awake and alert, I perish [all the same].

1b. Reason bids me give myself to study, but since love bids me do work of another kind, I am drawn in two directions; as reason wars with Venus, I suffer torture.

Refrain.

2a. As a leaf trembles on the bough, as a light boat is tossed on the sea, lacking the stabilizing weight of an anchor, and beaten by conflicting winds, so love from one side, reason from the other afflict me with a storm of doubt.

Refrain.

2b. On the scales I try to determine the better course, and anxiously debate with myself. First I call to mind the pleasures of Venus—the kisses my little Flora gives me, her smiles, her tender lips, her face, her forehead, her hair.

Refrain.

3a. Love entices and goads me with these delights. But reason sobers me, and arouses me to other pursuits.

Refrain.

3b. For [reason] thinks to solace me with the scholar's lonely life. But reason, begone! You are overcome by the sovereign power of Venus.

Refrain.

3. "Dionei sideris," ed. Wilhelm Meyer, *Die Arundel Sammlung mittellateinischer Lieder*, Abhandlungen der königlichen Gesellschaft der Wissenschaften zu Göttingen, Philosophische-Historische Klasse, N.F. 11: 2 (1908), 9–10.

1.
Dionei sideris
favor elucescit
et amantum teneris
votis allubescit.
Dum assistit non remota
sibi stacione,
celsiore fulget rota
filius Latone,
cuius aura gratiam
spondet non minorem.
Dum salutat Maiam,
his introcedens medius
Mercurius
devotus obtemperat
et aggerat
favorem.

2.
Renitenti pallio
Cybele vestita
flore comam vario
vernat redimita.
Ridet aula Jovialis,
ether expolitur;
senectutis Saturnalis
torpor sepelitur,
dum respirat tenere
gratus odor florum.
Florentis in ubere
campi canora residet
nec invidet
Talia sororibus
nec sedibus
sororum.

3.
Exulat pars acrior
anni renascentis.
spirat aura gratior
veris blandientis.
Rose rubor suis audet

nodis explicari,
aquilonem sibi gaudet
iam non novercari;
anni triste senium
ver infans excludit
Aquilonis ocium
terre depingit faciem;
temperiem
dans aura veneriis
imperiis
alludit.

4.
Brumali tyrannide
longe relegata,
sevit puer cuspide
Cyprius armata,
Ut nec Hermen caduceus
suus tueatur;
nec iam Liber est Lieus:
nominis negatur
Bacho privilegium;
stupet se servire.
Jactitat imperium
triumphans proles Veneris
de superis
cum cogatur iterum
rex superum
mugire.

5.
Ledit · urget · vulnerat
puer Cythereus.
lenit · mulcet · temperat
favor Dioneus.
Suo quemque donat pare
duo nectens diva,
duos gaudet inflammare
face relativa;
quo se nullus explicet,
implicat amplexu.
Et amor ne claudicet,
ignem bipertit nexibus
duplicibus.
bino nodus firmior
et certior
fit nexu.

PLACE OF SECULAR LATIN LYRIC 117

6.
In me telum miserat
Ciprius auratum.
igne ceco clauserat
pectus sauciatum.
Ambiebam prece · donis,
ambitu beato:
nil profeci, dum Choronis
aditu negato
me procul excluserat
mente · domo · thoris.
Et cui nil profuerat
illa felix ambicio,
nunc sencio
Dionei nimiam
clemenciam
favoris.

1. The benign star of Venus shines forth and gladdens the tender, yearning hearts of lovers. While she remains in a position that shifts only a little, the son of Lato shines in his higher orbit, diffusing a no less pleasing influence. When Mercury, passing between them, presents himself to Maia, he exhibits devoted obedience, and enhances the benign atmosphere.

2. Cybele, decked in her shining robe, flourishes, adorning her hair with flowers of all sorts. The court of Jove is happy, the air is bright; the sluggish old age of Saturn is laid to rest, as the pleasing scent of flowers breathes gently forth. On the bosom of the flowering earth Thalia sits and sings, unenvious of her sisters and their high dwellings.

3. The harsher portion of the newly reborn year has been exiled. The breath of the pleasant breeze of spring is sweet. The blushing rose dares to unfold its buds, rejoicing that the north wind no longer harasses her. The infant spring banishes the year's grim old age. The leisurely east wind brings color to the face of earth, and the breeze that bestows fair weather playfully conveys the commands of Venus.

4. When winter's tyranny has been driven far off, the Cyprian boy fiercely aims his pointed darts. Not even his caduceus can protect Mercury. The wine-god is no longer "Liber" [i.e., "free"]; Bacchus is denied the right to live up to his name, and is dumbfounded to find himself a slave. Venus's triumphant son flaunts his power over the gods, compelling the very king of the gods, again and again, to bellow like a bull.

5. The Cytherean boy strikes, goads, wounds, but Venus's favor soothes, sweetens, calms. Joining two together, the goddess grants the appropriate

gifts to each, rejoicing to kindle in both of them a similar flame. She involves them in an embrace whence neither can escape, and lest love progress haltingly, she divides her fire to ensure a mutual attraction. By this twofold bond the union is made firmer and more sure.

6. When Cupid had loosed a golden weapon at me, and my stricken breast harbored a hidden fire, I went round and round as if in a charmed circle, offering prayers and gifts. But I gained nothing, for Choronis, denying entry, held me far from her thoughts, her house, her chamber. And I, who gained nothing from this hopeful orbiting, now experience the surpassingly merciful favor of Venus [or perhaps "now recognize that to be spared can also be a mark of Venus's favor"].

4. "Amor habet superos," *Carmina Burana,* no. 88, ed. Alfons Hilka and Otto Schumann, vol. 1: 2 (Heidelberg: Winter, 1941), 78.

> 1.
> Amor habet superos:
> Iovem amat Iuno;
> motus premens efferos
> imperat Neptuno;
> Pluto tenens inferos
> mitis est hoc uno.
> *Refl.*   Amoris solamine
> virgino cum virgine;
> aro non in semine,
> pecco sine crimine.
>
> 2.
> Amor trahit teneros
> molliori nexu,
> rigidos et asperos
> duro frangit flexu;
> capitur rhinoceros
> virginis amplexu.
> *Refl.*   Amoris solamine . . .
>
> 3.
> Virgo cum virginibus
> horreo coruptas,
> et cum meretricibus
> simul odi nuptas;
> nam in istis talibus
> turpis est voluptas.
> *Refl.*   Amoris solamine . . .

4.
Virginis egregie
ignibus calesco
et eius cotidie
in amore cresco;
sol est in meridie,
nec ego tepesco.
Refl.   Amoris solamine . . .

5.
Gratus super omnia
ludus est puelle,
et eius precordia
omni carent felle;
sunt, que prestat, basia
dulciora melle.
Refl.   Amoris solamine . . .

6.
Ludo cum Cecilia;
nichil timeatis!
sum quasi custodia
fragilis etatis,
ne marcescant lilia
sue castitatis.
Refl.   Amoris solamine . . .

7.
Flos est; florem frangere
non est res secura.
uvam sino crescere,
donec sit matura;
spes me facit vivere
letum re ventura.
Refl.   Amoris solamine . . .

8.
Volo tantum ludere,
id est: contemplari,
presens loqui, tangere,
tantum osculari;
quintum, quod est agere,
noli suspicari!
Refl.   Amoris solamine . . .

9.
Quicquid agant ceteri,
virgo, sic agamus,

ut, quem decet fieri, ludum faciamus;
ambo sumus teneri;
tenere ludamus!
Refl. Amoris solamine . . .

1. Love possesses the gods above. Juno loves Jove; love gives orders to Neptune, curbing his fierce movement; and by the power of this god alone Pluto, who rules the underworld, grows mild.

Refrain. Pursuing love's reward, I play the virgin with a virgin; I plow without seed, and sin without blame.

2. Love governs tender spirits with a gentle bond, but breaks harsh and haughty natures to his cruel sway. Even the rhinoceros [conceived as a kind of unicorn] submits to a maiden's embrace.

Refrain.

3. I play the virgin with virgins, but I abhor women who have been tainted [by sexual activity], and dislike married women as much as harlots, for the pleasure one takes in such women is vile.

Refrain.

4. I burn with the fires of love for a special maiden, and my love for her increases day by day; the sun is at high noon, and I too am far from cool.

Refrain.

5. Nothing is more pleasing than the playfulness of this girl. Her heart is wholly without bitterness, and the kisses she offers are sweeter than honey.

Refrain.

6. Though I sport with Caecilia, fear not! I am a sort of guardian of her tender youth, lest the lilies of her chastity should be sullied.

Refrain.

7. She is still a budding flower, and it is a risky business to pluck such a blossom. I allow the grape to grow until it is ripe. Hope sustains me, happy at what will one day come to pass.

Refrain.

8. I wish only to play: to behold her, speak with her, touch her, eventually kiss her—but of the fifth stage, the act itself, have no fear!

Refrain.

9. Whatever others may do, maiden, let us behave in such a way that the game we play is a proper one. We are both very young; let us play youth's tender games.

Refrain.

NOTES

I am grateful to my friends Robert Edwards, Andrew Galloway, and Thomas Stillinger for useful comments on an earlier draft of this essay.

1. Peter Dronke, *Medieval Latin and the Rise of European Love-Lyric* (Oxford: Clarendon Press, 1965), 1:285n. For a useful orientation see Gerald A. Bond, "Latin Lyric Poetry," in *Medieval France: An Encyclopedia,* ed. William W. Kibler and Grover A. Zinn (New York: Garland, 1995), 526–28.

2. On this problem and its historical background, see Paul Zumthor, *Langue, texte, énigme* (Paris: Seuil, 1975), 108–14. The Latin *artes poeticae,* too, differ widely in their characterizations of lyric poetry; see Heinz Bergner, ed., *Lyrik des Mittelalters: Probleme und Interpretationen* (Stuttgart: PReclam , 1983), 1:11; and, in the same volume, Paul Klopsch, "Die mittellateinische Lyrik," 28–35.

3. Dronke's writings make almost no reference to the work of critics like Robert Guiette, Roger Dragonetti, Paul Zumthor, or Pierre Bec on the formal and "registral" characteristics of French and to a lesser degree Provençal lyric. His attitude is expressed in *Medieval Latin,* 1:55: "Of course there are epigones, schools of poets, literary fashions. But a poetry that is alive and richly varied cannot be 'explained' deterministically." A critique of the formalist view that complements Dronke's approach, though couched in largely postmodernist terms, is provided by Sarah Kay, *Subjectivity in Troubadour Poetry* (Cambridge: Cambridge University Press, 1990).

4. Dronke, *Medieval Latin,* 1:238.

5. On this last see especially Dronke, *The Medieval Lyric,* 2d ed. (Cambridge: Cambridge University Press, 1977), 142–43.

6. See, for example, the reviews of *Medieval Latin* by P. Boyde, *Medium Aevum* 36 (1967): 171–76, and Tore Janson, *Speculum* 42 (1967): 368.

7. Stephen G. Nichols, Jr., "Rhetorical Metamorphosis in the Troubadour Lyric," in *Mélanges de langue et de littérature médiévales offerts à Pierre le Gentil* (Paris: S.E.D.E.S., 1973), 569–85.

8. Jeffrey Peterson, "Writing Flowers: Figuration and the Feminine in *Carmina Burana* 177," *Exemplaria* 6 (1994): 1–34.

9. Peter Godman, "Literary Classicism and Latin Erotic Poetry of the Twelfth Century and the Renaissance," in *Latin Poetry and the Classical Tradition,* ed. Peter Godman and Oswyn Murray (Oxford: Clarendon Press, 1990), 149–69; Robert R. Edwards, *Ratio and Invention* (Nashville: Vanderbilt University Press, 1989), 59–66.

10. Peter Dronke, ed., *Bernardus Silvestris: Cosmographia,* Textus Minores, vol. 53 (Leiden: Brill, 1978). Winthrop Wetherbee, trans., *The Cosmographia of Bernardus Silvestris* (New York: Columbia University Press, 1973).

11. Bernardus is often credited with a lost treatise on the art of poetry, but Douglas Kelly has argued persuasively that the attribution is based on a misunderstanding of the sources, and that these refer to the *Cosmographia,* considered as a model of the art of composition. See Kelly, *The Arts of Poetry and Prose,* Typologie des Sources du Moyen Age Occidental, vol. 59 (Turnhout: Brepols, 1991), 57–65.

12. See Geoffrey of Vinsauf, *Poetria nova* 44–49, 60–61, 136–41, 214–18; edited by Edmond Faral, *Les arts poétiques du XIIe et du XIIIe siècle,* Bibliothèque des Hautes Etudes, vol. 238 (Paris: Champion, 1924), 200, 201, 203. English translations by

Ernest Gallo, *The Poetria Nova and Its Sources in Early Rhetorical Doctrine* (The Hague: Mouton, 1971), and by Margaret F. Nims, *Poetria Nova* (Toronto: Pontifical Institute of Mediaeval Studies, 1967).

13. Linda Lomperis, "From God's Book to the Play of the Text in the *Cosmographia*," *Medievalia et Humanistica* 16 (1988): 51–71.

14. "Ut mundus pulcrius poliatur." The phrase occurs in the *summa operis* which commonly precedes the *Cosmographia* in the manuscripts; see Dronke's edition (95, 156n). Though the *summa* may not be authorial, the aesthetic emphasis is equally marked in the opening section of the *Cosmographia* proper (Dronke, 97–98), which stresses the need for a cosmic *forma, decus, figura,* and for the unifying power of *artifices numeri.*

15. On the cultural significance of the aesthetic element in the *Cosmographia*, see Alfred Adler, "The *Roman de Thèbes*, a '*Consolatio Philosophiae*,'" *Romanische Forschungen* 72 (1960): 257–76; Gerhard Ladner, "Terms and Ideas of Renewal," in *Renaissance and Renewal in the Twelfth Century*, ed. Robert L. Benson and Giles Constable (Cambridge, Mass.: Harvard University Press, 1982), 1–33.

16. N. M. Häring, ed., "Alan of Lille, *De planctu naturae*," *Studi medievali*, ser. 3, 19 (1978): 797–879; James J. Sheridan, trans., *The Plaint of Nature* (Toronto: Pontifical Institute of Mediaeval Studies, 1980).

17. On the interplay of grammatical and sexual metaphor in the discourse of the twelfth-century schools, see Jan Ziolkowski, *Alan of Lille's Grammar of Sex: The Meaning of Grammar to a Twelfth-Century Intellectual*, Speculum Anniversary Monographs, vol. 10 (Cambridge, Mass.: Medieval Academy, 1985).

18. R. Howard Bloch, *Etymologies and Genealogies: A Literary Anthropology of the French Middle Ages* (Chicago: University of Chicago Press, 1983), 133–36; Alexandre Leupin, *Barbarolexis: Medieval Writing and Sexuality* (Cambridge, Mass.: Harvard University Press, 1989), 59–78.

19. Bloch, *Etymologies and Genealogies*, 136; compare Adler, "*Roman de Thèbes*," 257–58, 274.

20. *De planctu*, 1:47–50, in Häring, "Alan of Lille," 808.

21. Leupin remarks that for Alan true being "can be defined only in terms of an unspeakable virginity, a virginity eternally lost after the Fall" (*Barbarolexis*, 12).

22. The continuity is defined by Zumthor, *Langue, texte énigme*, 48–49; compare Peterson, who sees the *puella* of *CB* 177 as standing "at the intersection between a vernacular space of nature and the cultural space of Learned Latin" ("Writing Flowers," 28).

23. Bernart, "Can par la flors," edited by Moshé Lazar, *Bernard de Ventadour: Chansons d'amour* (Paris: Klincksieck, 1966), no. 24, lines 30–32.

24. Bernart, "Lonc tems a qu'eu no chantei mai," in ibid., no. 19, lines 28–30.

25. This aspect of twelfth-century literary language is well characterized by Peter Haidu, "Repetition: Modern Reflections on Medieval Aesthetics," *MLN* 92 (1977): 875–87; see also Zumthor, *Langue, texte, énigme*, 36–54; Sarah Spence, *Texts and the Self in the Twelfth Century* (Cambridge: Cambridge University Press, 1996), 85–86.

26. *De planctu*, 9, in Häring, "Alan of Lille," 842–44.

27. See esp. ibid., 18, in Häring, "Alan of Lille," 877–78. Alan's affinities with the troubadours may reflect his having taught for some years at or near Montpellier; see Marie-Thérèse d'Alverny, *Alain de Lille: textes inédits* (Paris: Vrin, 1965), 12–17.

On Montpellier in this period see Linda M. Paterson, *The World of the Troubadours* (Cambridge: Cambridge University Press, 1993), 188–95.

28. On the intellectual and religious background common to Latin and vernacular lyric, see Dronke, *Medieval Latin*, vol. 1, chaps. 2–3; and the pioneering study by Dimitri Scheludko, "Über die Theorien der Liebe bei den Trobadors," *Zeitschrift für romanische Philologie* 60 (1940): 191–234.

29. See Paul Zumthor, *Langue et techniques poétiques à l'époque romane (XIe-XIIIe siècles)* (Paris: Klincksieck, 1963), 27–49. As Zumthor remarks, "une poétique tient sa nature de la langue à laquelle elle s'applique, plus que d'une intention spirituelle générale" (47). See also Peterson, "Writing Flowers," 15–16.

30. Leupin, *Barbarolexis*, 22.

31. *De planctu*, 8, in Häring, "Alan of Lille," 837.

32. *Poetria nova*, 538–41, 545–48, 552–53; in Faral, *Arts poétiques*, 213–14.

33. "Troie post excidium" (*Carmina Burana* 98), stanza 9, as emended by Dronke, "Dido's Lament: From Medieval Latin Lyric to Chaucer," in his *Intellectuals and Poets in Medieval Europe* (Rome: Storia e Letteratura, 1992), 440. Compare Alfons Hilka and Otto Schumann, eds., *Carmina Burana*, vol. 1, part 2 (Heidelberg: Winter, 1941), 129.

34. For a very different reading see Dronke, "Dido's Lament," 440.

35. Peter Dronke, "Peter of Blois and Poetry at the Court of Henry II," in Dronke, *The Medieval Poet and His World* (Rome: Storia e Letteratura, 1984), 281–339.

36. See ibid., 283–85; Reto R. Bezzola, *Les origines et la formation de la littérature courtoise en occident*, 3:1 (Paris: Champion, 1963), 257–64.

37. That Peter may have been the pupil of Bernardus Silvestris during the early stages of his poetic career is suggested by Dronke, *Cosmographia*, 9.

38. On these aspects of vernacular lyric, see Pierre Bec, "Quelques réflexions sur la poésie lyrique médiévale: problèmes et essai de caractérisation," in *Mélanges offerts à Rita Lejeune* (Gembloux: Duculot, 1969), 2:1309–29; Bec, "La douleur et son univers poétique chez Bernard de Ventadour," *Cahiers de civilisation médiévale* 11 (1968): 545–71 and 12 (1969): 25–33; Paul Zumthor, *Essai de poétique médiévale* (Paris: Seuil, 1972), 189–285.

39. See Dronke, *Medieval Latin*, 1:163–263; Gerald A. Bond, "'Iocus Amoris': The Poetry of Baudri of Bourgueil and the Formation of the Ovidian Subculture," *Traditio* 42 (1986): 143–93.

40. *Carmina Burana* 67, stanza 1a, in Hilka and Schumann, *Carmina Burana*, 1: 2: 31; also Wilhelm Meyer, ed., *Die Arundel Sammlung mittellateinischer Lieder*, Abhandlungen der königlichen Gesellschaft der Wissenschaften zu Göttingen, Philosophische-Historische Klasse, N.F. vol. 11, part 2 (1908), 13; C. J. McDonough, *The Oxford Poems of Hugh Primas and the Arundel Lyrics* (Toronto: Pontifical Institute of Mediaeval Studies, 1984), 80. In translating I take "Natura," rather than an understood *rerum facies*, as the subject of "preconceperat." David A. Traill argues for the other reading on grammatical grounds ("Notes on '*Dum Diane vitrea*' (CB 62) and '*A globo veteri*' (CB 67)," *Mittellateinische Jahrbuch* 23 (1988): 149–50), but his alternative presents syntactic problems of its own, and so far as I can see this is true of any reading of the passage as it stands. On the topos of "Nature as the maker of beautiful human beings," see Ernst Robert Curtius, *European Literature and the Latin Middle Ages* (New York: Pantheon, 1953), 180–82. With the opening of *CB* 67

compare Bernard de Ventadour, "Lo tems vai e ven e vire," in Lazar, *Bernard de Ventadour,* no. 44, lines 50–59; "Be m'an perdut lai enves Ventadorn," ibid., no. 9, lines 43–45.

41. Raimbaut d'Orange, no. 30, lines 53–56, in Walter T. Pattison, ed., *The Life and Works of the Troubadour Raimbaut d'Orange* (Minneapolis: University of Minnesota Press, 1952), 172. See also the discussion of Raimbaut in Dronke, *Medieval Latin,* 1:98–112.

42. "Per vos am, dompn'ab cor vaire / Las autras tant co·l mons dura, / Car son en vostra figura" (It is through you, lady of the changing heart, that I love the others, while worldly existence lasts. For they are but *figurae* of you); no. 11, lines 64–66, in Pattison, *Life and Works of Raimbaut d'Orange,* 105.

43. Conversely a lyric relatively free of learned reference such as Peter's "Vacillantis trutine" (appendix 2) will show how much he can sound like Bernard de Ventadour when he is writing less pedantically.

44. This Acteon-like victimization by the consequences of gazing is, so to speak, the complement to the *effictio* Peter practices in this lyric, the detailed description of a beautiful woman prescribed by the *artes poeticae.* See A. C. Spearing, *The Medieval Poet as Voyeur* (Cambridge: Cambridge University Press, 1993), 35–48.

45. For a less precious variation, apparently by Peter of Blois, on the theme of virginity deliberately unravished, see "Ex ungue primo teneram," in Dronke, *Medieval Latin,* 2:378–80; for the attribution, Dronke, "Peter of Blois," 322. Godman suggests that this more obviously ironic poem may have been an answer to "Amor habet superos," which he regards as a straightforward celebration of continence ("Literary Classicism," 166).

46. *Carmina Burana* 58, stanzas 1–2, in Hilka and Schumann, *Carmina Burana,* 1: 2: 4.

47. On such thematic uses of the idea of aesthetic coherence, see Leupin, *Barbarolexis,* 66–67.

48. There are striking correspondences between "Si linguis" and Guillaume's poem. Dronke, noting that "Si linguis" shows signs of having been copied at least twice before the *Codex Buranus* appeared in the 1220s, suggests that the Latin poem is a generation earlier than Guillaume's, commonly dated 1225–30 (*Medieval Latin,* 1:323n).

49. On this affinity see Edwards, *Ratio and Invention,* 52–74.

50. Dronke sees the lover's wish as literally granted, and emends the final words of stanza 5, line 4, to "dum moraret icta" (*Medieval Latin,* 1:323).

51. The religious references are noted by Dronke (ibid., 1:318–31).

52. For Dronke the poem is a *summa* of courtly idealism, remarkable for "its high cult of the beloved, its awe before the mystery of love, . . . its faith in the sublimity of the courtly ideal" (ibid., 1:330). D. W. Robertson, Jr., views "Si linguis" as a parody of courtly love ("Two Poems from the *Carmina Burana,*" in his *Essays in Medieval Culture* [Princeton: Princeton University Press, 1980], 138–50). Divergent interpretations are discussed by P. G. Walsh, ed. and trans., *Love Lyrics from the Carmina Burana* (Chapel Hill: University of North Carolina Press, 1993), 68–69.

53. Toril Moi, "Desire in Language: Andreas Capellanus and the Controversy of Courtly Love," in *Medieval Literature: Criticism, Ideology and History,* ed. David Aers (London: St. Martin's Press, 1986), 24.

54. See Wetherbee, "Latin Structure and Vernacular Space: Gower, Chaucer and the Boethian Tradition," in *Chaucer and Gower: Difference, Mutuality, Exchange*, ed. R. F. Yeager (Victoria, B.C.: English Literary Studies, University of Victoria, 1991), 7–35.

55. *De vulgari eloquentia* 1.1.4; 1.5.1; 1.16.5–6; see also Roger Dragonetti, "La conception du langage poétique dans le 'De vulgari eloquentia' de Dante," in *Aux frontières du langage poétique* (Ghent: Romanica Gandensia, 1961), 29–35.

CHAPTER 4

On the Conventionality
of the Cantigas d'amor

JULIAN WEISS

Writing in 1959 about the apparent stylistic uniformity of the Provençal love lyric, S. C. Aston remarked that the prevailing view amongst recent scholars seemed to be that "all the troubadours are cast in the same mould but that some are mouldier than others."[1] He did not share this view, and argued that critics should look afresh at the ways medieval poets conformed to or broke free from their inherited poetic conventions. In doing so, Aston was participating in a larger trend of stylistic analysis, *Stilforschung,* which attempted to interpret European love lyrics as a far more dynamic interplay between the forces of originality and convention. One of the goals of this approach was to identify and rescue individual poetic talent, apparently rendered invisible by the methods of Ernst Robert Curtius, whose main interest was to study a culturally homogenous and essentially anonymous collection of topoi.[2] Although it is beyond the scope of this essay to summarize critically the various paths taken by scholars of the European love lyric during the past thirty or so years, in general they have led in two directions: some, like Paul Zumthor and Roger Dragonetti, have attempted to abstract paradigms for the whole corpus of a particular school, to lay bare the "deep structures" of its formal and thematic conventions.[3] Others, such as Peter Dronke, have been more interested in the elements that confer a sense of individuality, of difference within convention, upon the work of specific poets.[4]

But whatever the precise contours of these critical paths, they have led, almost inevitably, to a reexamination of the nature of the lyric "I," the subject of the poem, and a reassessment of its "sincerity" (to use a deeply problematic but readily understood term). I say "almost inevitably" because in humanist thought, the concepts of "originality" and "convention" on the one hand and the lyric subject, "sincere" (or not) on the other, are often linked in fundamental ways. What is held to be "conventional" is often thought of as "inauthentic," the product of artifice and learned rules (usually old ones); what is held to be "individual" or "original" is often implicitly thought of as the product of a "creative mind" working to throw off the "dead husk" of inert convention.[5] It is no coincidence that for Zumthor, for whom conventionality is the controlling principle of the *grand chant courtois*, the lyric subject of the Old French love song "n'a pour nous d'existence que grammaticale."[6] As a consequence, the love lyric is essentially self-referential, circular. More recently, there have been various attempts to move outside the circularity of the song by, amongst many others, Sarah Kay, Don Monson, and James Wilhelm, whose studies have in one way or another been concerned with the specific subjectivity of the Provençal and Old French love lyric, its various representations of an individual poetic self, and the nature of its social and historical referentiality.[7]

These issues are of obvious relevance to the Galician-Portuguese lyric tradition: a tradition which emerged in the Iberian peninsula in the very late twelfth century, flourished in the thirteenth, and gradually died out during the fourteenth, to become a self-consciously archaic lyric language in the early fifteenth century, having been supplanted by the cultural hegemony of Castilian. The recent scholarship in this field has attempted both to classify poetic conventions and to examine how they are manipulated by particular poets, within the three main genres of *cantigas d'amor* (male-voiced love song), *cantigas d'amigo* (female-voiced love song), and *cantigas d'escarnho e de maldizer* (satire and personal invective). Giuseppe Tavani's metrical inventory and Jean-Marie d'Heur's structural analyses have been complemented by a continuing flow of editorial work, done mainly by Italians, which has helped us to acquire a clearer picture of the conventions and different poetic personalities of this school.[8] Nonetheless, the related issues of originality within tradition, "sincerity," and the nature of the lyric subject need review, particularly with regard to the *cantigas d'amor*. This genre offers a perfect illustration of the increased homogeneity of the troubadour lyric as it developed from twelfth-century Provence, and it has received much less critical attention than its female-voiced counterpart, the *cantigas d'amigo*, precisely because of its perceived "conventionality," a code word for abstract artificiality or presumed lack of grounding in experiential reality. The received wisdom concerning the *cantigas d'amor* seems to be that their male composers all chorus their love in a conventional and utterly monotonous drone.

The critical consensus is voiced most clearly by Giuseppe Tavani, who considers the *cantigas d'amor* to be a pale imitation of a Provençal model: poetry which, because it has been uprooted from its native social context, is no longer dedicated to "una donna reale per esprimere sentimenti reali" (a real woman to express real emotions) but to a stylized abstraction; and which, in the process of "[l]a diluizione concettuale e l'affievolimento stilistico" (conceptual and stylistic enervation), has been rendered impersonal, stereotypical, and, finally, reduced to "puro gioco stilistico e ad esercitazione retorica" (pure stylistic play and rhetorical exercise).[9] Tavani's negative response is not wholly representative of *cantiga* criticism, but it is endemic; and the extent to which it has become so ingrained as to represent the "commonsense" view may be seen by a glance at many a literary manual.[10] Though they are more subtle and far more knowledgeable than most, the responses of Carlos Alvar and Vicente Beltrán in their popular 1985 anthology are typical. They recognize the need to approach the *cantigas d'amor* on their own esthetic terms, and make the fruitful observation that these poets dedicated themselves "al cultivo del matiz, del detalle, logrando un dominio preciosista de la lengua poética y del arte de escribir versos" (to the cultivation of nuance and detail, achieving a precious mastery of poetic language and the art of writing verses).[11] They also maintain that this genre "renovó considerablemente las pautas recibidas, tanto en la forma como en los contenidos" (substantially renovated their inherited models, both in form and content) (29). But these insights apart, they do not get beyond emphasizing the "empobrecimiento" and "monotonía" of this lyric mode, and confess, in a phrase of honest perplexity, that whatever formal and thematic renovation took place, it occurred "hasta el punto de dificultar la comprensión de su valor histórico y estético" (to the extent of obscuring its historical and esthetic value) (29).[12] It is significant too— for reasons I shall later explain—that they also hand down the other critical topos that some poets of this school invested their sense of identity in the concept of poetic sincerity (30).

More recently, however, a way out of this critical dead end has been opened up by Beltran himself and, from a different perspective, by Thomas Hart.[13] Beltran's thorough reevaluation of the *cantiga de amor* allows us to appreciate more clearly the esthetic basis of the form, especially its conceptual structure, which he maintains is unique within the corpus of the medieval Romance lyric. Whether or not Beltran's descriptive and largely formalist account has any impact upon the ingrained attitudes described above will depend in large measure upon the way we conceptualize conventionality. And this is the problem broached by Hart.[14] Drawing on the work of Paul Zumthor, Peter Haidu, and Giuseppe Tavani, Hart raises a number of esthetic and social issues concerning the Galician-Portuguese lyric as a whole, which deserve to be more fully explored. I therefore propose to reopen discussion of this genre's perceived conventionality, what Tavani called its "isomorfismo," both by looking at the ways in which homogeneity is established and put under pressure, and—more importantly perhaps—by reconsidering the way we conceptualize this literary fact. For what interests me most about conventionality is not so much a textual relationship—a matter of stylistic range—as a social one; not an idealist but a materialist problem. How does this highly repetitive, seemingly abstract, and nonreferential mode relate to a specific historical moment and to specific social formations? Before I elaborate on what I mean by a materialist reading of conventions, it is necessary to clarify the kind of reading I am arguing against, and this entails returning to Tavani's discussion of the esthetics of the *cantigas d'amor* published in the *Grundriss der romanische Literaturen des Mittelalters* in 1980.

Tavani structures his analysis around an account of four "campi semici" (semantic fields), which he believes mark out the boundaries of the genre: praise of the lady, the poet's love, the lady's reserve, the pain of love. As a general guide to the semantic field of the *cantigas d'amor*, this classification is stultifyingly narrow. Quite apart from the way Tavani seems to equate the semantics of a poem with its theme, Rip Cohen has convincingly argued that the scope of this fourfold division could be enlarged by reference to other thematic constants.[15] But although I think the semantic range of the *cantigas d'amor* is richer and more flexible than Tavani supposes, I am more interested at this stage in the way he deals with poems that seem to be variants on his semantic norms. Throughout his exposition, he lists examples of such variants (and a significant number it seems to me), from a wide range of poets and periods, which give rise to "testi anomali" (anomalous texts) that he finds hard to classify.

Tavani has a problem with variants: he calls them "deviazioni," "testi devianti," or "episodiche evasioni," referring on one occasion to a poet's "gioconda indisciplina per la tradizione" (playful irreverence toward tradition).[16] But lest we panic in the face of this indiscipline and textual deviance, he reassures us that this "tendenza deviante" does not disrupt the inner, or deep, structure of the genre as a whole. Variation in one area is always counterbalanced by a strict adherence to other stylistic and thematic norms in another. And he concludes on the calming note that in any case the medieval public "probabilmente" favored poems that most closely conformed to the traditional paradigm. From the point of view of medieval esthetics, Tavani argues, variants are of little overall significance: the examples he cites are "di minor conto" (of minor importance). In short, variants are not the mark of originality and modernity (that spurious pair), but merely the application of one of the rhetorical concepts of irony, "permutatio ex contrario ducta" (83).

Tavani's treatment of the conventionality of the *cantigas* is not so much a theory of medieval esthetics as a rationalization of his esthetic distaste, which is deeply rooted in the post-Romantic premise that a convention is a constraint, an obstacle to the expression of a unique, and hence authentic, experience. His is a form of idealist individualism, supported by an expressivist theory of language: this is to say that rather than considering language as a constitutive *activity,* indissoluble from the creation of human consciousness, he reduces it to being a transparent medium which expresses some previously experienced reality or emotion. And since these poems are not written to "una donna reale per esprimere sentimenti reali" (a real woman to express real emotions), their linguistic conventions must inevitably be discarded as "pure" rhetoric.

Idealism of a different kind is illustrated by the theorizing of medieval lyric conventions developed by Peter Haidu.[17] For him, the relationship between a concrete poem and its generic model is the same as exists between the Platonic worlds of Matter and Form: "Within the Neoplatonic view... each particular reincarnation of the abstract, of the ideal, serves merely to restate that abstract form. The content of each restatement will remain the same even though the particular concretizations may vary in detail from each other. Such variation from the norm represented by the predetermined content is discarded as non-meaningful variance" (883). The concept of nonmeaningful variance is one I find hard to accept; does Haidu really want us to believe that all verbal, thematic, and metrical variation should be ignored in order to produce a neat generic package, cleansed of inner contradictions, inconsistencies, and differences? Apparently he does, at least if we want to recapture medieval esthetic conventions which, he believes, were based on repetition "without the presence and presupposition of any consciousness" (876).[18] Haidu adopts a peculiarly narrow definition of consciousness, by which he means intentionality. We cannot establish with certainty the intentions of medieval authors and readers, he claims, because such explicit statements of purpose as exist "are almost invariably identifiable as part of a medieval convention, and hence represent a typical repetition rather than an authentic indication of authorial or even textual intentionality" (876). Leaving aside the old chestnut of whether "authentic" evidence for intentions can be recovered from any period, including the present, Haidu's reduction of medieval convention to unconscious repetition has several consequences. For what it produces is a kind of a formalist idealism, whereby fictional texts are trapped within a closed linguistic system from which all meaning emanates via an "unconscious" speaking subject. Moreover, because he claims that medieval fiction lacks divine purpose, its language becomes self-referential, falling "into a disconnected mode of autotelic existence" (885). Thus, he concludes, even exemplary fiction "is inherently subversive" of its own didactic intent (886).

The idealist approaches of Tavani and Haidu diminish the rich and often contradictory range of positions possible within conventions, ignore the different forms of consciousness to be found in writing, and effectively gut the ideological force that fiction exerts, in many complex ways, in shaping the social world. These shortcomings would be avoided by a materialist approach, one that explores the full consequences of the belief that "[a] definition of language is always, implicitly or explicitly, a definition of human beings in the world."[19] Such an approach would enable us to examine medieval lyric poetry not as a closed linguistic system or a pure medium for autonomous experience but as a specific shared social practice, encoding and contesting actual living relationships. To be shared this practice needed to be based on certain common agreements (which was, after all, one of the etymological meanings of "convention"). To quote Raymond Williams again: "it is of the essence of a convention that it ratifies an assumption or a point of view, so that the work can be made or received."[20] Given that the conventionality of the *cantigas d'amor* has itself become such a critical convention, it is about time that we began to confront the various assumptions and social contracts, or relationships, embodied in this highly ritualized use of language. And with an emphasis primarily on the social construction of class and gender, what follows are simply the first steps in that direction, an attempt to explore the ways in which generic conventions are, in the words of Laurie Finke, "producers as well as products of social meanings."[21]

Although during the past thirty years or so, there has been a considerable rise in interest in the complex nature of the medieval lyric persona, it is only in the past ten years or so that consistent attempts have been made to consider the speaking subject from the dual viewpoint of class and gender. Howard Bloch, Laura Kendrick, Sarah Kay, Laurie Finke, and Simon Gaunt, to cite just a few representative instances, have all explored the ways in which the love lyrics composed by the troubadours, *trobairitz*, and *trouvères* participated in the social construction of gender, both masculine and feminine, within concrete historical conditions.[22] These scholars have worked within the sociocultural confines of Provençal and Old French, but they raise questions of a general validity about the European love lyric as a specific, and historically variable, discourse of masculinity.

Just how that discourse functioned, and the problems involved in studying it, can be illustrated in particularly interesting ways by reference to Galician-Portuguese lyrics, because one of the most striking features of this branch of the troubadour tradition is its generic classification. Fully two-thirds of the corpus is divided into two roughly equal groups: the *cantigas d'amor* and the *cantigas d'amigo*, which though female-voiced were also composed by men (there are no surviving examples of female troubadours in the Galician-Portuguese tradition). Although there are of course male- and female-voiced love songs throughout the medieval European lyric tradition, the Galician-Portuguese school stands out precisely because a relationship between gender and genre is so deeply embedded within it. Although from a formal and thematic viewpoint, the *cantigas d'amor* and *cantigas d'amigo* overlap, enshrined in poetic convention is one simple premise: that the male poet could choose, with equal legitimacy, between a mode that allowed him to speak as a man and a mode that enabled him to appropriate the imaginary feminine, to speak as a woman (usually about himself, like Dustin Hoffman's Tootsie).[23]

Although this essay focuses on the ways that male poets constructed the masculine in the *cantigas d'amor*, a fuller understanding of the subject would require a detailed comparison with the male construction of the feminine in the *cantigas d'amigo:* in the words of Thelma Fenster, it would require us to ask "how the categories of man and woman in the Middle Ages determined each other as exclusionary, and how fixed or fluid the categories were."[24] The interplay of masculine and feminine in the Galician-Portuguese lyric as a whole can only be adumbrated here. Moreover, my reconstruction of the gender roles inscribed within these lyric poems should not be taken as an inflexible or unique paradigm. As some of the studies in *Medieval Masculinities* demonstrate, there were many models of masculinity available to men of varying rank and status within medieval court society, and lyric conventions encode just one of them. As such, the models sketched out below are not a monolithic and unchanging patriarchal structure, but part of a contested and dynamic cultural process. The hegemony of patriarchy lies in its ability constantly to renegotiate itself.[25]

In comparison with the *cantigas d'amor,* the *cantigas d'amigo* display a wider range of emotions, their vocabulary seems more concrete, and consequently (at least according to the received wisdom of modern criticism), the woman's lyric seems more firmly grounded in experiential reality than the male-voiced love song. For one thing, the feminine voice of the *cantiga d'amigo* is frequently localized: this is to say that the girl often speaks within the bounds of a specific place (in or by a church, by the sea, in a pine forest); or within the bounds of a specific time (at dawn); or in the company of other women (her mother, sisters, friends). And yet for all its relative concreteness and apparent specificity, feminine desire is still essentialized. As in other European lyric schools, the Galician-Portuguese women's love song is deeply imbued with the themes, settings, and voices of the "traditional" lyric. The feminine voice is the voice of nature.[26] So when male troubadours adopt the feminine voice to represent men (occasionally themselves, explicitly) as the objects of desire, that desire is imagined as a natural longing: it is amorous "speculation," both in the sense of a speculative longing and a narcissistic mirroring of male desire. On the other hand, when they are speaking subjects of the *cantigas d'amor,* men do not represent themselves as the object of women's desire (unlike the women of the *cantigas d'amigo,* who frequently boast of being the object of male passion). Thus, whereas for the feminine it is possible to present oneself as both speaking subject and the object of another's desire, for the masculine it is not. When they choose to speak in a masculine voice, the male troubadours cannot say "She loves me."

This inability to embrace both positions and to relinquish hold on the integrity of the subject is related to the fact that unlike the *cantigas d'amigo,* which are songs about a beloved, the *cantigas d'amor* are songs about love. The shift in emphasis in the generic labels is significant, and reveals a basic assumption about gender. Women sing about men, and though their song derives its essence and force from the ample powers of nature, it is ultimately channeled so that the feminine is both directed to, and circumscribed by, the male addressee. Men, on the other hand, sing about their own love, which is implicitly considered to be coterminous with the concept *amor* itself: masculine *coitas,* it is assumed, occupy the conceptual realm of the universal human emotion. As anyone who is familiar with this kind of courtly lyric will know, this "human emotion" is communicated in terms that are highly abstract and rational. The *cantigas d'amor* appropriate the center ground of love as a concept, and in the process they reproduce the Aristotelian division between the genders: feminine is nature, masculine is thought.[27]

This desire to participate in the sublime is also produced by the convention that the woman's beauty is unique and divinely ordained. Through a certain banal logic this obsession with the Unique reinforces unequal relationships between and within the genders. The woman's uniqueness is asserted, yet denied in poetic representation: save for the odd mention of her eyes, the woman is without body or face. The refusal to endow the lady with any individualizing features reduces her to a cipher of the man's own unique status.[28] And the denial of representation also means that this unique status cannot be demonstrably contested, only contradicted by similar assertions. As Jean-Marie d'Heur has remarked, the esthetic of the *cantigas d'amor* "aime l'universel et fuit le détail" (loves the universal and avoids detail) (*Recherches internes*, 469). And this refusal of detail in jostling pursuit of the universal accounts for both the stylistic conformity and the competitive edge of this lyric mode.

The relationship between conformity and competition may be traced through other forms of stylistic analysis. A preliminary survey of the *cantigas d'amor* shows that the repetition of certain syntactic and lexical formulas is exploited by a number of troubadours to impart an internal cohesion to their work. Indeed, this phenomenon parallels the way *cantigas d'amigo* are often grouped around an individual "signature"—an image, motif, situation—or arranged into a more or less coherent narrative sequence.[29] Some modern editors of the Galician-Portuguese school have recognized this stylistic cohesion in the *cantigas d'amor* they themselves edit, but the point has not been raised on the level of a general poetic practice, as it has been by Zumthor for the Old French *chansons*, or by Vickie Ziegler in her study of the German Minnesingers.[30] There is no space to document this point in any detail, but I can give one instance of what I mean, selected from the twenty-five extant *cantigas d'amor* composed by one of the earliest troubadours, Vaasco Praga de Sandin (active 1200–1225, hence at the very start of the Galician-Portuguese tradition). An upwardly mobile Galician, he married into the Portuguese landed aristocracy and, in the words of Carolina Michaëlis, wrote verse "d'um convencionalismo absolutamente incolor" (of an absolutely colorless conventionality).[31]

The appendix lists in decreasing order of frequency the most common formulaic phrases, syntactic constructions, and verbs of this man's work. None of these formulas, it should be emphasized, is exclusive to Vaasco Praga; they occur regularly throughout the corpus as a whole. The point, however, is that they occur in his work with a density that is specific to him. On a formal level, the first three formulas, "per bõa fé" (in good faith), "enquanto' eu vivo for'" (so long as I live), "dezir [etc.] ũa ren/cousa" (to say one thing), function as style markers, distinguishing this amorous discourse from that of his peers. But from a social viewpoint, they also signal his entry into the pacts and tensions of feudal relationships. The appropriation of a topos, in rhetorical terms a place from which to speak, marks out a personal space within the boundaries of accepted aristocratic discourse. The most frequent motif, "per bõa fé," acquires the status of a personal motto, similar in function to a heraldic device (it is perhaps no coincidence that the name Bonafé was used by one of the collateral branches of Vaasco Praga's family).[32] Like a heraldic device, the motif signifies membership of, and difference within, the social group. And here it is relevant to recall that for all their homogeneity, there are surprisingly few anonymous poems: it was obviously deemed important to assert paternity of the *cantigas* and preserve it in transmission.[33] In future research, the use of specific style markers, the internal cohesion, and the assertion of literary ownership will need to be set within the context of the important developments in aristocratic social formations during the late twelfth and thirteenth centuries. For it was at this time, according to the most recent research into Iberian patronymics, heraldry, and patterns of inheritance, that the basis was laid for the triumph of agnatic lines of descent in the later Middle Ages.[34] Howard Bloch has studied aspects of this in his book *Etymologies and Genealogies,* but his conclusions concerning the Provençal lyric and its relationship to changing aristocratic consciousness of lineage and kinship could not be transferred *tout court* to the specific conditions of Castilian and Portuguese feudal society.

What kinds of social relationships and situations are constituted in Vaasco's conventional love lyrics? Giuseppe Tavani describes the poems as purely platonic protestations of love, praise of an inaccessible and harsh lady, requests and pleas uttered in a tone of respect, humility, and discretion: "interminables litanies... d'une simplicité élégante mais monotone" (interminable litanies... of an elegant but monotonous simplicity).[35] As presented here, Vaasco Praga's verse does not disrupt the normative model Tavani had previously established for the genre as a whole, and this explains his choice of adjectives: "interminables litanies," "simplicité... monotone." This is the right choice, but for the wrong reasons.

The poems are consciously "interminable" because the poet's song ends only with his death (witness the common syntactic structure "enquanto' eu vivo for'" etc.). But that death is indefinitely postponed. Though he projects his song into the future, these lyrics occupy a continuous present, generated by the repetition of the temporal adverbs "today" (oje) and "now" (ora). This location in an eternal present is of course one of the most noted conventions of the masculine love lyric, and has been discussed for example by Howard Bloch in relation to the "easy style" (*trobar leu*) of the Provençal *canso*. What he calls a heightened awareness of the present is the result, in large measure, of the "overconventionalization" of an abstract poetic language: there is not just an "extreme stillness," a "fixity," in which no action takes place or is suggested but also a general passivity and linguistic self-referentiality.[36] But in spite of many close parallels, I would not say the same for the *cantigas d'amor*. Rather this insistence on the present denotes a process, rather than a fixed state: it is a process of constant self-renewal, whereby the poet constructs a masculine identity and forever projects it into the future. This process of self-reenactment is certainly carried out within a narrow set of linguistic registers and thematic situations, but it is not for that reason static: this would be to overlook Vaasco Praga's varied and original versification, which sets these restatements in motion from poem to poem.

Nor is Vaasco Praga's "overconventionalization" (to borrow Bloch's term) merely passive and self-referential, for conventions have an ideological function in establishing and mystifying a social relationship. One example of this is the repetition of groups of phrases built around the verbs *dezir* or *querer dezir* which communicate the truth, the unique sincerity of his love. When viewed as a whole, the insistent repetition of these entirely conventional phrases throughout about 80 percent of the poems undercuts the humility and respect which is their ostensible theme and sets up a conflict between submission and aggression. The assertiveness of his claims to be a vassal, the insistence on his desire to speak, to say "one thing" (ũa ren), endows his discourse with the qualities of a harangue (it reminds me of Toril Moi's brilliant reading of masculine discourse in Andreas Capellanus's *De amore*).[37] In this way, the courtier is able to act out a relationship which is cast in the passive terms of self-containment, but which is ultimately based on force (his words are a material "thing," "ũa ren").

The following poem offers a concrete example of the way a coercive relationship with the lady can be established from a position of alleged subservience:

> Como vos sodes, mia senhor,
> mui quite de me ben fazer,
> assi m'ar quit' eu de querer
> al ben, enquant' eu vivo for',
> se non vos. E sei ũa ren:

    se me vos non fazedes ben,
nen eu non vus faço prazer.
    E per bõa fé, mia senhor,
por quite me tenh' eu d'aver
vosso ben, enquant' eu viver',
nen al en que aja sabor.
Mais vos en preito sodes én,
ca me vus non quit' eu por én
de vosso vassalo seer;
    E quant' eu prendo, mia senhor,
de vos, quero vo-lo dizer:
ei mui gran cuita de soffrer
ca non prendo de vos melhor.
E pois mi-assi de vos aven,
ome seria eu de mal-sen,
se non punhass' en vus veer.[38]

    Just as you are, my lady,
quite free [from the obligation] of doing me good,
so I now free myself from desiring
any other good, as long as I live,
except for you. And I know one thing:
if you do not do me any good
nor do I cause you any pleasure.
    In good faith, my lady,
I consider myself free from having
your good, as long as I live,
nor anything in which there is pleasure.
But you are under obligation as a result,
because I do not therefore free myself
from being your vassal;
    And I wish to tell you
what I take from you, my lady:
I have to suffer much pain
because I take nothing better from you.
And since this happens to me because of you,
I would be a man devoid of sense
if I did not struggle to see you.

There is no space here to comment in detail on this tortuously paradoxical poem, so I shall simply emphasize the lack of symmetry in the respective freedoms and obligations on which this feudal love relationship is based; and how, in the last stanza, the poet conjures up the "rationality" of manhood out of a "right" to keep the woman within view, a "natural" right whose basis in force is revealed in the verb *punhar* (to struggle). And far from dismissing the abstract vocabulary (*fazer ben*) as an example of colorless conventionality, I would argue that this very abstraction is determined by the concrete need to sustain a gender relationship of dominance and subordination, and the identities and roles that rise from it, rather than find closure in specific demands.

This poem establishes a coercive relationship with the lady, but also through her with other men: for this and other poems like it are grounded in the self-assertive competitiveness of feudal courts. Male competition sheds light on the concept of sincerity, the prevalence of which as a conventional poetic theme is well known to scholars of the *cantigas d'amor*, and which is illustrated in Vaasco Praga's work by his continued emphasis on the truth and consistency of his verse (his ability to "say one thing"). It would be a simple matter to incorporate "sincerity" as another convention that goes into the construction of masculine identity, an identity that is "rational," self-renewing and self-coherent, but above all in control. But matters are not as simple as that. So by way of conclusion, I should like to look deeper into the ideological reasons why the theme of sincerity is so pervasive in this particular form of writing.

Poetic sincerity was the subject of a famous *cantiga d'amor* by the Portuguese king Dom Dinis, who at the end of the thirteenth century contrasted the unending authenticity of his love lyric with the shallow inspiration of the Provençal troubadours, who compose only in spring:

> Proençaes soen mui bem trobar
> e dizem eles que é con amor;
> mais os que trobam no tempo da frol
> e nom em outro, sei eu bem que nom
> am tam gran coita no seu coraçom
> qual m'eu por mha senhor vejo levar.[39]

> Provençal poets write fine verses
> which they say are inspired by love;
> but those who write verse only in spring
> and at no other time, I know full well
> that they do not experience the pain
> that I carry in my heart for my lady.

Clearly he is aware of belonging to an authoritative yet conventionalized tradition, one that contained some dead metaphors (love and poetic inspiration flower like the spring). He wants to inscribe himself within that tradition, yet not submerge himself in its potential anonymity. Several scholars have tried to explain on the basis of his actual poetic practice just how Dinis positions himself in relation to his Provençal models.[40] But whatever formal and thematic differences there may be, I do not think that enough has been made of the fact that the king distances himself from the tradition principally on the grounds of his own inner truth. The corollary of the view that the quality of writing (the Provençal's "bem trobar") does not guarantee the quality of experience is that experience cannot be proven in writing. Just as countless poets (Dinis included) claimed uniqueness simply by asserting the superiority of their beloved, so Dinis finds his own space by contrasting what others say ("dizem eles") with his own uncontestable experience ("sei eu bem" [I know well]).

The problems that could arise as a consequence of this recourse to the self are well illustrated by the literary satires directed against Roy Queimado, who was lampooned by his fellow troubadours because of his apparently insincere use of the convention "morrer d'amor."[41] This convention is one of the most basic in the corpus as a whole, and Queimado drew on it with an intensity that surpassed his peers, by constructing his *cantigas* around the constant repetition of the words "morrer" and "morte." This personal appropriation of what should have been a commonplace may on its own have been enough to unsettle his contemporaries; but there is more to it than that. As Manero Sorolla has remarked, he was "uno de los mayores genios satíricos de la lírica gallega, creador, al fin, de su propia parodia" (one of the greatest satiric geniuses of the Galician lyric, the creator of his own self-parody).[42] This *segrel*, perched on the social borders separating *juglar* from *trobador*, was also a writer of liminal verse. Forever on the verge of death, he draws attention to the boundaries between poetic fiction and authentic experience, and in doing so he destabilizes the association between gender and genre. His love lyrics challenge the agreement whereby the *cantigas d'amor* were a vehicle to convey the truth and consistency at the heart of masculine identity.[43]

The verses of Dom Dinis and Roy Queimado reveal a tension common in the Galician-Portuguese school. On the one hand, there is an awareness of the status that can be derived from subscribing to received poetic conventions; as Luciana Stegagno Picchio has observed, as a lyric language Galician-Portuguese seems "come blocco unitario, esente da particolarità regionali e personali, come se nella pratica di una koiné linguistica convenzionale un'élite letteraria volesse suggellare la propria appartenenza ad una comunità d'elezione" (like a homogenous block, lacking in regional or personal individuality, as if in the practice of a conventional linguistic koine a literary elite wanted to ratify its own membership in an elect community).[44] But the status achieved through conformity is counterbalanced by an awareness that by their very nature poetic conventions, through overuse and through dissemination amongst the various ranks of court society, could lose their power as markers of social privilege. A convention binds a group, but it also offers a point of entry; and the problem is how to police it. The most famous example of this anxiety over boundaries between men is the *Supplicatio* written by Guiraut Riquier around 1270 for King Alfonso X of Castile, in which the Provençal troubadour ranked into strict hierarchical order the possible range of lyric composers and performers.[45] He did this in response to the perception that Castilian court life had become chaotic, that there were blurred social distinctions between the troubadours, minstrels, jugglers, and the like, because everyone was writing in the same way. Guiraut's ranking was carried out using a number of criteria, located both outside and within writing: social status and function, versificatory skills, wisdom, and musicianship. And in this regard, his intervention echoes a number of contemporary satires (the *cantigas d'escarnho e de maldizer*) which also attempt to restore stability to the correlation between textual and social authority.[46] But Guiraut reveals his unease over whether such stability is in fact possible by declaring that ultimately his own authority rests firmly outside of writing, in his own divine status.

Guiraut's attempt to impose ordered conventionality upon Castilian chaos is a perfect example of the binding force as well as the social vulnerability of poetic conventions. Men of different ranks could participate in the conventions, and conformity of style could reproduce an unacceptable conformity in status. The need to belong produced, dialectically, the need to differentiate; but the most solid grounds for exclusion and ranking were found outside writing, in such metaphysical concepts as "sincerity," or in an ideal lady whose uniqueness is never represented, simply claimed. The assertion that their masculinity, rank, and status rest upon the absolute of an essence is related to the ideological strategy of universalization, which dehistoricizes the specific interests of class and gender. Future research must clarify how the *cantigas* promoted these interests within the specific social determinants of thirteenth-century Iberia, in ways that I have been unable to do here. But whatever the findings turn out to be, it should now be clear that though the troubadours may tacitly deny that they could be socially constructed, and hence subject to change, their actual practice indicates that they were not wholly unconscious of the strengths and limitations of writing within the circumscribed boundaries of the *cantigas d'amor.* And far from blandly assuming that they were constrained by the molds in which they cast themselves—what Dronke calls their "formidable fetters"— we should in fact regard their conventionality as a very creative practice.

APPENDIX
Formulaic Language in Vaasco Praga de Sandin, fl. *1200–1225 (Twenty-five* cantigas d'amor*)*

per bõa fé (14/25):
    (**2**,11,17; **4**,11; **6**,8; **7**,16; **10**,23; **11**,25; **12**,10; **363**,25; **364**,1, 22; **365**,5; **368**,16; **370**,1; **372**,6; **374**,18)

enquanto' eu vivo for' etc. (13/25):
    mentr'eu tal poder ouver'/ de viver (**1**,4–5); enquant'eu viver poder' (**1**,11); enquant' eu viver' (**368**,1); entanto com' eu vivo for' (**2**,19; **10**,22); entanto com' eu viver' (**363**,2); enquant'eu ja eno mundo viver' (**3**,9); enquant' eu no mundo viver' (**13**, refrain); enquant' eu vivo for' (**3**,23; **6**,4; **364**,13); enquant' eu viver' (**4**,13; **6**,10); enos dias que eu viver' (**4**,24); enos dias que viver' (**5**,19); esso pouco que eu poder'/ viver no mundo (**9**,9–10)

dezir [etc.] ũa ren/cousa (11/25):
    ũa ren vus direi (**2**,9); ũa cousa vus direi (**3**,12; **371**,21); direi-vus ũa ren (**3**,20; **12**,4); eu vus quer'ũa ren dizer (**367**,1)
    dizede-me ũa ren (**10**,13)
    creed'ora ũa ren (**4**,7)
    E sei ũa ren (**6**,5)
    ũa cousa vus preguntarei (**365**,22)
    rogar-vus-ia ũa ren (**366**,2)

quitar/tolher (10/25):
    quite (**6**, passim; **7**,2; **374**,12)
    quitar (**3**, passim; **4**,22; **7**, passim; **372**,19; **374**,23)
    tolher (**1**,2; **4**,6; **5**,6; **12**, refrain; **369**,23; **374**,27)

falar/parecer (7/25):
    Deus ... vus fez falar/ mui ben ... e mui ben semelhar (**2**,28–29); vus fez parecer melhor/ Deus ... e melhor falar (**3**,24–25); Deus, que vus fez melhor/ falar e mais fremoso parecer (**10**,8–9); mais fremoso parecer/ vus fez Deus, e mais fremoso falar (**364**,3–4); e quen a oje vir' falar/ e parecer (**370**, 24–25); Deus, que vus fez ... /mui ben falar e parecer (**371**,1–2); a dona, que eu vi falar/ nunca melhor nen melhor semelhar (**372**,4–5)

que farei? (5/25):
    (**10**,14; **363**,5; **365**,1; **366**,26; **371**,4)

querer dezir, direi, etc. (13/25):
    quero vo-lo dizer (**6**,16); do que vus eu quero dizer (**8**,9); mais vus quero dizer (**364**,11); al vus ar quero dizer (**369**,13)
    a verdade vus quer' eu dizer (**7**,6); pero verdade vus direi (**12**,16); gran verdade vus direi (**365**,15)
    ca inda vus eu mais direi (**4**,21); E inda vus mais direi én (**11**,12); mais vus direi én (**9**,8); mais eu vus direi (**368**,3); direi-vus én com' é (**368**,13); e direi-vus por que mi aven (**9**,18)

al vos direi/ que mi devedes a creer (**363**,15–16); vus ora direi (**364**,5); direi-lh'eu que faça (**8**,17)

NOTES

This chapter previously appeared in *La corónica* 26, no. 1 (Fall 1997): 225–45. Reprinted by permission of the editor.

1. S. C. Aston, "The Troubadours and the Concept of Style," in *Stil- und Formprobleme in der Literatur: Vorträge des VII. Kongresses der internationalen Vereinigung für moderne Sprachen und Literaturen in Heidelberg*, ed. Paul Bockmann (Heidelberg: Carl Winter Universitätsverlag, 1959), 142–47, at 143.

2. For a general overview of the relative positions of *Stil-* and *Toposforschung*, with abundant bibliography, see the preface and chap. 1 of Peter Dronke, *Poetic Individuality in the Middle Ages: New Departures in Poetry, 1000–1150*, 2d ed. (London: Westfield College, University of London Committee for Medieval Studies, 1986).

3. Roger Dragonetti, *La technique poétique des trouvères dans la chanson courtoise: contribution à l'étude de la rhétorique médiévale* (Bruges: De Tempel, 1960); Paul Zumthor, *Essai de poétique médiévale* (Paris: Seuil, 1972).

4. Peter Dronke, *The Medieval Lyric*, 2d ed. (London: Hutchinson, 1978); Dronke, *Poetic Individuality in the Middle Ages*.

5. See Raymond Williams, *Marxism and Literature* (Oxford: Oxford University Press, 1977), 173. The opposition between convention and the individual has its roots in Romanticism; see Lawrence Manley, *Convention, 1500–1750* (Cambridge, Mass.: Harvard University Press, 1980), 2–4, 8–9.

6. Zumthor, *Essai*, 192.

7. Sarah Kay, "La notion de personnalité chez les troubadours: encore la question de la sincérité," in *Mittelalterbilder aus neuer Perspective: Diskussionsanstösse zu amour courtois, Subjectivität in der Dichtung und Strategien des Erzählens, Kolloquium Würzburg 1984*, ed. Ernstpeter Ruhe and Rudolf Behrens (Munich: Wilhem Fink, 1985), 166–82. The ideas sketched here are richly developed in her *Subjectivity in Troubadour Poetry* (Cambridge: Cambridge University Press, 1990). Don A. Monson, "Lyrisme et sincérité: sur une chanson de Bernart de Ventadorn," in *Studia occitanica in memoriam Paul Remy*, ed. Hans-Erich Keller and others (Kalamazoo: Medieval Institute Publications, Western Michigan University, 1986), 1:143–59. James J. Wilhelm, "The Varying 'I's of Troubadour Lyric," in *Studia occitanica*, 1:351–61.

8. Giuseppe Tavani, *Repertorio metrico della lirica galego-portughese* (Rome: Edizioni dell'Ateneo, 1967); Jean-Marie d'Heur, *Recherches internes sur la lyrique amoureuse des troubadours galicien-portugais (XIIe–XIVe siècles)* (Paris: n.p., 1975).

9. Giuseppe Tavani, "La poesia lirica galego-portoghese," in *Grundriss der romanische Literaturen des Mittelalters*, vol. 2: *Les genres lyriques*, part 1, fascicule 6 (Heidelberg: Carl Winter Universitätsverlag, 1980), 61–62.

10. José Filgueira Valverde, for example, attributes the genre's insincerity to Provençal influence and claims that any signs of poetic authenticity ("muestras de verdadera poesía del corazón") derive from the Galician poets' contact with their native soil. See "Lírica medieval gallega y portuguesa," in *Historia general de las liter-*

aturas hispánicas, ed. Guillermo Díaz-Plaja (Barcelona: Barna, 1949), 1:576. Similar romantic nationalism may be found in Manuel Rodrigues Lapa's standard *Lições de literatura portuguesa, época medieval,* 9th ed. (Coimbra: Coimbra Editora, 1977), 129–41. Notable exceptions are Dronke, *Medieval Lyric,* and the suggestive essay by Thomas Hart to which I return below.

11. Carlos Alvar and Vicente Beltrán, *Antología de la poesía gallego-portuguesa* (Madrid: Alhambra, 1985), 32.

12. A remark that echoes Alan Deyermond's earlier (and at that time perfectly valid) observation: "It is possible that we do not yet fully understand the *cantigas de amor.*" See *A Literary History of Spain,* vol. 1: *The Middle Ages* (London: Ernest Benn, 1971), 14.

13. Vicenç Beltran, "La estructura conceptual de la cantiga de amor," in *O cantar dos trobadores: Actas do Congreso celebrado en Santiago de Compostela entre os días 26 et 29 de abril de 1993* (Santiago de Compostela: Xunta de Galicia, 1993), 53–75; Beltran, *A cantiga de amor* (Vigo: Edicións Xerais de Galicia, 1995). Thomas Hart, "New Perspectives on the Medieval Portuguese Lyric," *Estudos portugueses: homenagem a Luciana Stegagno Picchio* (Lisboa: Difel, 1991), 69–78.

14. I am grateful to Professor Hart for generously sharing an early draft of his study, and for discussing its contents with me.

15. See Rip Cohen's subtle analysis of three *cantigas d'amor* by Dom Dinis, in his *Thirty-two "Cantigas d'amigo" of Dom Dinis: Typology of a Portuguese Renunciation* (Madison: Hispanic Seminary of Medieval Studies, 1987), 1–11.

16. Tavani, "Poesia lirica," 82.

17. See Peter Haidu, "Repetition: Modern Reflections on Medieval Aesthetics," *MLN* 92 (1977): 875–87.

18. A certainty matched by Tavani: variants are not "violazioni *coscienti* dell'omogeneità di genere" (conscious violations of generic homogeneity) ("Poesia lirica," 82; my emphasis).

19. Williams, *Marxism and Literature,* 21.

20. Ibid., 179. Although Williams's definition of convention is not original, he brings to the fore its implications for cultural and ideological analysis. Contrast, for example, Douwe Fokkema, who adopts a similar sociological definition, but because he employs an untenably narrow definition of ideology, has nothing to say about the relationship between literary conventions and social structures; see "The Concept of Convention in Literary Theory and Empirical Research," in *Convention and Innovation in Literature,* ed. Theo D'haen and others (Amsterdam: John Benjamins, 1989), 1–16. Fokkema's article is included in a volume of collected essays on literary convention and innovation, and some of the theoretical and practical problems involved in studying these categories are surveyed in the editors' useful "Introduction: The Decline and Rise of Convention," vii–xxii.

21. Laurie A. Finke, "The Rhetoric of Desire in the Courtly Lyric," in her *Feminist Theory, Women's Writing* (Ithaca: Cornell University Press, 1992), 33. Like Williams, Finke adopts the materialist philosophy of language developed by Volosinov/Bakhtin (48–49).

22. R. Howard Bloch, *Etymologies and Genealogies: A Literary Anthropology of the French Middle Ages* (Chicago: University of Chicago Press, 1983); Laura Kendrick, *The Game*

of Love: Troubadour Wordplay (Berkeley: University of California Press, 1988); Kay, *Subjectivity in Troubadour Poetry;* Finke, "Rhetoric of Desire"; Simon Gaunt, *Gender and Genre in Medieval French Literature* (Cambridge: Cambridge University Press, 1995).

23. *Tootsie,* directed by Sydney Pollack, with Dustin Hoffman (Columbia Pictures, 1982).

24. Thelma Fenster, "Preface: Why Men?" In *Medieval Masculinities: Regarding Men in the Middle Ages,* ed. Clare A. Lees (Minneapolis: University of Minnesota Press, 1994), ix–xiii, at xii.

25. In spite of a tendency to simplification, the dynamism of patriarchy during the Middle Ages is well illustrated by Jo Ann McNamara's account of the restructuring of the gender system between 1050 and 1150; see "The *Herrenfrage:* The Restructuring of the Gender System, 1050–1150," in *Medieval Masculinities,* ed. Lees, 3–29. For a more general treatment of masculinities and their relation to "masculinism" (the ideology of patriarchy), see Arthur Brittan, *Masculinity and Power* (Oxford: Basil Blackwell, 1989).

26. See Janice Wright, "Nature and the *Amiga* in the Galician-Portuguese *Cantigas de amigo,*" *La Chispa '89: Selected Proceedings of the Tenth Louisiana Conference on Hispanic Languages and Literatures* (New Orleans, 1989), 345–55.

27. The assimilation of passion and thought is revealed in the play on the verbs *cuidar* and *coitar;* see d'Heur, *Recherches internes,* 473.

28. For a survey of the stock phrases that make up the "portrait" of the lady, see d'Heur, *Recherches internes,* 439–69. His stylistic analysis reveals that the *cantigas de amor* eschew the conventional *descriptio mulieris* found in other branches of the European tradition, and that the lady's features are often depicted by the substantivization of two verbs, *bel catar* and *bon falar.* Although I cannot adequately develop the point here, style conveys the ideology of masculinism since actions (verbs) are rendered immobile (as nouns), and since for all their emphasis on sight and voice, we neither see nor hear the lady.

29. See my study of "Lyric Sequences in the *Cantigas d'amigo,*" *Bulletin of Hispanic Studies* 65 (1988): 21–37.

30. See, for example, Luciana Stegagno Picchio, ed., *Martin Moya: le poesie* (Rome: Edizioni dell'Ateneo, 1968), 77; Matteo Majorano, ed., *Il canzoniere di Vasco Perez Pardal* (Bari: Adriatica Editrice, 1979), 8–9, 44. On the Old French *chanson,* see Zumthor, *Essai;* on the Minnesingers, Vickie L. Ziegler, *The Leitwort in Minnesang: Stylistic Analysis and Textual Criticism* (University Park: Pennsylvania State University Press, 1975).

31. For brief biographical details, see Carolina Michaëlis de Vasconcellos, ed., *Cancioneiro da Ajuda* (Halle: Max Niemeyer, 1904), 2:293–97. All subsequent quotations are from this edition (1:5–29 and 713–35). Incidentally, if this was one of the very first Galician-Portuguese poets, how "conventional" could he have been?

32. Michaëlis de Vasconcellos, *Cancioneiro da Ajuda,* 2:295, n. 4.

33. Drawing on the research of William Paden and Glynnis Cropp, Kay makes a similar point about Provençal verse; see "Notion de personnalité," 172–74.

34. See Isabel Beceiro Pita and Ricardo Córdoba de la Llave, *Parentesco, poder y mentalidad: la nobleza castellana, siglos XII–XV* (Madrid: Consejo Superior de Investigaciones Científicas, 1990), 29–60, 79–80.

35. See *Grundriss der romanische Literaturen des Mittelalters*, vol. 2: *Les genres lyriques*, part 1, fascicule 8 (Heidelberg: Winter, 1983), 55.

36. See Bloch, *Etymologies and Genealogies*, 122–24.

37. Toril Moi, "Desire in Language: Andreas Capellanus and the Controversy of Courtly Love," in *Medieval Literature: Criticism, Ideology, and History*, ed. David Aers (New York: St. Martin's Press, 1986), 11–33; see esp. 24.

38. Michaëlis de Vasconcellos, *Cancioneiro da Ajuda*, 1:15–16.

39. Cited from Thomas R. Hart, "The *cantigas de amor* of King Dinis: *em maneira de proençal?*" *Bulletin of Hispanic Studies* 71 (1994): 29–38, at 29. This is just one of several poems concerning Provençal verse; for bibliography see the following note.

40. In addition to Hart (ibid.), see Jean-Marie d'Heur, *Troubadours d'oc et troubadours galiciens-portugais: recherches sur quelques échanges dans la littérature de l'Europe au moyen âge* (Paris: Fundação Calouste Gulbenkian, Centro Cultural Portugués, 1973), 301–9, and X. Xabier Ron Fernández, "Os trobadores no tempo da frol," in *O cantar dos trobadores: Actas do Congreso celebrado en Santiago de Compostela entre os días 26 e 29 de abril de 1993* (Santiago de Compostela: Xunta de Galicia, 1993), 475–92.

41. See Maria da Conceição Vilhena, "A 'morte-por-amor' na lirica galego-portuguesa: reabilitação de Rui Queimado," *Cahiers d'études romanes* 3 (1977): 1–20; María del Pilar Manero Sorolla, "Aproximaciones a la lírica de Roy Queimado: en torno a las cantigas paródicas," *Anuario de estudios medievales* 13 (1983): 279–90; Carlos Pérez Varela, "Ironía fronte a sentimentalismo nas cantigas de amor de Roí Queimado," in *O cantar dos trobadores: Actas do Congreso celebrado en Santiago de Compostela entre os días 26 e 29 de abril de 1993* (Santiago de Compostela: Xunta de Galicia, 1993), 439–48.

42. Manero Sorolla, "Aproximaciones," 285.

43. In the fourteenth and fifteenth centuries, this obsession with the *omne esencial* is expressed in chronicles and moral treatises: a fact that underscores the changing relationship between gender and literary genre, as well as the dynamic nature of masculinism itself.

44. Stegagno Picchio, *Martin Moya: le poesie*, 81.

45. See Valeria Bertolucci Pizzorusso, ed., "La supplica di Guiraut Riquier e la risposta di Alfonso X di Castiglia," *Studi mediolatini e volgari* 14 (1966): 9–135.

46. See Manuel Rodrigues Lapa, ed., *Cantigas d'escarnho e de mal dizer dos cancioneiros medievais galego-portugueses* ([Vigo]: Editorial Galaxia, 1965), poems 53, 132–33, 285, 364, 377, 398, which conflate poetic with social or moral corruption.

CHAPTER 5

Traditional Genres and Poetic Innovation in Thirteenth-Century Italian Lyric Poetry

MICHELANGELO PICONE

Compared with the two centuries or more required for the expansion of the lyric in *langue d'oc*, in *langue d'oïl*, or in Galician, the medieval Italian lyric experience lasted for a relatively short period of time. In fact, little more than a century separates the poets of the Sicilian School from Petrarch. Nevertheless, this short period of time was sufficient for Italian lyric poets to achieve results that no other poets (Provençal, French, or Galician) had been able to achieve before: namely, the codification of the lyric genre in a form (the Petrarchan form) that would remain unchanged for centuries, at least until the Romantic era. My task in this essay is that of characterizing the Italian lyric tradition: firstly within its Romance context in general; and, secondly in its relationship with the founding tradition of the European lyric, that of the troubadours.

However, before tackling this problem of "generic" definition, I would like to indicate the main historical and cultural factors that, in my opinion, gave Italian poetry of the thirteenth century its distinctive character. While these factors have been acknowledged by literary historians of the period, their particular relevance to the formation and development of the Italian lyric tradition has not yet been duly emphasized.[1]

The first conditioning factor is the introduction of Aristotle into European culture, through the mediation of Arabic philosophy, Averroës and Avicenna in particular. As is well known, the Sicily of Frederick II had an important role to play in this *translatio* of Aristotle. Significantly, the creation of a new school of poetry in the vernacular language and the reception of Aristotelian thought occurred simultaneously in Sicily. For our perspective, there are two highly relevant consequences of the Aristotelian "vogue." The first applies to the level of lyric *content:* the Aristotelian-Arabic conception of the soul brought Sicilian poets first, and later the Stilnovisti, to develop a medico-philosophical theory of love, a theory that succeeded in strengthening the cognitive potential of courtly love.[2] The second consequence touches the level of lyric *form*. In fact, Aristotelian thought introduced the fundamental element of order in lyric discourse, by which love—an irrational passion—could be represented in rational (even syllogistic) terms.[3]

The second conditioning factor is the coming of the mendicant orders, the Dominicans and the Franciscans. This event bestowed a new spiritual dimension on Italian poetry. Not only did traditional love poetry become more spiritual in tone but an entirely new tradition of religious and moral poetry was introduced as well. Suffice it here to mention the names of Iacopone and Guittone, the "Guittone morale" of course. This constant interference of the sacred and profane registers, of *eros* and *caritas,* is characteristic of the medieval Italian lyric tradition.[4]

The third conditioning factor is the rise of the university. While the feudal court was the locus and focus of the troubadour lyric, the *aula* or classroom of universities such as Bologna or Naples became the center of irradiation for thirteenth-century Italian lyric poetry. Not only did most Italian poets from Giacomo da Lentini to Cino da Pistoia come from an academic background (more specifically in law) but also their poetry was imbued with the scholastic and encyclopedic mentality that could only be developed through a university education. The impact of scholastic culture on the medieval Italian lyric is immediately apparent when we consider how the troubadours' poetry is rewritten by their Italian counterparts.[5]

The fourth conditioning factor, and the one that in my view most deeply marked the destiny of the medieval Italian lyric, is the renewed interest in, and study of, classical *auctores*. This cultural element was responsible for the application of hermeneutical techniques previously used in thirteenth-century commentaries on classical authors to the construction of the Italian *canzoniere*. In fact, in the Italian *canzonieri* a typological organization of the lyric material becomes apparent: while Italian poets clearly imitated the *Liederbücher* of the troubadours, they also intended to emulate and challenge them; that is, they strove to reveal a new poetic *auctoritas,* parallel to that of the classics. This literary typology, present as a tendency in the *canzonieri,* will later be fully exploited by Dante in his *Vita Nuova*.[6]

The last conditioning factor, the sociopolitical factor, should be added to the ones that I have just analyzed; it has been especially emphasized by Marxist critical theory. Emperor Frederick's court more closely resembled the administration of a modern state than it did the feudal courts in which troubadours had lived and sung. The bourgeois society which surrounded Tuscan poets from Guittone to the Stilnovisti was quite the opposite of the courtly society which had surrounded their Romance predecessors. This totally different environment could not but provoke a radical shift in cultural attitudes toward lyric poetry. In effect, it changed both the function attributed to poetry and the role played by the poet. Almost all historians of the period have recognized the importance of this point. The Italian lyric poet of the thirteenth century was an intellectual who did not live by his art but by his profession as a bureaucrat or an administrator. He was a man who, far from using his artistic talent for economical and political gains, put his technical and scientific knowledge, his academic training, to use in the expression of his artistic passion. While troubadours had been professional poets, in general the Italians were amateur poets. In the place of the *companhos* to whom the troubadour had addressed his *cansos* and *sirventes,* we find the members of an intellectual community, the components of a poetic family or school, to whom the lyric message of the Italian poet was directed.[7]

Having discussed the main cultural and social factors that conditioned the development of the Italian lyric tradition in the thirteenth century, I would like to concentrate more on characterizing this tradition from the point of view of literary genres. In other words, I will attempt to determine how the Italian system of lyric genres differs from the system developed by the troubadours.[8]

The first element differentiating the two systems is a quantitative one. The number of lyric genres present in the Italian tradition is substantially reduced in comparison with its Provençal paradigm. In fact, some genres (for example the *sirventes*) disappeared altogether from the poetic practice of the Sicilian and the Tuscan poets. Therefore, the opposition *canso/sirventes,* which was central to the troubadours' system of genres, is neutralized in the Italian system. What that entails can be stated simply. Since the *sirventes* was a genre used by the troubadours either to represent passion other than love (for instance the passion of war), or to blame those who lived outside the boundaries of courtly love, its disappearance from the poetic horizon of Sicilian and Tuscan *rimatori* implies a greater concentration, on their part, on the matter typical of the *canso:* the theme of *fin' amor.* This did not result in the total exclusion of the *sirventes* themes from Italian lyric but rather in their treatment *sub specie amoris.*[9]

Similar observations can be made regarding the *alba,* or the metrical genre of the *sestina* invented by Arnaut Daniel. It is important to note that the *sestina* is used for the first time in Italian by Dante, and this only outside the *Vita Nuova.* Since this genre traditionally dealt with obsessive erotic passion, it could not enter the perimeter of the *Vita Nuova,* in which Dante discovers the truth about idealistic and rational love.[10] Petrarch's use of the *sestina* in his *Rerum vulgarium fragmenta* will, of course, stem from a totally different conception of love, one dominated by passion and drama.

This emphasis on the theme of *fin' amor* is, as we all know, asserted as an axiom in the important twenty-fifth chapter of the *Vita Nuova:* "E questo è contra coloro che rimano sopra altra matera che amorosa, con ciò sia cosa che cotale modo di parlare fosse dal principio trovato per dire d'amore" (This is an argument against those who compose in rhyme on themes other than love, because this manner of composition was invented from the beginning for the purpose of writing of love).

The thematic monotony that could ensue from a similar restriction is avoided due to the hypostatization of love (and chapter XXV of the *Vita Nuova* deals precisely with the rhetorical and literary problem of the personification of love). More than the *Donna* herself, love becomes for the Italian poets the true object of their existential and artistic quest. Love, which has become the privileged matter of Italian lyric, takes on the appearance of a character (the God of Love) and starts acting as the main partner in the poetic dialogue. Naturally the addition of this new character endows the Italian lyric with a narrative dimension; that is, the possibility of constructing a story in which the erotic impasse of traditional courtly lyric can be broken. Therefore Love, as personified by Italian poets, provides the solution to the *paradoxe amoureux* typical of the troubadours.[11]

In addition to reducing the number of genres, and consequently his thematic range, the Italian poet of the thirteenth century displays a different strategy in the way these genres are employed and appreciated. He sets off a process of homogenization and adaptation of single lyric genres to meet the demands of the macrogenre that includes them. This macrogenre, in which traditional lyric genres tend to dissolve or fuse, can be called the *libro di poesia* (as in the case of the *Vita Nuova*) or the *canzoniere* (as in the case of Petrarch's *Rerum vulgarium fragmenta*).[12] This trait, perhaps more than any other, differentiates the Italian lyric tradition from all other Romance traditions. In Italian songbooks, lyric genres tend to relinquish their literary specificity and formal autonomy in order to acquire a new function and a new meaning within the macrogenre. In other words, lyric genres become part of a new system, a system based on the narrative reconstruction of the poet's life as a lover and as an artist. The movement is therefore toward the unification of lyric genres, and at the same time toward the transformation of song into tale, and of lyric into narrative.[13]

A last distinctive feature of the Italian lyric tradition should be mentioned here, the divorce between poetry and music.[14] The impact of this phenomenon on the system of genres is evident. In fact, the elimination of musical accompaniment lessens attention to the formal aspects of the lyric text, and focuses attention on its content, on semantic and narrative values. Furthermore, the public performance of the troubadour's song gives way to the private reading of the Italian collection of poems. From the external "show" of the troubadour we come to the internal adventure of the Italian poet. From a lyric that is "acted out" we move to a lyric that is "lived in."

For the sake of brevity, instead of following the whole literary itinerary of the medieval Italian lyric, I have chosen to concentrate on two milestones of that itinerary, Guittone d'Arezzo and Dante Alighieri.

Guittone's *canzoniere* occupies a privileged position within the major manuscripts of thirteenth-century Italian lyric poetry. MS *L* (Laurenziano Rediano 9) is in fact a true *Liederbuch* of Guittone: a private collection of Guittone's poems, accompanied by poems (either by followers or predecessors) somehow linked to his poetic personality.[15] Such scribal recognition is a clear sign of the pivotal role which can be attributed to Guittone in the Italian lyric tradition. Indeed, Guittone's *canzoniere* is the first to be thematically and ideologically constructed; his collected poems are divided into two parts, the "rime amorose" attributed to "Guittone," and the "rime morali" attributed to "Fra Guittone." Canzone XXV ("Ora parrà s'eo saverò cantare"), occurring right in the middle, marks the split between the two parts. There are two guiding principles behind this new construction of a *Liederbuch:* on the one hand we have the Augustinian idea of *conversio*—the passage from *homo vetus* to *homo novus,* and from carnal love to divine love—and on the other we have the literary technique of *recantatio*—by which the poems of the second part of Guittone's *canzoniere* become a palinodic rewriting of the poems of the first part.[16]

The most important consequence of this new structure of the traditional *Liederbuch* is the fact that the lyric "I" of the troubadours acquires psychological and cultural depth with Guittone. The character that says "I" in Guittone's songbook is not only the lover engaged in an erotic adventure with no positive ending; he is also the teacher of morality projected in a spiritual adventure to discover the final truth about himself and the world around him. This double dimension granted by Guittone to the lyric "I" is clearly modeled on the allegorical *roman* (such as the *Roman de la Rose*). The *agens*, or protagonist of the erotic journey, and the *auctor*, or protagonist of the textual journey, establish a conflictual relationship with one another, in the sense that the *auctor* represents the correction and the rectification of the *agens*. Guittone's *canzoniere* is therefore the first embodiment of the tendency, typical of the Italian tradition, of transforming lyric discourse into a narrated story—a story with a negative beginning, a critical middle, and a positive ending.[17]

We come now to Dante's *Vita Nuova*. This work may be defined as an author's collection of poems by virtue of the fact that it demonstrates the achieved *auctoritas* of the person who has made the collection, the transformation of the protagonist into author. The *scriptor* of the "libello" becomes *auctor* because in the course of the work he also reveals himself as *commentator*, someone who, through the prose "ragioni," is capable of discovering the deep meaning of the poetic inventions contained in the collected poems, and who, as *compilator*, is capable of selecting poetic materials and prose explanations and ordering them in an exemplary tale.[18] The result of this process is a kind of "novel" of the poetic and spiritual formation of the protagonist.

The poems of the *Vita Nuova* reveal the presence of traditional lyric themes—from the *celar*, or lover's discretion, to the praise of the Lady; from the *gab*, or boast, to the death of the beloved. They also reveal the presence of traditional lyric genres—from the *sirventes* to the *canso*, from the *escondich* to the *planh*. The duty of the *commentator* and the *compilator* is that of linking these typical courtly situations to the personal development of the protagonist; their task is that of adapting these traditional genres to meet the demands of the new macrogenre, the "libro di poesia," the author's poetic autobiography.

In the outline provided in the appendix, I have tried to identify the pertinent lyric genre for each poem of the *Vita Nuova*. In the first column of this outline the reader will find the order in which the poems appear: short poems (mainly sonnets) and long poems (*canzoni* only) are distinguished by Arabic and Roman numerals respectively. In the second, closely related column, I have indicated meter. In the third column I have synthesized the theme of each poem, and I have indicated (within parentheses) the genre to which the particular poem belongs. In the fourth column I have indicated the chapter in which the poem is found.

I would now like to make a few observations on how to interpret this outline. I will try to see how lyric genres work within the system of the *Vita*

Nuova, and what kinds of relationships are established among the various genres on the one hand and between the genres and the macrogenre on the other.[19]

The outline makes the opposition between short poems and long poems quite clear. This opposition was operational in preceding *Liederbücher* as well. However, Dante introduces three innovations: he alternates short and long metrical forms instead of grouping them individually; he functionalizes this opposition to endow the *Vita Nuova* with a numerological meaning (notice the presence of the numbers 3 and 9, symbols of God and Beatrice respectively); and he uses the three *canzoni* as pillars to separate the three parts of the "libello."[20] Therefore, if in the traditional *Liederbücher* we find the metrical forms ordered according to an external taxonomy, in the *Vita Nuova* we see them ordered in a subjective, phenomenological manner.

Another element of interest is observable in this outline. A subject matter such as that of the second part (the praise of the Lady) can be treated either in a long metrical form (the *canzone*) or in a short metrical form (the sonnet); it can also be expressed in the conventional genre for love and praise (the *canso*), or in a less conventional genre such as the *tenso*. Here Dante clearly breaks the rigorous barriers that separated lyric genres in the troubadour tradition, in order to create a macrogenre capable of attributing new meaning to old poetic experiences.

A close look at the outline reveals that certain genres have disappeared from Dante's system. For instance, we do not find the genre of the *alba:* an empty case can be as revealing in interpreting the *Vita Nuova* as a full case. But let us consider another genre, the *sirventes*. The reader will have noticed that a *sirventes* in honor of the most beautiful ladies of Florence is mentioned in chapter VI of the *Vita Nuova,* but is not transcribed: evidently the *compilator* thought that it was old-fashioned and therefore omitted it.[21] Dante does seem to save at least one function of the *sirventes* in chapter XXIV, that of literary discussion and controversy. However, while the Provençal literary *sirventes* (for example "Cantarai d'aquestz trobadors" of Peire d'Alvernha) was an attempt to characterize a series of troubadours in a satirical and even grotesque way, Dante's sonnet "I' mi senti' svegliar" intends to insert the poets (more particularly Cavalcanti and Dante himself) into a literary typology of old poetry versus new poetry.

A similar observation can be made with regard to sonnets 7 and 11. In sonnet 7 Dante presents four theses on the nature of love: the *fin' amor* of the troubadours is contrasted with the *fol'amor* of the *roman;* the "amore dolce" of Guinizzelli is opposed to the "amore doloroso" of Cavalcanti. These theses, which obviously contrast with one another, find their solution in sonnet 11, where Dante offers his own thesis on the nature of love, a thesis that is partially consonant with that put forth by Guinizzelli. Here as well then, Dante uses a procedure inspired by biblical typology: the relationship that he establishes with his predecessors (from the troubadours to Cavalcanti) is analogous to the one established by Christ with the prophets of the Old Testament. As Christ realized and fulfilled the word of the prophets, so Dante realizes and fulfills the poetic word (that is, the images, the themes, and the genres) of the Romance poets.[22] The function of the biblical pattern is thus twofold: while it gives full meaning to the lyric genres represented in the poems, it also gives the *Vita Nuova* the dimension of a true book, a book modeled on that of Christianity, on the Bible.

APPENDIX
Lyric Genres in the Vita Nuova

Order	Meter	Theme (Genre)	Chapter
First Part (chapters I–XVII):			
1	sonnet	meaning of a vision (*tenso*) (only Dante's "proposta" is reproduced)	III
		list of the sixty most beautiful women ("serventese") (not reproduced)	VI
2	sonnet	"lamentanza" for the departure of the "donna-schermo"(*chanson d'absence*)	VIII
3	sonnet	death of a young woman (*planh*)	VIII
4	sonnet	*improperium* against Death (*planh*)	VIII
5	sonnet	meeting with Love in the countryside (*pastorela*)	IX
6	ballata	poet's defense against false accusations (*escondich*)	XII
7	sonnet	debate about the nature of Love (*tenso*)	XIII
8	sonnet	the Lady makes fun of the poet (*gab*)	XIV
9	sonnet	poet's reaction to the Lady's *gab*	XV
10	sonnet	effects of the Lady's *gab* on the poet	XVI
Second Part (chapters XVIII–XXVII):			
I	canzone	praise of the Lady (*canso*)	XIX
11	sonnet	definition of the nature of love (*tenso*)	XX
12	sonnet	praise of the Lady for her influence on others (*canso*)	XXI
13, 14	two sonnets	dialogue between the poet and some women about the Lady's conditions after her father's death (*tenso*)	XXII
II	canzone	vision of the Lady's death and transfiguration (*canso*)	XXIII

15	sonnet	vision indicating the poet's leading role (*sirventes*)	XXIV
16	sonnet	praise of the Lady (*canso*)	XXVI
17	sonnet	praise of the Lady for her influence on other women (*canso*)	XXV
18	*stanza*	praise of the Lady for her influence on the poet (*canso*)	XXVII

Third Part (chapters XXVIII–XLII):

III	*canzone*	death of the Lady (*planh*)	XXXI
19	sonnet	another complaint on the Lady's death (*planh*)	XXXII
20	*stanza*	final complaint on the Lady's death (*planh*)	XXXIII
21	sonnet	first "annovale" of the Lady's death (anniversary)	XXXIV
22	sonnet	meeting with the "donna gentile" (*chanson de change*)	XXXV
23	sonnet	meeting with the "donna gentile" (*chanson de change*)	XXXVI
24	sonnet	meeting with the "donna gentile" (*chanson de change*)	XXXVII
25	sonnet	meeting with the "donna gentile" (*chanson de change*)	XXXVIII
26	sonnet	poet's return to the Lady's memory (second anniversary?)	XXXIX
27	sonnet	passage of pilgrims through the sorrowing city (*canso de crozada*)	XL
28	sonnet	poet's spiritual pilgrimage toward his celestial Lady (*canso de crozada*)	XLI

NOTES

1. I have delved into this problem in my introduction to *L'enciclopedismo medievale*, ed. Michelangelo Picone (Ravenna: Longo, 1994), 15–21.

2. For discussions on this topic, see especially Giorgio Agamben, *Stanze: la parola e il fantasma nella cultura occidentale* (Turin: Einaudi, 1977), 105–55 (translated by Ronald L. Martinez as *Stanzas: Word and Phantasm in Western Culture* [Minneapolis: University of Minnesota Press, 1993], 63–131); and Manuela Allegretto, "*Figura amoris*," *Cultura neolatina* 40 (1980): 231–42.

3. Some interesting remarks on this topic can be found in Ulrich Mölk, "Le sonnet *Amor è un desio* de Giacomo da Lentini et le problème de la genèse de l'amour," *Cahiers de civilisation médiévale* 14 (1971): 329–39.

4. On the impact of the mendicants on thirteenth-century Italian literature see Roberto Antonelli, "L'ordine domenicano e la letteratura dell'Italia pretridentina," in *Letteratura italiana*, ed. Alberto Asor Rosa, vol. 1: *Il letterato e le istituzioni* (Turin: Einaudi, 1982), 681–728, and Corrado Bologna, "L'ordine francescano e la letter-

atura nell'Italia pretridentina," in ibid., 729–97. [On interference between sacred and profane in thirteenth-century French lyric see Huot in this volume; in Hebrew, see Brann.—Ed.]

5. For full discussion of this point I refer to the contrastive analysis of Giacomo da Lentini's canzone *Madonna dir vo voglio* and its Provençal intertext, Folquet de Marselha's *A vos midonz,* by Aurelio Roncaglia, "*De quibusdam provincialibus translatis in lingua nostra,*" in *Letteratura e critica: studi in onore di Natalino Sapegno,* ed. Walter Binni and others (Rome: Bulzoni, 1975), 2:1–36.

6. See Michelangelo Picone, "Dante e il canone degli *Auctores,*" *Rassegna europea di letteratura italiana* 1 (1993): 9–26; also in English, "Dante and the Classics," in *Dante: Contemporary Perspectives,* ed. Amilcare A. Iannucci (Toronto: University of Toronto Press, 1997), 51–73.

7. Most relevant for this issue are Roberto Antonelli, "Politica e volgare: Guglielmo IX, Enrico II, Federico II," in *Seminario romanzo* (Rome: Bulzoni, 1979), 9–109; and (with Simonetta Bianchini) "Dal *clericus* al poeta," in *Letteratura italiana,* ed. Alberto Asor Rosa, vol. 2: *Produzione e consumo* (Turin: Einaudi, 1983), 2:171–229, esp. 181–86. On the Sicilian School see Furio Brugnolo, "La scuola poetica siciliana," in *Storia della letteratura italiana,* ed. Enrico Malato, vol. 1: *Dalle origini a Dante* (Rome: Salerno Editrice, 1995), 1:265–337. [On professional bureaucrats as poets in fifteenth-century Spain see Gómez-Bravo in this volume.—Ed.]

8. See Erich Köhler and others, eds., *Grundriss der romanischen Literaturen des Mittelalters,* vol. 2: *Les genres lyriques* (Heidelberg: Carl Winter, 1979–90); Dieter Kremer, ed., *Actes du XVIIIe Congrès International de Linguistique et de Philologie Romanes Université de Trèves (Trier) 1986* (Tübingen: Max Niemeyer, 1988), 6:119–60; Pierre Bec, "Le problème des genres chez les premiers troubadours," *Cahiers de civilisation médiévale* 25 (1982): 31–47, reprinted in his *Ecrits sur les troubadours et la lyrique médiévale (1961–1991)* (Paris: Editions Paradigme, 1992), 87–103. Extremely helpful is the critical survey furnished by Luciano Formisano, "La lirica," in *La letteratura romanza medievale: una storia per generi,* ed. Costanzo Di Girolamo (Bologna: Il Mulino, 1994), 63–125.

9. See Brugnolo, "Scuola poetica siciliana," 319–27; also important are Henning Krauss, "Sistema dei generi e scuola siciliana," in *La pratica sociale del testo: scritti di sociologia della letteratura in onore di Erich Köhler,* ed. Carlo Bordoni (Bologna: CLUEB, 1982), 123–58; and Rinaldina Russell, *Generi poetici medioevali: modelli e funzioni letterarie* (Naples: Società Editrice Napoletana, 1982), 17–72.

10. See Michelangelo Picone, "'All'ombra della fanciulla in fiore': lettura semantica della sestina dantesca," *Letture classensi* 24 (1995): 91–108. For an overview of this metrical genre see Gabriele Frasca, *La furia della sintassi: la sestina in Italia* (Naples: Bibliopolis, 1992) and Marianne Shapiro, *Hieroglyph of Time: The Petrarchan Sestina* (Minneapolis: University of Minnesota Press, 1980).

11. An interesting analysis of this topic is provided by Paolo Cherchi, "Il tempo degli amanti e il carro di Febo," in *Studi di filologia e letteratura italiana in onore di Maria Picchio Simonelli,* ed. Pietro Frassica (Alessandria: Edizioni dell'Orso, 1992), 51–61.

12. See Marco Santagata's chapter "La preistoria del genere canzoniere," in *Dal sonetto al canzoniere: ricerche sulla preistoria e la costituzione di un genere* (Padua: Liviana, 1979), 131–54; Furio Brugnolo, "Il libro di poesia nel Trecento," in *Il libro di poesia*

dal copista al tipografo, ed. Marco Santagata and Amedeo Quondam (Modena: Edizioni Panini, 1989), 9–23; Furio Brugnolo, "Libro d'autore e forma-canzoniere: implicazioni petrarchesche," in *Atti e memorie dell'Accademia patavina di Scienze, Lettere ed Arti* 103 (1990–91): 259–90; Guglielmo Gorni, "Il canzoniere," in his *Metrica e analisi letteraria* (Bologna: Il Mulino, 1993), 113–34; Corrado Bologna, *Tradizione e fortuna dei classici italiani* (Turin: Einaudi, 1993), 1:3–156.

13. See Michelangelo Picone, "Rito e *narratio* nella *Vita Nuova*," in *Miscellanea di studi in onore di Vittore Branca*, vol. 1: *Dal Medioevo a Petrarca* (Florence: Olschki, 1983), 141–57; Michelangelo Picone, "Tempo e racconto nel *Canzoniere* di Petrarca," in *Omaggio a Gianfranco Folena* (Padua: Editoriale Programma, 1993), 1:581–92; Teodolinda Barolini, "The Making of a Lyric Sequence: Time and Narrative in Petrarch's *Rerum vulgarium fragmenta*," *MLN* 104 (1989): 1–38; Teodolinda Barolini, "'Cominciandomi dal principio infino a la fine' (*V.N.*, XXIII, 15): Forging Anti-Narrative in the *Vita Nuova*," in *"La gloriosa donna de la mente": A Commentary on the "Vita Nuova,"* ed. Vincent Moleta (Florence: Olschki, 1994), 119–40.

14. The expression is taken from Aurelio Roncaglia, "Sul divorzio fra musica e poesia nel Duecento italiano," in *L'Ars nova italiana del Trecento*, ed. Agostino Ziino (Certaldo: Centro di Studi, 1978), 4:365–97; also important are Joachim Schulze, *Sizilianische Kontrafacturen: Versuch zur Frage der Einheit von Musik und Dichtung in der sizilianischen und sikulo-toskanischen Lyrik des 13. Jahrhunderts* (Tübingen: Max Niemeyer, 1989); and N. Pirrotta, "I poeti della scuola siciliana e la musica," in his *Poesia e musica, e altri saggi* (Florence: La Nuova Italia, 1994), 13–21. [On fifteenth-century Spain see Gómez-Bravo in this volume.—Ed.]

15. See the important contribution by Lino Leonardi, "Guittone nel Laurenziano: strutture del canzoniere e tradizione testuale," in *La filologia romanza e i codici*, ed. Saverio Guida and Fortunata Latella (Messina: Sicania, 1993), 2:443–80.

16. I have developed this analysis in my article "Guittone e i due tempi del 'Canzoniere,'" *Rassegna europea di letteratura italiana* 3 (1994): 103–18.

17. The question of Guittone's role in the thirteenth-century Italian lyric tradition was dealt with in all its complexity at the 1994 Arezzo conference; see *Guittone d'Arezzo nel settimo centenario della morte: Atti del Convegno internazionale di Arezzo (22–24 aprile 1994)*, ed. Michelangelo Picone (Florence: Franco Cesati, 1995).

18. On this point, besides my article "Dante e il canone degli Auctores (Dante and the Classics)," see Albert Russell Ascoli, "The Unfinished Author: Dante's Rhetoric of Authority in *Convivio* and *De vulgari eloquentia*," in *The Cambridge Companion to Dante*, ed. Rachel Jacoff (Cambridge: Cambridge University Press, 1993), 45–66.

19. I have studied Dante's "libello" as the culmination of the entire Romance lyric tradition in my book *"Vita Nuova" e tradizione romanza* (Padua: Liviana, 1979), and in my article "La *Vita Nuova* fra autobiografia e tipologia," in *Dante e le forme dell'allegoresi*, ed. Michelangelo Picone (Ravenna: Longo, 1987): 59–69. The leading interpretation of Dante's "libello" is that provided by Domenico De Robertis, *Il libro della "Vita Nuova"* (Florence: Sansoni, 1970); for an up-to-date critical appraisal see Guglielmo Gorni, "*Vita Nuova* di Dante Alighieri," in *Letteratura italiana: le opere*, ed. Alberto Asor Rosa, vol. 1: *Dalle origini al Cinquecento* (Turin: Einaudi, 1992), 153–86.

20. All these observations can be found in Charles S. Singleton's seminal study, *An Essay on the "Vita Nuova"* (Cambridge, Mass.: Harvard University Press, 1949).

21. See Aldo Costantini, "'Compuosi una pistola sotto forma di serventese' (*V.N.*,

VI, 2): la narrativa spezzata e i *genres* della prima fase della *Vita Nuova*," in *"La gloriosa donna de la mente": A Commentary on the "Vita Nuova,"* ed. Vincent Moleta (Florence: Olschki, 1994), 37–60.

22. See my article "*Vita Nuova* fra autobiografia e tipologia." On the genre of the *tenso* see now Michelangelo Picone, "La tenzone *de amore* fra Iacopo Mostacci, Pier della Vigna e il Notaio," in *Il genere "tenzone" nelle letterature romanze delle Origini*, ed. Matteo Pedroni-Antonio Stäuble (Ravenna: Longo Editore, 1999), 13–31.

CHAPTER 6

Decir canciones:
The Question of Genre in Fifteenth-Century Castilian Cancionero *Poetry*

ANA MARÍA GÓMEZ-BRAVO

Standard histories of Spanish literature typically divide fifteenth-century Castilian *cancionero* poetry into two main and opposed genres, *cantigas* or *canciones* (songs) and *decires* (recited poems).[1] This distinction needs to be revised, however, since it is based on the uncontested assumptions that poetry has an ancillary relation to music and that the latter serves as the principal feature differentiating the two genres. It also overlooks the chronological boundaries of these genres, making possible anachronistic applications of earlier labels to later poems. I shall argue that evidence from late medieval music and late medieval literacy points to genre distinctions that rely on features that complement the distinguishing role traditionally attributed to music, and that the origin and evolution of the genres need to be taken into consideration in order to shed new light on fifteenth-century poetic genres. In considering the interplay of cultural movements and poetic practice, this viewpoint will also destabilize the current perception of these genres as self-contained static categories that remain unchanged through time.

In an important article on the strophic forms and metrical terms in the *Cancionero de Baena*, H. R. Lang defined the *cantiga* as a poem with a "fixed form" that "was intended to be sung."[2] He did not offer a definition of the *decir*. In an epoch-making and often-quoted book, Pierre Le Gentil distinguished the *cantigas* from the *decires* in the *Cancionero de Baena* in terms of "sung" and "recited" poetry. This theory was based on his unproven hypothesis that the Spanish poets of the period were, like many of their French and Provençal counterparts, also musicians and that, in late fourteenth- and fifteenth-century Castile, the process of writing a poem was intimately linked to that of setting it to music. For Le Gentil, the Castilian poet composed the music at the same time, or even before, the lyrics of his or her poem.[3] Both critics were transposing genre distinctions from earlier medieval poetic schools onto fifteenth-century Castile: Lang was thinking of Alfonso X's musical *cantigas* from the thirteenth century, and Le Gentil was thinking of the troubadour and, above all, the trouvère school.[4]

The lack of metrical unity among *cantigas*, other unsolved metrical and textual problems, and the fact that some of them are said to be "asonadas" or "set to music," caused these two scholars to use music as the single defining factor that would distinguish *cantigas* from *decires*. Old prejudices about "insincerity" and "drabness" also led critics to believe that music *had* to accompany this poetry in order for it to be at all attractive to a public.[5] The musical distinction between *cantigas* or *canciones* and *decires* thus became institutionalized, and the two critics' opinions have been followed consistently and uncontestedly up until this day. Furthermore, since the difference was deemed mainly musical, the terms *cantiga* and *canción* were regarded as synonymous, and the same differences that were found in the early pair *cantiga-decir* were applied to the later pair *canción-decir*.

However, current research on medieval music shows that the relation between words and music and the correlation between poet and musician changed in the late Middle Ages. In the earlier Middle Ages, since monophonic music was notationless, it was easy for a poet to compose his or her own melodies. The increasing sophistication and complication of medieval polyphony from the middle of the fourteenth century onward made it very difficult for anyone but an expert musician to compose music. In the fifteenth century musicians interested in complex secular polyphony had professional training and were often connected to a cathedral or large church choir; the minstrels had become professional musicians.[6] In the later Middle Ages, the poet rarely set his or her own poems to music[7] and these therefore were not written to fit a preexisting melody, with the obvious exception of the contrafacta.[8] Furthermore, even evidence from earlier secular music shows that, with a few exceptions, music did not necessarily precede words.[9] Evidence of the separation of music and words can be observed as early as the thirteenth century in Alfonso X's poetry. In the later Middle Ages the union of words and music had become optional, and thus one was not a requisite for the enjoyment of the other, as they could appear together, complementing one another, or independently. All this does not mean that music was unimportant or unattached to poetry or that it does not merit study.[10] On the contrary, because of its importance, studies must take into consideration its nature as a specialized discipline.

Although there exists evidence that some *cancionero* poems were set to music, it is not clear that a *cantiga* or a *canción* was always sung, or that they were always received with musical accompaniment by the audience. To the contrary, there are a number of indications in the texts themselves which lead us to the belief that music and poetry appeared together optionally in the *cantigas* and *canciones*.

It is only rarely that rubrics of the *cantigas* in the *Cancionero de Baena* say that the poems were set to music.[11] In fact, a strong case has been made that many of the *canciones* in the *Cancionero general* were not sung.[12] Moreover, most of the Spanish *cancioneros* do not include music; and in the few that do, the name of the poet and that of the composer are usually different.[13] Unlike the Provençal poetic treatises, the Spanish poetic treatises of the time never mention music as relevant or related to writing poetry. Whereas Provençal and French poets refer constantly to "mots et sons" (words and music),[14] the *cancionero* poets do not. Although Guiraut Riquier declared that the ability to compose music for their poems was a requirement for the troubadours,[15] the same was not true for *cancionero* poets. The situation in Castile at this time has a stronger parallel in contemporary fifteenth-century France and England than in troubadour poetry of the twelfth and thirteenth centuries.[16]

Authors of musical treatises also seem to disassociate the process of writing music from that of writing poetry.[17] When the Marqués de Santillana expresses admiration for the Catalan poet Jordi de Sant Jordi, since he set his poems to music himself, Santillana implies that this was an exceptional case and worthy of note.[18] The absence of any reference to music when Juan Alfonso de Baena describes the *gaya ciencia* in the introduction to his *Cancionero* is also telling.[19] In the introductions to their respective works, Santillana, Juan del Encina, and Gómez Manrique present their poetry as something that they expect to be *read* by the person to whom they are forwarding their poems. They never mention the act of listening to their songs with music. In the early sixteenth century, Juan de Valdés gives his judgment on *cancionero* poetry from a reader's point of view.[20] Enrique de Villena explains in his *Arte de trovar* how the poems were presented during the contest to the Consistorio de la gaya ciencia in Barcelona: the contestants stood and read aloud their poems; the jury deliberated and gave the prize to the poem that was considered the least flawed according to the rules of the Consistorio; only then did the jury allow the poem to be read and *sung* publicly.[21] The music was, therefore, added afterwards and did not accompany the poem during the judgment passed on the poem or its first reception by the public. In the *Crónica del condestable Miguel Lucas de Iranzo*, the chronicler tells us that the king wished to celebrate a victory of the constable over the Moors with a poem. He ordered a ballad to be written and *then* told his chamber musicians to compose music for it.[22]

By the fifteenth century the poem had become independent from its music to such an extent that the music was in many instances optional, whether the poem was later to be sung or, indeed, recited. Together with the evidence that some of the *cantigas* and *canciones* were sung, we find that some of the long narrative poems typically intended for recitation (or private reading), such as Juan de Mena's *Trescientas* and Jorge Manrique's *Coplas*, were also sung.[23]

The passage from song to poem, from "song to book," can be observed in late medieval Castilian lyric texts and presumably also in other areas of the Iberian Peninsula.

In order to determine the features relevant to a definition of these *cancionero* genres, we must consider evidence of current reading modes in a context of the state of literacy during the period.

Although the Middle Ages have often been represented as a period in which texts were transmitted orally, in some circles the orality attributed to the whole medieval period decreased during the last centuries. Current studies show that literacy and silent reading started growing in the twelfth century and increased significantly at the end of the fourteenth and in the fifteenth centuries among members of the clergy, the nobility, and the middle class. Texts in the vernacular do not address a "reader" but a "listener" until the twelfth century.[24] Of course, as most critics caution, the change is slow and gradual through the centuries. The lower classes remained illiterate in greater numbers and were more likely to "hear" a text until much later periods, although a certain degree of literacy must be granted to them. In the same fashion, some degree of orality is also present among the more literate groups. The survival of some oral formulas in written speech may also obscure the larger extent of literacy.[25] The intellectual group of the *letrados*, some noble men and women, some members of the middle class, and the clergy, were more likely to practice silent reading—and praying—in fifteenth-century Castile. *Cancionero* poetry circulated mainly within this group, at least in the beginning: the poets sent poems to one another or to other members at their social level and held debates through poetic exchanges. The authors themselves belonged to the literate group: to cite but a few of the most representative examples, the poets Marqués de Santillana and Jorge Manrique were members of the nobility; Fray Ambrosio Montesino and Fray Iñigo López de Mendoza were men of religion; and Juan de Mena and Juan Alfonso de Baena were members of the "intellectual class," secretaries to the king. The presence of poets of a lower social extraction, such as Alfonso Alvarez de Villasandino, is evidence of the growing extent of literacy in the late Middle Ages.

The shifting terminology used in the period to refer to the act of reading and the reader reflects this increased literacy and growth in silent reading. In the fifteenth century the intended public of a work was often addressed as "reader" (*lector*), not "listener" or "hearer" (*oidor*) as in the earlier Middle Ages, and the act of reading was expressed with *leer* (to read), rather than *oir* (to hear). The difference between reading and having someone read (*leer* and *fazer leer*) is readily recognized. For example, we read in the *Cancionero de Baena:* "Yo *non leo* bien *nin escriuo* / pero que *Oy leer* / angel fuste luzifer" (I *do not read* well, *nor do I write* / although I *heard someone read* that you were an angel, Lucifer) (PN1, ID1379, lines 1–3).[26]

It is in this fashion that we must understand references to *leer* in *cancionero* poetry, such as the one found in Juan Alfonso de Baena's dedication to John II of the *cancionero* he had just compiled. Baena tells the king that he will find enjoyment and solace from all his royal worries when he *reads* the book.[27] Significantly, the references to "oir" diminish sharply in the fifteenth-century manuscript of *El libro del cavallero Zifar.*[28] Visual vocabulary was also used in the late Middle Ages to refer to the act of reception of the text not only by means of terms such as "read" but also through references to "seeing," "looking," "eyes," and similar terms. The text was often received through the eyes rather than through the ear.[29] The *Invencionario* of Alfonso de Toledo defines "reading" as "looking with the eyes": "E commo el fin dela escriptura es para que se lea & *el leer es con los ojos acatar* . . . la escriptura a nuestros *ojos* presentada faze en nuestros *ojos* & ellos padesçen lo qual es claro. pues que dello resçiben daño" (And since the purpose of writing is that it be read and *to read is to examine with the eyes* . . . writing presented to our *eyes* does something to our *eyes* and clearly makes them suffer, since from that act they are injured). The references that we find in this text and in Bernardo de Gordonio's *Lilio de medicina* to the strain that reading small letters, "leer letras mucho menudas," can cause in the eyes, also point to the visual aspect of reading.[30]

Knowing how to read visually entails first learning the alphabet: "ninguno non puede *saber leer* si primero non sabe las *letras del a.b.c.*"[31] (no one can *know how to read* if they first do not know the *letters of the alphabet*). Reading is an acquired skill, which, therefore, must be taught and learned. Thus the references to teaching reading: "maestros que *enseñavan a sus fijos leer escrevyr* e fablar"[32] (teachers that *taught their children to read, write* and speak) and to learning or knowing how to read. As early as the thirteenth century in the *Siete Partidas*, knowing how to read silently is important for the king because of its political value: "Acuçioso deue el rey ser en aprender los saberes. ca por ellos entendera las cosas de rays & sabra meior obrar en ellas. & otrosi por *saber leer* sabra meior guardar sus poridades & ser señor dellas lo que de otra guisa no podria bien fazer"[33] (The king should be diligent in acquiring knowledge, for in that way he will understand the responsibilities of kings and will better know how to deal with them. And furthermore, by *knowing how to read* he will know better how to guard his secrets and be master of them, which he would not be able to do well in another manner).

Crucially, we find similar references in poetry from an early date. In the thirteenth century, poetry was often transmitted as a written text and therefore *read*. Because a poem was distributed and received as a written piece, it could "indelibly" tarnish the reputation of the ones who might be the butt of a poem. This is reflected in the legislature of the time. Thus in the *Siete Partidas*:

> Ley terçera. de la desonrra que faze un onbre a otro por canticas o por rimos
>
> Infaman & desonrran unos a otros non tan sola mente por palabras, mas aun *por escripturas* faziendo *cantigas* o rymos. o *deytados* malos de los que han sabor de enfamar. Esto fazen a las vegadas paladina mente. & a las vegadas encubierta mente echando aquellos *escriptos* malos en las casas de los grandes señores. o en las iglesias. o en las plaças comunales de las cibdades & de las villas. por que cada uno lo podria *leer.* (378r)
>
> (Third law: of the dishonor that one man does to another by *canticas* or *rimos*
>
> They defame and dishonor one another not only with words but also by *writings,* using offensive *cantigas, rymos,* or *deytados* of the kind that malign. This they sometimes do publicly and sometimes secretly, placing these offensive *writings* on the houses of great men, in the churches, or in the community plazas in the cities and towns so that everyone could *read* them.)

In fifteenth-century *cancionero* poetry we find references to seeing a text and calling on the reader's gaze, unambiguous references to the silent and visual reader. Thus in the *Coronación* by Juan de Mena: "espresare *por escripto* . . . por que tu *lector* tasonbres" (to express *in writing* . . . so you, *reader*, will be in awe) (PN13, ID0156, lines 48, 50), and in his *Laberinto de Fortuna:* "Las quales pasando conçedan *lectores* / Perdon a mi mano sy non son *escriptas*" (Passing those matters, I ask the *readers* to grant / pardon to my hand if they are not *written*) (PN5, ID0092, lines 287–88); Santillana in *Bias contra fortuna:* "Ya sea que los loores / en propia lengua ensordezcan / y por ventura me enpezcan / en *ojos* de los *lectores* / muy lexos de vanagloria" (Now it may be that praises / in one's own tongue become deafening / and by chance work to my detriment / in the *eyes* of the *readers* / very far from vainglory) (PN13, ID0148, lines 993–97); and Fernán Pérez de Guzmán: "*mira* discreto *lector* / qual es mas util dotrina" (*Look*, intelligent *reader* / which is a more useful doctrine) (PN5, ID0072, lines 2503–4). Francisco Vaca, poet of the *Cancionero general,* writes a composition against Antón de Montoro, because, he says, he could not believe his eyes when he *saw* the latter's *canción* praising Queen Isabel I and comparing her to the Virgin Mary: "Una cançion vuestra *vi*" (I *saw* a canción of yours). And afterwards, "De *leerla* muy cansado / con mil pensamientos tristes / yo quedo mucho turbado" (Very tired of *reading it* / with a thousand sad thoughts / I remain very disturbed) (11CG, ID6104, lines 1, 80–82). Similar references to the visual perception of other compositions, such as *coplas,* are also common (see for example the poems' rubrics in MH2, ID3100, ID3101, and ID3120).

It is true that references to *oir* are still found in the texts in the period, but the overwhelming development is the growing pervasiveness of *leer,* specially when found in specific contexts. Page setup became more visual: each verse was written on a separate line, paragraphs and poems were clearly marked, and rubrics and indices were provided, all of which also point to a private reader.[34] Scribes began to copy the poem not in the form of uninterrupted lines of text, in the form of prose, as it was customary until the fourteenth century, but rather in the form of verse, in which each verse is copied on a different line in the manuscript. This form of copying verse, generally adopted in the fifteenth century, was already considered outdated by some by the middle of the fourteenth century. In the *Cancionero de Baena* we find some remains of the hesitancy between the two systems, though the second one prevails in the extant manuscript. Although part of a different textual tradition, this hesitancy is similar to the one found in some epic texts, such as the *Mocedades de Rodrigo* so lucidly studied by Deyermond.[35] Later *cancioneros* are firmly grounded in the second system. As O'Keeffe has shown, the difference between the two models of transcription is closely related to the transition through the Middle Ages from orality to literacy, from an aural reception of the poem to a visual one, and from an oral to a written culture. The more importance and attention paid to the spatialization of the text inside the manuscript, the more literate and less oral is the culture within which it appears.[36] Juan Alfonso de Baena explains that he is providing a table of contents to his book so that the king and the members of his court can easily find the *cantigas* and *decires* that they would like to *read*.[37]

There are other innovations in the layout of the page that point to the "visual poetics" brought by heightened textuality and silent readership of this poetry. In a similar vein, in his *Universal vocabulario* Alfonso de Palencia explains textual devices that help the silent reader: "Hay otras señales en los libros que se ponen de fuera en las margines. para que do quier quel *lector* fallare la tal señal aya recurso al texto: & sepa la exposiçion de lo escripto: o del verso o quier que fallare otra señal de aquella semeiança"[38] (There are other signs in books that are placed outside in the margins, so that wherever the *reader* finds such a sign he may refer to the text and know the meaning of what is written, or of the verse; or wherever he may find another sign of that kind).

The strong tendency in the late Middle Ages toward silent and private discourse is also manifested in the shift to a different mode of praying, represented as silent and visual in the rubrics of late medieval books of hours. The iconography of reading and praying also changes to reflect the new reading mode. In addition, textual evidence of manuscript transmission suggests, as in the Spanish case, that poems were often intended for silent individual reading and more often had a written rather than an oral transmission.[39]

If music did not have an ancillary role in relation to poetry, and thus did not consistently operate as a genre designator during the act of poetic composition and reception, and if textual and contextual evidence points to silent and private reading, then other concerns, such as rhetorical and metrical ones, must have been the keys in creating the distinction between genres. Metrical and thematic differences between the two genres have already been noted,[40] but cannot account for all the differences among the texts. A promising avenue can be found in analyzing the terminology found in the rubrics and the poems in the *Cancionero de Baena*. When presenting the *cantigas* and *decires* in the introduction to his *cancionero* and in his rubrics to the poems, Baena describes the *cantigas* as *bien escandidas* (well scanned), and the *decires* also as *bien escandidos*, and *limados* (polished) as well.⁴¹ The concept of *limar* (to polish) is linked to the use of the *colores rhetorici* in the Latin rhetorical treatises.⁴² Thus, a higher incidence of rhetorical figures described in the Latin treatises might serve as one key distinction between *decires* and *cantigas*.

The terminology used to describe the *decires* does indeed signal a relation with medieval rhetoric. In fact, the actual meaning of the word *decir*, because of its current—and medieval—meaning in Castilian, has obscured its generic and rhetorical implications. In medieval texts, *decir* not only means "to say," "to state" but also serves as an equivalent to the terms *dictado* (also *deytado*) and *dictar*. *Dictado* consistently appears with the meaning of "poetic composition," and *dictar* with that of "to write poetry." Therefore, the same two meanings are found in *decir*. These meanings were evident to medieval writers, as is seen in medieval texts and vocabularies. Thus, the terms are closely related, for example, in Alfonso de Palencia's *Universal vocabulario:* "Dico ... & dictamen co<m>posiçion co<n> palabras plazenteras ... & del verbo dico vien<e> dicto.tas. Dictare es apuesta mente co<m>poner o escriuir" (*Dico ...* and *dictamen:* composition with pleasing words ... and from the verb *dico* comes *dicto, dictas. Dictare* is to compose or write elegantly), and in Santaella's *Vocabulario eclesiástico:* "Dicto.ctas. frequentatiuo de dico.cis Por dezir a menudo o dezir ordenadamente o componer escriptura"⁴³ (Dicto, dictas, frequentative of *dico, dicis:* To say frequently, to say in an orderly fashion, or to compose writing).

As evidenced by these definitions, the terms *dictado* and *dictar* reveal a relation with medieval *dictamen* and its art of writing pleasingly, "con palabras plazenteras," "apuestamente," "ordenadamente," following rhetorical precepts. It then follows that just as *dictamen* derives from *dicto, dictare,* so *dictado* comes from *dictar,* and *decir,* understood in its rhetorical sense, is used as the equivalent of *dictar* and *dictado*.⁴⁴ While *dictamen* is currently understood as the theory of prose letter-writing, in the treatises of *ars dictaminis* the term is used in the wider sense of "the whole of writing." And though instances where it designates exclusively "prose composition" can be identified, the *artes dictaminales* actually enumerate three types of *dictamen:* prose, rhythmic verse, and metrical verse. The authors of dictaminal treatises usually state that in their work they will only concern themselves with prose *dictamen,* and more specifically with the epistolary genre.⁴⁵ Therefore, *dictamen* may mean either poetic or prose composition. It is found in the sense of "poetic composition" both in Latin and, most often, in the vernaculars, with terms such as *dittato, dictats, dictié, dictado*.⁴⁶ Unfortunately the various studies on medieval Latin *dictamen* have not included the latter sense. The integrated study of both types of *dictamen* would help produce a deeper understanding not only of medieval dictaminal theory, but also of Latin and Romance rhetoric and poetic.

Dictamen relates to poetry because of the medieval tendency for dictaminal theory to be identified with rhetoric and for rhetoric and grammar, and thus the *ars poetriae*, to appropriate one another's field of competence. Teachers of rhetoric and grammar took over each other's discipline in their teaching and in their writing of prescriptive manuals.[47] In order to formulate the distinction between *cantiga/canción* and *decir* correctly, the dictaminal origin of the *decir* must be correctly traced and understood. The root distinction between the two might reveal a Latin rhetorical source for the *decir* and a vernacular origin for the *canción*, which might in turn explain the well-known "learned" character of the *decir;* a close relation of the *decir* to *dictamen* (see below) and of *canción* to *ars poetriae;* or a connection of each genre to a different level of rhetoric, of *decir* to *ornatus difficilis* and of *cantiga* to *ornatus facilis,* perhaps conveying "socio-poetic" differences similar to the ones that have been proposed to differentiate *vers* and *canso,* or any of these explanations in combination.[48] There is also a need for further studies relating to the analysis of the two terms as an operative pair through several centuries and of the pair's evolution as such, since it is already found in earlier texts, including one of Heloise's letters to Abelard, where she uses the pair *dictandi-cantandi* ("dictandi videlicet et cantandi gratia").[49] The study of the change in the nature of the generic designations of both terms as members of a pair and the shifts in meaning across languages and centuries is needed in order to fully understand their nature as well as their intersections.

It follows from its use in medieval texts that *decir* does not necessarily mean "to recite" or "to read aloud." Both *dictado* and *decir* are found designating "poetic composition" until the end of the Middle Ages. During the same period we find the verbs *dictar* and *decir* meaning "the act of writing poetry" (see above). Although all these terms are found at all times, *dictado* and *dictar* seem to have been favored until around the middle of the fourteenth century, when *decir* began to replace the other terms, then prevailed until around the middle of the fifteenth century. Evidence in support of this conclusion will be marshaled below; notice in particular the references to *leer* and *ver* in these examples.

In the thirteenth century the *Libro de Alexandre* uses *dictado* to refer to a poem: "qui lo uersifico fue ome bien letrado, / ca puso grant razon en poco de *ditado*"[50] (He who versified it was a well-lettered man, / and put so much thought in so little *ditado*). Alfonso X also uses the term with the same meaning profusely in his *Siete Partidas:* "por *cantigas* o por *rimas* o por *ditados*" (378v) (through *cantigas, rimas,* or *ditados*) (see other examples below).

In the fourteenth century, in his *Libro de buen amor,* Juan Ruiz, Archpriest of Hita, talks about including some *ditados* in his book, which, he states, is a sampler of different types of poetic compositions: "E conpóselo otrosí a dar algunos leçión e muestra de metrificar e rimar e de trobar; ca trobas e notas e rimas e *ditados* e versos fiz conplidamente, segund que esta çiençia requiere"[51] (141–44) (And furthermore I composed it to give lesson and example of *metrificar, rimar,* and of *trobar* to some; because I made these *trobas, notas, rimas, ditados,* and *versos* perfectly, as this science requires). He calls one of his poems a *ditado:* "a onrra de la virgen ofreçile este *ditado*" (in honor of the Virgin I offered her this *ditado*) (S1044-d). Pero López de Ayala uses the same term to introduce two of his poems in his *Rimado de Palacio:* "e por estar más firme, fize otro *deitado*"[52] (and to be more firm, I made another *deitado*), "a la cual muy deuoto, conpuse este *deitado*" (to whom I am very devout, I composed this *deitado*) (878c). In the *Cancionero de Baena,* Alfonso Alvarez de Villasandino refers to one of his poems with the same term, although the rubric calls it a *dezir:* "Yo vn vuestro natural / vos presento este *deitado*" (I, your servant, / present you this *deitado*) (PN1, ID1199, lines 5–6). In his answer to a poem written by Fray Lope del Monte in a debate on a theological matter, Diego Martínez de Medina calls Fray Lope's poem a *deytado:* "Non queriendo Replicar / vuestro *escripto* prolongado / contrallando tal *deytado*" (Not wanting to respond to / your lengthy *escripto* / contradicting such a *deytado*) (PN1, ID1451, lines 9–11). All of these poems appear under the rubric of *decir.* Juan Alfonso de Baena criticizes the art of Diego de Estúñiga, using the term *deitar* as meaning the act of writing poetry: "En buytrago o en villena / aprendiste El *deytar*" (In Buitrago or in Villena / you learned to *deytar*) (PN1, ID1553, lines 46–47). Fray Alfonso de la Monja states in response to a *decir* by Imperial: "En *ditado* apuesto, muy imperial / denuestas, Françisco, atán sin razón" (In an elegant *ditado,* very imperiously / you insult, Francisco, with no reason) (PN1, ID1380, lines 1–2). The same term is used to refer to the poetic *decir* in other compositions of the *Cancionero de Baena:* "que de otro fablan por las callejas / sino vuestros *deitados* d'aquesta caida" (they don't talk about anything else in the streets, but your *deitados* regarding this fall) (PN1, ID1267, lines 7–8).

Well into the fifteenth century *dictado* is still used. Juan de Mena calls his poem to the king a *dictado:* "Otu Rey questas *leyendo* / este mi simple *dictado*" (O king, who are *reading* / this, my simple *dictado*) (NH2, ID2389, lines 1–2). The marqués de Santillana, when discussing classical poetry in his *Prohemio,* talks about "aquellos *dictados* a que los poetas bucólicos llamaron"[53] (those *dictados,* called bucolic by the poets). Enrique de Villena mentions Santillana's enjoyment in writing poetry: "E quise dirigir este tratado a vos, honorable e virtuoso cavallero don Iñigo López de Mendoça . . . que vos delectaes en fazer *ditados y trobas*"[54] (And I wanted to direct this treatise to you, honorable and virtuous gentleman don Iñigo López de Mendoça . . . since you delight in making *ditados y trobas*). We also find *dictar* as the act of poem writing in Fernán Pérez de Guzmán: "David el santo cantor / asy lo quiso *dictar*" (David, the cantor saint, / thus wanted to *dictar*) (PN5, ID0072, lines 611–12).

Besides being used in cancionero rubrics to designate a poetic genre, *decir* may be found within the poetic composition itself, alternating with *dictado* to designate the poem. For example in the *Cancionero de Baena* we find: "Tienpo ha que he *leydo* / & sabido / vn *dezir* bien acoplado" (It has been a while since I have *read* / and known / a *dezir* in well-written stanzas) (PN1, ID1454, lines 1–3) in the same composition with *deitado* and *deitar:* "que leystes su *deytado*" (that you read his *deitado*) (PN1, ID1454, line 180), "Non yaze en *deitar* nota" (there is no note in *deitar*) (PN1, ID1454, line 13). *Decir* is used as a verb, often accompanied by the adverb *bien,* to mean "the act of writing poetry." It is often found associated with other verbs that carry a similar meaning, such as *trovar* or *cantar* or related terms. Thus, a poet can *decir cantares, canciones, trobas,* or even *decires* or *dictados,* as well as *coplas.* We find this usage already in the thirteenth century in the *Siete Partidas,* where King Alfonso X speaks against "*dezir* rymos nin *deytados*" (*dezir* rhymed verse nor *deytados*) if they are to tarnish someone's reputation (378r). In the fourteenth century, in the *Libro de buen amor, decir* is found with the same meaning: "Salvo en la manera del *trobar* e del *dezir*" (Save in the manner of *trobar* and of *dezir*) (S45-4); "siempre *dezir cantar* de tus loores" (always *dezir cantar* of your praises) (S1678-2), and also in the *Cancionero de Baena:* "Fablar de escripturas quando contesçiere / yo non contradigo con lengua sepista / nin yo manoscabo al que *bien dixere*" (To speak of writings when it is fitting / I do not contradict with an authoritative tongue / nor do I discredit him who *bien dixere*) (PN1, ID1407, lines 17–19). In the fifteenth century Fernán Pérez de Guzmán writes about "la corporal fortaleza / el apuesto Razonar / del palaçio la destreza / tan\<n\>er dezir e cantar" (the corporeal strength / the elegant reasoning / the dexterity of the palace / to *play music, dezir, and cantar*) (PN2, ID0038, lines 261–64). Santillana uses the expression in the same sense when he is making a judgment on the good poets of Castile: "En este Reyno de Castilla *dixo bien* el Rey don Alfonso el sabio, e yo *ui* quien *vio* dezires suyos" (In this kingdom of Castile, King don Alfonso the Wise *dixo bien,* and I know people who have *seen* his *dezires*), and "Alfonso Gonçales de Castro . . . *dixo asaz bien* e fizo estas cançiones" (Alfonso Gonçales de Castro . . . *dixo bien* and made these *canciones*). In his *Prohemio,* he also talks about "*dezir cantares.*"⁵⁵

Dictado, as an antecedent of *decir,* also appears coupled with *cantiga* in the sense of poetic composition. Thus in the *Siete Partidas* we find references to "malas cantigas o ditados" (328v), "malas cantigas & malos ditados" (408r), and expressions such as "por razon de cantiga o por razon de ditado" (by reason of *cantiga* or by reason of *ditado*) (329v), "por cantigas o por rimas o por ditados" (by *cantigas,* by *rimas,* or by *ditados*) (378v), and the like (378r, 380v, 408r).

The *dictamen* professional was a *dictator;* therefore the composer of *dictados* was a *dictador* as well, while the composer of *decires* was a *dezidor.* These two terms, *dictador* and *decidor,* were equivalent and generally meant "poet." In the *Primera crónica general:* "Et segund el latin nuestro et ell arte de la rectorica, que es el saber de fablar apuestamientre, *dictador tanto quiere dezir cuemo dezidor, que dize mucho et todauia bien et apuesto*" (And according to our Latin and the art of rhetoric, which is knowing how to properly speak, *dictador* means the same as *dezidor,* who says much while still being proper and elegant). In the *Morales de Ovidio:* "orfeo significa el predicador o el doctor o señor o *los cantares de palabras dictador*" (Orpheus means the preacher, doctor, lord, or *dictador of the cantares of words*) (176r).⁵⁶

The implications of this genealogy have to be further explored, since it links certain types of professionals—lawyers, secretaries to the king, and others—to poetry. And in fact, many of the better known poets in medieval Spanish literature held such positions: Gonzalo de Berceo was a notary; Juan Alfonso de Baena and Juan de Mena were secretaries to the king. The same link may be found in other literatures.⁵⁷ Going one step further, one must also consider the close relation of the *dictatores* and their literary interests and politics to those of their successors and the intellectual élite of the later Middle Ages and the Renaissance, the humanists, and the change in poetic taste and in the concept of poetry that the fifteenth century underwent.⁵⁸

❖

Another consequence of overlooking rhetorical considerations and viewing music's role as ancillary to poetry as the determining factor in genre distinctions is the lack of attention that has been paid to the chronological changes of genre labels in the poems' rubrics, since performance and reading mode were thought to be a main characteristic in creating genre distinctions, and those notions were deemed unchanged until the very end of the period. The opposition between *cantiga/canción* and *decir* is often applied to the whole range of *cancionero* poetry from the late fourteenth to the early sixteenth century.[59] The term *cantiga* appears only in the *Cancionero de Baena*, while *canción* appears in the rest of the later *cancioneros* and is applied to compositions that are formally different from the *cantigas*. In spite of this, since both *cantigas* and *canciones* were said to be sung, the two terms have been consistently considered interchangeable.[60] Moreover, the term *decir* gains wider use over *dictado* around the second half of the fourteenth century and is no longer used in rubrics around the second half of the fifteenth century, when it disappears and the term *coplas* prevails.[61] At this time we can no longer talk about *canciones y decires*, since, as Argote de Molina perceived some years later, the two main genres had become *canciones* and *coplas*.[62]

The typical characterization of *cancionero* genres as either *canción* or *decir* must then be modified to reflect the chronological evolution of these terms. Since we find *cantiga/cantar* and *dictado* in the thirteenth and fourteenth centuries in the works of Alfonso X, in the *Libro de buen amor*, and the *Rimado de Palacio*, and since we have established the relation of *dictado* and *decir*, the chronological transformations of the genre system become more elaborate and interesting. The chronology can be set forth roughly as follows:

1. *Cantiga* (or *cantar*) versus *dictado*, in the thirteenth century and until the last quarter of the fourteenth, as found in Alfonso X, the *Libro de buen amor*, and the *Rimado de Palacio*;
2. *cantiga* versus *decir*, at the end of the fourteenth century and the beginning of the fifteenth, attested in the *Cancionero de Baena*;
3. *canción* versus *decir*, in the last decades of the first half of the fifteenth century, for example in the *Cancionero de Palacio*;
4. *canción* versus *coplas*, in the second half of the fifteenth century and beginning of the sixteenth, for example in the *Cancionero General*.[63]

The trajectory of the terminology of these genres supports the idea that the *Libro de buen amor* and the *Rimado de Palacio* were individual *cancioneros* that could show the origin of *cancionero* poetry through an older Castilian tradition. Further research needs to be done in the area from this perspective.

We also need to take into consideration the fact that genre labels were not applied systematically. Many compositions do not have a genre label or appear under different labels depending on the manuscript. This is the case with Jorge Manrique's famous "*Coplas* por la muerte de su padre," which first appeared under the name of *Decir*.[64] Both titles, *coplas* and *decir*, often appear in the same manuscript and can appear in the works of the same poet. Presumably *coplas* would indicate a poem written or rubricated at a later date. Even though Santillana's consistent use in his prose *Prohemio* of the pair "canciones y decires" to refer to his own poetry and that of other poets is one important reason why those two genres have come to be known as the main *cancionero* genres, Santillana's labeling of his own works does not follow the pattern. In the original manuscript of his works (Salamanca: Universitaria, 2655, SA8), out of the ninety-two poems compiled, only three are labeled *decir* and only two are called *coplas*. The rest of the compositions belong to different genres—sixteen of them are *canciones*—or do not have any genre title at all. Two of the few manuscripts that are consistent in their genre labeling of *cantigas* versus *decires* and *canciones* versus *decires* are the *Cancionero de Baena* and *Cancionero de Palacio*, which have become "model" *cancioneros* even though for many reasons they are more like exceptions.[65]

This discussion and the established differentiation between *cantigas/canciones* and *decires* should not obscure the presence and nature of other lyric genres in *cancionero* poetry and their growth through the fifteenth century. Through the second half of the fifteenth century, the formal differences among the genres become more and more identified with their metrical profile. After the first half of the fifteenth century, genre labels are applied only to those poems that have a more fixed metrical scheme, such as the *canciones, villancicos, romances, esparsas, letras de justadores, motes*, and *glosas*. The poems that were not constrained by a certain metrical form seem to fall under the simple category of *coplas*, a term that one rarely finds in the earlier *cancioneros*.[66] Although the term *coplas* is generally used as a non-genre label that simply means "stanza," there is a need for further study of its poetics and its possible use in the second half of the fifteenth century as a genre designator.

The reasons behind the change in genre designators from the thirteenth to the sixteenth centuries are highly relevant, since they are related to the shifts in hegemonic rhetorical theories.[67] The predominance of dictaminal theory as the rhetorical theory of prestige explains the use of terminology such as *dictado, dictar,* and *dictador* when referring to poetry, the art of poetic composition, and the poet. The advent of humanism entails a major change toward Ciceronian rhetoric in its original form, which replaced *dictamen* as the theory of prestige. Several factors had a strong impact on the renewal of Ciceronian-inspired rhetorical theory. One of them was the discovery of new rhetorical texts, such as the Ciceronian *Brutus, Orator,* and *De oratore,* and the complete version of Quintilian's *Institutio oratoria*. Rhetoric, understood in its classical sense, took the place thus far occupied by *dictamen* and became a central point in the humanist movement.

The loss of prestige of *dictamen* has also been linked with the reform in rhetorical instruction that took place toward the end of the medieval period and with the slow but steady changes in poetry effected by poets like Petrarch. The "new" rhetoric was defined as the "ars bene dicendi," following Quintilian's definition in his *De Institutione oratoria* (2.17.37). The shift in terminology that accompanied the change in rhetorical theory and culture is apparent: the *dictado* written following the laws of *dictamen* was replaced by the *decir* inspired in the new *ars dicendi*. Although the defense of poetry figured as a central tenet of humanism, it wasn't until the latter was well established that poetry emancipated itself from its role as a subordinate of rhetoric. This second phase in which poetry gained its independence brought forth the disappearance of the term *decir* in favor of *coplas,* which no longer implied a relation to rhetoric's *ars dicendi* but to poetics in a narrower sense. Universities had been instrumental in the development and establishment of *ars dicendi* as a prestigious rhetorical theory, and they played a similarly important role in the acceptance of the "new rhetoric" in their curriculum. The humanists succeeded the *dictatores* as the intellectual elite. A chair of rhetoric first appeared in the university curriculum in Salamanca between 1405 and 1408, whereas the teaching of poetry began there later, around 1430. The new prescriptive treatises, such as those by Manzanares, Serra, and Martín de Córdoba reveal the shift in rhetorical theory, which had distanced itself from medieval *dictamen*, still the theory of choice in earlier treatises such as the *Summa rhetorice*. It must be underscored that the process was not one of mere substitution of one theory for the other, but rather one in which the close connection and similarities of the different hegemonic rhetorics gave way to shifts within the continuity of a system. This raises many specific issues, such as those regarding the cultural and political preeminence of the intellectual elite of the *dictatores* and their successors, the humanists, particularly since both groups occupied similar posts, both inside the university—in the chairs of grammar and rhetoric—and outside.

In summary, heretofore the distinction between the so-called two main *cancionero* genres in the fifteenth century has been based on whether or not they incorporate music. Since it appears to be clear that music and poetry did not play an ancillary role with respect to one another, and since the state of late medieval literacy and polyphony presents a strong case for the likelihood that this poetry was often read silently, scholars should seek genre differences in the poems' rhetorical and metrical features, while they research the rhetorical background of each genre. Moreover, the distinction between the two genres collapses on the basis of chronology as well. There are no *canciones* in the *Cancionero de Baena,* and the term *decir* disappears during the second half of the fifteenth century. The genre differences found in the histories of literature must, then, be revised in order to reflect the distinctions that were operative in the late Middle Ages, while at the same time we must present those distinctions in a chronologically faithful manner.

The disarticulation of the bases upon which former genre definitions were built enables a renewed study of genre and opens up new areas of research. Scholarship needs to emphasize the fundamental fluidity and instability of generic identity and the close interdependence between genres and their cultural context. Changes in genre formation point to related transformations in the cultural environment in which they grow, and conversely, shifts in genre labeling and evolution call attention to new developments in their intellectual milieu. Lyric genres should therefore not be considered in a textual vacuum, untouched by larger trends in ideas, culture, and society. The analysis of the shifts in genre designators developed here calls attention to the fact that those changes are significant and do not occur randomly or without a reason. They are not mere substitutions of new names, but respond to important innovations in literary theory and the context in which they develop.

The textual framework that must be considered key to changes in romance lyric genres is not only that of the vernacular but also that of contemporaneous Latin literature. The study of genre theory should, therefore, benefit from an approach that looks at both literatures in their—sometimes complex—intersections, and not as essentially separate genres in a hierarchical relation. This becomes even more clear if one looks at the number of influential authors writing in the vernacular within lyric genre conventions who were at the same time learned in the Latin tradition. In this regard, it is esential to consider the process of substitution of the vernacular for Latin that gradually takes place during the Middle Ages and is solidly established in the fifteenth century.[68] This "vernacularization" entails an appropriation of the Latin hegemonic discourse and its cultural privilege by the vernacular, as is evident within academic circles.

From the point of view of *cancionero* studies, one can no longer maintain the old approach that dismissed *cancionero* poets as a mere group of noble *dilettanti* irrevocably anchored in a medieval tradition that had become mummified and staunchly opposed to the breadth of new ideas brought by humanism. The charged value judgment implied by this view, according to which everything related to the medieval period appears negative and all that is connected to humanism and the Renaissance seems positive, is untenable, as is the sharply drawn periodization that this point of view defends. A brief look at the rhetorical and poetic theory of the time through their genres, together with evidence from the cultural environment of the period that presents many *cancionero* authors closely related to the sources of new esthetic and intellectual trends, questions that assertion and supports a view of genre constitution as something more fluid and permeable to complex influences stemming from the literary and cultural environment than has been defended in the past.

NOTES

1. See, for example, Francisco López Estrada, *Introducción a la literatura medieval española* (Madrid: Gredos, 1952), 396. For a further discussion of some of the ideas presented in this essay, see my "Cantar decires y decir canciones: género y lectura de la poesía castellana cuatrocentista," *Bulletin of Hispanic Studies* 76 (1999): 169–87.

2. H. R. Lang, "Las formas estróficas y términos métricos del *Cancionero de Baena*," in *Estudios eruditos in memoriam de Adolfo Bonilla y San Martín (1875–1926)* (Madrid: Imprenta Viuda e hijos de Jaime Rates, 1927), 485–523, at 505–6.

3. Pierre Le Gentil, *La poésie lyrique espagnole et portugaise à la fin du Moyen Age,* vol. 2: *Les formes* (Rennes: Plihon, 1952), 305–9. "Toutefois, si la chanson n'était plus ce qu'elle était aux origines, elle restait du moins une *chanson;* elle était normalement écrite et composée pour être *chantée*" (305). Le Gentil summarized his views in "Trayectoria de los cancioneros," in *Historia y crítica de la literatura española*, vol. 1: *Edad Media,* ed. Alan Deyermond (Barcelona: Crítica, 1980), 310–15. The important contribution and reputation of Lang and Le Gentil's work to the field, together with the lack of studies contradicting them, led later critics to accept these ideas without question. Dorothy Clotelle Clarke follows Le Gentil's explanation of the genres and their relation to music; see *Morphology of Fifteenth Century Castilian Verse* (Pittsburgh: Duquesne University Press, 1964), 42–45. Following Le Gentil, R. O. Jones and Carolyn R. Lee believe that the *cantiga/canción* is a musical genre not only for Juan del Encina, but for other poets as well, stating with Le Gentil that Villasandino set his own poems to music (*Poesía lírica y cancionero musical, Juan del Encina* [Madrid: Castalia, 1972], 8). Since Jones and Lee do not give the corresponding citation in the *Cancionero de Baena,* one must assume that they were thinking of the rubrics of a series of four cantigas by Villasandino that were sung before the town council in Seville (Brian Dutton and Joaquín González Cuenca, eds., *Cancionero de Juan Alfonso de Baena* [Madrid: Visor, 1993], ID1172, ID1173, ID1174, ID1175). The information is given by the rubrics of the four poems, all of which make statements similar to this: "Esta cantiga fizo Alfonso Alvarez a la dicha cibdat de Sevilla e fízogela cantar otra Navidat con juglares" (Alfonso Alvarez made this *cantiga* in the city of Seville and had it sung one Christmas with jongleurs) (ID 1174). It is not said, though, that Villasandino had composed the music, and the statement itself points rather to the exceptional character of a musicated performance; see Manuel Alvar, "La 'nueva maestría' y las rúbricas del *Cancionero de Baena,*" in *Miscellanea di studi in onore di Aurelio Roncaglia* (Modena: Mucchi, 1989), 1:17–18. Tomás Navarro Tomás also seems to accept the musical argument as a consideration for a

better understanding of the poem, whether problematic, as in the case of verse-length "irregularities," or not; see his *Métrica española* (Barcelona: Labor, 1991), 140–46. See also Alvaro Alonso, ed., *Poesía de cancionero* (Madrid: Cátedra, 1986), 26; Rudolf Baehr, *Manual de versificación española* (Madrid: Gredos, 1970), 114; Rafael Lapesa, *Los decires narrativos del Marqués de Santillana* (Madrid: Real Academia Española, 1954), 14; Lapesa, *La obra literaria del Marqués de Santillana* (Madrid: Insula, 1957), 21–23; and Francisca Vendrell de Millás, ed., *El cancionero de Palacio* (Barcelona: Consejo Superior de Investigaciones Científicas, 1945), 95–96.

4. See also Claudine Potvin, *Illusion et pouvoir: la poétique du Cancionero de Baena* (Montreal: Bellarmin, 1989), 65.

5. "Pero para ser enteramente justos, hay que poner esta poesía en su marco propio, y hacernos cargo de que los contemporáneos no la vieron como nosotros, en las rancias páginas de un códice donde se ha tornado letra muerta, sino rodeada de todos los prestigios que podían ofrecer las fiestas y saraos de una corte magnífica y ostentosa, en que estas poesías no se leían, sino que se cantaban, salvando sin duda lo gracioso del tono la insignificancia de la letra" (But to be entirely just one must place this poetry in its proper setting, and realize that the contemporaries did not see it as we do, in the stale pages of a manuscript where it has become dead letters, but surrounded by all of the delights that the festivals and dances of a magnificent and ostentatious court could offer, in which these poems were not read, but sung, with the gracefulness of the tune undoubtedly making up for the insignificance of the words) (Marcelino Menéndez y Pelayo, *Antología de poetas líricos castellanos* [Santander: Aldus, 1944], 5:xxiii). See also Romeu i Figueras's statement in n. 7, below. Similarly, C. S. Lewis thought that the only way to make the "drabness" of late medieval English lyric appealing was to think it accompanied by music and female charms; see his *English Literature in the Sixteenth Century, Excluding Drama* (Oxford: Clarendon Press, 1954), 222.

6. See Robert Murrell Stevenson, *Spanish Music in the Age of Columbus* (Westport, Connecticut: Hyperion, 1960), 50–306; for more on Spanish late medieval music, see Higini Anglés, *La música en la corte de los reyes católicos*, vol. 1: *Polifonía religiosa*, Monumentos de la Música Española, vol. 1 (Madrid: Consejo Superior de Investigaciones Científicas, 1941), and Higini Anglés, *La música en la corte de los reyes católicos*, vols. 2 and 3: *Polifonía profana: Cancionero musical de Palacio (Siglos XV–XVI)*, Monumentos de la Música Española, vols. 5, 10 (Barcelona: Consejo Superior de Investigaciones Científicas, 1947, 1951). For England see Julia Boffey, *Manuscripts of English Courtly Love Lyrics in the Later Middle Ages* (Dover, N.H.: D. S. Brewer, 1985), 87–112; also M. B. Parkes, "The Literacy of the Laity," in *Scribes, Scripts and Readers: Studies in the Communication, Presentation, and Dissemination of Medieval Texts* (London: Hambledon, 1991), 275–97, at 296.

7. On the relation of words and music in the late Middle Ages, see Rebecca A. Baltzer, Thomas Cable, and James I. Wimsatt, eds., *The Union of Words and Music in Medieval Poetry* (Austin: University of Texas Press, 1991), particularly James I. Wimsatt and Thomas Cable's introduction (1–14), and Lawrence Earp, "Lyrics for Reading and Lyrics for Singing in Late Medieval France: The Development of the Dance Lyric from Adam de la Halle to Guillaume de Machaut," 101–31; James Anderson Winn, *Unsuspected Eloquence: A History of the Relations between Poetry and Music* (New Haven: Yale University Press, 1981), 74–121; Claude V. Palisca, "Humanism and

Music," in *Renaissance Humanism: Foundation, Forms, and Legacy,* ed. Albert Rabil, Jr., vol. 3: *Humanism and the Disciplines* (Philadelphia: University of Pennsylvania Press, 1988), 450–85, at 471–72. In the Spanish Renaissance music followed words and the separation between poet and musician was complete. See Carmen Valcárcel, "La realización musical de la poesía renacentista," *Edad de oro* 7 (1988): 143–59. Josep Romeu i Figueras notes the disassociation between words and music in the *Cancionero musical de Palacio* and doubts that the relation between the two is as tight as it was thought to be in the previous decades: "Cada día creemos menos que la relación entre la música y texto sea lo cerrada, constante e inconmovible que pretende la metodología de ciertas escuelas de anteguerra" (Every day we believe less that the relationship between music and text is a closed one, unyielding and immobile, as the methodology of certain prewar schools claimed) (*La música en la corte de los Reyes Católicos,* vol. 4: *Cancionero musical de Palacio 3,* part 1: *Introducción y estudio de los textos,* Monumentos de la Música Española, vol. 14-1 [Barcelona: Consejo Superior de Investigaciones Científicas, 1965], 135, also 201). For early Spanish monophony and the polyphony in musical *cancioneros,* see Stevenson, *Spanish Music,* and entries "Spain" and "Sources, MS" in Stanley Sadie, ed., *The New Grove Dictionary of Music and Musicians* (London: Macmillan, 1980), vol. 17.

8. In *cancionero* poetry the poems that are supposed to be sung to a preexisting tune are a clearly marked group. These poems are generally introduced by a rubric indicating their nature as contrafacta, such as: "cántese al tono de" (sung to the tune of). In the beginning of the sixteenth century, these compositions may also be found in prints with the rubric "coplas para cantar." These "coplas" had an initial refrain.

9. This is the case for troubadour and trouvère compositions. Hendrik van der Werf finds a preeminence of words over music, with the exception of the *rondeaux,* and no strong interest in the correlation between words and music on the part of the poets except in the *clausulae* and *motets* (*The Chansons of the Troubadours and Trouvères* [Utrecht: Oosthoek, 1972]). He argues that troubadours and trouvères worried little about keeping a close relation between words and music, and finds no indication that this lack of attention to a tight relation can be blamed exclusively on the performers. The fact that many more lyrics than melodies of a poem remain strongly suggests that the first were far more important to poets and public. See van der Werf, "Music," in *A Handbook of the Troubadours,* ed. F. R. P. Akehurst and Judith M. Davis (Berkeley: University of California Press, 1995), 121–64. Grocheo, when writing about *modus componendi,* says that first somebody writes the text and *then* music is set to it; see Ernst Rohloff, *Die Quellenhandschriften zum Musiktraktat des Johannes de Grocheio* (Leipzig: Deutscher Verlag für Musik, 1972), 134. John Stevens, in *Words and Music in the Middle Ages* (Cambridge: Cambridge University Press, 1986), proposes an isosyllabic theory that words and music are synchronic physical realizations of a "numeric Idea," without a direct relation between the two in any way that is familiar to us now. He recognizes the chronological precedence of music in the case of contrafacta, and of words in cases where there are different melodies for a poem or direct references to the composition of music after that of the poem (498 and n. 19). The disassociation between words and music is already present, in the Iberian Peninsula, in the *Cantigas de Santa María* by the Castilian king Alfonso X el Sabio; see Carlos Alvar and Vicente Beltrán, *Antología de la poesía gallego-portuguesa* (Madrid: Alhambra, 1984), 61, and bibliography cited there.

10. The point of these pages is not to claim that music and poetry were unrelated, but to question the current assumptions regarding the nature of that relation during the late Middle Ages. Music was an integral part of courtly life, as was poetry. This is attested by musical *cancioneros* and other references found in a number of contemporary texts, such as chronicles. See, for example, the numerous references to music in the *Hechos del condestable don Miguel Lucas de Iranzo*, ed. Juan de Mata Carriazo (Madrid: Espasa-Calpe, 1940). The importance of music within a courtly setting may also be seen in special genres when performed in specific contexts. For example, some long religious poetic compositions that point to an incipient drama toward the end of the fifteenth century and that have genre labels that indicate their performative nature as simple plays (*diálogos para cantar, farsas, églogas, comedias, autos*) were often sung or contained songs. See, for example, ID2807 (in 14LF; see Lucas Fernández, *Farsas y églogas,* in Brian Dutton, *El cancionero del siglo XV c. 1360–1520,* Biblioteca Española del Siglo XV [Salamanca: Universidad de Salamanca, 1990–91], 6:240). See also Charlotte Stern, *The Medieval Theater in Castile* (Binghamton, N.Y.: Medieval and Renaissance Texts and Studies, 1996), esp. 175–89.

11. See n. 3 above.

12. Jane Whetnall, "Songs and *Canciones* in the *Cancionero general de 1511,*" in *The Age of the Catholic Monarchs, 1474–1516: Literary Studies in Memory of Keith Whinnom,* ed. Alan Deyermond and Ian Macpherson (Liverpool: Liverpool University Press, 1989), 197–207.

13. There are very few cases in which the poet was also a musician; the most famous example is Juan del Encina. For a list of *cancionero* poets, see Brian Dutton, *El cancionero del siglo XV c. 1360–1520,* Biblioteca Española del Siglo XV (Salamanca: Universidad de Salamanca, 1990–91), 7:321–473; for a list of musicians see 7:483–88.

14. See Pierre Bec, "Le problème des genres chez les premiers troubadours," *Cahiers de civilisation médiévale* 25 (1982): 31–47; Bec, *La lyrique française au Moyen-Age (XIIe–XIIIe siècles): contribution à une typologie des genres poétiques médiévaux* (Paris: A. & J. Picard, 1977–78), 1:19.

15. Lines 250–55 of his *declaratio*. See Valeria Bertolucci Pizzorusso, "La supplica di Guiraut Riquier e la risposta di Alfonso X de Castiglia," *Studi mediolatini e volgari* 14 (1966): 9–135; and Ramón Menéndez Pidal, *Poesía juglaresca y juglares: orígenes de la literaturas románicas* (Madrid: Espasa-Calpe, 1991), 33–41.

16. For a study of English poetry, see Boffey, *Manuscripts of English Courtly Love Lyrics,* 87–141. For French, see Sylvia Huot, *From Song to Book: The Poetics of Writing in Old French Lyric and Lyrical Narrative Poetry* (Ithaca: Cornell University Press, 1987).

17. See the anonymous fifteenth-century treatise on playing the lute, "Arte de tocar el laúd (de un anónimo del siglo XV)," in Marcelino Menéndez y Pelayo, *Historia de las ideas estéticas en España* (Santander: Consejo Superior de Investigaciones Científicas, 1946), 1:525. See also the later testimony of Francisco Salinas (*Francisco Salinas: De musica,* ed. Macario Santiago Kastner [Kassel: Barenreiter, 1958], 239 and passim) and Grocheo (Rohloff, *Quellenhandschriften zum Musiktraktat des Grocheio*).

18. "En estos nuestros tiempos floresçió mosén Jorde de Sant Jorde, cauallero prudente, el qual çiertamente conpuso asaz fermosas cosas, las quales él mesmo asonaua ca fue músico exçelente" (In these our times flourished Mosen Jorde de

Sant Jorde, a prudent gentleman, who certainly composed very beautiful works, which he himself set to music, for he was an excellent musician) (Francisco López Estrada, ed., *Las poéticas castellanas de la Edad Media* [Madrid: Taurus, 1984], 58). As López Estrada notes, Machaut also composed the music for his own poems. Santillana did not compose his own music. We find, for example, his "Señora qual soy venido" set to music by the composers Triana and Cornago in the *Cancionero musical de la Colombina*. See Miguel Querol Gavalda, ed., *Cancionero musical de la Colombina (siglo XV)* (Barcelona: Consejo Superior de Investigaciones Científicas, Instituto Español de Musicología, 1971). Santillana separates music from lyrics in the song: "las dulçes bozes e fermosos sones no apuesten e aconpañen todo rimo, todo metro, todo uerso, sea de qualquier arte, peso e medida?" (Do not sweet voices and beautiful sounds support and accompany all *rimo*, all *metro*, all *verso*, be it of any kind, meter or measure?). See his *Prohemio* in López Estrada, *Poéticas castellanas*, 57. The same sentiment is found in Dante: "Ad quod dicimus, quod nunquam modulatio dicitur cantio, sed sonus, vel tonus, vel nota, vel melos" (*De vulgare eloquentia*, liber II, viii, 5, quoted by López Estrada in *Poéticas castellanas*, 112).

19. Dutton and Cuenca, *Cancionero de Baena*, 7–8.

20. Santillana collected his own works in a volume to send to Don Pedro, constable of Portugal. He wished to teach Don Pedro about poetry and felt that sending his own poems would contribute to Don Pedro's learning. See the introduction to Santillana's *Prohemio* in López Estrada, *Poéticas castellanas*, 51–52. For Juan del Encina's *Arte de poesía castellana*, see ibid., 77–93. No music is mentioned as associated with the reading or writing. The art of poetry and the skill of the poet do not rely on any musical skills, but rather on metrics and rhetoric. Juan de Valdés discusses mainly metrics and style; see Cristina Barbolani, ed., *Juan de Valdés: Diálogo de la lengua* (Madrid: Cátedra, 1982), 240–44.

21. "E luego uno de los vergueros dezía que los trobadores allí congregados espandiesen y publicasen las obras que tenién fechas de la materia a ellos asignada. E luego levantávase cada uno, *e leía la obra que tenía fecha, en boz intelligible*" (And then one of the ministers asked the troubadors congregated there to expand and publish the works they had made with the material assigned to them. And then each one got up and *read the work he had made in an intelligible voice*). Afterwards, the winning poem "era asentada en el registro del consistorio, dando authoridat y liçençia para que se pudiese *cantar, e en público dezir*" (was placed in the registry of the council, giving authority and license so it could be *sung and publicly recited*). See Pedro Cátedra, ed., *Enrique de Villena: Arte de trovar*, in *Obras completas* (Madrid: Turner, 1994), 1:353–70, at 358.

22. "Por tan grande fue avido este fecho, quel rey nuestro Señor, porque mayor memoria quedase, le mandó facer un romance, el cual a los cantores de su capilla mandó asonar" (So great was the deed that the king, our lord, so that a greater memory would remain, ordered a *romance* be made, which he ordered the singers to set to music) (Carriazo, *Hechos del condestable*, 90).

23. See the testimony of Francisco Salinas, *De musica*, 329; and Nellie E. Sánchez-Arce, *Las glosas a las "Coplas" de Jorge Manrique* (Madrid: Sancha, 1956), 17.

24. On late medieval literacy, see M. Camille, "Seeing and Reading: Some Visual Implications of Medieval Literacy and Illiteracy," *Art History* 8 (1985), 26–49; Parkes, "Literacy of the Laity"; Paul Saenger, "Books of Hours and the Reading Habits of

the Later Middle Ages," in *The Culture of Print,* ed. Roger Chartier (Princeton: Princeton University Press, 1989), 141–73; Paul Saenger, "Silent Reading: Its Impact on Late Medieval Script and Society," *Viator* 13 (1982): 367–414; J. N. H. Lawrance, "The Spread of Lay Literacy in Late Medieval Castile," *Bulletin of Hispanic Studies* 62 (1985): 79–94. For background see Erich Auerbach, "The Western Public and Its Language," in *Literary Language and Its Public in Late Latin Antiquity and in the Middle Ages* (Princeton: Princeton University Press, 1965), 235–338; Peter Burke, "The Uses of Literacy in Early Modern Italy," in *The Social History of Language,* ed. Peter Burke and Roy Porter (New York: Cambridge University Press, 1987), 21–42; Carlo M. Cipolla, *Literacy and Development in the West* (Baltimore, Md.: Penguin, 1969); M. T. Clanchy, *From Memory to Written Record: England 1066–1307* (Cambridge: Blackwell, 1993); Ann M. Hutchison, "Devotional Reading in the Monastery and in the Late Medieval Household," in *De Cella in Saeculum: Religious and Secular Life and Devotion in Late Medieval England,* ed. Michael G. Sargent (Cambridge: D. S. Brewer, 1989), 215–27; James Westfall Thompson, *The Literacy of the Laity in the Middle Ages* (Berkeley: University of California Press, 1939). For an example of a useful approach to *cancionero* poetry from the viewpoint of reading practices within the framework of gender and poetic exchanges, see the recent study by Alan Deyermond, "Women and Gómez Manrique," in *Cancionero Studies in Honour of Ian Macpherson,* ed. Alan Deyermond (London: Department of Hispanic Studies, Queen Mary and Westfield College, 1998), 69–87. Paul Zumthor emphasizes that literary texts were received orally until the fifteenth century; see "Spoken Language and Oral Poetry in the Middle Ages," *Style* 19 (1985): 191–98. H. J. Chaytor, Margit Frenk, and William Nelson place an emphasis on orality and prefer to see the shift to silent reading in the sixteenth or seventeenth centuries, while admitting that the change is gradual. See H. J. Chaytor, *From Script to Print: An Introduction to Medieval Vernacular Literature* (Cambridge: Cambridge University Press, 1945); Margit Frenk, "'Lectores y oidores': la difusión oral de la literatura en el Siglo de Oro," in *Actas del Séptimo Congreso de la Asociación Internacional de Hispanistas, celebrado en Venecia del 25 al 30 de agosto de 1980,* ed. Giuseppe Bellini (Rome: Bulzoni, 1982), 1:101–23; Margit Frenk, "Ver, oír, leer... ," in *Homenaje a Ana María Barrenechea,* ed. Lia Schwartz Lerner and Isaias Lerner (Madrid: Castalia, 1984), 245–70; William Nelson, "From 'Listen, Lordings' to 'Dear Reader,'" *University of Toronto Quarterly* 46 (1976–77), 110–24. See also Alan Deyermond, "La literatura oral en la transición de la Edad Media al Renacimiento," *Edad de oro* 7 (1988), 21–32.

25. On early medieval popular literacy see Clanchy, *From Memory to Written Record.* The author of *Partenope of Blois* calls on the "letteryd" to read and on the "lewed" to listen to the stories in order for them to learn; see Ruth Crosby, "Oral Delivery in the Middle Ages," *Speculum* 11 (1936): 88–110, at 100, n. 3. Bernardo de Gordonio gives a recipe to aid friars and *letrados*—lettered people—to read hard-to-see small letters. He apparently thought of these two groups as the ones who engaged more actively in silent reading. See John Cull and Brian Dutton, eds., *Bernardo de Gordonio: Lilio de medicina* (Madison, Wis.: Hispanic Seminary of Medieval Studies, 1991), 333. On the levels of literacy among different groups at different times and illiteracy as a perennial, not exclusively medieval, phenomenon, see Cipolla, *Literacy and Development;* the same conclusion is reached by Thompson, *Literacy of the Laity,* 196–97. On the need to consider social group in literacy assessments see Franz

H. Bäuml, "Varieties and Consequences of Medieval Literacy and Illiteracy," *Speculum* 55 (1980): 237–65. Chaytor admits the likelihood of the formulaic nature of some expressions related to reading (*From Script to Print*, 145). Parkes warns that "The survival of these formulas, however, has helped to obscure the extent of the literate audience for such texts" ("Literacy of the Laity," 296–97).

26. The quotes from *cancionero* poems in the examples found below are given using the acronym chosen by Dutton for each manuscript in *Cancionero del siglo XV*, followed by the poem's ID number, also assigned by Dutton.

27. "Ca, sin dubda alguna, si la su merçed en este dicho libro *leyere* en sus tiempos devidos, con él se agradará e deleytará e folgará e tomará muchos comportes e plazeres e gasajados. E aun otrosí, con las muy agradables e graçiosas e muy singulares cosas que en él son escriptas e contenidas, la su muy redutable e real persona averá reposo e descanso en los trabajos e afanes e enojos" (Because without a doubt, if Your Mercy read in this book in his due time, it will please, delight, and relax him, and he will take much comfort in it, and pleasure and entertainment. And furthermore with the very pleasant and funny and very original things that are written and contained in it, your very redoubtable and royal person will find rest and repose from tasks, labors, and annoyances) (Dutton and Cuenca, *Cancionero de Baena*, 2). Baena uses the verb "leer" when he refers to the king. Only when he refers to the future enjoyment that the book will also bring to the rest of the people in the king's house does he also use the verb "oír": "E, finalmente, en general se agradarán con este dicho libro todos los grandes señores de sus reinos e señoríos, assí los perlados, infantes, duques, condes, adelantados, almirantes, como los maestres, priores, mariscales, doctores, cavalleros e escuderos, e todos los otros fidalgos e gentiles omnes, sus donzeles e criados e ofiçiales de la su casa real, que lo *ver e oír e leer e entender* bien quisieren. E porque la obra tan famosa d'este dicho libro sea más agradable e mejor entendida a los *leyentes e oyentes* d'ella" (and finally, in general, all the great lords of your kingdoms and dominions will be pleased with this book, and so the prelates, princes, dukes, counts, commanders, admirals, as the grand masters, priors, marshals, doctors, gentlemen and squires, and all the other hidalgos and gentlemen, their pages and servants and officials of your royal house, who might wish to *see and hear and read and understand* it. And so that the very famous work of this book may be more pleasant and better understood to its *readers and listeners*) (ibid.). Julian Weiss interprets the "leyere" in the first passage quoted above as "private reading"; see *The Poet's Art: Literary Theory in Castile c. 1400–60* (Oxford: Society for the Study of Medieval Languages and Literature, 1990), 47. There are some long religious compositions that may have been read aloud as part of a group prayer or religious ceremony. This can be seen, for example, in the rubric of ID2892 (ML1) (*Pasión trobada* by Diego de San Pedro), which also refers to those who would read and listen to the poem ("leyeran e oyeren"). As reflected by these quotes, public reading as a source of entertainment was a common occurrence and not in contradiction with silent private reading practices. See S. Coleman, *Public Reading and the Reading Public in Late Medieval England and France* (Cambridge: Cambridge University Press, 1996), and also Roger Chartier, "Leisure and Sociability: Reading Aloud in Early Modern Europe," in *Urban Life in the Renaissance,* ed. S. Zimmerman and R. F. E. Weisman (Newark: University of Delaware Press, 1989), 103–20.

28. See Roger M. Walker, "Oral Delivery or Private Reading? A Contribution to

the Debate on the Dissemination of Medieval Literature," *Forum for Modern Language Studies* 7 (1971): 36–42.

29. Rather than to the "hearer" of previous centuries, the address is generally to the "reader" in the popular texts of the fifteenth century, when references to hearers diminish. See Crosby, "Oral Delivery," 98–100. The vernacular texts written before the twelfth century always address a "listener" and not a "reader" (Auerbach, "Western Public," 284). In scholastic texts, *scribere* replaced *dicere* at the end of the Middle Ages, although the latter term had the sense of "to state" and did not imply an oral reading (Saenger, "Books of Hours," 143, 158, n. 11). Chaytor (*From Script to Print,* appendix B) presents examples of "lire" meaning "reading aloud"; however, many are examples of letters being read aloud. The reading mode of letters might not be transposed to other texts, since letters were frequently read aloud as public documents.

30. Alfonso de Toledo, *Invencionario,* Madrid: Biblioteca Nacional, 9219, transcription by Philip O. Gericke, *ADMYTE: Archivo digital de manuscritos y textos españoles,* CD-ROM (Madrid: Micronet, 1992–93), 1, fol. 13r. Cull and Dutton, *Bernardo de Gordonio: Lilio de medicina,* 140–42, 333. See additional evidence of literacy in late medieval Castile in Lawrance, "Spread of Lay Literacy."

31. *Tratado de la Música,* San Lorenzo de El Escorial: Monasterio, ç.III.23, transcription by Alan Hastings, *ADMYTE* 1, fol. 47r.

32. Jorge García López, ed., *Alfonso de la Torre: Visión deleytable* (Salamanca: Universidad de Salamanca, 1991), 1:316.

33. *Siete Partidas* (Sevilla: Meinardo Ungut & Estanislao Polono, 25 de octubre de 1491), transcription by Cynthia Wasick, *ADMYTE* 0, fol. 81r. Cited hereafter by folio number. We find other references to knowing how to read: "tu *non sabias letras & querias leer*" (you *did not know your letters* and *wanted to read*) (*Esopete Historiado* II, San Lorenzo de El Escorial: Monasterio, 32-I-13, transcription by Victoria A. Burrus, *ADMYTE* 1, fol. 62r); "*saber leer*" (*Sumas de la Historia Troyana,* Madrid: Nacional, 9256, transcription by Robert G. Black, *ADMYTE* 1, 259); *Siete Partidas,* fols. 83v, 85v, 87r, 88v, 123v, 216v; *Ordenanças sobre los abogados,* Salamanca: Juan de Porras, c. 1511, transcription by Aurora Martín de Santa Olalla Sánchez, *ADMYTE* 0, 5. For examples of *ver* and *leer* related to poetry, see below.

34. Significant to the understanding of these developments are Katherine O'Brien O'Keeffe's statements that "the cultural movement from orality to literacy involves the gradual shift from aural to visual reception," and that "such a shift is reflected in the increasing spatialization of a written text. The higher the degree of conventional spatialization in the manuscripts, the less oral and more literate the community." See Katherine O'Brien O'Keeffe, *Visible Song: Transitional Literacy in Old English Verse* (New York: Cambridge University Press, 1990), 25. See also Walter J. Ong, *Orality and Literacy: The Technologizing of the Word* (New York: Routledge, 1993), though Ong tends to consider the invention of printing as the "turning point" in the growth of literacy. For various effects of literacy on fifteenth-century Castilian manuscripts, see J. Weiss, *Poet's Art.*

35. See Alan D. Deyermond, *Epic Poetry and the Clergy: Studies on the "Mocedades de Rodrigo"* (London: Tamesis, 1968), 25–27, 54–58, 198–202 *et passim.*

36. See O'Keeffe, *Visible Song.* For these and other questions of visual poetics and the transcription of lyric poetry, see Wayne H. Storey, *Transcription and Visual Poetics in the Early Italian Lyric* (New York: Garland, 1993).

37. "Por qu'el dicho señor Rey e las otras personas que la *leyeren* fallen por ella [la tabla] más aína las *cantigas* o *dezires* que le agradare *leer*" (So that the king and others who read it sooner find in it [the index] the *cantigas* or *dezires* that they would like to *read*) (Dutton and Cuenca, *Cancionero de Baena*, 9).

38. Alfonso Fernández de Palencia, *Universal vocabulario en latín y en romance* (Madrid: Comisión Permanente de la Asociación de Academias de la Lengua Española, 1967), 306r.

39. The shift from oral to silent prayer from the middle of the fourteenth to the fifteenth centuries is reflected in the rubrics of the books of hours by more frequent references to vision and to the eyes (Saenger, "Books of Hours"). Mary is often depicted reading and teaching Child Jesus how to read; see Michael T. Clanchy, "Looking Back from the Invention of Printing," in *Literacy in Historical Perspective*, ed. Daniel P. Resnick (Washington: Library of Congress, 1983), 7–22, at 14; and M. T. Clanchy, "Learning to Read in the Middle Ages and the Role of Mothers," in *Studies in the History of Reading*, ed. Greg Brooks and A. K. Pugh (Reading: Centre for the Teaching of Reading, 1984), 33–39, at 36. This shift is also reflected in the way authors and the act of writing are depicted in medieval illuminations; see Saenger, "Silent Reading," 388–90, and Huot, *From Song to Book*. For a tradition similar to the Spanish one, see Boffey, *Manuscripts of English Courtly Love Lyrics*. For evidence on reading ballads in the Spanish Renaissance, see María Cruz García de Enterría, "Romancero: ¿cantado-recitado-leído?" *Edad de oro* 7 (1988): 89–104.

40. See, for instance, Navarro Tomás, *Métrica española*, and the bibliography cited in nn. 1–3 above. For a complete study of the *canción* genre and its metrical evolution, see Vicente Beltrán, *La canción de amor en el otoño de la Edad Media* (Barcelona: PPU, 1988). The fact that music was not a consistent genre designator does not imply that music did not add certain genre features when it indeed appeared, thus providing some added optional characteristics. For instance, we have genres such as the *romances*, with very distinctive metrical, thematic, and compositional genre features, whose music, when and if it appears, can often be "sad," depending on the theme.

41. Baena applies the term *escandidas* to both *cantigas* and *decires*. For the view of the opposition between *asonado* and *escandido* as key to distinguishing between the sung *cantigas* and the recited *decires*, see Francisco López Estrada, *Poesía medieval castellana: antología y comentario* (Madrid: Taurus, 1984), 188.

42. We find terms such as *politum, color,* and *ornatus* in medieval rhetorical arts. For example, Geoffrey of Everseley in his *Ars epistolarium ornatus:* "Item, si vis dictamen *politum* componere. . . . Universum officium artificis epistolaris *ornaturi* in tribus" (Valeria Bertolucci Pizzorusso, "Un trattato di *Ars dictandi* dedicato ad Alfonso X," *Studi mediolatini e volgari* 15–16 [1968]: 9–88, at 79). "Dictamen igitur est oratio prosaice et jta metris et metrorum aminiculis *colorata* mittentis desiderjum exprimens que conclusione panditur finem sorciens et assumens. A magistro B.us desscribitur: 'Dictamen est litteralis editio uenustate uerborum egregia sentencjarum *colorjbus adornata*'" (Ana M. Gómez-Bravo, "El latín de la clerecía: edición y estudio del *Ars dictandi Palentina*," *Euphrosyne, revista de filologia clássica* 18 [1990]: 99–144, at 126). See also the treatises published by Edmond Faral in *Les arts poétiques du XIIe et du XIIIe siècle: recherches et documents sur la technique littéraire du Moyen Age* (Paris: Champion, 1924).

43. Rodrigo Fernández de Santaella, *Vocabulario eclesiástico* (Seville: Juan Pegnitzer

de Nurenberga, Magno Herbst de Fils & Tomás Glockner para Juan Lorencio, 14 de febrero de 1499), transcription by Gracia Lozano and others, *ADMYTE* 0, fol. 56r. "Ditar. dezir lo que otro escrive {LAT. dicto.as}" (Antonio de Nebrija, *Dictionarium latino-hispanicum* [Salamanca: Impresor de la Gramática de Nebrija, 1492], transcription by Antonio Cortijo, *ADMYTE* 0).

44. For the etymology of *dictamen*, see James J. Murphy, *Rhetoric in the Middle Ages* (Berkeley: University of California Press, 1974), 195, n. 5; William D. Patt, "The Early 'Ars dictaminis' as Response to a Changing Society," *Viator* 9 (1978): 133–55, at 134, n. 2.

45. Thus, for example, the *Ars dictandi Palentina*, in Gómez-Bravo, "Latín de la clerecía," 126.

46. See Ernst Robert Curtius, *Literatura europea y Edad Media latina* (México: Fondo de cultura económica, 1984), 1:118; A. Ernout, "Dictare 'Dicter,' allem. Dichten," *Revue des études latines* 29 (1951): 155–61; the entry *deitado* in Walter Schmid, *Der Wortschatz des Cancionero de Baena* (Bern: A. Francke, 1951). Heloise writes to Abelard about the sweetness of the words of his love songs, which she calls "dictamen": "pleraque amatorio metro vel rithmo composita reliquisti carmina, que pre nimia suavitate tam *dictaminis* quam cantus sepius frequentata, tuum in ore omnium nomen incessanter tenebant," in *La vie et les epistres Pierres Abaelart et Heloys sa fame: Traduction du XIIIe siècle attribuée à Jean de Meun, avec une nouvelle édition des textes latins d'après le ms. Troyes Bibl. mun. 802,* ed. Eric Hicks (Paris: Champion, 1991), 1:51. Grocheo talks about *dictamina* when discussing how the lyrics of a poem are written before a melody is added to it (cited in Stevens, *Words and Music,* 498, n. 19).

47. For the relation between rhetoric and grammar through the Middle Ages, see Donald Leman Clark, *Rhetoric and Poetry in the Renaissance* (New York: Columbia University Press, 1922), 43–55; Rita Copeland, *Rhetoric, Hermeneutics, and Translation in the Middle Ages* (Cambridge: Cambridge University Press, 1991); Curtius, *Literatura europea,* 1:118, 217; Paul Oskar Kristeller, "Un' *Ars Dictaminis* di Giovanni del Virgilio," *Italia medioevale e umanistica* 4 (1961): 181–200; R. McKeon, "Rhetoric in the Middle Ages," *Speculum* 17 (1942): 1–32, at 26–29; Murphy, *Rhetoric in the Middle Ages,* 135–268; Francesco Novati, *La giovinèzza di Coluccio Salutati* (Turin: Loescher, 1888), 70–74; Louis John Paetow, *The Arts Course at Medieval Universities, with Special Reference to Grammar and Rhetoric* (Urbana-Champaign: University [of Illinois] Press, 1910), 67–91; Patt, "Early 'Ars Dictaminis,'" 151–53; Aldo Scaglione, *The Classical Theory of Composition from Its Origins to the Present: A Historical Survey* (Chapel Hill: University of North Carolina Press, 1972); Jerrold E. Seigel, *Rhetoric and Philosophy in Renaissance Humanism: The Union of Eloquence and Wisdom, Petrarch to Valla* (Princeton: Princeton University Press, 1968), 200–225; Ronald G. Witt, "Medieval 'Ars Dictaminis' and the Beginnings of Humanism: A New Construction of the Problem," *Renaissance Quarterly* 35 (1982): 1–35, at 23–26. For Latin and medieval French rhetoric, see Paul Zumthor, "Rhétorique et poétique latines et romanes," in *Grundriss der romanischen Literaturen des Mittelalters* 1 (1972): 57–91. Charles B. Faulhaber notes that for the study of medieval Spanish rhetoric, scholarship must turn mainly to the treatises on *dictamen* (*Latin Rhetorical Theory in Thirteenth and Fourteenth Century Castile* [Berkeley: University of California Press, 1972]). The teachers of grammar were also teachers of rhetoric and vice versa. Authors such as Geoffrey of Vinsauf, John of Garland, and Gervase of Melkley included both *ars dictandi* and

versificandi or *poetriae* in the same manual. Geoffrey of Vinsauf was both a *dictator* and a *versificator*. The authors of dictaminal treatises also wrote and taught about grammar and poetry and vice versa. For the influence of Latin rhetoric, grammar and *ars dictaminis* in medieval vernacular literary texts, see Douglas Kelly, *The Arts of Poetry and Prose,* Typologie des sources du Moyen Age, vol. 59 (Turnhout: Brepols, 1991), 146–79; J. Weiss, *Poet's Art;* Helene Wieruszowski, "'Ars dictaminis' in the Time of Dante," in *Politics and Culture in Medieval Spain and Italy* (Rome: Edizioni di Storia e Letteratura, 1971), 359–77; Ronald G. Witt, "Brunetto Latini and the Italian Tradition of *Ars dictaminis,*" *Stanford Italian Review* 3 (1983): 5–24, at 12, for a quote by Brunetto Latini equating *canzone* and letters as being treated equally by rhetoric; Zumthor, "Rhétorique et poétique." For the *dictatores*' interest in poetry, see, for example, Roberto Weiss, *The Dawn of Humanism in Italy* (London: H. K. Lewis, 1947).

48. Several authors who have characterized the *decir* by its reading mode assume that for lack of music, the genre must rely on rhetorical ornamentation. For this view, see Lapesa, *Obra literaria,* 46, 162, and Vendrell de Millás, *Cancionero de Palacio,* 97. The case defended in this essay is that the *decir* is defined from the beginning by its close relation with rhetoric, which does not result from its optional attachment to music, but helps explain it. On the difference between *vers* and *canso,* see Zumthor, "Rhétorique et poétique."

49. See the text in Hicks, *Vie et les epistres Pierres Abaelart,* 1:51. The terms are translated as "dicter" and "chanter" in the French manuscript.

50. Francisco Marcos Marín, ed., *Libro de Alexandre* (Madrid: Alianza Universidad, 1987), 330c–d.

51. Alberto Blecua, ed., *Juan Ruiz, Arcipreste de Hita: Libro de buen amor* (Madrid: Cátedra, 1992). Hereafter cited by stanza number and letter corresponding to the position of line within that stanza. Prose section numbers are also given.

52. Pero López de Ayala, *Rimado de Palacio,* ed. Germán Orduna (Madrid: Castalia, 1987), 727c.

53. López Estrada, *Poéticas castellanas,* 54.

54. Cátedra, *Enrique de Villena,* 1:355.

55. López Estrada, *Poéticas castellanas,* 59, 60. The same use can be found in the *Morales de Ovidio:* "los que saben tanto alegrar & *dezir* & por lisonjas asi dulçe mente cantar" (those who know so well how to please and *dezir* and by flattery sing sweetly this way) (175v); "los quales non pueden *dezir* o cantar" (those who cannot *dezir* or *cantar*) (189r); *Morales de Ovidio,* transcription by Derek Carr, *ADMYTE* 1. Dorothy Clotelle Clarke interprets Santillana's expression "deçir cantares" as referring to songs written in the form of a *decir* ("On Santillana's 'Una manera de deçir cantares,'" *Philological Quarterly* 36 [1957]: 72–76). However, as can be inferred from my analysis of this genre, *decir* must be interpreted in Santillana's expression as "poem writing," without a direct reference to *decir* as a *cancionero* genre. For "*dezir coplas,*" see, for example the rubric of ID2833 (MN14).

56. *Primera crónica general de España,* I, 85b.41–46, cited by Antoinette Letsch-Lavanchy, "Eléments didactiques dans la *Crónica general,*" *Vox romanica* 15 (1956): 237–38. The same use can be found elsewhere: "Este tono aplaze y es conforme a los que de continuo son muy alegres loçanos garridos / polidos/ *dezidores / trobadores / copleadores* / motejadores/ disimuladores / disfraçadores" (This tune pleas-

es and is agreeable to those who are continually very happy, lively, smart / polished / *dezidores* / *trobadores* / *copladores* / name-callers / deceivers / liars) (*Glosa sobre Lux Bella*, Madrid: Nacional, I-721, transcription by David G. Burton, *ADMYTE* 1, 77v); "poetas illustres y dezidores famosos" (*Crónica de Aragón*, Zaragoza: Pablo Hurus, 12 de septiembre de 1499, transcription by José Carlos Pino Jiménez, *ADMYTE* 0, 17v); "poetas e dezidores" (Dutton and Cuenca, *Cancionero de Baena*, 1); "dezidores e trobadores" (Santillana, *Prohemio*, in López Estrada, *Poéticas castellanas*, 59); "*dictador o conponedor que en Rimico estilo despues de veynte coplas*" (*dictador* or composer who in rhythmic style after twenty *coplas*) (Santillana, introduction to his *Proverbios*, PN12, ID0091, 144r).

57. See, for example, Seigel, *Rhetoric and Philosophy*, 208; Roberto Weiss, *Humanism in England during the Fifteenth Century* (Oxford: Blackwell, 1941), 181.

58. For the *dictatores* as predecessors of the humanists see Paul Oskar Kristeller, *Eight Philosophers of the Italian Renaissance* (Stanford: Stanford University Press, 1964), 160–61; Kristeller, "Humanism and Scholasticism in the Renaissance," *Byzantion* 17 (1944–45): 346–74. See also Witt's important observations on Kristeller's theory ("Medieval 'Ars Dictaminis'").

59. See the works cited in nn. 1 and 3, and Francisca Vendrell de Millás, "Los cancioneros del siglo XV," in *Historia general de las literaturas hispánicas*, ed. Guillermo Díaz-Plaja (Barcelona: Vergara, 1968), 2:63.

60. Le Gentil refers to both genres as "chanson," thereby implying that they designate a single genre. See the use of both terms, for example, in Navarro Tomás, *Métrica española*, 140. The metrical terminology of the time is generally considered as "loose." Nevertheless, the terminology is ambiguous only in prose or poetic texts that refer to poetry in a broad sense (see the terms used by Santillana in his *Prohemio*); it is generally less so in the manuscript rubrics.

61. Le Gentil, *Poésie lyrique*, 2:184. For the point of view that the *decir* was popular toward the *end* of the Spanish Middle Ages, see Potvin, *Illusion et pouvoir*, 167. For a development of the idea that the initial term that expresses *cancionero* poetic forms is *copla*, see López Estrada, *Poesía medieval*, 187.

62. "El marqués de Santillana, don Enrique de Villena y otros, de los quales *leemos coplas y canciones* de muy gracioso donayre" (Gonzalo Argote de Molina, "Discurso sobre la poesía castellana," in *La retórica en España*, ed. Elena Casas [Madrid: Editora Nacional, 1980], 207). The use of the verb "leer" here both for *canciones* and *coplas* should be noticed. The same term appears paired up in the successive printings of the *Cancionero general* and in the printed chapbooks, *pliegos sueltos*, of the sixteenth century; see Victor Infantes, "Los *Pliegos sueltos poéticos*: constitución tipográfica y contenido literario (1482–1600)," in *El libro antiguo español: Actas del Primer Coloquio Internacional (Madrid, 18 al 20 de diciembre de 1986)*, ed. María Luisa López-Vidriero and Pedro M. Cátedra (Salamanca: Universidad de Salamanca, 1988), 237–48.

63. The term *Obras* (Œuvres, Works) also appears frequently during this period to refer to the general works of a poet included in a general *cancionero*. A particular poem might be referred to as *otra* after that first main generic label. Although the French case seems to present different characteristics, see a study of the appearance of the term "œuvres" in the French Renaissance lyric collections in Nancy Freeman-Regalado, "Gathering the Works: The 'Œuvres de Villon' and the Inter-

generic Passage of the Medieval French Lyric into Single-Author Collections," *L'Esprit Créateur* 33 (1993): 87–100.

64. See Francisco Caravaca, "Estudios manriqueños: notas sobre el título: *'Coplas' de Jorge Manrique 'a la' muerte de su padre,*" *La torre* 73/74 (1971): 185–221.

65. Pierre Le Gentil (*Poésie lyrique*) and H. R. Lang ("Formas estróficas") studied mainly the *Cancionero de Baena,* while Francisca Vendrell de Millás edited the *Cancionero de Palacio.* Their statements on *cancionero* genres have been generally interpreted as valid for the whole *cancionero* corpus.

66. See the valuable study by Rafael Lapesa, "Los géneros líricos del Renacimiento: la herencia cancioneresca," in *Homenaje a Eugenio Asensio,* ed. Luisa López-Grigera and Augustín Redondo (Madrid: Gredos, 1988), 259–75. According to Juan del Encina, the only rules that applied to the *copla* were that it had to have a unity of meaning and should be comprised of four to twelve lines (though it was called a *canción* if it had four); see his *Arte de poesía castellana,* in López Estrada, *Poéticas castellanas,* 90. For an introduction to some of those genres see Navarro Tomás, *Métrica española,* 113–93.

67. For a full study of the reasons behind the changes in genre terminology described here and their relation to the rhetorical and poetic theory of the time summarized here, see Ana M. Gómez-Bravo, "Retórica y poética en la evolución de los géneros poéticos cuatrocentistas," *Rhetorica: A Journal of the History of Rhetoric* 17 (1999): 1–38.

68. For a study of several aspects of this process, see Copeland, *Rhetoric, Hermeneutics, and Translation.*

PART 2

Genre and Rhetoric

CHAPTER 7

The Poem as Art of Poetry:
The Rhetoric of Imitation
in the Grand Chant Courtois

DOUGLAS KELLY

Medieval poetics does not contain a theory of genres as such. However, current interest in this subject for medieval writing has led scholars to extrapolate generic features from the texts that we have today—that is, those features that tend to characterize groups of texts and that distinguish such groups from one another. In the lyric corpus this gave some validity to taxonomies developed in the nineteenth century using the language lyric poets themselves used to refer to different kinds of lyric pieces: *chanson, aube, chanson de malmariée, pastourelle,* and similar designations. However, this stable, comfortable system based on formal features like rhyme and stanza or content such as parting at dawn, abused wives, and women weaving and singing, does not always smoothly demarcate genres in ways more familiar from Renaissance and classical poetics. Given the absence of a medieval theory of genre or even recognizable principles of generic classification, scholars beginning with Hans-Robert Jauss began to speak of historical genres. By this they meant that public awareness of generic features of writing created an expectation that was constantly adapted as new works appeared, developing the potential of given forms and subjects for original rewriting. This points to a real, identifiable concern in medieval commentary on writing: the modus agendi or, in the French vernacular, a given work's *manière,* in its old sense of genus or species.

Modus agendi refers to the mode or modes or writing adopted in a specific piece of writing.[1] In the case of the *chanson* or *grand chant courtois* of the troubadours and trouvères with which I am concerned here the modus agendi was often rhetorical. This means that these poems are love poems written to persuade or dissuade a public or publics, including connoisseurs, patrons, and the loved one, on some amatory issue. But are vernacular poems rhetorical in the same sense that medieval Latin poems are when they are written according to the canons of the scholastic tradition in rhetoric?

Linda M. Paterson has distinguished between the rhetoric of the schools, whose medium was Latin, and "the rhetoric of the troubadours," which "was not necessarily the rhetoric of Dante"—Dante described their art as rhetorical: "fictio rhetorica musicaque poita"—"or of the medieval schools. It developed," she goes on to suggest, "*perhaps,* independently of these, to suit a secular courtly audience."[2] The statement is tentative. In any case, rather than embark on an in-depth study of medieval rhetoric as the troubadours might have known it and of the relation that may or may not obtain between that art and their practice, Paterson prefers to examine the eloquence of the troubadours as they themselves describe and practice it. Hence, in the five chapters she devotes to major twelfth-century troubadours, "No attempt is made to analyse in any comprehensive way the influence of Rhetoric on these poets, which is beyond the scope of the present study."[3] In this view, Paterson has probably read the troubadours much as they read one another. But, perhaps, such readers did not read in complete ignorance or neglect of the Latin tradition to which Dante likens that of the troubadours.

Ulrich Mölk has shown that some features of medieval rhetoric—for example, the distinction between easy and difficult ornamentation set forth systematically by Geoffrey of Vinsauf at the beginning of the thirteenth century—are present in the interventions and art of the early troubadours.[4] He goes on to argue that their rhetorical formation did in fact influence theoretical reflection and actual practice among the troubadours. Paterson, for her part, goes beyond such basic instruction to discover "Individual songs whose composition . . . illustrate[s] the ideas gathered from the poet's own literary observations, to see how far and in what way [the poet] puts them into practice."[5] The troubadours were not alone in learning and practicing their art in this way. Like most medieval writers who came up through or out of the school tradition, they began to read the elementary instruction in grammar and rhetoric, applying it, as Mölk suggests, to vernacular lyric. In doing so, they read their predecessors, reflected on their art in general and in specific pieces, and imitated them with originality, as Paterson suggests. They were able to do so because they brought to their practice conceptions and practices derived from study of the art of composition when they were learning to write in the schools.

In both Latin and vernacular traditions there was a tripartite approach to the study and practice of composition: study of treatises of composition, reading of predecessors to interpret their strategies of composition, and imitation of those strategies in new, original pieces.[6] This last stage evinces what Paterson calls their "individuality," but which I would prefer to term their "originality" or "adaptation."

Here I propose to look at some examples of this rhetorical background as it appears in several *cansos, chansons,* and ballades. In conclusion I will suggest ways in which my tentative findings might be applied to reading the corpus of lyric poetry in Occitan and French. Let us start by returning to the art of rhetoric.

In our times in which the term rhetoric has become something of a pejorative or catchall cliché, the art of rhetoric as the Middle Ages understood and practiced it must be properly understood before its use in medieval lyric can be appreciated.[7] Rhetoric is the art whereby one acquires eloquence so as to convince an audience as to the goodness or desirability of something. Eloquence for medieval writers is language so wrought as to sway an audience in matters of opinion or belief. Andreas Capellanus states that eloquence may move an audience to believe in the sincerity of the speaker's sentiments and to respond favorably to them. This is especially important when the audience is a loved one. "Sermonis facundia multotiens ad amandum non amantium corda compellit"[8] (Eloquence often compels the unloving heart to love). This is justification enough for knowing how to evaluate carefully a speaker's eloquence—that is, his or her language so articulated as to compel a listener's attention and convince him or her of the sincerity of the declaration and the sentiments that inspire it. Accordingly, language achieves this purpose when it is ornate. "Ornatum etenim amantis eloquium amoris consvevit concitare aculeos et de loquentis facit probitate praesumi"[9] (Eloquence, when it is ornate, often inspires love and makes one presume the speaker's worthiness). To illustrate this assertion Andreas introduces the eight dialogues that make up the bulk of the *De amore*'s first book. Book 1 thus illustrates ways by which eloquence serves to gain the love of another person. The reader is to study the examples and imitate the art and eloquence they illustrate. They teach the art of love and the art of courtly poetry through examples of eloquent language rather than by a treatise on rhetoric. Similar study is required in reading most *chansons,* usually designated *grand chant courtois*.[10] Both Andreas's dialogues and the *chansons* illustrate an art of love and an art of poetry by ornate language.

However, rhetoric is not first and foremost an art of ornamentation. The "ornate language" Andreas refers to completes the prior stages of invention and disposition from which ornate language, in the broad sense, derives and to which it refers. Ornate language expresses thought and emotion, the products of invention and disposition, making them convincing by the skill with which they are set forth and embellished. Rhetoric uses all these procedures—invention, disposition, ornamentation as well as the gesture and delivery implicit in troubadour performance—to make cases and resolve issues where a difference of opinion requires agreement. It does so not by logical demonstration but on the grounds of probability. These procedures determine the context (or the alleged context for those who cannot take medieval love poetry or Andreas Capellanus seriously) in and for which *chansons* were written. Therefore the *chansons* stage an implicit rhetorical performance before an audience.[11] The issues they raise have to do with love.

Let me insist on these points by rephrasing briefly the foregoing discussion.

Rhetoric as an art serves to resolve issues. An issue arises when agreement is lacking regarding a matter of opinion or belief. Judgment is the means to resolve an issue—the judgment of the speaker as well as that of the listener. How can the lover make his or her case convincing? How can he or she demonstrate the "goodness" requisite in the orator, that *vir bonus dicendi peritus,* or, in a number of cases, *femina bona dicendi perita* (good man skilled in speaking, good woman so skilled)? How may the audience evaluate the speaker's words and detect sincerity or deception in eloquent language? These are crucial problems, and thus issues in love, whether as courtship or seduction. To such questions rhetoric as an art provides means to find answers in specific instances. In the context of this volume, the specific examples of the art of eloquent persuasion are medieval love poems.

Before returning to Andreas Capellanus's *De amore* as an illustration, let me preface my comments by saying that I am not concerned as to whether Andreas's treatise is satirical or ironic in intent, nor convinced by arguments that it is—people in love usually look a little funny or silly, especially in love poetry from bygone times. But that does not matter here. For, even if the *De amore* were satirical or ironic in intent, there must have existed a recognizable object of the satire or irony, an object which was taken seriously by enough persons to warrant the satire and make it seem apt or noteworthy. Such persons must have made up the audiences of the *grand chant courtois.* Thus, even a mock *De amore* must show the lineaments of the object of mockery, even if it is ironically colored and, thus, more or less different from the serious or genuine object it mocks. And indeed, the *De amore,* especially its first book, contains numerous instances in which eloquence serves to incline a lady to consider the worthiness of various kinds of good men—that is, men whose love is allegedly good and worthy of the lady they love.[12] The scenario is commonplace, being analogous to that in love lyric, minus by and large the response of the woman.

In an important article, Frederick Goldin has shown how the troubadour adapts his or her "argument" to an implied audience.[13] To be sure, that audience may change from stanza to stanza, necessitating a restatement of the issues and the case for the new audience. Accordingly Goldin shows that the poet might assume different personae according to the implied audience for each poem or each stanza. These personae offer to the different intended audiences perspectives on the love-relation the speaker or singer is cultivating. Thus, to quote Goldin, "The courtly community is represented in the lyric by the audience; the directions that love may take, by the different kinds of persons in that audience and the conflicting impulses of the 'I,' the courtly lover, in the lyric." Accordingly, each poem sets out "a pattern of friends and enemies"—I would single out explicitly the person loved, whether friend or enemy—"radiating from a central love-relation upon which they are all intent."[14] Goldin points out that in lyric, as opposed to romance, the amorous relation is "static." This is true. But the argument register of the *chanson* intends a progression. Hence, a poem shows a stage in a *gradus amoris*. As is well known, the *gradus amoris* is a topical scheme that identifies the commonplace stages in love, from first encounter to consummation; it includes such moments as first sight, embraces, kisses, and prolonged thought on the object of love and on one's own emotions. The performance situation dramatizes one moment or the other in its relation to past and, more importantly for the lover, future stages.

We can see both audiences and issues in a rather straightforward case, the *canso* by Bernart de Ventadorn beginning "Lo gens tems de pascor."[15] In stanzas 1–6, the speaker addresses a nondescript, but presumably interested, male audience of noble birth, the "senhor" of line 9. In stanzas 7–9 he turns to the lady, or the "domna" (line 50) herself. To the "senhor" he describes his lady as "midons" (line 10). In so doing, he contrasts, on the one hand, her desirability as a beautiful, noble woman, "la gensor" (line 15) whose "cors blanc" (line 37) is a source of potential joy (line 35), with, on the other hand, her character as "traïdor" (line 11), "chamjan" (line 23), indifferent to his lot as expressed by her "no m'en chal" (line 44)—all of which makes her guilty of "pechat ... criminal" (line 48).[16] His language does not change in addressing the lady. To be sure, she retains her admirable traits: "bela ... et pros" (line 50), "faissos / e·ls bels olhs amoros" (lines 57–58), which justifies the *senhal* he gives her: "Bel Vezer" (line 65);

nor does he stint in criticism of the wrongs she has allegedly done him: "de mal respos" (line 60), "sembla·m trassios" (line 61), since she is "orgolhos" (line 63) when she affirms her dominion ("poderos," line 64) over him, that is, her *dangier* in the language of the *Roman de la rose*. These parallels contrast her with the speaker and lover ("amador," line 5).

What can he expect to gain by such evidently displeasing, *ad hominem* reproach? Among the men or *senhor* he might arouse pity by frequent references to his grief ("planh e plor," line 7; "viur' a dolor," 13; "Pen' e dolor e dan . . . gran," lines 17–18; "no vei a jornal," line 34), as well as his long-suffering ("sofert . . . ai tan," line 19) and constancy ("ben e . . . onor / c'ai faih," lines 14–15; "ses enjan," line 22; "Pois fom amdui efan," line 25; "d'amor coral," line 43). However, this description of his lot is reserved for the *senhor*. For the lady he speaks of himself only as "enveyos" (line 54), and of his song as being sustained only by her (lines 64–68). Thus, the first audience—the *senhor*—knows him and his suffering because of a treacherous woman; the woman knows only his protestations of constancy while hearing her own harshness blamed.[17] The credibility of the lover for the larger audience is his suffering; for the lady, it is his constancy and song contrasted with the treachery and pride that characterize her domination. To both audiences, however, he brands her conduct towards him deceitful. Could her shame because of such ignobility be the emotional response he is seeking from her? That is the issue.

I have attempted to illustrate in Bernart's *canso* rhetorical appeal to audiences, an appeal meant to be eloquent and thus sway them in his favor and towards approval of his love. Moreover, the performance is eminently rhetorical because it includes an advocate, a jury, and an accused. The advocate is the speaker, the jury the intended audience, the accused the lady herself. In Bernart's "Lo gens tems de pascor" they all appear. Each person is therefore represented in conformity with the argument being made. That argument is itself generic in character. It identifies the genre of the persona—what was termed *maneries/manière* in the Middle Ages.[18] The genre as persona could be a hybrid. We may return once more to Andreas Capellanus for cogent illustration.

The man-woman exchanges in Book 1 of the *De amore* illustrate what we call class distinctions among the interlocutors, but what the Middle Ages thought of as distinctions in social orders. The entire *De amore* shows a hierarchical classification of persons extending from the most noble (the *nobilissimi*), whom Andreas locates among the religious, down to peasants, prostitutes, and the ruttish. An analogous social hierarchy, from queens and princesses to prostitutes, informs Christine de Pizan's *Livre des trois vertus*, which suggests the general applicability of the scheme from the twelfth into the fifteenth century. Within this broad scheme, Andreas identifies the orders worthy of engaging in the kinds of love he ostensibly fosters—that is, love because of beauty, because of eloquence, and because of noble qualities. He admits the "middle class" (*plebei*) among lovers who are noble, more noble, and most noble.[19] In addition, other distinctions cut across orders and diversify issues and cases raised in the dialogues, such as age, blindness, charm, prowess, wealth, and profession or trade. The distinctions are by and large synonymous with the circumstantial topoi in description—that is, the elements out of which *manière* as defined above is elicited and identified.

Circumstantial topoi are those traits any class of beings has in common. Among humans these might be gender, age, nationality, language, habits of life, fortune, luck, family background, and affections. Among things and actions they might be cause, nature, quality, time, place, and antecedent, concurrent, and subsequent events, as in a *gradus amoris*.[20] "Might be" in both instances because the argument made will decide what features of persons, things, or actions—by features, I mean topoi or *loci, lieux*—require special identification and distinction, like male or female, young or old, or among actions, which stage in the *gradus amoris* has been reached and which is being sought after: a word, a kiss, or a lady "Quan l'ai despoillada / Sotz cortin' obrada."[21] To delineate topoi in *fin' amours* requires finesse.[22] The only topos that remains constant in Andreas Capellanus is that of social order. All lovers are in some way noble or ignoble. Yet even here argument is not excluded. In the *De amore*, nobility deriving from blood or from heart is an issue.[23]

The choice made between the topoi and the attributes assigned to them will determine the character of the person represented and his or her actions; it will also define the audience as one concerned with such persons and actions and their evaluation. In particular, the choice will define the quality of love and of the lovers. In Bernart de Ventadorn's *canso* "Lo gens tems de pascor," for example, the choice of physical features and the contrast between the lover's habitual constancy and the lady's deceptiveness illustrate topical attributes appropriate to the case being made. Such invention is successful if it convinces its audience—in the case of this *canso*, the *senhor* on the one hand and the *domna* on the other. There is no period in medieval literature in Occitan and French in which topical invention like this is not evident in the composition of lyric poetry, from Guillaume d'Aquitaine to Charles d'Orléans.

In the Middle Ages, the rhetorical term that designates the quality of such poetry is Material Style.²⁴ Material Style classes persons, things, and actions according to a social hierarchy and typology. The style is the dress, as it were. Thus, in Andreas Capellanus, a noble person may be young or old, handsome or ugly, accomplished in arms or a great preacher, male or female. Similar distinctions appear in lyric poetry. Striking examples are the *chanson* attributed to Jacques d'Ostun in which the poet evokes the child with which he has made his "Douce dame" pregnant,²⁵ or Thibaut de Champagne's oblique allusions to his exceptionally high nobility: "Ja par amors n'amera riches hom"²⁶ (No rich and noble man will love rightly), or so people say. But Thibaut states this only to contradict it. Elsewhere, the poet is anxious because of his ugliness, perhaps because of obesity:

> Toute biauté est en li aünee;
> Sousfrete en ot Deus a moi enbelir.
> Et quant biauté est toute a li donee,
> Deus, qui me fist a la biauté faillir,
> M'a doné cuer verai pour vous servir.²⁷

> All beauty is gathered up in her. God neglected to make me handsome. And since all beauty is given to her, God, who made me without making me beautiful, gave me nonetheless a true heart to serve you.

Translated into the lyric of troubadours, trouvères, the Second Rhetoric of the late medieval period, and their counterparts in other languages, the same conception of Material Style holds. The majority of lyric voices in these poems are those of lovers. All make a case for their love. In so doing, they describe or appeal to themselves (in monologues) and to their lady, as well as to others in their audiences like other lovers, jongleurs, spies, and *jangleors,* as Goldin has demonstrated.

Goldin believes that multiple audience perspectives are lacking among the trouvères.²⁸ In fact, quite the opposite is the case. For example, in one *chanson,* the Châtelain de Couci addresses alternately lovers in general once, love personified twice, God twice, and, finally, his lady once and for all in conclusion.²⁹ Other examples are not hard to find, although they may well be less frequent than in troubadour poetry.³⁰

Topical descriptions of *manière* as Material Style allow a perceptive yet critical audience to recognize the kind and quality of love being exemplified. Machaut's *chansons féminines* illustrate this. These feminine voices assert the commonplace that the woman in a love-relation should not request the love of a man—and yet they are doing just that, as in this stanza in which Machaut allows us to hear a lady beseeching her lover metamorphosed into a cold, marble phallus.

> Honteuse sui, quant je parole einsi,
> Et laidure est seulement dou penser,
> Qu'il n'apartient que dame à son ami
> Doie mercy ne grace demander;
> Car dame doit en riant refuser
> Et amis doit prier en souspirant,
> Et je te pri souvent et en plourant.
> Mais en toy truis, quant plus sui esplourée,
> *Cuer de marbre couronné d'aÿmant,*
> *Ourlé de fer, à la pointe asserée.*[31]

> I am ashamed to speak in this way, and it is awful even to have such thoughts, for it does not behoove a lady to ask mercy or a favor from her beloved. Rather she ought to turn down his entreaties with a smile while the beloved courts her with sighs. And I beseech your love often and in tears. However, in you I find when I am most racked with tears *a heart of marble crowned with a magnetic diamond ringed with iron and tipped with steel point.*

In fact, these poems are often found together with "*chansons masculines*" in exchanges that anticipate the ballade and rondeau cycles of Christine de Pizan, wherein the credibility of eloquence is acutely problematized for audiences attempting to discern honesty and deception in the lyric voices. On the other hand, in a *canso* by Azalais de Porcairagues, "Ar em al freg temps vengut" (Now have we reached the cold season), one stanza evokes the exceptional entreaty by a lady, including her concern because the man she loves (usually identified as Raimbaut d'Aurenga) is too highborn for her.

> Dompna met molt mal s'amor
> que ab ric home plaideia,
> a plus aut de vavasor,
> e si lo fai, ill foleia.[32]

> A lady does not place her love well if she becomes involved with a rich and noble man, if he stands higher than a vavasor; if she does so anyway, she has gone mad.

She and other troubadours treat the problem of what is decorous or appropriate, which surfaces as well in the *De amore*[33] and, as we have seen, in the *chanson* by Thibaut de Champagne cited above. It too is a matter of Material Style focusing on the topoi "physical appearance" (*natura a corpore*) and "age" (*aetas*) in Thibaut's case, on *sexus* in Azalais's.[34]

Material Style conforms to common medieval conceptions of rhetorical invention. The speaker is a lover. The author will have initially decided what kind of lover to represent in keeping with his or her conception of love itself. This may occur more easily if a personification of love takes on a specific Material Style. The personification's attributes will characterize the author's conception of love. To invent such a personification, the author will consider circumstantial topoi available in the personification's persona. Since circumstantial topoi are features that any class or genre shares, what will interest the poet is the argument to be made and how, therefore, to distinguish the image of his love by the choice and definition of appropriate topoi. As in Andreas. For example, age. Is the lover young, in the prime of life, or old? What deeds worthy of exciting love has the person of that age achieved or could he or she achieve? Is the lover a knight, a cleric, a merchant—and what does that vocation tell about the kind of love he is capable of and the good it might bring about?[35]

In lyric, the issues are more complex since, as we have seen, eloquence must convince of and by itself in order for progression in the *gradus amoris* to take place, including appropriate actions in the extradiegetic world. Such progression depends on the success with which the case is argued in the poem. The performance must be convincing. In fact, performance makes Andreas's aforementioned reference to ornate language assume greater importance: "Ornatum etenim amantis eloquium ... de loquentis facit probitate praesumi" (For a lover's fine eloquence argues for his worthiness).

Ornate language is style. Style is a matter of finesse, which itself is an attribute of the kind of love—*fin' amours*—the *chansons* promote. Let me illustrate this with the first stanza of Gautier de Dargies's "La gens dient pour coi je ne faiz chanz."

> La gens dient pour coi je ne faiz chanz
> Pluz legiers et meilleurs a retenir,
> Maiz ne sevent qu'Amours me fait sentir,
> Quar de celui u l'amours est pluz granz
> Convient mouvoir les chanz fors et pesans;
> Qui mainz aime de lui convient issir
> Les febles chanz que chascuns puet furnir;
> Qui ne le set demant le as fins amans
> S'Amours est si vertueuse et poissanz.[36]

People ask why I don't write simple songs that can be remembered more easily. But they don't know what feelings Love gives me. For from the one whose love is greater should issue difficult, weighty songs. From him whose love is inferior should come slight songs that anyone can write. If you don't know this, ask the courtly lovers—the *fins amans*—if Love has such force and power.

Perhaps an illustration of such weight (but not of obesity!) in verse would be Thibaut de Champagne's "De bone amor vient seance et bonté." This complex poem builds on semantically interdependent triangles of conventional courtly abstractions and commonplaces; the abstractions and commonplaces fit into concrete metaphors that articulate the functions of the triangles of abstractions for the audience. After the disquisition, both abstract and metaphorical, that makes up the body of the poem, the poet turns to his lady in the *envoi*, offering his poem as expression and image of his heart for her approval.

In the first stanza the three abstractions, *bone amor, seance,* and *bonté,* form a triune configuration from which issues an intention—a glance in the strict medieval sense of the word for vision—personified as *coreur* or "runners" whose way passes out through his heart as vision.

> De bone amor vient seance et bonté,
> Et amors vient de ces deus autresi.
> Tuit troi sunt un, qui bien i a pensé;
> Ja a nul jor ne seront departi.
> Par un conseil ont ensemble establi
> Li coreor, qui sont avant alé:
> De mon cuer ont fet leur chemin ferré;
> Tant l'ont usé, ja n'en seront parti.[37]

> From good love derive knowledge and goodness, and love comes from these two as well. All three are one thing if you consider them well. They will never be sundered from one another. The couriers who go on ahead have together agreed on a plan: they have made their roadway of my heart and have frequented it so much that they will never be separated from it.

Thibaut employs the medieval concept of extramission: the eyebeam meets the light emanating from an object of vision and brings the exterior image back along the same way.[38] In Thibaut's image the eyebeam brings the image through the heart to the speaker's love. The image carries over into the second stanza. In it too a complex metaphor is built on the lady's radiant beauty and her qualities or "bien" which shine forth at night, but are carefully obscured in the day. The triangulation here of "douz regart," assimilated to the runners, with beauty and the good qualities, explains the poet-lover's conventional dismay: "je m'en esbahi."[39]

> Li coreor sunt la nuit en clarté
> Et le jor sont por la gent oscurci:
> Li douz regart plesant et savoré,
> La granz biautez et li bien que j'i vi;
> N'est merveille se je m'en esbahi.
> De li a Deus le siecle enluminé,

> Car qui avroit le plus biau jor d'esté,
> Lez li seroit oscurs a plain midi. (lines 9–16)

> The couriers are illuminated by night and darkened in daylight because of people: they are the sweet glance, pleasant and delightful, and the great beauty and good I saw in her. No wonder I am overwhelmed by them. God has illuminated the world by her, for even the most beautiful summer day one might enjoy would be dark at noonday next to her.

That *ébahissement* becomes in turn the source of a third triangular disposition in stanza 3. Here the lady's "bien" seeks refuge in "grant valeur," which in turn is dependent on the triangle of love, fear, and courage that are constituents of the state of *ébahissement* in the lover. Love offers lodging to those who deserve it. But, since the poet-lover has failed to obtain such lodgings, he has become bewildered and uncertain: "si ne sai ou je sui" (line 24), a forerunner of Charles d'Orléans's "L'omme esgaré qui ne scet ou il va."[40]

> En amor a paor et hardement:
> Li dui sont troi et du tierz sont li dui,
> Et grant valeur est a eus apendant,
> Ou tout li bien ont retret et refui.
> Por c'est Amors li hospitaus d'autrui
> Que nus n'i faut selonc son avenant.
> G'i ai failli, dame, qui valez tant,
> A vostre ostel, si ne sai ou je sui. (lines 17–24)

> In love one finds both fear and courage. The two are three and the third derives from the two, while great worth depends on them in which all goods find harbor and refuge. That is why Love is the hostel for others, for no one lacks whatever he may merit. I have failed, lady of such great worth, to gain admittance into your hostel, which has caused me to lose my way.

Nothing remains in stanza 4 but to commend himself to his lady. She in turn now triangulates with his dual fates, happy and sad: "Ma bele joie ou ma mort i atent." The glance, or *coup* (*d'œil*) evoked at the beginning of the poem by an exchange of glances, is recalled with pleasure as he awaits his fate.

> Or n'i a plus fors qu'a li me conmant,
> Car touz biens fez ai lessié pour cestui:
> Ma bele joie ou ma mort i atent,
> Ne sai le quel, dès que devant li fui.
> Ne me firent lors si œil point d'ennui,
> Ainz me vindrent ferir si doucement

> Par mi le cuer d'un amoreus talent;
> Oncore i est li cous que j'en reçui. (lines 25–32)

> Nothing remains for me except to commend myself to her, for I have set aside all good deeds for her sake. I have been awaiting from this either wonderful joy or my death—I know not which—since I first came before her. Her eyes did me no harm then, on the contrary they came to strike me so gently through the heart with amorous desire that the blow I received then is still there.

The *coup* is restated in the final stanza as well as the arrow of love that translates the eyebeam of extramission.

> Li cous fu granz, il ne fet qu'enpoirier,
> Ne nus mires ne m'en porroit saner,
> Se cele non qui le dart fist lancier. (lines 33–35)

> The blow was great and it has grown ever worse, nor could any physician heal it except she alone who fired the arrow.

The wound is linked to the medieval commonplace of the beloved as healer, the mythic healer of the wound she herself has caused.

> Se de sa main i daignoit adeser,
> Bien en porroit le coup mortel oster
> A tout le fust, dont j'ai grant desirrier;
> Mès la pointe du fer n'en puet sachier,
> Qu'ele bruisa dedenz au cop doner. (lines 36–40)

> If she deigned to touch it, she could indeed remove the mortal blow together with the shaft—something which I desire very much; but the iron tip she cannot withdraw for it broke off when the blow was struck.

The transition thus reverts to the lady in a roundabout way, addressing her directly in the *envoi* in which the *chanson* personified becomes the messenger who goes out, like the couriers, to express the author's "heart." The solitary monologue, as poem, becomes "ornatum eloquium" and a gift for his lady.

> Dame, vers vous n'ai autre messagier
> Par cui vous os mon corage envoier
> Fors ma chançon, se la volez chanter. (lines 41–43)

> Lady, I have no other messenger by whom I dare send you my heart than my song, if you agree to sing it.

The *envoi* sends his *chanson* back to the source of the arrow, the lady herself and, implicitly, her eyes, with the hope that she might be willing to sing it. Words have replaced eyebeams.

I have analyzed this *chanson* in some detail in order to suggest how its art may function as an art of poetry. Not only does it provide original variants on commonplace themes and images, it shows by example how subsequent poets may imitate its procedures or strategies in adapting similar matter in their own poems. There is no direct influence, but the line of descent along exemplary lines between Thibaut's *chanson* and Charles d'Orléans's Ballade CV seems obvious:

> En la forest de Longue Actente,
> Chevauchant par divers sentiers,
> M'en voys, ceste annee presente,
> Ou voyage de Desiriers.
> Devant sont allez mes fourriers
> Pour appareiller mon logeis
> En la cité de Destinee;
> Et pour mon cueur et moy ont pris
> L'ostellerie de Pensee. (lines 1–9)

> In the forest of Long and Anxious Expectation I go riding along diverse paths this year on the voyage of Desire. My couriers went ahead to prepare my lodgings in the city of Destiny. For my heart they have taken the hostel of Thought.

The *puys*, consistories, or *chambres de rhétorique* of northern and southern France envisage by their very competitions the variant treatment of commonplace material whose art was available—and was said to be available—in the works of predecessors. Like the Latin tradition, the new vernacular tradition founded study of the art not only on treatises but also on antecedent works of art and imitative composition. But the works of art are chronologically prior to the treatises.[41] Like the Latin treatises, their vernacular counterparts do not constrain those who study them. Rather, they reveal the possibilities of poetic and rhetorical language, possibilities illustrated by the treatises and the predecessors imitable by those who came after them.

This means that those works, including the troubadour *cansos* and trouvère *chansons*, were read as intensely as Gautier de Dargies wished his poems to be read, and as seriously as we know, to take a later example, Machaut's own inventions were—as sources for a rhetoric.[42] From such works new authors drew an image which found ornate expression in their own original compositions: the art of rhetoric as twelfth-century authors knew it and learned it. The rhetoric allows for originality in traditional registers, as part of a tradition that could renew itself not with the clichés the art represented, but by finer and more exquisite expression of its ideals and art. This was an "illustrious vernacular," as Dante perceived and imitated it in his own traditional, yet original ways. By understanding the terms of that art and of that rhetoric, that is, by understanding the procedures of its practice, we can, as Paterson and Mölk show, interpret with some understanding and finesse medieval lyric poetry, despite the distances that separate us from it.

NOTES

1. The term comes from the *accessus ad auctores* but is also found in other works and in auctorial interventions. See Bruno Sandkühler, *Die frühen Dantekommentare und ihr Verhältnis zur mittelalterlichen Kommentartradition*, Münchner romanistische Arbeiten, vol. 19 (Munich: Hueber, 1967); Alistair J. Minnis, *Medieval Theory of Authorship: Scholastic Literary Attitudes in the Later Middle Ages* (London: Scolar Press, 1984).

2. Linda M. Paterson, *Troubadours and Eloquence* (Oxford: Clarendon Press, 1975), 1; emphasis mine. For the Dante reference, see Pier Vincenzo Mengaldo, ed., *De vulgari eloquentia*, II.iv.2, in Dante Alighieri, *Opere minori*, La letteratura italiana: storia e testi, vol. 5 (Milan: Ricciardi, 1979); cf. Mengaldo's translation, 161: "la quale poesia non è altro che invenzione poeticamente espressa secondo retorica e musica," and 161–63, n. 8.

3. Paterson, *Troubadours*, 6.

4. Ulrich Mölk, *Trobar clus trobar leu: Studien zur Dichtungstheorie der Trobadors* (Munich: Fink, 1968), esp. 177–99.

5. Paterson, *Troubadours*, 5.

6. See my *The Arts of Poetry and Prose*, Typologie des Sources du Moyen Age Occidental, vol. 59 (Turnhout: Brepols, 1991), 57–64, 159–63.

7. See Paterson's introduction, *Troubadours*, 1–2. The word "individuality" is too imprecise and unmedieval to be very helpful, presenting, as it does, the added risk of misunderstanding because of—individual—notions today of what constitutes the individual. Subjectivity, or the awareness of a conflict between one's own experience and tradition or authority, is more cogent. When personal experience takes precedence over tradition or authority, we have individuality. Christine de Pizan's discovery that her experience as a woman does not conform to traditional views of women places her on the borderline between subjectivity and individuality.

8. E. Trojel, ed., *Andreae Capellani regii Francorum De amore libri tres* (Copenhagen: Gadiana, 1892), 18.

9. Ibid., 18.

10. See Roger Dragonetti, *La technique poétique des trouvères dans la chanson courtoise: contribution à l'étude de la rhétorique médiévale* (Bruges: De Tempel, 1960; Geneva: Slatkine, 1979), 140–41, 542, 544.

11. I am using "performance" in Sylvia Huot's sense of the text which "stages" its own performance in manuscript and in the (medieval) imagination of the reader; see Huot, *From Song to Book: The Poetics of Writing in Old French Lyric and Lyrical Narrative Poetry* (Ithaca: Cornell University Press, 1987), esp. 3–4.

12. Some dialogues end with some slight encouragement, e.g., "Tuo Deus labori digna praemia ferat" (*De amore*, 53) (May God grant a worthy reward to your efforts),

or "si, ut verbis assertive proponis, facto curaveris adimplere, facile non posset accidere, quin a me vel alia retributionem susciperes abundanter" (80) (if as you claim you strive to do as you say, you can hardly fail to receive full and complete reward from me or some other woman). Others suggest indecision (218–19) or great difficulty in deciding (35), while another seems prepared to assent (108–9). None refuses outright.

13. Frederick Goldin, "The Array of Perspectives in the Early Courtly Lyric," in *In Pursuit of Perfection: Courtly Love in Medieval Literature*, ed. Joan M. Ferrante and George D. Economou (Port Washington, N.Y.: Kennikat Press, 1975), 51–99.

14. Ibid., 51–52.

15. Quoted from Moshé Lazar, ed., *Bernard de Ventadour: chansons d'amour*, Bibliothèque française et romane B4 (Paris: Klincksieck, 1966), *canso* 17.

16. There is an ambiguous reference to when she will be old (lines 31–32), but the attribute does not seem to be immediately relevant except as a reminder that *tempus fugit*.

17. Recent feminist criticism has suggested ever more subtle responses from the women in court audiences and from the lady herself; see, notably, Roberta L. Krueger, *Women Readers and the Ideology of Gender in Old French Verse Romance*, Cambridge Studies in French, vol. 43 (Cambridge: Cambridge University Press, 1993), and Helen Solterer, *The Master and Minerva: Disputing Women in French Medieval Culture* (Berkeley: University of California Press, 1995). Individuals or groups in intended medieval audiences might be quite diverse, depending on how the commonplaces or topoi of human beings and the times are articulated. For example, the sympathy of some members of a male public does not preclude the mockery of others for unsuccessful lovers, or scorn for their moral weakness.

18. On *maneries/manière* in this sense, see my "La spécialité dans l'invention des topiques," in *Archéologie du signe*, ed. Lucie Brind'Amour and Eugene Vance, Papers in Mediaeval Studies, vol. 3 (Toronto: Pontifical Institute of Mediaeval Studies, 1983), 107–13.

19. *De amore*, 18–19.

20. See Matthew of Vendôme, *Ars versificatoria*, §§1.38–116, in Franco Munari, ed., *Matthei Vindocinensis Opera*, vol. 3, Storia e letteratura, vol. 171 (Rome: Storia e Letteratura, 1988); on the *gradus amoris*, see §4.13.

21. Ernest Hoepffner, ed., *Les poésies de Bernart Marti*, Classiques français du moyen âge, vol. 61 (Paris: Champion, 1929), *canso* 3, lines 44–45.

22. See my *Medieval Imagination: Rhetoric and the Poetry of Courtly Love* (Madison: University of Wisconsin Press, 1978), 14–22.

23. See, for example, *De amore*, 22–25.

24. On this term, see the fundamental study by Franz Quadlbauer, *Die antike Theorie der Genera Dicendi im lateinischen Mittelalter*, Österreichische Akademie der Wissenschaften: philosophisch-historische Klasse, Sitzungsberichte 241 (Vienna: Böhlaus, 1962). Cf. as well Kelly, *Arts of Poetry*, 71–78; and, on applications to late medieval lyric, Daniel Poirion, "Jacques Legrand: une poétique de la fiction," in *Théories et pratiques de l'écriture au Moyen Age, Actes du Colloque, Palais du Luxembourg-Sénat, 5 et 6 mars 1987*, ed. Emmanuèle Baumgartner and Christiane Marchello-Nizia, Littérales, vol. 4 (Nanterre: Centre de Recherches du Département de Français de Paris X-Nanterre, 1988), 227–34.

25. See *chanson* 24 in Emmanuèle Baumgartner and Françoise Ferrand, eds., *Poèmes d'amour des XIIe et XIIIe siècles,* 10/18: Bibliothèque médiévale (Paris: Union Générale d'Editions, 1983).

26. Alex Wallensköld, ed., *Les chansons de Thibaut de Champagne, roi de Navarre,* Société des Anciens Textes Français (Paris: Champion, 1925), *chanson* 29, line 14.

27. Ibid., appendix: *chanson* 5, lines 25–29. Cf. the ugly king of Hungary in Andreas Capellanus, *De amore,* 62.

28. Goldin, "Array," 91–92.

29. Alain Lerond, ed., *Chansons attribuées au Chastelain de Couci,* Publications de la Faculté des Lettres et Sciences Humaines de Rennes, vol. 7 (Paris: Presses Universitaires de France, 1964), *chanson* 1: "amant" (line 1); "amours" (lines 6, 29), "Diex" (lines 9, 17), "dame" (line 41).

30. See, for example, the Châtelain de Couci, *chanson* 6: "amant" (line 23), "franche riens" (line 33); *chanson* 23: "Dame" (lines 25, 30), "Biauz sire Diex" (line 33); *chanson* 27: "Douce dame" (lines 17, 23, 33), "seigneur, qui proiez et amez" (line 31), "chançons" (line 41); *chanson* 29: "dame" (lines 36, 41), "chançonnete" (line 51), "Phelippe" (line 54). Alex Wallensköld, ed., *Les chansons de Conon de Béthune,* Classiques français du moyen âge, vol. 24 (Paris: Champion, 1968), *chanson* 4: "Amors" (line 1), "li grant et li menor" (line 13), 'you' [= knights who do not love] (line 39) and 'we' [= knights who do love] (strophe vi). Holger Petersen Dyggve, ed., *Gace Brulé, trouvère champenois,* Mémoires de la Société Néophilologique de Helsinki, vol. 16 (Helsinki: Société de Littérature Finnoise, 1951), *chanson* 42: "dame" (lines 15, 28, 33, 36), "Fins amorox" (line 43); *chanson* 44: "Amours" (line 11 and in each refrain), "Dame" (line 31), "sire Dex" (line 51), "Seigneur" (line 61); *chanson* 46: "Dame" (line 21, 34), "fause gent haïe" (line 57); *chanson* 55: "dame" (line 13) and "Bele" (line 17), "Amors" (lines 25, 41), "Beax compainz de Valeri" (line 45). Anna Maria Raugei, ed., *Gautier de Dargies: poesie,* Pubblicazioni della Facoltà di Lettere e Filosofia dell'Università di Milano, vol. 90: Sezione a cura dell'Istituto di Lingue e Letterature Neolatine, vol. 5 (Florence: La Nuova Italia, 1981), *chanson* 6: "felon plain de grant mautalant" (line 12), "Douce dame" (line 34). Guillame de Ferrières, le Vidame de Chartres, in Holger Petersen Dyggve, ed., "Personnages historiques figurant dans la poésie lyrique française des XIIe et XIIIe siècles, XXII (Suite): Chansons du Vidame de Chartres," *Neuphilologische Mitteilungen* 46 (1945): 21–55, *chanson* 8: "Dolce dame" (line 19), "traïtor" (line 32), "vos" [= public] (line 37), "Chançons" (line 50). Jean de Trie, in Holger Petersen Dyggve, ed., *Trouvères et protecteurs de trouvères dans les cours seigneuriales de France* (Helsinki: Société de Littérature Finnoise, 1942), 186–90: *chanson* 12: "Chaitive gent" (line 25), "Chançon" (line 33), "Dame de Blois" (line 41).

31. In Machaut's *La louange des dames,* ed. Nigel E. Wilkins (Edinburgh: Scottish Academic Press, 1972), *chant royal* 1, lines 31–40 (p. 47); refrain italicized by editor.

32. Quoted from MS *N* in Angelica Rieger, *Trobairitz: Der Beitrag der Frau in der altokzitanischen höfischen Lyrik, Edition des Gesamtkorpus,* Beihefte zur Zeitschrift für romanische Philologie, vol. 233 (Tübingen: Niemeyer, 1991), 481, lines 17–20; on Azalais and Raimbaut, see Rieger, *Trobairitz,* 494–504. On the commonplace of courtship by the lady, see Matilda Tomaryn Bruckner, "Fictions of the Female Voice: The Women Troubadours," *Speculum* 67 (1992): 886–88; cf. *De amore,* 113–14.

33. *De amore*, 11–12 (impotence), 25–27 (disproportionate ages).

34. See Matthew of Vendôme, *Ars versificatoria*, ed. Munari, §§1.80 and 1.82.

35. Examples from Andreas's *De amore* of some of the topical issues the attributes raise are: praise and social order of woman (20), prudence (*sapientia*) of non-noble woman (22), age (25–28), crossing social orders inside and outside nobility (36–37, 54–55, 70–71, 110–111), love as sin (122–23, 159–60), love and marriage (141, 171–72), love and the religious (185–86). Many of these issues are resolved by judgment in Book 2 (271–95).

36. *Gautier de Dargies*, ed. Raugei, *chanson* 2, lines 1–9.

37. Thibaut de Champagne, ed. Wallensköld, *chanson* 6, lines 1–8.

38. David C. Lindberg, *Theories of Vision from Al-Kindi to Kepler* (Chicago: University of Chicago Press, 1976); Gudrun Schleusener-Eichholz, *Das Auge im Mittelalter*, Münstersche Mittelalter-Schriften, vol. 35 (Munich: Fink, 1985).

39. See Dragonetti, *Technique*, 135.

40. Pierre Champion, ed., *Charles d'Orléans: poésies*, Classiques français du moyen âge, vols. 34, 56 (Paris: Champion, 1966), *Ballade* 63, refrain.

41. See Elena Landoni, *La teoria letteraria dei Provenzali*, Biblioteca dell'Archivum Romanicum, ser. 1: Storia-letteratura-paleografia, vol. 220 (Florence: Olschki, 1989); cf. Rupprecht Rohr, *Matière, sens, conjointure: methodologische Einführung in die französische und provenzalische Literatur des Mittelalters* (Darmstadt: Wissenschaftliche Buchgesellschaft, 1978), chap. 5.

42. Kelly, *Medieval Imagination*, 3–12.

CHAPTER 8

The Old Occitan Arts of Poetry and the Early Troubadour Lyric

RUPERT T. PICKENS

One characteristic of the Occitan chansonnier that sets it apart from other kinds of highly organized medieval codices is the wide variety of generic forms that are displayed and celebrated. In this the chansonnier differs radically from the cyclic William of Orange manuscripts, which are confined to epic narration, just as the chansonnier differs from single-genre collections of dramas. The generic variety manifested by the chansonnier also reflects the variety of experiences that might characterize lyric performance. Generic multiplicity abounds in troubadour song, then, and performative possibilities inherent in the spoken, prose *vida* and *razo* narratives suggest an even richer variety. The corpus of work by a very prolific troubadour might also reflect such variety.

The problem of genre, as it is conventionally understood in relation to the troubadour lyric, is so knotty in its complexity, however, that it may well seem to defy scholars' attempts to establish generic definitions that would be useful in discussing the troubadour corpus as a whole. On the one hand, the troubadour tradition itself generated an interest in generic distinctions that was to become, by the end of the thirteenth century, a veritable obsession with a system of intricate variety, as theoretical treatises Erich Köhler has called "klassifikations freudig[e] Poetiken der Spätzeit" bear witness.[1] Unfortunately for modern scholarship, from treatise to treatise there is much confusion and inconsistency in delineating generic terms.[2] On the other hand, modern scholars have extended the list of generic terms,[3] whether or not they actually conform with explicit or implicit medieval definitions,[4] and freely apply them to troubadour songs often in conflict with one another.[5]

Following the lead of John H. Marshall, Erich Köhler, and Pierre Bec,[6] I propose to explore the problem of genre in the early troubadour lyric from the perspectives of medieval poetics and modern critical practice. As we shall see, troubadours active before the last quarter of the twelfth century were, apparently, largely unconcerned about the kinds of literary distinctions that came to obsess their successors in the following generations—indeed, the impulse to categorize, manifest in the chansonniers organized during the thirteenth century as well as in the arts of poetry, is an essential feature of a "modern" poetics that developed after the 1170s. The study of troubadour lyric may well require criteria for generic distinction—*intergeneric* distinction[7]—that are different from the thematic and formal concerns that preoccupy theoreticians medieval as well as modern.[8]

The major Old Occitan arts of poetry evoke a dazzling constellation of troubadour genres that include, according to the *De doctrina de compondre dictats,* the *canso,* the *vers,* the *lays,* the *sirventes,* the *retroncha,* the *pastora* (or *pastorela*), the *dança,* the *plant* (or *planh*), the *alba,* the *gayta,* the *estampida,* the *sompni,* the *gelozesca,* the *descort, coblas esparsas,* and the *tenso.*[9] The *De doctrina de compondre dictats* dates undoubtedly from the last decade of the thirteenth century. Some twenty-five to thirty years later, the *Leys d'amors*—the "Laws of Love" designed to lay the groundwork for the Floral Games at Toulouse—offers means, implicitly and explicitly, for classifying the genres in that bewildering array. Certain forms are privileged as worthy of judgment for one of the floral prizes to be awarded by the Consistori de la subregaya companhia del Gay Saber. The single most accomplished *vers* or *canso* will receive the Golden Violet, as will the best *descortz. Dansas* will compete for the Silver Marigold. *Pastorelas, vergieras,* and "other like forms" (autras d'aquestas manieras)—that is, narrative accounts of a troubadour's encounter with a peasant woman—will vie for the Silver Rose.[10] Listed elsewhere among the major genres, but not mentioned as eligible for one of the floral prizes, are the *tenso,* the *partimen,* the *planh,* and the *escondig.*[11] Meanwhile, the *Leys d'amors* relegates some thirteen named genres, plus songs of similar form ("lors semblans"), to the minor status (or the non-status) of "other poems" (autres dictatz), among them the *somnis* (or dream-song), the *enueg* and the *desplazers* (songs of annoyance), and the *plazers* (a song about what pleases the troubadour). Other forms listed in the *De doc-*

trina do not seem worthy of mention in the *Leys d'amors* at all—nor, in fact, do they reappear in any other art of poetry; these include the *estampida*, a dance form; the *gayta*, a watchman's song, a love lyric associated with night; and the *lays*, which the *De doctrina* describes as similar to the *sirventes*.[12] Thus the troubadour genres worthy of consideration, according to the *Leys d'amors*, constitute a cluster, not of sixteen but of ten forms that include the *vers*, the *canso*, the *descortz*, the *dansa*, the *pastorela*, the *tenso*, the *partimen*, the *sirventes*, the *planh*, and the *escondig*.[13]

In defining a corpus of pertinent medieval critical texts, I would add to the *De doctrina de compondre dictats* and the *Leys d'amors*, not only the major and minor treatises edited by Marshall along with the *De doctrina*,[14] but also—and most especially—the *vidas* and *razos*.[15] The *vidas* and *razos* are important commentaries on troubadour poetry that predate every other medieval source except, perhaps, for the *Razos de trobar* of Raimon Vidal, which Marshall dates from the first third of the thirteenth century; the *vidas* and *razos* that can be attributed to Uc de Saint-Circ date from the early 1220s, while others found in the twin chansonniers *I* and *K* were in existence by the end of the middle third of the thirteenth century.[16]

I will focus attention on early troubadours, that is, poets who flourished before 1180, especially William IX, Cercamon, Marcabru, Jaufre Rudel de Blaya, Bernart de Ventadorn, and Guiraut de Borneill, all from the Aquitaine region, plus Peire d'Alvergne.[17] My main reason for restricting our view to these troubadours and some of their contemporaries is that the *vidas* and *razos* discuss with reference to them a poetics of the old order—"la uzansa antiga," as Cercamon's *vida* says.[18] This "antique style" is opposed, implicitly, to a more "modern" poetics associated with the time when the *vidas* and *razos*, as well as the more formal arts of poetry, were being written, that is, as we have seen, from the 1220s onward. But these texts explicitly situate the shift from "ancient" to "new" in the 1170s or 1180s.

The relatively early date of the troubadour corpus I have delineated will also enable us to set aside some of the generic terms in the privileged cluster already defined—for the simple reason that some of those terms apply only to troubadour practice after the turn of the century. Despite the prominence given to them in the *Leys d'amors* and other treatises, *dansas* consisting of three *coblas* with refrains developed too late to be of interest to us here; the *descort*, with its *coblas* of varying shapes, also seems to have been unknown to the early troubadours; nor do early troubadours seem to have practiced the *escondig*, a song of exculpation. It is perhaps significant that *dansas*, *descorts*, and *escondigs* are not mentioned in the *vidas* or *razos*. Relentlessly, the number of generic terms in the privileged cluster diminishes to seven which, tentatively, we can group under three headings: (1) lyrics (*vers, canso, sirventes, planh*); (2) dialogues (*tenso, partimen*); and (3) narratives (*pastorelas*).

Of the remaining terms, *vers* and *canso* are by far the most troublesome. In discussing *vers* and *cansos*, the *vidas* and *razos*, on the one hand, and the arts of poetry, on the other, are fundamentally at odds because each of the opposing sets of authoritative texts appears to distinguish between the *vers* and the *canso* on the basis of different principles of definition. In general, the *vidas* and *razos* posit a diachronic distinction—the *vers* gave way to the *canso*—while the arts of poetry discuss the two forms as existing simultaneously: we have seen how *vers* and *cansos* compete for the Golden Violet in the same category at the Floral Games at Toulouse. To complicate matters further, there are signs that the *vidas* and *razos* also, at times, intend the synchronic instead of the diachronic opposition.

Cercamon, we recall, "trobet vers e pastoretas a la usanza antiga" (composed *vers* and *pastorelas* in the ancient manner).[19] Peire de Valeira, according to his *vida*, was a jongleur from Marcabru's time: "e fez vers tals com hom fazia adoncs, de paubra valor, de foillas e de flors, e de cans e d'ausels" (and he made *vers* such as people made then, of poor quality, about leaves and flowers and about songs and birds).[20] Marcabru composed "De caitivetz vers e de caitivetz serventes" (miserable *vers* and miserable *sirventes*), while Jaufre Rudel made "mains bons vers ab bons sons, ab paubres motz" (many good *vers* with good melodies and poor words).[21] Peire d'Alvergne's *vida* is the most precise with respect to the old *vers* as opposed to the new *canso*:

> E trobet ben e cantet ben, e fo lo premiers bons trobaires que fon outra mon e aquel que fez los meillors sons de vers que anc fosson faichs.... Canson no fetz, qe non era adoncs negus cantars appelatz cansos, mas vers; qu'En Girautz de Borneill fetz la premeira canson que anc fos faita.[22]
>
> And he composed poetry well and sang well, and he was the first good troubadour from beyond the mountains and the one who made the best melodies for *vers* that were ever made.... He did not make a *canso*, for then there was no kind of song called a *canso*, but it was a *vers*; for it was lord Guiraut de Borneill who made the first *canso* that was ever made.

The version of Marcabru's *vida* in *AB* confirms that "En aquel temps non appellava hom cansson, mas tot qant hom cantava eron vers" (In that time people did not call [anything] a *canso*, but everything they sang was a *vers*).[23]

At least insofar as the earliest troubadours are concerned, the biographers' observation is surely based in part on the absence of the word *canso* in their works and their privileging of the term *vers*.[24] In these troubadours' exordial *coblas* and *tornadas* alone—privileged loci in troubadour and trouvère lyric for language evoking poetic technique—we find the word *vers* applied to the text at hand seven times in the ten authentic songs of William IX; the term *vers* is found three times in Jaufre Rudel's six songs, three times in Cercamon's eight, twelve times in Marcabru's forty-three, and eight times in Peire d'Alvergne's nineteen. These early troubadours never use the word *canso* in reference to their own work.[25]

What kinds of songs do the early troubadours themselves call *vers*?[26] In William IX's somewhat idiosyncratic corpus, we find the term applied to a variety of works: the ribald "Companho, farai un vers tot covinen"; the licentious Agnes-Ermessen narrative, "Farai un vers, pos mi sonelh," which P-C call a romance and Frank a *sirventes;* the parodic "Farai un vers de dreit nïen," which P-C call a *devinalh* but Frank a *sirventes;* the boastful *gap* (P-C) or *sirventes* (Frank), "Ben vueill que sapchan li pluzor"; the exquisitely courtly "Pos vezem de novel florir," a *canso* in P-C and Frank; and the elegiac "Pos de chantar m'es pres talenz," which Bond categorizes as a *planh,* P-C as a penitential song (*Busslied*), and Frank as a *chanson religieuse.*[27]

Among Marcabru's songs, their composer calls *vers* ten characterized by P-C and Frank as *sirventes* and one love lyric which P-C and Frank call a *canso.*[28] Significantly, Uc Catola invites Marcabru to debate in "Amic(s) Marchabrun, car digam" by proposing that they sing "Un vers d'Amor" (a *vers* about Love).[29] Cercamon's corpus displays greater variety: P-C term three songs which Cercamon calls *vers* a *planh* ("Lo plaing comenz iradamen"), a *canso* ("Assatz es ora oimai q'eu chant"), and "a kind of *sirventes-canso*" ("Pus nostre temps comens' a brunezir"), that is, a "satiric love song."[30] Jaufre Rudel's *vers,* which P-C and Frank describe as *cansos,* include a love lyric, "Quan lo rius de la fontana," and a parody in the manner of William IX, "No sap chantar qui so non di."[31] Peire d'Alvergne's corpus reflects the variety of Marcabru's: Peire designates as *vers* five songs modern scholars call *sirventes,* three love lyrics, and one ("Sobre·l vieill trobar e·l novel") which the earlier editor Rudolf Zenker classifies as a love lyric, but which P-C and Frank, as well as Del Monte, call a *sirventes.*[32]

These data suggest that, according to the actual "usanza antiga," the term *vers* had such broad application as to be utterly devoid of any generic specificity whatsoever.[33] Meanwhile, modern scholars' attempts—inappropriate attempts, I would argue—to categorize early troubadour lyrics according to criteria arising later in the tradition have resulted in a confused representation of the nature of the corpus. As we have seen, the variety of generic descriptors that have been employed in medieval and modern times with reference to the early troubadours' *vers* includes narrative "romance," companion song, love lyric, *canso, sirventes-canso* or satirical love song, love-lyric parody, *planh* or lament, *sirventes* or satire in a political, moral, or artistic vein, and *tenso* or debate song. To return to the cluster of important genres arrayed in the *Leys d'amors*, we find that the *vers* "in the ancient manner" embraces nearly all forms—and includes narrative, though without the precise plot requirements of the *pastorela*.

To be sure, it is the arts of poetry themselves, including the *Leys d'amors*, that have influenced modern scholars in their choices of generic descriptors. But the fact remains that the assignment of such terms by modern scholars can also be a matter of subjective interpretation of a song's thematic content and its emphases. In any case, it is clear, despite a modern critical commonplace, that the early *vers* is not the exact equivalent of what came later to be called the *canso* in the narrow sense of a refined love lyric. Thus a respected scholar's statement is a patent oversimplification: "*Vers* is the earlier term; gradually *canso* took precedence as the term used to designate this major lyric genre."[34]

The word *vers* "in the ancient manner" manifests a range of meaning comparable in its own way to the breadth of such non-genre-specific terms as the noun *cant* (song) and the infinitive *cantar* (to sing) used as a substantive. These latter terms occur with far greater frequency in early troubadour poetry than the word *vers*, yet scholars have not vested them with any kind of generic specificity—and rightly so—undoubtedly because the medieval arts of poetry do not use those terms to designate particular kinds of poetic compositions. I would suggest that the basic meanings of *cant* and *cantars*—that is, their basic meanings as words pertaining to the vocabulary of courtly poetics—are found in the common bird-song topos. As illustrated by Jaufre Rudel, for example, *cant* refers to song produced by a bird—not, I would stress, a song, which might suggest the rudiments of some kind of generic organization, but song consisting of music and an elemental love message conveyed through that music:[35]

> Quant lo rosignols el fuoillos
> Dona d'amor e·n quier e·n pren
> E mou son chant jauzen joios
> E remira sa par soven,
>   . . .[36]

> When the nightingale in the leafy wood gives of love, asks for it, and takes of it, and composes his song rejoicing and joyous . . .

In contrast to song in this sense, the substantive *cantars* denotes the process of musical production, that is, the art of singing:

E·l rossignoletz el ram
Volf e refraing et aplana
Son doutz chantar et afina,
. . .³⁷

and the little nightingale on the branch turns and modulates and polishes his sweet singing . . .

In a familiar extension of the bird-song topos, the troubadour produces his own *cant,* his singing, in imitation of the bird by exercising the art of *cantars* in his own way: "Pero mos chans comens' aissi" (wherefore my song begins thus), "Dreitz es q'ieu lo mieu [chantar] refraigna" (it is right that I should modulate my own [singing]).³⁸ Finally, the substantive *cantars* later came to mean also any kind of song composed by a troubadour, words and melody; this sense is common in the *vidas* and *razos* as well as in the arts of poetry.³⁹ In its emphatic reference to the song's verbal text, since the term is frequently linked to the word *so(n),* which designates a song's melody,⁴⁰ the term *vers* has a range of applicability of similar scope. As this is so, the later word that can be said to have replaced *vers* is not a narrowly generic *canso* but the broad term *dictatz,* a semi-learned word denoting any troubadour "poem" which occurs in the *De doctrina de compondre dictats* and is favored by the *Leys d'Amors.*

Margaret Switten reminds us that the term *vers* is a borrowing from the Latin *versus.*⁴¹ Medieval monastic *versus* are sung religious texts exemplifying a cultivation of original and highly refined, complex strophic forms; musically, the *versus* self-consciously creates and maintains an intimate relationship between verbal text and musical line. Of particular importance in the history of medieval Occitan poetry is the fact that the *versus* flourished at Saint-Martial in Limoges. I would suggest, following Switten, that Old Occitan *vers* used "in the ancient manner" refers broadly to any well-crafted troubadour song—and especially to the verbal text of that song; further, the *vers* is wrought in conformity with artistic principles that value the structure of the *cobla* and the intertwining of text and music. Such emphasis is reflected in Dante's insistence in the *De vulgari eloquentia* (II, ix, 2) on the stanza as the *gremium*—the heart, the soul, the matrix—of the song.

In historical context with the replacement of *vers* "in the ancient manner" by the "new" *canso,* Bernart de Ventadorn's usage appears to be transitional: seven of his forty-four songs he calls *vers,* while six are *cansos* and one a *cansoneta.*⁴² P-C and Frank term all fourteen of these songs *cansos.* Bernart's usage may be transitional. Or else he may be read as attempting some kind of synchronic distinction between *vers* and *canso* as the arts of poetry do. In his dialogue with Peirol, Bernart repeats a linking of the terms that was to become commonplace, remarking that his interlocutor has been for long "que no fezetz vers ni chanso" (without making either a *vers* or a *canso*); Bernart uses the expression again in a *canso,* "Era·m cosselhatz, senhor": "ja Deus no·m do / mais faire vers ni chanso" (may God not grant that I ever make a *vers* or a *canso*).[43] The commonplace recurs throughout the *vidas* and *razos*[44] and in the *Leys d'amors,* where, we recall, *vers* and *canso* together compete for the same floral prize.[45] Or else, perhaps, Bernart is expressing indifference as to whether his songs should be called *vers* or *cansos.*

A similar ambiguity marks Guiraut de Borneill's corpus. We recall, it is Peire d'Alvergne's *vida* that, in emphasizing Peire's "antique manner," credits Guiraut de Borneill with inventing the *canso.* Guiraut's own *vida* makes no such claim for him, but it does refer to his songs as *cansos.* More particularly it calls attention to the "maestrals ditz de las soas chansons" (masterful wording of his *cansos*).[46] And, in a famous passage praising Guiraut for his learning and his courtliness, it hails him as the "maestre dels trobadors" (master of the troubadours).[47] P-C, followed by Frank, identify forty-seven songs by Guiraut de Borneill as *cansos.*[48] Two of these the troubadour himself calls *cansonetas.*[49]

Three of his works Guiraut designates as *cansos* are dialogues,[50] that is, they are in some ways like *tensos* or *partimens.* Furthermore, six of the songs P-C and Frank identify as *cansos* the troubadour himself calls *vers.*[51] As in the other cases we have examined, P-C classify Guiraut's *vers* as *cansos* in an apparent attempt to apply to Giraut's songs medieval standards as reflected in his rival's *vida* and in the arts of poetry. Not the least significant indicator of imprecision in medieval technical language, however, is the closing to Guiraut's *vida* as it appears in the twin chansonniers *I* and *K:* "Et aici son escritas gran ren de las soas chansons" (and here are written a great many of his *cansos*).[52] Included in that corpus, characterized in *IK* as a collection of *cansos,* are not only the *vers,* dialogues, and *cansonetas* already mentioned but also, following P-C's and Frank's identifications, several *sirventes,* a number of *sirventes-cansos,*[53] two crusade songs, three *tensos,* a *pastorela,* a "romance,"[54] two *planhs,* and a *devinalh.*[55] The only significant omissions in the *IK* corpus are the *alba* "Reis glorios" and the romance/*pastorela* "L'autrier, lo primier jorn d'aost."[56] It is appropriate at this juncture to observe that Jaufre Rudel's *vida* (not in the version of *IK*, but in the closely related chansonniers *AB*) also calls *cansos* the three songs *AB* bear, the two songs Jaufre names *vers* plus "Lanquan li jorn."[57] To return to Guiraut de Borneill, it is noteworthy that he uses the term *canso* only once in reference to a particular song, in the *tornada* to "Ab semblan mi fai."[58] Elsewhere the word is found only in a general sense that may or may not include Guiraut's works.[59]

We can glimpse an important phase in the history of the technical terms *vers* and *canso* and their interrelationship thanks to Bernart de Ventadorn's apparent indifference to possible generic distinctions between *vers* and *cansos* and more particularly the nature of Guiraut de Borneill's corpus, both in the troubadour's conception of it and in the way it is presented in the manuscripts. It is clear that at some time in the 1170s the word *canso* was introduced as a term describing the troubadour lyric and that the word *vers* eventually disappeared as a meaningful term in opposition to *canso*. Already Arnaut Daniel is insistent in his exclusive use of the new term *canso*.[60] It is also clear, from the *vidas* and *razos*, that the word *vers* appropriately refers to songs composed "in the antique manner," while *canso* celebrates a new or a renewed poetics. Undoubtedly, one reason why the term *vers* was abandoned in favor of *canso* is because the former, despite its derivation from the monastic term *versus,* developed in Old Occitan an emphasis on the literary text at the expense of the musical line, or the *so(n);* the new term *canso,* with its obvious etymological association with *cant* and *cantar,* implicitly restores a balance in the exquisite interrelationship between the *cobla* and the melody it both shapes and is shaped by. Finally, it seems clear to me—and this is what I would like to propose in light of the evidence just presented—that the word *canso* may originally have taken the broad, non-genre-specific meaning of *vers* "in the ancient manner," but with a renewed emphasis on musical qualities. Subsequently, to be sure, the word *canso*—like the word *vers* simultaneously—was increasingly restricted to the very narrowest sense of refined love lyric. Thus, the term *vers* never had, among the early troubadours composing songs "in the ancient manner," a narrow, genre-bound meaning. Nor, at first, did the term *canso*.[61]

But, precisely, the new troubadour art which the term *canso* celebrates is itself partly involved in a process of categorization and increasingly strict generic definition. A predilection for description of poetic forms and, ultimately, for prescription and restriction is manifest in the arts of poetry and the *vidas* and *razos*. Although these critical texts have guided us in the theoretical approach I have proposed, we must understand the limits of their relevance to the early troubadour songs that predate them by decades. While the nonrestrictive *vers* "in the ancient manner" privileges verbal text in its relationship with melodic line, the arts of poetry reflect a new poetics stressing distinctions in content and strophic form as much as technique. A review of the members in the dazzling constellation of genres outlined in the *De doctrina de compondre dictats* suffices to prove the point. For example, as described in that treatise, questions of originality aside, the differences between the *canso*, the *planh*, and even the *sirventes* are not formal or structural but thematic.[62] Nor, for that matter, is any essential distinction made between the dialogue forms, the *partimen* and the *tenso*.[63]

The definitions of the terms *vers* and *canso* found in the *Leys d'amors* reveal limitations of another sort. In the arts of poetry, a veritable obsession with generic categorization seems to create the necessity to invent precise and restrictive meanings for every technical term in existence. Originally more or less synonymous, as I have suggested, both terms narrowed in meaning as generic classification gained prominence in troubadour art. In the *Leys d'amors* they are again synonymous, but of course in a very different way.

To summarize: (1) The *vers* "can treat of love, praise, or teachings for all who would keep themselves from blame"; the "*canso* is a poem that treats principally of love or praise, sung with pleasing words together with beautiful teachings; otherwise it would appear not at all refined." (2) The *vers* "contains from five to ten *coblas*"; the *canso* "is adorned with from five to seven *coblas*." (3) The *vers* "must have a long, well-placed melody, a new one with beautiful ascending, descending, and passing notes that are sweet, pleasing, graceful, harmonious [i.e., fitting the words], and melodious, developing with lively themes and drawing to an appropriate end"; the *canso* must have "a melody just like that of a *vers*. If it lacks in this (that is, the melody), it is denuded, or it is like a beautiful lady who is mute, so that it would appear utterly strange, for it would be undeserving of its name."[64] The only significant distinction here, other than the apparently trivial difference in the number of *coblas* permitted, is that the *vers* is said to have a *tornada*, whereas no mention of an *envoi* is made with respect to the *canso;* however, we know empirically that songs calling themselves *cansos* as well as *vers* were composed with and without *tornadas*.

The generic definitions of the *vers* and the *canso* in the *Leys d'amors*, augmented by a long disquisition on the *tornada*, seem fastidious in their obsession with descriptive precision—and prescription—but at the same time they are singularly uninformative. In their specificity, the hypothetical hyperrefined compositions called for in the fourteenth-century *Leys d'amors* bear little resemblance to the vigorous and richly inclusive *vers* as it was understood and put into practice by the early troubadours.

The kind of generic variety characteristic of troubadour lyric in the "new style" is lacking in the art of the *vers* in the "ancient manner." But, to recall my opening remarks about the generic richness in the chansonnier as well as in troubadour performance, generic variety abounds in the early lyric as well—retrospectively, in terms of the later arts of poetry or Bec's "virtual" genres, to be sure, but the posture is dangerously antihistorical.

Instead, I would propose as more fruitful in analysis of early troubadour song a classic structuralist three-genre paradigm, a model in some ways simplistic, even naive, but one which might well set the standards for discussion of poetic genres in the period. Recasting the paradigm in terms that recall the Dragonetti-Zumthor formulation of the *grand chant courtois*,[65] the grammar of genre is exemplified in the statement "I sing to you here and now"—*hic et nunc*—inscribing the subject of the sung discourse. The statement is completed by an expression of what constitutes the object of that discourse. Significantly, the predicate is likewise restricted by qualifications like *hic et nunc,* again, or its opposite, the "there and then." We commonly take such qualifications as being temporal and spatial, but Weinrich has taught us to think of them as referring to opposed conceptual worlds of narration and commentary. In any case, an "I sing," implicit or explicit, inheres in all sung discourse, just as "I tell" informs all spoken discourse. So, in oral performance, the particular *verbum loquendi*—"sing," "tell," et cetera—is not essential to generic distinction because each merely designates the mode of vocal delivery, although, to be sure, vocal delivery can enhance the message in very meaningful ways. Rather, generic distinction rests in the identity of the "you" to whom the poetic message is addressed as *destinataire,* in the nature of the object of that discourse, and, finally, in the nearness of singer and object, its "presentness" or presence, as opposed to the distance separating them, alterity—*hic et nunc,* there and then.

It is in terms of genre as distinguished according to these criteria that I propose to discuss troubadour song. In conformity with previous discussion of the *vers,* "troubadour song" will be defined as a sung discourse in a courtly style that is organized into more or less complex *coblas.* Although I believe that the generic distinctions have far wider significance, I seek to exclude from discussion at this point popular, religious, and didactic texts, on the one hand, and, on the other, extended works in laisses, rhymed couplets, and so forth.

1. *Pure lyric textuality.* Extracts from a song by Bernart de Ventadorn exemplify the most common type of troubadour song:

> 1.
> Non es meravelha s'eu chan
> mels de nul autre chantador,
> que plus me tra·l cors vas amor

e melhs sui faihz a so coman.
Cor e cors e saber e sen
e fors' e poder i ai mes.
Si·m tira vas amor lo fres
que vas autra part no·m aten.

It is no wonder if I sing better than any other singer, for my heart (*or* body) draws me closer to Love, and I am better suited to his command. Body and heart, knowledge and mind, strength and power I have committed to him. The reins so draw me toward Love that I can attend to nothing else.

7.
Bona domna, re no·us deman
mas que·m prendatz per servidor
qu'e·us servirai com bo senhor,
cossi que del gazardo m'an.
Ve·us m'al vostre comandamen,
francs cors umils, gais e cortes!
Ors ni leos non etz vos ges,
que·m aucizatz, s'a vos me ren.

Good lady, I ask nothing of you but to take me as a servant, and I will serve you as (I would) a noble lord, whatever reward may come to me. Behold me at your command, noble and gentle one, mirthful and courtly. You are not a bear or a lion that would kill me if I give myself over to you.

8.
A Mo Cortes, lai on ilh es,
tramet lo vers, e ja no·lh pes
car n'ai estat tan lonjamen.[66]

To "My Courtly One," there where she is, I send this *vers*, and may it never worry her that I have been away for such a long time.

In the opening *cobla*, Bernart establishes himself as a singer through the explicit statement "eu chan" of line 1, even though this is subordinated to the primary expression of wonderment. The object of the singer's sung discourse is his own lyric text, the very song he sings, although in this instance the song's status is not made explicit until the *tornada:* line 58, where it is called a *vers*.[67] Furthermore, and most particularly, the textual content of Bernart's song is like a mirror in which the singing subject is reflected: he sings about his body, his heart, his strength, his power, what pulls and drags him toward love, and what he himself has done to make himself susceptible to love's bidding.[68]

The question then arises: to whom is Bernart's text addressed? In *cobla* 7 we find the vocative "Bona domna" and imperatives and other verbs in the second person referring to her. Now, according to the language of *cobla* 7, as it so amply suggests, the singer seems to be subjected to this lady: he begs her to take him as her vassal, he promises to serve her, she will be as a lord over him, she might or might not kill him—"see, I am at your command," he cries (line 53). But subjection of this sort is purely conjectural: it is a projection of the signer's own desire, a futurity predicated upon her longed-for acceptance of him.

The singer naturally remains the subject of his own discourse and cannot be regarded as subjected to another's speech: it is the singing "I" that creates, controls, and, as it were, reifies the subject of verbs in the second person. In fact, if this text can be construed to be exhortative in any sense of the term, persuasion is only a secondary concern: the song may well express a desire for reciprocal discourse shared with the lady,[69] but its textuality is not that of a dialogic fragment or the one-sided remnant of unrealized conversation. It is the *tornada* that reiterates the song's primary status as discursive object: the lady is not here, but there (line 57) in a place to which the singer must transmit his *vers* (line 58). Her eventual reception of the text, like that of a letter, is also conjectural and depends upon its transmission by another voice, not the singer's own.[70] If the analogy between song and letter-as-finished-object is to stand, furthermore, we must admit, in fact, that the song being transmitted to the lady is like a letter addressed to someone else. She is beyond the range of the singer's voice; he aims his singing directly and primarily to auditors who are altogether distinct from her, those whom he informs of his act of transmission—the implicit "you" that constitutes the courtly audience. As the singer reengages himself with the implicit *destinataire* in the *tornada,* the "Bona domna" becomes once again the excluded, reified object *ilh* of line 57.

Other kinds of songs, in a different tonal register, illustrate a similar textuality; for example, a prototype "nonsense verse" by William IX, and its imitation by Raimbaut d'Aurenga. William IX:

> 1.
> Farai un vers de dreit nïen;
> Non er de mi ni d'autra gen,
> Non er d'amor ni de joven
> Ni de ren au,
> Qu'enans fo trobatz en durmen
> Sus un chivau.[71]
>
> I'll make a *vers* about nothing at all; it won't be about me or any other person, it won't be about Love or Youth or anything else, for it was composed a while ago when [I was] sleeping on horseback.

Raimbaut d'Aurenga:

> 1.
> Escotatz, mas no say que s'es,
> Senhor, so que vuelh comensar.
> Vers, estribot, ni sirventes
> Non es, ni nom no·l sai trobar;
> Ni ges no say co·l mi fezes
> S'aytal no·l podi' acabar,
> Que ia hom mays non vis fag aytal ad
> home ni a femna en est segle ni en
> l'autre qu'es passatz.[72]

> Listen, lords, but I don't know what it is, to what I want to begin (singing). It is not a *vers* or an *estribot* or a *sirventes*, nor can I find a name for it; I do not know how I might go about making it, unless I finished it like this: for never has anyone seen such made by man or woman in this age or in any other that has passed.

In these "pure lyric" songs, the singer is particularly self-conscious and the text is particularly self-reflexive. Pattison observes that Raimbaut d'Aurenga's song parodies William IX's *vers*.[73] But William's song is itself also a parody—if not of another lyric text, now lost, then of the lyric genre as a whole. For such parodies-in-the-negative all exemplify the lyric genre and are about lyric textuality. William implies, in lines 2–4 of his introductory *cobla*, that the discursive object in the kind of song his exemplifies must be himself and/or Love and Youth, which he embodies and illustrates as master of love-singing, or else other people and things filtered through his own subjectivizing consciousness.

In Raimbaut's joking response, the troubadour addresses genre in another way by introducing questions of form and content: *vers, estribot*,[74] and *sirventes* in the second line of the introductory *cobla* refer to "object-matter" (love, morals, politics) and mode of discourse (invective, satire). But Raimbaut's rejection of the term *vers* as inadequate to describe his poem also implies a concern for strophic form. The nature of subject matter and the "object-matter" in Raimbaut's text is identical with that of William's *vers*. As both songs are models of lyric textuality, they are generically similar as well. The only essential difference is that the *coblas* of William's *vers* are conventionally regular, while Raimbaut ends his *coblas* by extending the last line beyond the limits of troubadour artistry and into the realm of ordinary language: prose. Raimbaut does not know what to name his new form, so he calls it his "no-say-que-s'es" (line 36, not quoted) ("what's-it," "what-do-you-call-it"). In emphasizing the formal differences between his work and William's, however, Raimbaut also underscores the generic similarities.

2. *Reciprocal discourse.* I have rejected a reading of Bernart's lyric, "Non es meravelha s'eu chan," as designed to initiate a reciprocal discourse with the lady as primary addressee. But some troubadour texts represent true dialogic engagement, as is illustrated by a song involving Bernart de Ventadorn and a certain Peire:

> 1.
> Amics Bernartz de Ventadorn,
> com vos podetz de chant sofrir,
> can aissi auzetz esbaudir
> lo rossinholet noih e jorn?
> Auyatz lo joi que demena!
> Tota noih chanta sotz la flor,
> melhs s'enten que vos en amor.

> Friend Bernart de Ventadorn, how can you refrain from song, when you hear the little nightingale rejoicing night and day? Listen to the joy he feels! All night he sings beneath the flower: he is more adept in love than you.

> 2.
> Peire, lo dormir e·l sojorn
> am mais que·l rossinhol auzir;
> ni ja tan no·m sabriatz dir
> que mais en la folia torn.
> Deu lau, fors sui de chadena,
> e vos e tuih l'autr' amador
> etz remazut en la folor.[75]

> Peire, I like sleeping and idleness more than hearing the nightingale, and you couldn't say enough to me to make me turn to madness. God be praised, I am free of chains, while you and all other lovers have remained subject to folly.

This song is organized according to a "generic grammar" that functions differently from the self-reflexive textuality of "Non es meravelh s'eu chan." The text embodies two distinct voices that are engaged in a closed dialogic communication in which each voice functions alternately as discursive subject. As in conventional drama, moreover, the audience before whom the song is performed is excluded from the exchange, and is denied even the status of Bernart's reified Noble Lady, who may or may not receive in transmission a text addressed to someone else. Nor, for that matter, does the audience function as implicit *destinataire*. In fact the audience's role is reduced to that of a collection of eavesdroppers experiencing vicariously the pleasures of the debate and the beauties of the song. The dialogue is finished and closed off—objectified and itself reified—in ways that are quite distinct from true lyric text.[76]

Finally, I would argue that the generic nature of the dialogic exchange transcends critical questions such as single versus dual authorship, or the dominant versus the subordinate voice. In the Bernart-Peire model, for example, I am not prepared to discuss authorship.[77] However, it is worth pointing out that the song is very much *about* Bernart: Peire offers observations about Bernart's *état d'âme* and Bernart responds with reflexive self-analysis; and, as the introductory *coblas* demonstrate, Peire most often uses the pronoun "you," while Bernart answers with an authoritative "I." Thus, we can say that Bernart dominates the exchange, even that he is its major thematic subject, in that both participants focus attention on him and his particular feelings. Here I stress thematic, for, in terms of the song's structure, he is but one of two grammatical subjects. I would argue, therefore, that grammar in this sense determines genre and that theme constitutes a specific variable.

3. *Narrative textuality*. Two examples illustrate the third genre: Marcabru's classic pastourelle opening in "L'autrier, a l'issida d'abriu" and the beginning of William IX's dice-game seduction, in "Farai un vers, pos mi sonelh," which P-C and Frank call a "romance." Marcabru:

> 1.
> L'autrier, a l'issida d'abriu,
> En uns pastoraus lonc un riu,
> Et ab lo comens d'un chantiu
> Que fant l'auzeill per alegrar,
> Auzi la votz d'un pastoriu
> Ab una mancipa chantar.[78]

> The other day, at the end of April, in pastures along a river, at the beginning of singing that birds do to make merry, I heard the voice of a shepherd lad singing with a girl.

William IX:

> 1.
> Farai un vers, pos mi sonelh
> E·m vauc e m'estauc al solelh.
> Donnas i a de mal conselh,
> E sai dir cals:
> Cellas c'amor de cavalier
> Tornan a mals.

I'll make a *vers*, since I am dozing and going off and standing in the sun. There are ladies of bad counsel, and I can say which ones: those who speak ill of knight's love.

2.
Donna non fai pechat mortal
Qe ama cavalier leal,
Mais si es monges o clergal
Non a raizo!
Per dreg la deuria hom cremar
Ab un tezo.

A lady does not commit a mortal sin who loves a loyal knight, but if he is a monk or a cleric, she is wrong! People would be right to burn her with a torch.

3.
En Alvergnhe, part Lemozi,
M'en anei totz sols a tapi;
Trobei la moiller d'en Guari
E d'en Bernart;
Saluderon mi sinplamentz
Per Sant Launart.[79]

In Auvergne, beyond the Limousin, I made my way all alone as a pilgrim. I came upon Lord Garin's wife and Lord Bernart's. They greeted me affably in the name of St. Leonard.

In Marcabru's opening, the generically significant terms are those which situate the object of the singer's discourse not, as in the previous examples, in a *hic et nunc* that is coextensive with the time and place of his song, but in a "there and then" that is distinct and apart. These operative terms are the "L'autrier" of line 1 that fairly signals the pastourelle type and the preterit *auzi* of line 5; the "pastoraus lonc un riu" of line 2 are also meaningful in this context because they locate the narrated events spatially away from the court in which, we understand, the singer performs his song.

In William IX's less-refined avatar, the kind of distancing inherent to conventional narrative structure is delayed until the third *cobla;* it is noteworthy that the alterity of Auvergne is strictly maintained throughout the remaining eleven *coblas*. The textuality of the first two *coblas* stands in sharp contrast to the "otherworldly" narrative of the third. In fact, the opening manifests the self-reflexive "presence" that marks the generic distinctiveness of the "pure lyric." We could easily imagine these two *coblas* as opening such a song—satirical in mode to be sure—in which the singer might express personal observations about women.

Precisely, the opening *coblas* point to the textual complexity of the narrative. Elsewhere William's story manifests dialogic exchange not unlike that observed in the Bernart-Peire discussion; in narrative, however, such exchanges take the form of characters' words reported in direct discourse. Similarly, the troubadour-singer-as-narrative-artist employs text that looks like conventional "pure lyric" in order to make explicit his presence as narrator and to highlight the distance separating his "presentness" as singer-narrator and the "otherness" of the Auvergne where the prolonged dice game once took place. In this light, we see that the apparently lyric *coblas* begin to assume certain important functions of the conventionally self-conscious exordium. To return to Marcabru's introduction, we understand that the troubadour's reference to bird song in lines 3–4 also works as a kind of "exordial insertion" in which the poetic topos renews a conventional lyric image; in addition, thanks to the present tense *fant* (line 4), the "insertion" inscribes the "present" of the troubadour's narrative address.

It is also significant that sung troubadour narrative in strophic form is autobiographical in nature: the self-reflectiveness in character and event in the "then and there" is in many ways analogous to the specular lyric self-reflexivity of the here and now. The "I-me" textuality of troubadour lyric is so powerful that it can explode into autobiography—*pseudo*-autobiography, to be sure. Similarly, the *vidas* testify to inevitable transformation, not to say *translatio,* of I-centered lyric and narrative into third-person biography.[80]

Having established broad criteria for describing three basic types of troubadour textuality, *pure lyric, reciprocal discourse,* and *narrative,* I would like to return to the first category in order to explore possibilities of subgeneric distinctions. In fact, my earlier insistence on absolute self-reflexivity in the lyric does not account for all relevant texts—even though self-reflexivity may well constitute a generic standard: it informs nearly every *cobla* in the Rudelian corpus, for example, as well as the nondialogic works of Bernart de Ventadorn (forty-three songs in all). However, I would propose a generic variant in the lyric in which the singer's contemplation is at least partially deflected away from himself and from reflections of his own desires to include conditions and events lying beyond the limits of his closed world in the "here and now" that also embraces, as we have seen, his courtly *destinataire.* One form of such deflection is exemplified in the lyric textuality of Cercamon's *planh* on William X's death:

1.
Lo plaing comenz iradamen
d'un vers don hai lo cor dolen;

ir' e dolor e marrimen
ai car vei abaissar Joven:
Malvestatz puej' e Jois dissen
despois muric lo Peitavis.

I begin sorrowfully a lament in a *vers* wherein I have a grieving heart; I have sadness, grief, and sorrow, for I see Youth being cast down: Cowardice is rising and Joy waning since the Poitevin died.

3.
Del comte de Pitieu mi plaing
q'era de Proeza compaing;
despos Pretz et Donars soffraing
peza·m s'a longas sai remaing;
Segners, d'efern lo faitz estraing,
qe molt per fon genta sa fis.[81]

I lament the count of Poitou, who was a companion of Prowess; since Worth and Generosity are no more, it grieves me if I am left behind here for long. Lord, keep him far away from Hell, for his end was most worthy.

Quite a few preterits occur in the lament, yet the text does not threaten to slip into narrative. This is because the song does not seek to organize a *sequence* of narrated events. Significantly, the four references to the "other world" of Count William's life are scattered throughout the song: the Poitevin died (line 6), he was a companion of Prowess (line 16), his was a worthy end (line 19), he bequeathed his lands to the king (lines 38–39, not quoted). Those interspersed references to the "then and there" are like flashes bursting from without into the world of the lyric "here and now." They serve to inspire the singer's lament as, in accord with lyric self-reflexivity, he expresses a sadness and grief that are very personal. Like Bernart bending to his lady's will, however, he is only apparently subject to his bereavement—or he only apparently subjects himself to it: all the while he remains the controlling subject of his own lyric discourse: "Del comte de Pitieu mi plaing" (line 14) (literally: *it grieves me* about the count of Poitou), "peza·m" (line 16) (literally: *it weighs* on *me*), but *I begin* the *planh* (line 1), *I have* a grieving heart (line 2), *I see* Youth being downcast (line 3), *I stay* behind (line 16), and especially "Lo plaingz es de bona razo, / qe Cercamonz tramet N'Eblo" (lines 50–51, not quoted) (The *planh* has good subject matter, which [the *planh*] Cercamon transmits to Lord Eblo).

The *sirventes,* with its moral or political thematic content similar to some of the themes in Cercamon's *planh,* partakes of the same kind of lyric variance. For example, a song of Bertran de Born dated 1183:

1.
Seigner en coms, a blasmar
   vos fai senes faillia
car no·i ausetz anar
   pois ella o volia,
   a la dompna parlar.
Et al for de Cataloigna,
al vostr' ops eu n'ai vergoigna
car la·i fesetz fadiar.

My lord, it makes you blameworthy, there is no doubt, for you did not dare go to her, when she wished it, to talk to the lady. And, in the manner of Catalonia, I am ashamed for you because of it, for you kept her waiting there.

2.
E fis drutz no·is deu tardar
   si messatge·l venia,
mas que pens de l'anar
   e qe·is met' en la via,
   com non sap son affar
de sidonz, ni sa besoigna;
ben leu a talan que loigna
per que no·is deu aturar.[82]

And a refined lover should not tarry, if a messenger came to him, but may he think only of going and take to the road, as he does not know how his lady fares or what her plight is. Perhaps she wants him to stay away from her, which is why he shouldn't make the effort!

Unlike the *planh,* this song does not emphasize the singer's feelings with respect to events or conditions in the "other world" of contemporary history—lyric feeling is not always foremost in Bertran's poetry. But the *sirventes* generally represents a personal, subjective view of the external world that is expressed in "pure lyric" textuality: "eu n'ai vergoigna" (line 7) (I am ashamed about it), "so q'eu dizia" (line 26, not quoted) (what I have been saying), et cetera. Moreover, in self-conscious reflexivity, Bertran uses the vocabulary of love ("Fis drutz" [line 9], "sidonz" [line 14]) and singing ("Mon chant vir vas n'Azemar" [line 41, not quoted] [I aim my song at lord Azemar]), in reflection of his own status as a singer wise in the ways of love, in order to chastise Count Geoffrey of Brittany for hesitating to seize control of the revolt against Henry II after the death of the Young King.[83] And he contrasts his own successful practice of noble *fin' amors* with Geoffrey's ignoble fickleness: "Q'ieu non vuoil aver Bergoigna / sens temer e sens celar" (lines 31–32, not quoted) (I do not want to own Burgundy without

[=if I have to give up Love's] fearing and hiding), "Qu'ieu non vuoill ges esser bar / ... / per que·m reptar / nuills hom de vilania" (lines 33–36, not quoted) (I do not want to be a nobleman so that I might be accused of base behavior), "Mais am rir' e gabar / ab midonz" (lines 37–38, not quoted) (But I like to laugh and joke with my lady), et cetera.[84]

❖

According to the *usanza antiga,* during the period before about 1180 when troubadour song conceived of itself in terms of the all-inclusive *vers,* there were no troubadour "genres" in the sense understood by most modern scholars who base their view of early troubadour poetry on the retrospective and recapitulative major and minor arts of poetry written during the thirteenth and fourteenth centuries. In fact, Raimon Vidal's *Razos de trobar,* the thirteenth-century treatises associated with it, the *vidas* and *razos,* and the *Leys d'amors,* no less than the organized chansonniers themselves, are products of a "new" poetics concerned with expanding the horizons of troubadour song, but increasingly conscious of maintaining and transmitting a tradition. In response to these impulses were produced prescriptive, taxonomic documents which, because of their explicitness, have most strongly influenced scholars' views of early troubadour song, despite certain troubadours' expressions of quite different poetic concerns.

In speaking of troubadour genres, the most we can ascribe to works composed in the first two generations are the "virtual" genres proposed by Pierre Bec.[85] For example, one might discuss a Rudelian love lyric as a prototype of the *canso* or Marcabru's "Al departir del brau tempier," a *vers,* as a prototype of the *sirventes.*[86] Such categorization places the early works in context with later songs that are similar formally and thematically. As it is retrospective, however, it is more useful in understanding the nature of later poetry and in speculating about reception of the "ancient" troubadours than it is revelatory of their poetic essence.

A hypothetical negative case may make the point more clearly. William IX's three "companion songs" are unique examples of a certain strophic form, a certain ethos (the "law of *con*"), and a certain male-centered "courtliness."[87] There are no surviving imitations of these songs, nor do the arts of poetry or other theoretical works mention them. We could then speculate that the "companion song" is a genre that died aborning. While such a statement suggests a great deal about these songs' reception, about their future, it is virtually meaningless with respect to them as poetic texts, as *vers* produced in a particular time and place.

Many paths for future research in the area of troubadour genres seem to have emerged in the foregoing discussions. Among the most important I would single out the following:

1. Scholars need to establish a revised catalogue of the troubadour lyric that is more complete and more comprehensive than those of P-C and Frank. In addition to accounts by modern scholars, such a catalogue should include indications of the presence or absence of generic self-designation within songs, appropriate information about implicit and explicit generic identifications based on rubrics and the location of songs in chansonnier corpora, and generic descriptors applied to songs in arts of poetry, the *vidas* and *razos,* and elsewhere in medieval sources.

2. Scholars need to recognize and evaluate the historical implications inherent in such a catalogue. Internally, that is, as the troubadours judge their own works in their texts, generic identification can be a matter of conscious self-conception and laying claim to a place in literary history. In situating itself in the present within a particular generic tradition, a song both associates itself with an intertextual model, necessarily already in existence and identified as transmitted from the past, and projects itself into the future as a generic matrix involved in an ongoing process of renewal. Externally, that is, as the work is received by others—and particularly medieval theoreticians—generic evaluation is always a matter of retrospection. Moreover, as Köhler reminds us, each new genre (I would add: and each revival of a dead genre) owes its existence to certain social (including artistic) factors "whose continuity, transformation, and end determine as well the continuity, transformation, and end . . . of the genre."[88] For example, a *vers* composed in the period before 1180 is by no means the same thing as a *vers* written after 1250 by the antiquarian Guiraut Riquier, nor is it like the *vers* solicited for the Floral Games after 1330.

3. To return to the study of the early troubadours, further investigation of the relationship between the monastic *versus* and the Old Occitan *vers* promises to be productive in light of recent well-informed discussion of the marriage of lyric text and musical line.[89]

4. While it is helpful to regard the early troubadours' works as virtual generic prototypes whose potential may or may not have been realized through imitation in subsequent tradition, it would prove fruitful as well to emphasize other means of organizing the corpus by analyzing, in context with a revised catalogue and an awareness of historical implications, new generic constellations based in linguistic principles.

For example, the poetic qualities of Guiraut de Borneill's "Reis glorios, verais lums e clardatz," resonant in this song's association with troubadour genres, are not restricted to its identification with the *alba*.⁹⁰ How it participates in that tradition—how it compares with other *albas*—is also determined by its status as reciprocal discourse and thus by its rejection of description and other narrative elements. As an instance of early troubadour song, it compares with such other works in the corpus as Cercamon's debate poem "Car vei fenir a tot dia," Marcabru's *vers*-debate with Uc Catola, Bernart de Ventadorn's various exchanges, and especially Guiraut's own love-song dialogues.⁹¹

The last *cobla* of "Reis glorios" is crucial to any interpretation because it introduces a voice other than the watchman's, a voice attributable to the refined lover whom the watchman wishes to protect. Thus, the concluding *cobla* alone provides the reciprocity apparently sought in the watchman's repeated appeals to his "Bel companho" (lines 6, 11, 16, etc.) (dear companion). Meanwhile, this *cobla* furnishes the important structural elements that bind Guiraut's song to the conventional *alba:* in addition to the lover's voice we find references to his lady, to their night of love, and to the conventional *gilos* as her husband (line 35). Yet attribution of this *cobla* to Guiraut de Borneill has long been subject to scholarly debate.⁹² Whatever the case, discussion of "Reis glorios" must take into account the possibility of a nonreciprocated discourse as well, a circumstance that distances the song from the dialogic configuration and brings it into contact with univocal "pure lyric" textuality. In this light, our reading of the song is enriched by possibilities inherent in kinds of generic identification that are not afforded by retrospective description alone.

NOTES

For Karl D. Uitti in honor of his sixty-fifth birthday, December 10, 1998: "Bel dous companh."

1. Erich Köhler, "Zum Verhältnis von *vers* und *canso* bei den Trobadors," in *Etudes de philologie romane et d'histoire littéraire offertes à Jules Horrent*, ed. Jean Marie D'Heur and Nicoletta Cherubini (Liège: n.p., 1980), 205.

2. For example, the Ripoll treatises do not distinguish between *tenso* and *partimen;* see J. H. Marshall, ed., *The "Razos de trobar" of Raimon Vidal and Associated Texts* (London: Oxford University Press, 1972), 101 and 141, n. 12. It is also unclear whether the *planh*, the *tenso*, and other types should be set to original or to borrowed tunes (*Doctrina de compondre dictats*, in Marshall, 96, 97, and 138–39, nn. 58–60, 90–91). As I shall explain below, the treatises do not agree on grounds for distinguishing the *canso* from the *vers*.

3. For example, in the first few pages of Frank's catalogue of troubadour lyrics we find the terms *partimen, chanson, cobla, sirventes, tenson, planh, chanson religieuse,*

chanson de croisade, descort, échange de coblas, tenson fictive, sirventes-chanson, sextine, a list that is by no means exhaustive (István Frank, *Répertoire métrique de la poésie des troubadours* [Paris: Champion, 1953–57], 2:89–94). Frank follows Alfred Pillet and Henry Carstens, *Bibliographie der Troubadours* (Halle: Niemeyer, 1933), henceforth P-C. These generic terms distinguish songs on the basis of content (*canso*), form (*sestina*), or voice (*tenso, partimen*). The basic terms in the list are found in medieval arts of poetry; the permutations are, for the most part, modern inventions. Discussed below are instances, first, when modern scholars assign generic descriptors while ignoring terms used by the troubadours themselves and, second, when disagreement arises concerning the application of genre-specific terms.

4. Implicit definitions derive from terms the troubadours use in describing their own poetry; examples centering on *vers* and *canso* are discussed below. Explicit definitions are those found in the medieval arts of poetry. For example, discussion of the *alba* in the *De doctrina de compondre dictats* fits no modern definition of the genre: "Si vols far alba, parla d'amor plazentment; e atressi [deus] lauzar la dona on vas o de que la faras. E bendi l'alba si acabes lo plazer per lo qual anaves a ta dona; e si no·l acabes, fes l'alba blasman la dona e l'alba on anaves" (If you wish to make an *alba*, speak of love in a pleasing way, and you must also praise the lady to whom you are going or about whom you are making it [the *alba*]. And bless the dawn if you achieve the pleasure for which you went to the lady; and if you do not achieve it, make the *alba* blame the lady and the dawn when you went [to her]) (Marshall, *Razos de trobar*, 96; see 138, nn. 62–66). For successful comprehensive definitions of the *alba*, see Elizabeth Wilson Poe, "The Three Modalities of the Old Provençal Dawn Song," *Romance Philology* 37 (1984): 259–72, and Poe, "New Light on the *Alba:* A Genre Redefined," *Viator* 15 (1984): 139–50.

5. For example, in her edition *The Cansos and Sirventes of Giraut de Borneil* (Cambridge: Cambridge University Press, 1989), Ruth Verity Sharman groups Guiraut's songs under three headings: *cansos, canso-sirventes,* and *sirventes.* The category *sirventes* is the most controversial because, without explanation, it includes, in addition to eleven *sirventes* as commonly defined (songs on political, moral, or military themes or poetics), two *chansons de croisade,* a *chanson religieuse,* three *tensos,* a *pastorela,* a *pastorela-sirventes* (a term invented by Sharman), a *sirventes joglaresc,* a riddle poem, and an *alba* (359–62).

6. John H. Marshall, "Le *vers* au XIIe siècle: genre poétique?" in *Actes et Mémoires du IIIe Congrès International de Langue et Littérature d'Oc* (Bordeaux: Université de Bordeaux, 1965), 2:55–63; Pierre Bec, "Le problème des genres chez les premiers troubadours," *Cahiers de civilisation médiévale* 25 (1982): 31–47; Erich Köhler, "Zum Verhältnis von *vers* und *canso*," and "Die Sirventes-Kanzone: 'genre bâtard' oder legitime Gattung?" in *Mélanges offerts à Rita Lejeune* (Gembloux: Duculot, 1969), 1:159–83. See also Dietmar Rieger, "Zum *vers* der beiden ersten Trobadorgenerationen," in *Gattungen und Gattungsbezeichnungen der Trobadorlyrik* (Tübingen: Niemeyer, 1976), 185–245.

7. See Sara Sturm-Maddox and Donald Maddox, eds., *Intergenres: Intergeneric Perspectives on Medieval French Literature, L'Esprit créateur* 33, no. 4 (1993), esp. Sturm-Maddox and Maddox, "*Genre* and *Intergenre* in Medieval French Literature," 3–9.

8. At the Twenty-seventh International Congress on Medieval Studies (Kalamazoo, Mich., May 2, 1992), I participated in the program, sponsored by the Société

Guillaume IX, that inspired the Northwestern University conference devoted to medieval poetic genres. On that occasion I read a paper entitled "Form and Genre in Troubadour Song" which forms the second part of the present contribution.

9. Marshall, *Razos de trobar*, 95. On the arts of poetry, in addition to the introductory comments in Marshall, see Elena Landoni, *La teoria letteraria dei Provenzali* (Florence: Olschki, 1989), 121–46.

10. Joseph Anglade, ed., *Las leys d'amors: manuscrit de l'Académie des Jeux-Floraux* (Toulouse: Privat, 1919–20), 1:42.

11. Ibid., 1:30.

12. Marshall, *Razos de trobar*, 95.

13. *GRLMA* recognizes fifteen main genres, not all of them sanctioned by the medieval treatises: (1) *vers* and *chanson* combined, (2) *descort*, (3) *sirventes*, (4) *chanson-sirventes*, (5) *cobla*, (6) *chanson de croisade*, (7) *planh*, (8) *tenso*, (9) *jeu-parti*, (10) pastourelle, (11) *alba*, (12) *romance*, (13) *chanson de danse*, (14) *chanson religieuse*, (15) *salut d'amor*. See *Grundriss der romanischen Literaturen des Mittelalters*, vol. 2, t. 1, fasc. 3 (1987), 4 (1980), 5 (1979), 7 (1990); for subgenres of the *vers-canso*, see below n. 27.

14. Marshall edits Raimon Vidal, *Razos de trobar* (versions *B* and *H*, 1–25; version *CL*, 145–59); Terramagnino da Pisa, *Doctrina d'acort* (27–53); Jofre de Foixà, *Regles de trobar* (versions *H* and *R*, 55–91); the anonymous *Doctrina de compondre dictats* (93–98); and two anonymous treatises from Barcelona, MS. Ripoll 129 (99–105). Marshall mentions other treatises, edited and unedited (xi and n. 2).

15. Jean Boutière and A. H. Schutz, eds., *Biographies des troubadours*, 2d ed., rev. Jean Boutière and Irénée-Marcel Cluzel (Paris: Nizet, 1964); cited hereafter as Boutière-Schutz. See Elizabeth Wilson Poe, *From Poetry to Prose in Old Provençal* (Birmingham, Ala.: Summa Publications, 1984), and "Old Provençal *Vidas* as Literary Commentary," *Romance Philology* 33 (1980): 510–18.

16. Marshall, *Razos de trobar*, lxix. On the *vidas* attributed to Uc, see Boutière-Schutz, xli. P-C (xv–xvi) date both manuscripts from the second half of the century; they derive from an earlier common exemplar.

17. Gerald A. Bond, ed., *The Poetry of William VII, Count of Poitiers, IX Duke of Aquitaine* (New York: Garland, 1982); George Wolf, in Wolf and Roy Rosenstein, eds., *The Poetry of Cercamon and Jaufre Rudel* (New York: Garland, 1983); J[ean]-M[arie]-L[ucien] Dejeanne, ed., *Poésies complètes du troubadour Marcabru* (Toulouse: Privat, 1909); Rupert T. Pickens, ed., *The Songs of Jaufré Rudel* (Toronto: Pontifical Institute of Mediaeval Studies, 1978); Moshé Lazar, ed., *Bernard de Ventadour: chansons d'amour* (Paris: Klincksieck, 1966); Sharman, *Cansos and Sirventes of Giraut de Borneil*, used in conjunction with Adolf Kolsen, ed., *Sämtliche Lieder des Trobadors Giraut de Bornelh* (Halle: Niemeyer, 1910–35); Alberto Del Monte, ed., *Peire d'Alvernha: Liriche* (Turin: Loescher-Chiantore, 1955), used in conjunction with Rudolf Zenker, ed., "Peire von Auvergne," *Romanische Forschungen* 12 (1900): 653–924. Editions of other troubadours cited are William D. Paden, Tilde Sankovitch, and Patricia H. Stäblein, eds., *The Poems of the Troubadour Bertran de Born* (Berkeley: University of California Press, 1986), and Walter T. Pattison, ed., *The Life and Works of the Troubadour Raimbaut d'Orange* (Minneapolis: University of Minnesota Press, 1952).

18. Boutière-Schutz, 9.

19. Ibid., 9.

20. Ibid., 14. Peire de Valeira's *vida* continues: "Sei cantar non aguen gran valor, ni el" ("His songs did not have great value, and neither did he") (ibid., 14).

21. Ibid., 10, 16.

22. Ibid., 263.

23. Ibid., 12.

24. It is well known that the early troubadours consistently refer to their works as *vers* and that they use no other generic term; however, many implications of the fact have yet to be fully explored. Bec surveys William IX, Jaufre Rudel, Marcabru, and Cercamon and concludes: "Le *vers* lui-même n'est pas un genre lyrique. Vu en diachronie, il préfigure dès l'origine les grands genres qui viendront ['genres virtuels']; vu en synchronie, il en reste, pendant toute la durée du *trobar*, la référence paradigmatique" ("Problème des genres," 47). In "Zum Verhältnis von *vers* und *canso*," Köhler's more extensive corpus includes Aimeric de Peguillan, Bertran de Born, Elias Cairel, Gaucelm Faidit, Guiraut de Borneill, Guiraut de Cabrera, Peire d'Alvergne, Peire Rogier, Peire Vidal, Peirol, and Raimbaut d'Aurenga. Both Bec and Köhler had been anticipated by Marshall, "Vers au XIIe siècle."

25. One apparently inauthentic song attributed to William IX is called a *chansoneta*, "Farai chansoneta nueva" (Bond, *Poetry of William VII*, no. 8). The song's use of this generic term is only one of seven reasons listed by Bond ("Introduction," lxxviii) for dating the text from the end of the twelfth century and not from William's lifetime. The diminutive form *chansoneta* is also used in "Ans que·l terminis verdei," probably falsely attributed to Marcabru (Dejeanne, *Poésies complètes*, no. 7, l. 49). See Köhler, "Zum Verhältnis von *vers* und *canso*," 205, and Bec, "Problème des genres," 35 and n. 13.

26. In the following discussion, modern scholars' generic descriptions are attributed to P-C; to Frank, *Répertoire métrique*, vol. 2; and to editors and critics. P-C attempt to register the troubadours' use of the term *vers* in addition to their own genre descriptors such as *Kanzone*, but do not note all occurrences. Frank never acknowledges the term *vers*.

27. Bond, *Poetry of William VII*, nos. 1, 5, 4, 6, 7, 11. Köhler recognizes four subgenres in the *vers-canso*: (1) *gap*, (2) *devinalh*, (3) *escondit*, (4) "farewells" of two types, *comjat* and *chanson de change*. See Erich Köhler, "'Vers' und Kanzone," *Grundriss der romanischen Literaturen des Mittelalters* vol. 2, t. 2, fasc. 3 (1987): 45–176, at 147–76.

28. The ten *sirventes* are "Al departir del brau tempier" (Dejeanne, *Poésies complètes*, no. 3), "Al so desviat, chantaire" (no. 5), "Aujatz de chan com enans' e meillura" (no. 9), "Cortesamen vuoill comenssar" (no. 15), "Dirai vos senes duptansa" (no. 18), "Lo vers comenssa" (no. 32), "Lo vers comens quan vei del fau" (no. 33), "Hueymais dey esser alegrans" (no. 34), "Per savi·l tenc ses doptanssa" (no. 37), "Pos mos coratges s'es clarzitz" (no. 40). Dejeanne, who does not consistently use medieval generic terms to characterize Marcabru's songs, nevertheless describes "Al departir del brau tempier" (no. 3), as well as "A l'alena del vent doussa" (no. 2) (where the term *vers* does not occur), as "un chant de printemps et un sirventés" (216). P-C and Frank reserve the term *sirventes-canso* for no. 13 ("Bel m'es quan son li fruich madur"), which Dejeanne describes as "Chanson d'automne où Marcabru, contrairement à sa thèse habituelle, vante les bienfaits de l'amour, s'élève contre les superstitions, les présages, et, dans la VIe strophe, contre *l'amistat d'estraing atur*" (224–25). Meanwhile, P-C call "En abriu" (no. 24) a *sirventes-canso*, while Frank calls

it simply a *sirventes;* this song Dejeanne describes as "une satire assez grossière contre l'amour vair ou pie et contre son amie" (230). The love lyric is "Contra l'ivern que s'enansa" (Dejeanne, no. 14). See also Erich Köhler, "Die Sirventes-Kanzone," *Grundriss der romanischen Literaturen des Mittelalters,* vol. 2, t. 1, fasc. 4 (1980): 62–66, and vol. 2, t. 1, fasc. 7 (1990): 375–83.

29. Dejeanne, *Poésies complètes,* no. 6, line 3. Subsequently, Uc Catola asserts, "Per zo·us en mou e[u] la tenson / Qe d'Amor fui naz e noiriz" (lines 11–12) (I start the debate with you because I was born of Love and raised [by Love]). I would argue that the word *tenson* refers not to a song-form specifically but to debate in a more general sense, despite the parallel between "mou . . . la tenson" and the idiom *mover un chan* (to start singing).

30. Wolf, *Poetry of Cercamon and Jaufre Rudel,* nos. 1, 6, 8; Wolf's term. This song is discussed in Köhler ("Sirventes-Kanzone: 'genre bâtard,'" 178–79) as an early prototype of what is, for him, a short-lived *sirventes-canso* genre.

31. Pickens, *Songs of Jaufré Rudel,* nos. 2, 6.

32. The *sirventes* are "Cantarai d'aquesz trobadors" (Del Monte, *Peire d'Alvernha,* no. 12), "Bel m'es quan la roza floris" (no. 13), "Bel m'es qui a son bon sen" (no. 14), "Belh m'es qu'ieu fass' huey mays un vers" (no. 15), "Cui bon vers agrad' a auzir" (no. 16). The love lyrics are "Ab fina ioia comenssa" (Del Monte, no. 3), "L'airs clars e·l chans dels auzelhs" (no. 6), and "Deiosta·ls breus iorns e·ls loncs sers" (no. 7). "Sobre·l vieill trobar" is Del Monte, no. 11, and Zenker, "Peire von Auvergne," no. 3.

33. Bec, "Problème des genres," 47.

34. Margaret Switten, "Remarks on Versification," in Switten and Howell Chickering, eds., *The Medieval Lyric, Commentary Volume* ([South Hadley, Mass.: Mount Holyoke College], 1988), 73. The commonplace derives from Alfred Jeanroy, *La poésie lyrique des troubadours* (Toulouse: Privat, 1934), 2:66–67, and is based on the testimony of Cercamon's and Marcabru's *vidas* (Jeanroy, 2:63–64). It is monumentalized in the *Grundriss der romanischen Literaturen des Mittelalters,* vol. 2, t. 1, fasc. 7 (1990): 23–241; see also Köhler, "'Vers' und Kanzone."

35. Bec, "Problème des genres," 40–41. As Peire de Valeira's *vida* states, he made *vers; cans,* along with leaves, flowers, and birds, are what his *vers* are about (Boutière-Schutz, 14); see my discussion above.

36. Pickens, *Songs of Jaufré Rudel,* no. 1-1, 1–4.

37. Ibid., no. 2-1, 4–6.

38. Ibid., no. 6-1, 5, and no. 2-1, 7.

39. For example, "si com el dis en son chantar" (Boutière-Schutz, 10) (just as he said in his song), "Sei cantar no aguen gran valor, ni el" (Boutière-Schutz, 14) (His songs had no great value, neither did he), etc. But, in the earlier sense, "E lo vescons . . . s'abelli mout de lui e de son trobar e de son cantar" (Boutière-Schutz, 20) (And the viscount took a great liking to him, to his poetry-making, and to the way he sang).

40. For example, in Jaufre Rudel's "So sap cantar qui so non di," singing is apparently distinguished from the artistry of verbal composition: "Non sap chantar qui so non di / Ni vers trobar qui motz no fa / Ni connoys de rima quo·s va / Si razos non enten en si" (Pickens, *Songs of Jaufré Rudel,* no. 6-1, 1–4) (He cannot sing who does not produce a melody or compose a *vers* who does not make words or

recognize how rhyme goes if he does not understand the model in himself). See Jörn Gruber, *Die Dialektik des Trobar* (Tübingen: Niemeyer, 1983), 85–91. The distinction recurs in Marcabru's "Cortesamen vuoill comenssar": "Lo vers e·l son vuoill enviar / A·n Jaufre Rudel outra mar" (Dejeanne, *Poésies complètes,* no. 14, lines 37–38) (The *vers* and the melody I wish to send to lord Jaufre Rudel across the sea).

41. Switten, "Remarks on Versification," 73; see esp. Switten and Chickering, eds., *The Medieval Lyric, Anthology I*, 1–34: "Saint Martial of Limoges." Also Köhler, "Zum Verhältnis von *vers* und *canso*," 205. Essential background information is found in H[ans] Spanke, "St. Martial-Studien: Ein Beitrag zur frühromanischen Metrik," *Zeitschrift für französische Sprache und Literatur* 54 (1930–31): 282–317, 385–422; 56 (1932): 450–78, and Jacques Chailley, *L'école musicale de Saint Martial de Limoges* (Paris: Les Livres Essentiels, 1960), especially 260–319. For relationships with the troubadour lyric, see Chailley, "Les premiers troubadours et les versus de l'école d'Aquitaine," *Romania* 76 (1955): 212–39; see also Leo Treitler, "Musical Syntax in the Middle Ages," *Perspectives of New Music* 4 (1965–66): 75–85.

42. The *vers:* "Non es meravelha s'eu chan" (Lazar, *Bernard de Ventadour,* no. 1), "Chantars no pot gaire valer" (no. 2), "Ab joi mou lo vers e·l comens" (no. 3), "Ges de chantar no·m pren talans" (no. 11), "Be·m cuidei de chantar sofrir" (no. 13), "La dousa votz ai auzida" (no. 57). In the seventh, "Lo rossinhols s'esbaudeya" (no. 23), Bernart uses the expression "bo vers" (a good *vers*) in a general sense, but presumably the current song exemplifies what he is capable of composing: "e fatz esforz, car sai faire / bo vers, pois no sui amaire" (lines 7–8) (I am working hard at it—for I do know how to make a good *vers*—since I am not in love). In none of these cases do P-C record Bernart's own generic designation. The *cansos:* "E mainh genh se volv e·vira" (no. 8), "Pel doutz chan que·l rossinhols fai" (no. 10), "A! tantas bonas chansos" (no. 16), "Era·m cosselhatz, senhor" (no. 25), "Amors, e que·eu es veyaire?" (no. 27), "Bel m'es qu'eu chan en aquel mes" (no. 51). The *cansoneta:* "Conortz, era sai eu be" (no. 15).

43. Ibid., no. 35, line 2, and no. 25, lines 23–24. Köhler cites these examples and others from Guiraut de Borneill, Peire Vidal, and others in "Zum Verhältnis von *vers* und *canso*," 207.

44. Bernard de Ventadorn "fetz sas chansos e sos vers" (Boutière-Schutz, 20) (made his *cansos* and his *vers*) about the wife of the viscount of Ventadorn; the viscount liked "las chansos e·l vers d'En Bernart" (Boutière-Schutz, 21) (Lord Bernart's *cansos* and *vers*). Raimon Jordan "ac tal dol que pueys no fe vers ni canso" (Boutière-Schutz, 159) (had such grief that afterwards he did not make *vers* or *cansos*). Instead of learning his Latin letters, Uc de Saint Circ learned about "cansos e vers e sirventes e tensos e coblas" (Boutière-Schutz, 239). Peire Rogier fell in love with Ermengard of Narbonne, "e fetz sos vers e sas cansos d'ella" (Boutière-Schutz, 267) (and made his *vers* and his *cansos* about her). The husband of Guillem de Saint Leidier's lady took great delight "en sos chansos et en sos vers" (Boutière-Schutz, 280). Garin lo Brun "Non fo trobaire de vers ni de chansos, mas de tensos" (Boutière-Schutz, 299) (was not a troubadour of *vers* or *cansos*, but of *tensos*). Raimbaut d'Aurenga "fo bons trobaires de vers e de chansons" (Boutière-Schutz, 441) (was a good troubadour of *vers* and *cansos*).

45. For example, "verses, chansos et alcus autres dictatz" (Anglade, *Leys d'amors,* 1:38); "en verses, chansos et en autres dictatz" (1:81).

46. Boutière-Schutz, 39.

47. Ibid. For a comparison of the *vidas* of Guiraut de Borneil and Peire d'Alvergne as exemplifying these troubadours' reception in thirteenth-century Italy, see Gruber, *Dialektik des Trobar,* 22–28.

48. In her edition Sharman follows Kolsen in classifying seven of these as *cansos-sirventes:* "Ben deu en bona cort dir" (Sharman, *Cansos and Sirventes of Giraut de Borneil,* no. 49), "De chantar" (no. 42), "Ges aissi del tot son lais" (no. 45), "Ja·m vai revenen" (no. 44), "Jois e chans" (no. 46), "Qui chantar sol" (no. 40), "Si soutils senz" (no. 50); an eighth is a "*canso* of doubtful attribution": "Gen m'estava e suau e en paz" (no. 52). Thus Sharman recognizes thirty-nine of Guiraut's songs as *cansos.* Kolsen includes "Gen m'estava e suau e en paz" among Guiraut's forty *cansos* (*Sämtliche Lieder des Trobadors Giraut de Bornelh,* no. 34), but notes reasons why other scholars reject it (2:70).

49. "Aital cansoneta plana" (Sharman, *Cansos and Sirventes of Giraut de Borneil,* no. 32), "Leu chansonet' e vil" (no. 48). Guiraut uses the unusual term *chantaret* to characterize two of his songs, "Era si·m fos en grat tengut" (no. 29) and "Tot suavet e de pas" (no. 31); elsewhere he uses the word *chantaretz* in the plural to speak of his songs in general: "Deme / Mos chantaretz voidanz / De saluz e de manz" (no. 40, lines 19–21) (I sing my little songs emptied of greeting or commission). P-C do not recognize *chantaret* as a generic term.

50. "Ailas, co muer!—Qe as, amis?" (ibid., no. 5), "Mas, com m'ave, Dieus m'aiut" (no. 6), "Ar auzirets" (no. 7).

51. "Ben coven, pos ja baissa·ram" (ibid., no. 19), "Tostemps mi sol" (no. 21), "Chans embroil" (no. 23), "Quant la brun' aura s'eslancha" (no. 26), "Can vreis la fresca fueil' els rams" (no. 27), "A penas sai comenssar" (no. 33). P-C acknowledge that Guiraut calls nos. 19, 23, and 33 *vers,* but not nos. 21, 26 and 27. Frank does not attempt to record occurrences of the term *vers.*

52. Boutière-Schutz, 40.

53. By the standard of usage in the later arts of poetry, the *sirventes-canso* (or, as Sharman insists, the *canso-sirventes*) is a pseudo-genre, in that the arts of poetry do not mention such a hybrid. Sharman defines the *canso-sirventes* as "halfway between the courtly love-song of the *trobar leu* and the moralizing *clus* poem" (*Cansos and Sirventes of Giraut de Borneil,* 251), and she proposes that Guiraut may have been its inventor: "This was a genre, perhaps invented by Giraut, which counterpointed the poet's personal situation with moral comment on society" (36). On the *canso-sirventes* as a legitimate genre, see especially Köhler, "Sirventes-Kanzone: 'genre bâtard,'" who adduces slim manuscript and textual evidence to discuss *vers, canso, sirventes,* and the hybrid *sirventes-canso* in terms of the conflict between social reality and the ideal world of love and the court. P-C, followed by Frank, label four of Guiraut's songs *sirventes-cansos:* "Ben for' oimais dreigs el temps gen" (Sharman, no. 41), "En un chantar" (no. 51), "Leu chansonet' e vil" (no. 48), and "Los apleiz" (no. 43). Sharman, following Kolsen, swells the list to twelve by adding seven songs her predecessors identified as *cansos* and one they classified as a *sirventes,* "Be m'era bels chantars" (no. 47).

54. Sharman complicates the generic overview by calling a *pastorela* the narrative identified by P-C and Frank as a romance ("L'autrier, lo primier jorn d'aost," ibid., no. 55) and by inventing a pseudo-genre, the *pastorela-sirventes,* in order to catego-

rize the *pastorela* "Lo doutz chans d'un auzel" (no. 56); see *Cansos and Sirventes of Giraut de Borneil,* 359. Kolsen, however, calls the former a *pastorela* and the latter a romance.

55. At one point (ibid., 359) Sharman agrees with Kolsen and P-C in calling "Un sonet fatz malvatz e bo" (no. 54) a riddle-song, but elsewhere she follows Frank in labeling it a *sirventes* (372).

56. Ibid., nos. 53, 55.

57. Pickens, *Songs of Jaufré Rudel,* nos. 2, 6, 5.

58. Sharman, *Cansos and Sirventes of Giraut de Borneil,* no. 10. "Razon e luec" (no. 20) may or may not be an exemplification of "mas gayas chansos" (line 15) (my joyful songs) in contrast with the implicit *sirventes* he might have composed.

59. Most often in a general sense, not in reference to a particular work. In "Ar auziretz enchabalitz chantars" (ibid., no. 7), Guiraut observes that "Mou mas chansos e mos vers / Con fols de saber esters!" (lines 26–27) (I sing my *cansos* and my *vers* like a fool deprived of reason). In "Alegrar mi volgr' en chantan" (no. 17), he speaks of the *cansos* of his *destinataire:* "vostras *chanzos*" (line 23) (your *cansos*). In "Tot suavet e de pas" (no. 31), a *chantaret* which Guiraut is planing down to rid it of obscure words (of *trobar clus*), he remarks that "chanzos leu" (line 9) (an easy *canso*) is appreciated in Catalonia and Provence. In "A penas sai comenssar" (no. 33), Guiraut contrasts the *vers* he is singing with the "leu chansso" (18) (easy *canso*) he would need to compose if he wanted to make his *trobar clus* widely understood. In "Non puesc sofrir c'a la dolor" (no. 37), the troubadour predicts "E pueys auziretz chantador / E chansos anar e venir" (lines 41–42) (And then you will hear singers and *cansos* coming and going) when a dream his lord has interpreted for him comes true.

60. See James J. Wilhelm, ed., *The Poetry of Arnaut Daniel* (New York: Garland, 1981): "Lo ferm voler q'el cor m'intra" (no. 1), which P-C and Frank recognize as a *sestina;* "Chansson do·il mot son plan e prim" (no. 2); "Can chai la fueilla" (no. 3); "Lanquan vei fueill' e flor e frug" (no. 5); "Anc ieu non l'aic, mas ella m'a" (no. 7); "Doutz brais e critz" (no. 12); "Er vei vermeills, vertz, blaus, blancs, gruocs" (no. 13); "Sols sui que sai lo sobraffan qe·m sortz" (no. 15); "Ans que cim reston de branchas" (no. 16).

61. In "Zum Verhältnis von *vers* und *canso*" (206), Köhler dates generic definitions, including the term *vers* in opposition to other genres, from the 1170s. He posits an early distinction between *vers* and *canso,* exemplified, perhaps, in Guiraut de Borneill (see discussion above), as involving an association of *vers* with *trobar clus* and *canso* with *trobar leu* (209–10). In *Troubadours and Eloquence* (Oxford: Clarendon Press, 1975), Linda M. Paterson had observed the same trends in Peire d'Alvergne (83–85) as well as in Guiraut de Borneill (115–17, 132–36). Earlier, in "Sirventes-Kanzone: 'genre bâtard'" (179–83), Köhler had seen both the *sirventes* and the *canso* as deriving from the *vers,* as early as Cercamon (in what Bec was to characterize as a "virtual" state), in response to a courtly crisis wherein idealized love (evoked in the *canso*) becomes incompatible with the reality of feudal knightly service (the subject of the *sirventes*), and yet love is possible only in a courtly setting where the highest values of feudal service are maintained (a tension sustained by the short-lived *sirventes-canso*). In *Gender and Genre in Medieval French Literature* (Cambridge: Cambridge University Press, 1995), where he includes a chapter on twelfth-century troubadour

lyric ("Troubadours, Ladies and Language: The *Canso*, 122–79), Simon Gaunt uses the term *canso* anachronistically in the very narrow sense of refined verse incarnating *fin' amors*.

62. The *canso* "deu parlar d'amor plazenment, e potz metre en ton parlar exempli d'altra rayso, e ses mal dir e ses lauzor de re sino d'amor" (Marshall, *Razos de trobar*, 7–9) (must speak about love in a pleasing manner, and you may put into your speech bits of other subject matter, but without condemning or praising anything except love). In the *planh*, "d'amor o de tristor deus la raho continuar . . . E no·y deus mesclar altra raho sino plahien, si per comp[ar]acio no·y podies portar" (57, 60–61) (you must extend the theme of love or sadness . . . And you should not mix in any subject matter except grieving, unless you could bring it in for a comparison). In the *sirventes*, "deus parlar de fayt d'armes, e senyalladament o de lausor de senyor o de maldit o de qualsque feyts qui novellament se tracten. E començaras ton cantar segons que usaran aquells dels quals ton seventez començaras; e per proverbis e per exemples poretz hi portar les naturaleses que fan, o ço de que fan a rependre o a lausar aquells dels quals ton serventez començaras" (28–33) (you should speak of a military exploit, and especially either in praise of a lord or invective [against him], or about whatever events have recently transpired. And you will begin your singing [by naming] in their usual manner those about whom you begin your *sirventes*; and with proverbs and *exempla* you can bring in the alliances they make and what they do that is worthy of blame or praise) (see Marshall's note, 136–37). As for form, the *canso* must have at least five *coblas* and as many as nine (10–12); the *planh* may imitate any form except the *danza* (including, therefore, the *canso*) and may have as many *coblas* as the form being borrowed (57–60); the *sirventes* may have as many *coblas* as any song (including therefore the *canso*) (34–35). As for the melody, the *canso* must have a new one (15); the *planh* may have a borrowed tune (see especially Marshall's note, 138); the *sirventes* may either have an original melody or borrow one from a *canso* (35–36). See also Sturm-Maddox and Maddox, "*Genre* and *Intergenre*," and Jeff Rider, "Genre, Antigenre, Intergenre," *L'Esprit créateur* 33.4 (Winter 1993): 18–26.

63. The definition does not restrict subject matter or style: "Tenso es dita tenso per ço com se diu contrastan e disputan subtilmen lo un ab l'altre de qualque raho hom vulla cantar" (Marshall, *Razos de trobar*, 135–36) (A *tenso* is so called because two people must offer differing opinions or argue elegantly about whatever matter they wish to sing).

64. "Vers es us dictatz en romans, / De sen quar es verays tractans, / E quar dir se pot de virar. / D'amors yssamens pot tractar, / De lauzors o d'essenhamens, / E qui·s vol de reprendemen. / E conte de .V. a .X. cobblas; / E la tornada, si la doblas, / Far se pot neysh en tot dictat; / E deu haver long so pauzat / E noel am belas montadas / E deshendudas e passadas; / Doussas, plazens e graciozas, / Acordans e melodiozas, / Procezen am vivas razos / Et am leyals concluzios" (Anglade, *Leys d'amors*, 2:175–76). "Cansos es dictatz que d'amors / Principalmen o de lauzors / Tracta, recitan motz plazens / Am alcus bels essenhamens / Per dar a toz bona doctrina, / Qu'estiers del tot non appar fina. / De .V. a .VII. cobblas encara / Et aytal so cum vers ampara; / E si d'aquest defalh es nuda / Si que del tot appar estranha / Quar sos nonms am liey no s'afranha" (2:177).

65. Especially Roger Dragonetti, *La technique poétique des trouvères dans la chanson*

courtoise (Bruges: De Tempel, 1960); Paul Zumthor, *Essai de poétique médiéval* (Paris: Seuil, 1972), esp. 157–85, 189–243. Also Gérard Genette, *Figures III* (Paris: Seuil, 1972) and *Nouveau discours du récit* (Paris: Seuil, 1983); Emile Benveniste, *Problèmes de linguistique générale* (Paris: Gallimard, 1966), 237–50; and Harald Weinrich, *Tempus: besprochene und erzählte Welt,* 2d ed. (Stuttgart: Kohlhammer, 1971).

66. Lazar, *Bernard de Ventadour,* no. 1, lines 1–8, 49–56, 57–59.

67. In exordia of songs by Cercamon and William IX, for example, the object of the singers' discourse is explicitly stated as a kind of lyric text. William IX proposes a *vers:* "Companho, farai un vers tot covinen / Ez aura·i mais de foudatz no·i a de sen" (Bond, *Poetry of William VII,* no. 1, lines 1–2) (Companions, I'll make a *vers* just as it should be done, and there'll be in it more folly than sense). Cercamon begins a *vers* that is a *planh:* "Lo plaing comenz iradamen / d'un vers don hai lo cor dolen" (Wolf, *Poetry of Cercamon and Jaufre Rudel,* no. 1, lines 1–2) (I begin sorrowfully a lament in a *vers* wherein I have a grieving heart).

68. Jeanroy observes of all troubadours: "Le poète se prend lui-même pour sujet de ses chants.... Comme si l'amour était le seul objet qui pût nous intéresser, il nous montre ce cœur continuellement embrasé de flammes amoureuses" (*Poésie lyrique,* 2:62).

69. See Amelia A. Van Vleck, "'Tost me trobaretz fenida': Reciprocating Composition in the Songs of Castelloza," in *The Voice of the Trobairitz,* ed. William D. Paden (Philadelphia: University of Pennsylvania Press, 1989), 95–111.

70. Elsewhere Bernart addresses the transmitter directly: for example, "Messatgers, vai e cor, / e di·m a la gensor / la pena e la dolor / que·n trac, e·l martire" (Lazar, *Bernard de Ventadour,* no. 4, lines 73–76) (Messenger, go, run, and tell the Fairest One for me about the pain and the grief I endure because of her, and the martyrdom).

71. Bond, *Poetry of William VII,* no. 4, lines 1–6.

72. Pattison, *Life and Works of Raimbaut d'Orange,* no. 24, lines 1–7.

73. Ibid., 154; for other parallels between Raimbaut and William IX see Paterson, *Troubadours and Eloquence,* 163–68.

74. According to the Ripoll treatises, the *estribot* (usually defined as a satirical invective) is base and unworthy of courtly singing (Marshall, *Razos de trobar,* 103); Marshall notes (142, n. 84) that two Old Occitan examples survive, by Palais (P-C 315, 5) and Peire Cardenal (P-C 335, 64).

75. Lazar, *Bernard de Ventadour,* no. 28, lines 1–7, 8–14.

76. Dialogic exchange as a genre also characterizes troubadour forms such as the *tenso,* the *partimen,* and *cobla* exchanges; it can occur in interesting ways in other songs as well (see my discussion below).

77. Lazar (*Bernard de Ventadour,* 269, n. 1) and, implicitly, Del Monte (*Peire d'Alvernha,* 200) admit as probable Peire d'Alvergne's authorship as Bernart's interlocutor; but Zenker includes the *tenso* among the songs probably inauthentically attributed to Peire d'Alvergne ("Peire von Auvergne," 790–92). We should be prepared to consider the possibility as well that this is a "fictive *tenso,*" that is, with an invented interlocutor. Frank M. Chambers has suggested, for example, that Guiraut de Borneill's female interlocutor in "S'ie·us quier consseill, bell' Ami' Alamanda" (Sharman, *Cansos and Sirventes of Giraut de Borneil,* no. 57) is an invention

of the troubadour ("Las trobairitz soiseubudas," in *The Voice of the Trobairitz*, ed. William D. Paden [Philadelphia: University of Pennsylvania Press, 1989], 54).

78. Dejeanne, *Poésies complètes*, no. 29, lines 1–6.

79. Bond, *Poetry of William VII*, no. 5, lines 1–6, 7–12, 13–18.

80. Poe, *From Poetry to Prose*.

81. Wolf, *Poetry of Cercamon and Jaufre Rudel*, no. 1, lines 1–6, 13–18.

82. Paden et al., *Poems of Bertran de Born*, no. 16, lines 1–8, 9–16.

83. Ibid., 224; they suggest that the "lady" in question is a metaphor for the Limousin (227).

84. As Bertran de Born writes in the generation following the troubadours in the representative corpus, his is a *sirventes* in the "modern style." Unlike the textuality of the model "pure lyric," addressed to the courtly audience generally, this song, in its constant explicit address to Geoffrey, seeks to engage in a reciprocal discourse. Other, earlier *sirventes*-like songs, such as Peire d'Alvergne's "Sobre·l vieill trobar e·l novel" (Del Monte, *Peire d'Alvernha*, no. 11) and "Cantarai d'aquestz trobadors" (Del Monte, no. 12), a *vers* (line 85), are implicitly addressed to the wider courtly audience. It is evident to me that a similar kind of lyric variance is reflected in the connivance William IX seeks with his companions as he asks their advice in judging horses ("Companho, farai un vers tot covinen" [Bond, *Poetry of William VII*, no. 1]) and girls and women who are locked away ("Compaigno, non pus mudar qu'eu no m'effrei" [Bond, no. 2], "Companho, tant ai agutz d'avols conres" [Bond, no. 3]).

85. Bec, "Problème des genres," 45–46.

86. Dejeanne, *Poésies complètes*, no. 3.

87. Bond, *Poetry of William VII*, nos. 1–3; a three-line, mono-rhymed *cobla* with an 11–11–14 metrical scheme. See Frank, *Répertoire métrique*, 1:1.

88. "Jede literarische Gattung hat . . . ihren Ursprung in einer bestimmten gesellschaftlichen Gegebenheit, . . . deren Dauer, Veränderung und Ende auch Dauer, Veränderung und Ende . . . der Gattung bestimmt" (Köhler, "Sirventes-Kanzone: 'genre bâtard,'" 181).

89. Such as the program on "Medieval Lyric, Text and Melody" at the Seventh Triennial Congress of the International Courtly Literature Society, University of Massachusetts, Amherst, July 30, 1992. Speakers included Joel Cohen, Donna Mayer-Martin, Vincent Pollina, and Hendrik van der Werf.

90. Sharman, *Cansos and Sirventes of Giraut de Borneil*, no. 53. Poe, "New Light on the *Alba*."

91. Wolf, *Poetry of Cercamon and Jaufre Rudel*, no. 2; Dejeanne, *Poésies complètes*, no. 6; Lazar, *Bernard de Ventadour*, nos. 28, 32, 35; Sharman, *Cansos and Sirventes of Giraut de Borneil*, nos. 5–7.

92. On the appropriateness of including the final *cobla*, no. 7, see Sharman, *Cansos and Sirventes of Giraut de Borneil*, 367–68. The conclusion appears in two of six manuscripts, both of which are more or less corrupt; in *T* two extraneous *coblas* are introduced, and the song is not attributed to Guiraut de Borneill. Elizabeth Wilson Poe reasons that the conclusion was known to at least one other copyist (C), who rejected it; she concludes that it must be authentic ("La transmission de l'*alba* en ancien provençal," *Cahiers de civilisation médiévale* 31 [1988]: 339).

❖ CHAPTER 9

*Genre and Demonstrative Rhetoric:
Praise and Blame in the* Razos de trobar
and the Doctrina de compondre dictats

JOHN DAGENAIS

For most modern scholars, formal features of the Old Occitan corpus—meter, rhyme scheme, number of stanzas and *tornadas*—have seemed the logical place to start as we seek to distinguish and classify the various troubadour genres. The assumptions underlying this approach are illustrated rather neatly by István Frank in the introduction to his *Répertoire métrique de la poésie des troubadours*. For Frank, the Old Occitan corpus is a language, a language possessing its own unique grammar and lexicon: "Si un traité de versification est en quelque sorte une grammaire de la poésie, un répertoire où se trouvent classées toutes les formes métriques peut être consideré comme le dictionnaire des structures poétiques et de leurs éléments." Frank views the Old Occitan corpus, then, as *langue* and *paroles,* and his *répertoire* is a fascinating exemplum of how a system of minute differences works itself out in a "dictionary" of more than a thousand lexical items.

Implicit, however, in Frank's view is the project, not just of synchronic linguistics, but of diachronic linguistics as well. Armed with our grammar and dictionary we should be able, theoretically, to "speak" this dead language, the language of troubadour versification, once again. But like diachronic linguistics itself, Frank's system dodges or suppresses one key question: assuming that we can, in fact, speak a dead language, to whom will we speak it? Under what terms can a language be considered to be "spoken" if there is no one to speak it to? And this, in turn, suggests to me that as with dead languages we can speak to no one, an approach to the genres of medieval lyric purely through formal elements will be equally devoid of living response.

This idea seems already to have occurred to some of the writers who composed the late thirteenth- and fourteenth-century manuals of troubadour versification. They actively sought a means to reinscribe the genres of troubadour verse in a living language, in a moment of live performance. These manuals treat lyric not as a sung, spoken, or written *text* bearing specific formal characteristics but as an *act* of rhetoric, specifically demonstrative rhetoric, in which the poet addresses a real, or at least implied, audience, praising and/or blaming specific topics: love, ladies, feudal lords, for example. This view seems at first to shift the emphasis (our emphasis, anyway) from formal concerns to rhetorical and even ethical ones, but it is essential to keep in mind that the rhetorical act of praising and blaming also functions in these texts on versification as a quasi-formal mechanism for defining genres. Through this mechanism, the verse forms defined become once again active, oral, public, occasional, in a way which inevitably escapes us when we seek to understand genre through "dead" formal features alone.

It is not my goal to discover whether the rhetoricizing of the troubadour genres was a part of the twelfth- or thirteenth-century troubadours' idea of what they were doing when they created their verse. Rather, I seek to explore a significant feature of the late thirteenth- and fourteenth-century *reception* of troubadour lyric. Evidence shows that rhetorical concepts of praise and blame played a key role in shaping fourteenth-century poets' conceptions of how troubadour lyric should be written and in forming audiences' ideas of how it should be read or listened to. The rhetoricizing of classical troubadour verse breathes new life into it, restores in a slightly different key its original situation as act of public performance in a courtly setting, a setting in which the troubadour seeks the largesse of a lord and the favor of a lady before a courtly audience.

Before examining the treatise in which the epideictic classification of genres finds its maximum expression, I want to discuss briefly the first poetic and grammatical treatise on "Lemosí," or indeed, on any Romance language, the *Razos de trobar,* probably composed between 1190 and 1213 by the Catalan Raimon Vidal de Besalú. In the *Razos,* Vidal dramatizes what seems to have been a contemporary crisis of praising and blaming. It is precisely a misapplication of praise and blame, then, which founds the writing of poetic arts in the vernacular. Vidal offers a wry but rather suggestive twist upon the classical "scene of rhetoric": not only does the speaker deceive his audience but the speaker is equally misled by the audience's unsophisticated reaction. They lavishly praise a troubadour who sings a pretty song although they do not understand a word he has said.

> En aqest saber de trobar son enganat li trobador, et dirai vos com ni per qe: li auzidor qe ren non intendon, qant auzon un bon chantar, faran senblant qe fort ben l'entendon, et ges no l'entendran, qe cuieriant se qe·lz en tengues hom per pecs si dision qe no l'entendesson. En aisi enganan lor mezeis, qe uns dels maiors sens del mont es qi domanda ni vol apenre so qe non sap. Et sil qe entendon, qant auziran un malvais trobador, per ensegnament li lauzaran son chantar; et si no lo volon lauzar, al menz no·l volran blasmar; et en aisi son enganat li trobador, et li auzidor n'an lo blasme.[1]

> In this art of composing verse the troubadours are deceived, and I will tell you how and why: the listeners, who do not understand a thing, when they hear a good song, pretend that they understand it quite well and do not understand it at all, for they think that people will consider them stupid if they said that they did not understand. And so they deceive themselves, for one of the most sensible things in the world is the person who asks and wants to learn what he does not know. And those who understand, when they hear a bad troubadour, out of courtesy they will praise his singing; and if they do not want to praise him, at least they will not want to blame him. And thus the troubadours are deceived and the listeners are to blame.

The audience pretends to understand the troubadour for fear that it will be considered "pecs" (stupid). The result: the troubadours are deceived concerning the degree of their own artistic skill, and the audience is to blame. It is the unfortunate consequences of misapplied praise and blame which Vidal hopes to head off through his treatise. As he goes on to say, "una de las maiors valors del mont es qui sap lauzar so qe fa a lauzar et blasmar so qe fai a blasmar" (one of the greatest values in the world accrues to the person who knows how to praise what should be praised and blame what should be blamed).[2]

The goal of the treatise is, on the one hand, then, to teach a prospective audience how to apply praise and blame appropriately to the poems they hear. The audience will no longer be taken in by just another pretty voice. On the other hand, the treatise will provide troubadours some objective standards by which to evaluate their own poetic achievements, safe from the ignorance and lack of sophistication of their audiences. But what is most significant for us here is the way in which Vidal places the lyric moment not in the subjective outpourings of the feigned lover's heart but in a public performance in which audience feedback is an integral if often problematic feature.

Nearly a century later, but still in Catalunya, the *Doctrina de compondre dictats* was written. This brief treatise follows Vidal's *Razos* in the only manuscript in which it appears, currently Barcelona, Biblioteca Central, MS. 239. The treatise lacks the grammatical discussions found in the *Razos*. Instead, it is uniquely dedicated to a discussion of the various genres of troubadour verse. In it we find the traces of a system of genre definition which links troubadour verse to the vast medieval tradition of reading Latin texts for praise and blame. Here, for example, is the description of the *canso*:

> Deus saber que canço deu parlar d'amor plazenment, e potz metre en ton parlar eximpli d'altra rayso, e ses mal dir e ses lauzor de re sino d'amor. Encara mes, deus saber que canço ha obs e deu haver cinch cobles; eyxamen n'i potz far, per abeylimen e per complimen de raho, .vi. o .vij. o .viij. o .ix., d'aquell compte qe mes te placia. E potz hi far una tornada o dues, qual te vulles. E garda be que, en axi com començaras la raho en amor, que en aquella manera matexa la fins be e la seguesques. E dona li so noveyl co pus bell poras.³

> You should know that the *canço* should speak about love pleasingly, and you can put in your words examples from another topic, and without blaming and without praising anything except love. In addition, you must know that the *canço* requires and must have five stanzas; but you could also make six or seven or eight or nine in order to make it more beautiful or to complete the subject matter, in whatever number of stanzas you wish. And you can give it one envoi or two, whichever you prefer. And be careful that, since you will begin with the topic of love, you complete it well and carry it through in the same way. And give it a new tune, as beautiful a one as you can.

The description is fairly representative. The prime focus is on topical features in their relation to the activities of praising and blaming. Concern with formal features is limited to giving rather loose specifications for the number of *coblas* and *tornadas* and specifying whether a new or an old tune should be used. Little is said about meter and still less about rhyme.

I want to take a closer look now at how this little "system" works (see table 9.1A). The system functions by assigning genre designations to poems based on the presence of praise and/or blame and the specific topics which are praised or blamed in the poem. The emphasis is on the active role the poet takes in choosing a topic and then praising it or blaming it: "Si vols far alba, parla d'amor plazentment; e atressi [deus] lauzar la dona on vas" (If you want to write an alba, speak about love pleasingly; and you should also praise the lady you are going to visit).⁴ In these examples, the author of the *Doctrina* is clearly reading the act of creating troubadour verse in specific generic categories into the creative scenario defined for classical authors of

Table 9.1. Genres as Praise or Blame in the *Doctrina de compondre dictats*

Genre	Praise	Blame	"Rayso" (Materia)/Modus
A. Genres That Praise or Blame Their "Rayso"			
canço	ses lauzor	ses mal dir	de re sino d'amor
sirventez	o de lausor	o de maldit	de senyor o de qualsque feyts qui novellament se tracten
sirventetz	lauzan (o mostran)	blasman o castigan	de senyors o de vassals; o de faytz d'armes o de guerra o de Deu o de ordenances o de novelletatz
estampida	lauzan (o merceyan)	blasman	de qualque fayt vulles; qui·t vulles
alba			amor
	lauzar		la dona on vas
	bendi		l'alba (si acabes lo plazier)
		blasman	la dona e l'alba on anaves (si no·l acabes)
B. Genres with Praise as Their "Rayso"			
vers			de veritatz, de exemples e de proverbis *o de lauzor*, no pas en semblant d'amor
lays			de Deu e de segle, o de exempli o de proverbis, *de lausors* ses feyment d'amor
C. Genres That Praise or Blame Implicitly			
retronza	[plazen]	[cossiros]	amor, segons l'estament en que·n seras

Source: Written 1190–1213; Marshall, *Razos*, 96–98.
Note: Genres defined outside schema of praise and blame: *pastora, dança, plant, gayta, sompni, discort, cobles esparses, tenso.*

popular medieval school texts. Ovid, for example, was implicitly imagined to have sat down and determined to praise or blame certain ethical and unethical behaviors through the metamorphoses he portrays.[5]

We find the clearest articulation of this approach, as we might anticipate, in the definition of the satiric genre, the *sirventés*. The objects of praise and blame in the *sirventés* are lords, vassals, deeds of arms or war, God, decrees, or current events. Much of the standard medieval vocabulary of praising and blaming appears in the treatise's two definitions of the *sirventés: lausor, maldit, blasmar, castigar.* These verbs clearly echo the standard medieval Latin vocabulary of praise and blame. For "praise": *laudare, commendare, monere, hortari, suadere, approbare.* For "blame": *carpere, vituperare, reprehendere, dehortari, deterre, retrahere, invehere, damnare* (drawn chiefly from Ghisalberti, Huygens, Sedlmayer, and Young). It is also interesting to note the rather direct etymological link to *rhetorica demonstrativa* in the treatise's unusual use of the verb "mostrar" (table 9.1A).

This schema is not confined to the definition of the *sirventés*, however. The *canso*, too, as we have seen, is brought into it. In the *canso* the *materia* is love alone. The poet either praises love or blames it. The *estampida* takes the opposite tack. In it, you can praise or blame whatever you want or whomever you want. The description of the *alba* introduces new modalities. The *alba* may be divided into subgenres in which either praise or blame alone is present. The dawn is praised if the poet gets what he came for, presumably the lady. If the poet/lover is disappointed both the dawn and the *dona* get blamed. As Marshall points out,[6] this description seems to bear little resemblance to the events portrayed in most of the *albas* we know.

It would be a mistake to suggest that the approach to genre definition in the *Doctrina* was more systematic than it was. In fact, I think it is important that we allow ourselves to give consideration to ways of thinking about genre which do not quite crystallize into something we can legitimately call a "system." This embryonic set of structures and relations allows us, however, to extrapolate a could-be system in which the presence or absence of certain themes together with the act of praising or blaming these themes might become a reasonably precise means for distinguishing the most important troubadour genres.

What, in fact, were the goals of the author of this new classificatory scheme, a scheme which never quite gets off the ground? I think that he was attempting to bring the experience of the troubadour genres into line with what was the long-standing medieval practice of viewing all written texts as acts of demonstrative rhetoric in which an author or *auctor* uses praise and blame to commend virtue and condemn vice. Nearly every text which medieval people read, from the works of classical writers like Ovid to the Bible, was brought under the rule of praise and blame by someone, somewhere, at some time.

The very frequency of the appearance of "praise and blame" in medieval texts has led medievalists to miss how absolutely fundamental this pair was to medieval thinking about literature. For medieval academic commentators and their readers, praise and blame were constant companions as they read, were an essential part of the reading and writing processes. Praise and blame were as integral a part of the texts they read as was language itself. The burden placed on medieval readers, then, was to identify correctly what was being praised and what blamed in a given passage or work. And this was by no means as simple and reductive a task as it might first appear to us.

The origins of this way of reading are found in Aristotle, of course. Indeed, in the *Politics* Aristotle makes praising and blaming the defining characteristic of all human speech: "whereas mere voice is but an indication of pleasure or pain, and is therefore found in other animals . . . , the power of speech is intended to set forth the expedient and inexpedient, and therefore likewise the just and the unjust. And it is a characteristic of man that he alone has any sense of good and evil, of just and unjust."[7] Already, in the course of the discussion of epideictic in Book 1 of the *Rhetoric,* Aristotle makes the vital link between the binary pair "praise and blame" and another pair "virtue and vice." "We have now to consider excellence and vice, the noble and the base, since these are the objects of praise and blame."[8] This connection had, as I have just suggested, tremendous consequences for medieval thinking about literature. By the twelfth century we find praise and blame widely used in the *accessus ad auctores* to discuss the intentions of ancient authors—Ovid, Virgil, Horace, Homer.[9]

The basic binary pairs, praise and blame, virtue and vice, quickly spawn new sets of twins: persuasion and dissuasion, exhorting and discouraging, clinging and avoiding. Two brief examples must suffice. On Prudentius's *Psychomachia* the commentator says: "Intentio sua est nos hortari ad appetitum virtutum et contemptum viciorum" (His intention is to urge us toward the desire for virtue and the contempt for vice).[10] On Ovid's *Heroides:* "intentio huius libri est commendare castum amorem sub specie quarundam heroydum . . . vel vituperare incestum amorem sub specie incestarum matronarum" (The intention of this book is to commend chaste love through certain heroic ladies . . . or to criticize unchaste love through certain unchaste matrons).[11] We can even find it in the standard definition of the hymn as "laus Dei facta cum cantico," the praise of God using song.[12]

Abelard uses similar vocabulary in his commentary on Romans. In fact, Abelard explicitly reads the Holy Scripture as an act of divine rhetoric: "The intention of all Holy Scripture is to teach or move men in the same way as speech does in the sphere of rhetoric. It teaches when it advises what we should do or avoid. It moves us when, by dissuading us with divine admonitions, it makes our will draw back from evil; and by persuasion it brings us to the good, with the result that we want to do what we have learnt we ought to do, or avoid whatever is opposed to that."[13] By the thirteenth century a whole vocabulary of praising and blaming had evolved. In manuscripts, one often finds medieval readers going through their texts and sedulously annotating in the margins which particular laudatory or condemnatory activity an author was pursuing in a given passage. "Here the author shows, here he approves, here he chastizes, here he teaches, here he reprimands."[14] It seems to me, then, that in the first instance we can attribute the presence of praise and blame in the *Doctrina* to its author's familiarity with this widespread way of thinking about texts. Like classical, Christian, and biblical authors—Latin authors in other words—vernacular lyrics are now brought under the sway of academic commentary. They, too, are rhetorical acts of praise and blame.

This is surely an interesting phenomenon in its own right, suggesting that as troubadour lyric became more and more a written rather than a performance phenomenon, it also acquired the exegetical language borne by other written texts. I return to this point in a moment, because there is another development we should note first: Hermann the German's translation of Averroës's "Middle Commentary" on Aristotle's *Poetics*. This translation was made in Toledo a few decades before the *Doctrina* was composed. Averroës's "Middle Commentary" makes precisely the same move we find in the *Doctrina:* poetic activity is shifted wholesale into the realm of epideictic rhetoric. In the "Middle Commentary" poetic activity is associated with epideictic far more explicitly and insistently than it had been, even by Aristotle himself. I quote: "Aristotle says: Every poem, and all poetic utterance is either praise or blame."[15]

The renewed and newly explicit linking of all poetic activity to praise and blame in Hermann's translation of the "Middle Commentary" seems to have been fairly influential in Castile. Hermann's translation or the Arabic original may lurk behind a definition of the "versificador" (versifier) found in the Castilian *Libro de los cien capítulos,* a collection of proverbs put together around 1300: "El buen versificador es el que dize bien e ayna e sabe contar las maneras de quien quisier e sabe [denostar] vilemente e loar altamente"[16] (The good versifier is he who speaks well and quickly and knows how to recount the behavior of anyone he wants and who knows how to blame vilely and praise loftily). We may also glimpse the idea of poetic praise and blame in the boast made by Juan Ruiz, Archpriest of Hita, in his *Libro de buen amor:* he is one in a thousand troubadours who knows how to praise *and* blame subtly and elegantly, "que saber bien e mal dezir encobierto e doñeguil, / tú non fallarás uno de trobadores mill."[17] In the "Middle Commentary," then, we have another direction from which praise and blame may have entered the language of the *Doctrina,* this one more specifically concerned with lyric, vernacular lyric even, rather than standard Latin texts.

Even a cursory reading shows, however, that the *Doctrina* deviates somewhat from the common Aristotelian and medieval view which makes virtue and vice the exclusive objects of praise and blame. Instead of praising and blaming virtue and vice, it praises and blames love, ladies, and lords. The treatise's use of praise and blame stands outside the moral framework on which praise and blame was most frequently hung. But this shift, too, is well documented in the medieval tradition. Already in an early *accessus* to Maximian, praise and blame are transferred from purely moral concerns to become part of a schema for discussing the common *topoi* of youth and old age: "In hoc autem libro senectutem cum suis viciis vituperat iuventutemque cum suis deliciis exaltat" (In this book, old age with its vices is blamed and youth with its delights is exalted).[18] And in his *accessus* to that lyric of lyrics, the Song of Songs, Honorius of Autun outlines a system which comes closest to the one found in the *Doctrina:*

> In principiis librorum tria requiruntur, scilicet, auctor, materia, intentio. . . . Materia, ut scias utrum de bellis an de nuptiis vel de quibus rebus tractat. Intentio, ut cognoscas utrum rem de qua tractat suadeat vel dissuadeat, vel liber lectus quid utilitas conferat.[19]

> At the beginnings of books three things are investigated: author, subject matter, and intention. . . . The subject matter, so that you may know if it is about wars or marriages or whatever. The intention, so that you may know whether it persuades to or dissuades from the subject it treats, or what utility the book may confer once read.

This schema corresponds fairly closely to that found in the genre definitions (see table 9.1A): a subject matter—*rayso, materia*—is defined, and then we determine whether the author is arguing for or against this particular subject, praising or blaming it.

Honorius's *accessus* to the Song of Songs also allows us to observe another feature of medieval academic commentary: the tendency for categories to expand and collapse apparently at the caprice of the commentator. In Honorius's reduced tripartite scheme—*auctor, materia, intentio*—room is made for *utilitas,* normally a category of its own, under *materia.* Similar collapsing of categories occurs in the definition of the *vers* and the *lays* in the *Doctrina* (see table 9.1B). Praise is not so explicitly a particular rhetorical stance taken with regard to the subject matter, rather it is part of a broader grouping which seems to include both *materia* and some of the familiar *modi tractandi:* the *modus exemplorum suppositivus* or the *modus parabolicus,* for example. It is also interesting to note that these definitions introduce the notion of a negative *materia:* the *vers* and the *lays* forms must *not* be about love.

We find in the *retronxa* a final shift in these patterns (see table 9.1C). The *retronxa* also takes love as its subject matter, but in place of praise and blame of love, we find another binary pair vaguely reminiscent of it. The poet speaks according to his psychological or emotional state in the course of his love. Is he high on love or suicidal? That a pair of critical or definitional categories should reappear as psychological states is entirely typical of medieval thinking about literature and genre—the categories themselves get caught up in the play, reemerge wearing new masks.

This scheme—praise/blame/materia—goes on to play a significant role in the reception and creation of troubadour lyric in fourteenth-century Catalunya and Occitania. This is readily apparent in the genre definitions found in the *Leys d'amors* written between 1328 and 1337 (see table 9.2). Here, although praise and blame seem to have lost much of their force as creative *activities* which define genres, the language is even more strongly reminiscent of the language of praise and blame, virtue and vice, found in academic commentary. Praise and blame seem to have settled into specific generic categories of panegyric and invective. Their use is no less generic, perhaps, but it is less purely oratorical.

Another interesting development in the role of praise and blame in the reception of troubadour verse may be found in songbook *H,* copied in late thirteenth-century Italy.[20] In it the compiler presents a selection of first lines or isolated *coblas* under rubrics such as "cobla de lauzor" (*H,* fols. 47v and 48r), or "cobla de rancure" ([*sic*] *H,* fol. 49r). In some cases, the compiler gives a brief description of the *cobla* in question, using the language of praise and blame: "Aquesta cobla *repren* las dompnas que no uolen los ualenz fins amics, mas los no ualens menutz receben" (*H,* fol. 48r; emphasis mine) (This *cobla* reprimands those ladies who reject truly excellent courtly lovers but receive worthless and inferior ones). Or: "Aquestas coblas blasman dompna qes fai trop preiar" (*H,* fol. 49v) (These *coblas* blame the lady who makes her lover beg too much).

Clearly the ambience of the *canso* has its own set of values for virtue and vice, values that do not correspond, and, in fact, often oppose, those found in commentary on biblical texts or classical authors. Seen from the larger

Table 9.2. Genres as Praise or Blame in the *Leys d'amors*

Genre	Materia
vers	de sen (etymon: "verays")
	d'amors, *de lauzors, o de reprehensio, per donar castier* (etymon: "virar")
chanso	d'amors o de *lauzors*
sirventes	*de reprehensio o de maldig en general, per castiar* los fols e los malvatz, o . . . del fag d'alquna guerra
descort	d'amors o *de lauzors o per maniera de rancura* . . . o de tot aysso ensems
retroncha	de sen, de essenhamen, d'amors, *de lauzors o de reprendemen per castiar los malvatz*
plang	de lauzors de la cauza per la qual hom fay aytal plang
	del desplazer qu'om ha e de la perda que's fay per lo mescabamen de la cauza qu'om planh
	(cauzas: d'ome o de femna, . . . o d'autra cauza, coma si una vila oz una ciutatz era destruida e dissipada, per guerra o per autra maniera)
estampida	d'amors o de lauzors, a la maniera de vers o de chanso

Source: Written 1328–1337; ed. Carl Appel, *Provenzalische Chrestomathie mit Abriss der Formenlehre und Glossar,* 6th ed. (Leipzig: Reisland, 1930; Hildesheim: Olms, 1971), 197–201.

Note: Genres defined outside schema of praise and blame: *dansa, tenso, partimen, pastorela, escondig.*

perspective of medieval praising and blaming, *lauzor* in the courtly lyric is often *lauzenjar,* praising what should be blamed and blaming what should be praised. By approaching the courtly system of values as it was rendered into praise and blame by thirteenth- and fourteenth-century readers of troubadour verse, we might gain some interesting insights into how this system functioned within the larger medieval economy of praise and blame.

The system of genre classification through praise and blame found in the *Doctrina* it is at best a rudimentary one. The active application of praise or blame to thematic objects is limited to the definitions of the *canso,* the *sirventes,* the *estampida,* and the *alba.* Ironically, it is in the curious classification of the *alba* that we get our strongest suggestion that an idea of genre classification through praise and blame was indeed one of the author's goals. In his efforts to force the genre into this schema he manages to miss the nature of the *alba* itself, at least as we know it. In the other cases in the *Doctrina,* throughout the *Leys,* and in songbook *H,* the most we can observe, and it is an important observation nonetheless, is that praise and blame play an integral part in the thinking about troubadour genres which went on in late thirteenth- and fourteenth-century Catalunya, Occitania, and Italy. This is not the same thing as saying that praise and blame *defined* these genres, I know. But it is, at the same time, an important nuance which we must add to our understanding of how these genre conceptions functioned in a time not too distant from the composition of troubadour verse. In addition to the prosodic and thematic elements which have largely concerned modern scholars, we must take into account a view of the nature of this verse as rhetorical, oral, as a public performance in which persons present or absent are subjected in a collective setting to praise or blame by the troubadour *auctor.*

An important subtext of the preceding discussion is the shift which appears to occur in the course of the thirteenth century from an oral troubadour culture to a written one. This shift is suggested most obviously by the 150-year gap which separates the activities of the first known troubadour from the earliest troubadour songbook which has survived. There are many interesting issues which we might discuss in terms of this shift: the new importance of the written word over song, of private reading over public performance; a shift in authors' own view of the stability of their texts from one which participates, even willingly, in oral *mouvance* to one which relies on the fixity of the texts and the stability of stanza ordering. With this shift come new concepts of authorial property and new modes of composition and diffusion. Whatever the value of the *Doctrina* and the other texts I have discussed may be for understanding troubadour genres, they also serve as an important reminder of one of the numerous paradoxes which confront us as we seek to understand medieval orality and textuality. In moving troubadour song under the rubrics of Latin academic commentary, that is, under the same rubrics which had been applied to written texts for centuries, these authors and compilers were certainly participating in new understandings of troubadour verse primarily as written texts. But by the very act of transferring them to this realm, they also infuse in them a new type of orality, an orality characteristic of written, Latin, texts throughout the Middle Ages.

For the monk who confronted his Book-of-the-Year in his monastic cell or the student pouring over a copybook by smoky lamplight, the written page possessed a form of orality which our often too-simplistic division of orality and textuality suppresses. For most medieval readers, the written page was still an act of oration. The reader was an individual member of a collective audience, and the author spoke to the individual and the collective through the page, praising and blaming, persuading and dissuading. In this way, the *voces paginarum* re-create a moment which is quintessentially oral. And yet the author, for all his oral presence, is also textually absent. There is a gap in the midst of this oral moment which cannot be bridged. The orator's voice is faint. We are sure from the rhetorical/written setting itself that he is praising and blaming, but, as in the case of Ovid's *Metamorphoses,* we cannot always grasp just what the objects of praise and blame are. Although the orality of the moment implies the author's presence, the textuality of the page denies this presence to us. It is suddenly up to us as listeners and readers to fill this gap with our own system of values, to decide for ourselves what is praiseworthy or blameworthy in the text before us, that is, to decide what the physically absent author is praising in the rhetorically present moment. We should view the effort to assign genre designations to troubadour verse on the basis of praise and blame as part of an attempt to restore rhetorical presence to this verse, to bridge at once several gaps: between author and written text, between performance and reception, between the poet and his audience.

NOTES

1. J. H. Marshall, ed., *The "Razos de trobar" of Raimon Vidal and Associated Texts* (London: Oxford University Press, 1972), 4.

2. Ibid., 4. Vidal's *Razos* suggests that already in the late twelfth century, at least in Catalunya, there is a gap between the audience's ability to understand and ap-

preciate the linguistic and formal aspects of troubadour lyric and their ability to appreciate the musical aspects. This in turn suggests, not surprisingly after all, that music and individual vocal skills inevitably played a far larger role in the medieval reception of troubadour verse than the manuscript texts which are our only trace of it can possibly convey.

3. Ibid., 95.

4. Ibid., 96.

5. A great variety of medieval academic commentary on Ovid may be found in Fausto Ghisalberti, "Medieval Biographies of Ovid," *Journal of the Warburg and Courtauld Institutes* 9 (1946): 10–59; R. B. C. Huygens, ed., *Accessus ad auctores* (Leiden: Brill, 1970); Henricus Stephanus Sedlmayer, *Prolegomena Critica ad Heroides Ovidianas* (Vienna: C. Geroldi filium, 1878); and Karl Young, "Chaucer's Appeal to the Platonic Deity," *Speculum* 19 (1944): 1–13.

6. Marshall, *Razos,* 138, n. 62-6.

7. Jonathan Barnes, ed., *The Complete Works of Aristotle* (Princeton: Princeton University Press, 1984), 1253a, 10–17.

8. Ibid., 1366a, 23–24.

9. Huygens, *Accessus,* passim.

10. Ibid., 20.

11. Ibid., 32.

12. Madrid, Biblioteca Nacional, MS. 9240 (15th c.), fol. 6r.

13. A. J. Minnis and A. B. Scott with David Wallace, *Medieval Literary Theory and Criticism, c. 1100–c. 1375: The Commentary-Tradition* (Oxford: Clarendon Press, 1988), 100.

14. For an excellent late medieval example of the practice see Seville, Biblioteca Universitaria, MS. 331/175 (15th c.), G. de Trapezunde, passim.

15. Minnis and Scott, *Medieval Literary Theory and Criticism,* 289. The quotation attributed to Aristotle does not actually appear in the text of the *Poetics,* so far as I know. The commentary may also provide the framework for assigning certain subsets of each genre to praise or blame alone as we saw in the case of the *alba*. According to Averroës, some poets are successful in praising but not in bestowing blame. Conversely, others are successful in bestowing blame rather than praise (ibid., 292). Such a view seems to have provided the foundation for medieval views of the nature of satire. Clearly, in the case of the *sirventés* blame is more frequent than praise.

16. Agapito Rey, ed., *Libro de los cien capítulos* (Bloomington: Indiana University Press, 1960), 30.

17. Juan Ruiz, *Libro de buen amor,* ed. G. B. Gybbon-Monypenny (Madrid: Castalia, 1988), stanza 65cd. For a fuller discussion of praise and blame in the *Libro de buen amor,* see my *Ethics of Reading in Manuscript Culture: Glossing the "Libro de buen amor"* (Princeton: Princeton University Press, 1994), 91–103.

18. Huygens, *Accessus,* 25.

19. Jacques-Paul Migne, ed., *Patrologiae cursus completus [series latina]* (Paris: Migne, 1844–82), 172:347.

20. Rome, Biblioteca Vaticana, MS. lat. 1207 (late 13th c.).

CHAPTER 10

"Wa-hiya taklifu ghannat": Genre and Gender in Hispano-Arabic Poetry

VICENTE CANTARINO

The notion of genre is not unknown to Arab literary critics. Since early times in their history of poetic analysis, they have classified Arabic compositions in terms of notions very close to the Western, basically Aristotelian, concept. Yet scholars accustomed to Aristotle's formulation of genre will find its application to Arabic poetic concepts difficult. Arab critics, more often than not grammarians and rhetoricians, have tended to categorize the various poetic forms not on the basis of philosophical considerations but simply as a means to facilitate their inclusion and study in anthologies. Thus instead of searching for "the elements common to all or most of them," as any follower of the Aristotle's *Poetics* would put it,[1] they have tended to offer a simpler and more practical classification, often without regard for any generic common ground and without attempting any more technical or philosophical analysis.[2]

The most important genre, the *qasida*, is defined with reference to features of rhyme, meter, and content. It must be mono-rhymed, and accepts only one of the canonical meters (*tawil, kamil,* or *wasit,* and so forth), which are form-bound. On the other hand, it must also include three traditional parts, the *nasib* (lyrical introduction), the *rahil* (reference to travel), and the *madih* (praise), which, as their names indicate, are content-bound. Other genres are defined with reference only to the main theme, as are the genres of drinking poems (*khamriyyat*) or love songs (*ghazal, ghazaliyyat,* and so on).

More difficult to define are the poetic forms peculiar to Hispano-Arabic poetry. The *zajal,* which translates as "song," enjoys somewhat greater freedom as to meter with its rather short verses, and a broad range in its rhyme-schemes, which are often different from the canonical schemes allowed for the *qasida*. Another Hispano-Arabic form, the *muwashshaha,* is probably the only one that clearly responds to a formal notion, or range of possibilities, based on stanza and rhyme, yet the Arab literary critics insist that the *kharja* must be in a popular speech form (either romance or vernacular Arabic) and that it must be sung by a woman, requirements which, once again, combine linguistic forms and poetic concepts. In the *qasida,* moreover, with its *nasib,* as well as in the *muwashshaha* with its *kharja,* the lyrical content has, so it seems, a generative influence in the conceptualization of the poetic form.

Thus in Arabic poetry and poetics lyricism and its expression in poetic language become a natural pathway to take in a search for the meaning of poetic genre. I think we may accept for now, with Northrop Frye, that poetry is "an internal mimesis of sound and imagery."[3] Perhaps we should also assume that specific psychological, even cultural differences elicited by gender may also be manifested in the language that the poetic mimesis performs. Thus, in theory at least, poetic mimesis should be divided into two main categories, namely, one product of mimesis by men and the other of mimesis by women, the former constituting masculine poetry and the latter feminine. However, since a performer different from the author, and of the opposite gender, often accepts the poetic sound and imagery as mimesis of his or her own internal process, we must distinguish both the voice which proffers the poetry (the author) and the voice which transmits it (the performer) from the voice in the poetry itself (the persona). Mimesis by a performer, man or woman, could be assumed to carry, via the performer's acceptance and transmission, a formal connection with the internal process of the author.

For the sake of clarity I will reserve the more qualitative terms "masculine" and "feminine" to refer specifically to the gender of the persona as determined by the poetic discourse. In contrast I will call the poetic voice "man's" or "woman's" in direct reference to the gender identity of the performer, who assumes it as entirely his or her own. Thus in the majority of the *muwashshahas* the main voice in the body of the song is a man's, and in the *kharja* the man accepts a feminine persona, making a lyrical connection between the two moments which is required by the genre. This connection is expressed in terms of the generic form "I feel like the woman who sang . . . ," followed by the *kharja*.

So understood, women's or men's voices would appear to be the mechanics of sound and imagery which introduce the content, that is, feminine or masculine poetry. Sound and imagery may appear to be related in a necessary way to voice and content, and quite often are indeed deeply connected. But correspondence between the gender of a voice, man's or woman's, and the content, masculine or feminine poetry, is not the rule. No such correspondence is required as long as the poet who either proffers (as does the author) or produces (as does the performer) a mimesis of the opposite gender offers it with psychological validity. This is the crux of the matter.

It has been said that "Language not merely reflects sexual difference, it perpetuates it both subtly and overtly."[4] I propose to examine the agent which perpetuates sexual differences in the literary world of Andalusian Arabic poetry, and the manner in which that agent does so. I shall not ask whether or not there was a poetry in the Arabic literary world of al-Andalus which should be especially connected with women, either as the original authors of feminine poetry or as the singers endowed with the woman's voice. There is no question that there was a wealth of both. Instead I shall ask about the mimetic relevance of such authors and singers, and beyond that, whether or not we can detect that when Andalusian women wrote poetry, they used a literary or psychological vocabulary which is in any discernible way different from that used by men. I shall also ask whether or not women's voices, as created by men authors, are granted specific or distinctive qualities that differ from the ones granted to men's voices. I shall ask to what extent, if at all, women's voices in the poetry of al-Andalus are a definite and definable psychological reality—whether there is, so to speak, a feminine *gender-genre*.

Some of my observations on Hispano-Arabic lyric poetry are related to forms more or less common in the Iberian Romance tradition, and, beyond the peninsula, in Romance lyric poetry in general.[5] Other observations I will make in this connection could be easily extended beyond the Andalusian poetic world to include other forms, themes, and topics common to Arabic poetry in general. Extraordinary, and unique to the Arabic-Andalusian case, is the fact that we also see the Romance and Arabic traditions intermingling and influencing each other in some respects, yet in others performing back to back, taking hardly any notice of each other.[6]

Earlier and more clearly than its Romance counterpart, the Arabic literary tradition of al-Andalus reflects the importance granted in Arab society to refined and courtly behavior based on a code, *adab*, in which literary instruction and social grace were essential, and poetry and music were their two most important components.[7] Command of both was a sign of culture and social distinction not only for men but also, even more so, for women; the exercise of these skills in original composition or recitation was a favored occupation for men and women. By such means women slaves could find easy access to the households of the refined and wealthy; thus women skillful in singing and reciting poetry, including their own, achieved great distinction and became incorporated in both refined literature and folklore. In fact, as any reader of Arabic literary narrative can attest, women seem to have been able to assume a remarkable freedom of expression and action in the pursuit of love. Popular literature such as we find in the tales of *Alif layla wa-layla* (*The Arabian Nights,* as they have become known to the West), idealizing a wealthy and refined world for the urban lower classes, offers a multiplicity of situations in which the role of women is both idealized and exalted in contexts of social refinement. Thus we find a large number of women's voices introduced as the basis of the narrative, in a fashion that became a commonplace in literature.

Especially important in the literary tradition of the Iberian Peninsula, both for the Arabic and, later, for the Romance tradition, is the case of the beautiful, refined, wise, and loyal slave Tawaddud, a mirror of feminine moral and social virtues, an exemplar of intellectual talents, social education, and courtly behavior. As she herself tells us, she mastered all the arts and sciences:

> I learned the arts of poetry and music, and thus I am able to play all the various instruments that are plucked as well as those that are played with the fingers, and I mastered all the ways in which they are played throughout the world. I also learned the thirty-three different manners and ways that comprise the art of writing poetry and all the variations thereof, and know the names of each one. And in order that I might be even more expert in those arts, I also learned how to perform motets and how to sing and how to dance, including all the various steps that are required for and that belong to each dance. I know old pieces and new pieces, and I know both plain-song and part singing, including the upper and lower voices, and I know the old songs of heroes and many ballads that are sung. I know many canticles, both old and new, and I can perform them very well. And I know how to play the lute and the *vihuela,* with the most beautiful harmonies.[8]

In later versions the same training and abilities in the poetic and musical arts are always retained, even though they become less important to explain the events to follow or to underline the expertise and knowledge that the girl will be required to demonstrate. They undoubtedly are described in such detail in order to exalt Tawaddud's spiritual and social refinement.[9] The weight given to women's voices in the narratives gives the distinct impression that Arabic literary fiction derives from, or indulges in, a direct idealization of social reality.

If we move from the existence of women's voices in texts of fictional literature to the historical reality they may reflect, the Arabic historical tradition offers a similar situation. Not all these women's voices are products of a fanciful narrative. Arabic poetic tradition in general, and that of al-Andalus in particular, offers many cases (few if compared with that of male poets, but still a respectable number) of women who made a name for themselves as poets and recited their own compositions. Like many others, the famous Al-Maqqari (who died in 1631), for example, dedicates a chapter to women poets in his poetic anthology, *Nafh at-Tib*. (Nevertheless his reason for doing so results in a dubious compliment to women, since he declares that he has included them in his work "to make known that the superior literary excellence of the people of al-Andalus is an inborn quality that even women and children possess.")[10]

There are indeed numerous names of women poets that can be historically uncovered and identified, names of women belonging to all social classes, from a slave to a caliph's daughter. Hind, for instance, was slave to Abu Muhamma Abd Allah ash-Shatibi, and is quoted in the historical treatises on Arabic music as a skillful singer of poetry and lute player. Also famous for her singing and knowledge of poetry was Qamar, a slave brought from Baghdad to al-Andalus by Ibrahim ibn al-Hajjaj, who died at the beginning of the tenth century. The oldest was Hassana at-Tamimiyya, a poet born in the late eighth century. Maryam bint ibn Yaqubi was both a poet and a teacher in the early eleventh century. Representing the nobility there was Wallada, the daughter of the last Umayyad caliph of Cordova, known through her own lyrical verses as well as those dedicated to her by Ibn Zaydun, her most famous poet and lover. Others are Maryam bint abi Ya'qub al-Faysuly al-Ansari al-Hajja, who lived in Seville about the year 1000; Buthayna, daughter of al-Mu'tamid, king of Seville; Hafsa bint ar-Rakuniyya; Hamda bint Ziyad and her sister Zaynab, both from Guadix near Granada; and Nazhun bint Al-Qala'i, born in Granada near the middle of the twelfth century.[11]

As with male poets and their poetry, Arab anthologists and critics like to present the women's poetic texts within the context of their authors' biographies. Although the narrated events surrounding the poetry of men and women may be no more than literary fiction, it is noteworthy that the anthologists and literary historians made considerable efforts to provide those voices with a historical background. For that purpose they frequently related the composition of a poem and the nature of its content to specific and concrete events in the life of the poet. Quite often with lyrical verses, a woman is presented as answering a lover's poem with another famous love song, or an improvised gloss to it, with which she refers to her own situation as an expression of her own feelings. Such verses would seem to make a compelling case for women's voices expressing feminine poetry.

However, the scholar reading these poems in search of a distinctive note in texts ascribed to women may be disappointed, for they contain very little that is distinctive, even less than in the Romance tradition. Arabic verses written by women or attributed to them give the same impression of gender-neutrality as their counterpart, the poetry written by men, possibly for the same reasons, namely, the preponderant use of gender-neutral stereotypes in expression of feelings toward the beloved. Frequently we find no description of physical characteristics at all, or if we do find any, they are totally ambivalent.

An obvious case of literary stereotype is the lyrical poetry of Qamar. Although these verses are not about love but remembrance, they clearly show in the key of nostalgia the problems we confront when in search of the feminine in Arabic women's voices:

> Alas! I shed tears of longing for Baghdad and Iraq,
> for their women like gazelles,
> for the charm of their eyes,
> their languid stride by the Euphrates river,
> their faces rivaling the moon over a necklace;
> beauties, full of pleasure,
> delicately swaying
> as with hopeless love.[12]

More personal, but no less a product of rhetorical stereotypes, are the following verses by Hafsa bint Hamdun al-Hijariyya:

> Loneliness without my friends!
> Endless loneliness!
> That night, when I bid them farewell—
> sorrowful night!

or the following by the same woman, after a lovers' quarrel:

> My lover dislikes rebuke.
> When I left him he asked with arrogance,
> "Is there anyone my equal?"
> But I too asked him,
> "Have you ever found anyone who can cast a shadow over me?"[13]

Such gender-neutrality is further observed, on higher literary levels, in the not-isolated cases when anthologists attribute a composition to both a man and a woman, as in the following verses generally attributed to Ibn Zaydun, but also by some to his lover Wallada:

> Patience has departed
> from the parting lover,
> Revealing the secret love he offered you.
> He suffers, for there is no longer a path to you.
> Sister to the moon in brightness and splendor,
> May God protect the times you appear!
> If my nights seem long after you depart,
> Their shortness was painful when you were with me.[14]

In other cases of, perhaps, a more personal nature, we perceive a formulation of love and longing that may show a certain gender distinction, but may respond, too, to specific courtly love conventions. A case in point may be seen in the following verses by Wallada:

> After you departed, shall we ever meet again?
> Alas, lovers all lament their pains.
> I too waste away; the time we used to meet, as in winter
> by the burning fire of my desire. . . .
> Alas, we are apart![15]

These verses are attributed to Wallada and thought to be addressed to Ibn Zaydun during the time of their mutual love. Yet Ibn Zaydun uses the very same terminology and phraseology at the beginning of his famous *Qasida nunniya,* where he laments Wallada's absence after she rejected him, and where, consequently, separation should offer a completely different gender perspective. Gender-neutrality is further helped by grammatical rules created or imposed by courtly conventions which allow the use of the masculine forms when addressing a woman.[16]

There are, of course, many instances in which a feminine quality can be more easily determined, as in the verses by the slave Gayat al-Muna. When she was offered for sale to Ibn Sumadih, king of Almeria, he tested her literary refinement by asking her to continue his verses: "Ask about my passion for Gayat al-Muna / Who has dressed my body with such a pale garb," to which she responded: "He has shown me a lover / whose passion reveals that it is I."[17] The historicity of such an anecdote is of course doubtful, as is that of many other such stories so much to the liking of Arab anthologists; in fact, the anecdote is recorded elsewhere with other names and under different circumstances. Important for us is the poetic structure of the verse, in which the woman, with lyrical flirtation, calls her master "lover" and makes herself appear as the object, and cause, of his passion.

Quite often, also, in the Arabic lyrical tradition one may ask whether we are dealing with cultural stereotypes rather than with feminine feelings. Such is the case, for example, in the following verses by Qasmuna bint Ismail al-Yahudi, descendant (perhaps even daughter) of Yusuf ibn Nagrila, the famous Jewish poet and vizier to Badis al-Muzaffar, king of Granada:

> There I see an orchard, for which
> the time of harvest has arrived;
> yet there is no gardener
> to pick the fruits.
> Thus youth goes to waste,
> and only remains . . . what I may not say.[18]

The perception of one's own physical beauty and ripe sexuality as a fruit to be picked by a (male) gardener could very well be understood as a strictly feminine love-role. So too could the gazelle, alone and lonely in a garden, in the following verses (although the last line is merely a formalism which can be, and indeed is, also used by male lovers):

> You, gazelle, always in this garden,
> I am like you.
> Our loneliness, jet black eyes,
> we both alone, without a lover. . . .
> Let's endure a demanding fate.[19]

So too could these verses, which Wallada supposedly had embroidered on the hem of her robe, seem strictly feminine, although the historicity of this anecdote, too, is uncertain: "I allow my lovers to caress my cheek, / and bestow my kiss on whoever craves it."[20] If the historicity is uncertain, not so the seriousness with which anthologists have reported Wallada's proud and unconventional attitude toward love. However, the feminine quality of the verses rests on the assumption that it is the woman's role in the courtly game of love to allow caresses and grant kisses.

Of special interest, in spite of their rhetorical formalism, are the following verses by another woman poet, Nazhun:

> Pearls of the night, ever so beautiful!
> Even more, on the eve of Sunday
> if you were with me
> unseen by guardian's eyes,
> the sun one would see
> in the moon's embrace,
> or a Jazima gazelle in a lion's arms.[21]

There should not be a problem with the parallelism *sun-gazelle* for the woman and *moon-lion* for the man, as in Arabic the word for "sun" is feminine and "moon" masculine, although the moon as a term of comparison for feminine beauty and the woman as the moon's sister, in the meaning of equal, are also typical. (The metaphor of the moon as a woman, on the other hand, forces the poet to maintain the grammatical masculine gender instead of the corresponding feminine in reference to her.) Even more important than the situation or the poetic vocabulary used, the point in these verses is that the poet perceives her own role as passive, being loved and embraced by the lover in both images, with a more tranquil sensuality in the first and more aggressive action in the second. Stereotypes as they are, these images do indicate a feminine point of view, although, verse by verse, each has its parallel in others composed and used by men in their reference to women. Thus one could ask whether or not in these verses, as in all the preceding ones, we are dealing with simple cases of stereotypical role distribution, rather than with feminine poetry strictly speaking.

Quite often, also, the poetic vocabulary used in a woman's verses becomes so stereotypical that she uses descriptive physical characteristics of her male lover that are normally associated with a man's stereotypes of ideal feminine beauty—dark eyes, jet black locks of hair, smooth skin, rosy cheeks. This is, in fact, the stereotype of feminine beauty seen in popular literature such as the *Arabian Nights,* and attributed to al-Mutawakkil, caliph in Baghdad between 847 and 850: "In a woman four things should be black: the hair of the head, the eyelashes, the eyebrows, and the dark part of the eyes: four white: the complexion of the skin, the white of the eyes, the teeth, and the legs: four red: the tongue, the lips, the middle of the cheeks, and the gums."[22] Or as included in Tawaddud's own catalogue: "That woman is beautiful who possesses three white qualities, three black, three red; white body, teeth, and the white of the eyes; black hair, eyebrows, and pupils; red lips, cheeks, and gums."[23] The gender-neutrality of these attributes of ideal beauty is seen even more clearly in verses in which they are applied to the description of an ideally handsome man: "My lover has cheeks / beautiful as a red rose on lily-white."[24] Such application is also reflected in *The Arabian Nights,* where the narrator describes a man as he appeared to a sultan: "(a young man) fair to the sight, a well shaped wight with eloquence dight; his forehead was flower-white, his cheek rosy bright, and a mole on his cheek."[25] The narrator exemplifies this description with some verses, as so commonly in Arabic narrative style:

> A youth slim-waisted from whose locks and brows
> The world in blackness and in light is set.
> Throughout Creation's round not fairer show
> Not rarer sight thine eye hath ever met;
> A nut-brown mole sits throne upon a cheek
> Of rosiest red beneath an eye of jet.[26]

A similar instance is found in the following anecdote included in Nefzawi's *The Perfumed Garden,* probably written toward the end of the fourteenth century: "On a certain day, Abd al-Malik ibn Marwan went to see Leilla his mistress and put various questions to her. Among other things, he asked her what were the qualities that women look for in men. Leilla answered him: 'Oh my master, they must have cheeks like ours.' 'And what besides?' said Ben Merouane. She continued: 'And hair like ours; finally he should be like to you, O prince of believers, for, surely, if a man is not strong and rich he will obtain nothing from women.'"[27] In speaking of ideal beauty, those differences remain that are gender-descriptive and thus gender-bound. The phrase "ample hips along with a slender waist," referring to a palm above a sand dune, is used only in reference to women; so, of course, are references to breasts.

Despite the respectable number of poetic voices which are historically recognized as women's, there is hardly any case of authentically feminine poetry. Arabic poetic tradition obviously failed, or did not feel the need, to develop a feminine vocabulary or a type of expression which could be considered peculiar, if not essential, to feminine poetry. Frequently, in fact, we can assess the femininity of a lyrical lament or outburst only by the circumstances surrounding it, if they reflect attitudes and feelings which are general feminine stereotypes, or, as is more often the case, if the poetic dramatization reflects social stereotypes of women's role in Arab society. As a result, actions, circumstances, even feelings are quite often not as distinctively feminine in the Arabic poetic world as they would be in Romance.

In both the Arabic and Romance traditions of Iberia we are on sure ground as to the intended femininity of the poetry only when the person lamenting is talking to her mother (*ya mamma*), as often in the *kharjas,* or is working by the river, or laments that she has not married, or that she is unhappy with a forced marriage, or that she has been placed in a convent; or, of course, when she addresses her *amigo,* as in the Galician-Portuguese *cantigas de amigo*. In the Arabic tradition, however, most situations and actions, even phrases, are not gender-bound, and can only be interpreted as masculine or feminine after a careful analysis of the social and cultural stereotypes that may apply. Moreover, while an address to a beloved in the feminine gender would force the interpretation of the beloved's gender as feminine, not so with the use of masculine forms, which, as we have noted before, are often used when addressing a woman.[28]

Other cases must be subject to interpretation. For example, a lament for the lover's absence in a distant land or on a long journey tends to identify the voice as a woman's in Romance. This is not necessarily the case in the

Arabic tradition, where the absent lover may be identified as a man, and the solitude felt as that of a woman, but only if the journey is to distant lands and has been undertaken alone, or with only one companion, or to war, since the male poet might lament that the woman he loves has departed with her tribe in the reference to travel (*rahil*) in the introductory lines of the *qasida,* the most common stereotype since pre-Islamic times. Also, the lover's complaint about being sequestered and thus unable to join the beloved may express a woman's fate, but does not always do so since Ibn Zaydun uses such poetic vocabulary in his famous lyrical poems on solitude, possibly in reference to his yearning for Wallada during his alleged incarceration. The same could be said about the lover's decision to transfer his or her affection to a new beloved, which in Romance as well as Arabic seems to be a privilege reserved to the man. And yet in Arabic, there are frequent instances where a man complains in poetry about having been abandoned by a woman. Ibn Zaydun, decrying Wallada's betrayal, would be the most famous example. And yet, here too we may be dealing with semantic stereotypes; for, also in the Hispano-Arabic tradition, the *torto* (wrong) caused by *desvio* (capriciousness) is normally understood as feminine, while *deslealtad* (seeking another lover) is understood as a masculine trait.

Quite often too the woman's voice is no more than a secondary trait in a poem really based on the man's voice. This seems to be the case when the woman's voice is simply introduced as a *dramatis persona* in the lyrical setting of the poem. Thus not in every instance does a supposed woman's voice actually function as one, and consequently the poem cannot be considered feminine even though a woman may appear as main speaker or participant in a dialogue. At times we find a woman's voice, but hardly feminine poetry.

The most important cases of women's voices in Hispano-Arabic literature are found in the *kharjas,* the short verses or refrains found in some Andalusian poetic compositions of varied rhyme and stanzaic structure called *muwashshahas.* In most cases the language is Romance, and the content is more in consonance with the lyrical themes found in Galician-Portuguese poetry and the Castilian *romance* than in the Arabic poetic traditions. Yet these texts were preserved within the realm of Arabic literature, written with Arabic characters, and incorporated as a form into Arabic poetics, as the Arab anthologists and critics who discuss them make clear. These anthologists tell us that the *kharja* must always be introduced as a woman's love song and be appended to the Arabic composition as part of the *muwashshaha*'s overall structure.[29] The technique by which the Arab poet should, and in fact does, build up the lyrical nexus involves one of two different structures. In the first structure there is a direct and explicit reference to a woman's voice: "A girl sings as follows," "Wa-hiya gharaaman taklifu ghannat" (She in amorous yearning sang), and the following lines are explicitly addressed to either her mother or her lover. In the second form the poet, supposedly a man, attributes to himself the content of the woman's voice: "I lament like a girl who sings her grief"; within the following Romance text there may be no direct reference to the voice's sex, since the *kharjas* often reveal the femininity of their content only indirectly.

The *kharja* definitely portrays a woman's voice, and obviously tries to convey a feminine feeling; thus it seems to be a woman's voice conveying feminine poetry. Not all are quite as specific, but most of them indeed are. Without going into the debate about their interpretation, the following two examples should suffice:

> ke fareyu mamma
> mio al-habib ya bayshe
> kor le bol seguire
> shi tan non lo amashe

> What shall I do, Mama?
> My beloved is departing,
> and my heart wants to follow. . . .
> If only I did not love him so!

> ya mamma mio al-habibi
> bay-she e no me tornade
> gar ke fareyo ya mamma
> in no mio 'ina leshade.[30]

> Mama, my lover
> is gone, and will not return.
> What should I do, Mama,
> if my pain does not wither?

Arab anthologists and literary critics insist that the essential trait of the *kharja* is that it be put in the mouth of a woman; however, they add that the composer of the *muwashshaha* may compose a *kharja* himself if none to his liking are available. This is to say that the *kharja* must be spoken by a woman's persona, at least in the perception of Arab anthologists, but does not necessarily have to be a the work of a woman author. We have no way of knowing which of the existing *kharjas*, if any, were really authored by women.

The problem, however, is not with the feminine content of the *kharja*, but with the incorporation of the *kharja* into Hispano-Arabic poetic compositions. For if the presence of women's voices in the *muwashshaha* is evident, as either type of nexus ("A girl sings as follows" or "I lament like a girl") provides the necessary link between the Arabic part of the *muwashshaha* and its conclusion in Romance, this does not signify an equally evident acceptance of a Romance feminine poetry in the Hispano-Arabic tradition. A closer analysis of that nexus reveals that its function is merely the justification of their being joined together. Although the Arabic and Romance lyrical traditions are represented in the two parts of the composition, they are joined together by technical virtuosity rather than lyrical content. The real nexus is formal, incorporating features of verse, rhyme, and rhythm: the poet is required to structure a poem in Arabic using metrical and rhythmic patterns from another language, and from a language as different from Arabic as Romance.[31] That in itself is a great metrical, rhythmic, and linguistic achievement, but one that has little to do with the lyrical content, feminine or not, of the romance *kharja*.

Are these voices, put in the mouths of women, really women's voices? Do they express feminine poetry?

It seems to me that Arabic poetic traditions in general, and Hispano-Arabic in particular, do not recognize these questions or view them as problems. I referred earlier to the attitude that language does not merely reflect sexual difference but actually perpetrates it. My problem with this statement concerns the agent that perpetrates that sexual difference, and the manner in which it perpetrates it, in the literary world of Andalusian poetry. While Arabic and Hispano-Arabic traditions both seem to offer a curious gender-neutrality, the specifically Hispano-Arabic tradition, with the *kharjas* adopted for the purpose of an exercise in purely metrical virtuosity, failed to introduce the *kharja*'s feminine voice into the poetic content of Arabic poetry or even into the poetic content of the *muwashshaha* that is born from the *kharja*. So we are left, on the one hand, in traditional Arabic poetry, with lyrical genres without gender; and on the other, in the poetic world of al-Andalus, with a gender without lyrical genre.

But there is still another point. This gender-neutrality, so obvious in Arabic literary tradition, has inclined many contemporary readers to emphasize the many cases of a seemingly unhampered male homosexuality (actually pedophilia in most cases) apparent in the love poetry.[32] This interpretation is helped in many instances by the inclusion in the verses the name of a man to whom they are apparently directed. This is the case of the Andalusian Ibn Sahl, born in Seville about 1210, in whose Diwan we find several instances of poems with the use of the masculine in the singular: "How often I said to my lover [mahbubi]"; or in the plural, "All those to whose love I was guided " (ya man hudiitu li-hubbihi); or even after a dedication to a man's name, Musa, "You have bewitched my heart" (saharta fu'ady); or with reference to physical qualities normally attributed to women, for example, "When he looks at me from the side of eyes like a houri's."[33] More typical would be the case of the sometimes bawdy, mostly roguish and mischievous *zejel* verses by Ibn Quzman (who died in 1160), who is much inclined to offer in his poetry love situations in which attributes and phrases, gender-bound either by grammar or stereotype, are subject to ambiguity as to the specific gender of lover and beloved.

It could very well be, of course, that this gender-neutrality we perceive in the overwhelmingly male domain of classical Arabic poetry is not after all the result of open affectation of male homosexuality. It could very well be an unaffected application of a literary convention in lyrical poetry that leads a male poet to adopt the feminine voice even in his poetic references to a man, as if they came from a woman. If that is the case, while the conclusions I have arrived at remain valid, we should have to consider, in addition, for Hispano-Arabic, and for Arabic poetic conventions in general, something like a *gender-genre,* since the physical gender of the object would be the determinant factor of the poetic gender that the author, the performer, and the persona adopt.

NOTES

As a matter of editorial consistency, within this volume diacritics are not employed in Arabic or Hebrew.

1. So Averroës, the great Arabic Aristotelian in the introduction to his commentary to Aristotle's *Poetics.* See my "Averroes on Poetry," in *Islam and Its Cultural Divergence: Studies in Honor of Gustave E. von Grunebaum,* ed. Girdhari L. Tikku (Urbana: University of Illinois Press, 1971), 10–26; reprinted in *Classical and Medieval Literature Criticism,* ed. Jelena O. Krstovic (Detroit: Gale, 1991), 7:47–62.

2. On the Arabic concept of "poetics," see my *Arabic Poetics in the Golden Age* (Leiden: Brill, 1975).

3. Northrop Frye, *Anatomy of Criticism: Four Essays* (Princeton: Princeton University Press, 1957), 23.

4. Barbara Johnson, *The Critical Difference: Essays in the Contemporary Rhetoric of Reading* (Baltimore: Johns Hopkins University Press, 1980), 1, 12.

5. Doris Earnshaw, *The Female Voice in Medieval Romance Lyric* (New York: Lang, 1988).

6. See my "Lyrical Traditions in Andalusian Muwashshahas," *Comparative Literature* 31 (1969): 213–31.

7. This concept is familiar to students of Arabic; see F. Gabrieli, "Adab," in *The Encyclopaedia of Islam: New Edition,* ed. H. A. R. Gibb and others (Leiden: Brill, 1960–), 1:175–76.

8. "The Tale of Abu l-Husn and His Slave-Girl Tawaddud" extends over nights 437–62. See Richard F. Burton, trans., *The Book of the Thousand Nights and a Night* (New York: Heritage Press, 1934), from 3:1772 to 4:1842. The quote is a translation from the old Spanish *Historia de la Donzella Teodor*, ed. Walter Mettman (Wiesbaden: Verlag der Akademie der Wissenschaften und der Literatur in Mainz, in Komission bei F. Steiner, 1962), 109.

9. The admiration felt for the wise and refined girl is attested by a number of translations since the thirteenth century. In the Peninsula the most important was the comedy *La doncella Teodor* by Lope de Vega (1563–1635).

10. Ahmad ibn Muhammad al-Maqqari, *Nafh at-Tib min gusn al-Andalus ar-ratib*, ed. Ihsan 'Abbas (Beirut: Dar Sadir, 1968), 4:166.

11. Luis Gonzalvo, "Avance para un estudio de las poetisas musulmanas en España," *Revista de archivos, bibliotecas y museos* 13 (1905): 83–96, 200–214, 374–82; Teresa Garulo, *Diwan de las poetisas de Al-Andalus* (Madrid: Hiperion, 1986), with excellent bibliography. For a chronological survey from the late eighth century to the fourteenth, see Garulo, 24–26. Important anthologies for this study are Muhammad ibn Abd Allah ibn al-Abbar, *Kitab al-takmila li-kitab as-Sila*, ed. Francisco Codera y Zaidin (Madrid: Matbaat Rukhas, 1886–89); Al-Maqqari, *Nafh at-Tib min gusn al-Andalus ar-ratib;* and Ahmad ibn Yahya al-Dabbi, *Kitab bugyat al-multamis*, ed. Francisco Codera y Zaidin and Julian Ribera (Madrid: Matbaat Rukhas, 1885).

12. Ibn al-Abbar, *Takmila*, 2:114.

13. Al-Maqqari, *Nafh*, 4:286.

14. My translation from Karam al-Bustani, ed., *Diwan Ibn Zaydun* (Beirut: Dar Sadir, 1964), 6.

15. Al-Maqqari, *Nafh*, 4:205.

16. Ibn Zaydun, in this *qasida* dedicated to Wallada, uses both the masculine and the feminine forms when referring to her. This is a frequent occurrence with many other poets and is well known to readers of Arabic love poetry.

17. Ibn al-Abbar, *Takmila*, 2:872.

18. Al-Maqqari, *Nafh*, 3:530.

19. Al-Maqqari, *Nafh*, 3:530.

20. A. R. Nykl, *Hispano-Arabic Poetry and Its Relations with the Old Provençal Troubadours* (Baltimore: Furst, 1946), 107.

21. Al-Maqqari, *Nafh*, 4:295; Ibn al-Abbar, *Takmila*, 2:884.

22. The anecdote is attributed to the musician Ishak al-Mausili, who puts the words in the mouth of the caliph al-Mutawakkil, both well-known characters in the *Arabian Nights*. This attests to the importance that popular literature sees in such stereotypical descriptions of a woman's beauty. It is quoted by Edward William Lane, trans., *The Arabian Nights: A Selection* (London: Humphrey Milford, 1915), footnote to Night 352.

23. Hermann Knust, *Mitteilungen aus dem Eskurial* (Tübingen: Litterarischer Verein, 1879), 2:513–14.

24. Al-Dabbi, *Bugya*, 1586.

25. Burton, *Arabian Nights*, 1:78.

26. Ibid.

27. *The Perfumed Garden of the Shaykh Nefzawi*, trans. Richard F. Burton, ed. Alan Hull Walton (New York: Putnam, 1964), 72.

28. This peculiarity is well known to readers of Arabic poetry, and is made clear when the poets choose to alternate the use of the masculine and feminine form of the second person, as we saw earlier in Ibn Zaydun.

29. On the lengthy bibliography on this topic, see George D. Greenia, "Twenty-Year Index to *La Corónica*," *La Corónica* 20 (1992): 75–165, under *muwashshahat* and *kharjas*.

30. Josep M. Sola-Sole, ed., *Corpus de poesía mozárabe* (Barcelona: Hispam, 1973): *kharja* LVIII, p. 328; *kharja* VIIb, p. 100.

31. See my study, "The Composition of Arabic Muwashshahas with a Romance Kharja," *Kentucky Romance Quarterly* 21 (1974): 447–68.

32. Quite often this interpretation is forced on the text by a misunderstanding of Arabic poetic mechanics.

33. Arthur Wormhoudt, trans., *The Diwan of Abu Ishaq Ibrahim ibn Abu Aish ibn Sahl al Israili* ([Oskaloosa, Iowa]: William Penn College, 1981), 18, 19, 101, 24.

PART 3 ❖

Genre and Music

CHAPTER 11

Genre as a Determinant of Melody in the Songs of the Troubadours and the Trouvères

ELIZABETH AUBREY

As musicologists are fond of pointing out, the songs of the troubadours and the trouvères are not merely poems but must be accompanied by their melodies. One of the most often cited "proofs" of this is found in a *cobla* by Bertran Carbonel:

> Cobla ses so es enaissi
> co·l molis que aigua non a;
> per que fai mal qui cobla fa
> si son non li don' atressi;
> c'om non a gaug pas del moli,
> mas per la moutura que·n tra.[1]

> A *cobla* without a melody
> is like a mill that has no water;
> therefore, he who composes a *cobla* does badly
> if he doesn't give it a melody too;
> for one has no pleasure from the mill itself,
> but from the meal that one gets out of it.

The image evoked here implies that a poem is set in operation and driven by its melody—that both its meaning and its delivery are energized by the music. Because music is an aural phenomenon, the act of singing was central to the realization of the lyric songs. But we might wonder whether the poet-composers themselves consciously strove for what scholars sometimes refer to as a "wedding" between poem and melody, and if so, in what way.

Scholars have sought answers to this question in a variety of places, including the relation between the structures of poems and melodies, the possible connection of musical rhythm to text scansion, and overt melodic depiction of the meaning of words.

As for the last, it must be pointed out that a quest for musical text-painting in its more obvious form is difficult and perhaps unwise, because particular notes and particular words were not necessarily inseparable. The manuscript sources evince this, in that most melodies are transmitted with pitch variants of anywhere from one or two notes to entire phrases; this means that whatever composers might have intended, by the time songs were written down the notes easily could have shifted. Furthermore, in a strophic song the same series of pitches was used over and over for several different strophes, matching new words up with the notes each time. And the practice of borrowing a melody for different poems—creating what we call musical contrafacta—is attested both by surviving examples and by the sanction of contemporary theorists; in addition, sometimes a single poem was given more than one musical setting.

But if pitches and words are not necessarily inextricably linked in a song, surely the formal structures are interrelated. At least the number of syllables in the poem must be matched by an equal number of notes or note groups in each verse (although some manuscripts are not as careful about this as others). But beyond the syllable count, as musicologists have long been aware, structural correspondence between poem and melody does not always include an accord between the poetic rhymes and the musical cadences, nor do musical or textual repetition necessarily mirror one another.[2] Except for certain nonstrophic types, melodic structure in vernacular lyric does not become fixed until the late thirteenth century, with the rise of such genres as the rondeau and the virelai, in which the genre itself is defined by the interconnection of poetic and musical form. For the troubadours and the trouvères, however, poetic form and musical form were not necessarily intimately linked.

Some poetic and musical theorists of the twelfth and thirteenth centuries commented on the relationship between poem and melody, and their discussions suggest that composers conceived this relationship within the scholastic tradition of grammar and rhetoric. Specifically, the form, material, and oral delivery of both text and tune are interrelated with the song's genre, which itself is defined by its subject matter. Poetic theorists discussed not only the themes of various types of poems but also their structural building blocks, including rhyme, verse, syllable count, and strophic interrelationships.[3] They also sometimes alluded to how songs were delivered by singers. Music theorists, on the other hand, rarely discussed the musical structure, style, or performance of courtly lyric.[4] In fact, the only medieval treatise on music that included an extensive discussion of secular monophony at all was produced by a late thirteenth-century Parisian, Johannes de Grocheio.[5] One section of Grocheio's tract, quite familiar to musicologists, presents a complex and confusing classification system for secular monophony (*musica vulgaris*), including both vocal and instrumental pieces. Grocheio deals with poetic elements like verse and strophe structure, and discusses musical repetition schemes, cadences, and other formal ingredients. Numerous scholars have studied this passage in detail; let it suffice here to say that his descriptions of the various forms of secular music are neither altogether lucid in themselves nor easily accommodated to the structures of surviving pieces.[6]

But verse, rhyme, and strophe structure, and their musical counterparts, which by Grocheio's day were well on their way to becoming central elements in defining secular song, were not necessarily Grocheio's only—or even chief—concern. Music theorists of the thirteenth century barely acknowledged even the existence of secular music, devoting their attention rather to plainchant and to the polyphony that grew out of it. Grocheio was the first to include vernacular song in his typology, and in so doing he evidently felt it necessary to demonstrate its value and justify its existence. His descriptions of secular songs, as might be expected, call on concepts from the arts of poetry and prose, but they are cast in the language of Aristotelian thought; the resulting passages constitute a subtle and sophisticated synthesis between the specific art of rhetoric and the philosophy that underlay all scholastic thought. How a work is composed, according to the arts of poetry and prose, is determined by subject matter, speaker, audience, purpose, and mode of delivery.[7] Grocheio asserts that different types of French songs, which he calls *cantus* and *cantilena* (structurally distinguished, he says, mainly by the presence of a refrain in the latter), are set apart by differences in these rhetorical characteristics.[8] For instance, in his description of the *cantus coronatus,* the noblest lyric song in his typology, Grocheio invokes the rhetorical ideas of invention, style, structure, and performance. But the conceptual framework of his argument is Aristotelian:

> Cantus coronatus ab aliquibus simplex conductus dictus est, qui propter eius bonitatem in dictamine et cantu a magistris et studentibus circa sonos coronatur . . . , qui etiam a regibus et nobilibus solet componi et etiam coram regibus et principibus terre decantari, ut eorum animos ad audaciam et fortitudinem, magnanimitatem et liberalitatem commoveat, quae omnia faciunt ad bonum regimen. Est enim cantus iste de delectabili

> materia et ardua, sicut de amicitia et caritate, et ex omnibus longis et perfectis efficitur.⁹

> *Cantus coronatus* has been called by some a simple conductus, which on account of the goodness of its words and music is celebrated [wreathed] for its sounds [notes?] by masters and students . . . , which usually is composed by kings and nobles, and is sung in the court of kings and princes of the land, in order to move their spirits to boldness and courage, magnanimity and liberality, which all make for a good government. For this sort of *cantus* concerns delightful and difficult material, like friendship and charity, and is made from all sorts of longs, even perfect [ones].

These words explain a *cantus coronatus* as a product of the art of rhetoric, in which a song is judged by the social status of audience and speaker ("sung in the courts of kings and princes"), elegance of language and subject matter ("delightful and difficult matter"), and formal coherence ("made from all sorts of longs"). But Grocheio establishes the authority of his treatment of such vernacular songs by suggesting the four causes: *cantus coronatus* "concerns delightful and difficult matter" (material cause), "is made from all sorts of longs" (formal cause), and "is composed by kings and nobility" (efficient cause), "in order to move their spirits to boldness" and so forth (final cause).¹⁰

Further on, Grocheio insists that the rhetorical properties in the poem are determinants of an appropriate melody, and that a melody that works for one type of text is not suitable for another. In a well-known passage, he refers to how the text and melody of any *cantus* or *cantilena* are composed:

> Modus autem componendi haec generaliter est unus, quemadmodum in natura. Primo enim dictamina loco materiae praeparantur, postea vero cantus unicuique dictamini proportionalis loco formae introducitur. Dico autem *unicuique proportionalis,* quia alium cantum habet cantus gestualis et coronatus et versiculatus, ut eorum descriptiones aliae sunt, quemadmodum superius dicebatur. De formis igitur musicalibus, quae in voce humana exercentur, haec dicta sint.¹¹

> But the manner of composing these generally is one and the same, in the manner of (their) nature. For first the texts are prepared in the place of matter, but after this, the melody is introduced in the place of form in proportion to whatever text. But I say "in proportion to whatever (text)" because chanson de geste, or *cantus coronatus,* or *cantus versiculatus* (each) has a different (type of) melody, as their descriptions differ, in the manner that was said above. So then let these things be said concerning musical forms that are performed by the human voice.

This passage clearly says that the composer prepares the poem first, and then the tune. But its Aristotelian language does not suggest that the music is invented merely to serve as a vehicle for the poem,[12] rather something more fundamental. "Form" and "material" together comprise a song's substance, or its "being." Grocheio is saying that the particular thing called a *cantus* or a *cantilena* consists of a complex of text and melody—*dictamen* and *cantus*. The text occupies the place called matter, and the music, the place called form. In Aristotelian thinking, form (here the music) has no existence apart from matter (here the text); and matter (the text) is given shape by form (the music). Matter represents the potentiality of a thing, form its actuality, so a poem is potentially a song, while a sung text is actually the song. Aristotle's matter is indeterminate and limitless, requiring form to limit and define it.[13] In other words, music and text in a secular song together constitute its substance, and neither element alone constitutes a song, just as neither body nor soul alone, but both together, comprise a living being.

The concepts of "material" and "form," synchronic in an Aristotelian explanation of substance, play a crucial role also in the medieval art of rhetoric, where they have a diachronic meaning. The first step in the creation of a literary work is *inventio*, in which the material, or the idea or theme, is created. The material is given order (arrangement) in the next step, *dispositio*, and then the actual words are put together—given form and expression—in the process of *elocutio*, or style.[14] Working within the context of the Aristotelian intellectual system, Grocheio calls on the art of rhetoric to account for the various traits of secular songs.

The art of rhetoric is concerned with communication: the intent of the rhetor is to persuade the audience. In a secular song, two essential elements, the text and the music, together are the vehicle for this communication. Both text and melody appeal to the emotions: the text through verbal language, the melody through sung notes. When Grocheio speaks of a song's *dictamen*, he assumes that the theme or content (*materia*) of the song already exists as a *locus*,[15] and that the words expressing this material need but be prepared. When he speaks of the song's melody (*cantus*), he speaks of something that already exists in the *locus* of shape (*forma*), which then is introduced into the song. What gives a song form, according to Grocheio, is its audible delivery (*pronuntiatio*, as the art of rhetoric would put it) or its actuality (in Aristotelian terms), and this occurs only through music.

In short, Grocheio seems to be saying that a text and its melody are inseparable in that they arise from the same process of conception, and that the song itself does not exist except as a combination of both text and melody. A melody of a *cantus* or a *cantilena*, without its text, has no meaning; and a text, without music, has no form.[16] Furthermore, Grocheio indicates that the same rhetorical demands that dictate the composer's decisions about a poem's structure, language, and function also guide his or her musical choices, and that these decisions are circumscribed by what type of song it is. In other words, the melody, like the text, is dependent upon the song's genre.

❖

Grocheio was a northern music theorist writing at the end of the thirteenth century. Trained in Aristotelian logic, he appears to have been familiar also with teachings on medieval grammar and rhetoric.[17] Many passages in his treatise resonate with certain passages in the grammatical and rhetorical treatises on Occitan language and literature of the late twelfth through the mid-fourteenth centuries, which mention music in a variety of contexts.[18] One of the earliest of these treatises, Raimon Vidal's *Razos de trobar*,[19] written around the turn of the thirteenth century, begins with some observations about the social classes occupied by audiences and performers of troubadour songs, the topics addressed, and circumstances of their performance; while the account is a bit hyperbolic, its language is similar to that found in Grocheio's discussion of secular music:

> Totas genz cristianas, iusieuas et sarazinas, emperador, princeps, rei, duc, conte, vesconte, contor, valvasor, clergue, borgues, vilans, paucs et granz, meton totz iorns lor entendiment en trobar et en chantar, o q'en volon trobar o q'en volon entendre o q'en volon dire o q'en volon auzir; qe greu seres en loc negun tan privat ni tant sol, pos gens i a paucas o moutas, qe ades non auias cantar un o autre o tot ensems, qe neis li pastor de la montagna lo maior sollatz qe ill aiant an de chantar.[20]

> All people, Christian, Jewish and Saracen, emperors, princes, kings, dukes, counts, viscounts, lesser nobles, vavasors, clerics, bourgeois, and peasants, small and great, daily give their minds to verse-making and singing, whether they want to invent or listen, speak or hear; for you can scarcely be in a place so isolated or solitary, as long as there are a few people or many, that you will not hear one person sing, or another, or all together; even the shepherds in the mountains know of no greater joy than song.

Raimon later enjoins the poet to choose his theme carefully, and he implies that a song is defined—or constrained—by its theme or subject matter. This appears to be one of the earliest attempts to systematize a taxonomy of songs that relies mainly on subject matter.[21] Raimon offers a typical observation about the composition of a poem in accordance with an appropriate and unified theme (*razo*, Latin *ratio*) throughout:

> Per aqi mezeis deu gardar, si vol far un cantar o un romans, qe diga rasons et paraulas continuadas et proprias et avinenz, et qe sos cantars o sos romans non sion de paraulas biaisas ni de doas parladuras ni de razons mal continuadas ni mal seguidas.[22]

> In the same way he should take care, if he wants to make a song or a narrative [*roman*], to say themes and words [that are] sustained and proper and pleasing, and that his song or narrative not be of unsuitable words or of two [different] languages or of themes [that are] poorly sustained or poorly followed up.

While Raimon does not make a connection between a theme and a specific genre, later authors do. The Catalan theorist Jofre de Foixà, writing his *Regles de trobar* about 1290, echoes Raimon and asserts that the "rayso" is important in the concept of genre:

> Rayso deu hom guardar per ço cor la mellor causa que ha mester totz cantars es que la rasos sia bona e que hom la vage continuan, ço es a entendre que de aquella rayso que començara son cantar, perfassa lo mig e la fi. Car si tu comences a far un sirventesch de fayt de guerra o de reprendimen o de lausors, no·s conve que·y mescles raho d'amor; o si faç canço o dança d'amor, no·s tayn que·y mescles fayt d'armes ne maldit de gens, si donchs per semblances no o podiets aportar a raho.[23]

> One should take care with the theme, for the most important thing that all songs require is that the theme be good and that one continue with it, so it is understood that one will complete the middle and the end with the same theme that begins the song. For if you begin making a *sirventes* about deeds of war or about reproof or about praise, it is not appropriate to mix in a theme of love; or if you make a *canso* or a *dansa* about love, it is not appropriate to mix in deeds of arms or slander of people, if you cannot bring it back suitably to the theme.

As Occitan treatises on poetry began to address the differences among genres, they also began to include music in their discussions, characterizing the type of melody that is appropriate to each genre. Among the detailed descriptions of poetic genres in the anonymous *Doctrina de compondre dictats*,[24] written in the late thirteenth century, are found what appear to be the first prescriptions by a poetic theorist concerning the melodies of troubadour songs. The author suggests that certain standards of propriety attend different genres, especially whether or not it is acceptable to use a preexisting tune for a particular type of song. His statements imply that the character of a song's melody is in some way connected with the poem's genre, which is defined by its theme or subject matter.

The melody of a *canso*, reflecting the love theme that eschews anything evil, should be "as beautiful" as possible, and both *canso* and *vers* should have newly composed melodies:

> E primerament deus saber que cançó deu parlar d'amor plazenment, e potz metre en ton parlar eximpli d'altra rayso, e ses mal dir e ses lauzor de re sino d'amor. Encara mes, deus saber que cançó ha obs e deu haver cinch cobles; eyxamen n'i potz far, per abeylimen e per complimen de raho, .vj. o .vij. o .viij. o .ix., d'aquell compte que mes te placia. E potz hi far una tornada o dues, qual te vulles. E garda be que, en axi com començaras la raho en amor, que en aquella manera matexa la fins be e la seguesques. E dona li so noveyl co pus bell poras.
>
> Si vols far vers, deus parlar de veritatz, de exemples e de proverbis o de lauzor, no pas en semblant d'amor; e que en axi com començaras, ho prosseguesques e·u fins, ab so novell tota vegada. E aquesta es la differencia que es entre cançó e vers, que la una rayso no es semblant de l'altra. E cert aytantes cobles se cove de far al vers com a la cançó, e aytantes tornades.[25]

> And first you should know that a *canso* must speak pleasingly of love, and you can put in your poem examples of other themes, but without slander or praise of anything but love. Furthermore you should know that a *canso* needs and must have five stanzas; but all the same you can make six or seven or eight or nine, to adorn and perfect the theme, whatever number pleases you best. And you can give it one or two tornadas, whichever you wish. And take care that you continue and finish with the same theme with which you begin. And give it a new melody, as beautiful as you can.
>
> If you want to make a *vers*, you must speak of truth, of examples and proverbs, or of praise, but not in the guise of love; and just as you begin, you should proceed to the end, to a new melody every time. And this is the difference between a *canso* and a *vers*, that the theme of one is not like the theme of the other. And certainly one must give as many stanzas to a *vers* as to a *canso*, and as many tornadas.

This suggests that just as the poet manipulates his language, syntax, rhyme patterns, and so forth, to achieve the most eloquent expression of the song's theme of love, the composer should manipulate musical features of style, perhaps including motives, intervallic structure, melodic texture, and so forth, to produce an effective expression of the same theme. These musical ingredients, which rhetoricians did not explain with the analytical precision that we might desire, are described here and in other places as being beautiful or pleasing. Such qualities could take many guises, judging from the broad range of style found in the extant melodies.[26] But this is not inconsistent with the astonishing variety that poets used to express the theme of love in words.

Some passages of the *Doctrina,* however, hint broadly at certain elements of musical style or structure. For instance, the author says that the melody of the *lay* could be newly composed, in which case it should be pleasing, or it could be borrowed from a church piece or "another type":

> Si vols fer lays, deus parlar de Deu e de segle, o de eximpli o de proverbis, de lausors ses feyment d'amor, que sia axi plazent a Deu co al segle; e deus saber que·s deu far e dir ab contriccio tota via, e ab so novell e plazen, o de esgleya o d'autra manera. E sapies que·y ha mester aytantes cobles com en la canço, e aytantes tornades; e segueix la raho e la manera axi com eu t'ay dit.[27]

> If you wish to make a *lay,* you must speak of God or of the world, or of examples or proverbs, of praise without pretence of love, which thus would be as pleasing to God as to the world; and you should know that it must be done with contrition always, and with a new and pleasing melody, or one of the church or another type. And know that it needs as many stanzas as in the *canso,* and as many tornadas; and it follows the theme and manner as I have told you.

The suggestion that there is some affinity between the courtly *lay* and a certain type of church music is intriguing, because the double-cursus versicle form of the melodies of many vernacular *lais* is similar to that of the ecclesiastical sequence. A few Old French *lais,* in fact, actually borrow the melodies of sequences. In such songs, there is a closer structural interdependence between text and music than in strophic types, in that a new melody is required for each stanza since the stanzas do not share the same poetic structure. Two Occitan songs, the anonymous "Lai Markiol" and "Lai Non-par," have irregular repetition structures that are similar to those of late sequences; they also foreshadow the fourteenth-century French *lai* as it was standardized by Guillaume de Machaut, in that the poetic structure and the melody of the first stanza are repeated, with some variation, for the last stanza.[28] The subject matter of the four surviving Old Occitan *lays,* three of which survive with music,[29] is not didactic or religious, as this definition requires, but the themes of many Old French *lais* are.[30]

Many extant *descorts* also have a double-cursus poetic form, although the author of the *Doctrina* again does not specify that its stanzas should be so structured. There are two extant Occitan *descorts* that have been transmitted with melodies, one of which, "Qui la ve en ditz" by the late twelfth-century troubadour Aimeric de Peguilhan, survives in two manuscripts with two different melodies. One of these melodies does have a double-cursus musical form that is quite closely allied with its poetic structure, as does another Occitan *descort,* "Ses alegratge," by Guillem Augier Novella.[31]

The *Doctrina* includes a provocative statement about the style of a *descort* melody:

> Si vols far discort, deus parlar d'amor com a hom qui n'es desemparat e com a hom qui no pot haver plaser de sa dona e viu turmentatz. E que en lo cantar, lla hon lo so deuria muntar, que·l baxes; e fe lo contrari de tot l'altre cantar. E deu haver tres cobles e una o dues tornades e responedor. E potz metre un o dos motz mes en una cobla que en altra, per ço que mils sia discordant.[32]
>
> If you wish to make a *descort*, you must speak of love like a man who is distressed by it or a man who cannot have pleasure from his lady and lives in torment. And when this is sung, wherever the tune ought to rise, let it be low; and it does the opposite of all other songs. And it must have three stanzas and one or two tornadas and a refrain. And you can put one or two more words in one stanza than in another, to make it more discordant.

The text of a *descort* is supposed to speak of love's torment, reflecting the "disharmony" suggested by the genre's name.[33] This might explain the *Doctrina*'s instructions that "when this is sung, wherever the tune ought to rise, let it be low," implying that the contour of the melody, like its text, should develop in an unexpected or displeasing way. Whatever it means, the remark at least suggests that the *razo* of a *descort*, as well as its structure, produces a particular style of melody.[34]

In the *sirventes*, as is well known, structural imitation was a common practice. The theorist says that the troubadour could borrow the stanza and rhyme structure as well as the melody of another song, usually a *canso*, but that rare cases of newly composed melodies might occur:

> Si vols far sirventez, deus parlar de fayt d'armes, e senyalladament o de lausor de senyor o de maldit o de qualsque feyts qui novellament se tracten. E començaras ton cantar segons que usaran aquells dels quals ton serventez començaras; e per proverbis e per exemples poretz hi portar les naturaleses que fan, o ço de que fan a rependre o a lausar aquells dels quals ton serventez començaras. E sapies que·l potz fer d'aytantes cobles co la un d'aquestz cantars que·t he mostratz. E pot[z] lo far en qualque so te vulles; e specialment se fa en so novell, e maiorment en ço de canço. E deus lo far d'aytantes cobles com sera lo cantar de que pendras lo so; e potz seguir las rimas contrasemblantz del cantar de que pendras lo so, o atressi lo potz far en altres rimes.[35]
>
> If you wish to make a *sirventes*, you must speak of feats of arms, and in particular either of praise of a lord or of calumny or of some deeds that have been talked about recently. And you will begin your song following the custom of those with whom your *sirventes* began [i.e., using customary titles]; and by proverbs and examples you can bring in the allegiances

they swore, or what they deserve to be reproved for or praised for, those about whom you will begin your *sirventes*. And know that you can give it as many stanzas as one of the other songs I discussed. And you can make it to whatever tune you wish, exceptionally a new melody, but usually that of a *canso*. And you must give it as many stanzas as there are in the song from which you take the melody; and you can follow the rhymes corresponding to the song from which you take the melody, or you can make it on other rhymes.

The theorist describes the appropriate *razo* of a *sirventes,* then says that the melody can be whatever the composer wishes, and that the number of stanzas must be, and the rhymes may be, those of the song from which the tune is borrowed. Here and a little later the author seems to place some weight on the integrity of the melody, whose essence remains intact along with the rhyme scheme:

> Serventetz es dit per ço serventetz per ço com se serveix e es sotsmes a aquell cantar de qui pren lo so e les rimes, e per ço cor deu parlar de senyors o de vassalls, blasman o castigan o lauzan o mostran, o de faytz d'armes o de guerra o de Deu o de ordenances o de novelletatz.[36]

> A *sirventes* is so called because it serves and is subordinated to the song from which it takes the melody and rhymes, and because it must speak of lords or of vassals, blaming or chastising or praising or accusing them, or of feats of arms or of war or of God or of laws or of recent events.

The structure of the new poem can be determined only after the model song—with its melody—is chosen, and evidently the structure of the melody retains its shape even after it is separated from the original poem and joined with a new one.[37] The *Doctrina*'s remarks about the *tenso* suggest the same thing: "Si vols far tenso, deus l'apondre en algun so qui haia bella nota, e potz seguir les rimes del cantar o no. E potz fer .iiije. o .vj. cobles o .viij., si·t vols" (If you want to make a *tenso*, you must join it to some melody that has beautiful notes, and you can follow the rhymes of the song, or not. And you can make four or six stanzas, or eight, if you wish).[38]

In one extant pair of *sirventes,* we can see how one troubadour devised a new poem for a borrowed melody, modifying the music's structure but retaining its essential elements. The Monge de Montaudon used the melody of a *sirventes* by Bertran de Born, "Rassa, tan creis e mont' e puoia" (P-C 80,37), for his own *sirventes* text, "Fort m'enoja, so auzes dire" (P-C 305,10). Both songs survive in BN fr. 22543, Bertran's on folio 6v, and the monk's on folio 40r with the rubric "el so de la Rassa." The stanzas of Bertran's song have eleven verses, but the monk omitted verses 5–6, to create a nine-verse stanza.[39] The melody thus must be truncated:

Bertran:	a	a	a	a	a	a	b	b	b	b	b	rhyme
	8'	8'	8'	8'	8'	8'	8	8	8	8	8	syllables
	A	B	C	D	C'	D'	B'	C"	E	F	E'	melody
Monk:	a	a	a	a			b	b	b	b	b	rhyme
	8'	8'	8'	8'			8	8	8	8	8	syllables
	A	B	C	D			B'	C'	E	F	E'	melody

The musical phrases of these verses in Bertran's melody are simply varied repeats of the music for verses 3–4.[40] The essential material of the melody thus remains intact in the monk's adaptation. The truncation makes perfect sense if we assume that the monk adopted the tune first, choosing to eliminate the two repeated musical phrases (C' and D'), and then abbreviated his stanza form accordingly. He used the rhyme scheme of Bertran's poem but not the same rhymes, merely dropping the a rhymes of verses 5–6. In this case, the borrowing appears to have been as carefully planned as the author of the *Doctrina* urges, and the new song is as coherent a marriage of poem and tune, at least structurally, as is the model. Of course, because BN fr. 22543 is the only musical source for either song, it cannot be ruled out that it was the scribe who was responsible for the melodic adaptation as it appears in that manuscript.

The *alba* and the *retroncha,* says the theorist, must have newly composed melodies:

> Si vols far alba, parla d'amor plazentment; e atressi [deus] lauzar la dona on vas o de que la faras. E bendi l'alba si acabes lo plazier per lo qual anaves a ta dona; e si no·l acabes, fes l'alba blasman la dona e l'alba on anaves. E potz hi fer aytantes cobles com te vulles, e deus hi fer so novell.[41]

> If you wish to make an *alba,* speak pleasantly of love; and also you must praise the lady to whom you go or about whom you compose it. And praise the dawn if you have won the pleasure for which you went to your lady; and if you did not win it, make the *alba* censuring the lady and the dawn when you went. And you can make it to as many stanzas as you wish, and you must give it a new melody.

> Si vols far retronxa, sapies que deus parlar d'amor, segons l'estament en que·n seras, sia plazen o cossiros; e no·y deus mesclar altra raho. E deus saber que deu haver quatre cobles, e so novell tota vegada. E deus saber que per ço ha nom retronxa car lo refray de cada una de les cobles deu esser totz us.[42]

> If you wish to make a *retroncha,* know that you must speak of love, according to the state in which you will be, whether pleasant or thoughtful; and you must not mix in another theme. And you should know that it must have four stanzas, and a new melody every time. And you should know

that it is called *retroncha* because the refrain at the end of one of the stanzas must be used for all of them.

There are only three *retronchas* that survive with melodies, all by the late thirteenth-century poet Guiraut Riquier.[43] The extant examples have textual refrains consisting of the last two verses of each stanza, as required by the theorist's definition. The *Doctrina* does not require a musical refrain, nor do these three songs or the few extant French *rotrouenges* have one.[44]

The theorist remarks that a *pastora* melody can be new or borrowed:

> Si vols far pastora, deus parlar d'amor en aytal semblan com eu te ensenyaray, ço es a saber: si·t acostes a pastora e la vols saludar o enquerer o manar o corteiar, o de qual razo demanar o dar o parlar li vulles. E potz li metre altre nom de pastora, segons lo bestiar que guardara; e aquesta manera es clara assatz d'entendre. E potz li fer .vj. o .viij. cobles, e so novell o so estrayn ia passat.[45]

> If you wish to make a *pastora*, you must speak of love in the way I teach you, that is to say: if you meet a shepherdess and wish to greet her or woo or pursue or court her, or to ask or give or speak however you wish. And you can give it another name besides *pastora*, according to the animal that she keeps; and this genre is understood clearly enough. And you can give it six or eight stanzas, and a new melody or a borrowed melody that is no longer current.

The subject matter of a *pastorela*, vividly described here, obviously concerns the peasant class. But the song is still a courtly genre, and these songs entertained the upper classes as much as a *canso* did. If my translation of the phrase "ia passat" in the last sentence is correct, it might imply using a popular or folk melody that used to be widely sung. Using such a tune might have been heard as a conceit that added a flavor of the low class, even while staying within the courtly idiom.[46]

The *dansa*, on the other hand, according to the author of the *Doctrina*, requires a newly composed melody:

> Si vols far dança, deus parlar d'amor be e plasentment, en qualque estament ne sies. E deus li fer dedents .iij. cobles e no pus, e respost, una o dues tornades, qual te vulles; totes vegades so novell. E potz fer, si·t vols, totes les fins de les cobles en refrayn semblan. E aquella raho de que la començaras deu[s] continuar e be servar al començament, al mig, e a la fi.[47]

> If you wish to make a *dansa*, you must speak of love well and pleasantly, in whatever state you may be. And you must make it in three stanzas and no more, and a refrain and one or two tornadas, as you wish; every time [it has] a new melody. And you can, if you wish, make all the ends of the

stanzas on a similar refrain. And whatever theme with which you begin, you must continue and make serve well for the beginning, the middle, and the end.

But the melody of a *planh* may be borrowed:

> Si vols fer plant, d'amor o de tristor deus la raho continuar; e pot[z] lo fer en qual so te vulles, salvant de dança. E atressi potz lo fer d'aytantes cobles con la [un] dels damunt dits cantars, e en contrasembles o en dessemblants. E no·y deus mesclar altra raho sino plahien, si per comp[ar]acio no·y ho podies portar.[48]

> If you wish to make a *planh,* you must sustain the theme on love or on sorrow; and you can make it to any tune you wish, except that of a *dansa.* And likewise you can make it with as many stanzas as one of the other songs discussed above, corresponding or not [i.e., with the same or different rhymes]. And you must not mix in another theme besides mourning, unless you can introduce it through a comparison.

The author draws attention to the marked thematic difference between the two types by saying that a *planh* can use a melody borrowed from any kind of song except a *dansa.*[49] The mournful sentiment of the text of a *planh,* this suggests, would be ill served by a *dansa* melody. Only two Occitan *planhs* survive with music; both are somewhat melismatic, and both use a scale based on D, with its characteristic minor third.[50] The more famous of these, the lament by Gaucelm Faidit on the death of Richard Cœur de Lion, survives in four Occitan versions. The fact that its melody was borrowed for an Old French *plaint* text, "E, serventois, arriere t'en revas,"[51] might mean that the French poem's ascribed author, Alart de Chans, heard something in Gaucelm's music that struck him as being appropriate for his own lament.

The *dansa* consists of three stanzas plus a refrain, and one or two tornadas.[52] Any mandatory structural relationship between poem and music is not evident from this passage, nor do the four extant Occitan *dansa* melodies survive in a state that unequivocally elucidates their form.[53] Three of them survive with only one stanza, so whether or not there is a textual refrain cannot be determined. Their melodies, though, have a ternary structure, the first and last verses or pairs of verses being identical (giving an overall musical form of ABA); this feature has prompted some to regard them as early virelai types.[54] Moreover, in the stanzas of the songs that survive, the poetic rhyme schemes and the musical structures are closely parallel, just as they are in double-cursus *descorts* and *lais.* The *estampida* is similar to the *dansa* in that neither should have a borrowed melody, suggesting that their characters are quite distinct from those of the graver types—*canso, vers, retroncha, alba, tenso:* "Si vols far estampida, potz parlar de qualque fayt vulles, blasman o lauzan o merceyan, qui·t vulles; e deu haver .iiije. cobles e responedor e una o dues tornades, e so novell" (If you wish to make an *estampida,* you can speak of whatever matter you wish, blaming or praising or supplicating; and it must have four stanzas and a refrain and one or two tornadas, and a new melody).[55]

The *dansa* and the *estampida* are courtly types in theme, style, and structure, but their composition seems to have depended to some degree also on how they were to be performed, which according to the author of the *Doctrina* was as important to their identity as a punctiliously arranged structure and a coherent *razo*. He makes it clear, for example, that musical instruments played some role in the performance of a *dansa:* "Dansa es dita per ço com naturalment la ditz hom danca[n] o bayllan, cor deu [haver] so plazent; e la ditz hom ab esturmens, e plau a cascus que la diga e la escout" (A *dansa* is so called, naturally, because one performs it while dancing or leaping, so that it must [have] a pleasant melody; and one performs it with instruments, and it delights everyone who performs and hears it).[56] He also sets apart the *estampida* by its manner of performance: "Stampida es dita per ço stampida cor pren vigoria en contan o en xantan pus que null autra cantar" (An *estampida* is so called because it takes vigor in singing,[57] more than any other song).[58] The single surviving Occitan *estampida* with music, "Kalenda maia," by the late twelfth-century troubadour Raimbaut de Vaqueiras (P-C 392,9), was created about a hundred years before the *Doctrina*'s definition appeared. If we can believe an early fourteenth-century anecdote about the origins of "Kalenda maia," its melody preceded its Occitan poem. According to this famous *razo,* Raimbaut heard two French fiddlers playing the tune, to which the troubadour afterwards provided a text.[59]

Other twelfth-, thirteenth-, and early fourteenth-century texts, from north and south, associate the *estampie* with instruments.[60] Both the fourteenth-century *Leys d'amors* and Johannes de Grocheio refer to two types of *estampies,* one a vocal *cantilena* and the other an instrumental type.[61] Grocheio's description of the instrumental *stantipes* refers to the double-cursus structure, and indeed all of the surviving thirteenth-century untexted French *estampies* and the later fourteenth-century untexted Italian *istanpitte* have this paired form.[62] But no theorist to my knowledge explicitly says that the vocal *estampie* has this same structure. Grocheio and the *Doctrina,* in fact, both say rather that the poem has a refrain, and the latter says it should have four stanzas.[63] "Kalenda maia," however, has neither a textual nor a musical refrain; moreover, its text and melody do have the double-cursus structure that Grocheio calls for in the instrumental type.[64] In fact, very few vocal *estampies* in any language survive (nineteen in French and seven in Occitan), none of which has a verse refrain, although some have a word refrain. Five of the seven Occitan *estampidas*, including "Kalenda maia," have a double-cursus poetic structure, achieved by pairing groups of from two to six verses. The remaining two Occitan *estampidas* begin with paired groups of verses but conclude with several unpaired verses. The French vocal *estampies* tend not to have a regular double-cursus structure.

The instrumental *estampie* may have migrated from the north to the south during the late twelfth century.[65] The audibly repetitive musical form engaged the fancy of some meridional composers who apparently devised poems to match the music's structure. The anecdote about "Kalenda maia" is in this sense quite believable. The author of the *Doctrina* (and probably later Guilhem Molinier, compiler of the *Leys d'amors*), aware of the existence of the *estampie,* quite possibly had never actually seen or heard one, but he dutifully included the type among his courtly genres, ascribing to it a courtly theme. He even offered instructions on its form, similar to his instructions for the other types. A clear relationship between the vocal *estampie* and the instrumental type remains elusive.[66]

❖

These passages offer insight into how some theorists regarded the relationship between text and music in the songs of the troubadours and the trouvères, particularly as both were to be created within the context of the art of rhetoric. What is clear is that the interdependence between poem and tune is not so superficial as simply a relationship between rhyme scheme and musical phrase or between words and pitches, nor is it a monolithic concept that applies across all genres. The kinship between poem and melody is one of style, structure, sentiment, and delivery, as defined in the art of rhetoric. The melodies of the troubadours and the trouvères, by these accounts, served the same rhetorical purpose of expressing the song's theme—and hence its genre—that the poems did.

This hypothesis helps explain how a strophic poem that is essentially "through-composed" can be well served by a melody that is repeated five or six times in the delivery of the several stanzas. The words of a poem serve the larger rhetorical purpose of its author; each strophe, in fact, addresses the overall theme in some way, and the fact that different sources often disagree on the number of stanzas and their order suggests that there was not necessarily a diachronic constraint, but that each strophe has a certain thematic autonomy.[67] If the melody also serves the same rhetorical purpose, then its reiteration reinforces the theme. The poem's structure and theme remain the same in all stanzas, but its words change as they develop and unfold the subject matter to the listener. The melody's notes remain the same, but their impact on the listener changes as they carry forward each strophe's expression and shading of the theme.

A poem's effectiveness depends on an elegant arrangement of its matter; the cleverest rhyme scheme is mere pedantry without potent words artfully arranged to express the poem's theme. The music has its own expressive elements, such as rhythm and repetition patterns, motivic development, intervallic content, and texture. The song takes on audible form in its performance, bringing to fruition the rhetorical goal of moving the audience. Grocheio evidently believed this; for him a song was not an abstraction but came to life only when it was sung. In this sense, the songs of the troubadours and the trouvères embody the principles of the medieval art of rhetoric, and the music no less than the poem was an essential component in their realization.

NOTES

1. I am grateful to Elizabeth W. Poe for bringing this *cobla* to my attention and for this translation. The *cobla* is identified in Alfred Pillet and Henry Carstens, *Bibliographie der Troubadours* (Halle: Niemeyer, 1933; reprint, New York: Burt Franklin, 1968 [hereafter cited as P-C]), as item 82,33; for a recent edition see Martín de Riquer, ed., *Los trovadores: historia literaria y textos* (Barcelona: Planeta, 1975), vol. 3, no. 289. Gustave Reese quotes the first two verses of Bertran's *cobla* but attributes them mistakenly to Folquet de Marselha, in *Music in the Middle Ages* (New York: Norton, 1940), 205. See also Elizabeth Aubrey, "References to Music in Old Occitan Literature," *Acta Musicologica* 61 (1989): 112, n. 6.

2. See Theodore Karp, "Interrelationships between Poetic and Musical Form in Trouvère Song," in *A Musical Offering: Essays in Honor of Martin Bernstein,* ed. Edward H. Clinkscale and Claire Brook (New York: Pendragon, 1977), 137–61.

3. Important studies of the late medieval arts of poetry and prose, as disseminated by the theorists Matthieu de Vendôme, Jean de Garlande, Geoffroi de Vinsauf, Gervais de Melkley, Evrard l'Allemand, and others, include Douglas Kelly, *The Arts of Poetry and Prose* (Turnhout: Brepols, 1991); Edmond Faral, *Les arts poétiques du XIIe et du XIIIe siècle; recherches et documents sur la technique littéraire du Moyen Age* (Paris: Champion, 1924); Douglas Kelly, "The Scope of the Treatment of Composition in the Twelfth- and Thirteenth-Century Arts of Poetry," *Speculum* 41 (1966): 261–78; Kelly, "Theory of Composition in Medieval Narrative Poetry and Geoffrey of Vinsauf's *Poetria Nova*," *Mediaeval Studies* 31 (1969): 117–48; Kelly, *Medieval Imagination: Rhetoric and the Poetry of Courtly Love* (Madison: University of Wisconsin Press, 1978); and Linda M. Paterson, *Troubadours and Eloquence* (Oxford: Clarendon Press, 1975). See also John Stevens, *Words and Music in the Middle Ages: Song, Narrative, Dance and*

Drama, 1050–1350 (Cambridge: Cambridge University Press, 1986), and Jörn Gruber, *Die Dialektik des Trobar; Untersuchungen zur Struktur und Entwicklung des occitanischen und französischen Minnesangs des 12. Jahrhunderts* (Tübingen: Niemeyer, 1983).

4. The formal elements of a poem that limited musical borrowing, namely rhyme, verse, and strophe structure, are well known, thanks to the work of several scholars, especially Frank M. Chambers, "Imitation of Form in the Old Provençal Lyric," *Romance Philology* 6 (1952–53): 104–20; Friedrich Gennrich, "Internationale mittelalterliche Melodien," *Zeitschrift für Musikwissenschaft* 11 (1928–29): 259–96 and 321–48; Gennrich, *Der musikalische Nachlass der Troubadours*, Summa Musicae Medii Aevi, vols. 3, 4, 15 (Darmstadt: Friedrich Gennrich, 1958–65); Gennrich, *Die Kontrafaktur im Liedschaffen des Mittelalters*, Summa Musicae Medii Aevi, vol. 12 (Langen bei Frankfurt: Friedrich Gennrich, 1965); Hans Spanke, "Zur Formenkunst des ältesten Troubadours," *Studi medievali* n.s. 7 (1934): 72–84; and Spanke, *Untersuchungen über die Ursprünge des romanischen Minnesangs*, part 2: *Marcabrustudien*, Abhandlungen der Gesellschaft der Wissenschaften zu Göttingen, Philologisch-historische Klasse, 3d series, no. 24 (Göttingen: Vandenhoek & Ruprecht, 1940).

5. Ernst Rohloff, ed., *Die Quellenhandschriften zum Musiktraktat des Johannes de Grocheio, im Faksimile herausgegeben nebst Übertragung des Textes und Übersetzung ins Deutsche, dazu Bericht, Literaturschau, Tabellen und Indices* (Leipzig: Deutscher Verlag für Musik, 1972 [hereafter cited as Rohloff, *Grocheio*]).

6. See the attempt by Timothy J. McGee to reconcile Grocheio with extant works, "Medieval Dances: Matching the Repertory with Grocheio's Descriptions," *Journal of Musicology* 7 (1989): 498–517. See also a new edition and translation of these passages by Christopher Page, "Johannes de Grocheio on Secular Music: A Corrected Text and a New Translation," *Plainsong and Medieval Music* 2 (1993): 17–41.

7. These elements are most fully described in Jean de Garlande's treatise of around 1220, ed. and trans. Traugott Lawler, *The Parisiana Poetria of Jean of Garland* (New Haven: Yale University Press, 1974). See especially the first chapter, entitled "De Inventione." Two articles by Margot E. Fassler show how Garlande's discussion relates to the development of the late medieval sequence: "The Role of the Parisian Sequence in the Evolution of Notre-Dame Polyphony," *Speculum* 62 (1987): 345–74, and "Accent, Meter, and Rhythm in Medieval Treatises 'De rithmis,'" *Journal of Musicology* 5 (1987): 164–90. On the possible identity of the grammarian Jean de Garlande with the famous music theorist known as Johannes de Garlandia, see William G. Waite, "Johannes de Garlandia, Poet and Musician," *Speculum* 35 (1960): 179–95.

8. See Rohloff, *Grocheio*, 130–31, paragraphs 107–21.

9. Ibid., 130, paragraphs 112–13. The phrase "circa sonos coronatur" has excited extensive commentary among musicologists. My interpretation takes the words at face value, which I believe makes this sentence most consistent with the thrust of the surrounding text. Page translates the last clause "and it is composed entirely from longs—perfect ones at that" (Page, "Grocheio," 24; see also his n. 29). The interpretation hinges in large part on the meaning of "et"—whether it means literally "and," implies an antithetical delimitation (as in Page's translation), or provides emphasis (as in my interpretation).

10. Compare Jean de Garlande's suggestion of how students ought to invent their subject matter (Lawler, *Garland*, 28–32, lines 515–20): "They should not overlook

the four principal causes—the efficient cause, and so on—of any subject proposed to them. Thus, suppose one of them is treating of his book. He might praise it or criticize it through the efficient cause, that is, through the writer; through the material cause, that is, through the parchment or the ink; through the formal cause, as through the layout of the book or the size of the letters; or through the final cause, by considering for what purpose the book was made, namely, that in it and through it the ignorant may be made more knowledgeable" (non pretermittentes causes principales quattuor, scilicet causam efficientem, cuiuslibet rei sibi proposite. Ut, si tractet de libro suo, commendet eum uel uituperet per causam efficientem, idest per scriptorem; per causam materialem, idest per pargamenum et incaustum; per causam formalem, ut per libri disposicionem et litterarum protractionem; per causam finalem, considerando ad quid factus est liber, ad hoc uidelicet ut in eo et per eum nescientes scientes reddantur). See also Rohloff, *Grocheio,* 132–34, paragraph 127b: "Now the verse in a *cantus coronatus* is what is effected out of many phrases and concordances that produce harmony with one another. But the number of verses in a *cantus coronatus* has been set at seven, because of the seven concords. Indeed this number of verses must contain all of the sense of the material, no more and no less" (Versus vero in cantu coronato est, qui ex pluribus punctis et concordantiis ad se invicem harmoniam facientibus efficitur. Numerus vero versuum in cantu coronato ratione septem concordantiarum determinatus est ad septem. Tot enim versus debent totam sententiam materiae, nec plus nec minus, continere).

11. Rohloff, *Grocheio,* 134, paragraphs 130–32.

12. Albert Seay's translation, for example, implies this interpretation: "First, the words are prepared on the level of the raw material, afterwards a melody on the level of the formed material is adapted to the text in an appropriate way" (Albert Seay, trans., *Johannes de Grocheo, Concerning Music (De Musica),* 2d ed. [Colorado Springs: Colorado College Music Press, 1973]: 18–19). See also Patricia Alice Mitchell DeWitt, "A New Perspective on Johannes de Grocheio's 'Ars Musicae'" (Ph.D. diss., University of Michigan, 1973), 43–54. Page has come to a similar conclusion about the Aristotelian framework in this passage ("Grocheio," 29, n. 49), although his less literal translation deemphasizes this framework. I am grateful to Professors Katherine Tachau in the Department of History of the University of Iowa and Scott MacDonald in the Department of Philosophy of Cornell University for their help in translating and interpreting these critical passages in Grocheio.

13. Compare a later passage on the form of instrumental pieces where Grocheio says, "Just as in a certain way the material of a natural thing is bound by the form of a natural thing, so sound [i.e., the natural material of music] is bound by phrases, that is by the artificial form given it by the craftsman" (Quemadmodum enim materia naturalis per formam naturalem determinatur, ita sonus determinatur per puncta et per formam artificialem ei ab artifice attributam) (Rohloff, *Grocheio,* 138, paragraph 147).

14. See James J. Murphy, *Rhetoric in the Middle Ages: A History of Rhetorical Theory from St. Augustine to the Renaissance* (Berkeley: University of California Press, 1974), for a thorough treatment of Ciceronian rhetoric as it was understood in the Middle Ages.

15. A *locus* in Ciceronian rhetoric is defined as "the region of an argument." See ibid., 16.

16. Grocheio devotes some attention to untexted melodies, saying that every good fiddle player can perform any type of music, including *cantus* and *cantilena* (Rohloff, *Grocheio*, 136, paragraphs 139–47). The "materia" of such pieces is defined, evidently, by the purpose (dancing) and the performance (with marked beats). He also asserts in this section that the human voice can perform an untexted piece.

17. See ibid., 124, paragraphs 81–82. Although it seems unlikely that rhetoric was a central part of the university curriculum in the thirteenth and early fourteenth centuries (see Murphy, *Rhetoric*, 89–132), Cicero's *De inventione* and the *Rhetorica ad Herennium* were widely known.

18. It cannot be demonstrated that Grocheio or the authors of the Old Occitan grammatical treatises knew one another's work. Grocheio, in fact, says he is describing music "according to how the men of Paris use it" (qua utuntur homines Parisiis) (Rohloff, *Grocheio*, 124, paragraphs 77–79), deliberately avoiding the claim that his discussion pertains to music in other "regions," "languages," or "idioms." This has cautioned scholars against applying his comments about musical types or structures to the melodies of Occitania, certainly a prudent course. However, the philosophical attitude in his treatise is neither controversial nor parochial, and the rhetoricians of the Midi no doubt were as well versed as he in Aristotelian philosophy.

19. J. H. Marshall, ed., *The "Razos de trobar" of Raimon Vidal and Associated Texts* (London: Oxford University Press, 1972 [hereafter cited as Marshall, *Raimon Vidal*]).

20. Ibid., 2, lines 20–27. I am grateful to William D. Paden for his expert help and advice in my translations from Old Occitan.

21. Important studies of lyric genres and their themes include Hans Robert Jauss, "Littérature médiévale et théorie des genres," *Poétique* 1 (1970): 79–101; Paul Zumthor, *Essai de poétique médiévale* (Paris: Seuil, 1972); and Pierre Bec, *La lyrique française au Moyen-Age (XIIe-XIIIe siècles); contribution à une typologie des genres poétiques médiévaux* (Paris: Picard, 1977–78). See also Frank M. Chambers, *An Introduction to Old Provençal Versification* (Philadelphia: American Philosophical Society, 1985), 191–279; and Elizabeth Aubrey, *The Music of the Troubadours* (Bloomington: Indiana University Press, 1996), 84–85.

22. Marshall, *Raimon Vidal*, 22, lines 451–54.

23. Ibid., 56–57, lines 30–37. That this *razo* is the same as rhetoric's *materia* is confirmed in an anonymous treatise of the mid-fourteenth-century, now in Barcelona, the so-called Ripoll treatise, which consistently uses the word *materia* to refer to the subject matter of the poem, e.g.: "La materia de les cancons es de amor o de lahor de dones" (The subject of the *canso* is love or the praise of ladies) (ibid., 101).

24. Marshall argues convincingly on stylistic grounds that this treatise might have been written by the same Jofre de Foixà who produced the *Regles de trobar*; see ibid., lxxv–lxxviii.

25. Ibid., 95, lines 7–21. See Stephen G. Nichols, Jr., "Toward an Aesthetic of the Provençal Canso," in *The Disciplines of Criticism*, ed. Peter Demetz and others (New Haven: Yale University Press, 1968): 349–74, on the poetic content of the *canso*.

26. For examples from the troubadour repertoire, see Aubrey, *Music*, 86–95.

27. Marshall, *Raimon Vidal*, 95, lines 22–27. See Richard Baum, "Les troubadours et les *lais*," *Zeitschrift für romanische Philologie* 85 (1969): 1–44, and Jean Maillard, *Evolution et esthétique du lai lyrique des origines à la fin du XIVe siècle* (Paris: Centre de Documentation Universitaire, 1963).

28. Pierre Bec has argued that both of these melodies probably had northern origins (*Lyrique française,* 1:204–6).

29. They are listed in the index of P-C as 461,37; 461,122; and 461,124. See Elizabeth Aubrey, "Issues in the Musical Analysis of the Troubadour *Descorts* and *Lays,*" in *The Cultural Milieu of the Troubadours and Trouvères,* ed. Nancy van Deusen (Ottawa, Canada: Institute of Medieval Music, 1994), 67–98; and Aubrey, *Music,* 106–9.

30. See Bec, *Lyrique française,* 1:197, 201.

31. The other tune for Aimeric's poem is through-composed. The two Occitan *descort* texts are listed in P-C as 10,45 and 205,5. There is some disagreement about what to call "Qui la ve en ditz." Unlike other *descorts,* it has three stanzas with the same rhyme scheme (albeit not the same rhymes), and the double-cursus version is, in fact, strophic. István Frank considered the song to be a *canso* (*Répertoire métrique de la poésie des troubadours* [Paris: Champion, 1953–57], item 528:1), while both P-C and Gennrich (*Der musikalische Nachlass*) label it a *descort.* Following Frank, Richard H. Hoppin omitted it from his count of *descorts* and *lais* (*Medieval Music* [New York: Norton, 1978], 276). I regard it here as a *descort* because of its poetic structure and because double-cursus structure does appear in one version of its melody. See Ismael Fernández de la Cuesta and Robert Lafont, eds., *Las cançons dels trobadors* ([Toulouse: Institut d'Estudis Occitans, 1979], 402 and 531) for transcriptions of the three *descort* melodies. See also Jean Maillard, "Structures mélodiques complexes au Moyen Age," in *Mélanges de langue et de littérature médiévales offerts à Pierre le Gentil,* ed. Jean Dufournet and Daniel Poirion (Paris: S.E.D.E.S., 1973): 523–39, on "Ses alegratge"; and Aubrey, *Music,* 105–8, on "Qui la ve en ditz."

32. Marshall, *Raimon Vidal,* 97, lines 81–86. The structural similarity between *descort* and *lai* has prompted many scholars to reason that there is no substantive difference between the two courtly genres. See Bec, who argues in *Lyrique française* that the term *descort* was peculiar mainly to the south and *lai* to the north, while the only real difference between them was a closer association in the south of the genre with the courtly *canso:* "La seule différence entre les deux genres—qui n'est pas structurale—est peut-être la plus grande indépendance typologique du lai français par rapport à la *canso;* alors que le *descort* occitan, pourtant conçu au départ comme une sorte de repoussoir formel de la *canso,* ne parvient pas à s'en émanciper" (1:199–206, quotation on 202).

33. Compare the *Donatz Proensals* of Uc Faidit (c. 1240), which includes the word in its rhyme lists with the Latin translation "discordia, vel cantilena habens sonos diversos" (J. H. Marshall, ed., *The "Donatz Proensals" of Uc Faidit* [Oxford: Oxford University Press, 1969], 230, line 2861). Richard Baum, in "Le *descort* ou l'anti-chanson," labels the *descort* the "anti-canso" (in *Mélanges de philologie romane dédiés à la mémoire de Jean Boutière,* ed. Irénée-Marcel Cluzel and François Pirot [Liège: Soledi, 1971], 75–98). Christopher Page argues on the strength of this that the *descort* "lies on the edge of the troubadour art" and "subverts the High Style manner as represented above all by the *canso*" (*Voices and Instruments of the Middle Ages: Instrumental Practice and Songs in France, 1100–1300* [Berkeley, University of California Press, 1986], 23). Pierre Bec, however, points out that only in its structure, but not in its theme, is the *descort* different from the courtly *canso:* "Sa thématique en effet, quoi qu'on en ait dit, est la même que celle de la *canso,* c'est-à-dire courtoise et amoureuse dans sa grande majorité. . . . C'est par sa discordance formelle avant tout que ce type

de poème se caractérise et qu'il représente à ce titre une *anti-canso*. Genre très élaboré et aristocratisant, il pourrait être avec quelque raison intégré au registre du 'grand chant courtois'" (*Lyrique française*, 1:196). See further Erich Köhler, "Deliberations on a Theory of the Genre of the Old Provençal *Descort*," in *Italian Literature: Roots and Branches, Essays in Honor of Thomas Goddard Bergin*, ed. Giose Rimanelli and Kenneth J. Atchity (New Haven: Yale University Press, 1976), 1–13.

34. Marshall (*Raimon Vidal*, 139–40, nn. 81–86) points out that no *descorts* were being composed by the late thirteenth century, which could account for the inexactitude of the theorists' descriptions. Jean Maillard, "Problèmes musicaux et littéraires du *descort*," should be consulted for a thorough discussion of the music and structures of Occitan and French *descorts* (in *Mélanges de linguistique et de littérature romanes à la mémoire d'István Frank* [(Saarbrücken): Universität des Saarlandes, 1957]: 388–409).

35. Marshall, *Raimon Vidal*, 95–96, lines 28–39. In fact, there are a number of extant *sirventes* melodies that lack surviving models, notably thirteen by the late thirteenth-century troubadour Guiraut Riquier.

36. Ibid., 97, lines 104–8.

37. See Aubrey, *Music*, 111–12.

38. Marshall, *Raimon Vidal*, lines 90–92.

39. The number of stanzas is not the same, at least in manuscript BN fr. 22543.

40. The music of both songs is given in Aubrey, *Music*, 112–17.

41. Marshall, *Raimon Vidal*, 96, lines 62–66. An example of an Occitan *alba* with its melody is found in Aubrey, *Music*, 102–5.

42. Marshall, *Raimon Vidal*, lines 40–44.

43. P-C 248,57; 248,65; and 248,78; see Aubrey, *Music*, 127–29. Pierre Bec contends that the Occitan *retroncha* was imported from the north, where it was known as the *rotrouenge* (*Lyrique française*, 1:48 and 185). He points out that it does not appear in the south before c. 1220.

44. See Marshall, *Raimon Vidal*, 137, nn. 40–44. Despite the absence of musical repetition in the extant examples, Gennrich argued that it was musical structure that distinguished a *rotrouenge* from other lyric types (*Die altfranzösische Rotrouenge: Literarhistorisch-musikwissenschaftliche Studien*, vol. 2 [Halle: Niemeyer, 1925], 1–14).

45. Marshall, *Raimon Vidal*, 96, lines 45–50.

46. The only extant Occitan *pastorela* melody, by Marcabru, is given in Aubrey, *Music*, 96–99.

47. Marshall, *Raimon Vidal*, 96, lines 51–56.

48. Ibid., lines 57–61.

49. Marshall (ibid., 138, nn. 58–60) refers to two cases of melodic borrowing, but he apparently means poetic modeling; the poems he mentions do not survive with melodies, so musical borrowing cannot be substantiated.

50. P-C 167,22 and 248,63. See Aubrey, *Music*, 96–102.

51. Listed as item 381 in Hans Spanke, ed., *G. Raynauds Bibliographie des altfranzösischen Liedes, erster Teil*, reprinted with discography and alphabetical index of songs by A. Bahat (Leiden: Brill, 1980).

52. An internal refrain consisting of the last verses of each stanza is optional. See Marshall, *Raimon Vidal*, 138, nn. 52–56.

53. The songs are P-C 244,1a; 461,92; 461,196; and 461,230. See Page, *Voices and Instruments,* 24, 247, n. 22, and 43, example 8; and Aubrey, *Music,* 123–26.

54. Paul Meyer suggested that the Occitan *dansa* was the prototype of the northern virelai ("Des rapports de la poésie des trouvères avec celle des troubadours," *Romania* 19 [1890]: 21). Bec points out that the poetic structure of the *dansa* is more complex than that of the virelai. Its courtly theme and sophisticated structure cause Bec to place it, along with the *balada,* which has similar characteristics, in the "aristocratic register": "Il en est donc de même sans doute de la *dansa* que de la *balada,* genres qui se sont désolidarisés de leur possible origine popularisante et chorégraphique pour s'intégrer finalement (mais non sans quelque interférences) au registre du grand chant courtois" (*Lyrique française,* 1:239).

55. Marshall, *Raimon Vidal,* 97, lines 72–74.

56. Ibid., 98, lines 115–17.

57. See ibid., 141, nn. 124–25.

58. Ibid., lines 124–25.

59. See this *razo* in Jean Boutière and A. H. Schutz, eds., *Biographies des troubadours,* 2d ed., rev. Jean Boutière and Irénée-Marcel Cluzel (Paris: Nizet, 1964), 465–66.

60. See Bec, *Lyrique française,* 1:241–46.

61. Adolphe-F. Gatien-Arnoult, ed., *Las flors del gay saber, estiers dichas "Las leys d'amors,"* Monumens de la littérature romane, vols. 1–3 (Toulouse: J.-B. Paya, 1841–43), 1:350. Rohloff, *Grocheio,* 132, paragraph 120, and 136, paragraph 141.

62. See the edition of these pieces by Timothy J. McGee, *Medieval Instrumental Dances* (Bloomington: Indiana University Press, 1989).

63. In "Medieval Dances," Timothy J. McGee argues that the *Doctrina*'s "cobla" might be translated "couplet" instead of "stanza," which would make the description consistent with the paired-verse structure associated with the instrumental *estampie* (502–6). There are problems with this interpretation, however. In the first place, the author of the *Doctrina* uses the word "cobla" consistently throughout the entire passage on genres to mean "stanza," and nowhere else can it be taken instead to mean "couplet." Secondly, a *tornada* is usually at least two verses long, with the same structure as the final verses of the poem's stanzas. If the "coblas" in the *Doctrina*'s *estampida* are couplets and not stanzas, then the word *tornada* in the passage is meaningless.

64. Marshall suggests that the "responedor" mentioned in the *Doctrina* refers to some kind of musical rhyme at the ends of verses, as in the *descort* (*Raimon Vidal,* 139, nn. 72–74). But while most of the French and Italian instrumental pieces do have refrains concluding each musical section, the music for "Kalenda maia" only hints at musical rhyme. McGee attempts to explain the prescription for a refrain by suggesting "that there must have been a convention for selecting certain lines of each *estampie* to serve in that capacity," and that these lines would have been repeated in performance ("Medieval Dances," 503). Admitting that this is speculative, McGee goes on to demonstrate how it might have been done with "Kalenda maia." See also Lloyd Hibberd, "Estampie and Stantipes," *Speculum* 19 (1944): 222–49.

65. See Bec, *Lyrique française,* 1:243–44.

66. For further exploration of the differences between northern and southern

estampies, and between vocal and instrumental versions of the genre, see Elizabeth Aubrey, "The Dialectic between Occitania and France in the Thirteenth Century," *Early Music History* 16 (1997): 40–52.

67. Pierre Bec, among others, has pointed out that a lyric poem is more topical than narrative, so each strophe can express some aspect of the poem's theme (ibid., 1:21–2).

CHAPTER 12

Intergeneric Play: The Pastourelle in Thirteenth-Century French Motets

SYLVIA HUOT

The purpose of this essay is to examine the effects created when a well-established lyric genre, the pastourelle, was appropriated by a new form, the motet. As lyric genres, the pastourelle and the motet are very differently construed, the former being defined in terms of content—in Pierre Bec's terms, a "genre à pertinence thématique"—while the latter is defined by its polyphonic structure, placing it among Bec's "genres à pertinence lyrico-formelle."[1] The transposition of the pastourelle into the polyphonic format of the motet allowed for new ways of exploiting its stock characters and situations, reminiscent in some cases of the effects wrought in Adam de la Halle's dramatization of the pastourelle in the *Jeu de Robin et Marion*.[2]

Indeed, the appearance of vernacular polyphony in the thirteenth century opened up a whole new set of poetic possibilities. The monophonic *chanson* develops progressively from stanza to stanza, but there is only limited space for progression within the short motet text, which corresponds in length to no more than one or two stanzas of a chanson. The motet relies instead on juxtaposition and on the intertextual dialogue generated within its polytextual structure: the interplay among the upper voices, when there is more than one, and the interplay of the texted voice or voices with the tenor. Full appreciation of a motet additionally requires knowledge of its generic sources: for an audience familiar with the pastourelle tradition, for example, the mere mention of the names "Robin" and "Marion" conjures up associations that inform and enrich the sparse details offered by the motet texts themselves. Similarly, a vernacular motet with Latin tenor is most fully appreciated by those capable of identifying the tenor with its standard use in Latin sacred motets. Even the uninitiated could certainly enjoy motets musically and phonically, as Christopher Page has argued.[3] But it is in the complex juxtapositions of Latin and vernacular traditions, in the subtle textual and generic interplay of its component parts, that the real beauty and power of the motet lie.

The concept of "intergenre" or "intergeneric discourse" has been explored recently by Donald Maddox and Sara Sturm-Maddox, who propose "shifting focus from individual genres to multiple affinities within an intergeneric system."[4] Instead of judging a text according to its correspondence to some hypothetical generic norm, in other words, it is often more fruitful to acknowledge that a given text will resist classification in a single generic category, and that it in fact embodies a dynamic that operates "through and among *matières* and discursive registers in the system as a whole."[5] The hybrid nature of the vernacular motet makes it particularly well suited to this kind of intergeneric reading.

The vernacular motet arose in close relation to the corpus of Latin motets, as is shown by the high number of contrafacta linking the two corpora as well as by the existence of a certain number of bilingual motets. In particular, a feature common to Latin motets and shared by the vast majority of French ones is the use of a tenor, or *cantus firmus,* that ultimately derives from the liturgy.[6] The tenor, in other words, consists of a melismatic phrase that usually corresponds to no more than two or three words—sometimes to only one or two syllables from the middle of a word—taken from some part of the chant: usually an alleluia, responsory, or gradual. Although the chant is the immediate source, the liturgical text itself most commonly comes from the Bible. In this way the tenor can be seen as carrying with it associations from two originary contexts: sacred ritual and sacred scripture. In Latin motets there is a close textual relationship between the tenor and the upper voices, each of which is provided with a complete text, and of which there can be anywhere from one to three, known respectively as the motetus (or duplum), the triplum, and the quadruplum. The upper voices may expand on the tenor's source text, quoting or glossing it; supply a commentary on the feast day to which the tenor corresponds; or develop a devotional theme appropriate to that feast day. One might thus expect to find a hymn to the Virgin combined with a tenor from the feast of the Assumption, for example, while a tenor from the Christmas liturgy might be used in a motet devoted to the mystery of the Incarnation, the commemoration of Christ's birth, or the act of Redemption.

With vernacular motets the relationship is rarely so straightforward; although a few French motet texts treat devotional themes, most do not. Instead they draw on the vast and varied repertoire of vernacular lyric, including the *chanson courtoise,* the pastourelle, the rondeau, the *chanson de mal mariée.* A few even use vernacular refrains or rondeaux as tenors. Most, however, continue to use the Latin tenors, and many are musically identical to Latin motets—though it is often impossible to determine whether the Latin composition is a contrafactum of the French one or vice versa. It seems most likely that the process worked both ways. What this shows is that the French motets were cultivated in the same circles as the Latin ones; the composers of these pieces, as well as their original audience, would have been quite capable of recognizing the Latin tenors and would have had a level of education allowing for considerable literary and musical sophistication. The French motet stands quite literally at a linguistic, generic, and cultural crossroads: vernacular secular lyric meets Latin sacred polyphony. The result is truly a hybrid form.

While not in the majority, the body of motets drawing on the pastourelle represents a significant portion of the total corpus. Given that generic distinctions within Old French lyric are less than absolute, one may well hesitate in categorizing a given motet as pastourelle, *reverdie, chanson de mai,* and so on. I do not wish to address the question of precise generic definitions here, but rather to examine more generally the transformations that took place in the move from monody to polyphony. For the purposes of this essay, the pastourelle may be loosely defined as follows. It is a poem with a rustic setting, whether fields, orchard, or forest; the season is generally specified as spring or summer. Sometimes the poem describes the antics of shepherds or other rustics, often as narrated by an observer—the lyric "I"—who is not himself a member of the pastoral world. The shepherds' behavior may include amorous exploits ranging from a lament for an absent beloved, to flirtation, to explicit sex; or it may focus more on singing, the playing of rustic instruments such as bagpipes, and dancing. Often the pastourelle recounts an encounter between the first-person male persona—again, an outsider to the pastoral world, though it is often unspecified whether he is knight or cleric—and a shepherdess. This encounter may end with the shepherdess rebuffing her would-be suitor or with her shepherd lover arriving to chase away the intruder; or it may end with the fulfillment of the male persona's desires, either by force or by consent. Sometimes, in other words, the first-person lyric persona is an active participant—this type of poem has been designated as the *pastourelle classique*—while other times he is merely a witness and narrator, in what is generally known as the *pastourelle-bergerie* or *pastourelle désintéressée.*[7] These various elements are combined in Adam de la Halle's dramatic pastourelle, the *Jeu de Robin et Marion*, which includes an unsuccessful seduction and later an attempted abduction of Marion by a knight; episodes of flirtation and affectionate repartee with Marion and Robin; and scenes of rustic game-playing, song, and dance. The dramatic format allows for more voices than the strophic pastourelle, and for the development of various motifs and subplots; it is as though several different pastourelle poems, representing a range of generic possibilities, had been woven together.

When we turn to motets, we find that the polyphonic format also allows for a wider range of experimentation with the elements of the pastourelle. In the discussion that follows I will present examples illustrating several different ways that the pastourelle was used in polyphony. First, I will examine the contrast of the pastourelle world with that of the *chanson courtoise*; second, the distribution of elements among the various voices to create a quasi-dramatic version; and finally, the construction of a pastourelle scenario that corresponds either allegorically or parodically to the liturgical or biblical source of the tenor.

To illustrate the first possibility—the contrast of rustic and courtly love—I offer two examples: "Par un matinet l'autrier" (One morning the other day) (658) / "Hé, berchiers! si grant envie" (Hey, shepherd! such great envy) (657) / EJUS (Her) (O16), and "Encontre le tans de Pascour" (At Eastertime) (496) / "Quant fuellent aubespin" (With the hawthorn bush turning leafy green) (497) / IN ODOREM (In the odor) (M45).[8] In the first, a male persona—nothing indicates whether he is *chevalier* or *clerc*—expresses contradictory feelings about a shepherd who is evidently more successful in love. In the triplum, the lyric persona criticizes the shepherd for boasting of his sexual exploits, referring to him as "un fou berchier" (a foolish shepherd) (line 2) and to his behavior as "folie" (folly) (line 6) and "amour vilaine" (low-class love) (line 7). As counterexample the protagonist cites his own behavior, stressing that he, unlike the shepherd, is capable of steadfastness in love without need of physical gratification:

> Mais j'ains certes plus loiaument que nus,
> *car quant bele dame m'aimme,*
> *je ne demant plus.*
>   (lines 8–10)
>
> But certainly I love more loyally than anyone: since a beautiful lady loves me, I ask for nothing more.

In the motetus, however, the lyric persona seems to take less consolation in his lofty ideals; here he expresses envy for the shepherd, who finds more joy in love in spite of his lack of courtly idealism. The complete text of the motetus is as follows:

> Hé, bergiers! si grant envie j'ai de toi
> de ce que si bonne vie a envers moi,
> qu'onques loiautei ne foi
> trouver n'i poi
> la ou je l'ai deservie,
> et toi, qui de rien servie
> n'as amours joïr t'an voi
> et vanter t'oi *en l'aunoi:*
> "*Jui en l'aunoi es bras m'amie.*"

> Hey, shepherd! I have such envy for you because you have such a good life compared to me, who can never find loyalty or faith where I have deserved it; and you, who have not served love in any way, I see you take pleasure from it and I hear you boast in the alder grove: "I lay in the alder grove in the arms of my beloved."

From these contrasting statements there emerge two opposing ideas of what it means to be a successful lover: adherence to courtly ideals on the one hand, successful sexual conquest on the other. Through expressions of both envy and contempt the lyric persona attempts to distance himself from the shepherd, but at another level the carefree rustic represents the actualization of the singer's fantasies. On the one hand, the lyric protagonist acknowledges the frustrations inherent in the restricting code of courtesy that forces him to wait patiently for his lady's favors; he cannot help but long for the sexual freedom of the happy-go-lucky shepherd. On the other hand, however, these same frustrations are embraced as the sign of merit; whereas the shepherd sings boastingly of his sexual exploits, the protagonist actually flaunts his own failure as proof of his courtly refinement. Both personae, of course—the sexually charged shepherd and the lover who hopes only for a favorable disposition—are literary constructs, drawn from the pastourelle and the *chanson courtoise* respectively. Their juxtaposition in the motet allows for an intergeneric dialogue, as the two amorous codes associated with the two social classes are brought into confrontation. From the contrast between the two players, differently expressed in the two texted voices, there emerges a double message of desire and restraint.

The second example suggests a solution to this dilemma by allowing the lyric persona to participate in both worlds. In the triplum, the persona describes the beauty of the lady he has chosen and laments her refusal to yield to his wishes. The text is a conventional statement of courtly longing. The protagonist, noting that spring is a joyful time for lovers, wishes that he too could be "renvoisiés et plains de joie / et d'amour" (lighthearted and full of love and joy) (lines 8–9). But this, of course, depends entirely on the response of the lady he loves, and she has not been forthcoming:

> Ne por quant
> ma joie est tornee en plor,
> se ne puis avoir l'amor
> de cele, qui mon cuer a
> et qui toz jours mes l'avra.
>   (lines 12–16)

But my joy has turned to tears, for I cannot have the love of her who possesses my heart and who always will.

In conventional courtly fashion, the protagonist looks forward to his own death if the lady continues to reject him:

> Bele, que ferai,
> se vostre amor n'ai?
> Las, autrement
> sui a la mort
> sans resort.
>   (lines 39–43)

Fair one, what shall I do if I have not your love? Alas, otherwise death is my lot without recourse.

The motetus likewise is set in the springtime, and in this case the protagonist is successful in experiencing the amorous pleasures of the season. He describes his encounter with an attractive shepherdess who flees his advances, but is overpowered:

> Au col li mis
> mes bras et puis li dis:
> "Bele flour de lis,
> je sui vostre amis,
> a vous me rent pris."
> Tant fis et tant dis,
> qu'audesus me mis,
> ma volenté fis
> *tout a mon devis;*
> *dous ris ot et cler vis.*
>   (lines 32–41)

I put my arms around her neck and said to her: "Fair lily flower, I am your sweetheart and hand myself over, prisoner to you." With enough sweet talk and sweet gestures I was able to get on top of her and take my pleasure entirely as I desired; she had a sweet laugh and a bright face.

The pastoral world is a place where the languishing lover can satisfy his desires, for his code of courtly submission does not require him to acknowledge the wishes of a shepherdess.

The function of the pastoral world as a means of fulfilling the desires that are blocked in the courtly world is explicit in the *pastourelle classique,* which often begins with an allusion to the protagonist's predicament—sometimes he is merely "pensive," other times he is actively seeking relief from the pains of unrequited love—and proceeds to an actual or attempted seduction or rape of a shepherdess. The motet accomplishes a similar effect through juxtaposition of the different texts, allowing the sweet pain of courtly longing to form the backdrop against which the pastoral encounter takes place. The protagonist's words to the shepherdess stress the overlay of courtly ideology. She, not he, is in reality the one who has attempted to flee in fear and has been taken prisoner: "Esbahie / fu . . . / si torne a la fuie / et je apres. / Par la main l'ai prise" (She was frightened . . . she turned and ran, with me in pursuit. I took hold of her by the hand) (motetus, lines 20–25). When the protagonist proclaims himself the prisoner of the girl that he has just overpowered—addressing her as though she were a courtly lady, while otherwise treating her in accordance with her status as a shepherdess—it is clear that the frustrated desire of the triplum has been projected into an arena where it can be acted upon without restraint.

I turn now to the second type of pastourelle motet, that in which the distribution of elements between the two texted voices results in the dramatization of an implied narrative; again I offer two examples. In the first—"En mai, quant rosier sont flouri" (In May, with rosebushes blooming) (870) / "L'autre jour, par un matin" (The other day, in morningtide) (871) / "Hé, resvelle toi, Robin" (Hey, wake up, Robin)—each voice presents a self-contained pastourelle text.[9] The two upper voices, both examples of the *pastourelle-bergerie,* present simple narratives of the love of Robin and Marion. In the triplum, an unnamed shepherdess, observed by the narrator, sighs for Robin:

> . . . Aymi,
> Robin, mise m'avés en oubli
> pour Margot, la fille Tierri!
> Bien me doi descomforter et souspirer.
>   (lines 8–11)
>
> Alas, Robin, you have forgotten me because of Margot, Tierri's daughter! I must indeed lament and sigh.

Hearing her song, however, Robin bursts on the scene, playing his pipe, and the two go off together into the forest. The motetus, in contrast, focuses on the figure of Robin; again observed by the narrator, he laments the absence of his beloved:

> . . . Aymi!
> Quant vendra la bele au cuer joli,
> que j'atent ci?
> > (lines 7–9)
>
> Alas! When will she come, the fair one with the gay heart whom I wait for here?

Hearing this, like Robin in the triplum, Marion (Marot [lines 6, 10]) appears and offers her love. The tenor, finally, is a refrain alerting Robin to the attempted abduction of Marion; the same refrain is used for that very purpose in the *Jeu de Robin et Marion* (lines 358–60).

Together, the three voices of the motet imply a different sort of dramatization of the exploits of Robin and Marion, one with three scenes or subplots: Marion's fear, apparently unfounded, that Robin has left her for another woman; Robin's anxious search for Marion and his joy at finding her; the need for Robin to rescue Marion from abduction. The two upper voices form a symmetrical pair: in one Robin arrives to soothe Marion's fears, and in the other it is she who arrives to allay his anxiety.[10] Underlying these two scenes of amorous worry and consolation is the tenor with its allusion to yet another source of pastoral anxiety, one that involves intrusion from outside the pastoral world; and one can assume that, as in the *Jeu de Robin et Marion*, this one too will end happily, with no harm done. As a poetic construct, after all, the pastoral world is more a place of play, wish fulfillment, and comic relief than one of danger or trauma.

The motet does not, of course, function dramatically as does the *Jeu de Robin et Marion*, in which a variety of conventional pastourelle motifs are exploited as the basis for a coherent sequence of scenes. The upper voices are symmetrical, and could be imagined as distinct narrative episodes, but there is no narrative framework to link them. Due to the simultaneity of motet voices, the three scenarios that are invoked have a timeless quality that does not allow for the imposition of chronology. The motet offers a crystallization of three stock situations inherent in the pastourelle as a genre. And it is this generic frame, rather than a narrative or dramatic one, that gives the motet its unity as a polyphonic rendering of the pastourelle.

My second example—"L'autre jour par un matin" (The other morning) (200) / "Au tens pascour" (In springtime) (201) / IN SECULUM (Forever) (M13)—can also be compared to the *Jeu de Robin et Marion*.[11] The triplum, an example of the *pastourelle classique,* presents an encounter between the male lyric persona and an unnamed shepherdess, whom he finds singing of love. When he attempts to seduce her, however, she proclaims her preference for Robin:

> Sire, laissiés moi ester, ralés en vo contree,
> j'aim Robin sans fausseté, m'amor li ai donnee,
> plus l'aim que riens nee.
>   (lines 13–15)
>
> Leave me alone, sire, return to your land, I love Robin truly, and I have given him my love; I love him more than anyone.

The motetus, an example of the *pastourelle-bergerie,* describes a musical contest among five shepherds who play dance tunes on various musical instruments:

> Au tens pascour
> tuit li pastour
> d'une contree
> ont fait assemblee
> desous une valee.
> Hebers en la pree
> a de la pipe et dou tabour
> la danse demenee;
> Robin pas n'agree,
> quant il l'a esgardee;
> mais par aatie
> fera mieudre estampie.
> Lors a saisi son fourrel,
> prist son chapel,
> s'a sa cote escourcie,
> s'a fait l'estanpie
> jolie pour l'amour de s'amie.
>   (lines 1–17)
>
> In springtime all the shepherd folk from one region gathered together at the bottom of a valley. In the meadow, Herbert led the dance with pipe and tabour; Robin was not pleased when he saw it; but, out of defiance, would do a better estampie. Then he grabbed his drone, seized his hat, tucked up his tunic and did the jolly estampie for the love of his sweetheart.

The two texts are linked through the shared references to Robin, and again there is a symmetrical relationship. The triplum focuses on the shepherdess as both subject and object of desire, briefly alluding to Robin as her lover; while the motetus focuses on Robin and his male companions, with only one allusion to Robin's *amie* [motetus, line 17]—presumably to be identified with the shepherdess of the triplum. The motet, like Adam's play, comprises different elements of the pastourelle tradition: the encounter of knight and shepherdess and the depiction of rustic song and dance. But instead of recurring sequentially through alternating episodes, as in the play, the two vignettes of the motet unfold simultaneously. The shepherdess's firm protestations of love for Robin underlie his musical performance, executed out of love for her, while this inspired performance itself singles Robin out as worthy of her love.

As in the previous example, the love shared by Robin and Marion—one of the central features of the pastourelle genre—lies at the nucleus of the pastoral world, enabling it to resist disruption from the outside and informing its internal dynamics as well. The tenor, FOREVER, can be seen as an underlying echo of the eternal quality of the love that joins the rustic couple, a powerful generic constant: Robin and Marion surely will love one another forever, whether they appear in a monophonic *chanson*, a *dit*, a play, or a motet. And due to its origins in the Easter liturgy, the tenor additionally doubles the reference to Eastertide in the motetus, providing a musical reiteration of the conventional springtime setting.[12]

On this note, I turn to a third, somewhat different use of pastourelle motifs in the motet: as a means of recasting the sacred event celebrated in the liturgical text from which the tenor derives. Motets of this type present a fine example of intergeneric play, as vernacular pastourelle enters into dialogue with chant. In the first two examples discussed above, the polytextual format of the motet allowed for intergeneric coupling of the world of *fin' amors* with that of the pastourelle. What we encounter here, however, is a more complex play of genres and traditions, bringing into play not only the contrasting registers in the upper voices but also the Latin background of the motet itself as a genre.

The relationship between the pastoral scenario and the tenor could take various forms, both allegorical and parodic; I have selected three examples, illustrating a range of possibilities. The first—"Quant voi la fleur en l'arbroie" (When I see the flower in the wood) (250) / ET TENUERUNT (And they clasped) (M17)—represents a parodic use of the pastourelle.[13] The motetus recounts a short narrative scene in which a shepherdess plays her flute in order to summon Robin; when he hears her, he replies in song:

> Veez la, ma douce amie
> desouz l'olivier m'atent,
> la bele aus euz veirz, rians,
> au cors gent,

la bele, la blonde.
*Espringués legierement,
que li soliers ne fonde!*
   (lines 20–26)

> See her there; my sweetheart waits for me beneath the olive tree, the fair one with the bright, laughing eyes, the graceful one, the fair one, the blonde. Spring lightly so that your slipper be not weighted down.

The motetus can certainly be read as a conventional *pastourelle-bergerie*. But the scenario can also be seen as a parodic recasting of the encounter between the risen Christ and Mary Magdelene, as described in the Alleluia, used during Easter week and for the feast of Mary Magdelene, that is the source for the tenor: "Alleluia. Surrexit Dominus et occurens mulieribus ait: Avete; tunc accesserunt et tenuerunt pedes ejus" (Alleluia. The Lord arose and running up to the women, said: Hail. Then they came up to him and clasped his feet) (M17).[14] In both texts a maiden seeks her lover—in one case earthly, in the other heavenly—and when he calls to her, she runs up to him. The idyll presented in the motetus offers a secularized version of key elements of the biblical narrative, reconstructed in the familiar image of the amorous, singing shepherds of the pastourelle. And it is only through the contextualization within the motet that one sees the parallel between the vernacular text and the biblical model; the juxtaposition of motetus and tenor allows us to focus on common features that would otherwise go unnoticed.

My second example—"Chantez seri, Marot" (Sing brightly, Marot) (262) / PRAECEDAM VOS (I will go before you) (M19)—is somewhat more ambiguous.[15] The tenor is taken from an Alleluia used during Easter week, paraphrasing the words spoken by the angel to Mary Magdelene and her companion(s) on Easter morning: "Alleluia. In die resurrectionis meae, dicit Dominus, praecedam vos in Galilaeam" (Alleluia. In the day of my Resurrection, says the Lord, I will go before you into Galilee).[16] It is combined with a motetus in which a maiden—her name a popularized version of Mary—is summoned to meet her returning lover. The motetus reads in its entirety:

Chantez seri, Marot,
vos amis revient;
s'aporte un nouvel mot
de vous, car il convient,
que je de ce chant et not,
dont plus souvent me souvient.
Et je l'ai fet si mignot,

> que, quant on l'ot,
> il demande, qu'on le lot.
> *Donc chantez, bele, mignotement,*
> *que vos amis revient.*

> Sing brightly, little Mary, your sweetheart is returning; thus I bring a new poem about you, for I must sing and make music about that which I think of most often. And I've made it so pretty that whenever anyone hears it, he has to praise it. So sing prettily, beautiful one, that your sweetheart is returning.

Again, then, the text recasts the central idea—the return of the Heavenly Bridegroom—in imagery reminiscent of the pastourelle. Although the sparse text gives few details, the name "Marot" carries such strong generic associations with the pastourelle that it alone is enough to evoke a pastoral locus. And it is a commonplace of the characterization of Marion that she should be portrayed as awaiting her lover's return, and as singing to welcome him. In short, although the motetus does not identify the amorous couple as shepherds, there is nothing in its text to prevent our reading it as a pastourelle. The first-person voice of the motetus is that of Marot's returning lover, who sings of her in eager anticipation and invites her to do likewise as the moment of their meeting draws near. When read according to the conventions of the pastourelle, then, the motetus could be understood as the song of Robin as he approaches the waiting Marion, a motif found in the pastourelle and present also in the *Jeu de Robin et Marion* (lines 101–14).

At the same time, of course, the girl named Marot, eagerly awaiting the return of her shepherd lover, could be understood as Mary Magdelene, devotee of the Good Shepherd. The possible identification of Marot with the Magdelene is supported by the liturgical and biblical associations of the tenor. The motet can be understood either as a vernacular presentation of the angel's words or as a more thorough transposition of the Resurrection into the world of the pastourelle. The tenor supports this reading by doubling the use of first- and second-person forms found in the motetus. Here too the first-person voice [PRAECEDAM] is that of the returning male figure, the mystical lover; while the second-person pronoun refers to the female devotee who seeks him. It is the name "Marot," with its double associations—Marion or Sainte Marie—that provides the link between the two registers, sacred and secular, that are here brought together.

In my final example—"Au douz mois de mai" (In the sweet month of May) (275) / "Crux forma penitencie" (Cross, form of penitence) (274) / SUSTINERE (To bear) (M22)—the pastourelle text, though once again remaining within the conventions of the genre, is even more clearly allegorized through its contextualization within the motet.[17] Again, the piece operates not by means of linear progression but through the juxtaposition of texts and the interplay among them, producing a complex and beautiful meditation on the Crucifixion. The motetus, in Latin, stresses the Cross as a figure of life, joy, and consolation, locus of the marriage union of Christ and the human soul. The French triplum, on the other hand, describes the protagonist's encounter in an orchard with a shepherdess who laments inconsolably for Robin, whom she has lost. The tenor, finally, is derived from an Alleluia for the feast of the Finding of the Cross. Here are the complete texts of triplum and motetus:

>   Triplum
> Au doz mois de mai
> en un vergier flori m'en entrai,
> trovei pastorele desoz un glai;
> ses agneaus gardoit
> et si se dementoit,
> si com je voz dirai:
> "Robin, doz amis,
> perdu voz ai:
> a grant dolor de vos me departirai!"
> Lés li m'assis,
> si l'acolai;
> esbahie la trovai
> pour l'amour Robin,
> qui de li s'est partis:
> S'en estoit en grant esmai.

In the sweet month of May I entered a flowering orchard and found a shepherd girl beside a glen. She was watching her lambs and lamenting in this way: "Robin, my sweet beloved, I lost you; in great grief will I take leave of you!" I sat down beside her and put my arms around her. I found her overwhelmed with emotion on account of her love for Robin, who had left her. For this she was deeply distressed.

>   Motetus
> Crux, forma penitentie,
> gratie
> clavis, clava peccati, venie
> vena, radix ligni iusticie,
> via vite, vexillum glorie,
> sponsi lectus in meridie,
> lux plenarie
> nubem luens tristicie,

> serenum conscientie:
> Hanc homo portet,
> hanc se confortet,
> crucem oportet,
> si vis lucis vere
> gaudia sustinere.

> The Cross, shape of penance, key of grace, staff of sin, vein of pardon, root of the tree of justice, path of life, banner of glory, the Bridegroom's bed at midday, light that totally dispels the cloud of sadness, the bright sky of conscience—let mankind carry it, comfort itself with it. You must bear the Cross, if you desire the joys of the true light.

The encounter of a male protagonist and a sorrowful maiden is typical of the pastourelle; it is natural that the girl in question should be a shepherdess. As in previous examples, the world of the pastourelle is available for appropriation: as wish fulfillment, fantasy, entertainment, or allegory. Robin and Marion are quintessentially literary, stock figures with whom the French medieval audience was extremely familiar. Because their behavior is so predictable and so well known, they can readily become the basis for allegory, much like other stock figures—for example, those of the bestiary—whose salient features and allegorical significance are well established. Because part of Robin's standard identity is that of the anxiously sought, eagerly awaited lover, he can become an allegorical representation of Christ as Heavenly Bridegroom; because it is part of Marion's character to grieve for her absent lover, she can become a figure for Mary Magdelene, the Virgin, or Ecclesia, weeping over the crucified Christ or longing for his return.

Through its allegorical use of the pastourelle text, the motet presents the two sides of the Passion: human grief at the death of Christ and the (seeming) loss of the Beloved; the joyous transformation, in light of the Resurrection, of the instrument of death, bereavement, and pain into one of life, redemption, and glory. The dual aspect of the Passion is stated at the center of the motet, where two key phrases are sung simultaneously: "Robin, douz amis, perdu vos ai" (Robin, my sweet beloved, I have lost you) (triplum, line 7) and the characterization of the Cross as "Sponsi lectus in meridie" (Bridegroom's bed at midday) (motetus, line 6). Thus while the more limited human perspective of the triplum experiences the Crucifixion as bereavement, the theologically informed perspective of the motetus recognizes it as the moment in which the mystical marriage of Christ and his Church is consummated. Following this initial statement of the paradox of the Crucifixion, the opposing emotions unroll in tandem: the shepherdess's statement of "grant douleur" (great grief) (triplum, line 9) is sung against the characterization of the Cross as "Nubem luens tristicie" (dispelling the cloud of sadness) (motetus, line 8), and the narrator's unsuccessful efforts to comfort the sorrowful girl parallel the consolation and joy afforded by the Cross.

The polytextual format of the motet here allows for the intersection of two very different genres: the Latin hymn to the Cross, grounded in liturgical poetry and in theological doctrine, and the vernacular pastourelle, with its emphasis on the beauties of the natural world, on human emotion and erotic desire. The assemblage of attributes and allegorical figures that makes up the motetus is a conventional technique in Latin devotional poetry. There is no narrative and little integrated development, but rather a list of independent terms, each of which expresses an aspect of Christian doctrine regarding the Cross as an instrument of penance and redemption. The Cross is evoked in general terms in the first half of the piece, as a source of grace, life, justice; at the center is the figure of the marriage bed, a vivid reminder of the individual soul's access to the blessings that the Cross bestows; and the second half expands on the salvific effects available to those who submit to bearing the Cross. The triplum, on the other hand, presents an integrated narrative constructed out of familiar literary elements. The Passion is naturalized, vernacularized in the fullest possible sense of the word. In one sense, the two texts could not be more different. And yet they work closely together within the motet. The French triplum deepens the pathos of the Crucifixion as a human event of pain, loss, and incomprehension; the Latin motetus provides the all-important perspective that allows us to transcend the limited understanding of the shepherdess, moving from grief to joy.

The tenor, finally, invokes the conflation of grief and joy through its liturgical associations. The Alleluia from which it derives refers to the Instruments of the Passion: "Alleluia. Dulce lignum, dulces claves, dulcia ferens pondera, quae sola fuisti digna sustinere regem caelorum et Dominum" (Alleluia. Sweet wood, sweet nails, bearing the sweet weight, you alone were worthy of bearing the Lord, king of Heaven). The repetition of the word "sweet" reminds us that the Crucifixion, though bitterly painful, was ultimately the cause for the greatest rejoicing the world has ever known: the redemption of humankind. The motet as a whole captures perfectly the two perspectives that inform Christian meditation on the Cross.

❖

The pastourelle, which gives voice to female as well as male personae and which commonly presents both the separation and the reunion of lovers, the fulfillment of desire as well as the anxiety of absence, is fertile ground for the playful and suggestive allegorization that we have witnessed in the examples discussed above. It also provides a useful foil for the courtly discourse of the *chanson courtoise* tradition and readily lends itself to the contextualization, parody, or critique of the courtly lyric voice. Indeed, the encounter between the rustic figures of the pastoral world and the courtly narrator-protagonist is a well-established feature of the pastourelle. Finally, the pastourelle has always included a strong narrative element. The pastoral world is peopled with stock figures endowed with stereotypical rustic names and highly predictable in their behavior, attitudes, and relationships with one another and with the courtly persona who visits their world. With its standard narratives of revelry, rivalry, and desire, its witty, fast-paced dialogues, and its representation of shifting and sometimes conflicting emotions, the pastourelle has a dramatic quality that lends itself to the proliferation of voices, perspectives, and scenarios—and ultimately of different levels of meaning—typical of the vernacular or bilingual motet.

The phenomena that I have outlined are not entirely unique to the motet. The various lyric genres can also be brought into dialogue through the use of lyric insertions within a narrative frame; and the language and imagery of the pastourelle, as well as other lyric forms, can be transposed into a spiritual register through the composition of pious contrafacta, many of which retain a fairly substantial portion of the original text. The rise of vernacular drama also allowed new possibilities for the expansion and recombination of lyric models, as in the example of the *Jeu de Robin et Marion*.[18] But the simultaneity as well as the diversity of texts within the motet allows for particularly focused intertextual and intergeneric dialogue. Unlike a pious contrafactum, for example, the motet retains the secular text intact; instead of rewriting it, the motet composer simply embeds the text in a context that invests it with possible new meanings. Whereas the Latin motet tropes the chant and offers an expansion or commentary on it, the French motet expands on the vernacular lyric repertoire, exploring its dramatic potential, exploiting its points of contact with devotional models, and allowing the different lyric genres to comment on one another. Though more condensed and more tightly focused than a lyric-based play like the *Jeu de Robin et Marion* or a romance with lyric insertions, the motet can be categorized with such works as an example of thirteenth-century experimentation with the multiple forms of vernacular lyric.

NOTES

My ongoing study of thirteenth-century French motets has been funded by the George A. and Eliza Gardner Howard Foundation and by faculty research grants from Northern Illinois University, which I gratefully acknowledge.

1. Pierre Bec, "Genres et registres dans la lyrique médiévale des XIIe et XIIIe siècles: Essai de classement typologique," *Revue de linguistique romane* 38 (1974): 26–39.

2. Many critics have remarked on Adam's use of the pastourelle in a theatrical format. Paul Zumthor describes it as the dramatization not of a specific text but rather of the genre itself—"un montage opéré à partir du texte virtuel constitué par la tradition des pastourelles"—in *Essai de poétique médiévale* (Paris: Seuil, 1972), 446. Kevin Brownlee discusses the presence of the pastourelle in Adam's play in "Transformations of the Couple: Genre and Language in the *Jeu de Robin et Marion*," *French Forum* 14 (1989): 419–33. See also Ernest Langlois's remarks in the introduction to his edition of Adam le Bossu, *Le Jeu de Robin et Marion suivi du Jeu du pèlerin*, Classiques Français du Moyen Age, vol. 36 (Paris: Champion, 1965).

3. Christopher Page has argued against an intellectualizing interpretation of thirteenth-century French motets, asserting that they were intended as festive entertainment and not as texts for critical analysis; see, for example, his discussion in *Discarding Images: Reflections on Music and Culture in Medieval France* (Oxford: Clarendon Press, 1993), 46–85. To my mind, however, there is no conflict between the musical and phonic appeal of the motet and its quality of self-conscious textual play. Page does characterize the vernacular motet as "both playful and learned at the same time" in "The Performance of Ars Antiqua Motets," *Early Music* 16 (1988), 149. I have argued for the sophisticated literariness of the vernacular motet in *Allegorical Play in the Old French Motet: The Sacred and the Profane in Thirteenth-Century Polyphony* (Stanford: Stanford University Press, 1997); included therein are analyses of many of the motets discussed in the present study.

4. Donald Maddox and Sara Sturm-Maddox, "*Genre* and *Intergenre* in Medieval French Literature," *L'Esprit Créateur* 33, no. 4 (1993): 6.

5. Ibid.

6. For a concise discussion of the rise of the motet, see Jeremy Yudkin, *Music in Medieval Europe* (Englewood Cliffs, N.J.: Prentice Hall, 1989), 357–431. For fuller treatments, see Hans Tischler, *The Style and Evolution of the Earliest Motets (to circa 1270)*, Musicological Studies 40 (Henryville: Institute of Mediaeval Music, 1985); and Mark Everist, *French Motets in the Thirteenth Century: Music, Poetry, and Genre* (Cambridge: Cambridge University Press, 1994). For a convenient catalogue of motets, identifying French and Latin contrafacta and listing all French and Latin motets composed for each known tenor, see Hendrik Van der Werf, *Integrated Directory of Organa, Clausulae, and Motets of the Thirteenth Century* (Rochester, N.Y.: published by the author, 1989).

7. For an overview of the general development of the medieval pastourelle, see the following studies and editions: Karl Bartsch, ed., *Romances et pastourelles françaises des XIIe et XIIIe siècles: Altfranzösische Romanzen und Pastourellen* (Leipzig: Vogel, 1870); Maurice Delbouille, *Les origines de la pastourelle* (Brussels: Lamertin, 1927); Michel

Zink, *La pastourelle: poésie et folklore au moyen âge* (Paris: Bordas, 1972); William D. Paden, ed. and trans., *The Medieval Pastourelle* (New York: Garland, 1987).

8. Works derived from liturgy are identified by reference to the listing of Mass (M) or Office (O) numbers in Friedrich Ludwig, *Repertorium organorum recentioris et motetorum vetustissimi stili* (Langen bei Frankfurt: n.p., 1961–62); motet tenors are given the numbers assigned in Friedrich Gennrich, *Bibliographie der ältesten lateinischen und französischen Motetten* (Darmstadt: n.p., 1957). For the first motet listed, I cite Gordon A. Anderson, ed., *Compositions of the Bamberg Manuscript*, with translations by Robyn E. Smith, Corpus Mensurabilis Musicae, vol. 75 (New York: American Institute of Musicology, 1977), no. 41; the translation is mine, as no translation for this particular piece appears in Anderson and Smith's edition. For the second, I cite both text and translation from Hans Tischler, ed., *Motets of the Montpellier Codex*, with translations by Susan Stakel and Joel C. Relihan, Recent Researches in the Music of the Middle Ages and Early Renaissance, vols. 2–8 (Madison: A-R Editions, 1978), no. 95. The first also survives in a four-part version, published by Tischler (*Motets of the Montpellier Codex*, no. 22); in the additional voice the shepherd replies and insists that he too is an ardent and worthy lover. Throughout this essay, italicized passages in motet texts have been italicized by the editor, in indication that the words constitute a known refrain.

9. I cite text and translation from Tischler, *Motets of the Montpellier Codex*, no. 269.

10. The same effect is created in "Par un matinet" (295) / "Lés un bosket" (296) / PORTARE (M22) (ibid., no. 259).

11. I cite text and translation from Anderson, *Compositions of the Bamberg Manuscript*, no. 12.

12. The tenor derives from the Easter gradual *Hec dies. Confitemini Domino*, the text of which derives in turn from Psalm 118 (Vulgate 117). Here and elsewhere, I quote tenor sources from Tischler, *Style and Evolution of the Earliest Motets*. All translations of tenors and their sources are mine.

13. I cite text and translation from Tischler, *Montpellier Codex*, no. 241.

14. Mass and Vespers responsory for Tuesday of Easter week. It was also used for the feast of Mary Magdelene. The text is from Matthew 28:9. The women in question are Mary Magdelene and another Mary.

15. Hans Tischler, ed., *The Earliest Motets (to circa 1270): A Complete Comparative Edition* (New Haven: Yale University Press, 1982), no. 325. Translation mine.

16. In Matthew 28:7, the words are addressed to Mary Magdelene and the other Mary; in Mark 16:7, to Mary Magdelene and two other women. The angel's words recall Christ's own statement to his disciples in Gethsemane, just before his arrest (Matthew 26:32).

17. I cite text and translation from Tischler, *Montpellier Codex*, no. 41.

18. I have analyzed Adam de la Halle's transformation of lyric discourse in selected motets and in the *Jeu de la Feuillée*—though without specific reference to the pastourelle—in "Transformations of Lyric Voice in the Songs, Motets, and Plays of Adam de la Halle," *Romanic Review* 78 (1987): 148–64.

PART 4

Questioning Genre

❖ CHAPTER 13

"The Fire of Love Poetry Has Kissed Me, How Can I Resist?" The Hebrew Lyric in Perspective

ROSS BRANN

Precious little mystery surrounds the origins of medieval Hebrew lyric poetry. Even for readers distrustful of positivistic approaches to literary history it is nearly possible to pinpoint when, where, and how the Hebrew lyric first emerged, under what circumstances and subject to what influences.[1] More than a century before the appearance of the songs of Duke William IX of Aquitaine (1071–1126), members of the Andalusian Jewish elite set about producing and consuming Hebrew verse by appropriating the form, structure, themes, and rhetorical style of the culturally prestigious Arabic model. Poetic tradition for the Hebrew poets thus initially was embodied in a preexistent canon—the mono-rhymed Arabic poetry that functioned as the ultimate arbiter of Hebrew verse.

What exactly did Hebrew poetry in tenth-century al-Andalus inherit from Arabic in the way of lyric genres? Arabic critics largely held to the view that all poetry was derived from the rhetorical categories of praise and blame, corresponding to the Arabic themes *madh* and *hija'*.[2] In practice distinct lyric genres such as wine poetry (*khamriyya*), love poetry (*ghazal*), and lyrical complaint (*tazallum*) had long since evolved from brief thematic exercises called *qit'at,* and were reshaped and recast in the Muslim East during the ʿAbbasid age when Arabic poetry began to reflect the new urban environment of Islamic civilization.[3] The conventions for these occasional poems, "set pieces from a rather small inventory of themes," as Andras Hamori has called them,[4] were also derived from thematic blocks in the classical mono-rhymed *qasida* (ode) whose traditions are presumed to be the product of the pre-Islamic Arabian peninsula. In Arabic, then, an intergeneric mix in the form of the classical ode accompanied the development of distinct lyric genres. For its part, Hebrew poetry in Muslim Spain, its genres and their conventions, arose out of the dialectical relationship between a well-established yet still evolving Arabic tradition on the one hand and an emergent Jewish subcultural process on the other.

In order to understand some of the problems associated with the study of medieval Hebrew lyric genres, let us begin with testimony contemporary to the production of the poetry. The critic Moses ibn Ezra (c. 1055–c. 1135) refers to genres and verse-forms in *Kitab al-muhadara wa-l-mudhakara* (*The Book of Conversation and Discussion*),[5] one of two surviving Judeo-Arabic works he wrote on poetics and literary criticism. Yet Ibn Ezra does not bother to discuss genres at any length, presumably because they were self-evident categories of composition, each with its own structure, register, and formulation of themes, voices, and styles. Poetic tradition in the form of textual parodies also testifies to the recognition of genres and their conventions. A poem by Todros Abulafia (b. 1247), a devotee of Arabic culture and the Andalusian style who was active at the court of Alfonso el Sabio, begins a *qasida* (on which see below) with a long parody of a conventional passage in the Hebrew ode:

> Many [poets] sing only erotic verse
>   but dissipate their virility in desire.
> Another is always talking about wandering
>   and claiming he's ensnared,
> That he moans by day without respite
>   and tracks the stars by night. . . .
> Another swears his heart and soul
>   are hopelessly in tow to a beauty.
> He claims that a beauty stole his heart,
>   when he's actually pierced in the testicles![6]

Really a meta-ode on how to compose (or not compose) a poem, the parody naturally presupposes the existence of the genre and the reception of its thematic conventions.

Poetic genres also seem to have been recognized as an organizing principle in the transmission of a poet's literary corpus or *diwan*. For example the poetry of Samuel the Nagid (993–1056), one of two preeminent Hebrew poets of the mid-eleventh century and the highest fiscal and administrative officer of Granada from 1038 to 1056, was edited by his sons in three collections, roughly according to genre: *Ben Mishlei* (*The Little Book* of Proverbs; gnomic verse); *Ben Qohelet* (*The Little Book of Ecclesiastes;* reflective and meditative poems); and *Ben T^ehillim* (*The Little Book of Psalms*). The contents of *Ben T^ehillim* are varied and difficult to classify by genre but include many poems of an occasional and lyrical nature.[7] Notable among them are the Nagid's forty-one "war poems," idiosyncratic lyrics representing Samuel's forays into the world of Andalusian politics and his apparent involvement with the army of Zirid Granada on some twenty military expeditions.[8] Moses ibn Ezra, a poet absorbed by the Arabic literary tradition, also composed a book of *tajnis* (wordplay on homonyms and near-homonyms), each of whose ten chapters is devoted to epigrammatic rhetorical exercises within one of the distinct poetic genres Hebrew assimilated from Arabic.[9]

The question of genre in medieval Hebrew verse is further attested and complicated by the medieval editors' textual notes. The scribes who transmitted the poets' *diwans* often added Arabic superscriptions identifying the poem's "central theme," such as praise, love, or wine. Frequently the glosses of the manuscript tradition convey additional literary information or biographical data deemed relevant to the text. Until very recently readers of medieval Hebrew poetry were content to follow these textual notations as authoritative when it came to questions of genre, presumably on the assumption that historical proximity to textual production confers authenticity. The implications of this presupposition were obviously far-reaching, because for most readers, as E. D. Hirsch noted, "all understanding of verbal meaning is necessarily genre-bound."[10] The copyists' notes thus supplied the basis for seemingly "authoritative readings" of the lyrics.

Consider the Hebrew *qasida,* the mono-rhymed ode composed for recitation among the courtly class. Like the Arabic neo-*qasida* from which it is derived, the Hebrew *qasida* is more a verse-form than a genre. The *qasida* forms a continuous sequence of lines governed by a single meter and end-rhyme which are carried without variation through every line of verse. In terms of theme it typically consists of a panegyric dedicated to the poet's patron, yet more often than not the so-called panegyrical core of the poem is introduced by what the Arabs referred to as an "amatory prelude" (*nasib*). These introductory mood-pieces (which can be brief or go on for ten lines or more) do not differ significantly from the typically brief lyrics of, say, an independent wine song, love poem, song about the garden in spring, or lyrical complaint. One of Samuel the Nagid's longer wine songs that has come down to us in *Ben T^ehillim* incorporates verses transmitted as two independent compositions in *Ben Qohelet*.[11] The same can be said for one of his dirges, a war poem, and a panegyric respectively, as well as other poems preserved in *Ben T'hillim*.[12] Nevertheless, the aforementioned superscriptions to medieval Hebrew poems frequently identify the composite *qasida* with its panegyrical unit, ignoring as it were the often complex interplay between the poem's various thematic elements.[13] How odd it is to read of the irresistible charms of a merciless beauty whose daggerlike eyes and spearlike breasts skewer the poet, only to be told that the lyric is a poem of praise for the patron. For example, the introductory passage (lines 1–11) of a famous *qasida* by Joseph ibn Hisdai (eleventh century) relates a desperate, albeit conventional, seductive fantasy:

> And as he slept I plucked, with his consent,
>   that which he angrily refuses me when awake.
> With the hand of sweet sleep,
>   he gave me the nectar of his mouth to drink in ruby bowls.
> I lay down, and on my breast were locks
>   flowing with myrrh over blushing cheeks.
> My right hand embraced the white moon,
>   my lips kissed the warm sun.[14]

The superscription as well as Ibn Ezra's comments on the poem in *Kitab al-muhadara* are attuned to the laudatory sequence of lines 12–33 and present the poem as a panegyric for the renowned courtier, communal leader, poet, and rabbinical scholar Samuel the Nagid, to whom the lyric is addressed.[15]

A dazzling forty-four-line poem by Solomon ibn Gabirol (c. 1020–c. 1057) presents a different type of Andalusian fantasy and nearly the opposite problem of genre classification. Reminiscent of Keats's famous "The Eve of Saint Agnes," Ibn Gabirol's lyric—something of a descriptive floral poem in the Arabic tradition—invites us (lines 1–33a) into an exquisite palace and its resplendent courtyard garden, whose perfect opulence and lush setting are vividly rendered:

> Ah, come, my radiant friend, along with me,
> Let's lodge us in the villages. For see,
> The winter's past, and now on every hand
> We hear the voice of turtles in our land.
> We'll linger in the shade and take our ease
> Neath pomegranates, palms and apple trees;
> We'll stroll amid the vines, and peer to see
> The gentle folk who live in luxury
> Within a palace set upon a height,
> Built of finest stones, a splendid sight,
> On strong foundations firmly fixed, and bound
> With fortress-walls and turrets all around,

> With level galleries above, which show
> The fine display of courtyards far below.[16]

Appearances can be as deceiving as genre classifications. Despite the imposing nature of the structure delineated, the otherwise static palace is brought to life by the vibrant activity in the garden which is in turn abruptly frozen at the poet's command. The poet-observer fancies himself in complete control of the scene and thus the poem (lines 25–27, 31–34):

> And singing birds are glimpsed among the bowers
>   And in the beds below are fragrant flowers,
> As spikenards, roses, henna-plants and balms,
>   Which vie each with the rest to vaunt their charms, . . .
> Then up there rise the pretty boys and maids
>   Whose glory all the others overshades,
> And they too vie their splendors to disclose,
>   For they resemble young gazelles or roes.
> But as the sun began to sing their praise
>   I answered: "Silence, sun, deflect your rays,
> And praise instead the man who, with his light
>   Has darkened you and hidden you from sight."

The poet's immediate purpose is to enchant the listener by representing an ideal setting until he sings the required praises of his patron (lines 34–44). In this instance the textual superscription does not essentialize the patron-poet relationship in the production of poetry by focusing the reader's attention on the poem-concluding panegyric. Rather it offers a note of literary criticism having to do with the extended "lyrical prelude" and its centrality to the text: "The poem is called 'The Garden'; it is among his most exceptional lyrics." The limited usefulness of generic designations is also apparent in the tendency of the themes of the garden, wine, and love to be treated together. Furthermore most composite poems simply defy simple classification whatever the textual tradition may say. Moses ibn Ezra refers to an exceptional sixty-two-line epistolary *qasida* dedicated to a friend (according to the superscription) as a "wine song" (Arabic *khamriyya*).[17] The "wine song" actually serves as the poem's so-called prelude (lines 1–39) and is followed by a lyrical complaint (lines 40–62).

If Judeo-Arabic poetics and the textual tradition purport to identify and classify some Hebrew poems according to genre, how has criticism approached the question of genres? A major problem posed in any discussion of Hebrew genres is the distinction between the synchronic and diachronic approaches used to study and define them. Dan Pagis remarked that "[Hebrew] genres were an obvious but not strictly defined element in the poetic tradition; though often mentioned in poetical treatises, they were never imposed as strictly normative categories" in poetic practice.[18] Nevertheless Pagis attempted to make sense of medieval Hebrew poetry precisely by establishing rules for reading it. To that end he undertook an exhaustive inductive analysis of the structure, tone, attitude, and imagery in the poetry of Moses ibn Ezra, arguably the most conservative Hebrew poet of Muslim Spain.[19] In the most detailed study of the normative poetics of the school (a manifestly structuralist project as defined by Adena Rosmarin),[20] Pagis demonstrated that genres such as panegyric, lament, love poetry, and wine songs were stylized in form and conventional in content and tended to represent a static, idealized, and impersonal literary universe. Even occasional poems such as lyrical complaints (in which the poet laments his fate and vents feelings of grief and loss at his separation from family and friends), while open to a somewhat greater degree of self-expression, were also inclined to formulaic expression of conventional themes. Since they "implied a well-understood code" poets shared with their audience, what Todorov called recurrent, institutionalized "discursive properties,"[21] Pagis concluded that genre conventions served as the ultimate source of meaning in the production and reception of Hebrew verse.

Building upon Pagis's basic approach, Israel Levin too sought to elucidate the generic norms of medieval Hebrew verse, particularly in the comparative light of its Arabic models.[22] Somewhat more open to diachronic methods of research than Pagis in his early work, Levin also endeavored to describe in detail the characteristics of each genre and to utilize the results—his constructions of genre—as the standard for reading and evaluating individual poems. Levin adopted a somewhat more flexible view of the salient power of genre conventions in the production of Hebrew verse, perhaps because he drew upon texts composed by all the major figures of the school as well as their successors in twelfth- and thirteenth-century Christian Spain, rather than the oeuvre of a single poet.

Because they broke new ground in defining the formal and stylistic limitations imposed by poetic tradition upon the Hebrew poets of Spain, Pagis and Levin catalyzed new thinking about the complex relationship between individual creativity and poetic tradition in the making of Hebrew poetry. Subsequently readers of medieval Hebrew verse (including Pagis himself) sought to identify what was original in the work of inventive and imaginative poets by analyzing the ways in which they transcended the rules of their craft, transformed its stylistic prescriptions, and varied the formulation of traditional themes. Research in the field came to focus on aspects of the poets' "poetic experience," individuality, and originality, and the means by which they achieved distinctive expression while still observing the requirements of rhetorical style and working within the system of thematic and genre conventions. Raymond Scheindlin, for example, adopted a fresh approach to independent Hebrew wine and love poems. Examining the modality of their treatment of subject matter, Scheindlin views Hebrew lyric poetry as made up of a combination of descriptive, affective, and petitionary elements.[23] This insight proves to be especially significant in that it permits the reader to notice the ways in which Hebrew love songs function as dramatic monologues: they project a purely external image of the figure of the beloved, depict the poet/lover's anguished internal state, and frequently convey the poet's petition to the beloved. Integrating literary-critical readings of the texts with observations of a literary-historical nature, Scheindlin has focused attention on the interplay between conventional and unorthodox elements in the Hebrew lyric (the project that came to occupy both Pagis and Levin), and, most importantly, has situated the poems in historical relation to the cultural system they represent.

To illustrate the limitations of the formalist approach to genre studies, consider the distinctive tone and attitude evident in the following example from the love poetry of Solomon ibn Gabirol:

> Like Amnon sick am I, so call Tamar
>   And tell her one who loves her is snared by death.
> Quick, friends, companions, bring her here to me.
>   The only thing I ask of you is this:
> Adorn her head with jewels, bedeck her well,
>   And send along with a her a cup of wine.
> If she would pour for me she might put out
>   The burning pain wasting my throbbing flesh.[24]

As treated by Raymond Scheindlin, this distinctively Gabirolian lyric represents the realization of some of the darker impulses implicit in the conventional lyrics of love.[25] Yet Ibn Gabirol in effect reinvented the Hebrew love lyric by taking the full measure of its characteristic despair to the logical extreme and embracing suffering. Devotional lyrics by Judah ha-Levi that confront the breach between God and Israel provide an interesting parallel, since they too push a lyric theme to its absolute limit, as well as being a sign of the interpenetration of the secular love lyric and religious poetry. Like Ibn Gabirol's forlorn lover, the liturgical poet (speaking on behalf of Israel or as Israel personified) revels in abasement and represents his suffering as the ultimate sign of his love for God.[26] In the hands of many readers such exceptional variations on a theme as are evident in Ibn Gabirol and ha-Levi are more likely to be treated as departures from convention, as anomalous cases rather than as variations, end points on the continuum of lyrics governed by genre conventions. Similarly, structuralist methods do not sufficiently distinguish between love poetry of the conventional variety and the lyrics of spiritual love. Nor do they account for Moses ibn Ezra's mention of the idea of the latter during the eleventh century ("the soul's love for another soul, not the body's love for another body")[27] or its subsequent development in lyrics by Todros Abulafia in the thirteenth ("In my desire for her I do not want the pleasure of the body, Only the pleasure of the spirit").[28]

As Pagis's research turned to the literary history of medieval Hebrew poetry from Muslim Spain to Renaissance and Baroque Italy he came to appreciate more clearly the individuality of the Hebrew poets as opposed to their strict observance of rigid conventions.[29] This growing awareness necessarily reshaped his approach to genre. In what amounted to a major revision of his views on the overriding significance of genre conventions, Pagis noted that "it is not true that all of medieval poetry was impersonal stylization. Some genres were impersonal, even universal; others were emphatically personal, intended to be taken as self-expression and providing real and specific details. It is not just a question of themes but of genres."[30] Such reconsiderations have yielded more nuanced views of the production of Hebrew verse. They have shown that the poets' inventive treatment of conventional subject matter, novel formulations of traditional motifs, recasting of stock figures, and innovative use of rhetorical devices were no less dependent upon stylistic requirements and the system of genre conventions as conventional exercises and highly stylized formulations themselves. As Adena Rosmarin observes: "Genre, in other words, is a finite schema capable of potentially infinite suggestion."[31]

In general, then, the mono-rhymed Hebrew lyric, whether brief and independent or as a passage within the composite *qasida,* can be said to rest upon a set of delicate balances between formulaic and expressive lyrics, on one hand, and on the other, between representation of communal (that is, class) ideals and values and individual self-expression. Viewed in historical perspective, the tension between poetic tradition and literary creativity acted as a destabilizing force upon genre conventions and by extension upon the genres themselves.

In emphasizing the problematic aspects of structuralist discourse on genres and the significance of their conventions for mono-rhymed verse, I do not mean to give the impression that literary-critical and literary-historical study of the medieval Hebrew lyric has been without its difficulties or conflicts. On the contrary, how to give a contextually valid reading of secular Hebrew love songs has been among the most contested areas of scholarly discussion on medieval Hebrew letters. I am referring to the controversy over the figure of the beloved when the object of the poet's amorous intentions is a male (as in the poem by Joseph ibn Hisdai noted above). In this context it is worth recalling Paul Zumthor's keen articulation of the problem of reading medieval texts: "The ultimate term we aim for is really to bring the ancient text into the present, that is, to integrate it into that historicity which is ours. The pitfall is that in doing so we may deny or obscure its own historicity: we may foreshorten the historical perspective and, by giving an achronic shape to the past, hide the specific traits of the present."[32] Indeed, the rancorous polemics of two generations ago over the question of the male beloved in the Hebrew lyric seemed to have subsided only to resurface in recent Israeli scholarship with new extraliterary issues at stake.[33] Nevertheless it is now largely accepted that the prevalence of lyrics such as Ibn Hisdai's and Ibn Ghiyath's (see below) cannot be explained away as slavish imitation of Arabic literary style and taste. It is increasingly understood that the medieval Hebrew lyric attaches no particular importance to the beloved's gender and that love poetry signals the poets' (and their audience's) ritual appreciation of every manner of beauty.[34] The dispute over whether the lyrics of love actually set in relief the poets' social and sexual practice has recently given way to another discussion contingent upon historical concerns: the representation of women in medieval Hebrew literature.[35]

This observation brings us to the sole Hebrew lyric verse-form in which women are regularly permitted to speak. Here are several lines from a strophic poem by Todros Abulafia, who lived in thirteenth-century Christian Spain, in which a young woman is the object of the poet's affection. Notice that the etiquette of love poetry requires that the beloved be utterly cruel and the lover completely frustrated. The poet can demonstrate that he is truly a lover only if his anguish is absolute and he is prepared to sacrifice everything for love:

> Fire flows from my heart and a river from my eyes;
> there is a hell in my heart, but my eyes are like seas.
> My tears are pure, yet red as blood.
> Parting has set my bones on fire and mixed my tears with my heart's blood.

> They were purified in the crucible of anguish and leaped to my eyes
> as my heat rose.
> She burnt my heart, and there was no one who could help me.
> I said: "How can you, in the fire of your fury,
> Burn my heart that has always been your footstool?"
> To which she answered: "What concern is it of yours if I burn my own
> footstool?
> Sing out, my heart; rejoice as I burn it in my rage!"
> O come, my lovely doe, if only in a dream.
> Give yourself to me, if only in sweet speech.
> Even a few words would put out the flaming furnace within me.[36]

The reader must take care not to be misled by the figure of a young woman seemingly so empowered as to hold the poet's life in the balance. She is a woman as imagined by men, an ideal and objectified figure whose frequent appearance in Hebrew love poetry underscores the fact that real women were denied much of any voice in Hispano-Jewish society and were altogether silent in its literature.

Abulafia's poem offers an illustration of the *muwashshah* ("girdle poem"), the most important lyric verse-form Hebrew derived from the Arabic and the outstanding manifestation of lyrical sensibility among the Hebrew poets of Spain. Alongside the well-developed tradition of lyric genres (i.e., love and wine songs, floral poetry, and lyrical complaint) attested in monorhymed Hebrew verse as short poems or as passages in the composite *qasida*, the *muwashshah* was a strophic poem sung to musical accompaniment. Generally devoted to the theme of love but not infrequently to panegyric or their composite (with the panegyric introduced by an "amatory prelude" as in the *qasida*), the Hebrew incarnation of this verse form appeared during the eleventh century, apparently some one hundred years after the Arabic (c. 900). The Hebrew *muwashshah* flourished during the twelfth and thirteenth centuries, when Judah ha-Levi and Todros Abulafia each composed some fifty strophic songs that have come down to us.

Since publication of S. M. Stern's work on Romance *kharjat* preserved in Arabic and Hebrew script (1948, revised in 1953),[37] scholars have been preoccupied with demonstrating either the Arabic or Romance cultural provenance of the lyric verse-form. Claims put forward regarding the origins of the *muwashshah* and *kharja* and their metrical, linguistic, and sociocultural relationship have in fact rendered the *muwashshah* the most contested subject in all of Hispano-Arabic literature.[38] Remarkably, the literary form that seems to textualize the linguistic, musical, cultural, and social interaction among confessional communities on the western frontier of Islam and Europe is more often than not treated as evidence of the cultural hegemony of one Iberian community over another, rather than as testimony to their convergence. Readers of the Hebrew *muwashshah* have been far less concerned with the questions of genesis and cultural ascendancy than their Romanist or Arabist colleagues. They are unencumbered by these particular considerations because the Hebrew *muwashshah*, like all of the secular Hebrew poetry of Spain, was clearly predicated on an Arabic model. Recent work on the Hebrew *muwashshah* has suggested new strategies for rendering it intelligible. Combining structuralist methods with literary-historical and literary-critical analysis, Tova Rosen studies elements such as esthetic structure and style (e.g., strophic love songs may be descriptive, dramatic, and narrative) and examines how the *muwashshah* works as a lyric poem (e.g., how formulaic diction governs the thematic relationship between the penultimate strophe and the *kharja*).[39]

Because its prosody, form, and structure set it apart from the classicizing mono-rhymed poem transmitted in the poets' *diwans*, the Hebrew *muwashshah* was preserved in its own collections of verse. It employed the same quantitative meters as the mono-rhymed poem but frequently did so in an irregular fashion not in accordance with the strict canons of quantitative prosody or in syllabic meters. The *muwashshah*'s distinctive rhythms were further influenced by the tune to which the song was sung and undoubtedly by Romance stress-syllabic versification. One of the *muwashshah*'s two alternating rhymes (Arabic *ghusn*, the rhyme of the first part of each strophe) varies from strophe to strophe (usually five in the Hebrew); the second rhyme (Arabic *qufl*, that of the last part of each strophe) remains fixed throughout the poem (e.g., *aaabb, cccbb, dddbb*). Aside from its complex rhyme schemes and unusual metrical patterns, the distinctive feature of the *muwashshah* is its striking *kharja* ("exit" or envoi). The *kharja* of an Arabic *muwashshah* (frequently in the form of a quotation from a popular Mozarabic or Hispano-Arabic song) was composed in a colloquial language, either in the Arabic dialect of Muslim Spain or in Hispano-Romance. Hebrew *muwashshahat* conclude with either a Hebrew *kharja* (in the classicizing language since there was no vernacular) or with a Hispano-Arabic or Mozarabic *kharja* in Hebrew script. Underscoring the significance of form and structure in the production of strophic poetry, families of Hebrew *muwashshahat* are related by the widespread practice of *muʿarada* (contrafaction)—the deliberate imitation of the prosodic elements, tune, and *kharja* of another, usually well-known strophic composition. According to this tradition the incipit (*matlaʿ*) of a popular Arabic or Hebrew song might also serve as the concluding *kharja* for other *muwashshahat* in the family.

To move from formal considerations to thematic criteria and genres: the

Hebrew *muwashshah* presents a rather complicated picture. The formal and textual linkages we have noted among *muwashshahat* readily stretched across the generic boundary between love songs and panegyric, and bridged secular love lyrics and allegorical, devotional love poems. It should be noted that the latter transaction was considerably eased because all Hebrew love poetry, secular and religious alike, shared diction and imagery drawn from the biblical Song of Songs. Hebrew poets from the time of Solomon ibn Gabirol and Isaac ibn Ghiyath (1038–89) also utilized the form and structure of the *muwashshah* in devotional lyrics written for recitation by the precentor during the synagogue service. The corpus of liturgical *muwashshahat* further includes many compositions produced in direct imitation of Arabic and Hebrew love songs, indicating that worshipers were exposed to the secular music and textual associations of secular *muwashshahat* during the synagogue service.[40] Hispano-Arabic and Mozarabic *kharjas* were excluded from liturgical *muwashshahat*. But secular Hebrew *kharjat* in the form of piquant lines uttered by a young girl in the throes of love (a speaker new to the Hebrew lyric), or by the persona of the lover, seem to have found their way into liturgical poems. A *muwashshah* ascribed to Judah ha-Levi, for example, beginning and ending: "Come my love, come to the house of the nobleman's daughter, we will delight in love,"[41] bears an acrostic of the poet's name, a sign of its religious and allegorical character.[42] In this new context the *kharjat* served as the speech of figures involved in a fundamentally different kind of love affair, that between Catholic Israel and God, or between God and the individual soul.[43] On the one hand, these developments can be attributed to the prevalence of strophic verse forms in the traditional liturgical verse that the Hebrew poets of Spain inherited from the Muslim East; on the other hand, they parallel the tradition of penitential *muwashshahat* on religious themes developed by Arabic poets.[44]

In a secondary development unique to Hebrew, secular strophic love songs seem to have influenced the emergence of strophic epithalamia. In these compositions the form, structure, themes, and imagery of secular *muwashshahat* are absorbed by and recast in the lyrics sung at weddings, a sacred occasion with important textual links to the liturgy of the synagogue. A strophic epithalamium by Judah ibn Ghiyath (turn of the eleventh and twelfth centuries) exemplifies the fluid intergeneric production of the Hebrew *muwashshah*. The first two strophes of "Revive me with the wine of my fawn's lips"[45] detail the poet's failed efforts to be passionately kissed by his (male) beloved (lines 1–14). He proclaims that his lovesickness knows no cure and that he is prepared to die for love. In the third strophe the poet abruptly admonishes himself, uttering the rhetorical formula: "Drop the subject of love and start praising the paragon, Joseph!" (lines 15–16).

This figure is thus duly regaled in the third and fourth strophes (lines 15–26). When, in the fifth strophe (lines 27–32), the poet urges Joseph to rejoice on his wedding day, the lyric shifts to the theme of love's fulfillment, an essential element in epithalamia that is absent from conventional love poetry. The love song of the first two strophes, and the panegyric of the third, are thereby transformed into a legitimate wedding song. Then in the sixth strophe (lines 33–36) an enchanting girl appears (as in the penultimate strophe of a secular *muwashshah* and its *kharja*), apparently to encourage the groom. Although she has claimed many victims she tranquilizes her own beloved with kisses before singing the *kharja* (lines 37–38), which is the *matla'* (incipit) of an Arabic *muwashshah* by the court philosopher Ibn Bajja (d. 1139): "Drag your coat-tails whene'er you can / and add intoxication (of your beloved's kisses) to your debauchery!"[46]

We have seen that the two Hebrew verse-forms, the mono-rhymed *qasida* and the strophic *muwashshah*, accommodated lyric genres. Medieval audiences seem to have identified love poems or wine poems by genre without qualification. In this respect it appears that lyric genres were self-evident categories in the production and reception of Hebrew verse. Although formalist readers have endeavored to reconstruct the generic codes according to which the poems were understood, we have seen that the Hebrew lyric resists efficient generic mapping. The prevalence and sheer messiness of composite poems, the tendency for the themes of the garden, wine, and love to be grouped together in many poems so as to be undifferentiated, and the formal and textual linkages and generic transactions among various types of secular and religious *muwashshahat* complicate attempts to impose either stable or contingent definitions of Hebrew lyric genres. A way out of this quandary is available in Hans Robert Jauss's model for integrating diachronic and synchronic approaches to the texts: "It is . . . necessary to jettison the idea of a juxtaposition of genres closed in upon themselves; instead [one must] look for the interrelationships which help them to constitute a literary system at a historically given moment."[47] It remains for readers of medieval Hebrew lyric poetry to consider fully such a method and its balance of relativistic and noncontextual approaches.

NOTES

As a matter of editorial consistency, within this volume diacritics are not employed in Arabic or Hebrew.

1. "Esh ahavim nissqah vi w'-eikh et'apqah" ("The fire of love has kissed me, how can I resist?"), by Samuel the Nagid, is the opening line of one of the earliest strophic Hebrew love songs. Text from Dov Jarden, ed., *Diwan sh'mu'el ha-nagid (The*

Collected Poetry of Samuel the Prince, 993–1056) (Jerusalem: n.p., 1966–92), 1:314–15. See S. M. Stern, "An Arabic *Muwashshah* and Its Hebrew Imitations," *Al-Andalus* 28 (1963): 155–70.

On the emergence of Hebrew Lyric, see Raymond P. Scheindlin, *Wine, Women, and Death: Medieval Hebrew Poems on the Good Life* (Philadelphia: Jewish Publication Society, 1986), and Ross Brann, *The Compunctious Poet: Cultural Ambiguity and Hebrew Poetry in Muslim Spain* (Baltimore: Johns Hopkins University Press, 1991).

2. For a parallel in the reception of troubadour lyrics see John Dagenais's contribution to this volume.

3. M. M. Badawi, "From Primary to Secondary *Qasidas:* Thoughts on the Development of Classical Arabic Poetry," *Journal of Arabic Literature* 11 (1980): 1–31.

4. Andras Hamori, *On the Art of Medieval Arabic Literature* (Princeton: Princeton University Press, 1974), 6.

5. A. S. Halkin, ed., *Moses ibn Ezra: Kitab al-muhadara wa-l-mudhakara* (Jerusalem: Mekizei Nirdamim, 1975), 179–80 [94b–95a] = *qasida/nasib;* 106 [57a] = *ghazal* (love poetry) and *muwashshahat;* 277–78 [143a–b] = *ghazal;* 104 [56b] = *tazallum* (lyrical complaint), for example.

6. David Yellin, ed., *Todros Abulafia: Gan ha-mᵉshalim wᵉ-ha-hidot* (Jerusalem: Weiss Press, 1932–36), 1:173–74 ("Mᵉshorer lo' yᵉdabber raq hatulim"), lines 8–10, 12–13; the parody extends over lines 1–18. Also in Hayyim Schirmann, *Hebrew Poetry in Spain and Provence* [in Hebrew] (Tel Aviv: Mosad Bialik and Dvir, 1959–60), 4:418–20. The poem is discussed in Brann, *Compunctious Poet,* 153–56.

7. The problems surrounding the identification of the *diwan* with the collection *Ben Tᵉhillim* are discussed by Jarden, *Diwan shᵉmu'el ha-nagid,* 1:5–7 (introduction). For a different view see Nehemya Allony, "*Diwan u-ven tᵉhillim einam zehim,*" reprinted in his *Studies in Medieval Philology and Literature: Collected Papers* (Jerusalem: Rubin Mass, 1991), 4:97–112.

8. The nature and extent of this involvement, unattested in any Arabic source, are open to question. The texts and their Arabic superscriptions may be found in Jarden, *Diwan shᵉmu'el ha-nagid,* 1:3–145. Although the poems draw heavily upon the genre conventions of the Arabic (*al-hamasa*) the headings of many of the Nagid's "war poems" replicate superscriptions found in the biblical Book of Psalms (*tᵉhillah, zimrah, nᵉginah,* and *shirah*), apparently suggesting genre-correspondences with the psalms. For a discussion of the Nagid's reasons for evoking the correspondence between his poetry and biblical literature, see Brann, *Compunctious Poet,* 46–58.

9. Moses ibn Ezra, *Sefer ha-ᶜanaq,* in Heinrich Brody and Dan Pagis, eds., *Moses ibn Ezra: Secular Poems* [in Hebrew] (Berlin: Schocken Publishing, 1934–77), 1:295–404.

10. E. D. Hirsch, Jr., *Validity in Interpretation* (New Haven: Yale University Press, 1967), 76.

11. See for example, Samuel the Nagid, *Diwan (Ben Qohelet),* ed. Jarden, 3:23 (nos. 42 and 43) = *Diwan (Ben Tᵉhillim),* 1:291 (no. 147, lines 1–4 and lines 5–6).

12. Samuel the Nagid, *Diwan (Ben Qohelet),* ed. Jarden, 3:44 (no. 80) = *Diwan (Ben Tᵉhillim),* 1:251 (no. 105, lines 3–10); 3:15 (no. 27) = 1:117–21 (no. 35, lines 1–14, 48–51); 3:12 (no. 22) = 1:151–52 (no. 45, lines 3–14).

13. For example, forty-two of the sixty-three *qasidas* preserved in Moses ibn Ezra's *diwan* have introductory passages. Twenty-seven of these are lyrical complaints.

14. The so-called "Orphan Poem" or "Singular Song" is one of the most famous

poems in medieval Hebrew literary history. "Halisvi hen g^{e}vurat on w^e-^{c}osmah," in Schirmann, *Hebrew Poetry in Spain and Provence*, 1:172–75, lines 5–8; translated in T. Carmi, *The Penguin Book of Hebrew Verse* (New York: Penguin Books, 1981), 302.

15. Halkin, *Moses ibn Ezra: Kitab al-muhadara*, 69.

16. "L^{e}kha re^{c}i w^e-re^{c}a ha-m^e'orim," in Schirmann, *Hebrew Poetry in Spain and Provence*, 1:223–25, lines 1–7; translated by Raphael Loewe, *Ibn Gabirol* (New York: Grove Weidenfeld, 1989), 58–60.

17. Halkin, *Moses ibn Ezra: Kitab al-muhadara*, 246 (128b); "Esh qadhu uraw w^e-lo' nuppahu," in Brody and Pagis, *Moses ibn Ezra: Secular Poems*, 1:72–75, no. 72; partial translation by Carmi, *Penguin Book of Hebrew Verse*, 329.

18. Dan Pagis, *Hebrew Poetry of the Middle Ages and the Renaissance* (Berkeley: University of California Press, 1991), 21.

19. Dan Pagis, *Secular Poetry and Poetic Theory: Moses ibn Ezra and His Contemporaries* [in Hebrew] (Jerusalem: Mosad Bialik, 1970).

20. Adena Rosmarin, *The Power of Genre* (Minneapolis: University of Minnesota Press, 1985), 45.

21. Tzvetan Todorov, "The Origin of Genres," *New Literary History* 8 (1976): 162.

22. Israel Levin, *The Embroidered Coat: The Genres of Hebrew Secular Poetry in Spain* [in Hebrew] (Tel Aviv: Hakibbutz Hameuchad Publishing House, 1980), covers the *qasida*, "war poems," panegyric, boast, lyrical complaint, apology, reproof, and satire. Second and third volumes devoted to love poetry, wine songs, poems on ascetic themes, lament, and the *muwashshah* appeared recently (Tel Aviv: Hakibbutz Hameuchad Publishing House, 1995).

23. Scheindlin, *Wine Women, and Death*, 19–33, 77–89.

24. Translated by Scheindlin in ibid., 110. Text in Schirmann, *Hebrew Poetry in Spain and Provence*, 1:214.

25. Scheindlin, *Wine, Women, and Death*, 112–13. So too the poem "Y^{e}shureni w^e-^{c}af^{e}apo k^e-holeh," in Schirmann, *Hebrew Poetry in Spain and Provence*, 1:25, translated and discussed in Scheindlin, 130–34.

26. For example, Schirmann, *Hebrew Poetry in Spain and Provence*, 2:464–65 ("Ya-^{c}avor^{c}alai r^{e}sonkha" and "B^{e}khol libbi emet") and 2:467 ("Me-az m^{ec}on ha-ahavah"); translated by Carmi, *Penguin Book of Hebrew Verse*, 333–34.

27. Halkin, *Moses Ibn Ezra: Kitab al-muhadara*, 278–79.

28. Yellin, *Todros Abulafia, Gan ha-m^{e}shalim*, vol. 2 (part 1, no. 714), 124–25, line 21.

29. Pagis, *Hebrew Poetry of the Middle Ages and the Renaissance*, 7–23.

30. Ibid., 67.

31. Rosmarin, *Power of Genre*, 44.

32. Paul Zumthor, *Speaking of the Middle Ages*, trans. Sarah White, foreword by Eugene Vance (Lincoln: University of Nebraska Press, 1986), 33.

33. See Pagis, *Hebrew Poetry of the Middle Ages and the Renaissance*, 62–71, and the bibliography cited there.

34. See Brann, *Compunctious Poet*, 77–78, and the bibliography cited there.

35. Tova Rosen challenges the conventional assumptions about the supposedly charming and innocuous medieval Hebrew love lyric ("On Tongues Being Bound and Let Loose: Women in Medieval Hebrew Literature," *Prooftexts* 8 [1988]: 67–87).

36. Yellin, *Todros Abulafia, Gan ha-m^{e}shalim*, vol. 2, part 2, 41–42 ("girdle poems"); translated by Carmi, *Penguin Book of Hebrew Verse*, 412–13.

37. S. M. Stern, "Les vers finaux en espagnol dans les muwassahs hispano-hebraïques: une contribution à l'histoire du muwassah et à l'étude du vieux dialecte espagnol 'mozarabe,'" *Al-Andalus* 13 (1948): 299–346. Stern, *Les chansons mozarabes: les vers finaux (kharjas) en espagnol dans les muwashshahs arabes et hébreux* (Palermo: Manfredi, 1953).

38. S. M. Stern, *Hispano-Arabic Strophic Poetry: Studies*, ed. L. P. Harvey (Oxford: Clarendon Press, 1974). For a fresh look at the controversy see Maria Rosa Menocal, *The Arabic Role in Medieval Literary History: A Forgotten Heritage* (Philadelphia: University of Pennsylvania Press, 1987), 91–113.

39. Tova Rosen(-Moked), *The Hebrew Girdle Poem [Muwashshah] in the Middle Ages* [in Hebrew] (Haifa: University of Haifa Press, 1985), 170–78, 188–201. Of particular interest to students of the Romance lyric is Rosen's presentation of generic Hebrew expressions ("a maiden's song"; "a gazelle's song") in the penultimate unit that introduce the *kharja* and qualify it as a feminine lyric. She concludes that the *kharja*'s thematic material (especially Romance *kharjat* in Hebrew *muwashshahat*) differs radically from conventional Arabic and Hebrew love poetry and is closely related to romance lyric genres such as the *cantigas de amigo, cantica puellarum,* and *cantica amatoria*. See her "Towards the *Kharja:* A Study of Penultimate Units in Arabic and Hebrew *Muwassahat*," in *Poesía estrófica: Actas del Primer Congreso Internacional sobre poesía estrófica árabe y hebrea y sus paralelos romances (Madrid, diciembre 1989)*, ed. F. Corriente and A. Sáenz-Badillos (Madrid: Universidad Complutense, 1991), 279–88.

40. Some rabbinical authorities, notably Moses Maimonides, expressed opposition to this practice (as well as to the production and consumption of love poetry in Hebrew or Arabic in general). See Brann, *Compunctious Poet*, 77, 107. Yet more than two hundred religious *muwashshahat* by Abraham ibn Ezra (1092–1167) have survived; see Israel Levin, ed., *The Religious Poems of Abraham ibn Ezra* [in Hebrew] (Jerusalem: Israel Academy of Sciences and Humanities, 1975–80). In general the number of extant religious *muwashshahat* dwarfs the secular *muwashshahat* by comparison.

41. Heinrich Brody and A. M. Habermann, eds., *Diwan des Abu-l-Hasan Jehuda ha-Levi* (Berlin: Mekize Nirdamim, 1894–1930; reprint, Farnsborough: Gregg International, 1971), 2:320–21.

42. Zvi Malachi, "Observations on the Hargas in Hebrew Poetry," in *Poesía estrófica: Actas del Primer Congreso Internacional sobre poesía estrófica árabe y hebrea y sus paralelos romances (Madrid, diciembre 1989)*, ed. F. Corriente and A. Sáenz-Badillos (Madrid: Universidad Complutense, 1991), 256–57.

43. In addition to the thematic and formal connections between secular and liturgical *muwashshahat*, the persona of the beloved in secular love poetry known as "the gazelle" (male or female beloved) reappears in liturgical Hebrew *muwashshahat* (as well as in mono-rhymed liturgical verse). The connection was studied by Israel Levin, "I Sought the One Whom My Soul Loveth—A Study of the Influence of Erotic Secular Poetry on Hebrew Religious Poetry" [in Hebrew], *Hasifrut* 3 (1971–72): 116–49. See also Raymond P. Scheindlin, *The Gazelle: Medieval Hebrew Poems on God, Israel and the Soul* (Philadelphia: Jewish Publication Society, 1991).

44. See Stern, *Hispano-Arabic Strophic Poetry*, 81–91; Israel Levin, "A Survey of the *Muwashshah* and Its Various Strophic Variations in the Religious Hebrew Poetry in

Spain," in *Poesía estrófica: Actas del Primer Congreso Internacional sobre poesía estrófica árabe y hebrea y sus paralelos romances (Madrid, diciembre 1989)*, ed. F. Corriente and A. Sáenz-Badillos (Madrid: Universidad Complutense, 1991), 225–31.

45. "Samm^{c}khuni b^e-yein s^{e}fat^{c}ofri," ed. J. (Hayyim) Schirmann, "Poets Contemporary with Moses ibn Ezra and Judah ha-Levi" [in Hebrew], *Studies of the [Schocken] Research Institute for Hebrew Poetry* 2 (1936): 188–89. The outline of the poem follows Joseph Yahalom, "Love's Labour's Won: The Materialization of Love in Hebrew Girdle Poems," in *Circa 1492: Proceedings of the Jerusalem Colloquium*, ed. Isaac Benabu (Jerusalem: Misgav Yerushalayim, 1992), 197–200.

46. "Jarriri-l-dhayla ayyama jarri / wa-sili-l-sukra minhu bi-l-sukri"; S. M. Stern, "Imitations of Arabic *Muwashshahs* in Spanish-Hebrew Poetry" [in Hebrew], *Tarbiz* 18 (1946–47): 175, and *Hispano-Arabic Strophic Poetry*, 180–81.

47. Cited by Stephen G. Nichols Jr., "A Poetics of Historicism? Recent Trends in Medieval Literary Study," *Medievalia et humanistica* [n.s.] 8 (1977): 95.

❖ CHAPTER 14

Thwarted Expectations: Medieval and Modern Views of Genre in Germany

HUBERT HEINEN

Those who wish to utilize genre to understand medieval German songs are confounded by the paucity of evidence that the singers of and audience for such songs had any sense of it.[1] To be sure, we encounter certain subsets of the broad spectrum of song that are discernibly different from the remainder of the song corpus and have fairly consistent contemporary labels associated with them: the *Leich,* a nonstrophic form related to the sequence and the estampie;[2] the *Tagelied,* or "dawn song"; the *Kreuzlied,* or "crusading song";[3] and, very generally, *Minnesang.* The *Tanzweise,* or "dance song," and the *Reie,* or "dance," have names but lack clearly distinguishing characteristics beyond their function, which scholars have not generally accepted as sufficient cause to accept them as genres.[4] The German analogue of the Latin and Romance pastourelle lacks a medieval German appellation,[5] though a particular modification of it seems to have acquired the evanescent eponymous title *Neidhart,* a type now usually referred to as a Neidhart (or Pseudo-Neidhart) song.[6] There are no contemporary terms for certain types of song often discussed by modern scholars such as the *Spruch,* a commonly, though not exclusively, monostrophic didactic song roughly comparable to the Occitan *cobla;*[7] the *Frauenlied* (and/or *Frauenstrophe*);[8] the *Wechsel,* a particular type of dialogue;[9] the *Botenlied* or "messenger song."[10] To a degree, these types of song overlap; for instance, the *Wechsel* and the *Botenlied* always have at least one strophe in the woman's voice, as does the *Tagelied* for the most part. Women's voices play a prominent role in Neidhart's songs as well.

Before we push through the brambles of genre distinction, let us reflect briefly on what we mean by genre and why we should care about it. Perhaps we can, by doing so, avoid impaling ourselves on the thorns of misplaced precision.

The (originally) French word *genre* refers in English to a specific type of literature (art, music) set off from others by style, form, and/or content.[11] German has the same word with the same meaning, but most scholars use the term *Gattung* (genre, genus). The German word is not a precise match for the English one, and perhaps for this reason scholarly discussion has proceeded along somewhat different lines. As the biological term for *genus* coincides with the aesthetic one for *genre* in German as in French, there is a tendency among Germanists and Romanists to utilize biological taxonomic criteria in defining literary genres. Even where the literary term is used more loosely, *Gattung* implies a broad, overall concept and has often been equated with the triad epic—lyric—dramatic, with types of songs being treated as subgenres (*Untergattungen*). In common with the other scholars in this collection of essays, I prefer to use the term *genre* for the various recurrent types of song that we can discern rather than to restrict it to the broad meaning "lyric poetry." For medievalists the classical triad is not appropriate. To be sure, the object of all our reflections, "song," is one of several relatively discrete major categories of literature clearly recognized in the Middle Ages in Germany. We can, therefore, make a preliminary distinction between song and non-song. There is no unambiguous word for "song" in Middle High German; *sanc* or *gesanc* may mean either "song" or "singing" (or both simultaneously), and *liet*, which becomes the common Modern German word for song, means "strophe" (what we would term a song is referred to as *diu liet,* "the strophes"). Nevertheless, the texts we understand as songs are consistently presented in the manuscripts in a manner that differs from the presentation of works in rhymed couplets and even (less consistently) in epic strophes; although they may not have linked the broad genre of song with a specific word, medieval scribes did not confuse it with spoken or chanted genres; auditors, of course, would have heard the difference.[12] The extent to which a similar consensus applied to divisions within the broad group is less clear.

Taxonomy is a pursuit largely irrelevant to the German Middle Ages, where we find, to be sure, an increasing concern with lists (and, to a degree, compendia) from the thirteenth century on, but little or no interest in ordered classification. Theologians perused their *summae,* and those scholars trained in memorization tucked the items of an exposition into separate chambers for subsequent retrieval; however, we have little evidence that the producers or consumers of literature in German felt a need for pigeonholes. Although I doubt that a desire to classify engendered distinctions between genres, collectors do seem to have paid some (albeit scant) attention to genre in selecting and ordering the songs. Be that as it may, medieval Germans probably welcomed generic distinctions for another reason. If readers or, more appropriately for medieval song, auditors share expectations, based on specific signals in or about the text, these expectations influence how they comprehend what they read or hear. A song's creator can then fulfill or disappoint such expectations. The songs themselves provide ample evidence that poets did, in fact, make this sort of use of generic expectations. An art that delighted in thwarting expectations also was fecund in modifying the genres based on them; often genres were transformed almost beyond recognition from the very first time they were created or adopted. However, the fact that parameters for a genre change over time does not mean that its early manifestations can no longer be considered examples of it.[13]

As one "born and bred in the briar patch," I must return to the thorny question of what constitutes a genre, picking as my point of departure the well-attested dawn song.[14] There are more dawn songs in German than in the other languages: up to and including those by Oswald von Wolkenstein in the first quarter of the fifteenth century, around a hundred. Probably the first German example of the genre is a simple ditty ascribed in the sole manuscript containing it to Dietmar von Aist.[15]

1. "Slâfest du, vriedel ziere?	39,18 =
wan wecket uns leider schiere;	32 C
ein vogellîn sô wol getân	
daz ist der linden an daz zwî gegân."	
2. "Ich was vil sanfte entslâfen,	39,32 =
nu rüefestû, kint, wâfen.	33 C
liep âne leit mac niht sîn.	
swaz dû gebiutest, daz leiste ich, mîn vriundîn."	
3. Diu vrouwe begunde weinen:	39,26 =
"du rîtest hinnen und lâst mich einen.	34 C
wenne wilt du wider her zuo mir?	
owê, du vüerest mîne vröide sant dir!"	

1. "Are you sleeping, handsome lover? We'll unfortunately soon be awakened. A pretty little bird has flown onto the linden's branch."

2. "I had drifted away to sleep; now you call out the alarm, child. Joyful love cannot exist without sorrowful pain. Whatever you demand I'll do, my lady love."

3. The lady began to cry. "You'll be riding away and leaving me alone. When will you return to me? Alas, you're taking my joy with you!"

Although most scholars dispute the ascription, I agree with Günther Schweikle that the arguments against Dietmar as the song's author are specious.[16] Though the song, which can probably be dated around 1170 (give or take a dozen years), makes an archaic impression, it exhibits traits found in later dawn songs: a dialogue between a lady and her lover at the break of dawn; the lover's reluctance to be awakened; the lady's lament at her lover's imminent departure. We also find an echo of the *locus amoenus* not otherwise found in German dawn songs until the thirteenth century.[17] Despite its likely being at least a decade older than any other transmitted German song that betrays a knowledge of the dawn song tradition, two or more decades older than any other full-fledged German dawn song, its matter-of-fact use of features that prove to be constitutive for the genre would suggest that the genre was well established as a foil against which this example was understood. There may even be a rudimentary adumbration of the watchman, who so often wakes the lovers in later songs, if we understand the little bird to have warned the lady of the coming of the dawn. Possibly, however, we should not expect the lady to cry out, "It was the nightingale, and not the lark" (*Romeo and Juliet* 3.5), in a vain attempt to keep her lover from leaving. Dietmar is the most archaic German poet to be enamored of the *Natureingang* or "nature introduction," and his little bird may merely reflect this tradition.

Among the singers of the next generation or so, Reinmar der Alte and Heinrich von Morungen clearly know and play with the genre, though we have no straightforward examples of it from them.[18] Wolfram von Eschenbach, from the period around 1200, is the singer most closely associated, both in his own time and in ours, with the dawn song; of the nine songs attributed to him, four include the most impressive dawn songs in medieval literature and a fifth is an amusing revocation of the dawn song.[19] The final strophe of the latter song gives an impression both of Wolfram's characteristic humor and of the extent to which medieval poets and audiences were willing to play with generic expectations.[20]

2.
Swer pfliget oder ie gepflac, 6,1 =
daz er bî lieben wîben lac, 5 BC
   Den merkæren unverborgen,
   der darf niht durch den morgen
     dannen streben.
      er mac des tages erbeiten.
      man darf in niht ûz leiten
     ûf sîn leben.
   Ein offeniu süeze wirtes wîp
   kan sölhe minne geben.

2. Whoever is or ever was accustomed to sleep with dear ladies, not hidden from surveillants, need not, because of morning, leave. He can await the dawn. He need not be guided out to save his life. An open, sweet wife can give such love.

Wolfram turns the conventions of the dawn song upside down: if one sleeps with one's own wife, there is no need to fear the dawn. The dative plural of 2.2 is a dative singular in one of the two manuscripts, and that makes better sense, since he is surely not also praising polygamy.

Wolfram also alludes to the *merkære* or spies who, as the hapless suitor or the lovesick lady laments, keep the lovers separated. Such *merkære*, also called *lügenære* or "slanderers" (cf. the corresponding figures in Occitan and French), already appear in the earliest German songs as a shadowy group threatening to make secret love public knowledge. Their presence reminds us that although forms, motifs, and styles develop over several centuries, the courtly songs retain much the same set of attitudes: the lovers pine for each other, but usually dare not fulfill their desire for sexual union lest their secret be discovered. The marital status of the lovers is generally indeterminate; at no time in the German tradition is their love characterized as adulterous, but the recurrent references to secrecy suggest to us that it is illicit.[21] Though the suitor's lament usually decries a lack of fulfillment, often portraying the lady as recalcitrant or even haughty and disdainful, those songs and strophes in the woman's voice normally show the lady's hunger for fulfillment to be, if anything, greater than the man's, with the hindrance to intercourse being social pressures or the man's timidity. The dawn songs share the same basic view of love as other courtly songs; the difference is situational.[22]

A fairly mediocre dawn song by a minor poet, Bruno von Hornberg, can help us perceive what medieval audiences expected; in the thirteenth century (as in any age) we find ample evidence that epigonality fulfills a social need for a fixation of poetic norms.[23] As in most German dawn songs after

Wolfram's, a watchman sounds the alarm (the terms *tageliet* and *tagewîse*, which come to be used for dawn songs as we understand them, may initially refer to the song of the watchman or his functional equivalent signaling the breaking of day).

    1.
    "Swer tougenlîcher minne pflege,   3.1 =
    der sol nu wachen, wan ez wil âne zwîvel tagen.   11 C
    der ruowe er sich enzît bewege.
    er sol niht machen, daz man von im beginnet klagen;
    ein scheiden wil mir wol behagen:
    vil dicke ein man von lieben sachen
    vil grôziu leit beginnet *t*ragen."   *klagen*

    2.
    Der rede ein schoene wîp erschrac.   3.2 =
    ein umbevâhen tet sî ir gesellen dô.   12 C
    si sprach: "owê, ich wæne, der tac
    uns aber wil nâhen; des bin ich sendez wîp unfrô."
    diu reine süeze wachte alsô,
    daz grâwe lieht si beide an sâhen:
    si forchten melde und ouch den drô.

    3.
    Ir beider fröide ein trûren wart,   3.3 =
    do sî sich scheiden muosten, und der tac ûf brach.   13 C
    ein reine wîp in rehter art
    mit hôhen eiden ir lîbes im für eigen jach.
    der ritter dô mit triuwen sprach:
    "nieman kan dich mir geleiden.
    der himel segen sî dîn dach."

1. "Whoever may be enjoying secret love should now wake up, for dawn will surely break. Let him desist in time from his rest. He should not cause people to lament about him. A parting will please me best: often a man so happy with love then suffers great sorrows."

2. A beautiful lady was startled by these words. She then embraced her companion. She spoke, "Alas, I suspect the dawn will approach us again; I lovesick lady am sad about that." The pure sweet one thus lay awake; they both watched the grey light: they feared the threat of betrayal.

3. The joy both felt turned to sorrow when they had to part and dawn broke. A pure, high-born lady with solemn oaths declared fealty to him. Then the knight spoke loyally: "No one can diminish my esteem for you. May the blessings of the heavens be your roof."

    The first two strophes, at least, give the impression of what a large number of dawn songs, especially those composed (as were most in the thirteenth century) under the influence of Wolfram, would read like if they were stripped of extravagant imagery, passion, and the idiosyncrasies that typify Wolfram and can often be found to some measure in his imitators. Not only does the watchman wake the lovers, he also accompanies his warning with some general commentary on what discovery may bring. The lady first responds, lamenting the coming of day and initiating (or increasing the ardor of her) loving embraces. The knight replies and takes his leave. Even this song, however, derivative as it may be, has a few unusual accents. Hornberg, in stressing the fear of exposure both share, deviates from the usual pattern and adds a distinctive note, although the *hysteron proteron* "betrayal and the threat" is probably an inept poet's way of finding a rhyme rather than an elegant rhetorical flourish. The lady does not normally pledge fealty to the knight, nor does the knight, in parting, give such an ambiguous blessing. Entrusting the lady to the shelter of the heavens comes close to setting her out to the mercy of the elements; probably the plural *himel* is meant to signify "God's heaven" rather than "sky," but then *dach* is an awkwardly concrete word for "protection." Hornberg's variations on the basic pattern seem more likely to be infelicities of expression than marvels of poetic invention.

Although there are many trite and stereotypical love songs in medieval German, the overall variety and complexity of the lyrics is remarkable. Even against this background it can be said that invention or, as Alois Wolf remarks (in *Variation und Integration*), variation is a key characteristic of the dawn song. I have cited in full two of the some fifty German dawn songs of the twelfth and thirteenth centuries; it would be difficult to find many more that are as nearly typical. From the very beginning, the inversion implied by making day rather than night the time of danger elicited a wide range of responses.[24] Günther Schweikle (*Minnesang*) has sketched a number of the ways the poets diverged from what we might posit as *the* dawn song; here it may suffice to examine briefly one such divergence, a song by Ulrich von Singenberg that differs radically from his fairly conventional "Swer minneclîche minne."[25]

> 1.
> Wie hôhes muotes ist ein man,   7.1 = *21 A, 33 C*
> der sich zuo herzeclîchem liebe schoenem lîbe hât geleit!
> Zer vreude ich niht gelîchen kan:
> mir ist elliu vreude gar enniht gegen dirre, swaz mir ieman seit.
> Swer sich so wunneclîcher wunne wol für wâr gevreuwen mac,
> der hât die naht niht angest, wan daz in vertrîben sol der tac.

MEDIEVAL AND MODERN VIEWS OF GENRE 341

2.
Geselliclîcher umbevanc   7.2 = 22 A, *34 C*
mit blanken armben sunder wân tuot senede herze hôhgemuot.
Da wirt daz ungemüete kranc,
swa minneclicher minne kus so lieplîch liep anander tuot.
Swer sich . . .

3.
Der tac mich leider hât betaget   7.3 = *23 A, 35 C*
so selten nâch der êren sige, daz ich niht vreude mac verjehen.
Vil sælic man, der des niht clagit,
und ime sîn herze mac gesagen, waz ime ze leide ist geschehen!
Swer sich . . .

4.
Der süeze wehsel under zwein,   7.4 = *24 A, 36 C*
den werdiu minne vüegen kan, wie ruchet der daz herze enbor!
Diu beide ir muotes sint al ein:
ich kan nach wunsch erdenken niht zer welte sælde dirre vor.
Swer sich . . .

5.
"Der tac wil scheiden, ritter wert,   7.5 = *25 A, 37 C*
von liebe liep: ez muoz eht sîn. Wol ûf, lâz ir daz herze hie,
Diu dîn ze friunde hât gegert.
si wil och dir ir herze lân, diu triuwen dir gewankte nie:
Die leist och ir, als ez dîn werder lîp vil wol geleisten mac,
mit schiere komenne! ez mac niht langer hie gesîn: ich sihe den tac."

1. What courtly high spirits a man possesses who has joined himself to a beautiful body for the sake of hearty love! I have nothing to compare to this happiness: all happiness is nothing at all to me against what I am told of. Whoever in truth can please himself with such joyful joy has no anxiety at night except that dawn will drive him away.

2. A lover's embrace with bare arms lends lovesick hearts high spirits without a doubt. Despondency is weakened wherever a kiss of lovely love makes one another so fondly fond. Whoever . . .

3. Dawn has unfortunately so rarely broken for me after a glorious victory that I cannot claim happiness. He is blessed who does not lament of it when his heart can tell him what has happened to him to cause his sorrow. Whoever . . .

4. The sweet dialogue (exchange) between two people that worthy love can create, how it causes the heart to surge upwards! When they both are one in spirit, I cannot imagine or wish for an earthly bliss greater than this. Whoever . . .

> 5. "The day will separate, worthy knight, lover from lover; that must be so. Well then, arise, leave your heart here for her who desired you as her sweetheart. She who never faltered in her loyalty toward you will leave you her heart in return. Repay this loyalty as you in your worthiness can indeed do by returning soon! There is no remaining here any longer: I see the dawn."

Numerous motifs are played out here; we have an amalgamation of a lament that one has no cause to regret the coming of dawn—a variation on the dawn song we first have attested by Reinmar der Alte[26]—with a reverie on the joys of mutual love. Both are intensified and underscored by a refrain that links the first four strophes and suggests that the singer prefers the sorrow of parting to the anguish of never having come together. All is heightened by rhetorical flourishes utilizing *annominatio* with an added measure of the *figura etymologica*, only later codified by the theoreticians but gladly employed by the poets throughout the twelfth and thirteenth centuries. The series of strophes on the dawn song that could not be culminates with a citation of a dawn song yet to come. The watchman, far from introducing the song, concludes it. However, there is no real need for more; the convention, confounded, replays itself in echoes of the glorification of love and lamentation about its absence. To the typical elements of joining and separation, of coming together and taking leave, the watchman adds the well-known motif of the exchange of hearts, here made more profound because it follows a praise of mutual love. We have an ample sense of a deep awareness of genre, but little presented us fits the definitions we could deduce from most dawn songs.

As a matter of fact—as there is no mention of spies, of danger, of secrecy—there is no absolute need to assume that the love here glorified is illicit, and that the necessary parting is caused by a fear of discovery. This song would not be destroyed if Singenberg had added, in a final strophe, Wolfram's remark that one's own wife can grant such love. I doubt he would have; I suspect such a thought would not have even entered his or his audience's mind. After all, when Singenberg's younger contemporary Ulrich von Liechtenstein pauses in his ceaseless effort to win his lady's favors by prodigies of tournament prowess, he recounts that he took a few days off to have a pleasant visit with his wife. Love in marriage was perhaps not as impossible as some would have it, but it was clearly not what most singers and auditors had in mind when "my lady fair" was apostrophized. Furthermore, Dietmar's dawn song, with which I began these remarks, also lacks any reference to spies, danger, secrecy, or illicit love. Unless these elements are specifically denied, I would suggest, the audience's awareness of the genre provides them.

The terms *tageliet* and *tagewîse* are first unambiguously used around 1250 by Ulrich von Liechtenstein to designate the genre as we understand it. From the late thirteenth century on there are sporadic mentions of the genre (later sometimes called a *taghorn,* which stresses the aspect of warning of the coming of day). However, there seems to be no certainty about what the constituents of the genre are. Though Neidhart mentions, in a song plausibly dated around 1230, that he has written a *tagewîse*,[27] the strophe containing the word is transmitted only in a manuscript of the fifteenth century; in the same manuscript a song labeled *Ein tag weis* has none of the features we associate with the genre. In the Weingarten Song Codex (B), a later (probably fifteenth-century) reader labeled Wolfram's dawn-song parody a *[T]agwiß*. Far from becoming a *forme fixe* in the later Middle Ages, the dawn song appears to have lost whatever clear contours it may have had in its earlier, highly protean heyday in the thirteenth century.

Clear distinctions are also made, in practice more than in terminology, between minnesongs and didactic songs (*Sprüche*), and both in terminology and in practice between *Leichs* and strophic songs. Other types of song, both named and implicit, can be discerned. However, in the Middle Ages Germany never developed a system of genres. What generic expectations were aroused were as often thwarted as fulfilled. In addition, those genres such as the dawn song that clearly existed, that were utilized by the poets, and that were recognized by contemporary audiences, lack many of the qualities modern scholars find essential. Rarely do we find, as modern scholars would like to, a consistent marriage of theme and form in a given genre. For example, the refrain ending in *alba* or the like, so typical of Occitan and French dawn songs, occurs only sporadically in German. Singenberg's use of it may, in fact, be an allusion to the French tradition, and not to an indigenous German one (though Morungen's dawn song/ *Wechsel* also has a refrain, and several Alemannic singers use refrains). There are no absolute formal criteria to differentiate between a minnesong and a didactic song, although the latter are more likely to occur as single strophes and, conversely, less likely to be melded into multistrophic units. Peter Frenzel has suggested the melody may have given audiences an indication of which was meant;[28] perhaps there were other cues as well as to what sort of song was being performed. The *Leich*, which is formally quite distinct, can be used for any content. In other words, the expectations modern scholars bring to medieval German genres are consistently thwarted; in place of clear-cut distinctions we find a muddle. Amidst this muddle, in a delightfully playful manner, medieval singers used sprinklings of generic allusions to arouse and thwart their audiences' expectations.

NOTES

1. For a general discussion of the problem and of the possibility that Ulrich von Liechtenstein's *Frauendienst* does demonstrate such a sense, see Hubert Heinen, "Ulrich von Liechtenstein's Sense of Genre," in *Genres in Medieval German Literature*, ed. Hubert Heinen and Ingeborg Henderson (Göppingen: Kümmerle, 1986), 16–29. A recent anthology that gives a broad sampling of medieval German lyrics from the earliest through the fifteenth century is Ulrich Müller and Gerlinde Weiss, eds., *Deutsche Gedichte des Mittelalters* (Stuttgart: Reclam, 1993); for a collection of interpretations based more or less stringently on the notion of genre, see Helmut Tervooren, ed., *Gedichte und Interpretationen: Mittelalter* (Stuttgart: Reclam, 1993); see the introduction there.

2. See Karl Heinrich Bertau, *Sangverslyrik: Über Gestalt und Geschichtlichkeit mittelhochdeutscher Lyrik am Beispiel des Leichs* (Göttingen: Vandenhoeck & Ruprecht, 1964); Olive Sayce, *The Medieval German Lyric, 1150–1300: The Development of Its Themes and Forms in Their European Context* (Oxford: Clarendon Press, 1982), 346–407; and, with special attention to genre, Hermann Apfelböck, *Tradition und Gattungsbewusstsein im deutschen Leich: Ein Beitrag zur Gattungsgeschichte mittelalterlicher musikalischer "Discordia"* (Tübingen: Niemeyer, 1991).

3. See Günther Schweikle, *Minnesang* (Stuttgart: Metzler, 1989), 141–44.

4. See Heinen, "Ulrich von Liechtenstein's Sense of Genre," 20–22; for *reie*, Georg Friedrich Benecke, Wilhelm Müller, and Friedrich Zarncke, *Mittelhochdeutsches Wörterbuch* (reprint Hildesheim: Olms, 1963), 2.1.655, and Günther Schweikle, *Neidhart* (Stuttgart: Metzler, 1990), 22–23.

5. Gottfried von Strassburg uses the term *pasturele* together with other French terms: *rotuwange* (rotrouenge), *rundate* (rondeau), *schanzune* (chanson), *refloit,* and *folate* in *Tristan und Isold,* ed. Friedrich Ranke (Berlin: Weidmann, 1958), lines 8072–74. None of these terms would seem to refer to genres commonly utilized in German-speaking areas.

6. On the pastourelle see William D. Paden, ed., *The Medieval Pastourelle* (New York: Garland, 1987); Schweikle, *Minnesang,* 140–41; Schweikle, *Neidhart,* 22–23.

7. The word *spruch* has some currency in Middle High German, but clearly means "that which is said" and is not used in a generic sense (cf. Benecke, Müller, Zarncke, *Mittelhochdeutsches Wörterbuch,* 2.2.538–39); see also Helmut Tervooren, "'Spruch' und 'Lied': Ein Forschungsbericht," in *Mittelhochdeutsche Spruchdichtung,* ed. Hugo Moser (Darmstadt: Wissenschaftliche Buchgesellschaft, 1972), 1–25.

8. See William E. Jackson, "The Woman's Song in Medieval German Poetry," in *Vox Feminae: Studies in Medieval Woman's Songs,* ed. John F. Plummer (Kalamazoo, Mich.: Medieval Institute, 1981), 47–94; Schweikle, *Minnesang,* 126–28.

9. See Rolf Grimminger, *Poetik des frühen Minnesangs* (Munich: Beck, 1969); Schweikle, *Minnesang,* 131–32. *Wechsel* (dialogue) is a common word, but even when the thirteenth-century minnesinger Ulrich von Singenberg uses it to characterize an exchange between lovers, it has no generic significance (in fact, it is unclear whether the exchange is verbal or physical; see below); see Max Schiendorfer, ed., *Die schweizer Minnesänger,* vol. 1: *Texte* (Tübingen: Niemeyer, 1990), 7.4.1. The term *wechsell* is used for a variety of dialogue songs in the fifteenth-century Neidhart manuscript *c* (cf. Schweikle, *Neidhart,* 22–23).

10. See Franz Viktor Spechtler, "Die Stilisierung der Distanz: zur Rolle des Boten im Minnesang bis Walther und bei Ulrich von Liechtenstein," in *Peripherie und Zentrum: Studien zur österreichischen Literatur, Festschrift für Adalbert Schmidt*, ed. Gerlinde Weiss and Klaus Zelewitz (Salzburg: Bergland, 1971), 285–310.

11. I would add function (occasion) to this list of distinguishing criteria, but scholars do not tend to do so.

12. I treated the medieval German sense of "song" in a talk given to the Medieval Academy in Columbus, Ohio, in 1992; a revision of that talk will appear in my monograph in progress, *Mutability and Permutations*, vol. 1: *Minnesongs and Their Coherence* (Göppingen: Kümmerle, forthcoming).

13. My understanding of dynamic genres reflects Tzvetan Todorov, *Introduction à la littérature fantastique* (Paris: Seuil, 1970), as cited and interpreted in Ernst S. Dick, "Tradition and Emancipation: The Generic Aspect of Heinrich's *Crône*," in *Genres in Medieval German Literature*, ed. Hubert Heinen and Ingeborg Henderson (Göppingen: Kümmerle, 1986), 74–75, and Hans Robert Jauss, "Theorie der Gattungen und Literatur des Mittelalters," in *Grundriss der romanischen Literaturen des Mittelalters*, ed. Hans Robert Jauss and Erich Köhler, vol. 1: *Généralités* (Heidelberg: Carl Winter, 1972), 107–38.

14. On German dawn songs in the broadest possible context, see Arthur T. Hatto, ed., *Eos: An Enquiry into the Theme of Lovers' Meetings and Partings at Dawn in Poetry* (London: Mouton, 1965); see also the anthologies edited by Sabine Freund, *Deutsche Tagelieder: Von den Anfängen der Überlieferung bis zum 15. Jahrhundert* (Heidelberg: Winter, 1983); Renate Hausner, *Owe do tagte ez: Tagelieder und motivverwandte Texte des Mittelalters und der frühen Neuzeit* (Göppingen: Kümmerle, 1983); and Martina Backes, *Tagelieder des deutschen Mittelalters* (Stuttgart: Reclam, 1992). For a discussion of the genre, see Ioana Beloiu-Wehn, *"Der tageliet maneger gern sanc": Das deutsche Tagelied des 13. Jahrhunderts* (Frankfurt: Lang, 1989). In general, see Schweikle, *Minnesang*, 135–40.

15. Text according to Günther Schweikle, *Die mittelhochdeutsche Minnelyrik*, vol. 1: *Die frühe Minnelyrik* (Darmstadt: Wissenschaftliche Buchgesellschaft, 1977), 152–54; see also Hugo Moser and Helmut Tervooren, eds., *Des Minnesangs Frühling*, 38th ed. (Stuttgart: Hirzel, 1988), with the traditional and plausible emendations 2.4 "vriundîn mîn" and 3.2 "eine."

16. Schweikle, *Die mittelhochdeutsche Minnelyrik*, vol. 1: *Die frühe Minnelyrik*, 388–94.

17. See, for example, Otto von Botenlouben 3 and 14, in Carl von Kraus, ed., *Deutsche Liederdichter des 13. Jahrhunderts* (Tübingen: Niemeyer, 1952); Jakob von Warte 6, in Schiendorfer, *Die schweizer Minnesänger*. In Botenlouben 3 and Warte 6 a bird warns the lovers of the dawn.

18. Drawing in part from talks I have given over the past two decades, I treat Reinmar's and, to a lesser extent, Morungen's dawn song allusions in my *Mutability and Permutations*.

19. See, for example, Jonathan Saville, *The Medieval Erotic Alba: Structure as Meaning* (New York: Columbia University Press, 1972); Peter Wapnewski, *Die Lyrik Wolframs von Eschenbach* (Munich: Beck, 1972); Alois Wolf, *Variation und Integration: Beobachtungen zu hochmittelalterlichen Tageliedern* (Darmstadt: Wissenschaftliche Gesellschaft, 1979); and Marianne Wynn, "Wolfram's Dawnsongs," in *Studien zu Wolfram von Eschenbach: Festschrift für Werner Schröder*, ed. Kurt Gärtner and Joachim Heinzle (Tübingen: Niemeyer, 1989), 549–58.

20. Moser and Tervooren, eds., *Des Minnesangs Frühling*, 441.

21. There are few "mal mariée" songs in German, e.g., Reinmar 64 (ibid., 400; cf. Helmut Tervooren, *Reinmar-Studien* [Stuttgart: Hirzel, 1991], 130–39), and Burkhard von Hohenfels XV (Kraus, *Deutsche Liederdichter des 13. Jahrhunderts*, 45–46; cf. Susanne Staar in Tervooren, *Gedichte und Interpretationen: Mittelalter* [Stuttgart: Reclam, 1993], 233–50); as burlesques, they can scarcely inform us what medieval audiences perceived the status of the lady to be.

22. On woman's and men's roles, see Heinen, "Observations on the Role in *Minnesang*," *Journal of English and Germanic Philology* 75 (1976): 198–208; "Lofty and Base Love in Walther von der Vogelweide's 'Sô die bluomen' und 'Aller werdekeit' (L. 45,37ff and 46,32ff)," *German Quarterly* 51 (1978): 465–75; "The Woman's Songs of Hartmann von Aue," in *Vox Feminae: Studies in Medieval Woman's Songs*, ed. John F. Plummer (Kalamazoo, Mich.: Medieval Institute, 1981), 95–110; and "When Pallor Pales: Reflections on Epigonality in Late 13th-Century Minnesong," *Medieval Perspectives* 4–5 (1989–90): 53–68. On early conventionality see Heinen, "The Woman's Songs of Hartmann von Aue." The most outspoken proponent of the essential similarity between German dawn songs and other courtly genres is Eva Willms, *Liebesleid und Sangeslust* (Munich: Artemis, 1990), 200–14. [Most students of Occitan and French hold, in contrast, that the view of love in the *alba* or *aube* is fundamentally different from that in the *canso* or *grand chant courtois*.—Ed.]

23. I discuss certain aspects of this need for the epigonal in "When Pallor Pales." The song is cited, with some readings restored from the manuscript, from Kraus, *Deutsche Liederdichter des 13. Jahrhunderts*, 24. [By a similar logic the Occitan arts of poetry fixed poetic norms to facilitate imitation by late poets.—Ed.]

24. On the significance of the inversion, see Stephen L. Wailes, "The Erotic Realism of the German Dawn Song," in *Genres in Medieval German Literature*, ed. Hubert Heinen and Ingeborg Henderson (Göppingen: Kümmerle, 1986), 1–15; for a discussion of Ulrich von Liechtenstein's variations on the type, see my "Poetic Truth and the Appearance of Reality in Ulrich von Lichtenstein's Dawn Songs," in *From Symbol to Mimesis*, ed. Franz H. Bäuml (Göppingen: Kümmerle, 1984), 169–89.

25. "Swer minneclîche minne," no. 12 in Schiendorfer, *Die schweizer Minnesänger*, 103–5; "Wie hôhes muotes ist in man," no. 7 in Schiendorfer, 96–97.

26. Reinmar der Alte 154,32, versions A(C), BC, and E; see Heinen, ed., *Mutabilität im Minnesang: Mehrfach überlieferte Lieder des 12. und frühen 13. Jahrhunderts* (Göppingen: Kümmerle, 1989), 76–79.

27. Schweikle, *Neidhart*, 94.

28. Peter Frenzel, "Melody and Genre in German Courtly Singing in the Thirteenth Century," in *Genres in Medieval German Literature*, ed. Hubert Heinen and Ingeborg Henderson (Göppingen: Kümmerle, 1986), 30–46.

Contributors

Elizabeth Aubrey is a professor of musicology at the University of Iowa and the author of *The Music of the Troubadours* (Bloomington, 1996).

Ross Brann is a professor and chair of Near Eastern studies at Cornell University and the author of *The Compunctious Poet: Cultural Ambiguity and Hebrew Poetry in Muslim Spain* (Baltimore, 1991).

Vicente Cantarino is a professor of romance languages at Ohio State University and the author of *Arabic Poetics in the Golden Age: Selection of Texts Accompanied by a Preliminary Study* (Leiden, 1975).

John Dagenais is a professor of Hispanic studies at the University of California-Los Angeles and the author of *The Larger Gloss: The Ethics of Reading the Libro de Buen Amor* (Princeton, 1994).

Ana María Gómez-Bravo is an associate professor of Spanish at Purdue University-West Lafayette and the author of the *Repertorio métrico de la poesía cancioneril castellana del siglo XV* (Alcalá de Henares, 1998).

Hubert Heinen is a professor of German at the University of Texas-Austin and the author of *Mutabilität im Minnesang: Mehrfach überlieferte Lieder des 12. und frühen 13. Jahrhunderts* (Göppingen, 1989).

Sylvia Huot is a senior lecturer in French at Cambridge University and the author of *Allegorical Play in the Old French Motet: The Sacred and the Profane in Thirteenth-Century Polyphony* (Stanford, 1997).

Douglas Kelly is a professor of French at the University of Wisconsin and the author of *The Art of Medieval French Romance* (Madison, 1992).

William D. Paden is a professor of French at Northwestern University and the author of *An Introduction to Old Occitan* (New York, 1998).

Rupert T. Pickens is a professor of French at the University of Kentucky and the editor of *The Songs of Jaufre Rudel* (Toronto, 1978).

Michelangelo Picone is a professor of Italian at the University of Zürich (Switzerland) and the author of *Vita nuova e tradizione romanza* (Padua, 1979).

Elizabeth W. Poe is a professor of French at Tulane University and the author of *From Poetry to Prose in Old Provençal: The Emergence of the Vidas, the Razos, and the Razos de trobar* (Birmingham, 1984).

Julian Weiss is an associate professor and chair of Spanish at the University of Oregon and the author of *The Poet's Art: Literary Theory in Castile c. 1400–60* (Oxford, 1990).

Winthrop Wetherbee is a professor and chair of English at Cornell University and the author of *Platonism and Poetry in the Twelfth Century: The Literary Influence of the School of Chartres* (Princeton, 1972).

Index

Indexed here are terms relating to genre; names of authors, medieval, modern, and ancient; and medieval texts which are cited and translated at length, identified here by the first line of the citation. Anonymous works are listed by title. Authors are listed by first name until 1500 A.D., by last name thereafter.

Abelard, 167, 184n.46, 248
Abraham ibn Ezra, 332n.40
Abu Ishaq Ibrahim ibn Abu Aish ibn Sahl al Israili, 270n.33
Accessus ad auctores, 10, 205n.1, 248, 249, 250, 254nn.9–11, 254n.18
Adam de la Halle (Adam le Bossu), 176n.7, 297, 300, 304, 306, 308, 312, 313n.2, 314n.18
Adler, Alfred, 122n.15, 122n.19
Agamben, Giorgio, 154n.2
Ahmad ibn Muhammad al-Maqqari, 259, 269nn.10–11, 269n.13, 269n.15, 269nn.18–19, 269n.21
Ahmad ibn Yahya al-Dabbi, 269n.11
Aimeric de Peguilhan, 77, 82, 234n.24, 281, 293n.31
Akehurst, F. R. P., 60n.24, 63n.54
Alan of Lille, 7, 98–101, 104, 108, 109, 122nn.16–17, 122nn.20–21, 122nn.26–27, 123n.31; *De planctu Naturae*, 99, 101
Alart de Chans, 286
Alba (Occitan dawn song), 1, 6, 8, 21, 22, 30, 31, 38, 43, 69, 84, 86, 94n.93, 149, 152, 210, 216, 231, 232nn.4–5, 233n.13, 241n.90, 241n.92, 245, 246 fig. 9.1, 247, 252, 254n.15, 284, 286, 294n.41, 343, 345n.19, 346n.22; fragmentary *albas*, 58n.8; frequency of, 23–24, 28; religious *alba*, 58n.8
Albert Marques, 90n.53
Al-Bustani, Karam, 269n.14
Al-Dabbi, 269n.24
Alfonso X el Sabio, 159, 163, 167, 169, 170, 171, 177n.9, 182n.33
Alfonso Alvarez de Villasandino, 162, 168, 175n.3
Alfonso de la Monja, Fray, 168
Alfonso de la Torre, 182n.32
Alfonso de Toledo, 162, 182n.30
Alfonso Fernández de Palencia, 165, 166, 183n.38
Alfonso Gonçales de Castro, 169
Allegory, 12
Allegretto, Manuela, 154n.258
Allegri, Laura, 93n.82
Alleluia, 298

Allony, Nehemya, 330n.7
Al-Maqqari. *See* Ahmad ibn Muhammad al-Maqqari
Almqvist, Kurt, 90n.43
Almuc and Iseut, 91n.53
Al-Mutawakkil, 263
Alonso, Alvaro, 176n.3
Alvar, Carlos, 128, 143n.11, 177n.9
Alvar, Manuel, 175n.3
Alverny, Marie-Thérèse d', 122n.27
Ambrosio Montesino, Fray, 162
"Amor habet superos" (anonymous Latin poem), 105–6, 118–20
Amy, Robert, 51n to l. 46
Ancient manner. *See Usanza antiga*
Anderson, Gordon A., 314n.8, 314n.11
Andreas Capellanus, 9, 108, 193–94, 196, 197, 198, 199, 200, 205n.8, 205n.12, 206n.19, 206n.23, 207n.27, 207n.32, 208n.33, 208n.35
Anglade, Joseph, 92n.62, 233nn.10–11, 236n.45, 239n.64
Anglés, Higini, 176n.6
Anniversary (Italian genre), 154
Antón de Montoro, 164
Antonelli, Roberto, 154n.4, 155n.7
Antonio de Nebrija, 184n.43
Apfelböck, Hermann, 344n.2
Apology (Judeo-Arabic), 331n.22
Appel, Carl, 49n to l. 22, 60n.21, 61nn.30–32, 62n.46, 67n.88, 90n.50, 94n.97, 251 fig. 9.2
Arabian Nights, 11, 258, 263, 269n.22, 269nn.25–26
Argote de Molina, Gonzalo, 171, 186n.62
Aristotle, 4, 8, 10, 11, 15n.17, 134, 146, 147, 247, 249, 254nn.7–8, 254n.15, 255, 268n.1, 275, 276, 277, 278, 291n.12, 292n.18
Armitage, Linda H., 63n.51
Arnaut Daniel, 149, 217, 238n.60
Arnaut de Maruelh, 57n to l. 13, 67n.98, 83
Ars dictaminis. See Dictamen
"Arte de tocar el laúd" (anonymous Spanish treatise), 178n.17

Arts of poetry, 191–205
Arveiller, Raymond, 94n.93
Ascetic themes, Hebrew poetry on, 331n.22
Ascoli, Albert Russell, 156n.18
Aston, S. C., 126, 142n.1
"Au douz mois de mai" (anonymous French motet), 308–11
Aube (French dawn song), 191, 346n.22
Aubrey, Elizabeth, 11–12, 91n.56, 289n.1, 292n.21, 292n.26, 293n.28, 293n.31, 294n.37, 294nn.40–41, 294n.43, 294n.46, 294n.50, 295n.53, 296n.66
Audiau, Jean, 94n.93
Auerbach, Erich, 180n.24, 182n.29
Augustine, 150, 291n.14
Author as auctor, 151
Autobiography, pseudo-, in troubadour lyric, 226
Avalle, D'Arco Silvio, 89n.26, 89n.28, 90n.40
Averroës, 10, 146, 249, 254n.15, 268n.1
Avicenna, 146
Azalais de Porcairagues, 6, 22, 36–44, 69, 80; "Ar em al freg temps vengut," edition of, 44–55; mentioned, 199, 207n.32

Backes, Martina, 345n.14
Badawi, M. M., 330n.3
Baehr, Rudolf, 176n.3
Baena. *See* Cancionero de Baena; Juan Alfonso de Baena
Bal (Occitan dance song), 31, 32
Balada (Occitan), 31, 38, 295n.54; frequency of, 23–24
Ballad (Spanish), 161
Ballade (French), 193
Ballata (Italian), 153
Baltzer, Rebecca A., 176n.7
Barber, E. A., 67n.90
Barbolani, Cristina, 179n.20
Barnes, Jonathan, 254nn.7–8
Barolini, Teodolinda, 156n.13
Bartsch, Karl, 88n.9, 313n.7

Baudri of Bourgueil, 103, 123n.39
Baum, Richard, 292n.27, 293n.33
Baumgartner, Emmanuèle, 207n.25
Bäuml, Franz H., 180–81n.25
Beatritz de Romans, 63n.49
Bec, Pierre, 29, 44, 48n to ll. 2–3, 48–49n to l. 8, 49n to l. 9, 49–50n to ll. 23–24, 50n to l. 34, 60n.18, 60n.20, 62n.47, 65n.70, 65n.74, 66n.75, 94n.98, 121n.3, 123n.38, 155n.8, 178n.14, 210, 219, 229, 232n.6, 234nn.24–25, 235n.33, 235n.35, 241n.85, 292n.21, 293n.28, 293n.30, 293nn.32–33, 294n.43, 295n.54, 295n.60, 295n.65, 296n.67, 297, 313n.1
Beceiro Pita, Isabel, 144n.34
Bellet, Michel-Edouard, 51n to l. 46
Beloiu-Wehn, Ioana, 345n.14
Beltrán, Vicente, 128, 143n.11, 143n.13, 177n.9, 183n.40
Benecke, Georg Friedrich, 344n.4
Benveniste, Emile, 240n.65
Bergin, Thomas Goddard, 21, 23, 29, 35, 57n.1
Bergner, Heinz, 121n.2
Bernardo de Gordonio, 162, 180n.25
Bernardus Silvestris, 7, 97–98, 99, 101, 103, 104, 121nn.10–11, 122nn.14–15, 123n.37
Bernart Arnaut, 81, 91n.53
Bernart de Baseill, 74
Bernart de Ventadorn, 9, 30, 49n to l. 22, 59n.9, 60n.21, 63n.49, 65n.70, 94n.97, 99, 122nn.23–24, 123n.38, 124n.40, 124n.43, 142n.7, 195, 197, 206nn.15–16, 211, 215, 217, 223, 226, 227, 231, 233n.17, 236nn.42–44, 240n.66, 240n.70, 240n.75, 240n.77, 241n.91; "C'ab sol lo bel semblan que·m fai mal," 100; "Non es meravelha s'eu chan," 219–20; "Per la bocha·m feretz al cor," 100; "Quan la freid'aura venta," 86. *See also* Peire and Bernart de Ventadorn
Bernart Marti, 29, 75, 206n.21
Bertau, Karl Heinrich, 344n.2

Bertolome Zorzi, 79, 91n.59
Bertolucci Pizzorusso, Valeria, 62n.43, 145n.45, 178n.15, 183n.42
Bertoni, Giulio, 48n to l. 8
Bertran Carbonel, 80, 82, 84, 85, 88n.10, 88n.13, 289n.1; "Cobla ses so es enaissi," 91n.56, 273; "Per fol tenc qui s'acompanha," 69
Bertran d'Alamano, 83–84, 90n.53, 93n.85
Bertran de Born, 24, 30, 36, 41, 43, 48n to l. 8, 60n.22, 74, 91n.53, 233n.17, 234n.24, 241nn.82–84, 283–84; "Seigner en coms, a blasmar," 227–28
Bertran de la Tor, 91n.53
Bertran lo Ros, 88n.13
Bezzola, Reto R., 123n.36
Bianchini, Simonetta, 155n.7
Bible, 8, 247; Exodus, 14n.2; Mark, 14n.2; Matthew, 14n.2; Old Testament, 8; Psalms, 319; Song of Songs, 10
Biographies of Arabic poets, 259. *See also* Vida
Bishop of Clermont, 91n.53
Black, Robert G., 182n.33
Blanchot, Maurice, 2
Blecua, Alberto, 185n.51
Bloch, R. Howard, 99, 122nn.18–19, 132, 135, 136, 143n.22, 145n.36
Bluegrass music, 17n.24
Boast (Judeo-Arabic), 331n.22
Boethius, 97, 105, 125n.54
Boffey, Julia, 176n.6, 178n.16, 183n.39
Bologna, Corrado, 154n.4, 156n.12
Bond, Gerald A., 62n.43, 90n.40, 121n.1, 123n.39, 233n.17, 234n.25, 234n.27, 240n.67, 240n.71, 241n.79, 241n.84, 241n.87
Bossy, Michel-André, 64n.65, 66n.77, 67n.95
Botenlied (German messenger song), 13, 334
Boutière, Jean, 57n.2, 60n.17, 63n.50, 90n.47, 90nn.52–53, 93nn.73–74, 93n.81, 93n.84, 233nn.15–16,

233nn.18–19, 234nn.20–23, 235n.35, 235n.39, 236n.44, 237nn.46–47, 237n.52, 295n.59
Boyde, P., 121n.6
Braden, Gordon, 61n.38
Branciforti, Francesco, 91nn.59–60, 93n.86
Brann, Ross, 12–13, 155n.4, 330n.1, 330n.6, 330n.8, 331n.34, 332n.40
Brittan, Arthur, 144n.25
Brody, Heinrich, 330n.9, 331n.17, 332n.41
Brogan, T. V. F., 15n.17
Bromwich, James, 51n to l. 46
Brownlee, Kevin, 313n.2
Bruckner, Matilda Tomaryn, 44, 48n to ll. 2–3, 48–49n to l. 8, 49n to l. 9, 49–50n to ll. 23–24, 50n to l. 34, 62n.47, 66n.75, 66n.77, 207n.32
Brugnolo, Furio, 155n.7, 155n.9, 155–56n.12
Brunel-Lobrichon, Geneviève, 66n.81, 67n.86
Brunetto Latini, 185n.47
Bruno, Giordano, 2, 14n.4
Bruno von Hornberg, 13; "Swer tougenlîcher minne pflege," 338–40
Burke, Peter, 180n.24
Burkhard von Hohenfels, 346n.21
Burlesque, 346n.21
Burrus, Victoria A., 182n.33
Burton, David G., 186n.56
Burton, Richard F., 269n.8, 269nn.25–27
Buthayna, 259
Butler, H. E., 67n.90

Cable, Thomas, 176n.7
Cadenet, 90n.53
Camille, Michael, 179n.24
Canción (Spanish, "song"), 8–9, 158–75
Cancionero de Baena, 164, 165, 169, 171. *See also* Juan Alfonso de Baena
Cancionero de Palacio, 171
Cancionero General, 171
Canso (Occitan love song), 6, 8, 9, 10, 11, 16n.18, 21, 22, 23, 30, 31, 32, 33, 35, 36, 37, 38, 40, 41, 42, 43, 57n.2, 59n.13, 60n.22, 63n.49, 63nn.57–58, 64n.59, 64n.63, 65n.70, 65nn.74–75, 68, 71, 72, 75, 76, 78, 79, 82, 84, 86, 88n.16, 94n.96, 96, 136, 148, 151, 152, 153–54, 193, 195, 197, 204, 210, 211, 212, 213, 214, 215, 216, 217, 218, 229, 231–32nn.2–3, 232n.5, 233n.13, 234nn.24–25, 234n.27, 236nn.41–42, 236nn.44–45, 237n.48, 237n.53, 238n.59, 238–39n.61–62, 239n.64, 245, 246, 246 fig. 9.1, 251, 251 fig. 9.2, 252, 279, 280, 282, 283, 285, 286, 292n.25, 293nn.31–33, 346n.22; frequency of, 23–26, 28, 29
Cansoneta (Occitan, diminutive of *canso*), 63n.58, 215, 216, 234n.25, 236n.42, 237n.49
Canso-sirventes, 232n.5, 233n.13, 237n.48, 237n.53. *See also Sirventescanso*
Cant (Occitan, "song"), 30, 214, 215, 235n.35
Cantar (Occitan noun, "song"), 30; (Occitan verb, "to sing"), 214, 215
Cantar (Spanish, "song"), 171
Cantaret (Occitan, diminutive of *cantar*, "song"), 237n.49, 238n.59
Cantarino, Vicente, 10–11, 12, 268nn.1–2, 268n.6, 270n.31
Cantiga (Spanish, "song"), 8–9, 158–75
Cantiga d'amigo (Galician-Portuguese song in voice of woman), 7, 65n.75, 127, 132, 133, 332n.39
Cantiga d'amor (Galician-Portuguese song in voice of man), 7, 127, 128, 132, 140, 141–42
Cantiga d'escarnho e de maldizer (Galician-Portuguese satirical song), 127, 140, 145n.46
Cantilena, in Johannes de Grocheio, 275–77, 292n.16
Cantor, Norman F., 61n.36
Cantus (Latin, "melody"), in Johannes de Grocheio, 277, 292n.16; *cantus coronatus*, 275–76; *cantus versiculatus*, 276; in rhetoric, 277
Canzone (Italian), 35, 151, 152, 153–54

Canzoniere. See Macrogenre
Caravaca, Francisco, 187n.64
Careri, Maria, 92n.68, 93n.83
Carmi, T., 331n.14, 331n.17, 331n.26, 331n.36
Carmina Burana, 7, 97, 102, 106–8, 118–20, 123n.33, 123n.40, 124n.46, 124n.48, 124n.52
Carr, Derek, 185n.55
Carriazo, Juan de Mata, 178n.10, 179n.22
Carstens, Henry, 6, 22, 29, 35, 36, 38, 58n.3, 59n.15, 60n.15, 61n.2, 213, 215, 216, 224, 232n.3, 233n.16, 234n.26, 234n.28, 236n.42, 237n.49, 237n.51, 237nn.53–55, 238n.60, 289n.1
Castelloza, Na, 43, 55n to ll. 12–16, 63n.49, 66n.77, 240n.69
Cátedra, Pedro, 179n.21, 185n.54
Celar (Occitan, "discretion"), 151
Cercamon, 29, 65n.73, 211, 212, 213, 227, 231, 233n.17, 234n.24, 235n.30, 235n.34, 238n.61, 240n.67, 241n.81, 241n.91; "Lo plaing comenz iradamen," 226–27
Cerverí de Girona, 90n.51, 94n.93
Chabaneau, Camille, 92n.64
Chailley, Jacques, 236n.41
Chamard, Henri, 16n.21
Chambers, Frank M., 50n to l. 41, 50n to l. 42, 50n to l. 43, 57n.2, 60n.20, 63n.55, 67n.92, 93n.76, 240n.77, 290n.4, 292n.21
Chambres de rhétorique, 204
Champion, Pierre, 208n.40
Chan. See Cant
Chanson (French), 12, 96, 103, 191, 193, 194, 195, 203, 204; fragmentary, 58n.8. *See also Chanson courtoise; Grand chant courtois*
Chanson courtoise, 297, 299, 300, 301, 306, 312. *See also Chanson; Grand chant courtois*
Chanson d'absence, 153
Chanson de change (Occitan), 42, 65n.70, 154, 234n.27

Chanson de croisade. See Crusade song
Chanson de femme, 65n.75
Chanson de geste, 4, 276
Chanson de mai, 299
Chanson féminine, in Guillaume de Machaut, 198–99
Chanson leu, 38
Chanson plurilingue, 58n.8
Chanson religieuse. See Religious poetry
Chant, liturgical, 298. *See also* Liturgy
Chantar. See Cantar
"Chantez seri, Marot" (anonymous French motet), 307–8
Charles d'Orleans, 9, 197, 202, 208n.40; "En la forest de Longue Actente," 204
Chartier, Roger, 181n.27
Châtelain de Couci, 9, 198, 207nn.29–30
Chaucer. *See* Geoffrey Chaucer
Chaytor, H. J., 180n.24, 181n.25, 182n.29
Cherchi, Paolo, 155n.11
Chickering, Howell, 62n.39
Christine de Pizan, 16n.21, 196, 199, 205n.7
Cicero, 172, 291nn.14–15, 292n.17
Cino da Pistoia, 147
Cipolla, Carlo M., 180nn.24–25
Clancy, Michael T., 180nn.24–25, 183n.39
Clara d'Anduza, 63n.49
Clark, Donald Leman, 184n.47
Clarke, Dorothy Clotelle, 175n.3, 185n.55
Clausula (close of a period, in rhetoric), 177n.9
Cluzel, Irénée-Marcel, 57n.2, 93n.77, 233n.15, 295n.59
Cnyrim, Eugen, 49n to ll. 11–12, 49n to l. 22, 67n.91
Cobla, 6–7, 23, 30, 31, 32, 36, 38, 56, 58n.8, 61n.26, 63n.49, 64n.63, 68–87, 231n.3, 233n.13, 236n.44, 251, 273, 289n.1, 295n.63, 334; *cobla*-exchanges, 6, 58n.8, 60n.15, 61n.26, 68, 69–70, 71, 72, 73, 83, 88n.8, 88n.13,

89n.31, 92n.70, 232n.3, 240n.76; *coblas esparsas*, 6, 30, 68, 69, 70, 71, 73, 76, 78, 79, 80, 83, 87n.3, 88n.8, 88n.13, 94n.93, 210, 246 fig. 9.1; *coblas triadas*, 80–81; earliest use of word to name genre, 74; extracted, 6, 39, 68, 69, 87n.4, 88n.8; fragmentary *coblas*, 58n.8; frequency of, 23–25, 28; inserted, 6, 68–69, 87n.4; with an unknown poet (fictional?), 58n.8
Cobleiador (Occitan, "one who composes *coblas*"), 7, 79
Cobleiar (Occitan, "to make *coblas*"), 7, 79
Codera y Zaidin, Francisco, 269n.11
Cohen, Joel, 241n.89
Cohen, Rip, 129, 143n.15
Coleman, S., 181n.27
Coluccio Salutati, 184n.47
Comjat (Occitan song of leave-taking), 42, 65n.70, 234n.27
Commentary, as genre, 16n.23; in lyric genre, 219
Companion songs, 213, 229
Comtessa de Dia, 63n.49
Conceiçao Vihena, Maria da, 145n.41
Conon de Béthune, 207n.30
Conort (Occitan song of comfort), 31
Consistori de la subregaya companhia del Gay Saber, Toulouse, 35, 44, 210
Consistories, 204
Consistorio de la gaya ciencia, Barcelona, 160
Contrafacta, 12, 34, 60n.20, 63n.49, 159, 177nn.8–9, 274, 290n.4, 298, 299, 312, 313n.6. *See also* Mu'arada
Convention in genre, 3, 126–40, 142n.5, 322–24, 338, 346n.22. *See also* Gender in genre
Copeland, Rita, 184n.47, 187n.68
Copla (Spanish, "stanza, poem"), 9, 171, 172
Córdoba de la Llave, Ricardo, 144n.34
Cornago, 179n.18
Cortijo, Antonio, 184n.43
Cossir (Occitan song of care), 31
Costantini, Aldo, 156n.21

Count of Rodez, 70, 91n.53
Croce, Benedetto, 2
Crónica de Aragón, 186n.56
Crónica del condestable Miguel Lucas de Iranzo, 161
Cropp, Glynnis, 144n.33
Crosby, Ruth, 180n.25, 182n.29
Crusade song (Occitan), 21, 31, 32, 33, 154, 232n.3, 232n.5, 233n.13, 216; frequency of, 23–24, 28, 29. *See also* Kreuzlied
Cull, John, 180n.25, 182n.30
Curtius, Ernst Robert, 123n.40, 126, 184nn.46–47

Dagenais, John, 10, 254n.17, 330n.2
Dalfi d'Alvernhe, 90n.53
Dansa (Occitan dance song), 11, 12, 21, 22, 30, 31, 35, 38, 77, 84, 210, 211, 233n.13, 239n.62, 246 fig. 9.1, 251 fig. 9.2, 285–86, 287, 295n.54; *dansa d'amor*, 279; fragmentary, 58n.8; frequency of, 23–24, 28; parodic, 58n.8
Dansa-pastourelle, 58n.8
Dante Alighieri, 4, 7, 8, 109, 125n.55, 147, 149, 150, 151, 152, 153, 155n.10, 156n.19, 179n.18, 192, 204, 205n.2, 215
Daspol, 63n.51
Dawn song in German, 336–43, 345n.14. *See also* Tagelied; Tagewîse; Taghorn
De Lollis, Cesare, 88n.8, 92n.70, 93n.75, 93n.92
De Robertis, Domenico, 156n.19
Dechat (Occitan song of scorn?), 78
Decir (Spanish, "recited poem" or "poetic composition"), 8–9, 158–75
Dejeanne, Jean-Marie-Lucien, 60n.19, 90n.40, 233n.17, 234n.25, 234n.28, 235n.29, 236n.40, 241n.78, 241n.86, 241n.91
Del Monte, Alberto, 213, 233n.17, 235n.32, 240n.77, 241n.84
Delbouille, Maurice, 51n to l. 49, 313n.7

Derrida, Jacques, 2, 15n.7
Desconort (Occitan song of discomfort), 31
Descort (Occitan song of discord), 11, 21, 30, 38, 86, 94n.93, 210, 211, 232n.3, 233n.13, 246 fig. 9.1, 251 fig. 9.2, 281–82, 286, 293n.29, 293–94nn.31–33; frequency of, 23–24, 28
Desplazer (Occitan song of displeasure), 31, 210
Devinalh (Occitan riddle), 73, 213, 216, 232n.5, 234n.27
DeWitt, Patricia Alice Mitchell, 291n.12
Deyermond, Alan D., 143n.12, 180n.24, 182n.35
Dezidor (Spanish, "composer of *decires*"), 170
Di Girolamo, Costanzo, 49n to l. 22
Dia. *See* Comtessa de Dia
Dialogue genres in Occitan, 22, 212, 216, 224
Dick, Ernst S., 345n.13
Dictado (Spanish, "poetic composition"), 9, 166, 167–72
Dictador (Spanish, "composer of *dictados*"), 170, 172
Dictamen (medieval Latin theory of epistolary prose and writing in general), 9, 166–67, 173, 184n.44, 184n.47; "text," in Johannes de Grocheio, 277
Dictar (Spanish, "to write poetry"), 9, 166, 172
Dictat (Occitan, "written composition"), 10, 215, 236n.45, 239n.64
Didactic song (Middle High German), 334, 343
Diego de Estúñiga, 168
Diego de San Pedro, 181n.27
Diego Martínez de Medina, 168
Dietmar von Aist, 13, 342; "Slâfest du, vriedel ziere?" 336–37
Diez, Friedrich, 59n.14
Dinis, Dom, 139, 143n.15; "Proençaes soen mui bem trobar," 138
Diomedes, 4

"Dionei sideris" (anonymous Latin poem), 115–18
Dionysius Thrax, 4
Dirge (Hebrew), 319
Dispositio (arrangement, in rhetoric), 277
Dit (French genre), 306
Ditado (Spanish, "poetic composition"), 168
Divorce between poetry and music in Italy, 150
Diwan (Judeo-Arabic poet's literary corpus), 318, 319, 327, 330n.13
Doctor (as used by Guiraut Riquier), 84
Doctrina de compondre dictats, 7, 10, 11, 30, 32, 61n.28, 78, 210, 211, 215, 218, 231n.2, 232n.4, 233n.14, 245–50, 279–88, 295n.63
Dragonetti, Roger, 121n.3, 125n.55, 126, 142n.3, 205n.10, 208n.39, 219, 239n.65
Drama, 14
Drinking poetry. *See Khamriyya*
Dronke, Peter, 95–97, 103, 112–14, 121n.1, 121nn.3–6, 121n.10, 122n.14, 123n.28, 123nn.33–37, 123n.39, 124n.41, 124n.45, 124n.48, 124nn.50–52, 126, 140, 142n.2, 142n.4, 143n.10
Du Bellay, Joachim, 16n.21
Ducrot, Oswald, 15n.14, 16n.17
Duplum. See Motetus
Dutton, Brian, 175n.3, 178n.13, 179n.19, 180n.25, 181nn.26–27, 182n.30, 183n.37, 186n.56

Earnshaw, Doris, 65n.72, 268n.5
Earp, Lawrence, 176n.7
Eble d'Uisel, 94n.93
Edelman, Nathan, 62n.41
Edwards, Robert R., 97, 121n.9, 124n.49
Elias Cairel, 234n.24
Elias d'Uisel, 72, 89n.23, 91n.53
Elocutio (style, in rhetoric), 277
"En mai, quant rosier sont flouri" (anonymous French motet), 303

"Encontre le tans de Pascour" (anonymous French motet), 300, 301–3
Encyclopedic narratives, 4
Enrique de Villena, 160, 168, 179n.21, 186n.62
Ensenhamen (Occitan didactic genre), 86
Enueg (Occitan song of annoyance), 21, 22, 31, 210
Epic, 14, 16n.18
Epic-lyric-dramatic triad, 335
Epigons, epigonality, 338, 346nn.22–23
Epithalamium (wedding song), 13, 328, 329
Ernout, A., 184n.46
Escondich (Occitan song of excuses), 21, 31, 151, 153, 210, 211, 234n.27, 251 fig. 9.2
Esdemessa (Occitan song of effort), 21, 29
Esopete Historiado, 182n.33
Esparsa (Spanish genre), 172
Estampida (Occitan musical genre), 11, 21, 22, 30, 38, 210, 211, 246 fig. 9.1, 247, 251 fig. 9.2, 252, 286, 287–88, 295n.63; frequency of, 23–24
Estampie (French name of Occitan *estampida*), 287, 295n.64, 296n.66, 334
Estribot (Occitan genre), 21, 29, 37, 63n.55, 222, 240n.74
Everist, Mark, 313n.6
Evrard l'Allemand, 289n.3
Exchange of *coblas*. See Cobla
Exempla, 239n.62
Exercises, poetic. See *Qitcat*
Expectation, generic, 3, 191, 334–43
Extracted *coblas*. See Cobla

Fabla (Occitan fable), 21, 29
Fabliaux, 16n.18
Falquet de Romans, 94n.93
Faral, Edmond, 121n.12, 123n.32, 183n.42, 289n.3
Fassler, Margot E., 290n.7
Faulhaber, Charles B., 184n.47
Fenster, Thelma, 132, 144n.24
Fernán Pérez de Guzmán, 164, 169

Fernández, Lucas, 178n.10
Fernández de la Cuesta, Ismael, 293n.31
Ferrand, Françoise, 207n.25
Ferrante, Joan M., 67n.93
Ferrari de Ferrara, 34, 74, 83, 91n.53, 93n.80
Figures of rhetoric, 166
Filgueira Valverde, José, 142n.10
Fin' amor (Occitan or French), 8, 29, 34, 86, 100, 103, 108, 148, 149, 152, 197, 200, 228, 239n.61, 306
Finke, Laurie, 131, 132, 143n.21, 144n.22
Flabel (Occitan little fable), 21, 29
Floral Games, 230
Floral poetry (Judeo-Arabic), 326
Fokkema, Douwe, 143n.20
Folate (Middle High German name of a French genre?), 344n.5
Folena, Gianfranco, 88n.16, 89n.29
Folquet de Marselha, 6, 80, 83, 88nn.17–18, 89nn.19–20, 155n.5, 289n.1; "Vermillon, clam fos faç d'un'avol pega pencha," 71
Formisano, Luciano, 155n.8
Fowler, Alastair, 16n.18
Fragment (Occitan), 31, 58n.8; frequency of, 23–24
Francisco Vaca, 164
François Villon, 16n.20
Frank, István, 22, 23, 29, 30, 31, 32, 35, 36, 37, 38, 58nn.3–5, 58nn.7–8, 59n.12, 59n.15, 60n.23, 61n.26, 63n.58, 67n.83, 89n.31, 90nn.33–34, 213, 215, 216, 224, 231n.3, 234n.26, 234n.28, 237n.51, 237nn.53–54, 238n.55, 238n.60, 241n.87, 242, 293n.31; on titles, 92n.69
Frasca, Gabriele, 155n.10
Frauenlied, Frauenstrophe (German women's song), 13, 334
Freeman-Regalado, Nancy, 186n.63
Frenk, Margit, 180n.24
Frenzel, Peter, 343, 346n.28
Freund, Sabine, 345n.14
Frye, Northrop, 16n.18, 256, 268n.3

Gab (Occitan, "boast"), 151, 153, 213, 234n.27
Gabrieli, F., 268n.7
Gace Brulé, 207n.30
Gaita (Occitan song of a watchman), 30, 210, 211, 246 fig. 9.1
Gallo, Ernest, 122n.12
Gap. See *Gab*
Garber, Frederick, 15n.17
García de Enterría, María Cruz, 183n.39
García López, Jorge, 182n.32
Garden in spring, song about (Hebrew), 319
Garin lo Brun, 236n.44
Garip (Occitan melody), 31
Garulo, Teresa, 269n.11
Gatien-Arnoult, Adolphe-F., 61n.30, 295n.61
Gattung (German, "genre"), 335
Gaucelm Faidit, 72, 89n.22, 91n.53, 234n.24, 286
Gauceran, 73
Gauchat, L., 92n.63
Gaudairenca, 91n.53
Gaunt, Simon, 16n.18, 65n.69, 132, 144n.22, 239n.61
Gautier de Dargies, 204, 207n.30, 208n.36; "La gens dient pour coi je ne faiz chanz," 200
Gayat al-Muna, 261
Gazelle (male or female beloved in Judeo-Arabic poetry), 332n.43
Gehry, Frank, 13
Gelozesca (Occitan song of jealousy), 30, 31, 210
Gender in genre, 255–68
Gender-neutrality in Arabic poetry, 11, 12, 260, 261, 263, 267, 268
Genette, Gérard, 240n.65
Gennrich, Friedrich, 290n.4, 293n.31, 294n.44, 314n.8
"Genre" (English word), 335
Genre (French word), 335
Genres, lyric, in Dante's *Vita nuova*, 153–54
"Genus" (biological term), 335

Geoffrey Chaucer, 4, 125n.54
Geoffrey of Everseley, 183n.42
Geoffrey of Vinsauf, 7, 98, 101, 105, 121n.12, 123n.32, 184n.47, 192, 289n.3; *Poetria nova*, 102
Gericke, Philip O., 182n.30
Gervase of Melkley, 184n.47, 289n.3
Gesanc (Middle High German, "song" or "singing"), 335
Ghazal (Judeo-Arabic love song), 12, 255, 317, 319, 322, 323, 326, 329, 330n.5, 331n.22
Ghisalberti, Fausto, 246, 254n.5
Giacomo da Lentini, 147, 154n.3, 155n.5, 157n.22
Gioglaret, 92nn.71–72
"Gioglaret, quant passarez" (anonymous Occitan *cobla*), 81
Giovanni del Virgilio, 184n.47
Giraut. *See* Guiraut
Glosa (Spanish genre), 172
Glosa sobre Lux Bella, 186n.56
Gnomic verse (Hebrew), 319
Goddard, Eunice Rathbone, 14n.1
Godman, Peter, 97, 121n.9, 124n.45
Goethe, Wolfgang, 59n.14
Goldin, Frederick, 195, 198, 206nn.13–14, 207n.28
Goliards, 96
Gombrich, E. H., 2–3, 4, 15nn.9–11, 37, 63n.53
Gómez-Bravo, Ana M., 8–9, 155n.7, 156n.14, 175n.1, 183n.42, 184n.45, 187n.67
Gómez Manrique, 160, 180n.24
Gonfroy, Gérard, 58nn.2–3
González Cuenca, Joaquín, 175n.3, 179n.19, 181n.27, 183n.37, 186n.56
Gonzalo de Berceo, 170
Gonzalvo, Luis, 269n.11
Gorni, Guglielmo, 156n.12, 156n.19
Gospel song (in bluegrass), 17n.24
Gottfried von Strassburg, 344n.5
Gouiran, Gérard, 94n.93
Gower, 125n.54
Gradual, 298
Gradus amoris, 195, 197, 200, 206n.20

Grand chant courtois (French genre), 9, 16n.18, 96, 127, 191–205, 219, 294n.33, 346n.22. *See also Chanson; Chanson courtoise*
Gravdal, Kathryn, 17n.26, 65n.72, 66n.75
Greenia, George D., 270n.29
Grimminger, Rolf, 344n.9
Gröber, Gustav, 91n.57, 92nn.71–72
Grocheio, Grocheo. *See* Johannes de Grocheio
Gruber, Jörn, 236n.40, 237n.47, 290n.3
Grundriss der romanischen Literaturen des Mittelalters, 233n.13
Guglielmo IX. *See* Guilhem IX
Gui de Cavaillon, 77, 81, 88n.12, 91n.53
Guido Cavalcanti, 152, 153
Guido Guinizelli, 152, 153
Gui d'Uisel, 94n.93
Guiette, Robert, 121n.3
Guilhem IX (first known Occitan troubadour), 2, 24, 29, 34, 41, 62n.42, 68, 75, 90n.40, 155n.7, 197, 211, 213, 222, 223, 229, 233n.17, 234nn.24–25, 234n.27, 240n.67, 240n.71, 240n.73, 241n.79, 241n.84, 241n.87, 317; "Farai un vers de dreit nien," 221; "Farai un vers, pos mi sonelh," 224–26
Guilhem Ademar, 90n.43; "Deniers—pus 'deniers' mentaurai," 76
Guilhem Augier Novella, 281
Guilhem d'Autpol, 43, 63n.51
Guilhem de Berguedan, 73–74, 89n.31, 90nn.35–36, 90n.38; "Bernartz diz de Baseill," 74
Guilhem de Saint Didier. *See* Guilhem de Saint Leidier
Guilhem de Saint Gregori, 48n to l. 8
Guilhem de Saint Leidier, 49n to l. 21, 90n.42, 236n.44; "Aissi cum es bella cill de cui chan," 75–76
Guilhem del Baus, 72, 91n.53
Guilhem Magret, 78, 79, 90n.44, 90n.53, 91n.60; "Non valon re coblas ni arrazos," 76
Guilhem Molinier. *See Leys d'amors*

Guilhem Olivier d'Arles, 69, 80, 82
Guilhem Raimon, "N'Aimeric, qe·us par d'aqest novel marqes?" 82
Guillaume d'Aquitaine. *See* Guilhem IX
Guillaume de Ferrières, le vidame de Chartres, 207n.30
Guillaume de Lorris, 107, 108, 124n.48. *See also Roman de la rose*
Guillaume de Machaut, 9, 176n.7, 179n.18, 198, 204, 207n.31, 281; "Honteuse sui, quant je parole einsi," 199
Guillem. *See* Guilhem
Guiraut de Bornelh, 69, 75, 90n.40, 211, 216, 217, 230, 231, 232n.5, 233n.17, 234n.24, 236n.43, 237nn.47–51, 237nn.53–54, 238nn.55–56, 238nn.58–59, 238n.61, 240n.77, 241nn.90–92
Guiraut de Cabrera, 234n.24
Guiraut Riquier, 24, 34, 62n.43, 84, 93n.88, 140, 145n.45, 160, 178n.15, 230, 285, 294n.35
Guittone d'Arezzo, 8, 147, 148, 150–51, 156nn.15–17

Habermann, A. M., 332n.41
Hafsa bint ar-Rakuniyya, 259
Hafsa bint Hamdun al-Hijariyya, 260
Haidu, Peter, 122n.25, 129, 130, 131, 143n.17
Halkin, A. S., 330n.5, 331n.15, 331n.17, 331n.27
Hamda bint Ziyad, 259
Hamori, Andras, 317, 330n.4
Häring, N. M., 122n.16, 122n.20, 122nn.26–27, 123n.31
Hart, Thomas, 128, 129, 143n.10, 143nn.13–14, 145n.39
Hartmann von Aue, 346n.22
Hassana at-Tamimiyya, 259
Hastings, Alan, 182n.31
Hatto, Arthur T., 345n.14
Hausner, Renate, 345n.14
Hayes, Julia C., 66n.77
Hechos del condestable don Miguel Lucas de Iranzo, 178n.10, 179n.22

Heinen, Hubert, 13, 344n.1, 344n.4, 345n.12, 345n.18, 346n.22, 346n.24, 346n.26
Heinrich von Morungen, 337, 343, 345n.18
Heloise, 167, 184n.46
Hermann the German, 10, 249
Heur, Jean-Marie d', 127, 134, 144nn.27–28, 145n.40
Hibberd, Lloyd, 295n.64
Hicks, Eric, 184n.46, 185n.49
Hija' (Arabic, "blame"), 317
Hilka, Alfons, 109–12, 118–20, 123n.33, 123n.40, 124n.46
Hill, Raymond Thompson, 21, 23, 29, 35, 57n.1
Hind, 259
Hirsch, E. D., 319, 330n.10
Historia de la Donzella Teodor, 269n.8
Hoepffner, Ernest, 206n.21
Holmes, Olivia, 63n.51
Homer, 248
Honorius of Autun, 250
Hoppin, Richard H., 293n.31
Horace, 248
Hugh Primas, 123n.40
Huot, Sylvia, 12, 13, 155n.4, 178n.16, 183n.39, 205n.11, 314n.18
Hutchison, Ann M., 180n.24
Huygens, R. B. C., 246, 254n.5, 254nn.9–11, 254n.18
Hybrid forms, 299. *See also* Intergenre
Hymn, 311

Iacopo Mostacci, 157n.22
Iacopone da Todi, 147
"Iam ver oritur" (anonymous Latin poem), 106–7
Iannucci, Amilcare A., 16n.22
Ibn al-Abbar, 269n.12, 269n.17, 269n.21
Ibn Bajja, 329
Ibn Qusman, 268
Ibn Sahl, 267
Ibn Zaydun, 261, 265, 269n.14, 269n.16, 270n.28
Imitation, 191–205. *See also* Contrafacta
Imperial, 168

Improvisation, of Occitan songs, 81–82, 92n.71
Infantes, Victor, 186n.62
Iñigo López de Mendoza, Fray, 162
Iñigo López de Mendoza, Marqués de Santillana. *See* Santillana
Insertions, lyric, in French romances, 4, 12, 312
Intergenre, 12, 16n.20, 17n.26, 297–312, 318, 328. *See also* Hybrid forms
Inventio (creation, in rhetoric), 277
Iordan, Iorgu, 61n.36
Isaac ibn Ghiyath, 325, 328
Ishak al-Mausili, 269n.22
Istanpitte (Italian name of Occitan *estampida*), 287
Izarn, "E dic vos ben: Qan d'aqesta tenso," 77

Jackson, William E., 344n.8
Jacques d'Ostun, 198
Jacques Legrand, 206n.24
Jakob von Warte, 345n.17
Janson, Tore, 121n.6
Janzarik, Diether, 91n.57
Jarden, Dov, 329n.1, 330nn.7–8
Jaufre Rudel, 29, 211, 212, 213, 214, 216, 226, 229, 233n.17, 234n.24, 235nn.36–38, 235n.40, 236n.40, 238n.57; "E·l rossignoletz el ram," 215; "Quant lo rossignols el fuoillos," 214
Jauss, Hans Robert, 15n.15, 16n.18, 191, 292n.21, 329, 345n.13
Javanais (Occitan), 31, 58n.7; frequency of, 23–24
Javare, "E pois coblas sabes faire," 83–84
Jean de Garlande, 289n.3, 290n.7, 290n.10
Jean de Meun, 4, 7, 105, 108, 184n.46. *See also Roman de la rose*
Jean de Trie, 207n.30
Jeanroy, Alfred, 59n.9, 59n.14, 61nn.30–31, 64n.63, 65n.70, 67n.95, 85, 87n.2, 88n.10, 88nn.12–14, 89n.21, 90n.45, 91n.56, 93n.77, 93n.87, 93n.91, 235n.34, 240n.68

Jeffreys, Mark, 62n.40
Jewers, Caroline A., 66n.75
Joc partit (Occitan dialogue song), 30, 61n.24, 81, 233n.13
Jofre de Foixà, 11, 61n.28, 233n.14, 279, 292n.24
Johannes de Garlandia, 290n.7
Johannes de Grocheio, 11, 177n.9, 178n.17, 184n.46, 275–78, 287, 288, 290nn.5–6, 290nn.8–9, 291nn.10–13, 292n.16, 292n.18, 295n.61
John of Garland, 184n.47
Johnson, Barbara, 268n.4
Johnston, R. C., 67n.98
Jones, Nancy A., 64n.65, 66n.77, 67n.95
Jones, R. O., 175n.3
Jordi de Sant Jordi, 160, 178–79n.18
Jorge Manrique, 161, 162, 171, 179n.23, 187n.64
Joseph ibn Hisdai, 325; "And as he slept I plucked, with his consent," 320
Juan Alfonso de Baena, 160, 162, 165, 168, 170, 181n.27, 183n.41. *See also* Cancionero de Baena
Juan de Mena, 161, 162, 164, 168, 170
Juan de Valdés, 160, 179n.20
Juan del Encina, 160, 175n.3, 178n.13, 179n.20, 187n.66
Juan Ruiz, Archpriest of Hita, 168, 169, 171, 185n.51, 249, 254n.17
Judah ha-Levi, 323, 326, 328, 332n.41, 333n.45
Judah ibn Ghiyath, 328

Karp, Theodore, 289n.2
Kay, Sarah, 64n.69, 121n.3, 127, 132, 142n.7, 144n.22, 144n.33
"Ke fareyu mamma" (anonymous *kharja*), 266
Keats, John, 320
Kehrli, H., 92n.63
Keller, Hans-Erich, 67n.95
Kelly, Douglas, 9, 97, 121n.11, 185n.47, 205n.6, 206n.18, 206n.22, 206n.24, 208n.40, 289n.3

Kelly, H. Ansgar, 4–5, 16n.22
Kendrick, Laura, 132, 143n.22
Kendris, Theodore, 63n.51
Kerrigan, William, 61n.38
Khamriyya (Judeo-Arabic wine poetry), 12, 255, 317, 319, 321, 322, 323, 326, 329, 331n.22
Kharja (envoi in a *muwashshah*), 11, 256, 264, 265, 266, 267, 326–29, 332n.37, 332n.39, 332n.42
Klopsch, Paul, 121n.2
Knust, Hermann, 269n.23
Köhler, Erich, 57n.2, 60n.16, 60n.23, 65n.70, 94n.95, 155n.8, 209, 210, 230, 231n.1, 232n.6, 234nn.24–25, 234n.27, 235n.28, 235n.30, 235n.34, 236n.41, 236n.43, 237n.53, 238n.61, 241n.88, 294n.33
Kolsen, Adolf, 51n to l. 49, 90n.40, 90n.48, 93n.89, 94n.99, 233n.17, 237n.48, 237n.53, 238nn.54–55
Kraus, Carl von, 345n.17
Krauss, Henning, 155n.9, 346n.21, 346n.23
Kremer, Dieter, 155n.8
Kreuzlied (German crusade song), 13, 334
Krispin, Arno, 57n to Rubric, 64n.62, 66n.78
Kristeller, Paul Oskar, 184n.47, 186n.58
Krueger, Roberta L., 206n.17
Kuhn, Thomas, 3

Ladner, Gerhard, 122n.15
Lafont, Robert, 293n.31
Lai (Occitan) 11, 30, 31, 210, 211, 246 fig. 9.1, 250, 281, 286, 292n.27, 293n.29, 293nn.31–32; frequency of, 23–24. *See also Leich*
"Lai Markiol" (anonymous Occitan *lai*), 281
"Lai Non-par" (anonymous Occitan *lai*), 281
Lament (Hebrew), 322, 331n.22
Landoni, Elena, 208n.41, 233n.9
Lane, Edward William, 269n.22

Lanfranc Cigala, 60n.17, 79, 82, 84, 91nn.59–60, 93n.86
Lang, H. R., 158, 159, 175nn.2–3, 187n.65
Langlois, Ernest, 313n.2
Lanza Marques, 72–73, 89n.28, 89n.30
Lapesa, Rafael, 176n.3, 185n.48, 187n.66
Lauer, Philippe, 14n.1
"L'autre jour par un matin" (anonymous French motet), 304–6
Lawler, Traugott, 290n.7, 290n.10
Lawrance, J. N. H., 180n.24, 182n.30
Lay. See *Lai*
Lazar, Moshé, 122nn.23–24, 124n.40, 206n.15, 233n.17, 236nn.42–43, 240n.66, 240n.70, 240n.75, 240n.77, 241n.91
Le Gentil, Pierre, 158–59, 175n.3, 186nn.60–61, 187n.65
Lee, Carolyn R., 175n.3
Leich (German lay), 13, 334, 343, 344n.2. See also *Lai*
Leonardi, Lino, 156n.15
Lerond, Alain, 207n.29
Letra de justadores (Spanish genre), 172
Letsch-Lavanchy, Antoinette, 185n.56
Letter (Occitan genre), 21, 29
Leube(-Fey), Christiane, 58n.6, 64n.63, 65n.70, 87nn.1–2, 94nn.95–96
Leupin, Alexandre, 99, 101, 122n.18, 122n.21, 123n.30, 124n.47
Levin, Israel, 322, 323, 331n.22, 332n.40, 332nn.43–44
Levy, Emil, 67nn.87–88, 90n.50, 91n.59
Lewent, Kurt, 48n to ll. 2–3, 48n to l. 8, 51n to ll. 47–48
Lewis, C. S., 176n.5
Leys d'amors, 10, 31, 32–33, 36, 80, 92n.62, 210, 211, 214, 215, 216, 218, 229, 233nn.10–11, 236n.45, 250–52, 287, 288, 295n.61
Libro de Alexandre, 167, 185n.50
Libro de Buen Amor. See Juan Ruiz
Libro de los cien capítulos, 249, 254n.16
Libro del cavallero Zifar, 162
Libro di poesia. See Macrogenre

Liet (Middle High German, "strophe"), 335, 344n.7
Lindberg, David C., 208n.38
Linskill, Joseph, 89n.24, 93n.88
Literature, as genre, 33
Liturgy, 306, 311, 314n.8; Hebrew, 328. See also Chant
Locus (region of an argument, in rhetoric), 291n.15
Locus amoenus (topos of the pleasant place), 337
Loewe, Raphael, 331n.16
Lombarda, 81, 91n.53
Lomperis, Linda, 98, 122n.13
Lope del Monte, Fray, 168
López Estrada, Francisco, 175n.1, 179n.18, 179n.20, 183n.41, 185n.53, 185n.55, 186n.56, 186n.61, 187n.66
Love songs: *Cantica amatoria*, 332n.39
—: Judeo-Arabic. See *Ghazal*
—: Occitan, 213. See also *Canso; Chanson; Chanson courtoise; Fin' amor; Grand chant courtois*
Lozano, Gracia, 184n.43
Ludwig, Friedrich, 314n.8
Lügenaere (German, "slanderers"), 338
Lumsden-Kouvel, Audrey, 63n.51
Lyric (eighteenth-century term), 16n.19, 33
Lyric textuality, pure, in Occitan, 212, 219–23, 226–29
Lyrical complaint (Judeo-Arabic). See *Tazallum*

MacDonald, Scott, 291n.12
Machaut. See Guillaume de Machaut
Macrogenre, 149, 151, 152
Maddox, Donald, 17n.26, 232n.7, 239n.62, 298, 313nn.4–5
Madh (Arabic, "praise"), 317
Madih (praise in the Arabic *qasida*), 255
Mahoney, Georgina M., 66n.77
Maillard, Jean, 292n.27, 293n.31, 294n.34
Maimonides, Moses, 332n.40
Major genres (Occitan), 58n.3, 68

Majorano, Matteo, 144n.30
Malachi, Zvi, 332n.42
Malmariée (French song of an unhappy bride), 191, 299, 346n.21
Manero Sorolla, María del Pilar, 139, 145nn.41–42
Manley, Lawrence, 142n.5
Manzanares, 173
Marcabru, 25, 29, 57n.2, 60nn.19–20, 65n.73, 75, 80, 90n.40, 211, 212, 213, 226, 229, 231, 233n.17, 234nn.24–25, 234n.28, 235n.34, 236n.40, 241n.91, 290n.4, 294n.46; "L'autrier, a l'issida d'abriu," 224–25
Marcoat, 60n.20
Marcos Marín, Francisco, 185n.50
Marginal genres (Occitan), 24, 28
Marion, Marot (name of shepherdess in *pastourelle*), 297, 308, 310
Marshall, John H., 8, 35, 61nn.27–29, 62n.44, 79, 91n.5, 91nn.54–55, 210, 211, 231n.2, 232n.6, 233n.9, 233n.12, 233n.14, 233n.16, 234n.24, 239nn.62–63, 240n.74, 247, 253nn.1–2, 254nn.3–4, 254n.6, 292nn.19–20, 292nn.22–25, 292n.27, 293nn.32–33, 294nn.34–36, 294n.38, 294nn.41–42, 294nn.44–45, 294nn.47–49, 294n.52, 295nn.55–58, 295n.64
Martianus Capella, 97
Martín de Córdoba, 173
Martin Moya, 144n.30
Maryam bint abi Ya'qub al-Faysuly al-Ansari al-Hajja, 259
Maryam bint ibn Yaqubi, 259
Materia (content, in rhetoric), 250, 277, 292n.16, 292n.23
Material Style, 9, 198, 199, 200
Matfre Ermengau, 34, 69, 82, 93n.78
Matthieu of Vendôme, 103, 206n.20, 208n.34, 289n.3
Maximian, 249
Mayer-Martin, Donna, 241n.89
McDonough, C. J., 123n.40
McGee, Timothy J., 290n.6, 295nn.62–64
McKeon, R., 184n.47

McNamara, Jo Ann, 144n.25
Melody as an element in genre: in German, 343; in Occitan, 31, 91n.56, 239n.62, 245, 273–89; in Spanish, 158–75, 178n.10, 183n.40. See also *Son*
Meneghetti, Maria Luisa, 64n.66, 87n.4, 88n.16, 92n.68, 93nn.79–80
Menéndez Pidal, Ramón, 178n.15
Menéndez y Pelayo, Marcelino, 176n.5, 178n.17
Mengaldo, Pier Vincenzo, 205n.2
Menocal, Maria Rosa, 332n.38
Merkaere (German, "spies"), 338
Mettman, Walter, 269n.8
Meyer, Paul, 92n.67, 295n.54
Meyer, Wilhelm, 115–18
Michaëlis de Vasconcellos, Carolina, 134, 144nn.31–32, 145n.38
Miei-sirventes (Occitan half-*sirventes*), 21, 22, 29
Migne, Jacques-Paul, 254n.19
Minnesang (German courtly song), 334, 343
Minnis, Alastair J., 16n.23, 205n.1, 254n.13, 254n.15
Minor genres (Occitan), 24, 25, 28, 30, 58n.3, 68
Mocedades de Rodrigo, 164
Moi, Toril, 108, 124n.53, 136, 145n.37
Mölk, Ulrich, 51n to l. 46, 60n.18, 66n.75, 94n.94, 154n.2, 192, 205, 205n.4
Monk of Montaudon, 76, 89n.27, 90n.53, 283–84; "Senher, ieu tem que falhis," 75
Monophony, 12, 297, 299; secular, 275
Monson, Don, 127, 142n.7
Monumentarisation (Zumthor), 100
Morales de Ovidio, 170, 185n.55
Moser, Hugo, 345n.15, 346n.20
Moses ibn Ezra, 318, 319, 320, 321, 322, 324, 330n.5, 330n.9, 330n.13, 331n.15, 331n.17, 331n.19, 331n.27, 333n.45
Mote (Spanish genre), 172
Motet (French genre), 12, 177n.9, 297–312

Motetus (upper voice in motet, *duplum*), 12, 298, 301, 304, 311
Mouzat, Jean, 89n.22
Mu'arada (Judeo-Arabic contrafacture), 327
Muhammad ibn Abd Allah ibn al-Abbar, 269n.11
Müller, Ulrich, 344n.1
Müller, Wilhelm, 344n.4
Munari, Franco, 206n.20, 208n.34
Murphy, James J., 16n.23, 184n.44, 184n.47, 291nn.14–15, 292n.17
Muschamp, Herbert, 13–14, 17n.28
Music, 254n.2. *See also* Melody
Musical genres, in Occitan, 22
Muwashshah (Judeo-Arabic "girdle poem"), 11, 12, 13, 256, 265, 266, 267, 326–29, 330n.5, 331n.22, 331n.36, 332n.37, 332nn.39–40, 332nn.43–44, 333n.46

Narrative (as type of lyric), 10
Narrative genres, 16n.18
Narrative textuality, in Occitan genres, 212, 219, 224–26
Nasib (amatory prelude in Judeo-Arabic *qasida*), 255, 256, 319, 330n.5
Natureingang, 337
Naudieth, Fritz, 90n.44
Navarro Tomás, Tomás, 175n.3, 183n.40, 186n.60, 187n.66
Nazhun bint al-Qala'i, 259, 262
Nefzawi, 264
Neidhart (German poet), 343, 344n.4, 344n.9; name of German genre similar to the *pastourelle*, 334
Nelli, René, 50n to l. 37
Nelson, William, 180n.24
Nichols, Stephen G., 61n.36, 64n.65, 97, 121n.7, 292n.25, 333n.47
Nims, Margaret, 122n.12
Nonprincipal genres in *Leys d'amors*, 31–32, 33
Nonsense verse, 221
No-sai-que-s'es (Occitan anti-genre), 21, 22, 29, 37, 38. *See also* Raimbaut d'Aurenga
Novati, Francesco, 184n.47

Novella, 16n.18
Nykl, A. R., 269n.20

Occitan genres: relative frequency of, 23 fig. 1.1; absolute frequency of, 27 table 1.1
O'Connell, Terence, 63n.51
O'Keeffe, Katherine O'Brien, 182n.34, 182n.36
O'Neill, Barbara J., 66n.77
Ong, Walter J., 182n.34
Ordenanças sobre los abogados, 182n.33
Orduna, Germán, 185n.52
Ornatus difficilis (difficult ornamentaion, in rhetoric), 167
Ornatus facilis (easy ornamentation, in rhetoric), 167
Oroz Arizcuren, Francisco J., 60n.17, 90n.49
Orsini, G. N. G., 14n.4, 15n.17
Oswald von Wolkenstein, 336
Otto von Botenlouben, 345n.17
Ovid, 43, 56, 57, 57n to l. 13, 66n.78, 97, 100, 101, 103, 104, 123n.39, 246, 247, 248, 252, 254n.5

Paden, William D., 6, 9, 16n.21, 48n to l. 8, 55n to ll. 12–16, 59n.9, 59n.11, 60n.20, 60n.22, 62n.42, 62n.45, 62n.49, 63n.51, 64n.64, 65n.73, 66n.77, 66nn.79–80, 67n.97, 88n.6, 144n.33, 233n.17, 241nn.82–83, 292n.20, 314n.7, 344n.6
Paetow, Louis John, 184n.47
Page, Christopher, 290n.6, 290n.9, 291n.12, 293n.33, 295n.53, 298, 313n.3
Pagis, Dan, 321–22, 323, 324, 330n.9, 331nn.17–19, 331nn.29–30, 331n.33
Palais, 240n.74
Palisca, Claude V., 176n.7
Panegyric (Hebrew), 319, 322, 331n.22
"Par un matinet l'autrier" (anonymous French motet), 300–301
Parkes, M. B., 176n.6, 179n.24, 181n.25
Parody: in Arabic, 12; in French, 306; in Galician-Portuguese, 139; in He-

brew, 318, 330n.6; in Latin, 96, 124n.52; in Occitan, 58n.8, 86, 213, 214, 222
Partenope of Blois, 180n.25
Partimen (Occitan dialogue genre), 6, 10, 32, 38, 58n.8, 60n.15, 84, 210, 211, 212, 216, 218, 231–32nn.2–3, 240n.76, 251 fig. 9.2; frequency of, 23–24, 28, 29; with an unknown poet, possibly fictional, 58n.8
Pastora (synonym of *pastorela*), 30, 210, 246 fig. 9.1, 285
Pastorela (Occitan song about a shepherdess), 6, 10, 21, 22, 33, 43, 153, 210, 211, 212, 214, 216, 232n.5, 233n.13, 237n.54, 238n.54, 251 fig. 9.2, 285; frequency of, 23–24, 28; melody, 294n.46
Pastorela-sirventes, 232n.5, 237n.54
Pastoreta (synonym of *pastorela*), 212
Pastourelle (French song about a shepherdess), 12, 96, 191, 224–25, 297–312, 334; *pastourelle-bergerie*, 299, 303, 305, 307; *pastourelle classique*, 299, 303, 305; *pastourelle désintéressée*, 299; religious *pastourelle*, 58n.8
Pasturele (Middle High German form of the French word *pastourelle*), 344n.5
Paterson, Linda M., 63–64nn.58–59, 65n.71, 123n.27, 192, 193, 205, 205nn.2–3, 205n.5, 205n.7, 238n.61, 240n.73, 289n.3
Patt, William D., 184n.44, 184n.47
Pattison, Walter T., 49n to l. 13, 50n to l. 41, 50n to l. 42, 51n to l. 44, 63n.52, 63n.54, 63nn.56–58, 64nn.66–67, 124nn.41–42, 222, 233n.17, 240nn.72–73
Peire and Bernart de Ventadorn, "Amics Bernartz de Ventadorn," 223–24, 226
Peire Bremon, 88n.12
Peire Cardenal, 24, 59n.10, 82, 240n.74
Peire d'Alvernhe, 60n.20, 211, 212, 213, 216, 233n.17, 234n.24, 235n.32, 237n.47, 238n.61, 240n.77, 241n.84

Peire de la Mula, 90n.53
Peire de Maensac, 90n.53
Peire de Valeira, 61n.26, 212, 234n.20, 235n.35
Peire Guillem de Tolosa, 83, 90n.53
Peire Rogier, 234n.24, 236n.44
Peire Vidal, 72–73, 75, 80, 83, 89nn.26–28, 89n.30, 90n.40, 234n.24, 236n.43
Peirol, 216, 234n.24
Penitential song, 213
Pérez Varela, Carlos, 145n.41
Pero López de Ayala, 168, 185n.52
Persona, in rhetoric, 200
Peter of Blois, 7, 103–5, 123nn.35–37, 124nn.43–45; "A globo veteri," 103–4, 109–12; "Vacillantis trutine," 112–14
Petersen Dyggve, Holger, 207n.30
Peterson, Jeffrey, 97, 121n.8, 122n.22, 123n.29
Petrarch, 8, 146, 149, 155n.10, 156nn.12–13, 173, 184n.47
Pickens, Rupert T., 9–10, 58n.2, 232n.7, 233n.17, 235n.31, 235nn.36–38, 235n.40, 238n.57
Picone, Michelangelo, 8, 154n.1, 155n.6, 155n.10, 156n.13, 156n.16, 156nn.18–19, 157n.22
Pier della Vigna, 157n.22
Pillet, Alfred, 22, 29, 35, 36, 38, 58n.3, 59n.15, 60n.15, 61n.26, 213, 215, 216, 224, 232n.3, 233n.16, 234n.26, 234n.28, 236n.42, 237n.49, 237n.51, 237–38nn.53–55, 238n.60, 289n.1
Pino Jiménez, José Carlos, 186n.56
Pirrotta, N., 156n.14
Planh (Occitan lament), 6, 10, 11, 21, 30, 33, 38, 41–42, 43, 65nn.73–74, 151, 153–54, 210, 211, 212, 213, 214, 216, 218, 226, 227, 228, 231nn.2–3, 233n.13, 239n.62, 240n.67, 246 fig. 9.1, 251 fig. 9.2, 286; frequency of, 23–24, 28
Plato, 4, 15n.17, 98, 130, 135
Plazer (Occitan song of pleasure), 21, 22, 29, 31, 210
Poe, Elizabeth W., 6–7, 36, 39, 57n to

Rubric, 58n.6, 61nn.25–26, 64nn.62–63, 66n.78, 232n.4, 233n.15, 241n.80, 241n.90, 241n.92, 289n.1
Poetry (as genre), 14
Poirion, Daniel, 206n.24
Pollack, Sidney, 144n.23
Pollina, Vincent, 241n.89
Polyphony, 12, 297, 299, 300
Pons de Capdoill, 90n.53
Porcher, Jean, 14n.1
Potvin, Claudine, 176n.4, 186n.61
Praise and blame, 10, 242–52, 287, 291n.10; Arabic *madh* and *hija'*, 317
Primera crónica general de España, 170, 185n.56
Principal genres in *Leys d'amors*, 31–32, 33
Pronuntiatio (delivery, in rhetoric), 277
Propertius, 48n to l. 8, 67n.90
Prototypes of lyric genres in Occitan, 10, 65n.73, 221, 229, 230, 235n.30, 295n.54
Proverbs, 239n.62, 280, 281, 282
Prudentius, 248
Pseudo-genre, 237nn.53–54. *See also* Romance
Pure lyric, 10
Puy (French or Occitan literary association), 204

Qamar, 259, 260
Qasida (Arabic and Hebrew monorhymed ode), 12, 13, 255, 256, 265, 269n.16, 318, 319, 320, 321, 324, 326, 329, 330n.3, 330n.5, 330n.13, 331n.22
Qasmuna bint Ismail al-Yahudi, 262
Qitcat (Arabic poetic exercises), 317
Quadlbauer, Franz, 206n.24
Quadruplum (upper voice in motet), 12, 298
"Quan lo petz del cul venta" (anonymous Occitan *cobla*), 86
"Quant voi la fleur en l'arbroie" (anonymous French motet), 306–7
Querol Gavalda, Miguel, 179n.18
Quintilian, 172, 173

Rahil (reference to travel in the Arabic *qasida*), 255, 265
Raimbaut d'Aurenga, 22, 24, 36, 50n to l. 41, 51n to l. 44, 51n to l. 49, 55n to ll. 49–52, 63n.49, 63n.52, 63nn.56–59, 64nn.66–67, 65n.74, 104, 124nn.41–42, 199, 207n.32, 223, 233n.17, 234n.24, 236n.44, 240nn.72–73; death of, 49n to l. 13; "Escotatz, mas no say que s'es," 37, 222; genre in, 37–38
Raimbaut de Vaqueiras, 72, 78, 89n.24, 90n.53, 287
Raimon Berenger, count of Provence, 82
Raimon de Miraval, 83
Raimon Gaucelm of Béziers, 77, 81; "A penas vauc en loc qu'om no·m deman," 85
Raimon Jordan, 236n.44
Raimon Vidal, 30, 34, 72, 91n.55, 101, 111, 211, 229, 233n.14, 243–44, 245, 253nn.1–4, 254n.6, 278–79, 292nn.19–20, 292nn.22–23, 292n.27, 293n.32, 294nn.35–36, 294n.38, 294nn.41–42, 294nn.44–45, 294nn.47–49, 294n.52, 295n.55–58, 295n.64
Ranke, Friedrich, 344n.5
Ratio (theme, in rhetoric), 278
Raugei, Anna Maria, 207n.30, 208n.36
Raynouard, François-Just-Marie, 67n.96, 78, 89n.23, 90n.51
Rayso. See *Razo* (2)
Razo (1), Occitan prose genre, 9, 34, 74, 77, 78, 89n.25, 209, 211, 212, 215, 216, 217, 229, 230, 292n.23, 295n.59
Razo (2), *rayso*, Occitan, "theme" in rhetoric, 250, 278, 279, 282, 283, 287
Rebec (Occitan musical form?), 31
Reciprocal discourse in Occitan genres, 10, 223–24
Redondel (Occitan form of French *rondeau*), 31
Reese, Gustave, 289n.1
Reflective and meditative poems (Hebrew), 319

Refloit (Middle High German name of a French genre?), 344n.5
Refrain, 299
Regalado, Nancy Freeman, 16n.20, 17n.26
Reie (German dance song), 13, 334, 344n.4
Reinmar der Alte, 337, 342, 345n.18, 346n.21, 346n.26
Reiss, Timothy J., 62n.40
Relay (Occitan song of respite), 31
Religious poetry (Occitan), 31, 32, 33, 34, 213, 231n.3, 232n.5, 233n.13; frequency of, 23–24, 28, 29; reference to, 60n.17
Reproof (Judeo-Arabic), 331n.22
Responsory, 298
Retroncha (Occitan song with refrain), 11, 30, 31, 210, 246 fig. 9.1, 250, 251 fig. 9.2, 284–85, 286, 294n.43
Reverdie (French song of spring), 299
Reversari (Occitan song of antitheses), 31
Rey, Agapito, 254n.16
Rhetoric (as genre), 16n.23
Rhetoric, demonstrative, 10, 242–52
Ribera, Julian, 269n.11
Richter, Reinhild, 88n.7, 93n.78
Ricketts, Peter T., 93n.78
Riddle. *See Devinalh*
Rider, Jeff, 17n.26, 239n.62
Rieger, Angelica, 43, 44, 48n to ll. 2–3, 48n to l. 4, 48–49n to l. 8, 49n to l. 9, 49n to l. 16, 49n to l. 21, 49–50n to ll. 23–24, 50n to l. 34, 50n to l. 37, 50n to ll. 41–48, 50n to l. 42, 51n to l. 46, 51n to ll. 47–48, 51n to l. 49, 51n to l. 51, 52, 53, 55n to l. 29, 55n to l. 35, 55n to l. 44, 55n to ll. 49–52, 56n to ll. 49–50, 57n to Rubric, 58n.6, 62n.47, 63n.49, 64n.61, 54n.63, 64nn.67–68, 65nn.73–74, 66nn.76–77, 87n.3, 88n.8, 88n.13, 89n.23, 90n.45, 207n.32
Rieger, Dietmar, 58n.3, 60n.20, 73, 89n.32, 92n.71, 92–93n.72, 232n.6
Rimado de Palacio, 171

Rimas caras (Occitan, rare rhymes), 38, 64n.60
Ripoll treatises (Occitan), 30–31, 231n.2, 233n.14, 240n.74, 292n.23
Riquer, Martín de, 44, 51n to l. 44, 59n.9, 60n.20, 63n.49, 64n.67, 67n.85, 67n.94, 74, 89n.27, 89n.31, 90nn.33–34, 90n.36, 90nn.38–41, 90n.44, 90n.51, 93n.90, 94n.93, 289n.1
Robertson, D. W., Jr., 124n.52
Robin (name of shepherd in *pastourelle*), 297, 310
Rodrigo Fernández de Santaella, 183n.43
Rodrigues Lapa, Manuel, 143n.10, 145n.46
Rofian, 77
Rohloff, Ernst, 177n.9, 178n.17, 290n.5, 290nn.8–9, 291nn.10–11, 291n.13, 292nn.16–18, 295n.61
Rohr, Rupprecht, 58n.4, 208n.41
Roman (narrative), 279
Roman de la rose, 151, 196. *See also* Guillaume de Lorris; Jean de Meun
Romance, 4, 17n.23; French genre, 16n.18; Occitan genre, 23–24, 28, 29, 31, 32, 60n.16, 213, 216, 224, 233n.13, 237n.54, 238n.54; parody of, 58n.8; Spanish genre, 172, 183n.40
Romeu i Figueras, Josep, 176n.5, 177n.7
Ron Fernández, X. Xabier, 145n.40
Roncaglia, Aurelio, 155n.5, 156n.14
Rondeau (French), 274, 299
Rosen(-Moked), Tova, 327, 331n.35, 332n.39
Rosenstein, Roy, 65n.73, 233n.17
Rosmarin, Adena, 3, 14n.3, 15n.8, 15n.14, 17n.27, 322, 324, 331n.20, 331n.31
Rossi, G., 93n.80
Rotrouenge (French), 285, 294nn.43–44
Rotuwange (Middle High German form of French word *rotrouenge*), 344n.5

Index

Roy Queimado, 8, 139, 145n.41
Rundate (Middle High German form of French word *rondeau*), 344n.5
Russell, Rinaldina, 155n.9

Sadie, Stanley, 177n.7
Saenger, Paul, 179–80n.24, 182n.29, 183n.39
Saints' lives, 16n.18
Sakari, Aimo, 36, 44, 48n to ll. 2–3, 48n to l. 8, 49n to l. 16, 49n to l. 21, 49n to l. 22, 50n to l. 41, 50n to ll. 41–48, 50n to l. 42, 50n to l. 43, 51n to l. 46, 51n to ll. 47–48, 51n to l. 49, 56n to ll. 49–50, 62n.48, 64n.66–68, 67n.95, 90n.42
Salinas, Francisco, 178n.17, 179n.23
Salut d'amor (Occitan amorous epistolary genre), 58n.3, 86, 233n.13
Salverda de Grave, Jean-Jaques, 65n.70, 88n.14, 90n.45, 93n.85
Samuel the Nagid, 318–19, 320, 329n.1, 330n.8, 330nn.11–12
Samuelson, Edward J., 66n.77
Sanc (Middle High German, "song" or "singing"), 335
Sánchez-Arce, Nellie E., 179n.23
Sandkühler, Bruno, 205n.1
Sankovitch, Tilde, 42, 48n to l. 8, 60n.22, 65n.72, 66n.79, 233n.17, 241nn.82–83
Santa Olalla Sánchez, Aurora Martín de, 182n.33
Santaella, 166
Santagata, Mario, 155n.12
Santiago Kastner, Macario, 178n.17
Santillana, Marqués de, 160, 162, 164, 168, 169, 171, 172, 176n.3, 179n.18, 179n.20, 185n.55, 186n.56, 186n.60, 186n.62
Satire: Judeo-Arabic, 331n.22; medieval Latin, 96; medieval theory of, 254n.15
Saville, Jonathan, 345n.19
Savj-Lopez, P., 92n.65
Sayce, Olive, 344n.2
Scaglione, Aldo, 184n.47

Schanzune (Middle High German form of French word *chanson*), 344n.5
Scheindlin, Raymond, 323, 330n.1, 331nn.23–25, 332n.43
Scheludko, Dimitri, 123n.28
Schiendorfer, Max, 344n.9, 345n.17, 346n.25
Schirmann, Hayyim, 330n.6, 331n.14, 331n.16, 331nn.24–26, 333n.45
Schlegel, Friedrich, and August Wilhelm, 4
Schleusener-Eichholz, Gudrun, 208n.38
Schmid, Walter, 184n.46
School poetry (medieval Latin), 96, 108
Schultz-[Gora], Oscar, 44, 49n to l. 16, 67n.84
Schulze, Joachim, 156n.14
Schumann, Otto, 109–12, 118–20, 123n.33, 123n.40, 124n.46
Schutz, A.-H., 57n.2, 60n.17, 63n.50, 90n.47, 90nn.52–53, 93nn.73–74, 93n.81, 93n.84, 233nn.15–16, 233nn.18–19, 234nn.20–23, 235n.35, 235n.39, 236n.44, 237nn.46–47, 237n.52, 295n.59
Schweikle, Günther, 337, 340, 344n.3, 344n.6, 344nn.8–9, 345nn.14–16, 346n.27
Scott, A. B., 254n.13, 254n.15
Seay, Albert, 291n.12
Sedlmayer, Henricus Stephanus, 246, 254n.5
Seebass, Tilman, 14nn.1–2
Seigel, Jerrold E., 184n.47, 186n.57
Sequence (Latin liturgical form), 334
Serena (Occitan evening song), 21, 22, 29
Serra, 173
Serventese (Italian form of the Occitan word *sirventes*), 153
Sestina (Occitan metrical genre), 8, 21, 31, 38, 58n.8, 149, 155n.10, 232n.3, 238n.60; frequency of, 23–24
Shapiro, Marianne, 61n.28, 155n.10
Sharman, Ruth Verity, 232n.5, 233n.17,

237nn.48–51, 237nn.53–56, 238nn.58–59, 240n.77, 241nn.90–92
Shepard, Laurie, 44, 48n to ll. 2–3, 48–49n to l. 8, 49n to l. 9, 49–50n to ll. 23–24, 50n to l. 34, 62n.47
Shepard, William P., 93n.76
Sheridan, James J., 122n.16
"Si gais solatz ab bels ditz" (anonymous Occitan *cobla*), 84–85
"Si linguis angelicis" (anonymous Latin poem), 107–8, 124n.48
Siete Partidas. See Alfonso X el Sabio
Singleton, Charles S., 156n.20
Sirventes (Occitan satirical song), 6, 8, 10, 12, 21, 22, 23, 29, 30, 31, 32, 33, 34, 35, 37, 38, 58n.7, 60n.20–22, 65n.74, 68, 71, 72, 74, 76, 77, 78, 82, 84, 85, 86, 94n.93, 148, 151, 152, 154, 210, 211, 212, 213, 214, 216, 218, 222, 227, 228, 229, 231n.3, 232n.5, 233n.13, 234n.28, 235n.32, 236n.44, 237n.53, 238n.55, 238n.58, 238n.61, 239n.62, 241n.84, 246, 246 fig. 9.1, 251 fig. 9.2, 252, 254n.15, 279, 282, 283; frequency of, 23–25, 28; polyglot, 58n.8; religious, 58n.8
Sirventes (*tenson fictive*), 58n.8
Sirventes-canso (blend of Occitan genres), 30, 31, 32, 37, 60n.23, 213, 216, 232n.3, 234n.28, 235n.30, 237n.53, 238n.61; frequency of, 23–24, 28
Sirventes joglaresc (Occitan *sirventes* addressed to a *joglar*), 92n.72, 232n.5
Skalds, 5
Snyder, Jeri L., 66n.77
Sola-Sole, Josep M., 270n.30
Solomon ibn Gabirol, 328, 331n.16; "Ah, come, my radiant friend, along with me," 320–21; "Like Amnon sick am I, so call Tamar," 323
Solterer, Helen, 206n.17
Somni (Occitan dream song), 30, 31, 210, 246 fig. 9.1
Son (Occitan, "melody"), 215, 217. *See also* Melody
Song (with words, in bluegrass), 17n.24

Sonnet (Italian), 151, 152, 153–54
Sonnet (Occitan), 31; frequency of, 23–24
Sordel, 80, 90n.53
Spanke, Hans, 236n.41, 290n.4, 294n.51
Spearing, A. C., 124n.44
Spechtler, Franz Viktor, 345n.10
Spence, Sarah, 122n.25
Spodark, Edwina, 66n.77
Spruch (German didactic song), 13, 334, 343, 344n.7
Staar, Susanne, 346n.21
Stäblein, Patricia Harris, 48n to l. 8, 60n.22, 66n.79, 233n.17, 241nn.82–83
Städtler, Katharina, 50n to l. 37, 67n.93, 67n.95
Stantipes (Latin name of Occitan *estampida*), 287, 295n.64
Stanza (Italian verse form), 154
Stegagno Picchio, Luciana, 139, 144n.30, 145n.44
Stengel, Edmund, 92n.63, 93n.82
Stern, Charlotte, 178n.10
Stern, S. M., 326, 330n.1, 332nn.37–38, 332n.44, 333n.46
Stevens, John, 177n.9, 184n.46, 289n.3
Stevenson, Robert Murrell, 176n.6, 177n.7
Storey, Wayne H., 182n.3
Storme, Julie A., 66n.77
Streitgedicht (German debate poem), 96
Stronski, Stanislaw, 71, 88nn.17–18, 89nn.19–20
Sturm-Maddox, Sara, 17n.26, 232n.7, 239n.62, 298, 313nn.4–5
Subgenres, 14
Suchier, Hermann, 94n.93
Sumas de la Historia Troyana, 182n.33
Summa (theological treatise), 335
Swales, John M., 15n.12, 15n.16
Switten, Margaret, 62n.39, 214, 215, 235n.34, 236n.41
Systems of genre: general considerations, 4, 16n.18, 298; Grocheio's system for secular monophony, 275
—, French: names of lyric kinds treat-

Index 369

ed as system in nineteenth century, 191
—, German: no system developed, 13, 343
—, Hebrew, 323–24
—, Italian, 8, 148; development of macrogenre, 149; elimination of music, 150; *Vita nuova*, 151–53
—, Occitan: *cobla* provided release, 6, 7, 68, 86, 247, 252; development of genre system, 6, 21–67; late reception in terms of praise and blame, 10, 245–52; obsessive systematization in late arts of poetry, 209; taxonomy in Raimon Vidal, 278; versification system in Frank, 242
—, Spanish, 9; evolution, 171
—. See also Intergenre; Macrogenre; Prototypes; Virtual genres

Tachau, Katherine, 291n.12
Tagelied (German dawn song), 13, 334, 335, 336–43
Tagewîse (German dawn song), 339, 343
Taghorn (German dawn song), 343
Tajnis (Hebrew poems characterized by wordplay), 319
Tanzweise (German dance song), 13, 334
Tavani, Giuseppe, 127, 128, 129, 130, 131, 135, 142n.9, 143n.16, 143n.18, 145n.35
Tawaddud, 258, 263, 269n.8
Tazallum (Judeo-Arabic lyrical complaint), 12, 317, 319, 326, 330n.5, 331n.22
Tenor (lower voice in motet, *cantus firmus*), 12, 298, 311
Tenso (Occitan debate song), 6, 10, 12, 21, 22, 30, 31, 33, 36, 37, 38, 43, 58n.8, 59–60n.15, 68, 69, 71, 75, 77, 81, 86, 92n.70, 94n.93, 153, 157n.22, 210, 211, 212, 216, 218, 231–32nn.2–3, 232n.5, 233n.13, 235n.29, 236n.44, 239n.63, 240nn.76–77, 246 fig. 9.1, 251 fig. 9.2, 283, 286; fictional, 58n.8, 60n.15, 232n.3; frequency of, 23–24, 28, 29

Tenzone. See *Tenso*
Tenzone (Partimen), 59–60n.15
Terramagnino da Pisa, 233n.14
Tervooren, Helmut, 344n.1, 344n.7, 345n.15, 346nn.20–21
Teulié, H., 93n.80
Text-painting (madrigalism), 274
Theater, 16n.18
Thibaut de Champagne, 9, 198, 199, 204, 207nn.26–27, 208n.37; "De bone amor vient séance et bonté," 201–3
Thomas, A., 50–51n to l. 43
Thompson, James Westfall, 180nn.24–25
Thousand and One Nights. See *Arabian Nights*
Through-composed melody, 288, 293n.31
Tibors, 63n.49, 91n.53
Tischler, Hans, 313n.6, 314nn.8–9, 314nn.12–13, 314n.15, 314n.17
Titles of troubadour poems, 92n.69
Todorov, Tzvetan, 15nn.5–6, 15n.14, 16n.17, 322, 331n.21, 345n.13
Todros Abulafia, 324, 330n.6, 331n.28, 331n.36; "Fire flows from my heart and a river from my eyes," 325–26; "Many [poets] sing only erotic verse," 318
Toja, Gianluigi, 64n.60
Tolstoy, Leo, 3
Topoi in rhetoric, 199, 200; circumstantial, 197
Tornada (Occitan envoi), as element in genre, 32, 218
Traill, David A., 123n.40
Tratado de la Música, 182n.31
Treitler, Leo, 236n.41
Triana, 179n.18
Triplum (upper voice in motet), 12, 298, 300, 301, 303, 311
Trobairitz (Occitan woman poet), 6, 22, 36, 42, 43. *See also* Almuc and Iseut, Azalais de Porcairagues; Beatritz de Romans; Castelloza; Clara d'Anduza; Comtessa de Dia; Gaudairenca; Lombarda; Tibors

Trobar (Occitan, "to compose songs"), 79
Trobar clus (Occitan, difficult style), 34, 38, 63n.59, 205n.4, 237n.53, 238n.59, 238n.61
Trobar leu (Occitan, easy style), 34, 38, 63n.59, 136, 205n.4, 237n.53, 238n.61
Trojel, E., 205nn.8–9
Troubadour (as used by Guiraut Riquier), 84
Troyan, Scott D., 17n.23
Tune (in bluegrass), 17n.24

Uc Catola, 61n.26, 213, 231, 235n.29
Uc de Saint Circ, 71, 73, 77, 79, 80, 83, 88n.14, 88n.16, 89n.25, 90–91n.53, 91n.57, 211, 233n.16, 236n.44; "Seign'en coms, no·us cal esmaiar," 70
Uc Faidit, 34, 79, 91nn.57–58, 293n.33
Uitti, Karl D., 231n
Ulrich von Liechtenstein, 342, 343, 344n.1, 346n.24
Ulrich von Singenberg, 13, 343, 344n.9; "Wie hôhes muotes ist ein man," 340–42
"Un cavaler conosc qe l'altrer vi" (anonymous Occitan *cobla*), 86–87
Untergattungen (German, "subgenres"), 335
Usanza antiga, la (Occitan), 9–10, 65n.73, 211, 212, 213, 217, 218, 229

Vaasco Praga de Sandin, 7, 134–38, 141–42; "Como vos sodes, mia senhor," 136–37
Valcárcel, Carmen, 177n.7
Valla, 184n.47
van der Werf, Hendrik, 177n.9, 241n.89, 313n.6
Van Vleck, Amelia E., 67n.94, 92nn.71–72, 240n.69
Vanto (Occitan boast), 21, 29
Vasco Perez Pardal, 144n.30
Vega, Lope de, 269n.9
Vendrell de Millás, Francisca, 176n.3, 185n.48, 186n.59, 187n.65

Vergiera (Occitan genre), 210
Vers (Occitan song), 9, 21, 22, 29, 30, 31, 33, 36, 37, 38, 40, 41, 57n.2, 60n.20, 63n.57, 64n.59, 71, 76, 84, 210–17 passim, 220, 222, 225, 229, 230, 231n.2, 233n.13, 234nn.24–28, 235n.35, 236nn.40–42, 236nn.44–45, 237n.51, 238n.59, 238n.61, 239n.64, 240n.67, 241n.84, 246 fig. 9.1, 250, 251 fig. 9.2, 280, 286
Versus (monastic Latin, "verse"), 215, 230
Vezio (Occitan vision song), 31
Viaderes (Occitan dance song), 31
Viandela (Occitan dance song), 31
Vida (Occitan prose biography), 9, 34, 36, 42, 44, 57n.2, 60n.17, 69, 71, 78, 88n.16, 89n.23, 90n.53, 209, 211, 212, 215, 216, 217, 226, 229, 230, 233nn.15–16, 234n.20, 235nn.34–35, 237n.47
Villancico (Spanish genre), 172
Villasandino, 175n.3
Villon. *See* François Villon
Virelai, 274, 295n.54
Virgil, 102, 248
Virgin, Occitan song to the, 21, 29, 33
Virtual genres, 229. *See also* Prototypes

Wailes, Stephen L., 346n.24
Waite, William G., 290n.7
Walker, Roger M., 181n.28
Wallace, David, 254n.13
Wallada, 259, 261, 262, 265, 269n.16
Wallensköld, Alex, 207nn.26–27, 207n.30, 208n.37
Walsh, P. G., 124n.52
Walther von der Vogelweide, 346n.22
Wapnewski, Peter, 345n.19
War poems (Hebrew), 319
Warren, Austin, 15n.13, 17n.25
Wartburg, Walther von, 67n.89, 90n.37
Wasick, Cynthia, 182n.33
Wechsel (German song in dialogue), 13, 334, 343, 344n.9
Weinrich, Harald, 219, 240n.65
Weiss, Gerlinda, 344n.1
Weiss, Julian, 7–8, 144n.29, 181n.27, 182n.34, 185n.47

Weiss, Roberto, 185n.47, 186n.57
Wellek, René, 15n.13, 17n.25
Westrem, Scott D., 66n.77
Wetherbee, Winthrop, 7, 9, 121n.10, 125n.54
Whetnall, Jane, 178n.12
White, Sarah, 44, 48n to ll. 2–3, 48–49n to l. 8, 49n to l. 9, 49–50n to ll. 23–24, 50n to l. 34, 62n.47
Wieruszowski, Helene, 185n.47
Wilhelm, August. *See* Schlegel, Friedrich
Wilhelm, James J., 127, 142n.7, 238n.60
Wilkins, Nigel E., 207n.31
William IX. *See* Guilhem IX
Williams, Raymond, 131, 142n.5, 143nn.19–21
Willms, Eva, 346n.22
Wimsatt, James I., 176n.7
Wine poetry (Judeo-Arabic). *See* Khamriyya
Winn, James Anderson, 176n.7
Winter-Hosman, Mieke de, 58n.2–3, 60n.18
Witt, Ronald G., 184n.47, 185n.47, 186n.58
Witthoeft, Friedrich, 92n.72
Wolf, Alois, 340, 345n.19
Wolf, George, 65n.73, 233n.17, 235n.30, 240n.67, 241n.81, 241n.91
Wolfram von Eschenbach, 13, 337–38, 339, 340, 342, 343, 345n.19; "Swer pfliget oder ie gepflac," 338
Women poets, in Arabic tradition, 259–63. *See also* Trobairitz; Women's song

Women's song: *Cantica puellarum*, 332n.39; *Chanson de femme*, 65n.75; *Chanson féminine*, in Guillaume de Machaut, 198–99; in German, 13, 334, 344n.8. *See also* Women poets
Wormhoudt, Arthur, 270n.33
Wright, Janice, 144n.26
Wright, John, 17n.24
Wynn, Mariann, 345n.19

"Ya mamma mio al-habibi" (anonymous *kharja*), 266
Yahalom, Joseph, 333n.45
Yellin, David, 330n.6, 331n.28, 331n.36
Young, Karl, 246, 254n.5
Yudkin, Jeremy, 313n.6

Zaganelli, Gioia, 50n to l. 37, 63n.49
Zajal. See *Zéjel*
Zarnecke, Friedrich, 344n.4
Zaynab, 259
Zéjel (Arabic poetic form), 256, 268
Zenker, Rudolph, 92n.70, 213, 233n.17, 235n.32, 240n.77
Ziegler, Vickie, 134, 144n.30
Zink, Michel, 313–14n.7
Ziolkowski, Jan, 122n.17
Zufferey, François, 61nn.34–35
Zumthor, Paul, 16n.18, 35, 100, 121nn.2–3, 122n.22, 122n.25, 123n.29, 123n.38, 126, 127, 129, 134, 142n.3, 142n.6, 144n.30, 180n.24, 184n.47, 185n.48, 219, 240n.65, 292n.21, 313n.2, 325, 331n.32

Illinois Medieval Studies

Book and Verse: A Guide to Middle English
  Biblical Literature   *James H. Morey*
Medieval Lyric: Genres in Historical Context
  Edited by William D. Paden

ILLINOIS MEDIEVAL STUDIES IS A CONTINUATION
OF THE SERIES ILLINOIS MEDIEVAL MONOGRAPHS,
WHICH INCLUDED:

Celestina: Tragicomedia de Calisto y Melibea
  Fernando de Rojas, ed. Miguel Marciales
The *Nibelungenlied:* History and Interpretation
  Edward R. Haymes
The *Bugarštica:* A Bilingual Anthology of the Earliest Extant
  South Slavic Folk Narrative Song   *John S. Miletich*

Typeset in 10/13 New Baskerville
with New Baskerville display
Designed by Copenhaver Cumpston
Composed by Jim Proefrock
at the University of Illinois Press
Manufactured by Thomson-Shore, Inc.

University of Illinois Press
1325 South Oak Street
Champaign, IL 61820-6903
www.press.uillinois.edu